Russian Economic Reform

Attempts to portray the reform of the Russian economy as a disaster are misleading because they fail to take account of the complexities of the transition from socialism to capitalism. *Russian Economic Reform* brings a coherent view to the Russian transition, by focusing on the actual pre-reform conditions including the widespread private, informal economic activity. The framework that emerges highlights the similarities among many seemingly disparate aspects of the reforming Russian economy – from inflation to organized crime, from barter to military conversion. Throughout the emphasis is on real economic activity, rather than on formal plans for economic reform and the individuals behind them.

Perceptions of the pre-reform Russian economy are often inaccurate, primarily because the logic of a centrally planned economy is so different from a capitalist one that familiar economic phenomena, such as unemployment and inflation, take unfamiliar forms. Likewise, conventional statistics such as Gross National Product measured different things in socialist economies than they did in capitalist ones. Staggering amounts of black market and hidden private economic activity contribute to the difficulties in gauging the pre-reform state of affairs. The misconceptions about the starting point for Russian economic reform that result lead to an exaggeration of the costs of transition. Many of the costs associated with the transition process are not new, though during the reform process they may be borne in different forms and by different people. Meanwhile some of the costs which are new are the result of either partial reform measures or new problems caused by regional political upheavals. The short-term benefits of reform also tend to be exaggerated, however, due to an insufficient accounting of the pre-reform market economy.

Written in an accessible and lively style throughout, *Russian Economic Reform* sheds much new light both on changes within Russia and on the transition process in general. It will be essential reading for social scientists, college students and others interested in the economic transitions of the formerly-socialist world.

Jim Leitzel is Associate Professor of Public Policy Studies and Economics at Duke University.

Acknowledgements

Chapter 6, 'Monopoly', closely follows my article, 'A Note on Monopoly and Russian Economic Reform', that appeared in *Communist Economies and Economic Transformation* 6: 45–53, 1994. It is republished here with the permission of the Carfax Publishing Company, 875–81 Massachusetts Avenue, Cambridge, MA. An earlier version of the sidebar 'Parking and Perestroika' served as the first draft of an op-ed article that I wrote with Michael Alexeev and Clifford Gaddy, published in the *Journal of Commerce*, April 14, 1992, under the title, 'When Parking Meets Perestroika'. *The Brookings Review*, a quarterly publication of The Brookings Institution, published two short articles, that I co-authored with Michael Alexeev and Clifford Gaddy, 'Getting the Picture Right: Soviet Collapse, Transition Troubles, and Western Aid' (Winter 1992, pp. 14–17), and 'Mafiosi and Matrioshki, Organized Crime and Russian Reform' (Winter 1995, pp. 26–29). Early drafts of some of the material in this book served as a basis for those articles. Other material is drawn from 'Russian Economic Reform: Is Economics Helpful?', *Eastern Economic Journal*, 10, Summer 1993.

This book was begun when I was a National Fellow at the Hoover Institution on War, Revolution, and Peace, Stanford, California, during 1991–92. Many thanks to the Hoover Institution, and in particular Tom Henriksen and Wendy Minkin, for their support. Financial assistance from the National Council for Soviet and East European Research, for which I am grateful, contributed to this research. Comments on draft material were supplied by many individuals, including Michael Alexeev, Charles Clotfelter, Lydia Faulkner, Clifford Gaddy, Craufurd Goodwin, Simon Johnson, LynnErin McNeil, Kimberly Neuhauser, Will Pyle, Gertrude Schroeder, the late Jill Stuart, Vladimir Treml, and Erik Weisman. My deepest appreciation to them all.

This book is dedicated to my parents.

Russian Economic Reform

Jim Leitzel

London and New York

First published 1995
by Routledge
11 New Fetter Lane, London EC4P 4EE

Simultaneously published in the USA and Canada
by Routledge
29 West 35th Street, New York, NY 10001

© 1995 Jim Leitzel

Typeset in Garamond by LaserScript, Mitcham, Surrey
Printed and bound in Great Britain by
Mackays of Chatham PLC, Chatham, Kent

British Library Cataloguing in Publication Data
A catalogue record for this book is available from the British Library.

Library of Congress Cataloging in Publication Data
Leitzel, Jim.
  Russian economic reform/Jim Leitzel.
  p. cm.
  Includes bibliographical references (p.) and index.
  ISBN 0–415–12510–3. – ISBN 0–415–12511–1
  1. Russia (Federation) – Economic policy – 1991– . 2. Soviet Union
  Economic conditions. 3. Post-communism – Economic aspects –
  Russia (Federation). I. Title.
HC340.12.L45 1994
338.947 – dc20   94-24768
                                                                         CIP

ISBN 0–415–12510–3
ISBN 0–415–12511–1 (pbk)

Contents

Preface

AN ECONOMIC EXCURSION

A quaint Russian tradition governs the preparation for a journey. Immediately prior to embarking, travellers sit down to observe a brief moment of silence. The enforced calm provides a gentle counterpoint to the coming commotion and locomotion of travel.

Russia has now embarked on a monumental collective journey, that between socialism and capitalism. Perhaps the 'period of stagnation', as the late 1970s and early 1980s came to be known in Russia, represented the quiet moment that signalled the initiation of economic relocation. Imagine all of Russia sitting in silence in a huge living room, or more appropriately, around a large-scale kitchen table, scene of so many conversations with friends and family. What would be going through the minds of the apprentice travellers?

Hospitality is another cherished Russian tradition. At such a large table they would surely make room for unexpected visitors. This book represents my thoughts on the journey that the Russians are undertaking. I reflect on the starting point, the final destination, and potential transitional paths between today's and tomorrow's Russian economies. In the process, I hope to demonstrate that not all transitional paths are 'just as fair', and to illuminate desirable properties of reform programmes.

The stakes involved in choosing the best reform path are immense, with the lives and livelihoods of 150 million Russian citizens riding in the balance. Nor is the Russian journey a matter of indifference for those beyond Russian borders. There are humanitarian concerns. There is also self-interest, as the potential instability of a military superpower lends global significance to Russian economic reform. The humility requisite for entering the debate on Russian reforms brings to mind the words of Alexander Pope, 'in tasks so bold, can little men engage . . .?'. But it is to little men and women that the task of Russian economic reform has fallen.

The abrupt changes in Eastern Europe and the former Soviet Union caught economists in both the East and West unprepared for their new task. Most economists trained in the Soviet Union had little notion of the workings of market economies, or even how Western economists approached questions concerning markets. Simultaneously, the great majority of Western economists were similarly untutored in the ways of the centrally-planned economies of Eastern Europe and the Soviet Union. Those who were knowledgeable concerning socialist economies were inexperienced in analysing transitions from socialism to capitalism. Perhaps the closest parallel in Western experience is the return to peacetime economies from more centrally-controlled systems after the Second World War, but that analogy is far from unequivocal, and often misleading. The extent of central planning in Western war-time economies was never as large as in the socialist countries, and the return to the more decentralized world of consumer sovereignty occurred after an interregnum of just a few years. More than 60 years of extensive central planning in Russia have left generations of Russians unfamiliar with the workings of a widespread and legal market economy.

Furthermore, the economics discipline is limited in the insights it can bring to the analysis of economic transition. Western economic theory, which has found much success in analysing the properties of various equilibrium states, admittedly has very little to say about the paths between equilibria. Economic theory is also more developed with respect to efficiency concerns – the size of the economic pie – than with considerations about the distribution among individuals and groups of the shares of the pie. To the extent that successful reform depends on the actual or feared distributional effects of transition, economic analysis may be less useful than political or ethical analysis. Even many economists question the ability of their discipline to add constructively to the reform debate. One leading Western expert on the economic system of the former Soviet Union, Dr Ed Hewett, sounded this theme:

> Economists, Eastern and Western, excel in analyses and criticism of existing centrally planned economic systems, and in extolling the virtues of a decentralized system relying heavily on markets. But they are almost no help in devising a strategy for the transition from the old to the new system.'[1]

I contend that, even in its infancy, transitional economics is vital to successful Russian market reform. The complicated mathematical models that mark the pages of the leading economics journals are generally not the stuff of transitional economics, though some useful lessons can be taken from formal models. Rather, the core of transitional economics consists of the application of basic economic reasoning (some might call it common sense) to the situation faced by the transforming economies.[2] The trick, if there is one, lies in understanding the real initial situation – the main theme developed in the pages that follow.

One implication of the novelty of transitional economics is that the pedigree of an extensive economics education is neither necessary nor sufficient for contributing to the debate on Russian economic reform. There is room at the imaginary kitchen table for business people, lawyers, labour union officials, social scientists, politicians: fellow travellers are welcomed, not blacklisted. Wide-ranging input is necessary to avoid the pitfall identified by Pope: 'a little learning is a dang'rous thing'. Reform is too important to be left to the economists.

The discussion in the pages that follow presents an analysis that is far from definitive in formulating the best policies for a successful transition. Not all significant aspects of economic transformation, particularly those concerned with the politics of reform, receive the warranted attention. Nevertheless, the analysis is ambitious in another respect. The framework presented here, with its emphasis on private, often informal economic activity and the hidden aspects of the pre-reform situation, is designed to lend structure to the reform conversation. In adopting the perspective employed below, reform issues that usually appear to be unconnected are shown to have important similarities: similarities that can be exploited in the formulation and analysis of reform policies.

In attempting to help organize the reform conversation, this book, while written by an economist and adopting a distinctly 'economic' view of reform issues, is intended to be useful for non-economists interested in Russian reform. Economist Donald McCloskey notes that the 'opportunity cost of enchanting one's fellow economists is alienating non-economists. There is no such thing as a free argument.'[3] I have chosen to speak (not argue!) with non-economists, at the risk of (further) alienating my fellow economists. Nor is the discussion here aimed at specialists on the Russian economy, though perhaps they too may find some value in the framework that is offered. Indeed, while Russia serves as the case study, the approach to reform adopted in this book applies more generally to transitions from socialism, and even perhaps (though much less directly) to reforms within Western economies, such as corporate restructurings or defence industry conversion. For the ideas presented in this book, I share the hope that Russians have for their traditionally state-owned enterprises, namely, that they remain valuable long beyond the time frame of the current reform debates. Hope is not completely triumphant over experience; it must be recognized (and even welcomed) that the brisk pace of change in Russia guarantees the rapid obsolescence of many details in the exposition.

The nature of transition economics gives much of the discussion that follows the air of an introductory economics book. An unintended side effect of examining the reforming Russian economy is, for me at least, a better understanding of Western economic phenomena, and I hope that this side benefit will apply more generally. In the analysis that follows, the problems of Western market economies are often ignored, while the problems of central planning are closely examined. This omission is not a wholesale endorsement of market economies; rather, it simply reflects the fact that the discussion here pertains to the journey the Russians are committed, or appear to be committed, to undertaking, now that their silent interlude has passed.

Introduction

THE DESTINATION OF RUSSIAN ECONOMIC REFORM

Russia, where are you flying to? Answer!

Nikolai Gogol, *Dead Souls*, 1842[4]

An old saying has it that if you don't know where you want to go, any road will take you there. This saying could serve as the slogan for the first six years of perestroika, the restructuring that then General Secretary Mikhail Gorbachev announced for the Soviet economy in 1985. These years were marked by abrupt changes in the course of economic policy: from an acceleration in investment to an acceleration in consumer goods production; from a campaign to reduce the consumption of alcohol to efforts to sell more alcohol for increased tax revenue; from intensified legal restrictions on private economic activity to legal equality between private and state businesses.[5]

After these six years of confusion came three days that shook the world. The dramatic 72 hours of August 1991 that witnessed the victory of democratic forces in the Soviet Union also provided the future direction for the Soviet economy. Few voices were left calling for the reform of socialism: even the coup plotters made no appeal to Marxism–Leninism. Within the political mainstream, a Western-style market economy became the only goal in town, in St Petersburg, Russia, as in St Petersburg, Florida.

Since the failed coup attempt, a normal, Western-style capitalist country has remained the desired destination of the Russian economic transition, despite a steady diet of political twists, turns, and occasional upheavals. But there are several versions of 'normal' Western capitalism, including those of Sweden, Great Britain, Japan, and St. Petersburg, Florida. Which of these is the model that the Russians have, or should have, in mind? For the purpose of examining the journey between Russian socialism and Western capitalism, the precise Western model is irrelevant. Each of the Western models are sufficiently similar, and the current Russian economy is sufficiently dissimilar from all of them, that the transitional path can largely be plotted without exact knowledge of the destination. In driving from New York to Los Angeles, 99 per cent of the route can be determined without knowing whether the precise destination is Anaheim or Malibu. Similarly, the Russian economy must head West, and only upon arrival in the general vicinity of Tomorrowland need it concern itself with the local geography.

At this stage of the Russian transition, the precise destination is as unknowable as it is irrelevant. Countries are unique, and while we can be confident that a greater reliance on legal markets will be good for Russia, we cannot know what the best mix of market institutions will be. Many aspects of the final destination will only be learned through an evolutionary process. Given the unavoidable uncertainties, pre-commitment to a comprehensive map during the early phases of a transition to capitalism is unwise. (And of course, there is no 'final' destination. Institutions are continually evolving in Western market economies, too.) This reasoning, common enough in the West, is less familiar in a society where the primary organizing feature has long been, at least officially, the government's central plan – though the results of central planning may lend credence to the preceding argument. Western economist Richard Ericson notes that

> a final lesson for successful reform taught by the nature of the traditional Soviet-style system is to abandon the Faustian urge to control, to know in advance, and thus to allow economic outcomes to arise naturally as the unpredictable consequences of market interaction.[6]

There are some features of the destination that the travellers should understand before they embark, lest they be disappointed upon arrival – or even choose to turn back. First, as all Westerners know from an experience that Russians have not shared, Western capitalism is not without its own difficulties. Becoming a Western-style capitalist economy will not solve all of Russia's problems, and will even generate some new ones, such as open unemployment. Second, arrival at capitalism will not, at least in the near term, change the fact that Russia is a poor country relative to the United States, Japan, and most nations in Western Europe. Living standards in Russia are about one-fourth the level of the United States. (The 'precise' relationship between Russian and US living standards, obviously a chimera, is a matter of great controversy.[7]) If tomorrow Russia successfully completes the transition to capitalism, Russian living standards will still be about one-fourth of those in the United States. Capitalism holds the promise for faster growth rates, implying that Russians should live better than they would have had the economy remained centrally-planned, though they will not immediately achieve the economic levels of mature Western capitalist economies. This dose of pragmatism is not intended to be a counsel of despair. The rapid growth of West Germany and Japan after the Second World War, and of China in recent years, indicates that economic reform can yield tremendous achievements in relatively short periods of time. But these short periods of time are measured in years, not days.

THE THEME

> What we have to deal with here is a communist society, not as it has *developed* on its own foundations, but, on the contrary, just as it *emerges* from capitalist society, which is thus in every respect, economically, morally, and intellectually, still stamped with the birthmarks of the old society from whose womb it emerges.
>
> Karl Marx[8]

With a Western-style capitalist economy providing the destination, the starting point and the transitional path are the other elements of the journey that must be specified. The interaction between these two basic components of reform provides the theme for the analysis that follows. The theme begins with the contention that the pre-reform Russian economy is generally misperceived, both in the West and in Russia. The misperception arises for many reasons, most particularly because the logic of a centrally-planned economy is so different from a capitalist economy that familiar Western economic phenomena such as unemployment and inflation take on unfamiliar forms. Likewise, common statistics such as Gross National Product measure different properties in socialist economies than in capitalist economies. Significant (even staggering) amounts of black market and hidden private economic activity contribute to the difficulties in gauging the pre-reform state of affairs.

The common misperception of the starting point for Russian economic reform leads to an exaggeration of the costs of transition. Many, if not most, of the identified costs and difficulties that accompany a transition from socialism to capitalism are not new costs at all. The same or even greater costs were being borne in the unreformed Russian economy – though in a different form, and by different people, and somewhat less visibly. Meanwhile, some costs attributed to reform are indeed new costs, but are the result either of bad reform policies – more on this below – or of basically unrelated problems such as trade disruptions arising from regional political disputes. As Marx noted for transitions in the other direction, what the Russians have to deal with now is a capitalist society, not as it has developed on its own foundations, but rather, stamped with the birthmarks and even the deformities of the old socialist society from whose womb it emerges.

Correcting misperceptions of the pre-reform Russian economy does not imply that the transition path is free of thorns, or that all transition paths are equally efficient. It does suggest that a well-designed transition from socialism to capitalism can be accomplished without a precipitous short-term fall in living standards, while providing some guidelines for the properties that a 'well-designed transition' should possess.

IMPLICIT VERSUS EXPLICIT

Looking for a job, particularly if you are already out of work, is one of the more stressful, frustrating, and potentially demeaning tasks that accompanies life in a Western market economy. After repeated failures at finding a job, some people simply give up the search. Such people are called 'discouraged workers' in economics jargon, and there were an estimated one million discouraged workers in the United States in 1992.[9] Perhaps surprisingly, discouraged workers are *not* defined as unemployed, at least by the official compilers of economic statistics – even though discouraged workers would like to work and do not have jobs. The reason for this omission lies in the definition of 'unemployment' that is used by the US Department of Labour. To be officially unemployed (and, perhaps not incidentally, to collect unemployment benefits), a person has to be out of work *and* actively searching for employment. Since discouraged workers have given up the search for jobs, they are not officially unemployed.

Consider what would happen if the Department of Labour were to change its definition of unemployment to include any out-of-work person who would prefer to have a job, whether or not the person was actively searching for employment. Overnight, the number of 'unemployed' people would increase by one million.[10] Such an instantaneous jump in unemployment would be quite unprecedented, and to those who did not know that the definition of 'unemployed' had been altered, this increase in unemployment would be a signal of dramatically declining economic conditions. The signal would be misleading, though, because no real change in unemployment took place, despite the phenomenal change in measured unemployment, as implicitly unemployed workers are newly counted among the explicitly and officially unemployed.

In the current US economy, whether discouraged workers can be characterized as 'implicitly unemployed' may be largely a matter of semantics. Discouraged workers obviously share many important characteristics with officially unemployed workers. These shared circumstances are less conspicuous in the case of discouraged workers than they are for the explicitly unemployed, since discouraged workers are not getting turned down for jobs or collecting unemployment benefits. It therefore does no injustice, and perhaps is even illuminating, to signal the similarities between discouraged workers and explicitly unemployed workers by applying the term 'implicit unemployment' to discouraged workers. Likewise, in the Russian economy there are many phenomena that bear significant, though somewhat hidden, similarities with other, more widely recognized phenomena. The adjective 'implicit' (or 'repressed') will be used below to describe these aspects of the pre-reform Russian economy, in order to highlight the similarities with their more familiar, explicit (or 'open') siblings, which will emerge during transition to a market economy.

Inflation, private property rights, and monopoly power – like various non-economic features such as the degree of nationalist or religious sentiment – are phenomena that were previously present in Russia largely in a repressed or hidden form. For such phenomena, referring to the pre-reform situation as 'implicit' and the post-reform situation as 'explicit' seems natural. For other pre-reform conditions the appropriateness of the adjective 'implicit' is perhaps less apparent: many of the Russians whom I describe as 'implicitly unemployed' actually have jobs. The usage of the terms 'implicit' or 'repressed' may then grate some sensibilities. But these terms are only shorthand for the notion that, in judging the effects of reform, knowledge of the actual pre-reform conditions is indispensable. And the key to understanding the pre-reform Russian economic system, and hence the characteristics of a successful reform, lies in exposing disguised, 'implicit' elements.

During Russia's transition to a market economy, some implicit economic phenomena such as inflation or unemployment will automatically become explicit – indeed, the process is already well underway. In many cases, as in the parable of the discouraged worker, the transition from an implicit to an explicit form does not significantly alter reality, even as the economic statistics change precipitously.

PARTIAL REFORM

> Semi-effective, semi-actions push the half people back to the half rear
> From 'Half Measures', by Russian poet Yevgeny Yevtushenko[11]

There are still other economic phenomena in Russia that existed in implicit form under central planning, but that do not automatically metamorphose into an explicit form during the transition to a market economy. The old, implicit form of the phenomenon disappears and a new, explicit counterpart must be established. Two such phenomena are the methods of taxation and the social welfare system. Market-oriented reform undermines the implicit versions of these structures. Explicit systems of taxation and social welfare (unemployment benefits, etc.) then have to be specifically created during the transition. Economic reform runs into difficulties when the explicit forms of these systems fail to be created – when reform stops halfway.

Other varieties of partial reform measures also generate problems during a transition to a market economy.[12] Consider, for example, the impact of one type of 'halfway' reform, a selective price liberalization. If the price of milk is controlled by the government and kept low while the price of sour cream is freed, there is likely to be too much sour cream relative to milk. Producers of dairy products who are free to choose their product mix will find that they can do better by producing sour cream, because the high prices make sour cream production more profitable than milk production. Unless dairies are somehow forced to produce milk, shortages of milk may well increase during the partial reform period. Such partial controls can also be counter-productive if the remaining price controls are aimed at reducing inflationary pressure. Not having to spend much money on milk (because it is either unavailable or, if available, sold at a low fixed price), consumers will have more cash available to spend on other goods, causing the price of sour cream to be higher than it would be if all price controls were removed.[13] The milk–sour cream example is not merely a hypothetical scenario; the problems associated with this incomplete reform actually arose in Russia following a partial price liberalization on 2 January, 1992.[14]

Partial reforms create a second barrier to successful transition beyond the additional costs imposed on the reforming economy. This barrier to transition lies in the tendency for the controls on the economy that remain after partial reform to snowball into more and more controls. For example, increasing shortages of price-controlled milk and relatively high prices for sour cream following a partial price liberalization will lead to calls for either price controls on sour cream, or for commands to be given to dairies to increase their production of milk. With low fixed prices on their outputs, dairies become unprofitable. The likely next step is to regulate the prices of inputs used by dairies. But then the producers of the inputs will have to be commanded to sell at the low fixed prices, and the snowballing of controls continues.

Such a cascade of controls helped create Russia's centrally-planned economy in the first place.[15] During the New Economic Policy instituted under Lenin in 1921, most large industries were state-owned and their output prices were fixed, while small-scale economic activity soon became predominately private and was conducted via free markets. With high, free market prices for their inputs but low fixed prices for their outputs, state enterprises were unprofitable. In an attempt to make state enterprises more profitable, the Soviet government extended price controls to the inputs used by these enterprises. A private supplier of inputs then faced the choice of selling the inputs to the state at low prices or selling the inputs on free markets at high prices. Not surprisingly, the sellers preferred to transact on the free markets, leaving state enterprises without adequate supplies. The government then set voluntary quotas on the amount of supplies that private firms were to sell to the state; when there were insufficient volunteers, the quotas were made mandatory. The final result, unforeseen in the early years of the New Economic Policy, was a centrally-planned regime by 1930.

The snowballing of controls is not inevitable. Many other factors led to the Soviet centrally-planned economy. In particular, a single-party monopoly on political power played an important role, as the concerns of those who would be hurt by further economic restrictions were not well represented. Nevertheless, the tendency for price controls to propagate, and then lead to quantity controls, is unmistakable.

Related to the propagation of controls is the notion that, for all of its difficulties, the centrally-planned economic system in the former Soviet

Union was 'internally consistent'. Given that output prices were fixed, it was nearly a requirement that input prices be fixed; otherwise, firms would be unprofitable. But in order to induce sales of inputs at fixed prices, most economic activity had to be state-controlled. A state monopoly on foreign trade (an official Soviet policy) was also necessary. Consider what would have occurred had individuals been allowed to export. Entrepreneurs would have bought up goods that were relatively underpriced (at the fixed prices) in the USSR, and sold them abroad at world prices. While such entrepreneurs would have done well by this trade, the government would have found that the subsidies inherent in its fixed prices were benefiting only such entrepreneurs and the foreign buyers. In essence, it would have amounted to a large wealth giveaway by the government.

The internal consistency of the planning system and the tendency of controls to snowball into more and more controls, together imply that partial reforms can be particularly dangerous. Taking away one element of the old economic structure, such as the state foreign trade monopoly, can create large losses if not accompanied by other reforms, such as price liberalization. Despite an apparently strong desire in Russia for a fully-fledged market economy, the dynamics of partial reforms could lead to a gradual reinstitution of controls. For this reason, and because of the considerable costs generated by incomplete reforms, care must be given to the choice of the transition path, even if the initial conditions are accurately perceived.

PRE-REFORM STATISTICS

Economic statistics can be useful guideposts in locating the starting point for Russian reforms. Appropriately interpreting measures of economic activity is not always straightforward, though, and sometimes it is even difficult to collect accurate measures at the outset. Statistics can be misleading or perverse under any setting: recall the exclusion of discouraged workers from US unemployment statistics. But the difficulties in interpreting statistics tend to be appreciably greater in planned economies with large fixed-price state sectors.

One reason we cannot rely on pre-reform Russian economic statistics is that a large amount of private economic activity took place outside the official sector and was consequently not counted. The parallel in Western economies is traffic in illicit commodities such as narcotics, and transactions conducted surreptitiously for reasons of tax evasion. In Russia, though, such exclusion from official statistics arose to some degree for virtually all private activity.

Furthermore, pre-reform Russian statistics that were dependent on prices (i.e., statistics in value terms) generally used the official fixed state prices, which rendered them largely arbitrary. One hundred roubles worth of steel could just as easily be 200 or 50 roubles worth, if the government chose to double or halve the fixed price of steel. While free prices considerably reduce the scope of this problem in Western market economies, there are some analogues. Consider, for instance, tickets to popular Broadway shows or sporting events. The tickets have an official price, but are often purchased from scalpers at much higher prices. The original sale to the scalper at the official price is captured in Western economic statistics, but the next transaction, from the scalper to the Broadway or sports enthusiast, is not counted, even though the price of that transaction is a better measure of the value of the ticket than the official price. In pre-reform Russia, most consumer goods that were supplied via the official state sector were like scarce tickets in the West, in that their official prices were lower than their actual value on free markets. (Incidentally, this was true of tickets to productions at popular Russian theatres, where the majority of tickets were not sold through the normal box office channels, but rather distributed informally in exchange for scarce goods or services or at higher, black market prices.[16])

Economic statistics that did not incorporate prices, however, were immune to the arbitrariness of the centrally-determined pricing system. Accordingly, official Soviet statistics in terms of physical units, say tons of steel, traditionally were accepted in the West as fairly reliable, even as some problems with the statistics were acknowledged.[17] For example, there were obvious incentives for enterprises to exaggerate their production, because higher production meant higher bonuses for workers and managers. There were gaps in the availability of statistics: a dearth of information on the extensive defence sector comprised the most blatant omission. Nor were the statistics that were provided always easy to interpret. At one point, for example, Soviet statisticians began including sales of used cars in their figures for car sales, without documenting the methodological change.[18] Nevertheless, there was confidence in the general integrity of Soviet physical-unit statistics.

Recently, however, this confidence has been called into question. It now appears that the 'free invention' of statistics was perhaps quite considerable.[19] In fact, it is hard to escape the conclusion that output was grossly exaggerated, given Russian living standards in comparison with the claimed output growth over the years.

One story of falsified production figures demonstrates the scope of the potential distortions in official statistics. In a Soviet scandal of almost breathtaking proportions, the cotton output of the central Asian republic of Uzbekistan was systematically overestimated by hundreds of thousands of tons annually. Payments based on the non-existent output then flowed to Uzbekistan, providing the incentive to engage in such blatant misrepresentation. Official estimates indicate that between 1978 and 1983, the fictitious output came to 4.5 million tons of cotton, or more than twelve per cent of total state cotton purchases.[20] The overlord of the operation, which involved 'practically the whole population of the republic',[21] was the top Communist Party official in Uzbekistan. Soviet journalist Arkady Vaksberg, in relating the story of the scandal, notes that:

a commodity is not a thing, an object, something real, visible and tangible. It is a figure printed on paper, kept in an office in a statistical record. Since one eats bread not numbers, wears clothes not figures, it is possible and logical for the people to be destitute whilst the statistics demonstrate a country of riches and abundance.[22]

Compare this description, drawn from the real-life Soviet Union, with George Orwell's presentation of the fictional country of Oceania in *Nineteen Eighty Four*, where Winston Smith was called on to change, after the fact, the number of boots that had been planned to be produced:[23]

> Statistics were just as much a fantasy in their original version as in their rectified version. A great deal of the time you were expected to make them up out of your head. For example, the Ministry of Plenty's forecast had estimated the output of boots for the quarter at a hundred and forty-five million pairs. The actual output was given as sixty-two millions. Winston, however, in rewriting the forecast, marked the figure down to fifty-seven millions, so as to allow for the usual claim that the quota had been overfilled. In any case, sixty-two millions was no nearer the truth than fifty-seven millions, or than a hundred and forty-five millions. Very likely no boots had been produced at all. Likelier still, nobody knew how many had been produced, much less cared. All one knew was that every quarter astronomical numbers of boots were produced on paper, while perhaps half the population of Oceania went barefoot.

The extent to which official Soviet statistics generally masked the truth was boldly investigated by two Soviet citizens, the journalist Vasiliy Selyunin and the economist Grigoriy Khanin. In their 1987 article (appropriately titled 'The Cunning Figure') in the influential Soviet journal *Novy Mir*, Selyunin and Khanin provided alternative estimates of the growth of national income in the USSR.[24] Official statistics state that Soviet national income increased by a factor of 89 during the 1928–1985 period, while Selyunin and Khanin estimated that income increased by a factor of 6.6. The incredible difference between the estimates arose from a combination of different statistical techniques and 'corrections' made by Khanin to the official statistics. (It is perhaps even more surprising given that exaggerating growth rates requires an increased exaggeration of output *levels* over time, i.e., a constant 20 per cent exaggeration of output would have no effect on calculations of growth rates.[25]) While the analysis of Khanin and Selyunin may have painted too dire a picture – by taking insufficient notice of underground economic activity, for instance – the extent to which official statistics exaggerated Russian achievements was clearly extraordinary.

Even those at the highest levels did not have access to accurate information. Former Soviet leader Nikita Khrushchev noted in his memoirs his own distrust of Soviet statistics:

Having lived under Stalin, I tend to think that the figures for average yield which you read in the press these days reflect wishful thinking rather than reality. ... In other words, Stalin arbitrarily dictated the average yield. Nowadays [Khrushchev tape-recorded his memoirs between 1966 and 1971] it isn't that bad, but I still don't trust our bureau of statistics. I think there remains a tendency among our statisticians to conceal setbacks and tell the leadership what it wants to hear. ... They're clever at hiding the truth.[26]

Mikhail Gorbachev, likewise, had trouble getting reliable economic information, both as a Politburo member and later as General Secretary.[27] The Soviet penchant for secrecy combined with data distortions and limitations to provide a misleading economic view from the political summit. Such a situation would be troubling for economic policy-makers anywhere. But in a centrally-planned system, where all important economic decision making is concentrated at the highest political level, unreliable statistics represent a major disability.[28]

Completely reliable output statistics would not solve the task of correctly gauging the pre-reform Russian economy. The correlation between official economic activity and human welfare was less pronounced in Russia than in Western market economies. For example, if a Western company makes a product that few people want to purchase, the company will go out of business, and the resources used in making the product can then move to more highly-valued tasks. But if a state-owned enterprise in a fixed-price socialist state makes a product with little value, the enterprise need not go out of business. Indeed, increases in the enterprise's output will lead to increases in measured GNP, even if the output is not valuable relative to the inputs used in producing it.

STATISTICS AND REFORM

The catalogue of biases and mis-representations in pre-reform Russian statistics might suggest that economic transition would offer a more accurate statistical picture of the Russian economy. Unfortunately, in many instances the process of economic reform tends to add to the distortion of the statistical image.

The implicit-to-explicit conversion of economic phenomena that accompanies reform is one source of new difficulties in the interpretation of statistics. Inflation, for example, in the pre-reform era, took on its repressed or implicit form, and generally was not captured in official price statistics. With market-oriented reform, inflation becomes explicit, and price level changes are reflected in statistical measures of the price level. The post-reform price indices therefore are more accurate measures of inflation than they were pre-reform. During the transition itself, however, inflation statistics will be particularly misleading. The transformation during economic reform from implicit to explicit inflation will be recorded in statistics as a substantial increase in the price level, even if there is actually no new inflation during reform. More generally, changes in statistical measures during reform may not reflect real changes in conditions, as in the discouraged workers story; rather, the changes simply reflect the shift from implicit to explicit forms of previously-existing economic phenomena.

Reform also relaxes the legal constraints on private economic activity, which therefore blossoms. Nevertheless, such activity often remains undetected by the statistical authorities. Partly this under-counting of private economic activity results from the statistics-gathering resources inherited from the planning era. Under Soviet central planning, Goskomstat, the state statistical agency, was devoted to the collection of statistics on economic activity that was in accordance with the plan. Russian statistical practices are therefore not geared towards counting private economic activity. To effectively collect information in the emerging market environment will require a time-consuming restructuring within Goskomstat – its own mini-perestroika.[29] The transition period may be particularly hard on Russian statistics, as new opportunities in the private sector have drawn leading Russian statisticians away from Goskomstat.

Private activity is also under-counted because individuals and enterprises often prefer to conceal it. (This was true under central planning as well, but the amount of private activity has skyrocketed during reform.) Many conditions give rise to an incentive to hide private economic activity. First, much of it remains, to some extent, illegal. Second, taxes can be evaded by concealing private economic activity. Third, open activity might come to the attention of racketeers or simply envious neighbours.

The use of economic statistics as propaganda has become more complicated during the reform era. Under the Soviet regime, statistical methodology served political tasks.[30] The bias was clearly to paint a pretty picture, and information that reflected badly on the government was suppressed. In some instances this may still be the case, as Western and, in particular, International Monetary Fund support for Russia is conditional on certain economic criteria being met. The chairman of the Russian Central Bank has accused the government of deliberately understating the size of its budget deficit in order to mislead foreign lending institutions, and other accusations of 'two sets of books' have been raised.[31] On the other hand, two deputy prime ministers apparently exaggerated the inflation rate in order to convince the prime minister of the risk of hyperinflation, and the total amount of foreign aid is likely to be an increasing function of the amount of unfavourable economic dispatches from Russia.[32] There are now constituencies for both good and bad economic news.

Discrepancies between economic statistics and economic reality are not limited to centrally-planned economies. Former Prime Minister Andreas Papandreou of Greece once remarked that 'the figures prosper while the people suffer'.[33] This aphorism was generally applicable to pre-reform

Russia: the Uzbekistan cotton statistics being a particularly egregious example. Reform turns this message on its head, however, as statistics begin to capture changes from implicit to explicit forms of economic difficulties, but fail to capture much of the growth of private economic activity.

LIMITS TO UNDERSTANDING

Statistics concerning the Russian economy are often misleading, but this is just one aspect of a more general phenomenon. To an extent well beyond that of Western market economies, the Russian economy is, well, unknowable. First there is the obvious point that the term 'Russian economy' is itself ambiguous. Economic conditions vary widely across Russia, among individuals, enterprises, industries, and regions. While this has always been the case to some extent, the reform process has often multiplied the disparities. State-owned enterprises and localities that have enthusiastically embraced reform are in many instances doing better than their counterparts that have been slower to change. As is common in macroeconomics, a wealth of diversity is lost when speaking of 'the' Russian economy.

But the difficulty with understanding the Russian economy goes beyond the variance that is hidden in aggregate statistics. Almost any sort of information, statistical or otherwise, involves generalizing from individual, anecdotal accounts, as noted by economist Ed Hewett:

> The problem is one of weighting the various anecdotes, and there is no easy solution. Drawing inferences from a mass of anecdotes is a highly subjective enterprise and is not amenable to replication by others. The best one can do is to make prior assumptions (or biases) clear.[34]

My bias, as is probably already clear, is to focus on the informal, unofficial activity in the Russian economy, particularly during the years when the formal activity was prescribed in a central plan.

One reason that the process of aggregating individual bits of information seems more arduous for the Russian economy than elsewhere lies in the unofficial activity itself. Most Russians have developed informal methods for procuring goods or just generally 'beating the system'. Russians are naturally reluctant to discuss their own informal machinations; again, illegality, racketeers, and envy-avoidance all play a role in keeping the unofficial economy under wraps. Another important factor is that informal connections are often valuable only to the extent to which they are not widespread. If I have a good friend who occasionally can secure tickets to the Bolshoi for me, I do not particularly want all my acquaintances to also befriend this person, since then my access will be lessened. Publicity of informal economic relationships may create undesired competition.

For these reasons, Russians themselves may know little about the informal economic behaviour of other Russians. Susan Richards, a Western historian of the USSR, travelled to the Soviet Union four times between 1988 and 1990 and wrote a book about the lives of 'everyday' Russians.[35] Here is her description of this phenomenon:

> The economy that worked was subterranean, amenable neither to description nor, therefore, to reform. It consisted of a series of microscopic cells which, in a parody of revolutionary political tactics, were safe from control or infiltration because each cell knew nothing of the others. Beyond their own lives, or those of their friends, people knew little about how 'the system' worked. It was absurd not because it did not make sense, but because it was unknowable.[36]

The reluctance of Russians to disclose information concerning the reality of their economic lives, combined with the relative isolation of the Soviet period, implied that Western scholars of the Soviet economy faced a daunting task, which they not infrequently compared to archaeology.[37] How could one appraise the economic situation in the Soviet Union given such fragmentary information? One tendency in Western social science was to rely, perhaps too heavily, on almost the only source of information that appeared to be scientific, namely, the official statistics.[38] 'Anecdotal' or 'literary' evidence, such as the thousands of published letters in Soviet newspapers that exposed true local conditions, descriptions in Soviet novels, or firsthand accounts from émigrés, was discounted.[39] The basis for even the CIA's estimates of Soviet GNP was official Soviet statistics.[40]

(I am painting with too broad strokes myself here, in that there was a good deal of Western detective work that scrutinized Soviet statistics carefully, and took account of other sources of information. For many researchers, the Khanin–Selyunin recalculations of Soviet growth were newsworthy only in that they had been published in the Soviet press – similar, and perhaps methodologically superior, statistical work had long been accomplished in the West. My view of the Western consensus on the Soviet economy, however, to the extent a consensus existed, is that it took too little account of informal economic activity and relied too heavily on official statistics. A similar point probably applies to the consensus view of the US economy, but on a reduced scale.)

While the amount of subterranean economic activity remains substantial, the increased openness in Russia is allowing better pictures of 'the' Russian economy to emerge. But the ongoing reform generates many changes that require a continual updating of the picture. And with the pre-reform situation not well understood, the effects of reform are hard to discern, even as the current Russian economy becomes better known.

THE PATH AHEAD

The discussion in this introduction highlights three considerations that are helpful to keep in mind when attempting to understand Russian reform.

First, great care (and numerous grains of salt) should be directed at the interpretation of economic statistics during transition. Second, the interconnections between reform measures and the internal consistency of the pre-reform system render it unwise – even if, to a degree, unavoidable – to assess elements of reform on a piecemeal basis. Third, Russian conditions are so far removed from those in normal market economics that typical Western standards cannot be applied to the impact of reform; thus a fall in industrial production is not necessarily bad, nor is a large increase in measured GNP necessarily good, even though they generally would merit such interpretations in market economies.

Expediting a trip to the market requires (or at least is simplified by) knowing both where you are starting from and where the market is. Surprisingly, the quality of information in Russia on the location of the market is relatively better than the information on the starting point. Implicit economic phenomena and unreliable statistics combine to make delineation of the pre-reform Russian economy quite imprecise. Much of the remainder of this book is devoted to triangulating on the location of the pre-reform Russian economy, and the lessons for reform that can be drawn from an improved understanding of initial conditions in Russia. The next step on this journey is to review market and centrally-planned economies, in theory and practice.

Chapter 1

Markets and plans

The empirical evidence seems to be in: market economies generally out-perform centrally-planned economies in terms of living standards. But why? Could it not just as easily have worked out the other way around? This chapter provides a brief theoretical guide to market and centrally-planned economies which suggests that the answer is 'no': market economies have inherent advantages over centrally-planned economies.

Incidentally, looking at market and centrally-planned economies side by side generates a certain complementarity. Though there is some irony in the proposition, nevertheless it seems to be the case that a good way to understand free markets is to study societies where markets are suppressed – and vice versa. One final note before the tour of the wisdom of Adam Smith and his intellectual descendants begins: the relatively simplistic overview below will tax the patience of the economically sophisticated.

ECON 101

Economics 101 typically starts with a gloomy characterization of a post-Eden world of scarcity. Resources such as land, labour, buildings, and machines, that together can be used to produce goods, are limited. Meanwhile, human desires, if not infinite, at least exceed the current capacity for goods' production. Scarcity of resources implies that more of one good means less of some other good, so it is important to produce those goods that best satisfy human wants. An increase in the production of buggy whips is probably not going to do much to raise US living standards (unless the buggy whips can then be traded to foreign countries in exchange for goods more highly desired by US citizens.) What should be produced?

A question that should be answered along with the 'what to produce' question is 'how should it be produced?'. Various combinations of labour and capital (non-human goods such as machines that are used to produce other goods and are not immediately used up in the process) can be employed in the production of goods. An example familiar to paper pushers concerns copies of documents. Suppose you need thirty copies of a ten-page document. One way to get the thirty copies is the medieval method: put some monks to work with parchment, pens, and ink, and have them transcribe thirty copies. Alternatively, a typewriter and carbon paper (capital goods) can be substituted for some human labour. A photocopier substitutes for even more labour. And photocopiers themselves range in the amount of labour required to produce copies; some (the ones I like) will automatically collate and staple the copies.

In free enterprise market economies, the questions concerning what goods to produce and how to produce them are answered by individuals who respond to the prices in the marketplace. If the price of a good is high, and I can produce it cheaply, I will try to produce it in quantity. If lemonade were to sell for $1 million a cup (while the costs of producing it stay about what they are now, say 50 cents a cup), I would stop writing this chapter and be out on the street selling lemonade. So would you, though, and our competition to attract the occasional thirsty customer would eventually drop the price down to something close to the 50 cents a cup that it costs to make. As for how we would make the lemonade, well, we could probably buy some lemon soda at the grocery store, distil the lemon juice out of the soda, and then combine it with sugar to get lemonade; but, it is probably cheapest (based on those market prices) to procure lemons (from people who are growing them because it is worth it to them given the price of lemons and the alternative uses of their land, labour, and capital) and combine them directly with sugar, water, and cups.

An attractive feature of free prices is that people have incentives to provide what other people are willing to pay a high price for, i.e., what people value highly. There are also good incentives for producing goods in the least costly way. Entrepreneurs have inducement to develop new products that consumers will value, and to find innovative methods to lower production costs. Simultaneously, consumers are motivated to consume less of those goods that require relatively scarce resources to provide, since the prices of those goods will be high.

Another assumption has slipped into the discussion; namely, that people are free to respond to price signals and personally profit or lose by doing so. This 'private enterprise' part of the story is inextricably intertwined with free prices. The social value of goods generally gets reflected in free prices. Private ownership ties individual self-interest – making money – to social benefit, by inducing people to make decisions based on those social values of goods. There is little use, and maybe even disutility, in having either free prices or private enterprise in isolation, without its companion. For this reason, fixed-price regimes commonly find it prudent to restrict private enterprise. As we have already noted, the regulations within centrally-planned economies display a sort of internal consistency.

Two well-known examples help to illustrate the potential incompatibilities of free enterprise with fixed-prices. First, consider the situation of private agriculture in pre-reform Russia. While farming was collectivized into large state-owned farms in the Soviet Union in the 1930s, farmers were still permitted a small individual private plot and the right to own some livestock. These private plots, therefore, presented the possibility for free enterprise. Fixed prices created incentives for farmers to make perverse decisions in feeding their livestock. Price controls on bread meant that it was cheaper than the grain used to make it. Peasants chose to fatten pigs with bread rather than feed grain. Soviet statistics indicated that 10–13 per cent of bread sold in retail trade was fed to livestock. Despite legal penalties, the state could not eliminate such privately profitable activity.

A second example of incompatibility between fixed prices and free enterprise is drawn from the case of partial reform that recently existed in Poland. After private enterprise was allowed to develop, Poland maintained an extremely low price for coal. Despite Poland's cold climate, cheap energy led entrepreneurs to grow tropical flowers in Poland and export them.[41] The chief input into raising tropical flowers is heat, and since heat provided by coal was so inexpensive, growing tropical flowers was profitable for private producers. Simultaneously, the actual costs to society from this activity were quite large. Every tropical flower that Poland produced made Poland a poorer country relative to the situation that would have arisen if the price of coal reflected its actual scarcity. It would have been better for Poland to import tropical flowers than to grow them internally, and to put the coal saved in this fashion to some higher-valued use, such as home heating. Russia did not heed the Polish lesson and kept energy prices highly subsidized while most other prices, and foreign trade, moved towards liberalization in January 1992.[42] One Russian commentator noted in mid-1993 that 'Today a ton of coal is cheaper than an imported Snickers bar.'[43]

Returning to the Econ 101 lecture: By responding to the signals provided by free prices, the Adam Smith effect kicks in. One is 'led by an invisible hand to promote an end which was no part of his intention'.[44] That 'end' is benefit for society. Anarchic, individual action in a competitive market setting generally leads to good social outcomes – the miracle of the market.

This free price paradise is lost in some circumstances, however. There are some situations where decision makers don't face the full benefits or costs of their actions, even when prices are not fixed by the state (i.e., unlike the Polish tropical flowers story). Economists call these situations 'externalities'. One example is the air pollution that often accompanies industrial production. A more mundane example concerns talking in a movie theatre. While those conversing enjoy the benefit of their discussion, the costs – here, noise during the feature film – are borne by those around them. If, fully informed of the costs and benefits of various outcomes, the parties had bargained ahead of time and talkers paid the other theatre-goers a freely negotiated fee for the right to talk (or the others paid the talkers for silence), then the invisible hand argument applies.[45] Otherwise, talkers (or the others) are just being rude. They are imposing costs on other people without the consent of the others. But aside from those externalities that private bargaining is insufficient to control, free prices in competitive markets generally deliver the goods – the right goods, and made the right way.

SOVIET ECON 101

> The statesman who should attempt to direct private people in what manner they ought to employ their capitals would not only load himself with a most unnecessary attention, but assume an authority which could safely be trusted, not only to no single person, but to no council or senate whatever, and which would nowhere be so dangerous as in the hands of a man who had folly and presumption enough to fancy himself fit to exercise it.
>
> Adam Smith[46]

In a free market, private enterprise economy, the what to produce and how to produce questions are answered by individual initiative responding to price signals. What about in a Soviet-type, centrally-planned economy?

Before examining how these questions have been answered in the Soviet case, consider a thought experiment. You are the dictator of the world. No other countries or worlds exist that can serve as your guide. Command your people – what should they produce, and how should they produce it? Think hard, for the welfare of all the inhabitants on your world depends upon your answers.

The task is impenetrable. How can any one person, or any committee, or any Gosplan organization, know what goods should be produced and how they should be produced? At least with current technology, the answer seems to be that they can not. In theory, though certainly not in practice, there might be methods whereby central planners can mimic market pricing to make these decisions.[47] But then they might as well rely on markets, and put the central planners' time to more productive pursuits.

The Soviet Union was fortunate, though, because it did not have to answer the what and how questions de novo. It inherited a certain productive legacy from czarist times. More importantly, it was surrounded by a world that did rely on markets: the hostile capitalist encirclement. Because they continued to measure themselves against the West, Soviet planners could look to Western nations in order to determine what goods to produce and how to produce them. If personal computers were made in the West, then the Soviets would consider making them. If buggy whips were no longer being made in the West, maybe they should be discontinued in the Soviet Union too. But it was tougher to phase-out industries in a society where all industries were state-owned, just as it is hard to close government enterprises in the West.

So the Soviets looked to the West to help them answer the what and how questions of production. One difference between the Soviet Union and the West, however, is that the West is continually re-answering these questions. The Soviets found it much more difficult to innovate, to change the answers to the what and how questions.[48] That is why visitors to Soviet state industrial enterprises might be forgiven for thinking that they have been transported into the past. In a sense, they have been. For many Soviet enterprises, the what and how questions were answered during the industrialization drive in the 1930s, and only marginal changes have taken place since. Even official Soviet sources suggested that 48 per cent of the fixed capital in industrial production in 1989 was obsolete.[49] Two American researchers spent two months at a Moscow rubber goods production enterprise, Rezina, in early 1991, and wrote of their impressions:[50]

> To walk around these production departments is to be transported back to the last century. They are dark and dingy and the noise from the antiquated machinery can be deafening. The technology is so old – some of it harkens back to pre-World War II days – that many of its own employees liken it to an industrial museum.

The reluctance to innovate is partly a result of planning necessity. The overwhelming task of planning almost all of the production of a large country is made easier (or even made possible) by specifying only incremental changes. A declaration that 'This year's plan is last year's output, plus 3%', while rudimentary, is a feasible planning exercise. Reconsidering the what and how to produce questions from scratch, every plan period, is infeasible.

Incremental changes were also in the best interests of managers and workers. Enterprise managers lacked strong incentives to radically upgrade their existing facilities, because the short-term drop in output that such restructuring would entail would mean a loss of bonuses for workers and management, and the future benefits from the upgrading would largely accrue to the state, not the managers.

For these reasons, central planning tends to lock in an existing structure of production. This problem is less acute when the main task facing an economy is to recover production that has been temporarily lost, because of a war, say. But when the task is to increase productive capacity in unknown directions, as opposed to more fully utilize the existing capacity, planning is less successful.[51] While new investment is the area of economic activity over which central planners can exercise the highest degree of control, it is also an area in which planners are particularly poorly situated to make good decisions.

Dictating part of his memoirs in 1969, former Soviet leader Nikita Khrushchev favourably compared Japanese and West German science and technology with that of the Soviet Union:

technological knowledge is so advanced in Japan. Some say West Germany gives them competition. There's another country that was utterly destroyed in the war! These facts force us to look at the way we're organized and to think about the work our scientific research institutes do.

There is apparently some great defect in our system, for we have no fewer engineers, scientists, or mathematicians than West Germany or Japan. Statistics show that the number of scientists and technicians we produce is constantly increasing. How many master's degrees and doctorates do we have? Yet we still need to buy the best things overseas. It makes you think.[52]

The difficulty that central planners have in answering the what to produce question means that in the Russian official economy there are large discrepancies between what people want and what is produced. Also, there are large discrepancies between how a good gets produced and the least-cost method of producing it. A third problem is that citizens' demand for goods does not take into consideration the true costs of supplying those goods – witness the use of bread as animal feed.

Making and consuming the wrong goods in the wrong way – what economists term 'resource misallocations' – are at the heart of the economic difficulties in centrally-planned economies. Resource misallocations caused by fixed prices and state ownership of production have been a leading factor behind the difference in living standards between the economies of the two Germanys, Koreas, and Chinas, and are the main reason for Russia's relatively poor economic performance.

This description of the perils of central planning differs somewhat from conventional wisdom. When Westerners think about the problems of the Russian economy, they typically think of shortages, limited work incentives, wasteful production, and low-quality goods. But probably the main cost engendered by central planning is that the wrong goods are produced.[53] For example, beyond raw materials and (to a degree) military equipment, Soviet goods had trouble finding export markets. Many of the 'goods' found in Soviet state stores were barely recognizable to Westerners, and were often not strongly sought out by Soviet citizens, either. The peculiarities of goods from the former USSR, particularly their tendency to be too large and too heavy, are legion. 'We make the largest portable computers in the world!' brags a Soviet official in one version of a familiar joke.

That the major problem under fixed prices lies in deciding what to produce, as opposed to motivating people to produce efficiently and with high quality standards, was noted by Nobel prize-winning economist Friedrich Hayek in his classic 1944 critique of central planning, *The Road to Serfdom*. In the context of a worker choosing the right occupation, Hayek states:

The problem of adequate incentives which arises here is commonly discussed as if it were a problem mainly of the willingness of people to do their best. But this, although important, is not the whole, nor even the most important, aspect of the problem. It is not merely that if we want people to give their best we must make it worth while for them. What is more important is that if we want to leave them the choice, if they are to be able to judge what they ought to do, they must be given some readily intelligible yardstick by which to measure the social importance of the different occupations. Even with the best will in the world it would be impossible for anyone intelligently to choose between various alternatives if the advantages they offered him stood in no relation to their usefulness to society. To know whether as the result of a change a man ought to leave a trade and an environment which he has come to like, and exchange it for another, it is necessary that the changed relative value of these occupations to society should find expressions in the remunerations they offer.[54]

Central planners in a fixed-price regime face the same difficulties in determining what and how to produce, lacking any 'readily intelligible yardstick' with which to gauge their decisions.

Fortunately, there has always been a free market, a second economy, ready to step in where the resource misallocations in the first economy were most severe. As we will see, Soviet free markets were not the most efficient free markets in the world, but they nevertheless helped to overcome some of the more glaring central-planning mistakes. If Soviet consumers valued very highly a good that the Soviet official economy did not produce, entrepreneurs were there to supplement official activity. Second economy operators could either produce the good themselves, or, despite the official state monopoly on foreign trade, import the good from the West. If a Soviet factory produced a good in a high-cost way, the managers and workers had incentives to informally use a lower-cost production method, sell or trade the unnecessary inputs, and pocket the proceeds.

This discussion indicates the inherent difficulty that central planners have in answering the what to produce and how to produce questions for literally millions of goods. But what did Soviet planners do?

THE MYTH OF THE PLAN[55]

All this makes it perfectly clear that Soviet plans bear not the least resemblance to planning as we generally conceive it. Those plans are not prompted by the slightest intention of establishing a conscious, lucid management of economic life and thus eliminating the elements of anarchy and chaos.

Paul Barton, 'The Myth of Planning in the U.S.S.R.', 1957[56]

Not uncommonly, the Western image of the Soviet centrally-planned economy, at least until recently, was that of a workable, if not exactly a finely-tuned, machine. Economists at Gosplan, the State Planning Committee, trained in the latest mathematical, statistical, and computational techniques, sent orders out of Moscow, resulting in the systematic production and distribution of literally millions of goods. If a steel-making enterprise in Magnitogorsk needed more coal for its coke production, the planners would send the appropriate message to a coal mine in the Donbass, and soon the requisite coal would roll into the Magnitogorsk factory gates. Problems that arose in the system, such as a prevalence of low quality output, could be corrected (or at least improved) through minor administrative changes, such as adding quality control inspectors to state-owned enterprises, and giving the inspectors the power to reject low quality goods – to take just one example of an early Gorbachev-era reform.[57]

The reality of centrally-planned systems tells a markedly different story, however. Planning in practice was about as far removed from machine-like, high-tech precision as could be imagined. As Ed Hewett has written, 'The fact that plans are made and that economic activity then occurs need not mean that the two are closely linked in all, or even many, ways.'[58]

First, machine-like precision in central planning is simply not feasible. Central planners do not have the information to be continually re-assessing what goods would best satisfy consumers, or even what combinations of goods could be produced with the available resources, or even what the available resources are. The result, as noted in the previous section, is that instructions given to enterprises tend to be along the lines of 'produce the same things that you produced last year, only 3% (or 5% or 8%) more'.[59] The production profile within enterprises then tends to get locked in, and over time centrally-planned economies are inclined to fall further and further behind market economies in providing the mix of goods most desired by consumers. Second, even planning in growth rates does not work very well. Some enterprises fail to meet their plan, despite their managers' attempts to ply the underground economy for the needed inputs. But the plan must be fulfilled, and so it generally was in the Soviet Union, often by reducing, after the fact, the enterprise's target – another harkening of *Nineteen Eighty Four*.[60] Together, these two conditions indicate the extent that planning followed production, rather than the other way around.

The planners' relative lack of information regarding productive capabilities implied that plan formation, that three or five or eight per cent growth in output targets, became the object of an intense bargaining game between planners and firms and ministries, what Ed Hewett characterized as 'a ritualized battle for real resources'.[61] Writing in 1952 (based on information concerning the high-Stalin years of 1938–1941), Western economist Joseph Berliner noted that

The firm's output plan depends to a large extent upon what the plant officials have been able to bargain out of 'Moscow', the supply plan hinges upon how much can be haggled out of the functionary in the State Planning Commission, and the financial plan is based upon currying the favour of a minor official in the Commissariat of Finance [endnote omitted].'[62]

The endnote omitted from the previous quote discusses the convergence of senior enterprise officials from all over the USSR on Moscow in the months when a new plan was being finalized, in order to conduct the last round of bargaining. That such officials would not typically arrive in Moscow empty-handed goes without saying.

While existing production tended to become locked in, the central planners had considerable leeway in determining in what areas new investment would occur. Western researcher John Howard Wilhelm suggests that 'affecting the configuration of productivity capacity as it develops over time . . . [is] . . . the only meaningful type of planning' that the Soviets could carry out.[63] Thus the considerable resources devoted to the defence sector and heavy industry in the Soviet Union resulted from continued large investments mandated over the years by state and Communist Party officials.

The major day-to-day activity of Soviet planners was to ensure that the supply of inputs to state-owned enterprises more-or-less balanced the enterprises' demands, consistent with the output plans – a process known as 'material balancing'.[64] Most 'planning,' had little to do with 'what we in the West usually understand by this term, namely, the delineation of economic goals and the selection of strategies and instruments for their realization'.[65] The planners' necessity to ensure an adequate match of resources with plan requirements in turn required a focus on gross output such as tons of steel, while other objectives such as the quality or value of output became marginalized. When shortages developed, planners intervened in order to increase the supply or ration the demand. And since shortages were endemic to the system,[66] material balancing itself was an incredibly complex task. The planners alone could not ensure an equilibrium in the supply and demand for the myriad goods in the economy. Material balancing was only sustainable through the widespread resort to informal and illegal activity on the part of enterprise managers, their ministerial overseers, and local party officials.[67]

The dysfunctions of the planning system were legion. One of the most destructive and pervasive was 'storming', in which an enterprise would produce the bulk of its monthly output in the final few days of the month, in order to fulfil the plan – at least on paper – and thereby earn bonuses for the managers and workers.[68] The workers would then relax at the beginning of the next month – or work at their unofficial, private activities – only to repeat the supercharged production at the end of the month. Enterprises could hardly avoid such behaviour because often they did not receive their inputs until the end of the month, from suppliers that were likewise storming. The system of storming was not only disliked by workers, it also resulted in lower quality output produced at the end of planning periods. Soviet citizens were well aware of the problem, and tried to avoid purchasing major items that were produced at the end of the month or year.[69]

Problems that were identified in the planning system were addressed by marginal changes in the planning mechanism. Nevertheless, the problems remained. Minor adjustments were followed by further adjustments in a seemingly endless series of tinkerings, while the systemic problems such as low quality and waste continued unabated. This process was well described in a 1979 article by Professor Gertrude Schroeder, appropriately entitled 'The Soviet Economy on a Treadmill of "Reforms"'.[70]

Central planning has, since Marx (and earlier), been promoted as a rational alternative to the 'anarchy of the market'. But for sheer anarchy, planning in practice has few peers. As the director of a pharmaceutical enterprise in Chelyabinsk, Russia, told my colleagues and me in 1993, after the collapse of the planned system and the end of storming in his enterprise, 'It is only now that there is no plan that we can actually plan production.'

One of the most instructive lessons concerning the difficulties of central planning is provided by Russian economist S. A. Belanovskii, in an article entitled 'The Army As It Is'.[71] If any part of the Soviet system worked as a well-oiled machine, surely it was the Soviet army, the height of regimentation in a highly regimented society. But the army that Belanovskii describes is harrowing in its lack of formal discipline, particularly in those units that did not serve a high military purpose. The formal system of regulations was augmented, challenged, and in many cases surpassed by an informal caste system, which involved ritualized hazing that in some instances could only be termed torture. (Indeed, rape was a standard part of the hazing for those soldiers – 'snitchers' – who complained to the formal authorities about bad treatment in the informal system.) The weakness in the formal Army regulations that led to this state of affairs, was, according to Belanovskii, an inadequate system of incentives in the formal system – an almost exact (though unstated) parallel with the weakness in the formal economic system. The second factor that contributed to the elevation of the informal incentive system over the formal one in the Soviet military is also familiar in the economic sphere: the lack of a 'useful occupation'. Many soldiers had no important military duties, and were therefore assigned to civilian projects such as building construction. A final parallel between the informal incentive system in the Army and in the economy is the extent to which the official goals of the formal system were, in some circumstances, furthered by the informal system. Thus informal, underground dealing allowed enterprises to obtain the supplies necessary to fulfil their formal plan, and the caste system in the army helped to keep the equipment in militarily-important units in good repair.

Now that centrally-planned economies are largely a thing of the past, the gulf between central planning theory and practice might seem to be mainly of historical interest. But there are compelling contemporary reasons for understanding planning in practice. First, and most obvious, there remain important economies, China in particular, that still rely significantly on central planning. Second, the dynamics of intervention, the snowballing of controls, could bring other economies to widespread central planning, despite no prior intention to embrace this form of organization. Third, the starting point for Russian reforms is determined by the outcome of the planning system and its unofficial, parallel economy. Gauging the effects of reform requires knowledge of the actual pre-reform conditions.

Perhaps most important, though, the lessons that history takes from the experience of Soviet-type economies hinge on understanding the workings of planning in practice. One popular explanation for the collapse of the Soviet Union, for example, is that central planners put a high priority on military production, which therefore received a large share of economic resources. This priority of the armed forces eventually undermined civilian living standards. In some versions of this reasoning, it was the Reagan-era US arms build-up that was the final straw for central planning, since the additional costs needed for the Soviets to keep up were too much for the civilian economy to bear. In a sense, this argument holds that it was the effectiveness of central planning at mobilizing resources in the sectors favoured by the planners that led to its own demise: a Marxian-style contradiction of socialism. The difficulty of this explanation is that it seems to take central planning at face value, and implicitly suggests that a relatively minor adjustment, a diminution in the size of the defence complex, could have prevented the system from failing.[72]

The over-militarization of the Soviet economy may have played a role in the exact timing of the demise of the centrally-planned system. Nevertheless, as the root cause of the systemic failure, a more compelling explanation would focus on the resource misallocations that arise in a fixed-price system, and on the extent to which planning in practice diverged, of necessity, from an idealized version of central planning.

SUFFICIENT REFORMS?

O, reform it altogether.
William Shakespeare, *Hamlet*

Now that market and planned economies have been discussed in more detail, it might make sense to revisit the issue of partial reforms in the transition from plan to market. I have claimed that partial reforms are dangerous, because of the possibility of backsliding towards central planning and the imposition of new costs during transition. But almost all elements of Russian society require substantial change during the transition to a market economy. Not everything can change at once, so reforms cannot help but be both partial and gradual. From this perspective, an argument against partial reform is an argument against any reform.

But all hope is not lost, because not all partial reforms are dangerous. In order to give meaning to the notion of a partial reform, I need to outline what I would view as a sufficiently full reform, one that is capable of avoiding the problems of 'partial' reforms that have already been described. I believe, for reasons discussed throughout this book, that a full reform requires at least four elements, implemented quickly and more-or-less simultaneously: (1) near complete price liberalization; (2) a liberal environment for private economic activity; (3) an explicit social safety net; and (4) an explicit taxation system. Free prices (1) and free enterprise (2) are the cornerstones of any market economy. Explicit social welfare (3) and tax (4) systems must be established in Russia, because the reform process automatically undermines the pre-reform, implicit versions of these institutions. The traditional social safety net consisted in part of low-fixed prices for basic consumer goods in the state sector and full employment policies, both of which are doomed by reform. Taxes were raised in large measure through the administered price system and the claims of the government on the 'profits' of state-owned enterprises. Again, reform severely restricts the functioning of this implicit taxation system.

Of course, there are a host of other reform measures that would be beneficial to the Russian economy. The aim here, however, is to put forth the minimal set of reforms that is required for a fighting chance at a successful transition. Without these four measures, other reforms tend to be much more likely to fail, or to make matters worse: those dangerous partial reforms warned about earlier!

MORE ON THE PATH AHEAD

This chapter has provided a rough picture of market and planned economies. In trying to fix the starting point for Russian reforms, and some mileposts along the way, the next chapter will examine those numerous elements of the Russian economy that have already arrived at the market. For these portions of the Russian economy, the relevant reform question is not 'how to get to the market?', but rather, 'how can the market be made most effective?'.

Chapter 2

Russian market activity

> An international committee of experts charged with compiling a list of conditions that maximize the potential for a large underground economy would invent the Soviet Union.
>
> Western economists Gregory Grossman and Vladimir G. Treml, 1987.[73]

Russia has a market economy. It has had a market economy for decades. All told, private, capitalist-style behaviour accounted for perhaps as much as 25 per cent of all economic activity in the pre-reform USSR.[74] Some of it was even legal.

The legal part of the Soviet market economy was dominated by collective farm (kolkhoz) markets. Farmers who worked on the large state and co-operative farms also were permitted small private plots for growing produce and raising a limited amount of livestock. The output from these private plots provided the legal source for private sales of food on 'collective farm' markets in Soviet cities. Unlike the official state markets, the prices of goods at collective farm markets were more-or-less unregulated. In addition to private farming, some 100,000 Soviet citizens were legally involved in small-scale crafts and trades.[75]

The remainder of the Soviet market economy was technically illegal, and therefore to some degree hidden; hence, the 'underground economy'. Other terms used to describe this activity include 'second economy', 'parallel economy', and 'black markets'.[76] Ignored in official Soviet research or statistics, the second economy was nevertheless a pervasive element of Soviet life. Indeed, it is impossible to precisely delineate the second economy from the official planned economy, so intertwined were they.

In order to fulfil the plan, for example, managers of state-owned enterprises employed *tolkachi* (expediters or 'pushers') who would scour the country in search of needed inputs. Engaged to a large extent in technically illegal activity, Soviet tolkachi were nevertheless tolerated by the regime. The bribing and bartering that formed their stock in trade were required to keep the official economy running. But the market activity went beyond the acquisition of material inputs. It applied as well to labour, and to the disposition of output. Soviet second economy experts Gregory Grossman and Vladimir Treml noted that a 'very common practice, often on the scale of even a whole factory, is the use of a socialist facility by insiders as a facade for a private business'.[77] Private repair of automobiles in ostensibly state-owned garages was a recurrent example within the service sector.

The day-to-day activity within the Soviet official economy was therefore flush with private economic endeavours. Consider the case of a state-owned restaurant. The official version of how the restaurant operated is as follows. The restaurant would receive its inputs (food, equipment) from the state, and hire employees at wages that were state-controlled. It would then sell meals to customers, also at state-controlled prices. If it happened to make a profit (measured in terms of the fixed prices), then, for the most part, it would have to return the profit to the state. To encourage output, however, employees would generally receive a bonus if they served more than the number of meals called for in the restaurant's plan.

In practice, this ideal form of central planning worked much differently, as the earlier section on 'The myth of the plan' might suggest. As noted, the restaurant manager may have had to provide gifts or bribes to ensure that his or her restaurant actually received its needed supplies. Many of the food (and other) inputs were diverted into employees', or their friends', kitchens. There was little incentive to provide high quality meals or good service, and these dimensions of dining out suffered. A well-placed bribe could go a long way towards improving the availability and quality of a diner's meal, however.

The effect of all this informal activity was to turn the official command economy into a quasi-market economy. Bribes, whether paid in cash or given in the form of a favour or a non-monetary gift, lent flexibility to the fixed prices, and helped to equate supply and demand, just as free prices do in market economies. The theft of goods and time from work played a similar role, by adding flexibility to centrally-mandated wage scales.[78]

Market activity likewise thrived more far removed from the official economy. Individual artisans of all sorts operated illegally, either because their activity was prohibited or because they failed to procure the required licence (perhaps to evade taxes). Private seamstresses, handymen, middle-men, professionals such as doctors and teachers: all proliferated in the underground economy, though many of their inputs were obtained, legally or illegally, from the state-owned sector. Moonlighting outside of one's main job was engaged in by more than twenty million Soviet citizens.[79] Private production and sale of alcoholic beverages formed a useful supplement to the pension of many a babushka. Groups of cooperating individuals, from moonlighting private construction crews to full-scale underground factories, also dotted the Soviet economic landscape. The existence of the legal collective farm markets provided a handy outlet for agricultural goods illegally diverted from the state sector.

Any sort of visible, illegal activity that was not aimed at plan fulfilment was likely to require bribes to one or more patrons who could provide protection. Berkeley Professor Gregory Grossman, a pioneer in the study of the Soviet second economy, describes Soviet-era bribery:

> The patron, often some official, grants his permission, or at least his forbearance, and extends some measure of conditional protection. The client pays in cash or kind, and not infrequently buys his way into the particular niche. Indeed, second economy operations of even modest size require multiple and periodic payoffs – to administrative superiors, party functionaries or secretaries, law-enforcement personnel, innumerable inspectors and auditors, and diverse actual or potential blackmailers.[80]

The market economy of the Soviet era was an indispensable part of the overall economy. Consider once again the private agricultural plots. Despite accounting for only three per cent of the cultivated land, it is estimated that private plots traditionally contributed nearly one-third of Soviet agricultural output.[81] Much of this enormous productivity can be attributed to the improved incentives to work hard on private plots as opposed to state farms. Private plot output is magnified, however, by the diversion of state-owned inputs (fodder, fertilizer, tractors) to use on private plots, and by sale of illegally obtained state output on the private markets.

MARKET BEHAVIOUR DURING REFORM

The reform years have brought with them a partial surfacing of pre-existing economic activity, as well as a spurt in new private enterprise, both legal and illegal. Countless individual decisions to conduct private business have expanded enormously the Russian market economy. But the burst in private activity in the late 1980s did not occur simply because Russians suddenly developed a taste for entrepreneurship. Indeed, the extent of pre-reform private economic activity indicated that business acumen was long prevalent. The environment for private enterprise, as opposed to the nature of the Russian people, was what changed. Government economic reform policies since 1987 have played a major role in promoting Russian marketization, by increasing the scope of legal private economic activities and by simultaneously providing a cover for quasi-legal undertakings. Top-down pressure gave a further boost to free enterprise through the official privatization programme begun in 1992.

Mikhail Gorbachev succeeded Konstantin Chernenko as General Secretary of the Communist Party of the Soviet Union in 1985 and initiated a series of economic reforms that came to be known as *perestroika* (restructuring). The promotion of private economic activity was an important aspect of the *perestroika* reforms. In May, 1987, the Law on Individual Labour Activity took effect. This measure greatly enhanced legal private economic opportunities, permitting individuals to work alone or to unite into small groups called 'cooperatives'. Many restrictions remained in place following the Law on Individual Labour Activity, though. First, an individual or co-operative could not hire workers, reflecting the traditional Marxian prohibition against treating labour as a commodity. This meant that all individuals in a cooperative had to be 'owners', and not simply employees. Second, workers were not allowed to leave their state-sector employment in order to join a cooperative. The law was aimed at providing opportunities only for those who were not already in the labour force, such as housewives, pensioners, and students, and for moonlighters.

Restrictions on private activity were further eased in 1988, particularly by the Law on Cooperatives. Hired labour, generally illegal in the pre-perestroika Soviet Union, was permitted, and state enterprise employees could leave their jobs to work in cooperatives. State enterprises (or parts of state enterprises) could themselves become cooperatives, leasing the assets of the pre-existing enterprise. Joint ventures with foreign partners received government imprimatur, and cooperatives were given the right to sell their output at market-determined prices. In essence, cooperatives could operate like capitalist firms. The single remaining legal concession to the 'socialist' nature of cooperatives was a continued prohibition on outside investors. The only people who were supposed to receive income from a cooperative were those who actually worked there.

The cooperative sector mushroomed quickly following the liberalizing legislation. Starting from scratch in mid-1987, by June 1990 some five million Soviet citizens were working in cooperatives.[82] All indications pointed to a tremendous increase in unregistered private economic activity as well.

Following the abortive coup of August 1991, a further liberalization of economic activity took place. Land ownership, stock markets, commodity exchanges, free prices, and many other fixtures of normal market economies became commonplace. The liberalization thus far remains incomplete, and many steps backwards, including onerous licensing requirements and other central and local government restrictions on competitive markets, have been taken.[83] Nevertheless, the scope of the open Russian market economy of 1994 would have amazed a Russian transported forward in time from 1985. One rough estimate indicated that by mid-1994, half of Russian output and employment was in the private sector.[82*]

SPONTANEOUS PRIVATIZATION

The intensified market activity of the Gorbachev–Yeltsin years, like the extent of the pre-reform market economy, has probably received insufficient attention in the West. The reason for this situation is not solely the unavailability of information, though much private activity does evade official statistics. I believe that the main cause, rather, lies in the nature of the change that has led to *de facto* marketization of the Russian economy. It was a change that was not heralded in any government decree, not announced in any Kremlin press conference. Instead, it was brought about by widespread, 'grassroots' activity, whereby people took advantage of a few reform measures to further wrest control of the economy out of the state's hands and into their own pockets. 'Spontaneous privatization' is the name given to this change, and it gave many, if not most, Russian workers a chance to work for quasi-profit-maximizing, quasi-free-enterprise firms, even prior to the official privatization programme. In fact, as noted earlier in this chapter, much of the quasi-market economy was well-established long before the Gorbachev era.

Perhaps the simplest form of spontaneous privatization, common in the late 1980s and early 1990s, is known as the 'privatization of profits'. Under this process, the informal activity that constituted much of the actual working of state-owned enterprises moved completely to the forefront. Consider once again the example of a state-owned restaurant. With the privatization of profits, the restaurant managers and employees began to charge whatever prices the market would bear. The official menu and prices slipped further into meaninglessness. Diners negotiated over the constitution of the meal and the price. The restaurant accepted any inputs that it could acquire through official state channels, because those inputs remained low-priced. But since the suppliers of inputs also spontaneously privatized their enterprises, the restaurant probably had to pay quasi-market prices as well. In short, the restaurant began to operate like any restaurant in capitalist countries, except that the remains of the old state sector had not entirely disintegrated.

The process of spontaneous privatization has been pervasive in Russia. The 'liberal' Russian economist Vitaliy Nayshul' described the result in 1991, prior to official privatization: 'State property de facto is nearly non-existent. Somebody has made a common law claim to every piece of public property, and it would be impossible to take them away without force.'[84]

How were the managers and employees of the restaurant able to assert their common law claim, or to convert their enterprise from the state sector to the free market sector? They may have simply escalated the same illegal behaviour that they informally employed to some degree before. Alternatively, they may have tried to more-or-less legally commandeer the restaurant's assets for their own personal gain.

The more formal route to spontaneous privatization relied upon taking advantage of the legal possibilities that arose through Gorbachev-era reforms. The possibility of starting a cooperative enterprise and the possibility of leasing capital goods from the state provided the main sources of opportunities to spontaneously privatizing establishments.

One quasi-legal route to privatization worked something like this. A state-owned enterprise's employees and managers formed several overlapping cooperatives. Various stages of the state enterprise's production process were then controlled by the members of the cooperative that was established in the corresponding part of the plant. To acquire the legal right to use the state's productive assets, the cooperatives leased the productive equipment from the enterprise. This was far from an 'arm's-length' transaction, however; the people who determined the cost of leasing the equipment were generally the same people doing the leasing.[85] To the extent that higher-ups in the government apparatus who formally oversaw the state-owned enterprise could control the leasing, they were brought into the cooperative as well. Eventually, there existed a crypto-private enterprise, otherwise little different from the state enterprise that preceded it. The incentives to efficiently produce goods consumers actually valued highly were much greater, however, once the enterprise moved into private hands, since the new 'owners" well-being was tied closely to the enterprise's profits.

The account of spontaneous privatization presented above is much oversimplified. There were many other devices for shifting state assets into private hands, beyond the official privatization plan.[86] Some of these involved setting up a private bank and selling newly-created ownership shares of the enterprise to the bank. The owners of the bank, who thereby became de facto stockholders of the enterprise, were typically the managers, employees, and possibly higher level officials of the enterprise.

The details of how spontaneous privatization has been carried out remain obscure, and for good reason. Since the usual routes to spontaneous privatization were at best semi-legal, the participants had an incentive to muddy the waters as much as possible. Consequently, outsiders have frequently been at a loss to discover how privatization took place, and how cooperatives interacted within privatized firms. Recall the American researchers who spent two months at the Moscow rubber goods producer, Rezina, in early 1991. Despite their extraordinary access to the inner sanctum of a Russian state-owned enterprise, the machinations underlying the spontaneous privatization eluded them:

> Try as we might to disentangle the details of this network, we could not. Some cooperatives were empty shells or accounting devices, some were mainly connected to ventures outside Rezina, others were merely fronts for dispensing overtime. Different people gave us different accounts of the system as a whole, and the accounts from the same person might vary from conversation to conversation or even within the same conversation. It seemed that the network was designed, on the one hand, to make it impossible for outsiders to distinguish real from nominal transactions and, on the other hand, to create opportunities for flexible response to the barrage of decrees regulating the operation of cooperatives. The system was meant to remain a mystery.[87]

Glasnost' has not diminished the relevance of Winston Churchill's dictum concerning Russia, at least in the economic sphere: 'a riddle wrapped in a mystery inside an enigma'.

Whether a state-owned firm in Russia was spontaneously or officially privatized during the Gorbachev–Yeltsin years, or whether it remained in state hands, it very likely changed its behaviour in response to market conditions. New products, increased geographical distribution of output, and an unprecedented concern with costs and marketing, have all been among the strategies that enterprises have had to adopt – sometimes quite unwillingly – as market pressures, still limited, have developed. One survey indicated that between mid-1991 and mid-1993, '80% of enterprises had changed their circle of suppliers and customers to some degree or other'.[88]

MORE PRIVATE ACTIVITY

The conversion of existing state enterprises is only one route to privatization. A second route is the development of a private business de novo. Small-scale enterprises have been blooming throughout the former Soviet Union; by mid-1993, prior to most official privatization, some 40 per cent of the Russian non-agricultural work force was employed in the private sector.[89] Cooperative restaurants are one area of private activity. Private construction firms are widespread – they always were, but legality has made them more so.[90] Trade and services in general, undersupplied during the planning regime – in 1988, the USA had 61 retail shops per 10,000 residents, while Russia had only 20 – have been popular sectors for new private activity.[90*] In the industrial city of Perm', with a total workforce of slightly more than 600,000 people, as many as 100–125,000 had become involved in private street vending by mid-1992.[91] Some cooperatives have entered joint ventures with Western companies. Alas, even selling protection services to other private businesses appears to be an expanding industry. In short, there are many free market opportunities being seized upon by Russian entrepreneurs.

In agriculture, the average size of a Russian private plot increased by 80 per cent between 1991 and 1993, to nearly nine-tenths of an acre.[92] Small private agricultural plots farmed by town dwellers ('garden plots') are also common, and have enjoyed enormous recent growth: the amount of land devoted to the private plots of city dwellers doubled in 1991.[93] Official statistics indicate that in 1992, 54 per cent of vegetables and 78 per cent of potatoes were grown on private plots, while the corresponding figures for meat, milk, and eggs were near 40 per cent.[94] Private land 'ownership' is surprisingly common in Russia. In the late 1980s more than half of all Soviet families had access to a parcel of land.[95] This figure increased to nearly 90 per cent of households by mid-1993, when there were 41 million small plots of land in Russia alone (including those for summer cottages – dachas).[96] Included in this figure are more than 250,000 full-sized private farms (as of mid-1993); there were no such farms in the pre-reform period.[97]

COSTS OF DOING BUSINESS

Whether in small business, industry, or agriculture, many Russians are already active in the private sector, and often have been for years. It bears repeating – Russia has a market economy. But not all market economies are created equal, and the Russian version is substantially less efficient than its Western counterparts, even as it is considerably more efficient than the moribund state sector. The reason lies in what economists refer to as 'transactions costs'. The costs of conducting business are high in Russia, primarily because of difficulties with – another favourite phrase for economists – 'property rights'. The major stumbling blocks are uncertainty as to who are the actual owners of property, uncertainty as to what transactions are legal, a wide variety of restrictions that render much private activity clearly illegal, and little hope of state enforcement of private contracts. Together, these obstacles make it very difficult to enter enforceable, legally-binding business agreements.

Imagine that you are a Russian entrepreneur and you wish to start a construction business. You would like to enter an agreement with a timber supplier. If you deal with a state timber enterprise, precisely with whom do you transact? the managers of the enterprise? the Ministry in charge of timber? local government authorities, or the republic government, or (until the demise of the USSR in late 1991) the All-Union government? What happens if you pay a deposit for the timber, and then the enterprise fails to deliver? Is there any legal mechanism whereby you can recover your deposit and other damages arising from the breach? If instead you deal with a private timber producer, can you be sure that it is operating legally? Again, where do you turn in case of a dispute? Furthermore, government regulations concerning private economic activity are changing at a dizzying pace.[98] Today's legal agreement may be illegal or heavily taxed tomorrow, though it is probably impossible to discern even today's laws, regulations, and taxes, which themselves may be contradictory.[99]

All of this uncertainty over who owns what and what transactions are legal exacts a heavy toll on the Russian economy. Consider the ownership uncertainty. A Western analogy may be useful here. Say that you wanted to build a home. What would you do if the only land that was available could be leased for at most one year? It is unlikely under these circumstances that you would build any appreciable home, since after a year the landowner could greatly increase the rent or simply kick you off the land. To be willing to build the house, you would need either to own the land yourself, or to have a very secure long-term lease. But in Russia, the existing 'ownership' of many (if not most) assets amounts to a short-term lease.[100] The government or perhaps some other firm or individual could step in and challenge your ownership claim. Even if the ownership claims were undisputed, though, transactions would still be difficult, since the rights of owners remain unclear. For land, for example, owners generally cannot sell their claim to any prospective buyer at full market value, at least through the end of 1993.

Uncertain property rights and continuing state controls lead to massive corruption, perhaps exceeding that of the pre-reform era, since there is more private activity and even more state officials who might be able to stake a claim. The effect of this widespread corruption on foreign investment in Russia is described by two Western economists, Andrei Shleifer and Robert W. Vishny:

> To invest in a Russian company, a foreigner must bribe every agency involved in foreign investment, including the foreign investment office, the relevant industrial ministry, the finance ministry, the executive branch of the local government, the legislative branch, the central bank, the state property bureau, and so on. The obvious result is that foreigners do not invest in Russia.[101]

With unclear ownership claims, a restricted set of rights accruing to legitimate owners, and little protection offered by contract law, the incentives for even local owners to invest have been relatively paltry.[102] Credit is difficult to come by, since without clear ownership, assets cannot be utilized as collateral. Add to this the complication of trying to contract securely with a legitimate business such as a home builder, and the scope of the difficulties facing potential investors becomes almost overwhelming. Nevertheless, this state of affairs represents a considerable liberalization relative to the pre-reform situation. Then, the impediments to market activity were generally even higher, because most such activity was explicitly illegal.

CONDUCTING BUSINESS IN TRANSITIONAL RUSSIA

The barriers to doing business in Russia are therefore substantial. In most cases they go well beyond the market restrictions and imperfections in developed Western market economies. Nevertheless, the barriers to Russian private enterprise are not insuperable. A lack of legal safeguards does not preclude private business. Alternatives to a state-provided court system with a well-developed body of business law can be devised: they are simply more costly. That is one of the reasons why the Russian market sector, widespread as it is, is much less efficient than the market economies of Western countries. The costs of alternative arrangements to help ensure contractual sanctity are so high that only the most valuable transactions are worth the effort, and those transactions that do pass muster must still bear the high transactions costs.

One mechanism that business people turn to in highly uncertain environments is a reliance on the reputation of their contracting partners. Businesses that develop good reputations are likely to find many other businesses that are willing to transact with them. Enterprises that acquire a bad reputation will lose business. The importance of developing a good reputation may be sufficient to induce a firm to fulfil contractual bargains, even if it could breach without incurring any legal penalties. Reputation effects are so potent that many if not most business deals in the US are not strictly legally binding.[103] The development of personal relationships between business people complements the effectiveness of reputation in enforcing contracts.

Ironically, in the pre-perestroika, Brezhnevian 'period of stagnation', reputation effects among business partners were quite strong. Extra-legal activity in those days generally involved state officials. The trading on state resources under their control was well understood and generally accepted.[104] Long-term relationships could then develop in a stable environment. Furthermore, failures to live up to a bargain could be punished by selective official enforcement of laws against economic crime.[105]

The personal relationships that developed for sub-rosa private economic activity during the Communist regime have been useful in providing the trust that helps to promote exchange in the current, less constrained atmosphere. Ministers and other former government and party officials have moved into the private sector.[106] This move has occurred not only because such officials are well-placed to become owners via spontaneous privatization, but also because they have developed valuable networks of reliable trading partners.

Pre-existing personal relationships have been particularly valuable during the Russian economic transition because other factors have helped to undermine the capacity for reputation concerns to lead to good business behaviour. For reputation to effectively protect contracts, contracting parties must believe that by behaving well in a business deal today, they will get more opportunities in the future. Uncertainty regarding the future government policies toward Russian business is so great, however, that entrepreneurs have little confidence that they will even be allowed to operate in the future. Such uncertainty creates, quite rationally, an interest in short-term profits among Russian entrepreneurs. Given a chance to breach a contract profitably, entrepreneurs might well do so, since the value of a good reputation is likely to be negligible, particularly if close personal ties have not been established. Understanding this, contracting parties avoid deals that are supported only by considerations of reputation.

Even without established reputations or personal connections, there exist avenues to extra-legal contractual protection. They are all used to some extent in the West, but are even more valuable within the legal vacuum in reforming Russia. One such avenue is what economists call 'vertical integration', in which a downstream firm and its upstream supplier merge. If the construction firm cannot trust the timber company, it could buy the timber company – or vice versa. Then both stages of the transaction would be controlled by the same parties, greatly diminishing incentives to cheat. Russian enterprises, even prior to reform, tended to display a much greater degree of vertical integration than their Western counterparts, and not simply as a consequence of central orders. Without recourse to effective alternative forms of contractual protection, Soviet firms found vertical integration a useful means to govern transactions and ensure supplies. In the current environment, vertical integration is again being pursued as a way to organize new business relationships.[107]

Another method that contracting parties use to protect contracts is to take measures that commit the parties to actually carrying out the contract terms. For example, in a loan contract the borrower could put up collateral for the loan. If the lender could actually seize the collateral in the event of default, the borrower would have powerful incentives to repay, and the lender would face little risk in making the loan.[108] Barter exchanges between enterprises, which are quite common in Russia – one estimate indicates that 15 per cent of all inter-enterprise trade in 1991 was conducted via barter[109] – are one way of arranging a transaction to minimize the possibilities for a contracting partner to breach.[110]

The importance of barter as a method to mediate transactions gives firms an incentive to produce a wide array of goods, as this will expand their opportunities for barter.[111] As a result, conglomerates have been forming in Russia. The benefits brought from pre-existing personal relationships have the effect of making the new conglomerates look similar to the old ministry structure – often the same people are in charge. Both barter and the semi-private recreation of conglomerates are often viewed as negative developments in Russia, since they seem to harken back to the planning regime.[112] But in a high uncertainty, high transaction cost environment, barter and conglomerates are generally desirable features, increasing the degree of marketization of the Russian economy.

Without a functioning state legal system, private parties may create their own alternative legal system. Western researcher Kathryn Hendley, for example, documents how 'some Russian enterprise managers are responding to the current crisis by creating internally consistent legal regimes (within their enterprises) that meet their needs'.[113] In some instances, extra-legal systems may take the form of organized crime. Just as citizens receive some benefits for their tax payments to official governments, criminal organizations often offer services in exchange for their 'tax' revenue. Contractual protection, debt collection, a reduction in official interference, or a more stable business environment are benefits that organized crime can provide, at least in some circumstances. The pervasive bribes noted earlier likewise help to grease the skids of private business, though at a high cost.

Thanks to alternatives to court-enforced contracts, business can be conducted in Russia's market economy. And thanks to spontaneous as well as official privatization, productive assets are at the disposal of private Russian citizens, who generally have strong incentives to use those assets profitably. Together, these conditions have kept the Russian economy from collapse, and even ameliorated many of the problems that existed before the Gorbachev-era spurt in private enterprise.

AGRICULTURE

Take the case of agriculture. Throughout the 1990s there have been many reports of potential Russian famine during the wintertime. These fears have prompted calls from both Russian and Western leaders for Western food aid to Russia. Sometimes these calls are for very large amounts of food aid, and to some degree, these calls have been answered.

The agricultural problems that are often cited are not with Russian production, although the drop in grain production recorded in official statistics for 1991 is sometimes seen as a contributing factor. (The official 1992 harvest was considerably better, and 1990 brought a record grain harvest.) Rather the problems are suggested to lie in the harvesting, storage, and distribution system – the food infrastructure, if you will.[114] The food is said to rot in Russian fields and warehouses, without making it to market. In fact, the food-rotting problem may have been severe in the pre-Gorbachev Soviet Union, but de facto privatization and marketization has greatly reduced the scale of the difficulty.

Here is why. Under central planning, the farmers were paid based on their gross output (sometimes biased upwards by the weight of dirt and moisture), whether or not the food ever made it to market. Once the food entered the state distribution network and the farmers were credited with its production, they had no further interest in the crop. A similar story applied to the workers within the distribution system; as long as they were credited for moving so much food, they had little interest in the quality of the product, or whether it ever reached its intended destination. Consequently, food did rot in the field, in warehouses, and in railroad cars and trucks. Official Soviet sources indicated that at least one-third of the agricultural harvest was wasted before it reached the final consumer.[115] The free-price collective farm markets for food, though, made it likely that much of the food that was claimed to have rotted actually found an informal route to the market, just as in the current system.

Now, due to spontaneous privatization, any food that is lying around can be appropriated by someone and sold for private gain at market prices. Some of the nominally state-owned harvest can also be diverted in this fashion. Those who control the food can line their own pockets by ensuring that it gets to market. Ironically, this is particularly true if the reports of Russian food shortages are correct. If supplies are short, food will carry a high price, and people will be especially vigilant not to waste any food at their disposal.

Of course, the reports of Russian food shortages are misleading. The Russian state sector is (and in the past generally has been) experiencing food shortages, because its prices are fixed too low and state-sector suppliers would not keep the profits if there were any, at least prior to spontaneous privatization and price liberalization. But thanks to the legal free market in food, the increased production on private plots, and the large amount of food that has been shifted from the state sector to the private sector, there is not a shortage of food in the Russian economy overall.[116] The shifting of food from the state to the private sector even has public manifestations. Advertisements appeared in Russian newspapers in the fall of 1991 urging peasants to sell their crops at the private Moscow Commodity Exchange, instead of selling it to the state, and at prices ten times those the state would pay.[117] Russian farmers, both on the state-controlled collective farm fields and on the new private farms, are responding to market incentives.[118] This private activity, and not Western food aid, is why there has been no famine in Russia in the 1990s.

The agricultural sector demonstrates not just the amount of private economic activity in Russia, but also the considerable government intervention that limits the possibilities for development of the market economy. Consider some of the conditions in Russian agriculture at the end of 1993. Farmers continued to be compelled to deliver produce to state agencies at low prices. The allocation of farm inputs likewise remained to a large degree within the state sector. Access to credit is particularly important for private farmers, who incur many costs during the planting season but do not see much revenue until the harvest. Nevertheless, loans to farms were also 'monopolized by the Russian Agricultural Bank, which distributed state subsidies and shifted accounts among suppliers and buyers rather than acting as a banking system in the market-economy sense'.[119] Government officials can seize land that they determine is being used 'irrationally,' and over 162,000 hectares had been taken from peasant farmers in this fashion in the first nine months of 1993.[120] Though there has been a good deal of official 'denationalization' and privatization in the countryside – by March 1993, the state generally no longer had official title to the old state and collective farms – extensive government controls like the ones mentioned here continued to act as a brake on the transition to a normal market economy. Indeed, the controls made for a situation where many of the changes in agriculture were primarily cosmetic, and regulation had simply re-instituted the old system of central planning by other means.

CONCLUSIONS

The tradition of private activity within the Russian economy is quite extensive. Recent official and spontaneous reforms, such as de facto privatization and increased private agriculture plots, have greatly increased the scope of free-price, private enterprise activity. High transaction costs substantially hinder, but do not preclude, the workings of the Russian market economy. Here once again is Russian economist Vitaliy Nayshul': 'If one looks at our economy in this way [i.e., focusing on the substantial private activity] it changes one's approach to reform. We don't need to build a market, since a market already exists. We need to develop the existing market.'[121]

How can the Russian government 'develop the existing market'? The key is to lower the transaction costs associated with private economic activity. A more thorough liberalization, the further dismantling of state controls in the economy, is the most important step in lowering transactions costs. In this sense, the Russian economy could greatly benefit from some benign neglect from the government. Other, active measures would also be useful; for example, the development of a workable system of contract law would facilitate private economic activity.

Another lesson for reform that is drawn from a recognition of the extensive pre-existing market activity is less optimistic: the results that can be expected from market-oriented reforms are limited, at least in the short run. The reason, again, is that the most valuable market undertakings are already being carried out in Russia. While important, reducing transactions costs will probably not create a tremendous, rapid improvement in the state of the Russian economy. This negative point is counter-balanced by a positive one, noted in the Introduction and developed in the following chapters: just as many of the gains from a market economy are already being achieved in Russia, many of the costs of a market economy are already being paid. Reform will alter the nature of these costs from implicit to explicit forms, but the total costs need not increase.

THE RUSSIAN ECONOMIC PARADOX

Large-scale spontaneous market activity provides the answer to an old paradox that Westerners generally did not even acknowledge, much less attempt to unravel. The paradox concerned two contradictory images of Russian life, both frequently depicted on Western television and in Western newspapers during the Gorbachev years. The first image was that of Russian street scenes: seemingly well-dressed, well-fed people going about their daily business. One would have had to look hard to distinguish the pictures from those of the populace of any Western European country. The second image was that of state food stores, filled with only one item: empty glass cases.

How did Russian citizens generally dress nicely and get plenty to eat when there was little clothing or food in the state stores? The answer, of course, is that many Russian citizens did not rely extensively on state stores to procure their goods, and virtually all Russian citizens got some of their goods outside of the state sector. (The Western media focus on empty state stores was itself curious, since it could just as easily have provided photos of bustling, well-stocked, legal, and free price food markets that could generally be found just blocks from the empty state stores.) Recall that private plots accounted for approximately one-third of the agricultural products in the pre-reform system. Simultaneously, a good deal of the state-sector production was distributed outside of state stores, either directly through enterprises or through free markets. Thanks to both official and unofficial market activity, the condition of the state stores has not been a reliable indicator of the climate of the Russian economy. The Russian economic paradox was privately resolved.

ORGANIZED CRIME

a good many economic and business principles that operate in the 'upper-world' must, with suitable modification for change in environment, operate in the underworld as well – just as a good many economic principles that operate in an advanced competitive economy operate as well in a socialist or a primitive economy.

Economist Thomas C. Schelling[122]

One of the frequently-lamented results of Russian economic reform has been the emergence of 'the Mafia'. The market economy in Russia is lawless, like the 'Wild West', and organized criminals control the distribution of commodities. The old system was destroyed and the new system was not created to replace it, allowing the Mafia to fill in the power vacuum.

Applying the general method explained in the Introduction to the phenomenon of organized crime provides a rather different perspective. First, organized crime existed in implicit form in pre-reform Russia and is now becoming explicit. Second, the extent to which organized crime continues to prevail in Russia is largely due to the partial nature of the reforms that have been undertaken so far.

Corruption and organized crime have a distinguished history in the pre-reform Soviet economy. While central planning mandated that the production and distribution of goods be largely the state's prerogative, executing the plan required human intervention. Many individuals therefore had effective control over state resources, and they could (illegally) exchange these resources, often via barter, at prices that were essentially market-determined. The examples of trading on control of state resources are well-known and virtually endless. Butchers could sell choice cuts of meat 'through the back door', and nearly all retail clerks could engage in similar activity.[123] Consumers could bribe officials to move to the front of queues for scarce commodities such as automobiles. Tolkachi, the supply expediters employed by state enterprises, used connections and bribes to secure supplies. Even housing, which was constitutionally guaranteed in the USSR to be distributed on the basis of need and with very low rents, nevertheless was allocated in large measure via formal and informal markets.[124]

As we have seen, the old system was one of near total corruption. The 'ring leaders' of this activity were party and state officials. They controlled access to the jobs (enterprise managers, for example) that led in turn to more direct access over goods. Just as important, party officials controlled the judicial system.[125] Bribes thus tended to flow up through the party and state hierarchy. Indeed, the privileges and access to goods and bribes that accompanied important state and party posts were well established, and the term 'mafia' was used freely.[126] Professor Gregory Grossman described the situation this way in 1977:

> At the very least one can deduce that the purchase and sale of positions for large sums of money signifies the profound institutionalization in the Soviet Union of a whole structure of bribery and graft, from the bottom to the top of the pyramid of power; that considerable stability of the structure of power is expected by all concerned; and that very probably there is a close organic connection between political-administrative authority, on the one hand, and a highly developed world of illegal economic activity, on the other.[127]

The systemic corruption in the former USSR thus can be characterized as an implicit form of organized crime, where the organization was provided through the Communist Party power structure. The bribes that flowed up the Communist Party hierarchy formed the tribute, the extortion money, or the informal taxes, that were a necessary part of doing business in the USSR.

Organized crime does not prosper in all environments. Mafias that are in the business of offering protection require a monopoly; otherwise, clients may be subject to competing claims for tribute, and less powerful mafias cannot actually provide protection. Organized crime likewise thrives under conditions where good substitutes for Mafia protection are not available. This is the role that illegality plays. An honest operator of a legitimate business in the US is less vulnerable to extortion because he or she can turn to the police.[129] An operator of an illegal bookmaking service cannot do likewise. The hold that organized crime had on the distribution of liquor in the Prohibition-era US did not survive the legal competition that emerged following the repeal of Prohibition.

Pre-reform Russia presented almost ideal conditions for organized crime. The Communist Party had a legal (and even supra-legal) monopoly on power and the judiciary, and there were few competitors willing to challenge it. Furthermore, virtually all private business was illegal. Bribes could thus be demanded for any private economic activity, and even legal activity within the confines of the plan was not exempt. In many instances, in order to receive timely supplies of sufficiently high quality, state enterprises had to bribe representatives of their suppliers, which were other state enterprises.

Economic reform has, to a degree, undermined both the monopoly and illegality conditions that help to promote organized crime. The expected stability of the power structure, noted by Grossman, unravelled during perestroika. The monopoly on power held by the Communist Power has disappeared. 'Private' protection rackets can now compete, among themselves and with the remnants of the old system, to attempt to gain monopoly rights. This competition is more visible – explicit – than was the stable environment of the pre-reform system. The new competition in racketeering can more accurately be described as an increase in 'disorganized' crime, a breaking down of the old organizing structures, the Communist Party and the central economic plan. Simultaneously, the increased visibility of corruption is further enhanced by the new journalistic freedom.

The extent of Russian economic crime, whether organized or disorganized, is fostered by continuing controls over private enterprise, i.e., by partial reforms. It is virtually impossible for a Russian entrepreneur to operate entirely in accordance with the laws – in fact, the laws are themselves conflicting. While private economic activity remains to some degree illegal, organized crime has an opportunity to exploit business people, as they cannot generally turn to the police. And state officials continue to play a role in organized crime. Russian economist Valeriy Rutgaizer reports on a survey of 542 adults in Kiev, who were asked to choose one of seven 'definitions' (including 'no opinion') of the mafia. 'A criminal network with accomplices in law-enforcement agencies and governmental organizations' was the answer chosen by 80 per cent of the respondents, while no other answer received more than a seven per cent share.[130] The former head of government anti-monopoly efforts in Russia, Valery Chernogorodsky, in comparing Russian with Western corruption, has said 'Corruption encompasses more people at the top [in Russia], not just a few. It goes in all directions, from the bottom to the top of ministries – through bribes – and from the top to the bottom – through power.'[131] State controls have tremendous staying power, owing to the large profits that powerful state officials can glean from them.[132]

Slow movement on the development of contract law also contributes to the prevalence of organize crime in Russia. If the state is unable to enforce private contracts, business people must look elsewhere. Substitutes for state enforcement include barter, collateral, or a reliance on personal connections and reputation. Another alternative, however, is the mafia, and under some conditions, this may be the best of the feasible options. Organized crime can provide the contractual security that business people need to enter into deals in the first place.

During a transition period in which the amount of private economic activity increases sharply – despite a measure of illegality – organized criminal activity can increase. More private economic activity means that there are more potential victims for criminals to extort. Eventually, however, the competition among potential extortionists – the increased difficulty in maintaining a monopoly position – and better methods of defence for private businesses, will reduce the amount of organized crime. The evolution of some protection rackets into Western-style security firms is already apparent in Russia. (It should be kept in mind that in the US, the number of private security guards far exceeds the number of public police officers. Security is a normal, and often substantial, business expense.) With more complete reform, private entrepreneurs will no longer be forced to behave illegally, and thus they will make less attractive mafia clients.

In at least two other respects partial reform has served to promote corruption indirectly. First, to the extent that the remaining regulations and controls make it difficult to create new businesses, the monopoly position of the old system cannot be successfully challenged. For example, the flower market in Moscow is widely rumoured to be controlled by 'the Mafia'.[133] This seems almost impossible, since there are seemingly thousands of small-scale flower sellers throughout Moscow street corners and subway stops. But the flowers are not grown in Moscow; rather, they are grown in more temperate climes, and transported to Moscow. The transportation stage is dominated by lingering monopoly elements of the old command system. By controlling the means of transportation, an organized network can set monopoly-level prices when it sells flowers to individual street corner entrepreneurs, without caring what prices are then charged by the sellers to their customers. (This account is indirectly substantiated by seasonal changes that appear to take place in the Moscow flower markets. Mafia control of the market for flowers is suspected during the winter months; in the summer, flowers can be grown in the Moscow area, undermining the transportation monopoly, and Moscow flower markets appear to be competitive.)

The second route by which partial reforms indirectly foster corruption follows from their deleterious effect on total income in Russia. While the mechanisms by which partial reforms reduce the size of the Russian economic pie will be examined later, the detrimental impact itself will encourage corruption. With low incomes and the impediments that continued state ownership place on the rapid adjustment of wages to market conditions, the temptation to augment one's income by corrupt means increases – particularly in occupations where direct non-monetary compensation is not a large part of income.[134] A traffic policeman in Moscow, in an interview where he claimed that the majority of his fellow workers took bribes, explained his own reasons for doing so[135]: 'You understand, in order not to take bribes you have to earn a normal salary. A salary that enables you to live decently so you don't have to wrack your brain about how you're going to feed your family.' The inertia of the old system ensures that the corruption continues. Even if he wanted to stop taking bribes, a policeman may not be able to refrain from doing so, as his superior will continue to expect a cut.[136]

Inertia contributes to continued corruption in one other respect as well. As corruption became institutionalized, it lost much of its moral taint. Russians are surprisingly tolerant of employee theft, for example. A December 1989 survey indicated that a majority (52 per cent) of respondents did not condemn workplace theft.[137] Sociologist Vladimir Shlapentokh notes a 1983 study showing that 79 per cent of the Moscow workers surveyed refused to condemn pilfering of state property from the workplace.[138]

Nevertheless, Russians are quite apt to believe that the mafia is the cause of their difficult economic conditions.[139] During economic reforms in which the distribution of income is changing rapidly, people who find their relative position slipping – or fear such a slip – are likely to ascribe the relative success of others to nefarious means, and the visibility of corruption suggests an obvious scapegoat. Ethnic hostilities and the perceived ethnic homogeneity of 'mafia' groups may also contribute to such charges. And the perception of extensive organized crime is itself undoubtedly harmful to the Russian economy, as potential entrepreneurs refrain from opening businesses, or limit the scope of their business activities, in order to avoid dealing with 'the Mafia'.

The presence of organized crime is virtually dictated by the continuing illegality that plagues private enterprise, the absence of contract law and the difficulty of privately challenging state monopolies. Further liberalization of economic life will leave less, not more, scope to organized criminals, dependent as they are on government monopoly and the illegality of private economic activity. Organized crime, like its companion government monopoly, will see its sphere of influence dwindling to 'normal' Western levels as reform proceeds.[140] In the meantime, a corrupt market is probably preferable to no market.

Chapter 3

Price liberalization and inflation

TRANSITION ECON 101

Free the Prices!

While not exactly the kind of slogan that is going to inspire crowds, this nostrum is a rallying cry for development and reform economists. There's an old joke that says 'If you laid all the world's economists end-to-end, they wouldn't reach a conclusion.'[141] 'Free the Prices' is one bit of economic wisdom that gives the lie to the jest. Economists differ about when in a reform prices should be liberalized (before or after privatization?), and whether some prices should remain fixed for a while (say, food and gasoline), but within the Western economics fellowship, it is widely believed that almost all prices should be free, somehow, some day.

The theoretical economic argument in favour of free prices is both compelling and now familiar, being the chief narrative of Economics 101. Controlled prices in centrally-planned economies lead to resource misallocations, most particularly, the production of the wrong goods. Such resource misallocations can be partly ameliorated through second economy activity. A more complete solution, however, lies in that most basic of reforms – freeing prices. Then the advantages to individuals of various alternatives would be related, through the invisible hand, to the usefulness of the alternatives to society.

Prices can be freed at a single stroke. All it requires is a government declaration to that effect. (The Russians came close to implementing immediate price freedom on 2 January 1992, as part of the reform measures undertaken by then Deputy Prime Minister Yegor Gaidar.[142]) With complete price freedom, the only other reform that is necessary to secure most of the benefits of free markets is that people be allowed to respond to those prices. There is no sense in freeing prices while constraining the reactions of entrepreneurs and managers to those prices. Like the former Soviet Union's contingent at the 1992 Olympics, free enterprise and free prices are a unified team, split up only at the economy's peril.

If this Transition Econ 101 wisdom is so potent, why are not all economists, politicians, and everyday people in favour of immediately freeing prices? There are two types of reasons. One is concerned with the potential distributional impact. While freeing prices may be a good thing on average, there may be some deserving or politically influential people who are made worse off by the action, and there may be some disreputable people who would benefit greatly from free prices. The other type of objection to freeing prices is the fear of inflation. If prices are free to change, then open inflation – a rise in the prices of goods generally – may occur, and typically does occur in modern market economies. Both of these objections are rendered much less powerful when the alternative of continuing to control prices during a market-oriented reform is examined closely. The thrust of the counter-argument is that the concerns of inflation and distributional impact apply, perhaps with even more force, in the pre-reform, fixed-price setting.

INFLATION, REPRESSED AND OPEN

First, consider the inflation argument from the perspective of a Russian economic policy-maker in the fixed-price regime. In other words, play the economist's game, and assume that you did not know that Russian inflation following price liberalization approached hyper-inflationary levels. (This suspension of knowledge will become more difficult to sustain as you encounter the arguments of the next few sections. If you are impatient for a discussion of the inflation that actually did occur, you may want to skip ahead to the 'Causes of inflation' section.) What should you expect to happen following price liberalization?

The most frequent concern was, in fact, that a massive inflation, perhaps 1000 per cent or more, would immediately follow price freedom. When price controls were lifted, so the story went, Russian citizens would show up at stores, 'waving fistfuls of roubles'.[143] Their subsequent spending spree would result in too many roubles chasing too few goods, rapidly pushing up prices and fuelling inflation.

The logic behind the inflationary scenario starts with the 'rouble over-hang'.[144] The amount of roubles in the hands of the Soviet population grew substantially in the 1980s and early 1990s – much faster than the amount of goods in the state stores. Therefore, with fixed prices in the state stores, the ratio between the public's cash holdings and the total value of goods in the state stores, measured at the fixed prices, rose. Citizens of the former Soviet Union had the ready means to purchase any goods that became available in the state stores at low fixed prices. When goods were available in the low-price state sector, Soviet shoppers would rush to buy them (if only for resale at higher free prices), except for goods that were so undesirable that even at rock bottom prices, no one wanted them. The result of this rush to buy engendered by the ready cash was reduced availability of goods in the state sector, and longer queues when goods were available.

(Incidentally, on a smaller scale, a similar phenomenon sometimes occurs in Western markets. A bagel shop in Durham, North Carolina, for instance, offers free bagels to customers who say 'Happy Birthday' to the clerk on the anniversary of the store's opening. Although I am a regular customer of the store, I have yet to procure a free bagel: the queue on such days usually winds outside of the store, and a person might have to wait half an hour or more for a couple of 'free' bagels.)

Diminished availability of goods in the fixed price sector, and long queues when goods are available, are symptoms of what economists call 'repressed inflation'. It is repressed, instead of US-style open inflation, since the official Soviet prices were fixed. The inflationary concern with price liberalization is that the 'rush to buy' evidenced in the fixed price regime would suddenly get converted into a massive open inflation, with seemingly no limit on the upward path of prices.

The inflation scenario that has just been described has apparently been borne out in the reality of post-price liberalization Russia. Many prices were liberalized, and a galloping inflation ensued. But this appearance is somewhat deceiving. The inflation that Russia experienced after price decontrol is not a direct result of liberalization. Liberalizing prices simply ensured that the inflationary pressures would manifest themselves in an open, as opposed to repressed, manner.

The argument that price liberalization did not create inflation turns, not surprisingly, on the understanding of the relevant prices facing Russian consumers prior to price liberalization. The actual prices for goods were not simply the nominal state prices. In general, Russian consumers were not guaranteed that goods would be available at the nominal state price. Uncertainty in the supply of goods forced consumers to engage in extensive searching, which is itself costly. These high search costs represented additional payments that consumers had to make to purchase goods in the state sector, and should be included when determining the actual prices facing shoppers. Nor was finding a good in the state store the end of the story. Russian consumers, as is well-known, often had to endure long queues to purchase goods. Like searching for goods, waiting is an activity that is costly to shoppers. The costs of waiting in lines should also be considered when judging the pre-reform prices facing Russian shoppers – likewise when judging the prices of 'free' bagels facing Durham breakfast aficionados.

Virtually all goods that were occasionally in state stores were also available on free markets, though at prices that customarily were higher than the nominal prices in the state stores. These free markets included both legal markets, such as the collective farm markets for food, as well as illegal but tolerated black markets. A Russian consumer interested in buying a good decided whether to purchase the good on the free market or in the state sector. If the good was cheaper to purchase in the state sector, when all the non-pecuniary costs of searching and queuing were taken into account, then no one would ever use the free market, and the free market price would fall. Since people shopped in both the state sector and the free markets, on average the free market price reflected the true costs of shopping in the state sector. This is a point worth repeating – free market prices were good indicators of the actual costs of goods facing Russian consumers, even prior to price liberalization. In the free markets, these costs were paid in roubles (or foreign currency); in the state sector, the costs were borne partly in roubles, and partly in time for searching and queuing.

What happens to actual prices when price controls are lifted? The nominal rouble prices in the state sector by and large rise. Simultaneously, though, the costs of queuing and searching nearly disappear. The actual costs of purchasing goods, measured by free market prices, need not increase with market freedom. The official price reform that occurred in the Russian state sector on 2 April 1991, raising state-controlled prices by an average of 60 per cent, bears out this contention. Free market prices did not rise when the nominal prices in the state sector were raised. A similar story applies to the 2 January 1992 partial price liberalization – free market prices did not jump upward on 2 January 1992, despite large increases in the prices charged in state stores.[145] The fear of an immediate inflation accompanying price liberalization was unfounded and unrealized.

The measured rate of inflation in the Russian economy for April 1991 and January 1992 was very high (63.5 per cent and 245 per cent, respectively), reflecting the large increase in state-controlled prices.[146] Nevertheless, the actual costs of acquiring goods did not rise substantially, as witnessed by the relative price stability in free markets. The conventionally-measured rate of inflation is therefore not a good indicator of whether actual prices consumers pay are rising during a market-oriented transition. Price indices are an example of how misleading statistics can be when starting from a centrally-planned system.

ONE-TIME PRICE INCREASES VERSUS CONTINUING INFLATION

Sometimes a distinction is drawn between a one-time price increase and a continuing inflation. If all prices were to double tomorrow in the US, and remain more-or-less constant after that, the episode would be characterized as a one-time price increase. A continuing inflation, on the other hand, consists of an ongoing increase in the price level.

A common suggestion is that price liberalization in a reforming socialist economy consists of a one-time adjustment in the price level. The trick, then, is to prevent the one-time increase from initiating a continuing inflation. The point of the previous section, however, is that price liberalization does not really represent an increase, even a one-time increase, in the price level. Nominal state prices do adjust upwards, but the relevant prices facing consumers do not. Liberalization brings a one-time measured price increase, but not a one-time actual price increase. Still, the admonition to prevent liberalization from launching a continuing inflation remains relevant, regardless of the view taken towards the initial price liberalization.

COSTS OF OPEN INFLATION

The inflationary argument against price liberalization (or perhaps the one-time price increase argument against price liberalization) might still be compelling if the costs of pre-reform repressed inflation are lower than the costs of open inflation. But, as I hope to demonstrate, the opposite case is more likely, particularly when the amount of inflation is substantial: repressed inflation is more costly than open inflation.

What are the costs of open, Western-style inflation? Perhaps surprisingly, it is not easy to identify social costs resulting from open inflation. Here is why. Imagine you wake up tomorrow, and find that all prices in the economy have gone up by a factor of ten. Simultaneously, though, your earnings increase by the same factor. The currency that was in your pocket miraculously has a face value ten times what it was yesterday. All of your assets (and liabilities) are worth ten times as much – your car, your house, your savings account, your credit card payments, your pension, your insurance policy. What is the net result, in terms of your budget, of this virtually unprecedented inflation of 1000 per cent in one night? Precisely nothing. You can still afford the new car that you were planning to buy. Paperback books still cost about the same as movies, though the books are still better. You still make less money than your spouse. Nothing has changed, except the price level is ten times higher.

Of course, inflation does not raise the prices of everything by the same percentage, and this is where some of the difficulties enter. First, the face value on currency has an unfortunate tendency to remain unchanged even as prices rise, so inflation undermines the value of cash. The value of savings in banks, to the extent that the interest paid does not keep track with inflation, is also prone to dwindle during inflationary periods. Savers might therefore not be very pleased by inflation. The bank is a little more pleased, because it was able to use the savings when they were worth more, and when depositors withdraw money, the bank can pay out cheaper dollars. Because all prices and values do not rise by the same percentage, inflation redistributes wealth; in the example given, it redistributed some savers' wealth to the bank. The savings scenario is one example of a common redistribution brought about by inflation, that from lenders to borrowers. If loans are not indexed, i.e., the amount to be repaid is not multiplied upwards by the inflation rate, borrowers get to pay back their loans with less valuable dollars. So, the bank won't be all that pleased with inflation, even if it does gain from savings accounts, because it loses out on all of its outstanding, non-indexed loans.[147]

Because of such wealth redistributions, people will be reluctant to hold cash if they expect inflation to be high in the future. They will, rather, rapidly convert their cash into goods: both consumer goods and assets that will be expected to rise in price as the price level rises, such as stocks, gold, jewellery, and art. Alternatively, they may convert their domestic currency into foreign currencies that are not expected to suffer from high inflation. Furthermore, people will only loan money (or enter into other long-term commitments) if the agreement is indexed to the future inflation rate. (The indexing could be implicit, i.e., the interest rate charged could include a premium for expected future inflation.)

While one individual can unload cash by buying goods, the cash must go to someone else, so society as a whole will still have the same amount of cash. If the person from whom I buy jewellery is also afraid of future inflation, she will try to quickly convert her new cash holdings into some other good. This continual process of attempting to unload cash because of fears of future inflation will result in a 'run' on goods, and the run itself will cause prices to rise. The widespread expectation of future inflation results in future inflation, just as the expectation of a shortage of toilet paper will cause people to quickly stock up on toilet paper, perhaps creating (at least in the short run) the feared shortage. Extensive fears of inflation are well-grounded, because of the self-fulfilling nature of such fears.

The story above suggests another cost of inflation, namely, having to think about it. In a high-inflation environment, people have to continually evaluate how best to shield themselves from losing wealth via inflationary redistribution. This may result in minor changes such as more frequent trips to the bank to minimize cash held in hand (assuming the bank interest partially compensates for the inflation), or in major changes such as a complete abandonment of the local currency in favour of either foreign currencies or barter transactions.[148] Greater concern by individuals over matters financial then translates into more financial services firms; more of society's labour and capital are devoted to financial management under conditions of high inflation. Perhaps, as a famous economist once said of monopoly profits, the best feature of a non-inflationary environment is a quiet life.[149]

There is yet another element of a quiet life that inflation undermines. Consider again the story of the overnight rise in all prices, wages, and values by a factor of ten. The fact that nothing changes under these circumstances, other than the price level, indicates that the level of prices is not important for decision making. What is important, rather, is the relative price of goods, the price of a movie relative to the price of a paperback. Candy bars once cost a quarter, and now they cost 50 cents, but I still eat about the same number of candy bars, since the price of candy bars relative to other goods has remained roughly the same. If no other prices (or my income) had changed, but the price of candy bars increased by a factor of two, then I would eat more ice cream and fewer candy bars. In a low inflationary environment, when I walk into the store and see that the price of candy bars has increased significantly, I can be fairly sure that the price of candy bars relative to ice cream has gone up, since the general price level is stable. It is then easy to process the information concerning the increased relative price of candy bars, and appropriately adjust my consumption of ice cream and candy bars. In a situation of high and variable inflation, though, when I see that the price of candy bars has gone up, I do not know whether that increase reflects a general price rise, or whether the relative price of candy bars has indeed risen. I have to check other prices, such as those for ice cream, other food products, and even my earnings, to determine to what extent the increased nominal price for candy bars represents a relative increase. Inflation therefore undermines, to some degree, the information contained in price changes.[150] The information is still there, but it requires more effort to ferret out and process. Lives are less quiet.

The variability of inflation rates and the different timing of price increases among goods and services is the source of another cost that can be attributed to open inflation. As Western economist Rudiger Dornbusch has noted, 'An environment of high and unstable inflation deters productive economic activity. . . . Spurious gains and losses related to the vagaries of inflation rather than to effort and productivity become the rule.'[151] Why bother to work hard when the return you receive depends more on something outside your control – the 'vagaries of inflation' – than on your labour input? Investment, then, can be undermined by persistent inflation, hindering long-run economic growth.[152]

There is one more important cost associated with open inflation in a market economy, and that is the cost of reversing the inflationary process. Nothing in inflation is more unbecoming than the leaving it. Substantial reductions in inflation in market economies are generally accompanied by a recession. The costs of recessions, with their reductions in output and their increased unemployment, are quite high. It is estimated that the cost of a reduction in the US inflation rate of one per cent requires a four per cent reduction in one year's output.[153] For a meagre one per cent reduction in the inflation rate, our country, by this calculation, must pay a sum that is currently equal to nearly $230 billion.

COSTS OF REPRESSED INFLATION

In contrast to open inflation, repressed inflation takes various forms, all of which were present in the pre-reform Russian economy. These forms include: (1) lessened availability of goods in the state (fixed-price) sector, (2) longer queues when goods are available in the state stores; (3) deterioration in the quality of state-sector goods; (4) disappearance of low-priced varieties of the output assortment in the state stores; and (5) higher prices (i.e., open inflation) in the parallel, free markets. Lowering the quality of a good while maintaining the same fixed price (repressed inflation (3)) represents a hidden price increase. Getting rid of low-price varieties (4), for example, by representing a product that is only marginally changed as an 'improvement' and therefore deserving of a higher fixed price, is another form of hidden price increase. Along with the open inflation in the free markets (5), these varieties of hidden price rises are not uncommon in Western market economies.

Repressed inflation is costly. Lessened availability of goods in the state sector means that the time and effort devoted to search for state sector goods increases. Finding goods in the Russian state sector, in fact, became an increasingly difficult task during perestroika. 'By October 1990, of the 115 consumer goods that the State Committee on Statistics (Goskomstat) follows, not one was still freely available.'[154] Once state sector goods are located, the time spent waiting in queues to purchase them expands with an increase in repressed inflation. A large amount of repressed inflation results in almost mind-boggling shopping costs. An unofficial Soviet source estimated that, on average, 25 per cent of the waking time of every Soviet adult was spent in queues.[155] Repressed inflation in the state sector therefore results in an enormous waste of time, as searching and queuing costs rise. The simultaneous open inflation in the free market sector of centrally-planned economies has costs similar to the costs of open inflation in market economies discussed above. The incentive to get rid of currency by shifting into goods and assets, a characteristic of open inflation, also occurs under repressed inflation. Not only does currency lose its value as free market prices rise, but the longer queues and dwindling availability in the state sector induce consumers to buy as large a quantity as possible when they finally get the opportunity to make a state-sector purchase. While the incentive to buy in bulk is a feature of the economy whenever state-sector prices are fixed below market-clearing levels, it becomes more prominent as repressed inflation increases the differential between state and free market prices. Inventories move out of state warehouses and retail outlets into private homes and apartments. A frequently-cited paradox of the Russian economy was that the stores were empty but refrigerators were filled.

One additional feature of repressed inflation worth noting is the increase in corruption that accompanies it. As the fixed prices in the state stores fall further and further behind prices in the free market sector, the incentives for individuals to divert goods from the state to the free market sector increase. Misappropriation of state goods and assets – a form of spontaneous privatization – increases in situations of continuing repressed inflation.

The existence of channels to evade state price controls has some interesting implications for the costs of repressed inflation associated with the time wasted on searching and queuing for goods. Some goods such as cigarettes, meat, clothing, and most other everyday consumer goods, can be fairly easily, if illegally, diverted into the free-price sector. Other goods are more difficult to divert. It is not easy, for example, to resell electricity supplied to your home, even if the electricity would command a high price in a free market. (Electricity could be implicitly resold, though, through the production and sale of goods produced using the cheap electricity, à la energy prices and Polish tropical flowers.) Nor can many services, such as haircuts, be resold, though perhaps the providers of services can spontaneously privatize.

As repressed inflation becomes severe, two competing effects emerge. In the markets for goods where diversion is not extremely costly, more and more diversion will occur, until the state sector becomes largely irrelevant.[156] In these markets, the 'time' costs of repressed inflation are shaped like the Gateway Arch in St. Louis, when plotted against the degree of repressed inflation. Low levels of repressed inflation are not that costly (one end of the arch) because the queues are short. Moderate levels of repressed inflation become quite costly (the middle of the arch) because of the long queues and search costs imposed on shoppers. High levels of repressed inflation do not carry high time costs, however (the other end of the arch). At high levels of repressed inflation, the goods disappear from the state sector, so the queues also disappear, and the repressed inflation is informally converted into open inflation. Of course, the costs of diverting these goods out of the state sector must also be borne. These costs are not inconsequential, else the diversion would have occurred even at low levels of repressed inflation.[157]

For goods that cannot easily be diverted out of the state sector, however, the situation is different. Higher levels of repressed inflation impose higher and higher costs in terms of the misallocation of resources. People continue to use electricity as if the costs were, say, one rouble per kilowatt hour (the fixed nominal price), when the actual costs are, say, 100 roubles per KWH. The state subsidy that is required for the electric utility to remain operating continues to increase as repressed inflation increases. While the information carried by relative prices in a market economy is a bit noisier with open inflation than with a stable price level, at least the information is there. With repressed inflation, the official relative prices cannot adjust at all, and resources become increasingly misallocated.

INFLATION COSTS AND PRICE LIBERALIZATION

Price liberalization, i.e., freeing state sector prices (as opposed to simply raising their fixed levels), converts repressed inflation into open inflation. Will such a conversion increase the social costs of inflation? The 'flight from domestic currency' is similar under both regimes. The unquiet life, the necessity to think about strategies to best shield oneself from inflation, and the difficulties in assessing relative prices, are likewise similar in situations of repressed and open inflation. The major differences between these two types of inflation, in terms of net social cost, are the time and other resources wasted under repressed inflation. A conversion from repressed to open inflation frees up most of the hours spent in an effort to procure consumer goods. This time can then be put to other productive uses, which include remunerative employment as well as relaxation with friends or family. A switch from repressed to open inflation also reduces the misallocation of resources endemic to fixed price regimes. Putting aside potential effects on the distribution of income, an economy is better off with open inflation than with the equivalent amount of repressed inflation, at least when the rate of inflation is moderate to high.

DISTRIBUTIONAL IMPACTS

While the argument above suggests that society as a whole is better off with open rather than repressed inflation, some (and perhaps even most) individuals may be better off in a regime of repressed inflation than they would be in a regime of open inflation. In the pre-reform Russian state sector, the full price of a consumer good was paid partly in roubles and partly in time spent searching and queuing for goods. Under free prices, almost the entire cost of goods is paid in roubles. People with few roubles but with a good deal of time are therefore likely to be better off (at least in the short run) with fixed prices than they would be with free prices. Given the enormous movement away from the state sector that occurs at high levels of repressed inflation, and given that those who choose to wait in state sector queues have the lowest-valued alternative uses of their time, possibly even a majority of the remaining state store shoppers may find that they are temporarily made worse off by a movement to market prices.

For consumer goods that can be easily diverted into free markets, the distributional impact of moving from repressed to open inflation is less pronounced the higher the rate of repressed inflation. Perhaps this is why the much feared social unrest that was predicted to follow price liberalization never took place in Russia, following the 2 January 1992 price liberalization. In fact, the popularity of President Boris Yeltsin's economic programme rose after the price reform.[158] Repressed inflation had reached such proportions, and goods were so widely unavailable in the state shops, that relatively few people actually lost in the conversion to open inflation, at least in the realm of consumer goods. Simultaneously, the large resource misallocation costs that occur for those goods that cannot be easily diverted are such an obvious hindrance to economic growth that popular support for price freedom increases. It was claimed at the beginning of this chapter that the slogan 'Free the Prices' was not likely to inspire crowds. But in late 1991 there were demonstrations in Moscow by supporters of radical reform who favoured price liberalization.

Still, price liberalization hurts some people. While it is impossible to know precisely who will be hurt by price liberalization, some groups are more likely to suffer than others.[159] People with low monetary incomes, those without access to consumer goods through channels other than retail shops, and those who had a relatively large amount of time available for state-sector shopping, were liable to be hurt by the move to free prices. Retirees, known as 'pensioners' in Russia, were particularly likely to exhibit these characteristics. (Individuals who were able to make large profits by diverting state sector goods to the free market also benefited from repressed inflation.) Low official state sector prices therefore served as a safety net, albeit a frustrating one in light of the searching and queuing costs, for those with low monetary incomes – an implicit welfare system. The conversion to open inflation will leave these people in dire circumstances, unless this implicit welfare system is replaced with an explicit system. As noted in the introduction, moving from implicit to explicit inflation requires a movement from an implicit to explicit welfare system, if the poorer and most vulnerable members of society are to see their living standards protected.

ALTERNATIVES TO PRICE LIBERALIZATION

Repressed inflation occurs when the fixed state sector prices fall ever further behind market-clearing levels. In these circumstances, the demand for goods by consumers (measured at the fixed prices) is growing faster than the supply, creating shortages in the state sector. Price liberalization, the elimination of price controls, almost immediately ends the bulk of repressed inflation by replacing it with its open sibling. State-sector nominal prices increase until demands and supplies balance. The movement to free prices is a necessity in nurturing a productive and above-ground market economy, and the Russians and Eastern Europeans have indeed largely embraced price liberalization. But there are strategies other than price liberalization that can be employed to reduce repressed inflation, and the Soviet government tried at least three of them in 1991.

One obvious method of reducing repressed inflation is to increase the supply of goods, as opposed to decreasing the demand. Not surprisingly, in the Soviet Union there was continuous pressure on workers and enterprises to increase output. Exhortations to accelerate production, which were once able to motivate dedicated Communists to tremendous efforts, had with time lost most of their impact. (Incidentally, Stalin noted that the pressure to produce brought about by repressed inflation had its advantages: 'The increase of mass consumption [purchasing power] constantly outstrips the growth of production and pushes it forward.'[160]) Without material rewards for doing so, or punishment for failure to do so, workers had little incentive to increase output. Material incentives, in the form of paying workers more money for greater output, were also insufficient, since without corresponding increases in the supply of consumer goods, the higher wages simply fuelled repressed inflation. Furthermore, increased output is not always good, if the output that is being produced is not particularly valuable. Thus, the opportunities to battle repressed inflation under the planning system through increased state sector production were fairly limited by the time of the Gorbachev era. The eventual emphasis on price liberalization and privatization in Russian reform is partly explained by the dearth of palatable alternatives.

Two other strategies adopted by the Soviet government in 1991 to battle repressed inflation focused on the demand for goods in the state sector. One strategy involved raising the state-sector prices, and the second strategy entailed an effort to reduce the level of market-clearing prices.

The Soviet government raised (but did not liberalize) the fixed prices in the state shops by an average of 60 per cent on 2 April 1991. Simultaneously, savings accounts, pensions, student stipends, and other nominal accounts were indexed upwards to partially compensate for the higher prices.[161] For example, savings account balances were increased by 40 per cent.[162] This reform was somewhat successful in reducing repressed inflation. Queues in the state shops were fewer and shorter, the availability of goods increased, and there were many complaints about high prices. Continued inflation (brought about by factors discussed later in this chapter), however, undermined these temporary gains in the battle against repressed inflation, and by the fall of 1991 the condition of the state shops was as bad as it was prior to the 2 April price reform.

The controlled price rise of April 1991 was actually the second reform made by the Soviet government that year attempting to reduce the amount of repressed inflation. The earlier effort was aimed at lowering the level of market-clearing prices by taking purchasing power out of the hands of Soviet citizens. In January 1991, a monetary reform sought to withdraw from circulation all 50 and 100 rouble notes. (These were the highest denominations at the time.) Individuals who had more than a small number of these bills had to verify that their currency was legally obtained in order to exchange it for other denominations of roubles. Since many black marketeers were suspected of having high rouble balances that were illegally earned, there were hopes that this reform would eliminate some 40 billion roubles from circulation. The monetary confiscation was an abject failure, however. Only seven billion roubles were collected (about one per cent of the existing money stock), and what little faith there had been in the rouble was undermined.[163] And as with the 2 April 1991 price rise, even had the monetary confiscation been more successful, the achievement would have been short-lived, as the continual printing of roubles throughout 1991 guaranteed further inflation.[164]

COMPARING STRATEGIES TO COMBAT REPRESSED INFLATION

Reducing repressed inflation by controlled price increases or monetary reforms shares one desirable feature with price liberalization. All of these reforms tend to reduce the demand for goods. Price liberalization and controlled price rises reduce demand simply because nominal state sector prices are higher. A well-designed and implemented monetary reform (unlike the Soviet attempt at currency confiscation) reduces demand because with fewer roubles and the same amount of goods, each of the existing roubles is more valuable. With each rouble worth more, the old fixed prices appear more expensive. (An important qualifying point is that the monetary reform must be viewed as a one-time adjustment, lest people think that the government will confiscate their currency again in the future, reducing the incentive to hold the currency.)

Despite the similar impact on the demand for goods, in other respects price liberalization is preferable to price or monetary reform. Controlled increases in prices do not allow relative prices to adjust, so resources are still misallocated as people respond to the economically-meaningless fixed relative prices. State-owned enterprises, to the extent that their behaviour remains centrally-controlled, may not even be able to respond to the price changes at all. Continuing price controls imply that desirable future changes in the answers to the 'what goods to produce' question will not be forthcoming. The higher prices that result from price or monetary reform do reduce demand, but there is little supply response, and what response there is may not be beneficial, since relative prices remain inappropriate. Alternatively, price liberalization coupled with free enterprise provides strong incentives for producers to respond to the higher prices in socially-valuable ways.

One interesting comparison between price liberalization and other price reforms is with respect to the distributional impact. Presumably, raising state-controlled prices on 2 April 1991 harmed the same people who were later harmed by the 2 January 1992 partial price liberalization – primarily those who had relatively more time than roubles.[165] Alternatively, the distributional impacts of the January 1991 monetary confiscation were quite arbitrary. While ostensibly aimed at black marketeers and shady foreigners who allegedly (and nonsensically) had spirited hoards of roubles abroad, those who were harmed were likely to be just average citizens who, through thrift and hard work, had managed to garner some savings. The black marketeers had probably diversified into jewellery, art, foreign currency, etc., long before the 50 and 100 rouble note confiscation. At the Rezina plant in Moscow, American researchers Michael Burawoy and Kathryn Hendley noted that 'For three days, the enterprise almost came to a standstill while everyone worried about how they were going to change their money.'[166] The two eventually useless 1991 reforms aimed at combating repressed inflation without price liberalization were not exempt from generating distributional changes, and yet they were implemented. Arguments against price liberalization based on its potentially adverse distributional impacts were therefore somewhat undermined in Russia. The Soviet government had already demonstrated its willingness to impose distributional costs in hopeless reform attempts.

It is far from obvious that price liberalization is any more unpopular than the alternative methods of combating repressed inflation. The prolonged Soviet experience with fixed prices conditioned Russians to believe that nominal state-sector prices were simply decided by the government, because, of course, they were. High prices, then, were perceived as being due to bad government decisions. When the price of a good rises in the West, people do not usually blame the government.[167] But in the Soviet Union, people did, and the government was so fearful of this blame that it generally avoided increasing the prices of important consumer goods.[168] A reform plan announced in May of 1990 by then Soviet Prime Minister Nikolai Ryzhkov proposed future increases in the price of bread. The plan was quickly scuttled due to the hoarding and popular discontent that it prompted. Without the supply response and improved resource allocation that price liberalization offers, the demand reduction that accompanies administered price rises has limited popular appeal. Swedish Sovietologist Anders Åslund quotes a prominent Soviet journalist: 'An increase in prices has never led to anything good.'[169] While some people may rally behind a 'Free the Prices' banner, 'Raise the Prices' is unlikely to attract comparable support.

The perception that higher prices are simply a result of bad government policy poses a problem for price liberalization as well, since the first obvious effect of price liberalization is a large increase in most state-sector nominal prices. In the city of Barnaul in Siberia, President Yeltsin felt compelled to explain to shoppers who were distressed by higher prices a few months after the price liberalization, 'As for the prices – Moscow does not dictate them any more. It is the market price.'[170] A well-implemented price liberalization should highlight this message – before the liberalization. The message may carry more weight if liberalization is viewed by the populace as a dramatic break with the past, as was the case in the Polish 'big bang' of 1 January 1990. Government responsibility for prices can then be relegated, in the minds of consumers, to the dustbin of history, a feature of the 'old system'. Nevertheless, the Soviet administered price rise of 2 April 1991 and the Russian partial price liberalization of 2 January 1992, were not met with widespread protests. As noted, this suggests that the pre-reform situation had itself become intolerable, and that some of the benefits of price liberalization, such as the ending of queues and the return of goods to the shops, were themselves advantageous enough to limit popular discontent.

CAUSES OF INFLATION

If inflation, either open or repressed, is so bad, why is it so common? In a market economy, continuing inflation is fuelled by government monetary policy.[171] In attempting to reduce unemployment and keep interest rates low, the government may increase the money supply so quickly that inflation eventually results. But a short-term economic stimulus is indeed likely. So one cause of inflation is government monetary policies that, consciously or not, trade off perceived short-term gains for long-run inflation. There is also a pro-inflation constituency. The redistributions created by inflation imply that many individuals, such as borrowers, may benefit from an unanticipated inflation. As a large borrower, the government may itself have an additional incentive to inflate, in order to reduce the real value of its loan repayments.

The monetary policies that lead to inflation can be artefacts of a government's fiscal policy. Governments require resources in order to operate. To gain control over resources, the government in a market economy has three basic weapons – other than direct confiscation – at its disposal. First, it can collect taxes from private citizens.[172] Second, it can borrow money from the public (including foreigners) through the issue and sale of government bonds. (To pay back the money in the future, the government can again resort to one of the three methods of gaining control over resources.) Third, the government can print new money, and spend the money on goods from the private sector. This printing of money will allow the government to gain the resources, and the loss of resources coupled with the increased cash held by the private sector results in inflation. The money that people hold will be worth less as the government prints new money for its own purposes. This sort of inflation is an implicit tax, and it may be a particularly attractive tax from a government's point of view, in that it does not require the passage of a tax bill in order to take effect.[173]

If a government collects enough money from explicit tax revenues to cover its expenditures, then it will not be compelled to fuel inflation by printing additional currency.[174] (It may still choose to inflate, perhaps to influence the unemployment rate or interest rates.) But if government expenditures exceed government revenue, that is, if the government runs a budget deficit, then the shortfall will have to made up either by borrowing or by printing money. If the government elects to print money, then the budget deficit will lead to inflation.

BUDGET DEFICITS AND INFLATION DURING TRANSITION

Why should there be a budget deficit, money creation, and inflation in a fixed-price, centrally-planned economy? The government would seem to be able to control the value of goods relative to the amount of money in the economy by fixing wages and prices at the appropriate levels. The government's needs for additional money can be met simply by raising the prices of the goods its enterprises sell to consumers, or by lowering the wages of its employees. Consequently, there is no apparent reason for the government of a centrally-planned economy to run a budget deficit.

Nevertheless, budget deficits existed in the former Soviet Union through-out the 1980s, and probably a good deal earlier.[175] Even in Communist societies leaders are not eager to take measures that are sure to be un-popular, such as raising the prices of consumer goods or lowering wages. The tendency in the USSR was for wages to grow over time, and for official consumer good prices to be held nearly constant. (Some prices were even occasionally lowered.) If the productivity of workers increased sufficiently quickly, the upward wage drift would not have created a problem, since the higher total wages would have been matched by the higher total value of consumer goods at official prices. But productivity in consumer goods production did not match the wage increases, partly because of the Soviet emphasis on the production of defence and other non-consumer goods.[176]

The total wage bill in the Soviet Union therefore tended to increase over time, more quickly than the total amount of money spent on consumer goods at official prices. One manifestation of this process was increased nominal savings on the part of the Soviet population. More important, though, was the effect on the government budget. Since wages are a cost to the government and the prices paid for state-sector consumer goods are revenues to the government, Soviet budget deficits tended to increase.

Not surprisingly, budget deficits in the pre-reform Soviet system can be characterized as implicit. Fixed prices imply that calculating real government revenues and expenditures is impossible, but even employing those fixed prices the deficit was hidden. Gorbachev himself said that 'The heaviest burden we have inherited from the past is the budget deficit, which was carefully concealed from society, but nevertheless existed.'[177] Though the existence of budget deficits in the Soviet Union was hidden, the economic effects of those deficits was tangible.

As noted, deficits that are financed via borrowing, the issuing of bonds, need not be inflationary. But the budget deficits in the former Soviet Union were not compensated for by the issuing of bonds.[178] Instead, deficits were 'monetized', i.e., the government essentially printed new roubles to cover its budget deficits. With each rouble less valuable, free prices would tend to increase as more roubles were printed. Since state-sector prices were fixed, the inflation resulting from Soviet monetized budget deficits was of the repressed variety, with reduced availability of goods in the state sector.

Russian economic reform converted budget deficits from implicit to explicit form. But the changes of perestroika increased the size as well as the visibility of budget deficits. The culprit was – again no surprise – partial reform. Because reforms that would lower government expenditures and increase (or at least limit the decrease in) government revenues were not sufficiently pursued, Soviet budget deficits worsened during the Gorbachev years.[179]

On the government revenue side of the economic ledger, the problem was that the main element of pre-reform taxation consisted of the earnings of state enterprises above their costs. Higher retail prices for state-produced goods would increase state enterprise revenue, which was largely appropriated for the government budget. In this sense, a higher price for a state good was simply an implicit increase in taxes. As perestroika gave state enterprises more autonomy, the enterprises themselves were able to keep more of their own revenue (with which they could, for example, increase the wages of their workers.) Similar changes occurred in the agricultural sector.[180]

The increased autonomy of enterprises undermined another implicit tax as well, one based on foreign exchange. In the pre-reform Soviet economy, any foreign currency that a state-owned firm earned by exporting its product went to the government. In exchange for its foreign currency, a firm received roubles, with the amount it received based on the official (centrally-controlled) exchange rate. This rate greatly overvalued the rouble, so that the foreign currency the government received was worth considerably more than the roubles that the enterprises received in exchange. This system of confiscating foreign exchange earnings was an implicit tax on the enterprise. With reform, firms received increased rights to retain their foreign currency earnings, further diluting the state's system of implicit taxation.[181]

One feature of a transition to a market economy, increased autonomy for state-owned enterprises, thus directly undermined the implicit tax system.[182] To maintain its revenues during reform, the Soviet government would have had to effectively implement, at an early stage, new, explicit taxes – a step it failed to take.[183] To be fair, this is a difficult step to take, since the entities that become available for new taxes are largely in the emerging private sector. The pre-reform government apparatus had almost no experience with taxing private businesses, so the administration of new private-sector taxes must start from ground zero.

Increased budget deficits could have been avoided, despite the fall in government revenues, had government expenditures been similarly reduced. The reforms that would have accomplished reductions in government expenditures would have been to cut or eliminate subsidies to state-owned enterprises, perhaps in concert with privatization. In other words, if the increased autonomy for state-owned enterprises, which was responsible for reducing government tax revenues, had been matched by more enterprise accountability for their financial situation, increased budget deficits could have been avoided. Reductions in the investment and defence components of the government budget would also have been helpful, and were to some degree implemented.[184] These expenditure reductions, however, were offset by continued subsidies to state-owned enterprises: by the end of 1992, no large state enterprise had yet been forced to close for financial reasons.[185]

In fact, partial reforms tended to increase government expenditures at the same time that the decay of the implicit taxation system was reducing government revenues. Under the Soviet system, new roubles were added to the money supply when workers received their wages. Transfers of goods within the state sector did not add to the money supply; while the supplying firm acquired an accounting credit and the receiving firm's financial balance changed by the corresponding debit, no actual money changed hands. In other words, official exchanges within the state sector were non-monetary, except for payments to workers. Early reforms such as the Law on Co-operatives, however, expanded the possibilities for money creation within the state sector. New businesses as well as parts of state-owned enterprises could be organized as cooperatives. Purchases by state-owned firms from cooperatives involved money creation. The purchasing firm would provide a receipt to the cooperative, which then could legally acquire the corresponding rouble payment from the state. Exchanges that in the old system did not involve the use of money thereby became monetized during perestroika. In allowing state-owned enterprises to deal with private cooperatives, without subjecting the enterprises to strict financial discipline, perestroika led to large monetary emissions and inflation.

CREDIBLE DISINFLATION

Inflation is not an inevitable accompaniment of a transition to capitalism. It was the failure to fully reform, in the sense of effectively implementing an explicit taxation system or of limiting government subsidies to enterprises, that resulted in new inflation during Russia's economic transformation.

Russia is now faced with the task of reducing its inflation, which has largely been converted from repressed to open form. (In some localities, however, extensive controls on prices remain.) As noted, getting rid of inflation can be a costly endeavour. Recent high levels of inflation create expectations of continued high inflation in the future. Since inflationary expectations tend to be self-fulfilling, Russia appears to be caught in a cycle of high inflation.

The situation is not hopeless, however, and some policies could help smooth the transition to a lower inflationary path. The key is to alter the expectations of high inflation. And the way to lower inflationary expectations is for the government to clearly embark on an economic plan that is non-inflationary. In Russian circumstances, a non-inflationary economic programme requires a balanced (or nearly balanced) government budget. The more apparent it is that the government is committed to such a plan, the more quickly inflationary expectations will be revised downwards, and the less costly the disinflationary episode.

The first order of business, then, is to commit to reducing the government budget deficit, presumably by a combination of increased tax revenues and lowered spending. Other policies could complement the deficit reduction package. A currency reform, for example, wherein 'old' roubles are exchanged for new ones, perhaps at a ratio of 1000 old roubles to one new rouble, could in these circumstances have an effect beyond reducing nominal prices by a factor of 1000. Combined with a credible government budget deficit reduction package, the new currency might not carry the weight of the old currency's inflationary expectations. The path to a low inflation regime could then be accomplished without the severe output declines that often accompany disinflationary policies.[186] Currency reforms tied to credible regime shifts have worked elsewhere, with the German monetary reform of 1948 being one of the most conspicuous successes.[187] Another success was the Soviet NEP-era currency reform of 1922, which introduced a gold-backed parallel currency, the 'chervonets'. Combined with tax increases, the monetary restraint derived from the gold-backed currency resulted in a balanced government budget by 1923-4, following years of high and even hyperinflation.[188]

How can a deficit reduction policy be made credible? After all, the government can always resort to printing more roubles, old or new, tomorrow, and it would even appear to have incentives to do so. Under these circumstances, no disinflationary programme can be completely credible. Nevertheless, some plans are more believable than others. One way to enhance credibility of a plan to reduce the deficit is to tie the currency reform to privatization. Once in private hands, enterprises no longer have claims to government subsidies – or at least their claims are less compelling. Privatization, therefore, is in itself a disinflationary policy.[189]

There are other means of achieving credibility of a disinflationary policy, such as a commitment to a conditional International Monetary Fund aid and reform programme.[190] Poland had been experiencing large budget deficits in the late 1980s. The Polish 'big bang' reforms of 1 January 1990, which liberalized prices and made the Polish currency, the zloty, convertible, also resulted in a government budget surplus in 1990, without a currency reform.[191] The Polish experience indicates that a currency reform is not an essential element of a transition to a market economy. What is essential is some reform that will introduce a believable disinflationary regime. By making a very visible break with the past (in the manner of the Polish big bang), a currency reform combined with deficit-reducing policies has the potential to quickly erase inflationary expectations.[192]

PARKING AND PERESTROIKA

It is difficult for Westerners to understand the nature of some of the changes accompanying economic reform in Russia. Strange as it may sound, one area of Western life that presents a useful analogy to conditions in centrally-planned economies is that of automobile parking in major metropolitan areas. Consumer behaviour responds to similar circumstances in pre-reform Russia as in Western parking.

On-street public parking in the West generally involves either no monetary payment, or a relatively small fee collected via parking meters. It often takes a long time to find a public parking space in crowded downtown areas because the price is fixed below market clearing-levels. This is the Western analogue to the search for goods and long queues that awaited Russian shoppers in pre-reform state stores, where the monetary costs of goods were also held artificially low.

Once a driver finds a parking space, moreover, he or she can generally not claim it for ever. There is usually some time limit, ranging from a few minutes to a few hours, beyond which the same car cannot remain legally parked, even if the meter price is continuously paid. The Russian analogy here is with the quantity restrictions that await shoppers when they finally get to the front of the line in the state stores. They cannot buy all they want of the good at the low fixed price, but instead are often limited to a certain small quantity. (Incidentally, this is another illustration of the tendency for economic controls to snowball. Since higher prices cannot be used to ration the demand, quantity controls become necessary.)

Public parking on the street at below market rates is only one parking option. An alternative is to park in privately-operated parking lots and garages that charge whatever the market will bear. Here, the waiting time is generally minimal, but the price can be many multiples of the price for public street parking. In Russia, goods sold in state stores were also available at free market prices in 'parallel' markets, which are now largely legal, and in the case of food have been legal for decades. Russian consumers buying food, like Westerners attempting to park, could use the subsidized public sector or the free market private sector.

An important difference between the public and private parking alternatives should be noted. When a driver pays a private garage owner, the driver gets the parking and loses the cash, but the garage owner receives the cash. That is, the cash payment for the parking space is a transfer of purchasing power from the driver to the garage owner. In the state sector, the time that goes into searching for a space is 'spent' by the driver, but does not benefit anyone else. Instead of a transfer of resources, time spent in search uses up a valuable resource: the driver's time. By using up resources, the allocation of goods by low fixed prices and waiting lines is more costly to a society than free markets. Thus repressed inflation tends to be more costly than open inflation, and the blatant waste of resources is partly to blame for the frustration that often accompanies the search for a parking space.

Reform has witnessed an increase in the process of 'spontaneous privatization' in Russia. This activity occurs when private citizens (workers and managers) simply usurp the state ownership rights – quasi-legally, at best – and operate enterprises for their own profit. Interestingly, spontaneous privatization also occurs in particularly congested Western parking markets. Large men will step into public parking spaces when automobiles leave and then 'offer' the spaces at market prices to others wishing to park. The driver can either pay the market price, continue to search for another parking place, or attempt to park anyway – a strategy that will likely be met with violence (or at least the implicit threat of violence) either to the car or the driver. An alternative device to achieve the same ends involves a protection racket. Here a private citizen will offer, for a fee, to keep an eye on the car of a newly-parked driver.[193] (Thus the protection rackets that have become widely remarked upon in Russia also have their – pardon the pun – parking parallels.) If these sorts of spontaneous privatizations seem disreputable, imagine how the Russians feel about their similar, and much more widespread, phenomenon.

One point that the parking analogy suggests, however, is that spontaneous privatization can occur in situations of excessive shortage, even without reform. Much of the spontaneous privatization now under way in Russia represents a more visible version of a long-standing practice, that of diverting state sector goods to private markets: once more, the implicit–explicit distinction. (A similar point applies to protection rackets.) While state-sector shortages increased during perestroika, and thus the incentive to spontaneously privatize also increased – and reform measures simultaneously reduced the costs of such privatizations – reform did not directly cause spontaneous privatization.

Information plays a key role in parking. A local who knows the location of difficult-to-find public parking spaces can more easily discover a place to park at the low fixed price than can a tourist. Businesses that trade on this information can even spring up, by offering 'valet' parking in public spaces. Information about local 'market' conditions is likewise invaluable to Russian shoppers. By knowing which state stores are likely to have which goods at which times, local consumers can often procure the goods, and perhaps without large amounts of time spent in searching and queuing. Specialists become professional shoppers, collecting fees for buying goods for others in the state sector.

Now consider Russian economic reform. Full reform will mean that state sector prices will match the parallel market prices, and searching and queuing will largely disappear. For those who have relatively more time than roubles, and who have good information about the current state sector, the reforms will be unwelcome. The social costs of time wasted waiting in queues, however, will virtually disappear, and quantity restrictions will become unnecessary.

Likewise, imagine a reform to raise the prices for all public parking to market levels. (In some areas, this could involve a more than ten-fold increase in prices.) Again, for those with relatively less money than time, and with relatively good information about the availability of public parking spaces, parking will become more onerous. Simultaneously, however, the search for parking would be virtually eliminated, as would the restrictions on the amount of time in a parking space.[194] Suddenly, drivers would have no trouble finding parking, and no socially wasteful time would be spent searching for parking spaces! Such a reform would raise the quality of life for many drivers, even if it came at a higher monetary price. But the Russians put up with the equivalent of parking problems in virtually all of their everyday, state sector transactions. For many Russians, full price liberalization offers a very significant increase in welfare.

ARE ROUBLES WORTHLESS?

The question 'Are roubles worthless?' has been answered in the affirmative so many times in the Western media and by Western economists that there seems to be little reason to pursue the issue further.[195] The worthlessness of roubles is viewed as being responsible for the rise in barter and the lack of incentive to work – why work if the roubles that you are paid cannot buy anything? Nevertheless, the notion that roubles are worthless is a complete myth. It has been the case throughout the reform era that you could buy virtually anything you desired in Russia, including dollars, with roubles, if you had enough of them. Roubles are valuable. In his seminal paper on the Soviet second economy in 1977, Gregory Grossman noted that he had been told by a Moscow resident that 'In this city you can get anything for money, though sometimes it takes a lot.'[196] This characterization of the Russian market economy remains accurate, and the money involved need not be foreign currency.

The perpetuation of the myth that roubles are worthless stems from an over-emphasis on the official component of the Russian economy. The low fixed prices in the state sector and the accompanying shortages gave the appearance that the binding constraint on Russian shoppers was not the number of roubles that they had, but rather the amount of time that they were willing to invest to procure goods. This appearance matched reality only within the fixed-price state sector, however. Parallel markets with free prices also existed, and Russians could buy goods in these outlets as well. Many Russians did not purchase a substantial amount of their goods on the free market because of the high prices. (Young people, however, were reported to buy 40 per cent of their goods on the black market.[197]) But this is precisely the point. High prices only deter shoppers if they cannot afford the high prices, i.e, if additional roubles would be valuable to them.

After the recent reforms that increased state sector prices, complaints concerning high prices were voiced by many Russian shoppers. Nevertheless, the 'roubles are worthless' myth continued to be perpetuated, sometimes even in articles that simultaneously reported discontent over high prices![198]

The related myth that Russians have no interest in working hard in order to earn their worthless roubles has also proved persistent. Actually, the incentives to work for roubles are quite intense, and perhaps ironically, the more difficult the economic situation, the greater these incentives become. Indeed, the amount of effort devoted to earning roubles in cities like Moscow is eye-opening. Entrepreneurs have been running enormous risks in Russia – in 1988–9, 34,000 Soviets were punished for 'speculation'[199] – to earn roubles. Of course, workers are happy to work directly for consumer goods as well – maybe even happier. But they will also willingly work for roubles, if they are paid enough of them. They are less eager to work in state-sector jobs that pay only low rouble wages, or if they get paid the same amount whether they work hard or not.

The notion that roubles are worthless is connected to the idea of a rouble overhang, which has its origins in the concept of 'unsatisfied demand' in the Soviet economics discipline. Unsatisfied demand is calculated as the amount by which the value of consumer goods produced in the economy, measured at fixed state prices, exceeds the income earned by households, minus a small amount of desired savings. If households have more income than there are consumer goods, they will be forced to save the money, or so the theory goes. The total amount of such forced savings, accumulated year after year, represents the ominous-sounding rouble overhang.

Again, the difficulty with the concepts of unsatisfied demand, forced savings, and the rouble overhang is that they ignore the free price, parallel markets. 'Forced' savings are actually voluntary; individuals choose not to pay the high prices on the free markets, and save the money instead.[200] Westerners engage in similar behaviour; for example, shoppers might wait until a sale before making a desired purchase. This is the Western equivalent of a Russian postponing a purchase until he or she luckily comes across some low-priced goods in a state-sector shop.

The concept of a rouble overhang is not itself worthless, because it represents a good indicator of repressed inflation. The greater the rouble overhang, the greater (in general) the amount of repressed inflation, and the greater the difference between free market prices and the official state-sector prices. But the rouble overhang does not directly portend doom. As a measure of repressed inflation, the rouble overhang gives some indication of the amount by which fixed state sector prices will rise with price liberalization, though prices in existing free markets probably provide a better guide. The rouble overhang does not create any new inflation, however. Russians will not suddenly show up 'waving fistfuls of roubles', because they could have done so before in the free market sector but chose not to. And in fact, the rouble overhang came crashing down after the 2 January 1992 partial price liberalization with barely a whimper. There is always a new crisis on the horizon, though. The crisis following the partial price liberalization was a tremendous *shortage* of roubles that was preventing Russian workers from getting paid![201]

Chapter 4

Employment and unemployment

Our unemployment is the highest in the world. But unfortunately, all our unemployed get salaries.

Russian economist Pavel Bunich[202]

It is no secret that even now many people get their pay only for reporting to work and hold positions regardless of their actual labour contribution. And the most surprising thing is that this hardly worries anyone.

Mikhail Gorbachev[203]

INTRODUCTION

For Russians long accustomed to a high degree of price stability in the state shops, the rapid increases in prices during the reform era must have come as something of a shock. But that shock may be relatively minor compared with what transition holds in store for them with respect to employment. Finding a job was not difficult in the Soviet Union, maybe even easier than finding desirable consumer goods. Western-style unemployment was virtually unknown. A transition to a market economy will end this situation, and many Russians will be faced with potentially long periods of involuntary unemployment for the first time in their lives. Government assurances that basic needs will be met and that eventually everyone will be better off might provide little solace. A rough US analogy might be a reform to quickly eliminate the Social Security system. Given the amount of controversy engendered by minor proposed changes in Social Security, sudden abolition of the programme could ignite a revolution. Will a rising unemployment rate cause Russians to man the barricades?

The themes that emerged during the discussion of price liberalization – pre-existing markets, misleading statistics, implicit versus explicit phenomena, and the dangers of partial reform – re-emerge in the transitional employment sphere. For example, implementation of the Soviet government's full-employment policy resulted in substantial underemployment, or 'repressed unemployment', as evidenced by the quotations that open this chapter. Such repressed unemployment continues in present day Russia. Wages are also partly hidden, as Russian enterprises generally provide scarce goods and social services to their employees, in addition to monetary compensation. These benefits, combined with the full employment mandate, formed part of the implicit welfare system in the pre-reform setting, complementing the low fixed prices in state stores for most everyday consumer goods. There was no system of unemployment benefits under the Soviet regime, because there was little need for one. But during market-oriented reform, the repressed unemployment becomes open unemployment, and the implicit welfare system formed in the employment sphere ceases to operate. An explicit unemployment benefits system therefore becomes a high priority during reform. The economic costs of the new open unemployment need not exceed the costs of the old repressed unemployment, however, and the implicit social welfare system can be replaced with an explicit one that includes unemployment benefits: conclusions familiar from the examination of price liberalization and inflation.

The major benefits from market-oriented reforms of state-owned enterprises derive from changes in the answers to the 'what goods to produce?' question. Making the right goods will require that workers who are currently making the *wrong* goods change their jobs. Finding a new job is not always easy, though, particularly in a society where people have little experience in searching for work while unemployed. Some of the people who have to change jobs, and some new entrants to the Russian labour force, will go through spells, perhaps prolonged spells, of open unemployment. This is standard operating procedure in Western market economies; some unemployment is accepted as necessary to allocate labour efficiently, though governments typically try to cushion the adverse economic consequences of unemployment for out-of-work individuals. Such acceptance of open unemployment cannot be taken for granted in Russia, however; polls indicate that most Russians believe that it is the duty of the government to provide everyone with a job,[204] and the cushions in the form of unemployment benefits are not yet well developed. But a reluctance to generate open unemployment during transition carries a cost beyond the continued misallocation of labour. If enterprise reform does not keep pace with price reform, the potential benefits of market prices are themselves partially undermined. In disbanding the 'unified team' of free prices and free enterprise, the entire reform process runs the risk of being run aground.

THE LABOUR SECTOR UNDER THE ANCIEN RÉGIME

'Implicit contract theory' is a branch of Western macroeconomics and labour economics theory that bears some relationship to conditions in the pre-reform Russian economy. Implicit contract theory is based on the notion that workers tend to be more averse to risk in the amount of their pay than firms are to risk in the amount of their profits.[205] In these circumstances, firms might provide implicit insurance to workers, by maintaining wages and salaries even during economic downturns, at the cost of sharing fewer of their profits with workers during an upswing. The Russian state employment sector operated roughly in accordance with implicit contract theory. Workers were implicitly insured in the form of near guarantees of employment and relatively stable pay.

The Soviet government announced the official end of unemployment in October 1930, and there was no mass open unemployment during the years of central planning.[206] (This provided quite a contrast with Western market economies during the Great Depression, and to a lesser degree since.) A small amount of unemployment did exist, however, due to what economists call 'frictional factors'. These include situations that are specific to individuals, and that result in temporary unemployment: quitting, getting fired, or newly entering the job force. Unemployment due to more widespread factors, such as the decline of an entire industry or an economy-wide recession, was not a feature of the centrally-planned system. Typical estimates of the Soviet pre-perestroika frictional unemployment rate are on the order of 2–3 per cent.[207]

The maintenance of full employment was an explicit goal of the Soviet regime. The Soviet constitution recognized the right and duty of a citizen to work, and the duty of the state to provide citizens with jobs.[208] Able-bodied adults without a working spouse or family responsibilities who did not have an official job were potentially subject to prosecution under 'anti-parasite' laws.[209]

Participation in the Soviet labour force greatly exceeded typical Western levels: about 80 per cent of adults of working age were active in the labour force, as compared to approximately 70 per cent in the US[210] This relative labour force activity was most pronounced for Soviet women, who held jobs at a higher rate than women in any other industrialized country.[211] Part-time work, at least officially, was virtually unknown: almost all Soviet workers held full-time jobs. Unofficially, though, opportunities to work less than 40 hours a week were widely available.[212] In contrast to the high labour participation rates, official retirement ages were relatively young. Most Soviet workers could retire with a state-provided pension at the age of 60 for men and 55 for women.[213] Many pensioners continued to hold formal or informal jobs, however.[214]

The Soviet employment realm was an amalgam of planned and market elements, and the conditions that arose from this combination have continued into the post-planning period in Russia. At a general level, planners determined the allocation of labourers between occupations and enterprises – how many workers were needed in what jobs requiring what skills in what industries.[215] The official 'demand' for labour was thus guided, though not precisely determined, by the plan. Wage rates were centrally determined, varying with job classifications. Other aspects of the employment relationship, such as the working conditions, were also centrally regulated.

The planning system exerted less influence over the supply of labour than it did over the demand for labour. The leverage over labour supply operated through the anti-parasite laws, official education and training opportunities, retirement policies, military service, and, alas, forced labour camps. The distribution of workers among individual enterprises, however, generally involved the conscious decisions of individual Russian citizens. The great majority of Soviet workers were hired simply by applying at the local factory, without any centralized allocation.[216] (The major exception involved initial jobs for school graduates, who were often placed in employment.) To some degree, despite the anti-parasite laws, there was even a choice over whether or not to enter the work force.[217] (The relative freedom that workers had in the labour market became particularly important in the post-Stalin era. Under Stalin, labour was 'militarized', and during the war, a single late arrival or absence from work could result in a five-year term in a labour camp.)

Because of the relative freedom in labour supply, planners had to respond to workers' preferences by raising wages or bonuses for jobs in which it was otherwise difficult to attract workers, such as those in remote areas.[218] Planners in Moscow had limited information on local conditions and limited control over individual enterprises, though, so their actions alone could not come close to matching labour supply with labour demand. Action on the part of the managers of individual enterprises was therefore necessary to attract good workers. Since the official wage rates were fixed by the planners, it was impossible for managers to directly raise wages in response to local conditions. Enterprise managers had to find ways to circumvent the central wage controls in order to attract and retain workers.[219] Among the devices for informally increasing compensation were spurious upgrades of positions, management complicity in the mis-appropriation of time or materials from work, and the distribution of highly sought-after goods through the work place.[220] The amount of such informal compensation was surprisingly extensive; one conservative estimate indicates that 12 per cent of total working time was 'stolen' from state employers in the late 1970s.[221] Large enterprises took on the role of benevolent company towns, supplying food, consumer goods, housing, schools, and even vacation retreats to their employees.

Soviet planners understood the opportunities for informal compensation on the job, and they responded, perhaps unintentionally, by fixing lower official wages for jobs that offered particularly lucrative additional sources of funds – another case where planning followed practice rather than vice versa. Butchers and retail trade employees, for example, had fairly low official wages, implicitly recognizing the opportunities in these professions for informal wage supplements. Retail trade workers could easily supplement their official pay by selling state-sector goods 'through the back door', at free market prices paid either in roubles, gifts, or favours.[222]

Soviet state-owned enterprises, unlike private Western firms, were not motivated to earn high profits. Their main official goal was simply to fulfil, and if possible to overfulfil, their output plan, which as previously noted, could be revised downwards if they were in real danger of severe underfulfilment. Lacking a strong profit motive, enterprises also lacked incentives to ensure that they operated efficiently and at low cost, or that they produced high quality output.

The relative unimportance of profits was perfectly reasonable in a fixed-price regime. If prices are centrally-determined, then profits are, to a large extent, also centrally-determined. By raising the price of a firm's output or lowering the price of its inputs, the planners could generally raise a firm's profits. High profits in a Western economy are a signal that a firm is providing something that its customers find particularly attractive. In a centrally-planned economy, high profits signal planners' whims, not consumer satisfaction. Indeed, urging enterprises to increase profits in a fixed-price regime is dangerous – it is the Polish tropical flowers story, or the feeding bread to livestock tale. By focusing on output rather than profits, the centrally-planned system maintained a degree of internal consistency.

The internal consistency of the pre-reform system is also demonstrated by the seeming lack of work place discipline. Workers would drink, steal goods and time, and generally lack industriousness at their official jobs at levels that apparently far exceeded those of the West. Why would managers tolerate and even in some cases condone such behaviour? Much of the answer lies in the official reward structure. Since plan fulfillment was the most meaningful success indicator, managers could primarily focus on meeting their output plan. As long as the plan was fulfilled, management had little interest in controlling other aspects of employee behaviour.[223]

With few incentives to minimize costs but strong incentives to fulfil the gross output requirements of the plan, enterprise managers had a tendency to demand more labour, as well as more of other inputs, than the planners deemed necessary.[224] This incentive reflects the situation of 'soft budget constraints', whereby firms that lost money simply received state subsidies; that is, there was no bankruptcy.[225] Again, subsidizing money-losing firms is perfectly reasonable, even essential, in a fixed-price economy, since profits are largely determined by the pricing decisions of the planners.

The general result of soft budget constraints has been a situation in which a firm, at the official wage rates, wanted to hire more workers than the enterprise could actually entice at that wage. From a firm's point of view, labour was another good that was in chronic shortage in the USSR. These strong enterprise incentives to hire workers in the Soviet economy played a major role in implementing the stated goal of full employment.[226] Even in the absence of excessive firm hunger to accumulate labour, though, an aggregate labour shortage probably would have existed, as total planned manpower requirements consistently exceeded the supply of labour.[227]

Soft budget constraints therefore led Soviet state-owned firms, in general, to hire more workers than a similar private firm in a market economy would have chosen to hire. This tendency was particularly apparent in Soviet factories that were purchased from the West, and thus had nearly identical Western analogues:[228]

> in 1969 it was reported that the [Soviet] chemical plants bought from abroad employed considerably more workers than needed in the countries of purchase: one and a half times as many in the case of basic blue-collar workers, three and a half times as many in the case of white collar workers, and eight times as many in the case of auxiliary blue collar workers.

The giant Magnitogorsk steel mill employed 60 thousand employees to produce sixteen million tons of steel per year, while USX's modern plant in Gary, Indiana produced eight million tons with only seven thousand workers.[229] This relative overstaffing of enterprises was reinforced by legal barriers that firms faced in getting rid of unwanted employees. While workers could be fired for disciplinary reasons, workers who simply were not needed were more difficult to let go. Legally, enterprises had a duty to find a new job for a redundant employee.[230]

It is easy to overestimate the amount of overstaffing in Soviet firms, however, because many seemingly excess workers were actually producing inputs or goods unrelated to a firm's main line of production for distribution to employees or for barter, or were engaged in second economy activity.[231] Furthermore, relative to Western market economies, the USSR was labour-rich and capital-poor, at least with respect to modern capital goods. A higher labour intensity therefore may have been sensible. Despite these reservations concerning the interpretation of statistics, though, Soviet enterprises probably were overstaffed relative to the employment levels that would have existed under private ownership and market conditions.

The Soviet full employment system and overstaffing brought with them underemployment, which took many forms, such as frequent periods of idleness and worker over-qualification. Since the choice of what goods to produce in the state sector was not driven by market prices, many workers produced goods that were not valuable to consumers. These workers were also underemployed relative to their potential productivity in market settings. (Perhaps the frequent periods of idleness were, in some instances, socially beneficial. More industrious workers may simply have turned out an increased supply of useless goods – another example of the internal consistency of the centrally-planned system?)

Incentives to work hard were notoriously paltry within the Soviet state sector. With near guarantees of employment, relatively low official pay differentials between employment grades, and official compensation that was tied mainly to plan fulfilment, employees had little reason to exert much effort at work.[232] Nor could workers easily turn to alternative employers when they were dissatisfied with their jobs, despite the usual Soviet condition of 'excess demand' for labour. It was generally illegal for workers to move to major cities like Moscow and St. Petersburg to look for work: the Catch-22 was that they already had to have a job offer in order to move there.[233] The chronic housing shortage further limited worker movement, since arranging for housing in a new area was extremely difficult. In-kind benefits that were distributed through the work place, often including housing, served as another barrier to changing jobs, because the potential loss of such benefits (unless they could be quickly replaced by similar benefits from the new enterprise) was nearly intolerable. Even the *possibility* of in-kind benefits limited worker mobility. Workers at an enterprise often had a place on a waiting list for enterprise-provided housing; waits of more than 10 years were not uncommon.[234] By leaving their enterprise, workers would also lose their place on the waiting list. Similarly, the importance of networks of personal connections for informal and corrupt activity served as a barrier against shifting jobs or location. And the option of openly entering business for oneself was available only in a few trades.[235]

Constraints on outside opportunities available to good workers diminished incentives for employees to distinguish themselves at their current jobs. Amid these difficulties, the amount of labour turnover, while lower than US levels, was surprisingly extensive, with 12 per cent of industrial workers leaving their jobs in 1987.[236] Simultaneously, absenteeism far exceeded Western levels.[237] The effects of substantial turnover and absenteeism on the value of production may not have been particularly severe, however, given the overstaffing and mis-production within the state sector.[238]

FROM IMPLICIT TO EXPLICIT UNEMPLOYMENT

In moving to a market economy, Russia will have to force most state-owned enterprises to make it (or not) on their own: in economics jargon, to face a hard budget constraint. The essential reform is that subsidies to state-owned enterprises cease (or at least be severely restricted), whether or not the enterprises are formally privatized. This reform is only sensible, however, if prices are liberalized and firm managers' decisions are not controlled by the state. Under these circumstances, profits become a function of enterprise behaviour and not planner decree: once again, free prices and free enterprise are a unified team.

The ending of subsidies to enterprises will be accompanied by the possibility, indeed, the near certainty, judging from East European experience, of widespread open unemployment. Without the implicit subsidies (low prices on inputs, including subsidized credit) and explicit subsidies (direct transfers from the state budget) that they currently receive, many enterprises will become bankrupt.[239] But prior to the cut-off of subsidies and the freeing of prices it cannot be determined which enterprises or how many enterprises will be unable to cope in a market setting, since only then will profits be a good measure of a firm's solvency. And even those enterprises that can make it under market conditions may need to reduce their work force, further adding to open unemployment.[240] As state-owned enterprises lose their access to state subsidies, the state-guaranteed 'implicit contract' will no longer operate. Instead, the employment sector will be marked by the familiar Western situation where workers bear some of the risk of economic downturns, by possibly becoming unemployed during recessions.

What is the potential size of the open unemployment that could accompany reform? An unemployment rate of 10 per cent, similar to that prevailing in some East European countries in the years following the implementation of major reforms, would leave more than seven million Russian citizens unemployed.[241] Other estimates of Russian unemployment can be generated by measuring the extent of pre-reform overstaffing. Relying on an over-staffing figure of 25 per cent drawn from a survey of more than 500 factories, the International Labour Organization suggested that 15–45 million workers in the former USSR could become unemployed during reform.[242] Such a large amount of unemployment would not be in accord with Eastern European experience. Nevertheless, even much lower levels of unemployment appear daunting, particularly since there were so few openly unemployed Russians in the pre-reform situation.

If the Russian labour force participation rate were to decrease to levels more typical of Western market economies, the increase in open unemployment during reform could be lessened. This may already be happening, as employment has already begun to fall, even without significant increases in official unemployment.[243] Participation rates may not fall sharply, though. Expanded opportunities for part-time work may attract some new workers into the labour force – though some workers who now hold full-time jobs may elect to reduce their work hours.

In any event, reform is quite likely to result in a substantial increase in open unemployment. Open unemployment is economically detrimental for two reasons. First, unemployed workers are not producing goods and services that other members of society can enjoy. This is a cost that society as a whole pays for unemployment. Second are costs that the unemployed workers themselves must bear. These include reduced income, as well as the psychological costs that often accompany the state of unemployment.

The social costs of open unemployment, though, are already being borne in the unreformed Russian economy. Consider a firm that becomes bankrupt post-reform. Bankruptcy in a market economy indicates that the firm's inputs are more valuable than its outputs. A Russian enterprise that is forced to close during market-oriented reform therefore reveals that it was being subsidized prior to the reform. The subsidy may have been implicit, being hidden in favourable pricing or priority access to inputs. Indeed, the firm may even have made positive 'profits', calculated according to the fixed state sector prices. Whether the pre-reform subsidies were explicit or implicit, closing the firm and ending the subsidies represent a net benefit to society; in other words, the economic pie gets bigger.

A rise in measured unemployment in Russia during the transition therefore need not represent a rise in de facto unemployment; the increase in the measured unemployment rate is misleading in terms of costs imposed on the economy, because the pre-reform unemployment rate failed to capture the repressed unemployment. As Nobel Prize-winning economist James Tobin once noted, 'If people are at unproductive work, whether as hired wage earners, family farm hands, or self-employed, the best statistical symptom of this social malady is low per capita income, not unemployment.'[244]

Shutting down unprofitable firms is just one of the routes to social gains via labour market reform. Another benefit that will accompany the introduction of hard budget constraints is the improved incentives to work on the part of those who remain employed. Even absenteeism can be expected to fall abruptly, as it has elsewhere when workers were faced with the prospect of reform.[245] In the longer run, the switch to the production of goods that are highly desired by consumers will also increase the size of the social pie.

Some job opportunities for newly (and openly) unemployed workers will continue to arise in the nascent legal private sector, particularly as burdensome government restrictions are removed.[246] As noted earlier, some 50 per cent of the Russian work force was employed in the private sector by mid-1994.[247] The process of privatization, both spontaneous and official, whereby state assets have been converted to private use, has allowed many workers and managers to supplement their wages with de facto profit shares.[248] Private employment may rise particularly quickly in those areas that were relatively neglected under Soviet central planning. Housing construction and maintenance, and the service and consumer goods sectors are candidates for rapid growth. The former Soviet Union had only one-third the number of workers in trade occupations as the US had in retail trade alone.[249] The retail sales kiosks that have sprung up on busy street corners throughout Russia can thus be seen as filling a particularly wide niche left unfilled in the old system.

It is likely that the total social costs in the Russian employment realm will go down during a comprehensive market-based reform, even as open unemployment rises. But the decrease in total social costs is largely irrelevant to those individuals who are forced to newly bear the costs of open unemployment. To shift some of the costs of unemployment that otherwise fall on the unemployed, Western governments typically provide explicit unemployment insurance, in the form of benefits to laid-off workers. The Russian government should do likewise during the transition, explicitly restoring, in part, the previous implicit contract. And indeed, the Russian government is attempting to implement a new system of explicit unemployment benefits.[250] Shifting the costs of unemployment away from the unemployed individual involves a difficult trade-off, though. The higher the level of unemployment benefits, the less unemployed workers suffer, but the lower the impetus to find work and stay employed. The incentive to work hard fuelled by the threat of potential unemployment becomes attenuated as unemployment benefits rise. Simultaneously, employers may be more willing to let workers go if the employers know that substantial unemployment benefits are available.

Payments to 'unemployed' workers are basically a fixed cost in the Russian economy.[251] These payments can be made just as easily to explicitly unemployed workers post-reform, in the form of unemployment benefits, as they can be made to implicitly unemployed workers pre-reform, in the form of wages and in-kind benefits. The unemployment benefits of Russian workers who lose their jobs during a full market-oriented reform do not represent new costs for society to bear. Since Russia can afford its pre-reform, implicit social safety net, which was relatively inefficient because it required wasteful production and was not targeted at the most needy individuals, it can easily afford a targeted, explicit social safety net during transition to a market economy. With labour costs only some 20 per cent of total production costs, the gains from eliminating wasteful production while paying explicit unemployment benefits are in fact quite substantial.[251*] Boris Fedorov, then the Russian Minister of Finance, estimated in 1993 that it cost three times as much to keep a person employed at an unproductive job through industry subsidies than it would cost to pay unemployment benefits.[252]

The argument that unemployment and its costs simply change from implicit to explicit form during the transition may understate the difficulties that reform poses in the employment sector. There are two potential sources of new costs – i.e., costs that were not already being borne in the unreformed system – associated with open unemployment. One is the non-monetary strains suffered by unemployed workers. Other new costs, examined in the next section, may arise as a result of partial reforms.

One Western expert on Soviet labour lists some of the individual non-pecuniary consequences of open unemployment[253]:

> a change in role and status, changes in social contacts outside the home and in the sphere of intrafamilial relationships, an increase in free time, idleness, a lack of purpose, boredom, the feeling of not being wanted, a sense of deprivation and alienation, demoralization, resignation, despair, apathy, hatred of immigrants, and enmity between the sexes.

These non-pecuniary costs can be quite substantial, as anyone knows who is familiar with unemployment in Western industrialized nations. But the extent to which these represent new costs in the Russian employment sphere is uncertain. Many of these negative consequences of open unemployment are 'reproduced' in the full employment Russian setting.[254] People can generally tell when they are engaged in unproductive work. The implicitly unemployed are therefore already susceptible to the non-monetary costs of open unemployment. Taking the general disappearance of job security into account makes it likely that the non-pecuniary costs of open unemployment during transition will exceed the analogous costs of repressed unemployment in the pre-reform Russian system. But the magnitude of the additional costs is not calculable.

PARTIAL REFORMS AND ECONOMIC DISTORTIONS

Beyond the psychological costs of open unemployment, there is a host of other potential sources of economic distress that could accompany a market-oriented reform of the enterprise sector. For the most part, the roots of increased costs in the employment realm during transition can be characterized as partial reform measures. This section examines two of the potentially most damaging partial reforms, those associated with incomplete price liberalization and credit market restrictions.

Consider the difficulties that partial price liberalization brings to the employment realm. As noted, in market economies without major distortions, a firm becomes bankrupt when the value of the inputs the firm uses – e.g., raw materials, machinery, and labour – exceed the value of its outputs. When the firm goes out of business, the inputs can be redeployed to other, more highly-valued activities. Bankruptcies, then, are beneficial to the economy as a whole, even as they are quite painful to the workers, owners, and creditors of the defunct company. This logic, though, rests on the assumed lack of major 'distortions' in the economy.

An economic distortion is a departure from competitive conditions. Common distortions include unregulated externalities such as pollution, monopoly power, and anti-competitive government regulations such as tariffs. All economies are distorted, and there is no theoretical reason why a 'more' distorted economy should work less well than a 'less' distorted economy, because additional distortions could in some sense be offsetting.[255] A previous example illustrates this point: given the distortions caused by fixed prices in centrally-planned economies, restrictions on private enterprise were necessary to prevent individuals from responding to the distorted price signals. Nevertheless, as conditions in centrally-planned societies indicate, economies that are extremely far removed from competitive conditions are unlikely to perform as well as those that rely primarily on the market mechanism for answers to the what to produce, how to produce, and for whom to produce questions.

One important source of distortions, particularly in centrally-planned economies, is fixed prices. The distortions generated by fixed prices can result in substantial costs in the employment realm during reform. When some prices remain fixed, profits, which are a noisy indicator of the social valuation of productive activity under the best conditions, will be unreliable signals of which firms are and which are not socially viable. Then the wrong firms, and perhaps too many firms, will go bankrupt. Thus Polish tropical flowers formed a viable industry when the energy price was subsidized.

Excessive layoffs may have occurred in Eastern Germany, where real wages – the price of labour – were maintained at artificially high levels after reunification.[256]

Distortions related to the price of labour may be common, even in market economies. A key feature of Keynesian economics is the presumed difficulty money wages have in falling – the 'downward rigidity' in wages. Since wages represent a price, if there is some mechanism that prevents them from fully adjusting to market conditions, then wages resemble the fixed prices of centrally-planned economies. If wages are not flexible downward, insufficient demand for goods and services can lead to increased unemployment.[257] The Russian economy has two features, though, that lessen the relevance of this Keynesian predicament. First, recall that Russian workers receive a large amount of employment compensation in non-monetary and informal fashion. Even if monetary wages are not flexible downwards, such informal elements of compensation are generally more adaptable. Second, inflation remains rampant in the Russian economy, and a high inflation rate will exist for the foreseeable future. In an inflationary environment, monetary wages can rise even as their purchasing power – real wages – decline.

Another potential distortion that is frequently cited as a source of additional unemployment during reform stems from the credit market. In a well-functioning market economy, productive firms do not have to continuously generate enough cash to pay their current bills; rather, if they are temporarily short of funds, they can borrow money from banks, and repay the loan later. Banks are willing to make such loans if they are confident that the firm will eventually be able to settle its accounts, because the loans are repaid with interest. In a well-functioning market economy, temporary illiquidity does not force an otherwise valuable firm to close down.

Russia does not have a well-functioning market economy, though. Consider the plight of a Russian enterprise that has to change its product mix to survive under market conditions – presumably, a very common situation. Such changes are costly, and they have to be borne now, whereas the benefits of the adjustments will not occur until later.[258] Adjustment costs may cause temporary illiquidity in some firms that would be solvent in the long-run. The problem is that in the absence of a well-developed banking sector, such firms may not be able to secure bank loans. Without credit, these potentially viable firms may nevertheless close when their budget constraints are hardened.

While the theoretical point that credit market imperfections can lead to increased bankruptcies and economic distress is compelling, the empirical relevance of this potential problem remains unknown. Though there is not a well-developed capital market in Russia, the private banking sector is growing, and should increase with further reform. The large conglomerate enterprises that are springing up in Russia also help to ease the credit crunch, because they can internally allocate funds to the branches of the firm that offer the best returns.[259] Barter deals and inter-enterprise credits can also allay liquidity constraints during the transition. It is therefore not clear that illiquid but otherwise solvent firms will be unable to borrow. Certainly many new firms have been able to open and grow during the reform years, despite any credit market imperfections.[259*]

Concerns have been raised about the presumably high price of credit – the interest rate – as well as credit availability. While nominal interest rates have been high – in late 1992, over 100 per cent per annum – after adjusting for inflation, real interest rates have not been particularly high, and were even negative until November 1993.[260] As long as interest rates are market-determined in the absence of other major distortions, it is not clear that the price of credit is a problem. If interest rates are high, that reflects the real costs of borrowing money in Russia – precisely what free interest rates are supposed to do to achieve the best mix between current consumption and investment. The expectation of continued inflation implies that market-determined nominal interest rates will remain high (by US standards) in the near future, but this does not in itself portend doom for the Russian economy.

ENTERPRISE DEBT

As opposed to shortages of credit, the more salient concern in the reforming Russian economy is an *excessive* amount of credit, either explicitly or implicitly provided by the government, and interest rates that are too low. For the most part, interest rates and access to credit in Russia have been determined by political, not economic, factors. Credit is therefore likely to be used to sustain state-sector firms that should be downsized or eliminated, as opposed to being channelled to the emerging market-oriented firms.[260*]

The Russian government can avoid closing state-owned enterprises by providing loans to money-losing firms, either through banks, other enterprises, or to the troubled firms directly. Inter-enterprise loans suddenly became widespread in Russia during the early months of 1992 (i.e., following price liberalization): debts between state-owned enterprises rose by a factor of 80 between January and July 1992.[261] While market-based credit is generally a good development, these non-market loans, which may never be repaid, have the same effect as direct state subsidies – postponing the day of reckoning, when firms have to make a go of it (or fail to) in the marketplace. Furthermore, the interest rates applied to loans backed by the Russian Central Bank are held below the market-clearing levels, and real interest rates, as noted, were actually negative throughout 1992.[262] With subsidized interest rates, it is not surprising that credit must be administratively rationed. What enterprise would not want to borrow money if it was getting paid to do so, which in effect is the situation when real interest rates are negative?

There is little risk to individual banks or enterprises in dispensing such credit, provided that the practice is widespread, even if there is no explicit government insurance. When most state enterprises have debts they cannot repay, the state almost certainly will step in with additional funds, rather than risk massive shutdowns. Such considerations are one key to the build-up of trillions of roubles in credit.[263] Another important factor in dispensing inter-enterprise credits is that a firm that does so, and is not repaid, does not appear to suffer any major negative consequences. Even if the firm is not being paid by its customers, it generally is given access by the state to funds with which to pay the wages of its own employees.

Banking in the pre-reform Russian economy was passive – dare I say implicit? – and was largely devoted to accounting for the flows of goods and services that were determined by the plans.[264] Soviet banks were not in the business of evaluating potential borrowers and making loans for those projects that appeared most promising. During the transition, independent commercial banks should emerge that will explicitly take on the job of funnelling investment funds to high-valued users. But the unwillingness to impose hard budget constraints on enterprises slowed the development of the commercial banking sector. Writing in early 1993, Russian researchers Sergei Aukutsenek and Elena Belyanova concluded that 'in many respects the Russian financial system has not changed since the reforms began. . . . [T]he old system of credit allocation by the state continues to exist and is concealed behind the visible credit market.'[265] Also in 1993, the Russian government affirmed the right of privatized firms to receive access to sub-sidized state credits on an equal footing with state-owned enterprises, thereby indicating that privatization alone would not lead to a market allocation of credit.

Whether funnelled through banks or state enterprises, low interest, state-provided credits have the unfortunate end result of the printing of roubles to make good the loans, and the continued fuelling of inflation. This is another instance of the damage that can be caused by partial reforms; in this case, reforms that do not harden budget constraints and produce market interest rates. With the continuing availability of state-subsidized credit, which is often assured through personal connections between enterprise managers and bank officers (the bank may even have been established by the enter-prise, ensuring its access to loans), enterprises that continue to produce even useless output receive the financial means necessary for production.

A goal of price liberalization and free enterprise is that profits become useful indicators of the social value of the activities of enterprises. But if subsidies remain available and budget constraints remain soft, profits during the transition become even more unreliable signals of a firm's performance than they were under central planning. Firms can have profits on paper at the same time that they are not being paid by their customers. The real value of an enterprise's accumulated accounts receivable is unknown, and prob-ably unknowable. If the money to match the accounts receivable is forth-coming from the central bank (and the value of the roubles to be paid has not been undermined, relative to expenses, by inflation), then the firm may indeed be profitable, but perhaps only because its customers are being propped up. If the funds are not forthcoming, then the enterprise's paper profits are worthless.

LESSONS FOR REFORM

The recognition that the unreformed Russian employment regime involved repressed unemployment and an enterprise-centred social welfare system bolsters one conclusion from the examination of price liberalization: to implement a successful reform, an explicit unemployment and welfare system must be created, since the rise in open unemployment that will accompany reform undermines the old enterprise-based social welfare system. This explicit welfare system will take a different form than the old implicit system, but it can be substantially less costly, as subsidies can be made available only to those individuals who are truly needy.

Other lessons for reform also emerge from examining the employment sector. For example, unemployment benefits should not be tied to past wages, because of the tremendous uncertainty as to what actually constitutes the wage rate in Russia. Given that official and unofficial wage components were generally inversely related – butchers had low state wages but high informal compensation – basing unemployment benefits on only the official portion of the previous wage would result in new inequities among workers from different industries. Brookings Institution economist Clifford Gaddy has argued that labour unrest during the reform era by coal miners, who traditionally have the highest official wages of any category of Russian industrial workers, has been sparked by the limited opportunities for coal miners to earn additional income informally. There is little to steal in a coal mine, and literally underground workers have a tough time producing for the 'underground' economy during official working hours.[266]

The extent of open unemployment can be minimized if reforms are led by freeing new economic activity. Emerging private enterprise can attract workers away from the state sector on a significant scale, as has happened in China and Eastern Europe, and is already taking place in Russia. The state sector can then wither away (as opposed to attempts at rapid privatization) as long as the government can resist demands for higher state wages. Resisting such demands may be quite difficult, however. Wages for employees in private businesses are typically 1.5 to 3 times the wages of comparable state employees.[267] Much of this difference can be explained by the non-wage compensation available in the state sector, but it is still probably the case that private-sector employees have higher real earnings, on average, than comparable state employees. (Part of the differential may also represent a 'risk premium', since private-sector employees may still enjoy less job security than state-sector employees.) If Russia were to remove the substantial legal barriers to entry into private enterprise, these wage differentials would draw labour out of the state sector until the wage rates equalized. But in the meantime, the remaining state sector workers are likely to press demands for higher wages, which if met will contribute to the government budget deficit and inflation, and slow down the withering away of the state sector.

Instead of raising state wages, the government may choose to limit private incomes in order to maintain the existing relationship in the remuneration between private and state employment. Like raising state-sector pay, though, wage limitations on the private sector, whether they take the form of direct wage controls or indirect levers on earnings such as high income tax rates, would prevent the gradual development of the private enterprise economy. To encourage the movement of labour into the private sector, therefore, the wage controls that are applied to state-owned enterprises should not be extended to private firms.[268] This is another instance of the undesirability of partial reforms, or rather policies that run counter to market-oriented reform.

The main danger of partial reforms in the employment realm, however, has already been discussed: partial reforms that maintain pre-existing economic distortions could result in the wrong firms adjusting, and adjusting in ways that are not socially beneficial. To prevent the costs of unemployment from rising, most market restrictions should be lifted before state enterprises are given unlimited managerial discretion and are cut off entirely from state subsidies. Price liberalization makes for a good start, and tariffs that remain fixed by the state, such as energy prices, should be raised to reduce or eliminate subsidies. Enterprise profits will then be a strong guide as to which firms will be solvent in the marketplace.

Freeing prices is the easy part. It is the next step, that of cutting state-owned enterprises off from government subsidies and tolerating the open unemployment, that has proved more difficult. Of course, for political purposes, after imposing hard budget constraints, the Russian government can elect to subsidize some of the insolvent firms. As long as this is not a pervasive phenomenon, it need not be particularly costly to the economy – at least not as costly as the unreformed system, where the government propped up all insolvent state-owned enterprises, without even knowing which firms were net recipients of subsidies.

The partial reform of price liberalization in the absence of hard budget constraints on state-owned enterprises, as occurred in Russia in 1992, also generates new problems. Under these circumstances, thanks to the easy availability of loans, enterprises do not have to alter their behaviour in response to the free prices. 'Free' prices then are similar to higher but administratively fixed prices, in that they discourage demand but induce little supply response, at least from the state sector. (The private sector, not dependent on subsidies, may respond to free prices all the more quickly, if the potential state sector competitors are not interested, particularly if government constraints do not severely limit or preclude private market activity.)

The final implication of the implicit/explicit approach in the employment realm echoes an earlier contention: the initial gains to even a well-designed reform are not monumental. Just as many of the costs of unemployment were already being borne in the unreformed economy, many of the benefits of reform were already being captured. The large amount of de facto private activity, which has increased markedly in the Gorbachev–Yeltsin years through spontaneous privatization, implies that the most flagrant wastes of labour were informally curtailed long ago. While the partially reformed nature of the Russian economy channels some activity into endeavours that are not socially valuable – e.g., the continuing energy subsidies lead to great waste in that area – the existing private market ameliorates the problem. People are not likely to waste even subsidized gasoline if they can easily sell it at high market prices.

DISTRIBUTION AGAIN

> It must be remembered that there is nothing more difficult to plan, more doubtful of success, nor more dangerous to manage than the creation of a new system. For the initiator has the enmity of all who would profit by the preservation of the old institutions and merely lukewarm defenders in those who would gain by the new ones.
>
> Machiavelli[269]

Increasing the size of the social pie is not necessarily a good thing if the slices of the pie that some individuals receive get smaller. Workers who lose their current jobs because of enterprise bankruptcies or downsizing are strong candidates to be among those who are harmed by reforms – though sensing this, many Russian workers have already left enterprises with poor prospects. It is important to (at least partially) compensate unemployed workers, if only to ensure that popular discontent with reform does not become sufficient to scuttle reform efforts. Markets may well be viewed as being unfair if some industrious workers lose their jobs and incomes while others prosper post-reform, merely as an artefact – albeit an important artefact – of market prices. Of course, the pre-reform fixed-price system created economically-arbitrary winners and losers. With reform, alternatively, 'strong' enterprises and industries will be those that efficiently produce socially-valuable products.[270] Nevertheless, unfavourable movements from the status quo for some people surely will be perceived as particularly unfair, providing yet another reason to create an explicit social welfare system.[271]

There has been concern expressed about the rise of an ownership class, on the grounds that Russians are not ready to accept such a development.[272] Reform will allow some entrepreneurs to earn large profits: there is already a Russian millionaires' club. (That is a million dollars, not a million roubles.) A significant share of total income will then represent a return to the ownership of capital (interest and profits). Capital income seemingly entails a profound change from the pre-reform situation, when almost all household income was earned as a payment to labour in the form of wages, bonuses, and in-kind compensation. There were no (open) capitalists collecting profits or interest payments. Once again, though, the unreformed system is misleading when taken at face value. Productive assets were controlled by individuals, even if they were not the 'owners'. Often, these individuals could extract a return from their control of capital, via bribes, favours, or simply free market sales. Capital did earn some positive return (even above the low nominal interest rates applied to individual savings accounts), and there were millionaires in the pre-perestroika Russian economy.[273] Still, reform is likely to increase the number of individuals who are substantially more wealthy than the average. Under the planning regime, the necessity of keeping illegal private economic activity fairly well hidden limited the scale of such endeavours – hired labour, for example, constituted only a small fraction of labour inputs into the pre-reform second economy.[274] With reform, the scale of successful private enterprises will increase, and the owners should therefore reap greater returns.

The return to various skills will undergo a tremendous re-alignment during transition. Some professions that require substantial education and training, such as the medical profession, were poorly paid under the Soviet regime, though again, informal mechanisms for increasing the pay of doctors abounded.[275] The hours invested in Marxian studies or the Marxian version of social sciences, which were well rewarded under the old system, will become relatively worthless. Simultaneously, highly-trained engineers and technical workers may increase their standing, perhaps by participating in joint ventures with Western firms, though the relative over-supply of technical workers may make some engineering skills less valuable under free markets.[276] Incentives to accumulate human capital in business fields such as accounting and finance are already increasing dramatically. Traders skilled in the ways of free markets can also reap large returns, as the new system of free relative prices develops and stabilizes.[277]

Just as the elimination of Social Security in the West would tend to harm older citizens relative to younger citizens, Russian reforms are biased towards the young. Younger people will have more time to enjoy the eventually increased living standards, and they have committed fewer resources to the pre-reform system. They have more time and incentive to invest in high-return education and training. Not surprisingly, younger Russians are much more prepared to enter the private sector than older workers.[278] A 1993 survey indicated that younger people were more likely to have seen an improvement in their economic situation from the previous year, and to be more optimistic about their future economic prospects.[279] Older Russians, particularly those on fixed incomes, may find themselves relatively worse off with reform. One mitigating factor is that older people have generally been able to accumulate some wealth in the form of housing and durable consumer goods. Difficulties that arise during transition can then be overcome by liquidating some of this wealth, an option that younger people, most of whom did not have an opportunity to acquire a substantial holding of consumer goods, do not share.

REAL WAGES

What is the wage of an average Russian worker? Thanks to the wide-scale provision of goods like housing and food through the work place and informal opportunities to supplement the basic wage and bonuses by taking bribes or stealing time, calculations of a Russian worker's compensation are complex. Inflation further complicates the determination of a worker's wage.

When there is inflation, wages tend to go up along with other prices, though not by the same percentage. Higher wages and higher prices are not necessarily preferable to constant wages and constant prices, because a dollar of wages will buy less as the prices of goods in the shops inflate. Increases in wages that only match the price inflation do not make workers better off.

Economists attempt to account for the illusion of prosperity when inflation raises wages by taking out the component of wage increases that reflect generally higher prices. The resulting wage statistic is called the 'real wage', and it serves to measure the actual purchasing power of wages, simultaneously providing a proxy for the standard of living of a worker. The real wage is calculated by dividing the nominal money level of wages (what a worker actually receives in his or her pay cheque) by a price index that measures inflation. The price index equals 100 in some specified base year, so real wages are expressed in dollars (or roubles) of that year. As an example, US wages in private nonagricultural industries averaged \$7.68 per hour in 1982, and averaged \$10.50 per hour in December 1991. If the US price level is defined to be 100 in 1982, it would be about 140 in 1991: in other words, prices on average went up 40 per cent in the US between 1982 and 1991. Real wages in December 1991 were \$10.50/140 = 7.48 per hour measured in 1982 dollars – actually lower, in real terms, than they were in 1982.[280]

While the procedure for determining real wages is straightforward, the results can be quite misleading in the circumstances of a reforming socialist economy. The numerator of the real wage calculation, the nominal monetary wage, is rendered nearly meaningless unless in-kind and informal components of compensation are also included. The denominator, the price index, is even more problematic. Price indices capture the change from repressed to open inflation as though it represented new inflation, because the original (base year) prices are understated when the official state prices are used: for example, the costs of searching and queuing for goods are not reflected in the pre-reform price

Average annual rate of growth (%) of the average real wage, USSR

Year	Growth rate
1986	0.9
1987	2.4
1988	7.7
1989	7.2
1990	8.2
1991	−2.1

Source: IMF (1992a, p. 62)

index. But even if corrections for this understatement could be made, determining the pre-reform price level is exceedingly difficult, since there were multiple official prices for each good. The prices that a person had to pay depended on the person's official position, with high official positions generally associated with lower prices.[281]

Thanks to all of these complications, the calculation of real wages in Russia using the official price and wage data is ludicrous. (See the table above.) The early years of perestroika (1988-90), according to the official statistics, were marked by tremendous increases in the real wage. These large increases in real wages should have been associated with a tremendous economic boom. Later, the sharp drop in real wages in 1991 would seem to signal an economic crash.

In reality, neither the boom nor the crash took place.[282] Actual prices facing consumers during the early years of perestroika increased much faster than the official price index, because of the increased amount of repressed inflation. This trend was reversed in 1991 and 1992, when the repressed inflation was largely converted to open inflation. The total growth in real wages evidenced by the table is more than 25 per cent between 1986 and 1992 – an equally nonsensical figure, signalling an elusive prosperity. Nor can the usual association of real wages with living standards be maintained during the Russian transition, as moonlighting and multiple job holdings increased significantly. The real wage is a textbook example of how statistics from an economy undergoing a transition from socialism to capitalism can be particularly misleading.

MISLEADING UNEMPLOYMENT STATISTICS

Price indices and the real wage are not the only statistics that tend to be misleading during transitions. Changes in unemployment rates are also suspect. The large rise in measured unemployment that will accompany a successful reform does not signal economic deterioration; rather, it reflects a shift in unemployment from the repressed to the open variety.

Not only is the change in the measured unemployment rate during reform not indicative of actual economic changes, the level of unemployment may itself be misleading. Officially unemployed workers often hold jobs in the informal economy. Anecdotal evidence suggests that unrecorded second economy jobs in transitional economies can result in immensely overstated measured unemployment rates. A leading spokeswoman for the poverty lobby in Hungary reportedly has said that eight out of 10 registered un-employed Hungarians have other sources of income. The same report tells of a Hungarian agricultural cooperative that declared its work force 'un-employed', bussed them to the unemployment benefits office, and then bussed them directly back to work.[283] The official unemployment rate in Poland is thought to overstate unemployment by approximately one-third.[284]

The effects of increasing second economy activity on economic indicators such as the unemployment rate can have serious and deleterious ramifi-cations. Policy-makers will be tempted to change policies in response to a perceived worsening economic situation, even as the actual situation is not deteriorating.[285] This is particularly true of transforming socialist economies, as the initial levels of the indicators are themselves quite distorted.

While unfavourable statistics can sometimes mask positive developments, favourable statistics can likewise conceal less favourable movements. Poten-tially, one such statistic is the exceedingly low official unemployment rate in Russia, remaining under two per cent throughout 1993.[286] This figure could be understated for a variety of reasons, including the fact that Russian citizens have little incentive to register as unemployed, when unemployment benefits are relatively modest. A person registered as unemployed is also subject to government efforts to place the worker in a new job, which some people view more as a penalty than a service. Furthermore, the official unemployment rate excludes workers who are on short time or forced variations, or who are not paid their full salary in a timely fashion. But the most likely cause of the low unemployment rate is that decisive restructuring has yet to take place within state-owned enterprises – a conclusion bolstered by the almost total lack of plant closings. Of course, important gradual changes have occurred since perestroika began, both in the new private sector and the privatized state enterprises. But the transition from repressed to open unemployment that is almost sure to accompany the imperative state-sector restructuring has yet to appear. As one Russian economist, perhaps overly pessimistic, told me in the summer of 1992, 'Reform cannot be said to have begun until the unemployment rate is three per cent'.

Finally, it is the effect of unemployment on human welfare, and not the amount of unemployment in itself, that matters most. For this reason, Western economists often focus on the duration of unemployment, and persistently high unemployment rates among socio-economic groups such as minority teenagers. In transitional Russia, the welfare losses from un-employment have tended to be low. It is extremely rare for a Russian household not to contain at least one employed person, even if some member of the household is unemployed. (This could change, however, if large firms in 'company towns' close down.) Participation in informal economic activities, such as self-provision of food, also limits the impact of unemployment. Based on annual surveys of Russians conducted since 1992, British economist Richard Rose concludes that in Russia, 'the effect of unemployment upon a household's economy tends to be temporary and marginal'.[287]

Chapter 5

Privatization

In this sense, the theory of the Communists may be summed up in the single phrase: Abolition of private property.
Karl Marx and Friedrich Engels, *The Communist Manifesto* [288]

INTRODUCTION

Socialism is frequently defined as an economic system in which capital goods, the 'means of production', are state-owned, as opposed to capitalism, where private individuals own capital and can employ it for their own gain. Accordingly, the privatization of capital goods is a leading issue in the Russian transformation from socialism to capitalism, and an official privatization programme is ongoing. Treatises on economic reform in formerly socialist countries typically devote a good deal of attention to such privatization programmes.

The discussion here has so far been notable for almost completely skirting the issue of official privatization. Voucher schemes, auctions, multi-coloured coupons and the other paraphernalia of various official privatization schemes have been honoured here only in the breach, while the somewhat shady spontaneous version of privatization has uncustomarily received the observance. This madness is partly thrust upon, as Russian reality had seen a good deal of spontaneous privatization prior to any official privatization; and it is partly achieved of method, reflecting my view that official privatization is not an indispensable element, particularly in the early stages, of a successful transformation. What is indispensable, as previously argued, is the freeing of *new* economic activity and the provision of a relatively undistorted economic environment. Combined with the privatization of small-scale state-owned enterprises such as restaurants and retail outlets, new private endeavours and the emergence of pre-existing market activity have already created a substantial open market economy in Russia. With time, this emerging private activity can swamp the state-owned sector, so that official privatization of large state-owned industries becomes a desirable but not too pressing policy. The state-owned sector can wither away instead of being 'big-banged' out of existence.

At the same time, within the traditionally state-owned sector, what matters is not so much whether assets are state-owned or privately-owned, but rather the environment in which the ownership claims exist and the performance incentives that accompany ownership. State ownership is not prima facie 'worse' than private ownership. Under Soviet conditions, though, state ownership and fixed prices resulted in poor incentives to create economic wealth.

The improved economic environment in Russia, most particularly the liberalization of prices and the partial hardening of enterprise budget constraints, has led to improved performance from many state-owned enterprises even prior to privatization. Recall that during 1991 and 1992, one survey indicated that 80 per cent of enterprises had changed their suppliers or customers to some extent.[289] Product innovations and the shedding of excess labour have also been common.[290] A new concern with the sale of output, as opposed to the production of output, has become widespread.[290*]

Nevertheless, at some point privatization of the 'commanding heights' of the economy, those large-scale industrial enterprises, must be addressed. Once again, the issue of privatization is clarified by understanding the pre-reform situation. Not surprisingly, the ownership structure in Russia during the pre-reform era involved many implicit, repressed elements. As discussed in the previous chapter, de facto ownership claims by individuals over capital goods existed under Russian socialism, despite de jure state ownership. Since the de facto property rights were not recognized in pre-reform official statistics, assessments of reform based on the number of state-owned firms that have been 'privatized' are inadequate and even misleading indicators of the extent of private ownership and marketization in the Russian economy.

Partial reform measures in the privatization sphere, as elsewhere, can raise the costs of transition. Privatization is not a desirable policy unless accompanied by complementary reforms. Recall that a partial reform that includes privatization and free foreign trade but not price liberalization, for example, would be dangerous. Entrepreneurs would purchase goods that are underpriced in Russia – oil, for instance – and export them, reaping the economic rent created by the price controls while the Russian government pays the subsidy. Or, they might purchase a cheap input like energy, and produce a final product like tropical flowers for export. A reform that includes privatization but does not include the establishment of an explicit social safety net may also be undesirable, as newly unemployed workers may suffer unduly.

PRIVATIZATION GUIDELINES

By enlisting the aid of various partial reforms, it is comparatively easy to design detrimental, even disastrous privatization schemes. But what properties should be exhibited by a potentially successful privatization programme for large-scale industrial enterprises? I will mention five such properties, though not all would receive universal assent, nor would a failure to exhibit all of these properties clearly spell doom for a privatization programme: they are desirable, not essential. Two of the features concern the destination of enterprise reform. The first, near to the heart of economists, is that at the end of the process, clear, explicit property rights should be established. Informality (of property rights) breeds contracting problems, so informality should be limited by reducing ownership uncertainty. A second desirable property for the destination of a privatization programme is related to the first: not only should clear ownership claims be established, but the owners should in general have strong incentives to take socially-valuable actions. A law that stipulates that everyone gets paid an identical amount no matter what his or her actions would surely provide poor incentives for 'owners' and, for that matter, everyone else.

Three other markers of successful privatization concern the nature of the transition path to private ownership. First, the privatization scheme should largely validate pre-existing ownership claims. Taking away what people regard (often for good reason) as their property is bound to generate resentment and opposition. (There may be competing 'ownership' claims pre-reform, but the system was so well-established and stable in Russia that I believe this complication is relatively unimportant.) It can be argued that the pre-existing ownership structure is unfair, and should not be respected. But it can also be argued that the pre-existing claims are no more unfair than other distributions, and that there are better ways of dealing with unfairness than through the privatization scheme – with progressive taxation, for instance, or an improved social safety net.[291]

Beyond the respect for pre-existing claims, I believe that 'fair' access is a second desirable property for the transition to private ownership. A privatization programme should not be systematically biased against classes of people who are identifiable prior to the programme. (After the fact, there are bound to be relative winners and losers.) In general this property would seem to require widespread access to the privatization programme, so that pensioners, for example, are not sure to be excluded from the benefits of privatization. And the final desirable feature of ownership transition is that the privatization programme be relatively swift, both to generate improved enterprise performance and to limit the amount of special pleading that enterprises and individuals can engage in to try to garner more of the benefits for themselves.

PRE-REFORM PROPERTY RIGHTS

By informal property right we mean legally unsanctioned and even illegal, yet in reality effective, control over assets for private profit or other form of access to future streams of informal/illegal income and consequent wealth. Such an informal right may be an expected and de facto accepted by-product of a legitimate job (a very common situation).

Gregory Grossman[292]

'State ownership' of the means of production, in itself, leaves a host of questions unanswered. (So does 'private ownership'.) Sometimes it is said that state ownership of an asset means that everybody owns it, which means that nobody owns it: ownership, like 'priority', cannot accrue equally to all without eviscerating the concept in the process. But it is not really the case that state ownership is the same as no ownership. Some person or group of people controls the uses and returns to capital goods, even in a socialist society. Economist Yoram Barzel makes this point quite emphatically:[293]

> The distinction between the private and the public sectors is not a distinction between the presence and absence of private property rights. Such rights are necessarily present in both systems. The distinction lies in organization, and particularly in the incentives and rewards under which producers tend to operate. In the private sector, producers are more readily given the opportunity to assume the entire direct effects of their actions. In the government sector, people assume a smaller portion of the direct effects of their actions.

State ownership, then, is associated with relatively weak incentives for the owners, whomever they are, to take actions that are socially valuable, since the owners' rewards are not tied closely to 'the direct effects of their actions'. It is these poor incentives that have sullied the reputation of state ownership. But this is not to say that state ownership *requires* poor incentives.

As an example of state ownership, it might be useful to broaden the earlier discussion of the operation of a Russian state-owned restaurant to state-owned enterprises more generally. Under an ideal version of central planning, an enterprise would receive its output plan and requisite inputs from the state, and hire workers at wages that were state-controlled. It would then deliver the planned output to the centrally-specified downstream customers, at prices – accounting entries, basically – that were also state-controlled. If the enterprise happened to make a profit (measured at the fixed state prices), then the profit would be returned to the state. Under this ideal centrally-planned system, workers have the property right to their centrally-determined wages: a fixed payment, largely independent of the 'direct effects of their actions'. Downstream customers have property rights to their share of the planned output at the fixed prices, and the state is the 'residual claimant', receiving whatever is left over after the claims of the other parties are satisfied.

The official Soviet system did not attempt to implement such an extreme form of central planning. Rather, official compensation was tied somewhat more directly to the effects of employees' actions, at least as measured by the plan indicators. To provide better incentives for workers, bonuses were available for above-plan output, with the bonus fund depending on a host of indicators of enterprise performance.[294] Similarly, some profits could be retained by enterprises for investment purposes.[295] Wages were supplemented in areas with poor working or living conditions, such as for coal miners or for jobs in the Far North. The administratively-set prices were, in general and relative terms, not inconsistent with market-based scarcity prices.[296]

Of course, the actual operation of a state-owned enterprise in Russia bore little relationship to either the ideal version of central planning or the de jure system. Extra-plan, informal activity generally moved the economy towards the form of organization associated with private property, with compensation tied more closely to the direct effects of actions. (And the measures of the effects of action in the informal economy were no longer plan indicators, but real market values, and hence more in tune with consumer preferences.) Bribes to official and unofficial suppliers, theft of goods and time from work, second economy production on the official job, bribes from customers, and bribes to secure employment: all formed the part and parcel of 'really existing' socialism.

The de facto system of property rights therefore differed considerably from the de jure system. Workers and managers were, to a degree, residual claimants of their enterprises' profits – in some sense, owners. The central government was likely to receive close to a fixed payment, the 'planned profit' for the enterprise. High officials in the planning or party networks, who controlled either supplies or the jobs that controlled supplies, received bribes, and presumably higher bribes for increased supplies. Customers generally could not convert roubles to goods at the fixed prices, but could do so at higher prices, paid either in roubles or partly in time and partly in roubles. There was even a substantial, illegal 'capital market', where underground firms could be bought and sold.[297] And of course, the shadow system of property rights was closely tied to Communist Party positions.

The pre-reform system thus had many elements of a private ownership, market economy, where producers had opportunities to serve as residual claimants. As Gregory Grossman noted in 1977, the Soviet second economy was 'a kind of spontaneous surrogate economic reform that imparts a necessary modicum of flexibility, adaptability, and responsiveness to a formal setup that is too often paralyzing in its rigidity, slowness, and inefficiency. It represents a de facto decentralization, with overtones of the market.'[298]

THE REFORM PERIOD

The market overtones of the Soviet second economy amplified considerably during the Gorbachev era via spontaneous privatization. Three factors helped to promote marketization during the perestroika years. First, the degree of repressed inflation increased, simultaneously raising the benefits available from diverting state-sector goods to the private sector, since the free prices in the private sector rose, while the state prices remained, for the most part, fixed. In the language of property rights theory, the value of assets that were previously 'in the public domain' appreciated, increasing the incentives for private individuals to garner control of those assets, legally or illegally.[299] The second factor promoting marketization was that legal routes to garner control of state goods and assets were expanded. For example, the Law on Cooperatives provided one quasi-legal route to divert state-sector goods into private hands. Reform provisions thereby lowered the costs of diverting state-sector goods to free markets at the same time that the benefits from so doing were increasing. The third factor driving spontaneous privatization might be termed an 'insurance incentive'. As the stability of the old system began to be undermined during the late 1980s, individuals saw that their implicit property rights were threatened by reform. They had an incentive, then, to insure their ownership claims by converting their implicit property rights into explicit rights that would be more likely to survive the reform process. Together, these three factors led to marketizations that in many cases were complete enough to merit the now familiar term 'spontaneous privatization'.

But the increasingly formal private property rights in Russia did not translate into an efficient economy. High transaction costs, as discussed in Chapter 2, are a major impediment. Furthermore, the extent to which reform has brought rewards that are closely related to the direct effects of actions has been limited by government policy. The owners of privatized firms do not necessarily become residual claimants. Because the Russian government has been unwilling to cut off subsidies to unprofitable enterprises, owners do not face significant penalties for failure.[300] The up-side potential for private activity within the former state-owned enterprises may also be limited, as it was in the pre-reform system, to the extent that successful enterprises will be the source of subsidies for the unsuccessful firms. The 'partial reform' of continuing state subsidies has reduced the value of the shift from repressed to open private property rights.

This reflects the more general point noted above, that privatization is not an end in itself. (For that matter, neither is a Western-style market economy, but it appears to be the best means to the higher living standards that presumably are an end.) The important conditions for the efficient operation of a market economy are generally free prices, and strong incentives to respond to those free prices. Residual claimant status provides the strong incentives for owners, and free prices enhance the probability that the privately profitable decisions will be socially valuable, whether the state or an individual is the official owner. In the absence of generally free prices and strong incentives to respond, the Russian economy is unlikely to markedly improve, irrespective of the extent of privatization. Indeed, some privatized firms operate exactly as they did under state ownership.[301]

OFFICIAL RUSSIAN PRIVATIZATION

The ongoing Russian privatization plan includes three variants for large enterprises.[302] Under two of the variants, large firms (more than 1000 employees or a book value exceeding 50 million roubles) are being converted into capitalist-style joint-stock companies. Ownership shares are then distributed, with the two variants distinguished by the amount, type (preferred or common), and price of stock available to employees and management. In each of these distributions, no less than 25 per cent of the stock would go to 'insiders', the workers and managers of the enterprise. A third, considerably less popular, alternative is for the employees of part or all of an enterprise to submit a reorganization plan that requires some additional investment on their part. After one year, if they have lived up to the terms of the agreement, employees then have some priority in purchasing common stock. Remaining shares are slated to be auctioned off to the general public. In practice, workers and managers of a privatized enterprise are likely to control no less than 40 per cent of the shares under any of the privatization schemes, and early results indicated that some 70 per cent of shares were initially procured by enterprise insiders.

Not all of the shares are being sold for roubles, however. By early 1993, nearly every Russian citizen had received a 'privatization cheque', a small piece of paper with a serial number and a face value of 10,000 roubles printed on it. At least 29 per cent of the shares of large enterprises are slated to be auctioned off using privatization cheques.[303] The purpose of privatization cheques is to widen the scope of privatization and render it more fair. Teachers, doctors, pensioners, and others who do not work for privatizing state-owned enterprises can still take part in privatization, and at no monetary cost, by purchasing ownership shares of an enterprise with their privatization cheques.

Privatization cheques counter the bias towards enterprise insiders in the privatization process, but they certainly do not eliminate insider advantages. Indeed, there are further aspects of privatization that favour existing workers and managers, beyond the privileged access to ownership shares. Employees who spontaneously privatized their enterprises by leasing their assets prior to 3 July, 1991, the date of the original Russian Federation law on privatization, can now become employee-owned. Firms in fields such as R&D and defence are exempt from mandatory privatization, though spontaneous privatizations are taking place among enterprises in these industries. Finally, the auctions of the remaining shares of enterprise stock, whether for privatization cheques or cash, are tainted by a seemingly large informational advantage of insiders. How can an outsider have a good sense of the value of a privatizing firm, relative to insiders? One mechanism that helps outside investors is the development of a 'market for information'. Russians can sell their privatization cheques to other individuals or for shares of mutual funds, that then invest the collected cheques on the funds behalf. The funds – there are more than 500 in Russia – presumably are better positioned to learn about the enterprises in which they invest than are individual shareholders. Still, insider advantages are not overcome by these contrivances, and the remaining insider bias may be large enough to chill the competitive nature of the share auctions.[304] A similar phenomenon exists in the West, where it is feared that widespread insider trading makes stock market transactions less attractive to outside investors.

How does the Russian official privatization programme measure up against the privatization 'success indicators' promulgated earlier in this chapter? As for creating clear ownership claims, the official Russian pro-gramme appears to accomplish this goal straightforwardly: the shareholders are the owners of firms. The protection of pre-existing de facto ownership claims is also largely achieved in the privatization programme, via the preferences given to enterprise workers and management. Thanks to this policy, there has been virtually universal voluntary compliance with the privatization programme. And except for the desirable bias towards existing workers and managers, there appears to be little discrimination against identifiable social groups in privatization. The mass distribution of vouchers gives all Russians a stake in privatization, though worker-manager control appears to be the likely short-term outcome. Furthermore, the speed of the Russian privatization programme compares favourably with that of Eastern Europe. By privatizing most non-defence state-owned enterprises more-or-less simultaneously, special pleading has been held to a minimum. Creat-ing privatization cheques and stock markets out of thin air has required some time, of course, particularly in comparison with the alternative of simply turning firms over to their workers, but the generally perceived increase in fairness may have been worth the extra time.[305]

It is with respect to the incentives for the new owners that the Russian privatization programme is most vulnerable. The first obstacle, familiar in the West, is that in the absence of a single controlling owner, individual share-holders have limited incentives to actually monitor the activities of the firms that they 'own'. Most employees in the US who own shares of firms via their pension plans do not pay close attention to the management decisions in the firms in which their pensions are invested, though perhaps the pension fund managers do. Wide distribution of vouchers virtually rules out a controlling owner in the short term. Again, however, much of the ownership is accruing to workers and managers, who should have the interest, information, and ability to exercise effective ownership control. Incentives for worker-owners should be fairly 'high-powered', since their wages and profit shares will directly depend on the performance of the enterprise – unless continuing state subsidies provide adequate compensation irrespective of performance.

Worker ownership is not necessarily ideal, however. Workers do not have the same incentives that outside owners might have; in particular, workers might be reluctant to hire more employees, since another employee not only receives wages but also dilutes the ownership shares of those already working. (An outside owner would not be similarly reluctant since the new worker would not get a stake in ownership.) Worker-owners also face some diversification problems, since both their labour income (their wages) and their investment income are tied up in the same firm. In general it might be thought that individuals would prefer to invest in firms other than the one in which they work, to minimize their exposure to bankruptcy of the firm.

The empirical evidence on worker ownership is not encouraging. First, the practice was institutionalized in Yugoslavia, without much success. Second, worker ownership is rare in Western market economies, where it is perfectly legal and feasible. If worker ownership were economically beneficial, would there not be more of it in the West?

Perhaps. But the West is not undergoing a transition from socialism. As Harvard economist Martin Weitzman argues, during transitions worker ownership can play a valuable role, particularly in maintaining employment.[306] With relatively free stock markets, over time more efficient ownership structures can evolve to replace worker ownership – workers can sell their ownership shares to outsiders. The official Russian privatization programme therefore has the virtue of not fixing a final ownership pattern – unlike the Yugoslavian precedent – but rather allows for the evolution of the form of 'normal market economy' that best suits Russian conditions.

The Russian privatization programme, taken in isolation, seems to offer fairly good incentives for new enterprise owners. But privatization is not taking place in isolation. It may well be the environment created by other policies not directly related to the privatization scheme that could undermine the programme. One such policy would be an unwillingness, perhaps because of concerns with extensive monopoly power, to extricate the government from its old duty of price setting. Whatever the incentives that the owners would then have, there would be little reason to suspect that they would be well aligned with social benefits. A second stumbling block has already been mentioned, that of continuing government subsidies to privatized firms because of fears of open unemployment: in 1993, the Russian government indicated that privatized firms would receive the same access to subsidized state credits as state-owned enterprises![307] Without penalties for failure, incentives to respond well to free prices are reduced, though not necessarily eliminated. Third, excessive taxation of successful enterprises, perhaps to raise revenue for subsidies to poorly-performing firms, will similarly limit the incentives for private sector firms to engage in socially valuable activities. Fourth, slow movement on the development of state-enforced contract law will keep transaction costs high. Finally, it is competitive markets that seem to provide good incentives. Constraints on new private activity, such as the onerous licensing requirements, will reduce the degree of competition faced by privatized firms in the Russian market economy, and thereby reduce the benefits of privatization.

Chapter 6

Monopoly

INTRODUCTION

Monopoly, the control of an industry by a single seller (or perhaps a small group of sellers) is one situation in which free markets are likely to result in socially undesirable outcomes. Monopolists in market economies produce too little output from a social point of view, in order to sustain high prices and profits, and so they at least partially deserve their bad public image. The high profits, in turn, attract competitors. Unless there is some barrier preventing the entry of new firms, monopolies in market economies tend to be short-lived.

Central planning in Russia, however, was invested with the legal authority to sustain a highly monopolistic industrial structure. Thirty to forty per cent of manufactured products, including sewing machines, freezers, and colour-photography paper, had a single producing enterprise within the USSR.[308] Presumably, the planning task was made easier by dealing with a relatively small number of big firms than with a host of little firms: the enforcement of price controls and centralized rationing could be streamlined. Market-oriented reform in Russia, it is often argued, holds the danger of creating an economic system dominated by large monopoly producers. Some observers suggest that privatization should be postponed until after the forced de-monopolization of Russian industry, in order to forestall the detrimental effects of monopoly firms operating in a market environment.[309]

The existence of monopoly in the pre-reform Russian economy holds implications for the analysis of reform and the role of demonopolization. Monopoly 'rents', or excess profits, were available in the pre-reform Russian system, though not in the usual market economy form of excessive profits arising from prices that are high relative to costs.[310] Rather than focusing on how best to combat post-reform monopoly or on how to demonopolize prior to reform, the initial question for reform becomes whether the social costs attributed to monopoly are higher in the pre-or post-reform setting. In other words, to what extent is monopoly a *reform* problem? This chapter argues that the costs of monopoly were substantially greater in the pre-reform Russian economy than they will be in the fully reformed system, though the reduction in the costs of monopoly that will accompany reform can be slowed or reversed if anti-competitive measures – partial reforms – are adopted. From this perspective, excessive industrial concentration is not an important issue for a comprehensive market reform, irrespective of concentration's detrimental impact on the Russian economy. Russia would be lucky indeed if the only economic problem that it had to worry about was monopoly.[311]

MEASURING MONOPOLY

For a change of pace, I would like to begin this section by talking about the ease in interpreting the reliable Soviet statistics on monopoly power. But, of course, I can't. Plus ça change . . . As with inflation and unemployment, measures of the degree of monopoly power in Russian industry may be misleading. Consider, first, measures based on 'concentration ratios', the percentage of a good's production that derives from the one, two, three (or more) largest producing enterprises. (Concentration ratios are typical measures of monopoly power employed in the West.) In 1988, the market share of the single largest Soviet producer exceeded 50 per cent for over 60 per cent of product groups; for the US in 1982, the four largest producers exceeded a 50 per cent market share in less than 30 per cent of manufacturing industries.[312] This appears to be rather unambiguous evidence that the pre-reform Soviet economy was more concentrated than the US economy.

One problem with concentration ratios, however, derives from the extreme amount of vertical integration in Russian firms.[313] Because of the near-impossibility of disciplining state-owned monopoly suppliers, Russian enterprises (and ministries) produced many of their own inputs, as noted earlier. Dr Ed Hewett wrote that in the planned Soviet economy, 'the successful enterprise is the vertically integrated enterprise, and the successful ministry, the vertically integrated ministry'.[314] As a result, in the situations where an enterprise (or a ministry) was particularly dependent on a single supplier, vertical integration (perhaps conducted informally) probably occurred prior to reform. A second factor suggesting that concentration statistics yield a distorted view of the extent of monopoly power in the pre-reform system consists of the defence sector. Production in the defence complex was virtually a black box, with what happened inside a fairly closely-guarded secret. Goods that were produced by a single civilian seller may also have been produced in the defence sector, though the defence production would generally not be reflected in official concentration statistics. And in making comparisons between Russia and Western market economies, it should be kept in mind that the planned imports in Russia – the state had an official monopoly on foreign trade – rarely offered effective competition to domestic producers in the Soviet system, whereas imports often provide important competitive elements in the West.

Another type of statistic that is used to document the extent of monopoly power in the pre-reform Russian economy focuses on the large size of enterprises, often as measured by the number of employees. For example, 73.4 per cent of the (Soviet) work force was employed in enterprises with more than 1000 employees.[315] The average size of industrial enterprises in Soviet-type economies, in terms of number of employees, exceeded that of developed market economies by more than a factor of ten.[316] The interpretation of such statistics must be conditioned on the range of activities that occurred within Russian enterprises, however. The extent of horizontal conglomeration, as with vertical integration, was immense in the pre-reform Russian economy. As previously noted, an industrial enterprise was often involved in providing its workers with food, schools, hospitals, apartments, and a host of other goods and services that were outside the enterprise's main line of business. Concentration statistics that are based on the number of employees at average enterprises are then particularly suspect, as many of the employees were engaged in these sideline activities.

Incidentally, it is perhaps worth noting that the size of individual enterprises is not directly related to monopoly power, at least as monopoly is understood in the West. Monopoly power has to do with the extent of competition in the market for a firm's output, not with how big the company is. Duke University is a large employer (the biggest in Durham, North Carolina!), but its students choose among many competing schools, so Duke is not a monopolist. In the former Soviet Union, however, the monopoly problem associated with capitalism consisted of more than just high prices for the monopolist's output. Another problem associated with monopoly was the propensity of big, powerful enterprises to exploit their workers through low wages and benefits and poor working conditions. The number of employees at a firm is a useful indicator of these kinds of 'monopoly' problems, which approximates the Western notion of 'monopsony'. A monopsonist is a firm that represents the only purchaser of a good. Large firms may have monopsony power in the purchase of labour, as in the case of company towns (like Durham?). Nevertheless, the association of large enterprises with monopoly may be lingering into the post-Soviet era.[317]

The discussion so far indicates potential biases in the usual measures of monopoly power, but the difficulties of using the 'usual measures' in centrally-planned systems are even more fundamental. Concentration ratios or employment ratios calculated at the enterprise level are inappropriate measures of monopoly power in the pre-reform Russian setting, since the former industrial branch ministries provided a built-in cartel structure for the production of many goods.[318] Five producing enterprises that were all subordinated to a single ministry may have had as much monopoly power as a single firm, if the ministry could effectively act as a cartel ringleader. The number of competing ministries in the production of a good probably provides a more accurate guide to the degree of monopoly power than the number of producing enterprises. There was also a good deal of regional specialization, where a geographical area was supplied with a commodity from a single enterprise in the region. (A relatively poor transport infrastructure continues to provide more geographical insulation than is typical in Western market economies.) The number of producing enterprises nationwide would then serve as a poor indicator of the extent of competition.

Most importantly, however, the nature of the central planning system itself renders any statistic irrelevant as a measure of the extent of monopoly. Under Russian planning, virtually all producers were monopoly providers from the point of view of their customers. Downstream users were tied to individual suppliers by the plan. If an enterprise was dissatisfied with the performance of one of its suppliers, and the firm could not vertically integrate, it had little recourse.[319] At another level this was even the condition in retail trade. While Russian citizens could choose to shop at different outlets, the state was generally the only legal seller.[320] Monopoly power, though 'repressed', was nevertheless extensive.

The Russian planned economy therefore resulted in an industrial sector that was much more monopolized – irrespective of industrial concentration statistics – than its Western counterparts. How does the existence of monopoly pre-reform influence the Russian transition to capitalism?

MONOPOLY RENTS, PRE- AND POST-REFORM

The 'dead-weight loss', the net social value of output that monopolists choose not to produce but that would be produced under competitive conditions, is the usual focus in identifying the social losses from monopolies in market economies. (Other social losses may arise from the money that enterprises spend on lawyers and lobbyists in an effort to obtain government support for a monopoly position.[321]) High prices relative to costs are then the most important indicators of social losses from monopoly. Under central planning, alternatively, almost all prices in the Russian state sector deviated significantly from real costs, which can not even be ascertained without free prices, anyway.[322] Fixed prices result in their own dead-weight losses; in fact, the inefficiencies of the fixed-price system are probably the major reason that Russia is undergoing economic reform. But the fixed-price regime indicates that the criterion of the deviation of price from (marginal) cost cannot easily be applied in assessing monopoly power in pre-reform Russia. The dead-weight loss of monopoly can not be distinguished from the efficiency losses and misallocations associated with fixed prices.

The social costs of Russian monopoly are indirectly indicated, however, by the nature and extent of the excess profits, 'rents', that accrue to monopolists. In a centrally-planned setting, monopoly rents take on different (and perhaps less visible) forms than in market economies. Large state monopolies in the pre-reform setting had a great deal of bargaining power in dealing with planners. They were therefore in a position to receive more inputs and lower output targets than firms in worse bargaining positions. Likewise, such firms had bargaining power with respect to customers, even those who were legally entitled via the plan (and the corresponding contract) to the monopolist's output. Large monopoly suppliers could then perform poorly with impunity, letting quality, output assortment, or delivery schedules slip.[323] Alternatively, the monopolists could informally solicit payments in cash or kind for their output – those high prices generally associated with monopoly. The inefficiencies of excessive vertical integration brought on by a firm's attempts to shield itself from unreliable suppliers should also be counted as a cost of monopoly in the pre-reform system. As Ed Hewett noted, 'The result [of excessive vertical integration] is costly for society: large quantities of goods and services produced in small batches at very high cost and probably of variable quality.'[324]

With privatization and price liberalization, monopoly assumes its market economy guise of reduced output (relative to hypothetical competitive levels). Monopoly rents will be generated by prices that are higher than costs. But now the familiar argument applies: the new form of monopoly during transition does not imply higher social costs. Indeed, the emergence of competitors (including imports) will almost certainly mean that the social costs of monopoly will be lower post-reform than pre-reform, even in the absence of any official anti-trust activity.

The basic reason is that the Russian economy can hardly become less competitive during reform, since it started with so little competition relative to that in market economies. With free enterprise, barriers to entry will disappear. Suppliers who dissatisfy their customers will see competitors spring up to take away their business. The Russian economy is quite large, making the prospects for the development of competitors bright relative to those in smaller, closed economies. With the 'emergence' and conversion of military industries, defence enterprises may surface as new competitors. Competition will also be given a boost to the extent that reform increases the participation of foreign firms in the Russian economy. The only monopolies that seem destined to survive reform will be natural monopolies – those monopolies that can produce any given level of output at lower cost than could competitive firms. Temporarily, perhaps some collusion among enterprises could restrict competition in sectors that are not natural monopolies. (Such collusion is difficult to sustain because it is generally in any individual firm's best interest to quietly break the collusive agreement.) But in any case, the post-reform situation will represent quite a departure from the pre-reform system, where nearly every producer was invested with a degree of monopoly power.

Of course, partial reform measures contain the possibility of worsening the monopoly situation during reform. First, some prices, particularly those of the outputs of producers deemed to be monopolists, could be controlled, undermining the incentive for competitors to emerge. Simultaneously, the combination of enterprise autonomy (making it possible for firms to respond to prices) and some fixed prices (as for energy) can result in the Polish tropical flowers problem. Second, government barriers to legal entry, such as a complex licensing system, could likewise prevent competitive pressures from coming to bear. (Private barriers to entry, perhaps due to organized crime, could also limit competition.) Third, the possibility of legal action against firms that raise their prices 'unfairly' could also act to 'fix' prices, and bring on the associated resource misallocations. In other words, government anti- monopoly policy could itself sustain monopoly. With a fairly comprehensive reform, however, monopoly power and the associated costs will fall.

MONOPOLY AND PRIVATIZATION

Since the social costs of monopoly will automatically be reduced during a comprehensive reform, anti-trust activity would appear to have a low priority on the reform agenda. The best policy would seem to be to implement reasonably complete market-oriented reforms, let competition develop and conditions improve, and then tinker around the edges with regulations and anti-trust legislation for the few remaining monopolists. One potential problem with this happy scenario, though, is that the existence of monopolies may itself hinder the reform process. A common contention is that privatization is made more difficult by the presence of monopolies, implying that demonopolization must precede privatization.[325]

There are three main arguments. The first is that privatization, especially through sale, is more difficult for large enterprises than for small enterprises. The second is that demonopolization may be more inconvenient post-reform, and reform itself may increase industrial concentration. The third argument suggesting that industrial concentration hinders reform is that a large enterprise has bargaining power. Enough large enterprises may be able to bargain exceptions for themselves that privatization becomes meaningless.

Why should larger enterprises be more difficult to privatize than small enterprises? The possibility generally considered is that there are not enough wealthy citizens to become owners of huge enterprises. Of course, the enterprises will be sold in shares, not as indivisible units. The new owners do not have to consist of a few wealthy individuals. Another consideration is that the social consequences of bankruptcy are much greater for large enterprises than for small enterprises, so that privatization and the imposition of hard budget constraints are not credible policies. Government bailouts of major corporations in the US, for example, have occurred precisely because of the perceived social consequences of bankruptcy. Once again, however, this monopoly problem – actually a problem of large enterprises, not necessarily monopolists – is worse in the unreformed Russian economy.

No doubt many large enterprises are candidates for bankruptcy, but until prices are free and private ownership is established, it cannot be determined which ones. Now, all of the potentially bankrupt companies are being sustained by the government. Post-reform, failing companies that are deemed worthy may see increased infusions of cash from the private sector. Those that will still be non-viable will then become known. As previously noted, the government can then choose on an individual basis which ones to aid and which ones to let falter.

The concern that monopoly will increase during reform is prompted by reports of enterprises attempting vertical integration and horizontal conglomeration during the transition. In general, however, these types of transactions do not increase monopoly power. If large previously-competing producers attempt to merge, then perhaps some government oversight is desirable, but I know of no evidence of this occurring in Russia. So far, the concern that monopoly power will increase with transition appears to be empirically unjustified.

Preceding privatization with demonopolization may be sensible if the ability to implement anti-trust measures is likely to be greater in the pre-reform setting than after private ownership is established. In market economies, it appears that it is easier to prevent mergers from occurring than it is to break up firms that have already merged.[326] But in Russia, to the extent that new competition-reducing mergers are not taking place, the choice is between breaking up existing monopolies before or after reform. Since market-oriented reforms would seem to do much of this work automatically, and expose those firms that are truly viable monopolists, postponing anti-trust activity until after privatization would appear to be a more efficient strategy for combating monopoly. This point is amplified by a consideration of the limited number of trained personnel available to help manage the transition. Given the importance of such tasks as privatization and military conversion, devoting significant human resources to antitrust policy during the early stages of reform comes at a high cost.[327]

The argument that large enterprises may bargain exceptions for themselves to avoid privatization may well be correct. It is perhaps even more likely, however, that the exceptions they bargain for will be better terms for privatization or continued subsidies. In any case, the bargaining power already exists, and it might also prevent the implementation of demonopolization decrees. Reform and the increased competitive pressures are the best way of counteracting this bargaining power. As Russian economist G. Kazakevich has said, 'Every act of privatization is simultaneously an act of demonopolization.'[328]

Political and nationalistic problems are creating barriers to interregional trade in the former USSR. Regional economic policies that restrict the 'export' of locally-produced goods to other parts of Russia present another barrier.[329] By keeping out competitors, these trade barriers help sustain monopoly power. (The possibility that such barriers reduce trade and output, irrespective of their effect on monopoly power, is probably more significant.) But again, the increase in monopoly power due to trade disruptions is neither caused by economic reform nor worsened by reform, and some of the decreased competitiveness is clearly the result of local anti-reform policies. Political barriers to trade are unfortunate, but are not a problem for market-oriented reform per se.

Finally, two elements of monopoly may actually be beneficial for reform efforts. First, if monopoly pricing practices would generally be available after reform, and these high prices translate into high profits, then sales of monopoly firms during privatization should find plenty of buyers. Foreign firms should also be relatively eager to enter such potentially lucrative markets. (The high profits of monopolies also present a trade-off with the concern over the increase in open unemployment, as profitable monopolies will not go bankrupt.) Second, the breakdown in economic coordination that is sometimes feared from reform is ameliorated by industrial concentration. Downstream firms know precisely what supplier they will have to continue to deal with, and new enterprises should also be able to quickly learn where inputs are available.

ANTI-MONOPOLY POLICY

It has been argued here that anti-trust policy should be accorded low priority in the design of market-oriented reform policies in Russia, and that the more appropriate time to consider anti-trust action is after market reform has been fully implemented and new competitors have had a chance to emerge.

There are two anti-trust measures that may be appropriate for the transitional era, however. First, a watchful eye could be kept on mergers of previously-competing enterprises. In cases where such mergers can be shown to involve large social costs, they should be prevented. Second, price fixing among competitors should be proscribed.

Anti-monopoly policy in Russia during reform has gone well beyond the relatively limited role that I think is desirable. Subsequent to the 2 January 1992 price liberalization, lists of enterprises designated as monopolists were established, at both the national and local levels. An enterprise was eligible for the anti-monopoly list if it produced more than 35 per cent of the output of a good, though in practice inclusion was rather arbitrary.[330] This criterion was even applied at local levels, where almost any large firm would exceed 35 per cent of the locally-produced output of its main products. Note also that the lists were based on local production, not on local sales. So vodka producers, for example, who faced stiff competition from many other vodka makers, including importers, were frequently on local anti-monopoly lists.

The outputs of an enterprise deemed to be a monopolist are subject to price regulation, and overall profitability limits can also be established. An enterprise that exceeds those limits can have its excess profits confiscated, even if they are not attributable to the goods for which it is considered to have a monopoly position. Since most large enterprises are considered monopolists, anti-monopoly policy has provided a mechanism to continue price controls and other features of the planning mechanism. Depending on the level of the price controls and profit ceilings, the monopolists may have little incentive to increase output. Other firms may also be reluctant to increase their market share for fear of being labelled a monopolist. Furthermore, price controls provide a rationale for money-losing firms to demand state subsidies. On balance, Russian anti-monopoly policies seem to be effectively serving as anti-reform measures.

Chapter 7

Income and living standards

if you can know but one fact about a man, knowledge of his income will
probably reveal most about him. Then you can roughly guess his political
opinions, his tastes, and education, his age, and even his life expectancy.

Nobel Prize-winning economist Paul A. Samuelson[331]

CRISIS, CHAOS, COLLAPSE . . .

and Consensus. Virtually all observers in recent years appear to agree that
the Russian economy is or will soon be in a state of crisis, chaos, and
collapse:

> The economy is in a free fall with no prospects for reversal in sight. Severe
> economic conditions, including substantial shortages of food and fuel in
> some areas, the disintegration of the armed forces and ongoing ethnic
> conflict will combine this winter [1991–92] to produce the most significant
> disorder in the former U.S.S.R. since the Bolsheviks consolidated
> power.[332]
>
> Robert M. Gates, Director of the CIA in 1991–2

> The collapse of the Soviet Economy following the August coup is an event all
> but unprecedented in recent economic history. . . . The rapidity of the
> upheaval and the magnitude of the Soviet economic decline have been
> especially spectacular. In two to three years' time, the economy moved from
> positive growth to a drop in the GNP exceeding 20 percent and from relative
> price stability to a yearly inflation rate approaching 1000 percent.[333]
>
> Marshall I. Goldman, Associate Director of the
> Russian Research Center at Harvard University

This [Soviet] crisis is often described as a deeper version of the Great
Depression in America. In fact, the ex-Soviet Union is in much worse
condition, nearer to that of post-World War II Germany and Japan. Its

infrastructure is crumbling. Aeroflot no longer has adequate fuel, its planes decrepit and disintegrating; the collapse of the railroads is not far off; the oil industry is in a similar shambles.[334]

> Martin Malia, professor of Russian history at the
> University of California, Berkeley

the situation of the real economy remains grave. The depression has deepened and is already much worse with respect to output reduction than the Great Depression in the West; living standards have fallen sharply; officially registered foreign trade has been greatly reduced; the foreign debt is increasing; and income distribution has become very unequal.[335]

> Michael Ellman, professor of economics at Amsterdam University and a
> specialist on the Russian economy

And finally, former President Richard Nixon:

> Russia is going through an economic downturn worse than the Great Depression of the 1930's in the United States. In 1992 inflation was 25 percent a month, the gross national product was down 20 percent, and living standards were down 50 percent.[336]

Nor are the reports of economic crisis new. Marshall Goldman's 1983 book, *USSR in Crisis*, subtitled 'The Failure of an Economic System', had already pointed to economic deterioration, as had many predecessors. And in some sense, a crisis began with the introduction of central planning in the late 1920s, as suggested by the previous discussion of the resource mis-allocations endemic to centrally-planned systems. As time passed and the czarist productive legacy became less relevant, the state-sector difficulties perhaps increased, though simultaneously, second economy activity expanded. But there is remarkably little evidence to indicate that average material living standards in Russia have declined significantly, if at all, in the recent years of reform. The consensus view of Russian economic collapse, like virtually every other aspect of the conventional Russian economic story, is misleading.

Exponents of the collapse scenario muster both theoretical and empirical arguments to support their views. The empirical evidence centres on the large fall in measured GNP, and includes secondary phenomena such as declining industrial production, high inflation, and barter. The bulk of this chapter will be devoted to a closer examination of the fall in GNP and the other empirical evidence offered in support of the view that Russian living standards have fallen drastically.

The theoretical arguments cited by the purveyors of Russian doom often focus on coordination problems (a.k.a. 'chaos' or 'anarchy') that arise during reform. These problems are rarely spelled out, but the arguments typically invoke either the costs incurred in changing long-term economic relationships (the adjustment costs discussed earlier), or the lack of individual, private incentives to take actions that, collectively, would result in an improved economy.[337] Neither of these forms of coordination problems provides a persuasive source of economic collapse, however.

First, consider again the costs involved in changing existing connections among enterprises. When will the established relations be severed? Existing economic relationships will not be changed on the whole, unless the new relationships are more efficient. (Political problems associated with the dissolution of the Soviet Union have caused inefficient breakdowns, but these unfortunate developments are not the consequence of economic reform.) A breakdown in existing economic relationships is not a necessary by-product of reform, and as long as partial reform measures do not result in the wrong relationships being severed, the economy is helped by the rearrangement of economic ties. The benefits of the rearrangement may not accrue until the future, though, while the costs of establishing the new economic relationships are borne immediately. But exchanging immediate costs for future benefits is the profile of any investment. And just as with any other investments, the immediate costs should not be viewed as signalling a worsening of economic conditions. Freely choosing to save and invest (your own resources, at least!) in the hope of higher consumption in the future does not make a person, or an economy, worse off, even at the cost of a reduction in current consumption. For this reason, investment expenditures are included in calculations of GNP.

The second type of perceived coordination problems are those associated with situations where the private incentives of individuals result in poor social outcomes. For example, in escaping a burning building, any individual viewed in isolation should get out as quickly as possible. (Economic game theorists might say that there is a 'first-mover advantage'.) Applied to all individuals, however, these incentives can cause panic and tragedy. In the case of economic reform, there may be a 'second-mover advantage'. While society might be better off if people embraced capitalism, the first individuals to do so might, for example, find their personal gains expropriated by the government through selective taxation. Everyone has an incentive to let others go first, and capitalism never takes root. The problem with this argument (and its siblings) is that it just is not so. There are plenty of incentives to be successful in the free market sector in reforming Russia, though the incentive is less for state-owned enterprises, which through 1993 basically remained immune to bankruptcy. The 'second-mover advantage' is a theoretical possibility, but not a major practical concern.

While coordination problems are unlikely suspects, other factors may work to reduce Russian incomes during reform. As argued in the previous chapters, economic reform threatens living standards in two respects. First is the difficulty in expeditiously replacing the implicit tax and social welfare systems with explicit counterparts. Second is the problems that accompany partial economic reforms, such as free enterprise combined with some fixed prices. Partial reforms, for example, weaken the link between enterprise profits and the social desirability of production. Increases in unemployment may then represent more than simply a movement from repressed to open unemployment.

Many Russians are apprehensive that lower incomes will accompany reform. A September 1990 survey of Soviet citizens indicated that 75 per cent feared that their material well-being would fall during the transition.[338] These fears have not been put to rest by the experiences of Eastern Europe, nor by the further economic reforms in Russia.[339] In 1994, a majority of Russians surveyed indicated that they believed their living standards had fallen during the previous five years.[340]

MEASURING LIVING STANDARDS

As with inflation and unemployment, the initial step in understanding the effects of economic reform on living standards is to evaluate the pre-reform situation. But first we must investigate how to measure living standards. Incomes, perhaps the premier data in assessing a society (or a person, as Paul Samuelson suggests in the opening quotation), must be determined – and there is the rub. The measurement of income is full of pitfalls, even in market economies, and is much more problematic in centrally-planned economies.

Of the frequently-employed indicators of income, perhaps the single most comprehensive statistic is *Gross National Product* (GNP), particularly in per capita terms.[341] A nation's GNP measures the total market value of all final goods and services produced in the nation during a given time period, typically one year.[342] Since for every good sold there is a payment to someone, there are two avenues to computing GNP. One route, the income method, is to measure the incomes accruing to workers and owners; alternatively, the product method consists of adding up the value of the final goods sold, capital investment and additions to inventory, government outlays, and net exports.[343] This approach results in the well known identity $Y \equiv C+I+G+(X-M)$: GNP (Y) equals the consumption expenditures of households (C) plus investment (I) plus government expenditures (G) plus net exports (X–M).[344] Price indices are used to offset the effects that rising price levels (inflation) have on GNP measured in current values of the national currency; i.e., real GNP is calculated by deflating nominal GNP by the relevant price index.[345]

Of course, income is just one element of the standard of living. Defining and measuring the quality of life is notoriously difficult, resulting in a panoply of indicators being employed to provide a more-or-less satisfactory portrait of living standards. Important indicators include life expectancy, literacy rates, and rates of infant mortality.[346] The 'noise' inherent in using GNP as a signal of living standards must be borne in mind. Some of the shortcomings associated with the use of real GNP to measure welfare were eloquently addressed by Robert F. Kennedy[347]:

> For the gross national product includes our pollution and advertising for cigarettes, and ambulances to clear our highways of carnage. It counts special locks for our doors and jails for the people who break them. The gross national product includes the destruction of the redwoods, and the death of Lake Superior. It grows with the production of napalm and missiles and nuclear warheads, and it even includes research on the improved dissemination of bubonic plague. The gross national product swells with equipment for the police to put down riots in our cities; and though it is not diminished by the damage these riots do, still it goes up as slums are rebuilt on their ashes . . .

One other important component of social welfare that is inherently absent from aggregate measures such as GNP is the distribution of income. A nation can have a relatively high GNP if all the people enjoy moderate earnings, or if a small number of people have phenomenally high incomes while everyone else is poor. The quality of life is likely to differ markedly between these two scenarios, even as per capita GNP is unchanged.

Interpreting GNP simply as a yardstick of economic output or income or material living standards, as opposed to an indicator of human welfare, does not avoid difficulties. Measuring economic output is hard. Major issues include: (1) market vs non-market output; (2) final vs intermediate production; (3) the constituents of 'investment'; and (4) the valuation of output.[348] These issues, discussed here in the context of market economies, will later be shown to be even more germane with respect to pre-reform Russia.

The national product accounts are geared towards transactions that occur in legal markets. Needless to say, many activities that generate economic benefits are thereby excluded from the calculations. Illegal transactions such as those involving contraband drugs, prostitution, or illegal gambling are not counted. Off-the-books employment, often paid for in cash, also are ignored. Barter agreements, such as when a dentist treats the teeth of an investment broker in exchange for financial counselling, are missed. Housework, which provides large benefits in terms of cleaner homes and laundry, is not counted, except if you hire someone to do your housework for you – and the transaction is properly reported and taxed.[349] Above all, the benefits of leisure time are not directly included in the national accounts.

Theoretically, only 'final' goods and services should be included in GNP. Sales of new automobiles are included, but the steel that goes into the car door is not directly counted. 'Intermediate' goods, i.e., those goods (like steel) that are used to produce other goods, are excluded, because otherwise they would be double-counted. The value of the steel is captured in the value of the car. To count the steel separately is to count it twice. Many goods that in practice are included in GNP nevertheless appear to have a large 'intermediate' component; a common example is the gasoline that is consumed in commuting to work. The government sector is particularly susceptible to the intermediate goods problem. Government expenditures (excluding transfer payments such as unemployment benefits) are included in the calculation of GNP, yet many of these expenditures are for intermediate goods and services. The nearly $300 billion US defence budget, for example, provides national security, which primarily represents an intermediate good that helps to promote the enjoyment of other goods and services such as birthday parties, beach vacations, and deodorants. Alternatively, some intermediate goods, such as services provided by businesses to their employees, are in reality final goods, and should be included in theoretically-pure calculations of GNP.

'Investment' goods are problematic in calculating GNP because many transactions that represent investment are either excluded from GNP calculations, or counted in other categories such as household consumption or government purchases.[350] When you buy a new car, it counts as a consumption good in this year's GNP, even though it will provide you with driving services for many years: i.e., it is largely an investment (and, a large investment!). Cars, like washing machines and other durable goods, are counted as consumption goods if purchased by households, are counted as government expenditures if purchased by the government, and are intermediate goods and thus excluded (directly) from GNP if purchased by businesses (laundromats or taxi companies, say). Expenditures for education and training also are generally not considered to be 'investment' in national income accounting. And the investments that do get counted are risky, in the sense that they are not guaranteed to bring future rewards.[351]

Market prices are used to aggregate GNP. But what is a market price? Taxes, subsidies, monopoly, and unpriced externalities all drive prices away from the Econ 101 conceptual ideal of prices formed in perfectly competitive markets. But that is only part of the problem. Seemingly identical goods (say, boxes of Tide laundry detergent) often have different prices even among stores in the same supermarket chain in nearby locations, though in competitive markets such price differences are generally small. The opposite problem is also a concern in calculating GNP; specifically, goods that differ in terms of consumer satisfaction may have the same measured price. Consider, for example, the benefits of shopping in pleasant surroundings with polite salespeople, as opposed to shopping in a dingy and hostile environment. The same pomegranate purchased for the same money price in the pleasant store as in the uncongenial store represents varying 'output', due to the differential quality of the shopping experience. But the addition to GNP is the same regardless of which store you buy your pomegranate in. (Alternatively, this 'market price problem' may be viewed as resulting from the 'non-marketed' production of service quality – a positive externality.)

This concludes our brief tour of major obstacles in measuring the nominal or 'dollar' value of economic output. There is one further piece of potentially disappointing news, however. The dollar value of GNP, as it happens, is not particularly useful in itself. The problem is that a rise in dollar GNP (or, in France, franc GNP) could be due either to inflation or to more output or to a combination of the two. In order to remove the effects of inflation and thereby get a better measure of changes in output, dollar GNP must be divided by a price index to generate 'real GNP'. The price indices used to convert dollar GNP to real values can be very inaccurate, though, as was demonstrated in the discussion of real wages. For inflation to be accurately reflected in real GNP, prices of goods and the quantities produced in some 'base year' must be known, as well as the current prices and quantities. But many common items such as microwave ovens, VCRs and personal computers did not exist twenty years ago, and hence had no relevant prices, making it hard to account for these items in price indices. It was noted in the discussion of real wages that in the US, real wages in manufacturing jobs fell slightly between 1982 and 1991. Hardly any of the people holding those manufacturing jobs in 1982 owned microwave ovens, CD players, or laptop computers, but today, many do. While measured real wages have fallen, it is not clear that the real consumption those wages buy has also fallen, because access to new products is not adequately accounted for.

The problems that new products cause for the measurement of real GNP arise in less drastic form for products that undergo quality improvements. Higher prices may reflect, well, higher prices for the same goods, or higher prices for better quality goods. Consider a bottom-of-the-line 1993 car, and a bottom-of-the-line 1972 car, both in their brand-new, showroom-floor incarnations. Though the price in real terms for the 1972 car in 1972 and the 1993 car in 1993 are likely to be about the same, the 1993 car is undoubtedly higher quality. Such quality improvements are often missing from GNP statistics, since separating out the quality-increase component of a price rise is hard.[352] As quality improves over time, measures of real GNP will generally understate the actual increases (or overstate the decreases) in the value of output, as some quality improvement is masked while the corresponding price rises enter the price deflator.

Thus far the discussion has focused on measures of GNP that count the value of outputs. As noted, it is also possible to generate GNP by counting the payments to workers, owners, and lenders, since every dollar spent by one person goes into another person's pocket. These 'income-side' calculations of GNP are, not surprisingly, also full of complications. Please permit just one example. Measuring income requires that the compensation received by workers be recorded. The problem is that a good deal of compensation takes place not as simple wage payments, but rather in some non-monetary forms, such as fringe benefits. The value of non-wage compensation, though, is hard to accurately measure. How much is it worth to an employee to get an office with a big window? How much is it worth to an employee to make personal calls at work, or to 're-allocate' office supplies to home use?

No matter how you calculate it, on the output side or the income side, GNP (or any related measure) is pretty hard to interpret, for all the reasons given above, and more. But often the next step is still more risky: comparing one country's GNP with another country's GNP. The most obvious problem is that they will be measured in different currencies, so direct comparisons are of the apples and oranges variety. Fortunately, there are (imperfect, of course) methods to convert GNPs to the same currency, resulting in a comparison more akin to Mackintosh apples and Delicious apples.[353] A second problem is that a GNP of $100 billion means one thing in a country with good roads, plenty of streetlights, an efficient government, and a large stock of other public goods, but $100 billion means another thing in nations less favourably bestowed. Still more difficulties in cross-country comparisons of GNP are likely to crop up in the pages ahead . . . (an old soap opera ploy!)

GNP AND LIVING STANDARDS IN THE FORMER SOVIET UNION[354]

It is at least as hard to assess the standard of living in the former Soviet Union as in Western market economies. Nevertheless, a useful first step is to calculate GNP. Only shortly before its demise did the Soviet Union begin to provide an annual estimate of GNP, however. The main measure of aggregate economic activity that the Soviets employed was called 'Net Material Product'. This statistic includes final material goods but excludes 'unproductive' activities such as most services.[355] The West therefore had to rely on its own statisticians to compute GNP for the Soviet Union. The major source of estimates was the US Central Intelligence Agency, which was particularly interested in Soviet military potential. The CIA's annual calculations included the USSR/US GNP ratio; for 1989, the CIA estimate of this figure stood at 51 per cent.

Throughout the 1980s CIA estimates of Soviet GNP became increasingly controversial, with most critics suggesting that the CIA estimation approach overstated, perhaps by a large margin, Soviet GNP relative to US GNP.[356] The report on the Soviet economy prepared at the request of the G7 summit in Houston in 1990 estimated the USSR/US GNP ratio at 8.5 per cent, though this estimate employed a rather dubious method of converting Soviet GNP measured in roubles to a dollar figure using the then-prevailing 'market' exchange rate.[357] Nevertheless, many other observers have provided estimates well below that of the CIA. Russian economist Victor Belkin, for example, estimated the USSR/US GNP ratio at 14 per cent.[358]

The CIA methodology in calculating Soviet GNP in roubles was based on 'adjusted (average) factor costs'.[359] These costs, for labour and other inputs, take the fixed state-sector prices as their starting point. The effects of explicit Soviet taxes and subsidies were then removed. Because Soviet enterprises received machinery and equipment without paying market prices, the costs of using these machines were not included in the official Soviet prices. So, the CIA methodology imputed payments (interest charges) for the use of capital goods, and added them into the factor costs.[360] Adjustments were also made to reflect the fact that many Soviet goods had multiple prices, with preferred customers like heavy industry or the defence sector typically paying lower prices.[361] The adjustments to the fixed Soviet prices generally did not make a large difference, however; that is, estimates of Soviet GNP based on official costs and those based on adjusted factor costs are similar.[362]

Given an estimate of Soviet GNP, common currency units must still be employed to make international comparisons. The CIA used a 'purchasing power parity' approach. The dollar estimate of Soviet GNP was prepared by examining Soviet production, and asking how much it would have cost in the US, in dollars, to produce the same things. Comparing this figure with US GNP measured in dollars resulted in one US/USSR GNP ratio. Alternatively, the cost in roubles that the Soviets would have faced in generating US output, and comparing this with Soviet GNP measured in roubles, provided a second estimate.

The dollar approach to the US/USSR GNP ratio gave markedly different results from the rouble approach. For example, in 1989, the dollar approach suggested that Soviet GNP was 66 per cent of US GNP, while the rouble approach yielded an estimate of 39 per cent.[363] A country's GNP tends to be overestimated when calculated in another country's prices. Goods that were relatively high priced in the US, for example, tended not to be made in large quantity in the US – the high price discouraged demand. If the same goods had relatively low prices in the Soviet Union, though, they may have been produced and consumed in great quantities there. Accounting for such Soviet goods at the high US price therefore produced a higher measure of Soviet GNP than using the lower Soviet price.

To produce its final estimate of the US/Soviet GNP ratio, the CIA simply took an average (the so-called geometric average) of the estimate calculated on the dollar side and the estimate calculated on the rouble side.[364]

Criticism of the CIA approach has focused, and rightly so, on the validity of employing Soviet official statistics, both on prices and quantities. Quality deterioration and fabricated product improvements are suggested as having led to price increases that do not reflect increases in output value; i.e., there is hidden inflation. Revelations during the years of reform have also undermined the traditional view that Soviet data expressed in physical units was basically trustworthy. Finally, the relationship between what is produced, and what is actually used, has been questioned. For example, output that spoils or is destroyed in transport is included in CIA calculations, despite being unavailable for use.[365] Some commentators suggest that these losses were staggering. 'Every year approximately 40 per cent of agricultural output . . . and half of industry's output . . . is lost.[366]

Stephen Rosefielde, an economics professor at the University of North Carolina, Chapel Hill, has reviewed the controversy between the CIA and the critics of its Soviet GNP calculations. Professor Rosefielde concludes that their differences '. . . are due almost entirely to disparate perceptions of free invention [i.e., made-up Soviet output statistics], hidden inflation, waste and forced substitution . . . [367] and that 'The problem primarily lies in our inadequate access to the facts, not in the inherent shortcoming of the national income accounting methodologies at our disposal.[368] The 'limits to knowledge' discussed in the introduction suggest that calculations of Soviet-era GNP will remain controversial.

CENTRAL PLANNING AND THE MEASUREMENT OF GNP

Consider the situation that would arise, though, if we had access to the 'facts' that separate the CIA from its critics. Assume for a second that Soviet official statistics met world standards, and all experts agreed on the calculation of Soviet GNP. What would such a figure tell us? I believe that we would learn little or nothing of value about Soviet output or living standards. The nature of the centrally-planned system, with fixed prices, questionable investment, over-production of intermediate goods, and a large share of output traded outside official channels, inherently reduces the correlation, tenuous in the best of circumstances, between measured GNP and welfare, or even between GNP and material well-being. The obstacles, identified in the previous section, encountered when calculating GNP – market vs non-market production, final vs intermediate goods, the nature of investment, and the valuation of production – are substantially more sizeable in the pre-reform Russian economy than in Western market economies. Coupled with the actual statistical limitations and distortions, these obstacles render any calculation of Russian GNP or living standards extremely precarious, or worse, meaningless.

First and foremost is the 'legal market' criterion for the inclusion of output in GNP. Prior to reform almost all Soviet private economic activity, except for the food sold on collective farm (kolkhoz) markets, was not transacted on a legal market, and hence not counted as part of GNP. As discussed earlier, the size of this shadow economy was enormous: perhaps 25 per cent or more of Soviet GNP. While Western industrialized countries have shadow economic production as well, the phenomenon is generally on a significantly smaller scale in the West.

Another area of non-marketed 'production' is environmental degradation. A worldwide problem, pollution of the environment nevertheless achieved momentous proportions in the USSR. From the drying up of the Aral Sea to ocean dumping of nuclear waste to Chernobyl, the Soviet environmental legacy is harrowing.[369] An inclusion of the environmental impacts of economic activity into GNP statistics would surely lower the former USSR's relative standing.[370]

The second factor that makes Soviet output statistics questionable measures of aggregate economic activity is the distinction between final and intermediate production. In theory, only final goods should be included in GNP calculations, but government spending is counted even when the spending is for intermediate goods or services. An important component of government spending in the West is for defence (primarily an intermediate service); for example, defence spending represents about 4 per cent of US GNP. But this figure is dwarfed by the comparable Soviet figure, which was estimated by the CIA to be 15–17 per cent in the late 1980s. Many outside critics (including citizens of the former Soviet Union) put the defence share of Soviet GNP at even higher levels: 25 per cent is not an uncommon estimate, and some figures are as high as 40–50 per cent.[371]

Another intermediate vs final product issue arises because of Soviet fixed prices and second economy activity. Recall the feeding bread to livestock story, where price controls on bread rendered it profitable for Soviet farmers to feed bread instead of grain to livestock; for this reason some bread became an intermediate good. A similar story applies to sugar that was purchased for use in home alcohol production. Generally, inputs that go into finished products should not be counted as part of GNP. Nevertheless, the production of inputs carried great weight in CIA estimates of Soviet output.[372] This practice was particularly misleading because of the tremendous Soviet inefficiency, relative to Western standards, in turning inputs into useful outputs.[373] The Soviet Union had 'a steel output per dollar of GDP fifteen times higher than that of the United States in 1988'.[374]

A third consideration that undermines the relevance of Soviet GNP calculations is the nature of the investment component. A striking feature of the Moscow landscape to many Western visitors is the amount of building cranes that are visible in the skyline. Construction appears to be going on everywhere in Russia. And construction was everywhere: there were some 350,000 construction projects throughout the former Soviet Union in the late 1980s, though the official statistics concerning construction were quite unreliable.[375] In the absence of economic reform, it would have been likely that the building cranes would have remained in place for quite some time, since the average construction project took 10 years to complete in the planned system. With or without reform, many construction projects may never be completed. While GNP calculations included this investment at cost, the real economic value of much of the Soviet investment was questionable. Other components of investment are also dubious. Soviet payoffs from extensive research and development were notoriously small. Increases in inventories of goods during the Soviet era are similarly suspect in terms of economic value. Swedish economist Anders

Åslund quotes former Soviet Deputy Prime Minister, the economist Leonid Abalkin: 'The warehouses are overloaded with unnecessary production, and [enterprises] continue to produce more and more of it: for the sake of the growth rate!'[376] Since investment formed over 30 per cent of Soviet GNP (as measured by the CIA), versus about 15 per cent in the US in 1990, reservations concerning the value of this investment are particularly serious.[377]

(Partly because of the difficulties with intermediate production and investment goods, attention is sometimes focused on Soviet *consumption* instead of Soviet GNP. CIA figures put Soviet per-capita consumption at approximately one-third of US levels, but again, many observers believe this to be an overestimate.[378] Consumption statistics are themselves not immune to criticisms almost as severe as those levelled at GNP statistics. For example, as with investment goods, not all Soviet consumption goods were valuable.)

The fourth factor that tends to thwart the interpretation of Soviet GNP statistics is the formerly fixed prices in the state sector. Fixed prices added a good deal of arbitrariness to value calculations of Soviet output. An additional refrigerator that officially 'cost' 100 roubles to produce and sold for 150 roubles, represented a 100 rouble increase in CIA calculations of Soviet GNP (assuming that the adjustments made to official costs in calculating adjusted factor costs had no net effect). The real value of resources used in producing the refrigerator, though, may actually have been 1000 roubles. But before it is concluded that 1000 roubles is the appropriate addition to GNP, what if no one was willing to pay more than 200 roubles for the refrigerator? In the West, as noted above, an increase in crime may lead to more resources being devoted to police and security services, which could raise GNP – though welfare in the usual sense has fallen. In the USSR, fixed prices meant that many goods, perhaps even refrigerators, had this perverse property. One Soviet economist estimated that as much as 25 per cent of Soviet output was 'unnecessary'.[379]

There are other difficulties with valuation. Consider the problem of estimating household income (or the labour factor cost), which requires the calculation of wages. As previously noted, in Soviet circumstances, the determination of a 'wage' for a given occupation is as difficult as determining a 'price' for a given commodity.

Institutional differences also make GNP calculations less meaningful as welfare measures in centrally-planned economies than in market economies. Four areas where Soviet (and now, to some extent, Russian) conditions differed substantially from Western conditions are queues, quality of housing, working environments, and public transport.[380] All of these factors tend to paint a bleaker picture of Soviet living standards than the CIA's per capita GNP figures might suggest. The enormous amount of time spent searching and queuing for goods in the pre-reform situation has already been mentioned, perhaps ad nauseam. As for housing, according to one Soviet economist in an article published in 1992 (though written when the USSR was extant), 'Among industrial nations the USSR is currently among the worst regarding housing standards', and she provides many telling statistics.[381] Working conditions in ageing Soviet industrial enterprises were also a cause for concern. Soviet emigré sociologist Vladimir Shlapentokh noted a 1981 survey that found that only 34 per cent of the adult population in big Soviet cities was satisfied with conditions at work.[382] The same source reported similar dissatisfaction with public transport. Only 30 per cent of the inhabitants of large cities (and only 15 per cent in Moscow) found the mass transit acceptable – a statistic that is understandable to anyone who has spent much time crammed on to Soviet buses. While such findings add to the picture of Soviet living standards presented by GNP calculations, they provide a far from definitive representation.

For the purposes of Russian or Western policy, an inability to get an accurate reading on pre-reform Russian material welfare via the usual GNP statistics is not immediately disabling. Russia appears committed to a transition to a market economy, regardless of whether the CIA or its most strident critics are correct about the measurement of Soviet GNP. Furthermore, Western aid will be forthcoming for the reform effort, independently of the initial Russian living standards. The problems in measuring Russian pre-reform living standards, however, can lead to policy mistakes down the road, since without understanding the initial situation, assessing the welfare effects of the transition is nearly impossible.

RUSSIAN INCOMES DURING THE TRANSITION

It has been argued above that the evaluation of Russian pre-reform living standards via the usual calculation of GNP (or per capita consumption, or any other method, for that matter) is problematic, even relative to the considerable difficulties involved in similar evaluations of Western market economies. Changing institutions such as the move to free prices implies that the complications are compounded during a transition to a market economy. With both the pre-reform and transitional positions difficult to judge, so too are the effects of reform. In the Russian case, basically unrelated events such as trade disruptions, civil unrest among the former republics, and falling world oil prices also influence living standards, making the marginal impact of economic reform even harder to disentangle.

As noted at the beginning of this chapter, there seems to be a near consensus in Russia and the West that economic conditions have worsened significantly in the past few years. Again, declining output and increased inflation are the most prominent signals of Russian economic decline.

The output and inflation statistics do not present a prima facie case for economic deterioration, however, for the by now familiar reason that during a transition, typical measures of economic activity take on entirely new meanings. Thus the change from repressed inflation to open inflation creates a large jump in price indices, even if there has been no increase in the underlying amount of inflation. This not-so-subtle point frequently goes unremarked upon. Thus the IMF reports an inflation rate of 140.7 per cent in the former USSR in 1991.[383] But the reported inflation rate for April 1991 is itself 55 per cent, due to the 2 April 1991 raising of administered state sector retail prices. This state-controlled price rise simply validated previous repressed inflation in open form; i.e., it did not represent new inflation.[384] Replacing the April 1991 inflation rate with the average monthly rate (excluding April) from 1991 changes the overall figure of 1991 inflation to 62 per cent – quite substantial, but less than half of the reported figure. And, as previously noted, determining the actual economic costs of such inflation is another matter. While there is the potential for large redistributional effects, efficiency losses are harder to pinpoint – though extremely high rates of inflation, and particularly hyperinflation, are quite costly.

Presumably the output decline is unambiguous evidence of significant economic deterioration. Measured industrial production in Russia fell by more than a third between 1990 and 1993.[385] But once again, the analysis is complicated by the pre-reform situation, which included an over-production of industrial goods, a prevalence of worthless output, the non-existence of some claimed output, and waste of output that was produced. Falling output figures alone are therefore not a sign of collapse; in fact, any successful transition will probably require a large drop in industrial output. The official statistics even indicated a six per cent increase in the production of consumption goods between 1987 and 1992.[386]

Statistics on actual consumption (as opposed to the production of consumption goods) can similarly be misleading during a transition. The Russian economy now involves widespread legal markets for most goods and services. This presents a marked change from the pre-reform situation. Different skills are being rewarded. In order to prosper in this new environment, many Russians are engaged in acquiring those skills that have seen their relative value increase: market business skills, for example. To some extent, then, a transition brings a temporary shift from consumption to investment, and hopefully to investment in skills that are both privately and socially profitable.

Many positive economic developments that arise with reform are not reflected in official statistics at all. Most obvious is the significant diminution in time spent queuing that followed the 2 January 1992 partial price liberalization. Nine-tenths of Russian households had at least one member queuing for goods at least an hour per day in early 1992; two years later, only one in six households spent that much time in line.[387] Western economist Bryan Roberts estimated the change in average welfare brought about by the price liberalization to be positive and quite substantial, with decreased queuing more than offsetting the measured fall in consumption.[388]

Increased private economic activity appears to be only partially reflected in the official statistics, which were traditionally geared to determining state sector production. Changed incentives to misreport output have also arisen with reform. Previously, virtually all parties involved in the official economy were interested in exaggerating the amount of output produced. With new taxes and relatively unrestricted wage funds, these incentives have been reduced, and in some cases replaced by motivations to understate output. Russian statistics also have a new role to play as data influences negotiations with Western aid agencies such as the IMF.

In summary, recent economic statistics that indicate severe decline in Russia in the 1990s are extremely misleading, as are the statistics indicating substantial growth in 1988-90. The regime change of economic reform results in economic statistics measuring different phenomena than they did in the pre-reform economy. Changes in these statistics during reform cannot then be trusted to signify similarly changed economic circumstances.

MOSCOW AND ST. PETERSBURG

One difficulty in judging the economic situation in Russia is that there is no single economic situation. Regions and localities differ markedly in the strength of their economy, just as they did in the pre-reform system. There have also been widely varying responses to economic reform, with local leaders often playing decisive roles in the speed and form of reforms. Nevertheless, much of the reform discussion focuses on Moscow and St. Petersburg, Russia's two largest cities.

Moscow and St. Petersburg have traditionally been better supplied with food and other goods within the official state distribution system than other regions of the former Soviet Union. This situation was not entirely accidental, as these cities were officially accorded the highest priority status within the state distribution network. (The priority standing of Moscow and St. Petersburg extended to non-economic phenomena under the old system. Former convicts, for example, could not settle in these cities.) The high priority of Moscow and St. Petersburg has been undermined in recent years, as the state distribution system has deteriorated. Residents of these cities have found their economic standing, relative to their fellow citizens, falling.[389] (In some cases, of course, their absolute standard of living has fallen as well.) Real wage statistics, as unreliable as they are in the Russian setting, seem to bear this out. Of the 76 'administrative units' in Russia, Moscow city and the Moscow region ranked 73 and 74 in terms of measured real wage growth between mid-1991 and mid-1992, with about a 35 per cent reduction. (Many regions had positive measured real wage growth.[390]) The relative decline in the prosperity of Moscow and St. Petersburg has engendered discontent among the citizens of these cities – discontent which can now find a voice in the liberalized political climate. Since the vast majority of Western foreign correspondents within the borders of the old Soviet Union are in Moscow and St. Petersburg, the complaints have been widely reported.[391]

The Moscow–St Petersburg slant on Western news from Russia is pervasive. Here is a quiz that even well-informed Westerners often have trouble with – at least I did. What is the third – or fourth, or fifth – largest city in Russia?[392]

Reform is creating other difficulties for the major Russian cities, particularly Moscow, which are then incorrectly extrapolated to the country as a whole. As the relative value of food has increased, rural areas have been prospering relative to Moscow. Smaller cities, many of which had not seen any meat from within the official state supply system for years, are no longer systematically discriminated against. Simultaneously, some of the major 'goods' produced in Moscow have seen their market dry up. Most obvious is the central management of the economy and of the Soviet empire. The reduction in the defence budget also harms Moscow and St. Petersburg relative to most other Russian regions. One-quarter of Moscow's workforce is involved in military production, accounting for a third of the city's industrial output. St. Petersburg also employs about one-quarter of its workforce in defence production.[393]

The loss of the special privileges accorded large cities in the official distribution of goods is new to Moscow. A lack of those special privileges forced remote areas long ago to find alternative methods to 'beat the system', a process that Moscow is now learning. Furthermore, the transactions costs of engaging in private business, while still quite substantial, have fallen significantly relative to the pre-reform situation in which most private activity was illegal. With high costs of doing business, it makes sense to engage only in high volume operations, since many of the transactions costs would be the same for both small and large operations. Therefore, rather than have flourishing markets in every town, big cities like Moscow became the focus of trade; people from rural areas and smaller towns would travel tremendous distances to come to Moscow to participate in both the state and private markets. (This situation was facilitated by the low fixed prices on internal travel in the Soviet Union. Farmers found it profitable to fly thousands of kilometres to large cities in order to sell a couple of bins of fruit.) As the costs of doing business fall, local markets are developing. The special status of Moscow as a trading post is therefore diminishing, particularly in the realm of consumer goods. But with the journalistic focus on Moscow, this positive development is likely to be overlooked, or worse, misperceived as a fall in living standards, as some trade that would have previously occurred in Moscow is diverted to other regions.

DISTRIBUTION REVISITED

Along with changes in the geographic distribution of economic goods, Russian economic reform has brought changes to the distribution of income.

Once again, determining the effect of transition on income distribution requires knowledge of the pre-reform situation. This is a particularly difficult task, both because of the widespread informal activity and the former Soviet government's unwillingness to provide substantial information on the distribution of income. What does seem clear is that the Soviet Union did not have an income distribution substantially more equal than in many Western market economies. The findings of British economists Anthony Atkinson and John Micklewright, for example, indicate that the Russian household income distribution in 1986 was slightly more equal than that of Great Britain, while the distribution of individual earnings was slightly less equal in Russia than in Great Britain.[394] Since these calculations exclude second economy earnings, it is likely that Russia was comparatively even less egalitarian. Such evidence suggests that it cannot be taken for granted that economic reform will lead to wider dispersions in the Russian income distribution. It is highly probable, however, that increased legality of private economic activity is leading to more people in Russia who are very well-off relative to the average. Also, the massive inflation accompanying economic reform has led to a major change in the distribution of wealth, as the value of pre-existing rouble savings has been almost completely eliminated.

At the same time that reform influences income distribution, pre-existing income differentials are becoming more visible. The great wealth accumulated by important Party members in the pre-reform system was pretty well hidden from public view. Now, fancy restaurants, casinos, and expensive foreign cars are on open display. Repressed differences in living standards have become increasingly open; the result would likely be a perception of more inequality, even without any underlying changes.

Changes in income distribution, or the perception of changes, might create popular unrest that would scuttle reform efforts. So far, though, that does not seem to be the case in Russia. There is even some evidence that distributional concerns may not be all that great in Russia. Survey results reported in 1992 by Western Sovietologist Ellen Mickiewicz found that 84 per cent of the respondents in Russia believed that the government should not reduce differences in income among people. Comparable figures for Ukraine and Uzbekistan were 81 per cent and 58 per cent, respectively.[395]

There are also theoretical reasons for believing that distributional concerns are less compelling during large systemic changes than they are in other circumstances. With most policy changes in the West, the major distributional effects (which generally fall on a narrow group of individuals) are substantial relative to the social gains from increased efficiency, which are diffuse. For example, import barriers on Japanese automobiles are very beneficial to the relatively small number of owners and workers of US automobile companies, while the much more numerous American consumers of automobiles pay somewhat higher prices because of the trade restraints. When the entire economic system is being restructured, however, these factors can be reversed. Potential efficiency gains are large relative to the distributional effects.[396] Changes in the size of the pie become more meaningful relative to how the shares of the pie are distributed.

Distributional changes are continuously occurring, with or without reform.[397] Not all distributional changes have to be counteracted. The major concern is to ensure that the worst-off members of society do not suffer further. But protecting the worst-off citizens is comparatively inexpensive and easy, at least relative to counteracting all downward changes in distribution – though identifying the most needy represents a new task in Russia.[398] On balance, Russia appears well-equipped to provide an explicit social safety net, thanks to the existence of state stores and long experience with ration coupons.

PERCEPTIONS OF DECLINE

The previous sections have suggested that Western (and possibly even Russian) perceptions of the Russian economy are more pessimistic than the actual situation merits. There is indirect evidence that for many Russians, the economic situation is not as dire as many news reports imply. American economists Robert McGee and Edward Feige, writing on the US economy, note that 'Survey results suggest that individuals appear to be much more optimistic about their personal economic situation than about the general economic situation. This is precisely what would be expected when aggregate data based on false reporting produce the statistical illusion of economic malaise'.[399] Similar survey results have been reported for the transitional Russian economy. A Russian economist describes a survey in which residents of the former Soviet Union considered the economic situation of their own republic to be better than that of the union as a whole.[400] American researchers Anthony Jones and William Moskoff report on a late-1989 poll of Muscovites in which 82 per cent of the respondents thought that the overall economy had worsened under the policy of perestroika, though only 33 per cent of the respondents felt that they were personally less well off.[401] Distributional changes may help to create a perception of general decline, even if average living standards are not falling.

The limited availability and reliability of economic information in the pre-reform situation also helps to create perceptions of increasing economic misery. Russian researchers noted in an article originally published in 1991 that 'Only in the last year or two has the fact that a large number of people are living in poverty in [the Soviet Union] been recognized.[402] According to the same source, 64 per cent of the respondents to a September 1990 poll believed that there are many poor people in the Soviet Union.[403] Misinformation about living standards was surprisingly pervasive in the pre-reform Soviet Union. Sociologist Vladimir Shlapentokh reports on a late 1960s and early 1970s survey in the town of Taganrog, conducted by Boris

Grushin, 'According to Grushin's survey of Taganrog residents . . . [o]nly 2 per cent thought living standards were "very high" in the United States, France, and Great Britain; the figures for Czechoslovakia and Bulgaria were 63 and 49 per cent, respectively'.[404]

Under glasnost' there has been an upsurge of information available to citizens of the former Soviet Union, both about their own and other countries. In particular, information that paints the former Soviet Union in a negative light is newly available. The extent of environmental damage, for example, is now amply reported – there is even a Soviet branch of Greenpeace.[405] To the extent that increased reporting of negative phenomena is mistaken for an increase in the phenomena themselves, the transition may be blamed for pre-existing problems.

Perceptions of the economic situation matter, even if they do not well reflect reality. First, as mentioned, the government may respond to perceived economic problems in ways that are inappropriate for the actual situation. Second, perceptions and expectations are inter-related, and expectations influence current economic activity. What is the incentive to undertake a long term investment in an economy perceived to be on the verge of collapse? 'Real wealth', while impossible to accurately measure, surely depends to some degree on expected future income (or consumption) streams. But the perceptions of economic decline, combined with high inflation and general economic and political uncertainty, render future income streams highly uncertain, and perhaps highly discounted in current calculations of economic well-being. Economic pessimism, even when otherwise unfounded, has a disturbing propensity to be self-justifying.

BARTER

One phenomenon that is frequently taken as a sign of Russian economic deterioration is the significant number of transactions that are conducted via barter. Yale University economist Merton Peck, for example, comments that 'The rise of bartering is the most obvious and pervasive indicator of an economic crisis.'[406] A reversion from monetary to barter exchange is harmful because the level of economic activity is almost sure to fall precipitously during such a switch. Barter is inefficient relative to the use of money to conduct exchange because there is no reason for the person who supplies the goods that I want to buy to be interested in buying the goods I can offer. My grocer may have little use for books about economic reform, even though I would like to obtain some groceries. By using money that is widely accepted, I can buy groceries without my grocer simultaneously having to buy my economic reform ramblings. The use of money makes it easier to find appropriate trading partners – in fact, it makes almost anyone an appropriate trading partner. More deals are then worth the effort, and fewer resources are devoted to arranging each exchange.

In a Western industrial economy, virtually the only circumstance in which barter would replace monetary exchange on a large scale is if people lost confidence in the currency, perhaps because of massive inflation or expected inflation. In such conditions, barter will be associated with economic collapse. But Russia has not seen a 'reversion' to barter: a good deal of barter has always been there. Furthermore, despite the substantial inflation during the reform era, there has not been an enormous movement to barter. The vast majority of transactions in Russia (and throughout the rouble zone) continue to utilize roubles. Most important, though, some of the barter that is appearing actually promotes the development of a market economy. When legal enforcement of contracts is largely unavailable, barter becomes a useful device for governing exchanges.

Barter played a substantial role in the pre-reform Soviet system, driven by legal restrictions on monetary market relationships, and the low fixed prices in the state sector. Official exchanges between state-owned enterprises did not employ direct monetary payment; rather, accounting transfers were recorded to match exchanges that took place in accordance with the state's central plan. The accounting roubles that governed these exchanges were unrelated to the roubles used to pay wages and for households to purchase consumer goods. (The accounting roubles were even called 'non-cash' roubles.) Therefore, the wholesale market, the market for capital equipment, or the market governing any official inter-enterprise trade was in essence one large barter system, separated from the rouble-employing retail market.

Recall also that informal transactions were frequently conducted through barter. Enterprise supply expediters would barter goods in order to get necessary supplies. As noted previously, workers at state enterprises would receive much of their pay in kind, and large enterprises would provide housing, kindergartens, and a host of other goods and services to workers and their families. Individuals would barter vodka for privately provided services such as plumbing or auto repair. The exchange of favours and gifts for scarce commodities has been well-documented. No description of life in the Soviet Union can be complete without a discussion of 'blat', the use of connections and gifts to obtain such goods as high quality meat or theatre tickets.[407] Soviet foreign trade with both the East and the West involved barter arrangements; for example, Pepsi Cola was provided to the USSR in exchange for Stolichnaya vodka.

The increased reports of barter that have accompanied reform are therefore not surprising: the implicit system, particularly with respect to inter-enterprise trade, is becoming explicit. And partial reform contributes to the use of barter. It remained illegal throughout 1992 for state-owned enterprises to sell intermediate goods for cash.[408]

One factor promoting barter is the enormous amount of price uncertainty, and general economic uncertainty, prevalent in Russia. Under the ancien régime there were no legal markets for outside-of-plan inter-enterprise exchanges, and hence there were no established prices for legal transactions. (And many illegal exchanges were themselves conducted via barter.) In the US, it is fairly easy to learn the approximate price of almost any traded commodity. In Russia, there may not be a 'typical' price. 'In a society where no one knows the fair value of anything, everyone suspects he is being cheated all the time', is how one journalist has described the situation in Russia.[409]

Some firms engage in barter precisely to keep the actual 'price' of a transaction hidden. Disguising prices by engaging in barter can be a way to practice what economists call 'price discrimination', which simply consists of charging different prices to different customers for an identical good. For example, airlines price discriminate when they sell seats on airplanes for high prices to business travellers, but sell at low prices to vacationers. (The familiar Saturday night stay-over requirement for a lower fare helps to implement this form of price discrimination.) It is hard to price discriminate in selling an identical good, though, if a market price is well-established, because then no customer will be willing to pay more than that price – she can always go to a competitor and pay the market price. Price discrimination is also prevented if goods can easily be resold. For example, if kids' tickets to movies were the same colour, shape, and size as adult tickets, kids would buy all the tickets at the children's price and resell to the adults. The movie theatre would then be forced to either differentiate the tickets or sell them all at the same price. Thanks to the old planning system, many enterprises in Russia have some degree of monopoly power. These firms can earn more money by engaging in price discrimination. But if the price discrimination becomes well-known, those customers that are charged the lower price will begin to resell to the other customers. Price-discriminating enterprises therefore have an incentive to conceal prices through barter deals. (Incidentally, price discrimination, even in non-barter deals, is widely practised by Russian enterprises. Traditional contracting partners are typically charged lower prices for goods than new private enterprises.[410])

The semi-reformed nature of the Russian economy contributes to barter in other ways. For example, the possibility of further currency reforms encourages barter, because the government may confiscate roubles in the future. This is not an idle threat, given the January 1991 confiscation of 50 and 100 rouble notes and the July 1993 reform that invalidated some 'old' roubles. Threats by some former republics to issue new currency operate similarly to make roubles less attractive. The continuing lack of government enforcement mechanisms for private contracts also induces barter, as such direct exchanges (particularly when conducted with long-time trading partners) enable enterprises to ensure that they are not swindled in transactions.

Finally, barter deals fall largely outside of any centralized regulation; as long as the government remains completely enmeshed in the economy, firms will engage in barter as a way of circumventing government controls. A fair number of price controls remain in place in Russia. Barter remains a means of evading such controls, and has also become useful in avoiding the value-added tax.[411]

Barter trade in the reforming Russian economy is not an unambiguous sign of economic collapse. Much of it occurred in the old system, and there are good reasons for Russian enterprises to engage in barter transactions. As reform proceeds, barter will become increasingly less common, as the factors associated with partial reforms – including the inflationary budget deficit – diminish in importance.

THE SOCIALIST VICE

Consumption is the sole end and purpose of all production.
Adam Smith, *The Wealth of Nations*, 1776[412]

What do We Need Most of All? Most of all we need machines.
New Russia's Primer, The Story of the Five Year Plan, 1931[413]

quasi-humorously . . . [s]teel happens, in the minds of Communists, to be more beautiful and desirable than saucepans or even guns. This is how their minds work: the tradition has very deep roots.
Western economist PJD Wiles[414]

A friend at a party introduces you to Nina, explaining that she's a Soviet economist. Then your friend runs off to the punch bowl, and you attempt to strike up a conversation with Nina. The ambiguity of the phrase 'Soviet economist' presents a small difficulty, though. You are not sure whether Nina is an economist from the former Soviet Union, or a Western-trained economist who studies Soviet-type economic systems. Attempting not to appear too obtuse, perhaps you are unwilling to come right out and ask Nina for clarification. Fortunately, there is an indirect method of ascertaining Nina's economic background that is extremely reliable – until a few years ago, nearly 100 per cent reliable. Explain to Nina that you have heard that there is a shortage of, say, steel plate, in some exotic country, and since Nina is a professional economist, you would like her suggestion as to how this shortage should be dealt with. If Nina is a Western-trained economist, her most likely response will be 'Raise the price of steel plate.' If Nina learned economics in the former USSR, she will probably respond, 'Increase the production of steel plate.'

Production, production, production. The Soviet Union led the world in the production of steel, coal, steel, tractors, steel, nickel, steel, wheat, steel, . . . but for all its production, the Soviet official economy was clearly out-performed by many Western market economies. The focus on production was a mistake – though perhaps an inevitable mistake within a planned economy – since living standards are dependent on consumption, not pro-duction. It is this production fetish that I call 'the socialist vice'.

But surely, it might be thought, production and consumption are just two sides of the same coin. The more you produce, the more you consume, and if you do not produce, you cannot consume. Focusing on production should amount to pretty much the same thing as focusing on consumption. Production is probably easier to monitor and control than consumption, since there are relatively few producing firms and farms and relatively many consumers and mouths.

Such reasoning is fallacious. First, production and consumption are not always intimately connected. A potato that is harvested adds to production statistics, but if it rots before making it to a consumer, then it has not added to consumption. And such waste was rampant in the centrally-planned USSR; in fact, a European Bank for Reconstruction and Development report concluded in 1991 that 50 per cent of Soviet potatoes never made it to consumers.[415] Nor are all potatoes created equal. Potato quality, like 'potato' pronunciation (and spelling?), varies, and once again, low quality within the Soviet state sector was a persistent problem. But more importantly, the relationship between production and consumption depends on what goods get produced. You cannot eat steel, even if you have more of it than anyone else in the world.

But steel and other intermediate goods were accorded high priority within the Soviet production profile. Partly the over-attention paid to intermediate goods derives from the lack of a direct link between consumer satisfaction and the production of intermediate goods. Consumer satisfaction being difficult to achieve in a centrally-planned way, the planning system itself is better suited to the production of intermediate goods relative to consumer goods. Furthermore, as the opening quotation suggests, there is an ideological attachment to heavy industry in many socialist societies. In the Soviet Union, the primacy of industrial production grew from an unfortunate 'law' of socialism derived from Marx, which stated that economic growth required a more rapid expansion of industrial goods than consumer goods.[416] In a sense then, Soviet planners did eat steel, even as Soviet consumers continued to find it unappetizing. As an epigram attributed to eminent Western economist Abram Bergson put it, 'Steel was a final good to Stalin, and bread an intermediate one.[417]

The focus on industrial production was successful in producing high measured growth rates. The 1962 book by P. J. D. Wiles that has served as a source for much of the discussion in this section contains a chapter entitled 'Why They Have Grown Faster'. The relatively high Soviet growth rates continued into the 1980s, even as absolute growth rates declined. But more production does not mean higher living standards, though the output numbers may well increase – a point occasionally overlooked.[418] In fact, it is only within a market setting that production can serve as a rough proxy for consumption or living standards, since only then can it reasonably be expected that production that is not valuable will be curtailed.

Consider the situation with tractors in Russia, as described by Western economists Ed Hewett and Clifford Gaddy[419]:

> In the early 1980s the USSR produced tractors at a rate of 550,000–580,000 a year – 40 per cent of world tractor production – of which approximately 350,000 went to agriculture. US farmers purchase 50,000–60,000 tractors a year, which is one-sixth of the Soviet figure. Yet the USSR still had to devote 19 percent of its labor force, or 30 million workers, to agricultural production, and almost three-fourths of those were working manually. [Shades of Orwell's Oceania.] The apparent low productivity of tractors (and other agricultural machinery) seems linked to frequent breakdowns and long downtimes, which in turn were due to poor servicing and a shortage of spare parts. Twenty percent to 45 percent of all Soviet tractors were out of service at any one time.

Petr Aven, a Russian-trained economist, noted that in 1991 the production of tractors continued to increase, though there were insufficient numbers of tractor drivers for the existing tractor stock – itself many times the size of the stock of tractors in the US – and there was almost no demand for many brands of tractors.[420] In the Russian city of Chelyabinsk, home of a major tractor factory, parking lots and vacant areas near the factory were jammed with unsold and unsaleable tractors in 1993, while production continued. (The tractors tended to be too large for the emerging private farms.[421]) A resident of Chelyabinsk described the situation as 'a tractor hanging from every tree'.

The misplaced concentration on production permeated all facets of Soviet economic life. Economic problems were engineering problems: given a shortage, how could production be increased? Where was the bottleneck in production? If the constraint on increased production was too few trucks for transport, then the solution appeared to be to produce more trucks. Without free prices in the state sector, the cost of the increased production was neglected, though it may well have exceeded the value of the additional output. Environmental costs were particularly likely to be insufficiently taken into account.

The focus on production was not limited to officials in Gosplan, the State Planning Committee. One of the features of the Soviet planned economy was that leaders at the highest level were involved in mundane decisions concerning such issues as the number of children's shoes to produce. General Secretaries would give speeches about production problems in various industries, and initiate campaigns to increase production or decrease waste. Newspaper and television reports of production figures and plan fulfilment were a daily, mind-numbing exercise.

The early Gorbachev-era reforms also reflected the socialist vice in bringing a technological approach to economic problems. 'Intensification' and 'acceleration' were the major themes of reform in the mid-1980s. Together with the anti-alcohol campaign, they were designed to increase production – and in particular, in an echo of the socialist law concerning the primacy of industrial goods, to increase the production of machine tools, machines that could make other machines.[422]

In taking this approach, Gorbachev was applying the best wisdom available within the Soviet economics discipline, which was itself held hostage to the socialist vice. Most Soviet economists were employed in industry, and their job was to think of ways to increase production or to increase the technological efficiency of production. (Enterprise managers were not always willing customers of the economists' suggestions, however, since increased output would lead to increased plan targets in the future, and increased technological efficiency might mean fewer inputs.) The collection of official statistics also focused heavily on production, 'with distribution, consumption, and income data accorded much lower priority'.[423] Market-oriented solutions to problems were almost unthinkable, and would have branded the perpetrator as ideologically suspect. So it is unsurprising that Gorbachev's early fixation with increased production of machine tools was the pet programme of his main economic adviser at the time, Abel Aganbegyan, who had a strong reputation as a reformer.[424]

The technological approach to economic problems remains very popular in Russia.[425] In the transition another phenomenon has arisen, though, which itself is a legacy of the old regime. Under a planning system, people are likely to assign responsibility for the success or failure of the economy to decisions made by high government officials and their economic advisers. After all, such officials are explicitly responsible for all major economic decisions. (This assignment of responsibility also happens, though to a lesser extent, in market economies such as the United States, where the president has very limited influence over the economy.) Upon learning that the economies of market countries outperformed their own economy, many Russians have apparently attributed the difference to the better economists in the West, and leading Russian reform economists have emerged as popular politicians. An undue appreciation of the powers of economists is a touchingly (at least I am touched) ironic outcome of six decades of central planning.

Chapter 8

False hopes

The focus on implicit elements in the pre-reform economy has tended to paint a picture of Russian economic reform that is significantly rosier than that provided by the standard commentaries. The flip side of this generally positive assessment of the reforming Russian economy, however, is a greater degree of scepticism with respect to the short-term benefits from the implementation of some reform measures, such as official privatization, that are widely viewed as important for the transition to a market economy. Three reform elements that are typically deemed to be promising in lifting the Russian economy are military conversion, rouble convertibility, and Western aid. Chinese-style gradual market reforms have been similarly highly-touted. While such reforms do offer some benefits to the Russian economy, I believe that like official privatization, all have generally been overvalued. This chapter attempts to demonstrate why these reforms, for the most part, present false hopes.

MILITARY CONVERSION

> more and more evidence points to the fact that in the area of defense expenditures, as in many other areas, the Soviet leadership operated for years and continues to operate in the dark, without a solid database.
>
> Western economist Vladimir Treml, 1992[426]

It may seem a bit disingenuous to view the defence sector of the former Soviet Union, an acknowledged military superpower, as being largely implicit, but there were a host of hidden elements. Most important was simply the burden that national security placed on the economy, which because of hidden subsidies and fixed prices was probably unknown even at the highest levels of the Soviet government – though the CIA's estimate of 15–17 per cent of GNP in the mid-1980s can serve as a lower bound. One form of hidden subsidy to defence was price discrimination: defence enterprises were charged less for some inputs, such as electricity, than non-defence enterprises. A priority system in which the defence complex received preeminent access to inputs, including skilled labour, likewise masked a subsidy. An extreme penchant for secrecy also led to other hidden attributes in the defence sector, including entire towns, comprising hundreds of thousands of people in toto, that were closed not just to foreigners but even to the rest of the Soviet population, and were omitted from Soviet maps. (Residents of these towns, which could not publish newspapers, were discouraged from venturing 'outside' the town limits, and visits from outside relatives were strictly controlled.[427])

A final, less hidden feature of the pre-reform situation in the defence sector is that the production of civilian goods has long been an important component of the activities of defence enterprises. (Any Soviet enterprise that was subordinate to one of the ministries in the 'defence complex' was typically considered to be a defence enterprise, even if it exclusively produced civilian goods.) Defence enterprises produced 100 per cent of Soviet televisions, radios, and VCRs, and the majority of washing machines, vacuum cleaners, and refrigerators.[428] Almost all high technology consumer goods were produced in the defence sector. In total, consumer goods accounted for 40 per cent or more of the output of defence enterprises, and defence enterprises accounted for some 25 per cent of all consumer goods other than food.[429]

The large percentage of Soviet output that was devoted to the military has made this sector a natural target for reformers. And indeed, the conversion of military industry to civilian production has been an important part of Soviet (and later Russian) reform efforts since Mikhail Gorbachev called for demilitarization at the United Nations in December, 1988. An official Soviet defence conversion plan was approved in December 1990. The plan was marked by two important features. The first feature was that physical 'conversion' of productive assets from military to civilian production was not the major thrust of the conversion effort. Rather, the major part of the conversion programme was a call for an increase in the production of those civilian goods that were already made within the defence complex. The second feature of the official conversion plan was, well, that it was a *plan*, i.e., it involved a centralized approach to conversion. Defence enterprises were to be told by central planners the type and quantity of consumer products to produce.

The dissolution of the Soviet Union left the fate of military conversion uncertain, and there was little progress through 1992. Furthermore, there is only a small basis for optimism concerning the outcome of conversion. Any centralized conversion plan, particularly if implemented in the absence of accompanying market-oriented reforms, can be expected to exhibit all the problems that are characteristic of centrally-planned economies. Without free prices, there is no yardstick to measure how highly consumers value goods, nor how much goods actually cost to make. As we have seen, producing more centrally-determined consumer goods does not necessarily lead to a rise in living standards. Centralized control of conversion in state-owned enterprises will also result in poor incentives to efficiently produce high quality consumer goods.

But military conversion need not be planned in Moscow; rather, it can be undertaken in a decentralized fashion. While defence enterprises were, at first, generally exempted from the official privatization programme, spontaneous privatizations still took place in the defence sector.[430] The extent of private ownership in the defence sector was further augmented by an acceleration of official privatizations in 1993.[431] Private businesses utilizing the assets of defence firms can make their own decisions concerning what to produce. As long as prices are free and the Russian government continues to adequately provide for its defence needs, there is not much that can be said against conversion of productive assets from military to civilian uses by de facto private firms. Profit-maximizing entrepreneurs in free markets have wide scope in deploying their assets, and if the 'owners' of defence firms view conversion as profitable, they should be given free rein.

Western experience with decentralized military conversion has been dismal. In the words of Martin Marietta Chairman Norman Augustine, US defence conversion efforts have been 'unblemished by success'.[432] China, alternatively, has apparently enjoyed successful military conversion during its ongoing reforms.[433] In Russia, the large amount of civilian goods already made within the defence complex might suggest that Russia is relatively well-positioned for successful military conversion. But many of these goods are the same low-quality products that are legendary in Russia: 2,000 fires a year in Moscow have been blamed on exploding colour televisions produced by defence enterprises.[434] On balance, conversion schemes that involve the actual physical conversion of assets from defence production to consumer goods production are relatively unpromising, whether undertaken in a centralized or decentralized fashion.

Nor is it the case that privatized defence enterprises are sure to be interested in the production of consumer goods. The owners may view their best opportunities to make profits as the production and export of military goods – a stance shared by many Western defence companies that are faced with similarly declining demands for their main products. Indeed, foreign trade may be the most effective way for the Russians to turn guns into butter: sell the guns and buy the butter. Privatization alone is not certain to result in physical conversion of assets to the production of civilian goods, if export opportunities exist. But the actual export options for Russian arms appear quite limited. First, Western arms producers provide formidable competition, and the Persian Gulf war has increased the perception that Western arms are higher quality than Russian weapons. Second, advanced weapons systems require ongoing maintenance and spare parts. In the midst of economic and social turmoil, Russian arms producers cannot credibly commit to being able to service weapons in the coming decades.

One conversion-type reform with the potential to improve the economy in Russia is simply to reduce the size of the defence budget. While it remains difficult to gauge the amount of resources that go to defence, there probably has been some reduction during the reform era.[435] State orders for military procurement were said to fall by two-thirds during 1992, and the number of uniformed personnel has apparently also been reduced, perhaps by 500,000 or more men.[436] The defence sector's previous priority access to material inputs and skilled labour has also been undermined during the reform era, in itself representing a diminution in the value of resources that are devoted to the Russian military.

To the extent that the resources freed by significant declines in defence expenditures are redirected towards the private sector, improvements can occur in Russian living standards. (Even if Russian military production could be sold abroad for consumer goods, a reduction in the number of troops would increase the manpower available to the civilian economy.) It still remains to be seen, however, to what extent such defence reductions actually occur and will be maintained. One commentator, writing in 1994, noted that only three million Russians were actually producing arms, and declared that military conversion had, to a large extent, already succeeded.[436*]

The expectation that military conversion in isolation can bring large improvements is unwarranted. This expectation appears to be implicit in the common view, noted in 'The myth of the plan' section, that the necessity of matching Western arms spending eventually proved so costly to the Soviet Union that the only way out was to embrace reform. If excessive military spending brought the Soviet Union down, presumably cutbacks in such spending could have revitalized the Soviet economy. As argued above, however, it was fixed prices and the concomitant paraphernalia of central planning that resulted in the resource misallocations and waste that kept Soviet living standards low. A reduction in the amount of resources devoted to defence could have postponed reform, but the underlying causes of the inefficient economy would have remained. It is systemic economic reform, not military conversion, that holds the hope for higher living standards in Russia's future.

On another level, it could be said that the entire official Soviet economy was militarized. Fixed prices, rationing, and government requisitions mark Western-style wartime economies and the official Soviet economy. The movement from a command to a market economy in Russia could be likened to converting from a wartime to a peacetime economy. In this sense, de-militarization and conversion are the essential reform elements, irrespective of the final size of the Russian defence sector.

ROUBLE CONVERTIBILITY

Under Soviet central planning, Soviet citizens were generally not allowed to trade roubles for foreign currencies, nor could foreigners legally take roubles out of the USSR. (Tourists in both directions were allowed to exchange small amounts of currency at a rate determined by the government.) The market for foreign exchange was suppressed. In other words, the rouble was not a convertible currency: it could not be freely exchanged for other currencies.

In parallel with the currency restrictions, planners controlled virtually all Soviet foreign trade.[437] What goods to import, and what goods to export to pay for the imports, were both centrally-determined, as were the ultimate recipients of industrial imports. The primary exports to non-socialist countries were energy products (oil and natural gas) and weapons. While the Soviet Union was not a large player in world trade – even including trade with the socialist world, the immense Soviet Union was less than two Hong Kongs in terms of value of exports – as a share of its own measured GNP, Soviet foreign trade was significant.[438] In 1988, the value of imports was roughly 12 per cent of measured Soviet GNP, near the comparable US figure.[439] The actual economic value of trade with the socialist countries is difficult to interpret, however, because of the fixed prices involved, but much of this trade involved implicit Soviet subsidies to its allies. Trade with market economies of necessity relied on market prices, though concessions were made for political reasons in some cases, e.g., arms exports were frequently subsidized.

During the reform period, Russia has greatly liberalized the system of foreign trade. Trade in foreign currencies at market-determined rates is allowed, so the rouble has achieved a good deal of convertibility. Most restrictions on imports have been removed, though exports generally require a licence, and trade taxes exist for some goods.[440] Oil exports, for example, are heavily taxed, as are imports of automobiles and vodka.

The convertibility that Russia has largely adopted is referred to as 'current-account' convertibility.[440*] This means that roubles can be exchanged for foreign currencies for the purposes of trading goods and services and for tourism. It does not mean, however, that foreigners can exchange their currencies for roubles in order to buy Russian factories, or that Russians can exchange their roubles to buy foreign assets. The international exchange of asset ownership, rather, requires 'capital-account' convertibility.[441] Convertibility for capital transactions has been argued to be unwise until macroeconomic stabilization is achieved.[442] One fear of capital account convertibility is that it will lead to 'capital flight', whereby assets are moved to less volatile foreign economies. Even in the absence of capital account convertibility, estimates of capital flight from Russia are in the range of $20 billion annually, possibly exceeding the aid inflows.[443]

How important has the partial liberalization of foreign trade and the foreign exchange market been to reforming Russia, and what can be expected from a more complete, current-account liberalization? Many commentators suggested that rouble convertibility would play an important, and perhaps essential, role in marketizing the Russian economy.[444] The reasoning is that convertibility, combined with a largely unrestricted trade regime, promotes three desirable consequences: increased foreign trade, increased foreign investment, and the importation of world relative prices.

Indeed, the liberalization of foreign economic relations has led to a good deal of new foreign trade with Western countries and foreign investment during the reform era.[445] Simultaneously, the break-up of the Eastern trading bloc COMECON and the dissolution of the USSR have reduced official Russian trade with countries in Eastern Europe and the other countries of the former USSR. As noted, the fixed prices involved in that trade made the value of it uncertain. On balance, the reduction in trade with the former East Bloc has probably been beneficial to Russia.[446] Breakdowns in intra-USSR trade, however, may have contributed to production declines that are not economically justified.

The trade and investment benefits that would accompany full rouble convertibility, while desirable, are not indispensable. Foreign investment generally plays a minor role in promoting economic growth, despite its potential to promote technology transfer. Foreign trade confers gains on both trading partners, so the trade-creating aspect of rouble convertibility would benefit the Russian economy. But Russia has a huge internal economy. Policies that rationalize this internal economy are almost sure to produce gains that swamp the effects of improvements in foreign trade.[447] Simultaneously, internal decontrol of economic activity, and a stable legal environment, will serve as perhaps the best attractor of foreign partners.

Beyond the trade and investment benefits, rouble convertibility is viewed as desirable because of its ability to 'get prices right', both in the direct sense of ensuring that world prices are relevant in Russia, and in the indirect sense of providing commitment to a domestic price liberalization. Russian enterprises, monopolies or otherwise, will not long be able to charge excessive prices if foreign firms can offer competition. In itself, however, the importation of world relative prices may not confer large gains on Russia. There is evidence that the state-controlled relative prices were largely consistent with world prices, though with some notable exceptions such as the prices of housing and energy.[448] Again, the more important reform is to ensure that domestic producers have strong incentives to respond to market-determined prices, as opposed to simply 'getting prices right'.

The 'commitment' argument suggests that rouble convertibility, combined with unfettered foreign trade, necessitates internal price decontrol. If prices remain fixed when trade is freed, arbitragers would purchase Russian goods that are relatively underpriced, export them, and receive the higher world price. Such arbitrage activity would result in a huge wealth giveaway by the Russian government.[449] (For this reason, the Soviets required joint ventures operating in the USSR to use world prices even for domestic transactions, as opposed to the fixed state prices.[450]) To avoid this outcome in a regime with rouble convertibility and free foreign trade, the Russians would have to free prices internally. Adopting a policy of rouble convertibility, so the story goes, therefore commits the Russians to price liberalization.

The significant degree of price liberalization that has occurred since the beginning of 1992 renders this credibility argument largely moot in a policy sense. But there were good reasons to distrust this 'convertibility-implies-price liberalization' logic anyway. If the Russians truly were committed to full price liberalization, they could achieve this convincingly without rouble convertibility, simply by decontrolling prices. Without governmental commitment to price liberalization, a policy of rouble convertibility is not credible – the government will simply back off from convertibility as its losses mount – so convertibility cannot provide any commitment to a price liberalization policy. ·

Rouble convertibility has often been tied to Western aid programmes. The logic is that if foreign trade is to be liberalized and the rouble made convertible at a fixed exchange rate, balance-of-payments assistance (i.e., provision of foreign exchange or other measures to subsidize Russian imports) or a 'rouble stabilization fund', or both, may be necessary to maintain the exchange rate.[451] For example, the Russian government could declare that roubles are fully convertible at, say, 3000 to the dollar. Any person who presents one dollar to the Russian government would receive 3000 roubles, and perhaps more importantly, vice versa – the government would be willing to give one dollar in exchange for 3000 roubles. In order to credibly make such a commitment, the Russian government, which can print roubles but not dollars, must ensure that the 'market value' of 3000 roubles is not less than $1; otherwise, there will be a 'run' on the government, as people try to exchange 3000 roubles for the more valuable dollar.

To prevent such a run, then, the government must not allow people to think that 3000 roubles are less valuable than a dollar. By 'committing' to a fixed exchange rate, governments presumably tie their hands not to inflate the domestic currency more quickly than world inflation; otherwise, the run would eventually occur. The fixed exchange rate therefore serves as a 'nominal anchor', i.e., it anchors the domestic price level by restricting the government's ability to profligately print roubles. Indeed, the stabilization of expectations – convincing people that you are committed to a non-inflationary policy – is the main argument for employing a fixed exchange rate during a transition.

Expectations that the fixed exchange rate will hold can perhaps be purchased by a stabilization fund of foreign exchange, which indicates to holders of the domestic currency that the opportunity to obtain foreign currencies at the fixed rate will continue to be honoured. If they adopt such expectations, there will not be a run against the domestic currency, and the stabilization fund remains intact.[452]

Once again, however, commitment arguments in reform are not completely persuasive. It is true that with a fixed exchange rate, government budget deficits that are paid for by printing money quickly come to the attention of the government, by a run against the domestic currency. But this outcome is not so dire that no government would ever choose not to print money. Instead, faced with a run, the government can simply devalue the supposedly 'fixed' exchange rate. A fixed exchange rate can be viewed as providing an incentive to alter the rate when domestic inflation mounts, as opposed to providing a nominal anchor. Stabilization funds do not provide free commitment to an otherwise uncommitted government policy.

A fixed exchange rate is not a necessary component of rouble convertibility. Many market economies (like the United States) employ floating exchange rates, whereby the value of the currency is determined in the market in which it is exchanged with other currencies. As opposed to a fixed exchange rate regime, maintaining a floating exchange rate does not require that the government have substantial foreign currency reserves. (It was the lack of such reserves that probably prompted the move to a floating exchange rate in Russia.)

The government of a transitional economy that implements sound fiscal and monetary policies has little to fear, in terms of inflation, from either fixed or floating exchange rates.[453] Simultaneously, a government that implements inflationary policies will face a rapid depreciation of its currency in a floating-rate regime, or a run against domestic currency and eventual devaluation in a fixed exchange rate regime. It is sound monetary policies, and not the exchange rate regime, that are important for improving a transitional economy's price stability.

Nevertheless, short-term balance-of-payments support has become a part of the received aid wisdom.[454] To the extent that Russia meets the usual requirements for such support, Western aid in the form of a rouble stabilization fund and balance-of-payments support may be a desirable policy. This is not a pressing issue, however. While full rouble convertibility would undoubtedly be beneficial, the most advantageous trade (such as oil exports and food imports) is generally already taking place. Furthermore, market-oriented reforms can proceed and generate large improvements in Russia, even without rouble convertibility.

WESTERN AID

And, as we hear you do reform yourselves,
We will, according to your strength and qualities,
Give you advancement.

William Shakespeare, *King Henry IV*, Part II

On 1 April 1992, Western leaders announced a $24 billion aid package to the states of the former Soviet Union.[455] While this programme has been amended and augmented since, major components of planned Western aid remain balance-of-payments support and a rouble stabilization fund. Once again, the pre-reform situation is a crucial determinant of the potential impact of Western aid.

Consider first the balance-of-payments support, which is equivalent to giving the former Soviet states Western goods. What form the goods take, whether food or clothing or medical supplies, is largely irrelevant. Such direct aid is fungible, in the sense that aid received in the form of food, for instance, frees internal Russian resources for other purposes.

The pre-existing debt owed by the former USSR to the West greatly alters the impact of Western aid. The states of the former Soviet Union owe some $60–85 billion to the West – a debt that they are having difficulty servicing. Indeed, the repayment of principal due on this debt was postponed in December 1991.[456] The situation is further complicated by the disappearance of the entity – the USSR – that was the original borrower.

The existence of this potentially unrecoverable debt implies that Western aid to Russia may largely be returned to the West in increased debt repayment.[457] Aid effectively transfers funds from the IMF, World Bank, or Western governments to Western banks, simply passing through Russia.[458]

As opposed to balance-of-payments support, the rouble stabilization fund is designed to work in an indirect fashion. If a rouble stabilization fund achieves its purpose, it will not actually be used – with a stable rouble, the extra foreign exchange comprising the stabilization fund will remain in place, since there will be no run against the rouble. Such forms of indirect assistance are therefore conceptually different from direct aid. As noted in the previous section, however, a rouble stabilization fund is neither necessary nor sufficient for achieving rouble convertibility, which itself will bring limited benefits to Russia in the short-term.

The current instability in the rouble, however, results in Russian aid to the West, of a sort. Because of high inflation and the possibility of another currency confiscation, many people in Russia hold foreign currency, chiefly dollars and deutschemarks, instead of roubles. But how do Russians originally acquire the foreign currency? They must sell something to the West, that is paid for, say, in dollars. Instead of using the dollars to buy US goods, however, the dollars circulate (or are hoarded) in Russia. The US has therefore acquired Russian goods, and, until the dollars actually return to the United States, has not had to provide any goods in exchange. In essence, the use of dollars in Russia represents an interest-free loan from Russia to the United States. The US does not have to repay the loan until the Russians finally divest themselves of their dollars by purchasing US goods. In the meantime, the widespread use of foreign currency in Russia is a form of Russian aid to the West.

The existence of widespread formal and informal market activity in Russia, as described in the previous chapters, does not imply that the Russian economy is in good shape, or that Western aid to Russia and other states of the former USSR is inappropriate. While there are many countries that are poorer than Russia, aid to the Russian economy could have a sustained impact. Systemic change such as Russia is undergoing holds out the possibility, not just for temporary improvements in living standards, but for movement to a higher growth path that will raise living standards in the future. Aid that helps to ensure successful systemic change will benefit both current and future generations of Russians. There is little possibility of creating a long-term dependence on aid, as can occur with assistance to developing countries, nor will other nations be enticed to embrace socialism as a means of qualifying for Western aid. For these reasons and because of the strategic importance of the former USSR, the Russian claim to Western aid is strong.[459] Also, because of the pre-existing debt, aid can be a useful measure to promote market reforms, without actually imposing significant net costs. But not all forms of aid are equally useful, and some may be detrimental.

Government involvement in economic production and distribution in the former Soviet Union remains extensive, despite many years of partial reforms and widespread private activity. An anecdote from post-coup, independent Lithuania illustrates this point. A police officer confiscated the goods of a seller at a flea market. Her crime was speculation. She had purchased some chocolates in Moscow and was selling them for a higher price in Vilnius.[460] The economic reform most needed in the former Soviet Union is for the government to allow the private sector to bloom, while clamping down on coercive private impediments to business: organized crime.

Economists differentiate between private goods, everyday items such as apples, where one person's consumption of an apple effectively rules out another person's consumption of the same apple, and public goods like national defence, where one citizen's 'consumption' does not interfere with another citizen's consumption. There is little reason for the government to be in the business of producing private goods, because private actors in free markets generally do a good job in ensuring good social outcomes. Public goods, however, involve an externality, and hence their provision can potentially be improved by government intervention. The pre-reform Soviet government dominated the production of both public and private goods. In reforming Russia, state provision of private goods such as food and consumer goods should diminish – the private sector is much better placed to efficiently produce the right private goods. State provision of some public goods, however, should continue.[461]

Western aid to the former Soviet Union should therefore be aimed at promoting private provision of private goods, and continued (or improved) state provision of public goods. Aid that enables continued state control of the economy is counterproductive, whether the aid is directed at the national, regional, or local level. Aid provided at the national level that allows, for example, Lithuania to continue to harass chocolate 'speculators' is obviously misplaced.

Private economic activity in Russia can be promoted either by directly helping private economic agents, or by helping the state provide the public goods – the legal system, the banking infrastructure, etc. – that indirectly promote private activity. Aid to private economic agents is difficult to implement, however, in an official aid programme. This type of 'aid' is probably best left to private economic agents in the West, in the form of undertaking profitable ventures within Russia and possibly with Russian partners.

Official Western aid should therefore focus on helping the Russian state sector provide public goods that promote private market activity. The Russian government's economic policy forms one such public good. Conditioning aid on the removal of price controls on gasoline, for example, would be an example of subsidizing the provision of a public good. The danger of unconditional aid, and to a degree conditional aid, bears re-iterating – aid directed at the state sector could inadvertently foster continued state interference in economic affairs best left to private actors.

Technical assistance for improving public goods such as the legal system or communications infrastructure is obviously important, though not always straightforward. Technical assistance in the economics realm may differ substantially depending on who provides the assistance. Transformations from socialism remain sufficiently complex that disagreements persist among Western economists. In other areas, say, in setting up accounting procedures or other elements of market infrastructure, 'appropriate technology' is an issue. With per-capita income approximately one-third of the US level, Russia may want to rely less extensively on computerization of accounting procedures than the US does, for instance.

One state-provided public good that will require significant revamping has already been mentioned – the implicit welfare system must be replaced with an explicit system, and a similar transformation must take place in the realm of tax collection. It has been argued in previous chapters that the costs of these systems need not rise during reform. Nevertheless, technical assistance will be valuable in both of these areas, is relatively inexpensive, and is, in fact, being provided.

Another public good that has been suffering with the collapse of the state sector is in the area of training and research. Western aid can be quite useful here. First, there are some fields, particularly the social sciences, where traditional Soviet training is clearly irrelevant. Few qualified teachers exist. While individuals are proving to be quite industrious in teaching themselves, Western aid in the form of textbooks and graduate student fellowships could help restore these fields much more quickly. Even in areas such as mathematics and the natural sciences where Russian research remains world-class, talented researchers have been enticed into private market, non-research activity, because of the financial incentives there and because of the diminished resources of the Academy of Sciences. While such labour movements are not entirely undesirable, grants to particularly talented researchers could return them to productive research.[462] Russian research fields are also suffering from an inability to attract young entrants, again because of improved alternatives. Fellowships provided by Western foundations, or possibly by Western governments, could support talented young graduate students.

Military conversion, as noted earlier, is not promising from an economic point of view. Western aid aimed at improving Russian living standards should not be directed at such types of physical conversion. Nevertheless, individual defence enterprises that are seeking to convert to consumer goods production, and that are working for their own account, may be good candidates for Western technical assistance, and possibly for private co-operation with Western companies.

One important 'aid' component is a reduction in Western trade barriers. This would involve both opening Western markets to goods from Russia (and other former socialist countries), and in reducing some of the trade controls that have existed because of Western security concerns. Unlike other forms of Western aid, reducing such trade barriers generally has the desirable property of making both Russia and the West better off in a direct way, since the existing trade restrictions tend to be welfare-reducing. Unfortunately, this suggests that the likelihood that trade barriers will be reduced for Russian exports is relatively small. (Alternatively, Western export restrictions to the former Soviet Union based on security considerations are already being dismantled.[463]) Domestic producers in the West have managed to secure protection from imports to the detriment of Western consumers. It is unlikely that their claims to protection will be eroded by the interests of emerging Russian exporters.

Aid may have other purposes than promoting the marketization of the Russian economy. Assistance for centralized Russian military conversion, a policy proposed by Senator Sam Nunn and others, may make sense from the perspective of Western security interests.[464] Money and technical assistance for the dismantling of nuclear weapons, and for the continued employment of Russian nuclear scientists, could be similarly motivated. Assistance in the environmental sphere, such as help in improving the safety of nuclear reactors, can also flow directly from Western self-interest.

Finally, an implicit sub-text of this chapter warrants explicit re-telling. The ultimate success or failure of Russian market-oriented reform is in the hands of the Russians. While Western aid can be useful, most of the gains from Russian reform can be secured without any help from foreign governments.

GRADUAL REFORM, CHINESE STYLE

Beginning with agricultural reform in 1978, the Chinese have gradually moved towards an increased use of markets. Following agriculture, China has extended its liberalization, first to foreign trade, and then to industry.[465] By all reports, the gradual approach to economic reform in China has been a huge, virtually unprecedented success, with impressive growth in agriculture, industry, and services, and an overall growth rate averaging 8.8 per cent per year between 1978 and 1992.[466] China is therefore exhibit A for the gradualist side in the debate between those who favour gradual transitions from socialism and those who prefer a more rapid introduction of legal markets.

The question then arises, is the Chinese success story of more general applicability? Does China indicate that a gradual transition from socialism, one sector at a time, is preferable to a relatively rapid, broad-based transition? A first step in answering this question requires an examination of the possibility of maintaining a market-based sector (e.g., agriculture), within the larger framework of a centrally-planned economy. This question was addressed by Western economist Gregory Grossman in 1963, and his framework of analysis remains serviceable.[467]

Grossman identifies three potential reasons for failure of an attempt to marketize one sector within a command economy. First, planned sectors may depend on the output of the market sector, and if the availability of that output is unpredictable, the planned portion of the economy may be harmed. Agriculture, therefore, may be particularly well-suited for marketization, since the production of industrial goods and other consumer goods does not generally require direct inputs from the agricultural sector. Simultaneously, the greater the extent to which the unplanned sector requires inputs from the planned sector, the lower the benefits of liberalization are likely to be, since the market sector's growth will be constrained by the availability of planned inputs. Second, according to Grossman, the result of production in the market sector may not accord with the government's values. Increased income differentiation in the market sector, for example, could result in a re-imposition of planning by authorities not accustomed to large, visible discrepancies in living standards. Third, the market sector may not fully utilize its resources. Unemployment, for instance, could again create pressure for more extensive planning.

As noted, these considerations suggest that marketizing the agriculture sector within a planned economy is relatively likely to succeed, if the planning regime can tolerate the distributional impacts both within the agricultural sector and between the agricultural and planned sectors. If the agricultural sector is large relative to the size of the overall economy – in China, 71 per cent of the labour force was involved in agriculture in 1978 – the economic benefits from such a marketization can be significant. In Russia, with only 14 per cent of the work force in agriculture at the beginning of perestroika, the gains are likely to be substantially smaller.[468] Furthermore, Russian farms average 40 times the size of Chinese farms, and Russian agriculture is much more highly industrialized than Chinese agriculture.[469]

The Grossman-style links, therefore, between the planned sector (agricultural machinery) and the unplanned sector (agriculture) are greater in Russia, again suggesting that an agriculture-first market reform is less likely to succeed in Russia than in China.

A successful reform in a single sector such as agriculture is only the beginning, however. Problems will arise as the agricultural sector prospers. The greater productivity brought about by the marketization of agriculture will eventually tend to create new resources and perhaps free other resources employed in the agricultural sector. What new activities will these freed resources undertake? If the only option is for them to enter into the planned sector, then the productivity gains in agriculture would, in all likelihood, not spread to the rest of the economy, which will still be marked by all the usual shortcomings of central planning. The economic boom arising from the liberalization of agriculture will be a useful, but one-time, affair. The agricultural reforms in China led precisely to such a one-time jump in productivity, though the ensuing liberalizations in other sectors allowed growth to spread.[470]

A second method of separating out a market sector in an otherwise planned economy – and a method also pursued in China – is to make the division along geographical lines, by declaring certain areas 'special economic zones'. Within these zones, as with the 'empowerment zones' established in American cities, economic conditions are then liberalized relative to other areas. The Grossman criteria apply as well to this type of partial reform. The importance of links between the controlled and liberalized areas, in particular, are once again quite important. Consider, for example, what might happen if price controls are lifted in a special economic zone, but not in other parts of the country. Typically, nominal prices will then be higher in that zone relative to the planning areas. Firms in the planning areas, to the extent possible, will then prefer to sell their goods in the free zones; i.e., the free zones will tend to draw resources away from the unplanned zones. This argument applies to labour as well. Wages are likely to be higher in the free market sector, so workers will tend to migrate to these zones. Non-market regions will then either have to tighten controls – by forbidding 'exports' of food to the special economic zone, for instance – or by freeing their own prices. In Russia, local controls on the movement of goods became the response of many localities to the situation that arose following central price liberalization but locally-imposed price controls.[471]

Related to the issue of gradual vs rapid transition is the extent to which economic liberalization should be conducted in a centralized or a decentralized manner. The centralized variant of reform involves the mandating of reforms, more-or-less uniformly, from the political centre. The official privatization plan in Russia is an example of such a reform. Decentralized reforms, alternatively, would let localities choose their own rates of transition. The Chinese agricultural reforms were largely of the decentralized variety – in many instances, they were spontaneous, not official reforms – with the central government stepping in only to prevent local officials from squelching the reforms.[472]

Centralized reforms have the advantage that they can perhaps overcome the intransigence of local officials. The related disadvantage, however, is that local resistance might be sufficient to scuttle the reform efforts – and perhaps rightly so, if the central reform plan was not sufficiently sensitive to local conditions. Decentralized reforms, as noted before with respect to regionally gradual reforms, would seem to work best if they create a reinforcing momentum for reform: one region liberalizes quickly, and other regions, noting the flow of resources into the liberal region, respond with liberalizations of their own. Decentralized reforms are less likely to work, however, if the response to a flow of resources out of one region is the strengthening of controls to prevent such a flow.

Decentralized reforms, then, like gradual reforms, are most likely to succeed under two sets of circumstances: either there are few links between the liberalized region and other regions, or, if there are extensive links, they are such as to promote a virtuous cycle of reform. 'Agriculture first' reforms in Russia are not promising on either of these counts, given the important links between the agricultural machinery (and fertilizer) industries and the agricultural sector, and the frequency of locally-imposed price and trade restrictions. The decentralization of more broad-based reforms is also problematic in Russia. Here, the difficulty is that the most pressing reform that remains is to reduce subsidies to state-owned enterprises. Every locality, however, has an incentive to press for centrally-directed subsidies to its own industries. The virtuous cycle of reform may therefore have a hard time getting underway.

CONCLUSIONS

So many reforms, so little time. The Russian economy is sufficiently distant from a normal market economy that there is scarcely any aspect of the economy that does not require significant change, or that could not benefit from Western assistance. Nevertheless, some reforms have higher priority than others. The most important reforms are those that I have identified with a sufficient reform package: free prices, free enterprise, and explicit systems of taxation and social welfare. The gradual introduction of these reforms, in the Russian context, seems to hold many pitfalls relative to rapid implementation. Other desirable reforms, such as rouble convertibility, military conversion, or, as noted in a previous chapter, large-scale privatization, are of decidedly secondary importance. Indeed, if these subordinate reforms are implemented prior to the more basic measures, they will almost surely fail, and may well worsen the economic situation. Western aid will also tend to have a limited impact unless the basic reform measures are in place. But once the basic reforms are implemented, significant Western aid is probably unwarranted. The main role for Western aid, therefore, is to help promote and cement the fundamental reform measures – measures which Russia should take irrespective of foreign assistance. After Russia implements the basic reforms, Western participation in the Russian economy can be as a partner, not a patron, like standard economic links among market economies.

Conclusions

In the relations of a weak Government and a rebellious people there comes a time when every act of the authorities exasperates the masses, and every refusal to act excites their contempt . . .'
John Reed, Ten Days that Shook the World, 1919[473]

It's a very serious risk to do nothing. It is a very serious risk to do anything unpopular. It is even a very serious risk to do something popular because everyone understands that really popular measures will lead you nowhere.
Yegor Gaidar, 1991[474]

[T]o catch or destroy five rats and ten mice . . .
Part of the 'plan' proposed to Soviet children to further the first 5-year plan, from New Russia's Primer. The Story of the Five-Year Plan[475]

China's economic reformer, Deng Xiaoping, is noted for his claim that 'It doesn't matter whether the cat is black or white, as long as it catches mice.' Presumably his point is that as long as an economic system delivers the goods, labels such as 'socialist' or 'capitalist' are irrelevant. The traditional Soviet system was, in many ways, not a planned system at all. Similarly, the market economy that is now growing in Russia, from extensive and largely subterranean pre-existing roots, remains far removed from any notion of what a normal market economy might look like. The difficult task that remains is for the Russian government to nurture the market economy that already exists, by providing the conditions under which the private behaviour of individuals will by and large mesh with the social good – mice will then be caught.

The analysis presented in this book has argued that a useful way to think about Russian reform is as a movement from implicit to explicit versions of pre-existing economic phenomena. A partial list of some of the phenomena that are undergoing such a conversion would include: inflation; unemployment; monopoly power; economic crime; private property rights; taxation; and the social safety net. Many of these economic phenomena more or less automatically revert from implicit to explicit form during any effective transition to a market economy. Since free prices are a sine qua non of a market economy, inflation, for example, of necessity will become largely open in a market-oriented reform. Alternatively, some of the formerly repressed economic phenomena, such as tax and social welfare policy, become open only as the Russian government consciously creates new, explicit systems that accomplish these functions.

The two pillars that underlie the conducive conditions for 'growing' a market economy are free prices, and good incentives to respond to the free prices. The major obstacles to overcome in building these pillars can be characterized as partial reform measures, particularly in the form of keeping some important prices fixed (generally at levels well below the market rate), continuing to subsidize unsuccessful firms or confiscating surpluses from successful firms, providing undue legal restrictions on private enterprise, or failing to provide workable explicit versions of the tax and social welfare systems. A lack of stability in the legal environment also militates against the establishment of a well-functioning market economy. Furthermore, in gauging the effects of reform, traditional indicators of economic performance must be carefully assessed, as such statistics will begin to measure different things when economic phenomena move from repressed to open form. With a reasonably comprehensive market-oriented reform, most of the costs that appear to accompany reform will simply represent more open versions of costs that were being paid surreptitiously under the old system.

None of this is to suggest that the transition from socialism to capitalism is child's play, or to appropriate a phrase of Lenin's, could be accomplished by any kitchen maid. If such a transition were simple and painless, it probably would have taken place in Russia many years ago. But as the quotations that open this section intimate, systemic reform is hard to accomplish.

The difficulty of transition means that countries tend to postpone reform until the pre-reform conditions get nearly intolerable, to the point where those who are clearly better off with the status quo become small in number and influence. But the initiation of reform is, of course, only the beginning; there will be those who are harmed by reforms, as well as others, perhaps responding to the inappropriate statistical measures of the effects of reform, who will succumb to what the historian Edward Gibbon called 'the propensity of mankind to exalt the past and to depreciate the present'.[476] The legacy of the old system in Russia is such that despite a near decade of bad economic news and many voices of despair accompanying reform, there appears to be little interest in turning back.[477] The danger is not so much from a conscious decision to re-impose central planning as it is from the temptation to meet every seeming (and in some cases, real) economic 'crisis' with a government control, until a planned economy arrives more-or-less accidentally.

The road of Russian reform is therefore difficult to traverse, and there will be frequent retreats. In the end, it is likely that Russia will arrive at the destination of a normal market economy, if only because other endpoints are either unstable, or, like the previous system, clearly undesirable. But the timetable for the journey involves years, and with bad economic policies, decades. All is not pessimistic, however. Another Chinese saying is that a journey of a thousand miles begins with a single step. The Russian economy has already taken many steps, even giant leaps, in the direction of a market economy, and in a relatively short period of time. It was only at the end of 1991 that the Soviet flag came down from the Kremlin. Russian streets are alive with private market activity, private farms are blossoming, many state-owned enterprises have been 'privatized'. Russians are not sitting silently, anxiously anticipating their journey to the market economy. They are well on their way.

Notes

Notes denoted by an asterisk have been added since the text was first completed.

1 Hewett (1989a, p. 18).
2 Evidence for the positive contribution that economic reasoning can bring to the reform debate comes, ironically, from Dr. Hewett's own work (Hewett (1988)), among other sources. Kornai (1990) is an outstanding example of the application of basic economic reasoning to Eastern European reform.
3 McCloskey (1985, p. 131).
4 Gogol (1972 [1842], p. 259).
5 Some of the Gorbachev-era reform flip-flops are chronicled in Goldman (1992).
6 Ericson (1991, p. 26).
7 On the controversy regarding Russian living standards, see Rosefielde (1991), Bergson (1991), and the 'Income and Living Standards' chapter below.
8 From Karl Marx's 'Critique of the Gotha Program'. Feurer (1959, p. 117).
9 *Economic Report of the President* (1992, p. 104).
10 In January 1994, the survey used by the Department of Labor to calculate the unemployment rate was revised. The new survey revealed some unemployment that was previously uncounted, so that the reported unemployment rate increased in January 1994, although calculated on a consistent basis, unemployment actually fell from December 1993.
   A sudden 'loss' of 640,000 US jobs in the first quarter of 1991 was discovered, two years later, to be merely a statistical artefact reflecting a change in how the number of jobs was tabulated. See 'Labor Dep't Overstated Jobs Lost in Last Recession', Durham (NC) *Herald-Sun*, 4 June 1993, p. 16.
11 The full poem appears in Hewett (1989b, pp. 104–106).
12 Wolf (1991) chronicles the many years of difficulties with partial reform measures in Hungary and Poland.
13 This effect on the price of sour cream ignores the supply shift noted earlier in the paragraph. With both the supply and demand of sour cream increasing, the net effect on the price is ambiguous.
14 See, e.g., 'Puzzle of Moscow Milk: Prices Soar, Still Scarce', by Celestine Bohlen, *New York Times*, 7 February 1992, p. A8, and National Public Radio, *Morning Edition*, 'Yeltsin Receives Harsh Criticism, Moscow,' 16 January 1992.
15 This description of the evolution of Russian central planning is drawn from Sedik (1991). A hint of this reasoning also appears in Grossman (1963, p.107).
16 Shlapentokh (1989, p. 210, and endnote 4, p. 244).
17 Nove (1986, p. 364f). Ofer (1987, pp. 1770–1775) provides a good overview of

Soviet statistics. Treml (1988, 1992a) discusses the changes in Soviet statistics, and Western interpretations of the statistics, under perestroika.

18 The undocumented change involving the inclusion of used car sales in the automobile sales statistics was uncovered by Vladimir Treml. See *Radio Liberty Research*, RL 177/77, 26 July 1977.

19 See, e.g., Alexeev and Walker (1991, p. 4f).

20 Åslund (1990, pp. 19–20).

21 Vaksberg (1991, p. 115). The Uzbekistan cotton story is also related in Boyes (1990, p. 149f).

22 Vaksberg (1991, pp. 113–114).

23 This passage from Orwell (1983, p. 37) was brought to my attention during a talk at the Hoover Institution by Robert Conquest in 1992.

24 On the Khanin and Selyunin article, see Treml (1988) and Ericson (1990). Belkin (1993) provides a brief history of Khanin's work.

25 That growth rates will be unaffected by a consistent falsification of output levels is known as the 'Law of Equal Cheating'. See, e.g., Nove (1986, p. 374).

26 Khrushchev (1974, p. 131).

27 Goldman (1992, pp. 97–99). On Gorbachev's announcement of the previously hidden budget deficit, see Birman (1990, p. 25).

28 Incidentally, unreliable statistics at the highest levels are indicative of the types of problems that would render even 'ideal' central economic planning ineffective.

29 Hanson (1991, p. 290f).

30 The political purposes of statistics collection were noted by the last chairman of the USSR State Committee for Statistics (Belkin (1993, p. 59)). Of course, statistics can be used for propaganda purposes in market economies, too.

31 See 'Light at the End of the Tunnel?', by Keith Bush, *RFE/RL Research Report*, 14 May 1993, p. 64, and 'The Russian Budget Deficit', by Keith Bush, *RFE/RL Research Report*, 9 October 1992, p. 31.

32 'Leaders Said to Have Exaggerated Runaway Inflation Risk in Russia', by Steven Erlanger, *New York Times*, 3 March 1993, p. A7.

33 Quoted in Bronfenbrenner, Sichel, and Gardner (1984, p. 9).

34 Hewett (1988, p. 160).

35 Richards (1990).

36 Richards (1990, pp. 76–77). See also her discussion of the inability to generalize on pp. 72–73.

37 On the limits to knowledge, and an analogy to archaeology, see, e.g., Nutter (1969, pp. 70-71, 109–11).

38 Susan Richards (1990, p. 73) also notes how a (perhaps reluctant) reliance on the official story by Western Sovietologists failed to convey the realities of daily economic life.

39 Conquest (1991). See also 'The Party in the Dock', by Robert Conquest, *Times Literary Supplement*, 6 November 1992, p. 7, and the letter by émigré sociologist Vladimir Shlapentokh to the *AAASS Newsletter*, May 1993, pp. 5, 7.

40 Interviews and surveys of émigrés provided much of the systematic information that has become available concerning informal economic activity during the Soviet era. The Berkeley–Duke Project on the Second Economy in the USSR has produced more than 30 papers based largely on a survey of émigrés. Thousands of Soviet émigrés were also interviewed for the aptly-named 'Soviet Interview Project'. Millar (1987) provides a compendium of research based on this source (see p. 17).

40* Treml and Alexeer (1993, p. 18n)

41 See, e.g., 'Capitalism or Bust', *Economist*, 8 February 1992, and Wellisz (1991, p. 212).

42 The state price of oil and natural gas remained at 10%–20% of world prices in mid-1993. 'Light at the End of the Tunnel?', by Keith Bush, *RFE/RL Research Report*, 14 May 1993, p. 65.

The 'tropical flowers in Poland' sort of waste can only occur when based on products that are relatively plentiful in a centrally-planned economy; otherwise, for example, the greenhouse owners could not actually procure energy at the low official price.

43 'Free Market Prices For Coal Could Strengthen Russia's Economy, or Blow it Apart', by Sergei Leskov, *Izvestia*, 23 June 1993, p. 1. Condensed text translated in *Current Digest of the Post-Soviet Press*, Vol. XLV, No. 25, 1993.

44 Smith (1991 [1776], p. 400).

45 The notion that the invisible hand applies as long as all affected parties can costlessly contract in advance is known as the 'Coase theorem' in the economics world. The argument appeared in Coase (1960).

Complete information is important in leading to desirable outcomes because without it, bargaining may be inefficient. Farrell (1987) provides an excellent discussion of the relative merits of bargaining versus 'planning' in the presence of incomplete information.

46 Smith (1991 [1776], pp. 400–401).

47 Lange and Taylor (1938) present one approach to equilibrium pricing under socialism. From a systemic perspective, the informational advantages of markets seem substantial, as argued by Hayek (1945). In more limited arenas with incomplete information, however, planning may offer improvements over free markets. Again, see Farrell (1987).

48 Berliner (1976).

49 Khanin (1992, p. 14).

50 Burawoy and Hendley (1992, p. 373), endnote omitted. Rezina's operations in Moscow began in 1915.

51 Ericson (1991, p. 21).

52 Khrushchev (1990, p. 93).

53 Incidentally, the 'wrong goods' problem probably lies at the heart of difficulties in planned sectors, such as the defence industry, of Western economies. See, e.g., Leitzel (1993a).

54 Hayek (1972, pp. 124–125).

55 *The Myth of the Plan* is the title of a fine, balanced book by Peter Rutland (1985), though its focus is on the extent to which the Soviet command economy served political as opposed to economic objectives. An early contribution examining the reality of Soviet planning is Barton (1957).

56 Barton (1957, p. 43).

57 Goldman (1992) provides a description of the quality-control reform, which established State quality-control committees ('Gospriemka').

58 Hewett (1988, p. 184).

59 Birman (1978). Other important contributions that shed light on the actual workings of centrally-planned systems include Grossman (1963), Powell (1977), Zaleski (1980), Ellman (1983), Wilhelm (1985), and Hewett (1988, chapter 4). For a discussion of planning in a Western economy during wartime, see Devons (1950).

60 Powell (1977, p. 65n) reports on the frequency of plan changes, which for a single enterprise could be as often as 30 times a year. See also Hewett (1988, pp. 188–189).

61 Hewett (1988, p. 190).

62 Berliner (1952, p. 358).

63 Wilhelm (1985, p. 127).

64 Grossman (1963, pp. 108-112).
65 Grossman (1963, pp. 108).
66 See, e.g., Kornai (1992, chapters 11 and 12).
67 Powell (1977) discusses some of the informal methods whereby information on shortages was conveyed and balancing actions were taken in the Soviet economy.
68 Storming is described in Berliner (1956), and is further analysed in Alexeev (1991).
69 Smith (1984, pp. 287–288).
70 Schroeder (1979).
71 Belanovskii (1992).
72 A more sophisticated version of this theory would suggest that there is something inherent in central planning – perhaps the relative ease in measuring technical characteristics as opposed to consumer satisfaction – that results in a large share of official economic activity being devoted to defence.
73 Grossman and Treml (1987, p. 285).
74 General Accounting Office (1991, p. 22) cites one expert's estimate of the second economy in 1988 at 25 per cent of GNP. Grossman (1987) suggests that more than one-third of the income of Soviet urban dwellers in the late 1970s was earned in the second economy. Gaddy (1991) discusses the growth of second economy incomes during the 1980s. Income measures of second economy activity are more reliable than GNP measures because of difficulties in measuring GNP (see the 'Incomes and living standards' chapter) and connections between the first and second economy – some goods produced in the official economy and hence already counted in GNP can be double counted if they serve as intermediate inputs in the second economy. State-sector sugar might become an input into second economy alcohol production, for example.
75 Jones and Moskoff (1991, p. 3). Grossman (1977, 1979) are relied upon heavily throughout this section.
76 The term 'second economy' was defined by Grossman (1977) to include any activity that is conducted for private gain, or is undertaken in knowing, non-trivial contravention of the law, or both. The legal collective farm markets thus formed an important component of the Russian second economy. Sales on these markets would generally not fall under the rubric 'black markets', however, since these were legal markets. Shlapentokh (1989) documents a vast array of activities conducted for private gain in the pre-reform USSR.
77 Grossman and Treml (1987, p. 285).
78 On the theft of time from work, which generally occurred with the connivance of management, see Gaddy (1991), Treml (1992b), and Shlapentokh (1989, p. 52).
79 Shlapentokh (1989, p. 192).
80 Grossman (1989, p. 81).
81 Shlapentokh (1989, p. 191).
82 Jones and Moskoff (1991, p. 16).
83 Åslund (1993) notes many of the ways in which the Gaidar reforms of 1992 fell short of a full liberalization. Starodubrovskaya (1994) discusses many of the remaining barriers to the development of free markets (see p. 30).
83* European Bank for Reconstruction and Development (1994, p. 34)
84 'Byurokraticheskiy rynok. Skrytyye prava i ekonomicheskaya reforma', by Vitaliy Nayshul'. *Nezavisimaya gazeta*, 26 September 1991, p. 5. Translated by Clifford Gaddy.
85 Jones and Moskoff (1991, p. 58) describe the conflict of interest in the leasing of equipment by medical cooperatives.
86 For various routes to spontaneous privatization, see Johnson and Kroll (1991).

87 Burawoy and Hendley (1992, p. 379). The authors do not refer to the confusing array of cooperatives as constituting a form of spontaneous privatization.

88 Starodubrovskaya (1994, p. 9), and the references cited therein.

89 Starr (1993).

90 Shlapentokh (1989, p. 193) notes that private construction crews were much more productive than the state crews; indeed, in the springtime official state crews were almost deserted because workers migrated around the country as private builders.

90* Sachs (1993b, p. 153).

91 Gaddy (1993, p.4).

92 Prosterman, Hanstad, and Rolfes (1993, p. 3).

93 Prosterman and Hanstad (1991).

94 Gaddy (1993, p. 12).

95 Shlapentokh (1989, p. 161).

96 Prosterman, Hanstad, and Rolfes (1993, pp. 18-19), and Gaddy (1993, p. 11).

97 'Rural Reform in Russia', by Stephen K. Wegren, *RFE/RL Research Report*, 29 October 1993, pp. 43–53, on p. 48.

98 The extent and instability of government regulation of cooperatives is detailed in Slider (1991). See also Litwack (1991a).

99 Some examples of contradictory laws are provided in *Delovoy Mir*, 18 February 1993, p. 13.

100 Ownership uncertainty with respect to land, in particular, remains a problem in Russia. For a review of reform-era legislation in the agricultural sector, see 'Yeltsin Decree Finally Ends "Second Serfdom" in Russia', by Don Van Atta, *RFE/RL Research Report*, 19 November 1993, pp. 33–39.

101 Shleifer and Vishny (1993, p. 615).

102 de Soto (1989, p. 24) indicates that in Peru, the value of a house with a secure legal title exceeded the value of a house without legal protection by a factor of 9, on average. This source, Hernando de Soto's acclaimed book about the informal sector in Peru, *The Other Path*, details both theoretically and empirically the high costs associated with market activity, formal and informal, in situations where government restraints on private business are pervasive. Much of the discussion in *The Other Path* is directly relevant for the case of Russia.

103 A classic account of the degree to which business in the United States is actually conducted without legal protection is provided in Macauley (1963).

104 Simis (1982).

105 Rutgaizer (1992, p. 31, endnote 26), touches on this aspect of enforcement of laws against economic crimes.

106 See, e.g., Johnson and Kroll (1991), Burawoy and Krotov (1992), and 'From Soviet Minister to Corporate Chief', by G. Bruce Knecht, *New York Times Magazine*, 26 January 1992, pp. 24–28.

107 Johnson and Kroll (1991, p. 293). Kawalec (1992, p. 133) gives some Polish examples of de facto vertical integration.

108 Incidentally, the prospect to supply collateral for loans helps to underscore the importance of privatization of land and housing in a transition to a market economy. This point, for the case of land ownership, is noted by Prosterman and Hanstad (1991).

109 Aven (1991, p. 191n).

110 Johnson and Kroll (1991, p. 294).

111 See the discussion of barter in the chapter on 'Income and Living Standards'.

112 Burawoy and Krotov (1992) offer a description and generally negative assessment of 'parastatal conglomerates'.

113 Hendley (1992, p. 131).
114 For grain output statistics, see 'Agriculture and Food Supply in the Former Soviet Union', by Timothy N. Ash, *RFE/RL Research Report*, 13 November 1992, pp. 39–45.
115 Shlapentokh (1989, p. 92).
116 Individual Russians in particularly dire economic straits may have trouble affording food – or any other goods – and their plight may fuel the alarmist cries of food shortages. (The distribution of economic costs and benefits during reform is discussed in the chapters that follow.) Some of the voices proclaiming the potential for imminent famine have been raised by Russians, not Westerners. While it is understandable that Westerners might overestimate the importance of the state sector, it is unlikely that Russians would similarly misperceive the situation. Russians who are calling for food aid are generally representatives (and beneficiaries) of the state sector. It may be the state-sector crisis, not the overall condition of agriculture, to which they are responding.
117 See, e.g., *Izvestiya*, 9 September 1991. 'Ending Russia's Bread Lines', an op-ed by Leon Aron, *Wall Street Journal*, 18 December 1991, notes that '[l]ast summer the peasants were paid 200 roubles by the state for a ton of wheat delivered as part of the plan quota, and 400 roubles for each ton above the plan. At the same time, on the black (i.e., free) market, a ton of wheat cost 5,500 roubles!'
118 See 'Free Market Ideas Grow on Russian Farms', by Serge Schmemann, *New York Times*, 6 October 1992, pp. A1–A4.
119 'Yeltsin Decree Finally Ends 'Second Serfdom' in Russia', by Don Van Atta, *RFE/RL Research Report*, 19 November 1993, pp. 33–39, at 36. This article serves as a source for the discussion of remaining government interventions in Russian agriculture.
120 'Rural Reform in Russia', by Stephen K. Wegren, *RFE/RL Research Report*, 29 October 1993, pp. 43–53, at 51n.
121 'Byurokraticheskiy rynok. Skrytyye prava i ekonomicheskaya reforma', by Vitaliy Nayshul'. *Nezavisimaya gazeta*, 26 September 1991, p. 5. Translated by Clifford Gaddy.
122 Schelling (1984a, p. 158).
123 Thanks to opportunities for second economy activity, people employed in trade and services were more likely to own such prestige items as colour TVs than workers in other industries who had higher official salaries, but less control over state goods. See Shlapentokh (1989, pp. 79–80) and Rutgaizer (1992, p. 31, endnote 25).
124 Alexeev (1988b).
125 Simis (1982) and Vaksberg (1991) detail Communist Party control of the judiciary. See also Richards (1990, pp. 331–332), on the extent to which people believed that the Party controlled the law.
126 Shlapentokh (1989, p. 204f) notes the frequent use of the term 'mafia'. Simis (1982) and Vaksberg (1991) detail corruption and organized crime in the Soviet Union. The extent to which this system was known and understood is highlighted by former Moscow mayor Gavriil Popov's advocacy of legalizing the established bribes that are received by civil servants. See 'The Criminal Economy', by Mikhail Glukhovsky, *Delovie Lyudi*, No. 26, September 1992, pp. 14–16.
127 Grossman (1977, pp. 32–33).
128 The discussion of the importance of monopoly and illegality to organized crime draws heavily on Schelling (1984a,b).
129 It is more difficult to avoid paying tribute if the would-be extortionists are the police themselves, or if the business can be easily damaged in ways that are difficult to protect against. Schelling (1984b, p. 189) gives the example of

restaurants, where '[n]oises and bad odors and startling events can spoil the clientele, and even physical damage cannot be guarded against'.

130   Rutgaizer (1992, pp. 45–6).
131   Quoted in 'Wolf at the Door', by Maggie Mahar, *Barron's*, 19 October 1992, p. 20.
132   Valery Chernogorodsky, the former head of government anti-monopoly efforts in Russia who was quoted earlier, left his post when the anti-monopoly committee was put under the jurisdiction of the state committee on real estate. 'The real estate committee is itself a state monopoly . . . From the beginning of privatization, all of the corrupt forces gathered around the real-estate committee. . . . The anti-monopoly committee was supposed to be, in all ways, the opponent of everything the real estate committee stood for'. Quoted in 'Wolf at the Door', by Maggie Mahar, *Barron's*, October 19, 1992, p. 20. In a similar vein, the Russian Tax Service, which has been given the responsibility of registering all large bank accounts in order to fight corruption, has a reputation for being particularly corrupt itself. See 'The Russian Civil Service: Corruption and Reform', by Victor Yasmann, *RFE/RL Research Report*, 16 April 1993, p. 21.
133   See, e.g., Åslund (1993, p. 21).
134   In the West, it has been suggested that high wages are the prime deterrent against employee theft. See Lipman and McGraw (1988, p. 58).
135   '"We Need Bribes to Survive", Traffic Cop Says', *The Moscow Times*, 12 June 1992, p. 7.
136   Richards (1990, p. 332). Pre-Soviet Russia was also marked by a good deal of corruption. These words appear in one of the last chapters of Gogol's (1972, p. 382) famous uncompleted novel *Dead Souls*: 'The dishonest practice of taking bribes has become a necessity, something that even people who were not born to be dishonest cannot do without'.
137   Reported in Rutgaizer (1992, p. 47).
138   Shlapentokh (1989, pp. 90–91).
139   See the poll results reported in Rutgaizer (1992, pp. 42–44).
140   Vaksberg (1991, p. 251) makes a similar point.
141   The alternative resolution of the joke is 'it would be a good thing'.
142   The departures from price freedom in the 2 January 1992 Gaidar reform were: (1) some 10 basic goods such as gasoline and milk remained under explicit government price control, though the levels of their fixed prices were raised; (2) state retailers were allowed to mark-up goods by only 25 per cent over their wholesale prices; and (3) in some areas, local controls continued to be placed on prices. See Fischer and Frenkel (1992). Åslund (1993) documents the substantial extent to which the January 1992 Russian reforms fell short of complete liberalization, and Sachs (1994, p. 46), lists the major price controls that remained in mid-1993.
143   The quotation is from an editorial in the *New York Times*, 24 January 1991.
144   This analysis is developed in more detail in Alexeev, Gaddy, and Leitzel (1991).
145   Kolkhoz market prices rose by 7.5 per cent in April 1991, less than the inflation rate for any of the preceding three months. A rise of 53 per cent was recorded for January 1992, somewhat higher than the 33.2 per cent and 39.3 per cent increases in the previous two months. See Koen and Phillips (1993, p. 33). In neither case, however, was there a sudden, overnight surge in free market prices. The monetary compensation that accompanied the price reforms was one source, however, of new inflationary pressure.
146   The inflation figures are the Consumer Price Index for all goods and services. Koen and Phillips (1993, p. 33).
147   Taxes are also not neutral with respect to inflation, so the real amount of taxes

that people pay and hence the real amount of government tax revenues are altered by inflation, even if there is no change in economic activity.

148   Another cost of inflation consists of the resources that are used up in physically re-changing prices. Economists refer to these expenses as 'menu costs', since menus have to be redone as prices rise.

149   John R. Hicks made the comment 'The best of all monopoly profits is a quiet life', in Hicks (1935).

150   Strictly speaking, this information-processing cost arises only to the extent that the inflation is unanticipated; any positive rate of inflation, though, makes relative price change calculations dependent on the approximate date at which the shopper last checked the price in question. The actual amount of inflation is harder to anticipate when inflation is high than when it is low because the variance of inflation rates tends to be higher at high levels of inflation than at low levels. See, e.g., Schultze (1992, p. 127).

151   Dornbusch (1993, p. 6).

152   Yakir Plessner, a deputy governor of the Bank of Israel during years of high inflation, provides a nice account of the perceived costs of inflation from that vantage point in a letter to the *Journal of Economic Perspectives*, Spring 1994, pp. 204-206.

153   See the discussion of the 'sacrifice ratio' in Dornbusch and Fischer (1994, pp. 547–548).

154   Aven (1991, p. 198).

155   Cited in Shleifer and Vishny (1991, p. 6). Russian repressed inflation pre-dates perestroika. Shlapentokh (1989, p. 66) cites sociological studies in 1983 indicating that the average Soviet citizen spent 4–5 hours per day in search of consumer goods and services – though presumably not all of this time was spent in queues.

156   Strictly speaking, repressed inflation should refer only to a situation where the fixed state-sector prices are falling further behind free prices, as opposed to just being at a lower level.

157   The increased diversion of goods from the state sector as repressed inflation worsens is modelled in Leitzel (1993b).

158   'Russians Put Anxiety Aside and Try to Eke Out a Living', by Celestine Bohlen, *New York Times*, 1 March 1992, pp. 1, 9.

159   Uncertainty over who will benefit from reform can serve to delay or prevent reforms that would be socially beneficial. Fernandez and Rodrik (1991).

160   Quoted in Nove (1982, p. 313).

161   As previously noted, indexation of savings and other accounts is itself a source of new inflationary pressure.

162   For a brief commentary on the 2 April 1991 price reform, see Dyker (1992, pp. 207–208).

163   On the currency confiscation see Hewett and Gaddy (1992, p. 142n) and Goldman (1992, pp. 196–197).

164   In July 1993 a similar rouble confiscation scheme was implemented, this time under a regime of largely open inflation.

165   Differences in the pattern of accompanying compensation may have altered the types of people harmed by the two price reforms.

166   Burawoy and Hendley (1992, p. 397).

167   The extent to which people in the West look for government intervention when the price of an important good rises is not inconsiderable. Prices rose for such goods as timber and flashlights in the areas of Florida stricken by Hurricane Andrew in the late summer of 1992. Government efforts to combat 'price gouging' included threats of criminal prosecution against those who sold at prices that were 'too high'. See 'Price Gouging is Widely Cited in Storm Region', by Joseph B.

Treaster, *New York Times*, 30 August 1992, and 'Lessons From a Hurricane: It Pays Not to Gouge', by Steve Lohr, *New York Times*, 22 September 1992.

168   The government fears were well-founded. Increases in meat prices ignited a civil revolt in the southern Russian city of Novocherkassk in 1962. Khrushchev had the uprising forcibly suppressed by the army, and 22 lives were lost in the struggle. See 'Soviet Archives Provide Missing Pieces of History's Puzzles', by Serge Schmemann, *New York Times*, 8 February 1993, p. A6.

169   Åslund (1990, p. 24).

170   'Yeltsin Contemplates Prices, Stress, and His Plans to Retire', *New York Times*, 28 May 1992, p. A8.

171   'Supply shocks' like the Arab oil embargo may also lead to generally higher prices, though in the absence of an accommodating monetary policy, such an effect is not certain, nor could general price increases continue for long. Ball (1993) provides a nice discussion of the causes of inflation.

172   Another method whereby a government can gain control over resources is through voluntary donations, including receipts of foreign aid.

173   All three of the methods that the government can employ to garner resources from the private sector are limited. If taxes become extremely high, people will reduce their amount of taxable activity. Likewise, individuals will eventually become reluctant to buy government bonds as the government becomes further and further indebted, relative to its capacity to repay. Finally, if the government prints too much money, individuals will refuse to accept the rapidly-inflating currency in exchange for goods.

174   Money creation in itself does not necessarily imply inflation. First, productivity may be going up, so the supply of goods can be increasing as fast or faster than the nominal demand. Second, people could choose to hold more currency. It has been argued, for example (Sachs and Woo (1994, p. 128)), that increased money demand in China during transition has allowed the Chinese government to essentially print money without overly severe inflationary consequences. Government interest rate policy affecting the return on monetary assets held in savings accounts can thereby influence inflation through its effect on monetary demand.

175   Émigré economist Igor Birman (1990, p. 27) notes that his research indicates that Soviet government budgets have been in deficit since the Second World War.

176   Together, investment and defence comprised roughly half of Soviet GNP; in the US, these components form about one-quarter of GNP. On Soviet investment in GNP, see Pitzer and Baukol (1991, p.5); on the defence share of GNP, see Rowen and Wolf (1990). Statistics for the US in 1991 can be found in the *Economic Report of the President* (1992).

177   *Izvestiya*, 8 and 24 January 1989, p. 1, as quoted in Birman (1990, pp. 25, 40).

178   There were government bonds in the former Soviet Union, but sales of such bonds were economically inconsequential, though useful for citizens to launder second economy earnings (Malyshev (1987)). The first Russian government bond issue of the post-Soviet era took place in May 1993, but planned bond sales remain very small relative to the size of the Russian state budget deficit. See *RFE/RL News Brief*, 18 May 1993. Foreign aid could also have been employed to finance the budget deficit in a non-inflationary manner, but through the first quarter of 1993 foreign financing was basically used to supply subsidies for imports, and not used to finance the domestic budget deficit (Fischer (1994, p. 16)).

179   On the budget deficit, see Birman (1990), McKinnon (1990b), IMF (1992a, p. 67), and 'The Russian State Budget', by Erik Whitlock, *RFE/RL Research Report*, 23 April 1993, pp. 32–36.

180 Desai (1992, p.51).

181 Hewett and Gaddy (1992, pp. 83–88).

182 McKinnon (1990b).

183 A value-added tax was part of the reform package adopted in January 1992. See IMF (1992b, pp. 89–91, 101–115), and 'The Russian State Budget', by Erik Whitlock, *RFE/RL Research Report*, 23 April 1993, pp. 32–36. Enforcement of the value-added tax was weak in the initial months, with only one-half of the levied tax actually collected during the first quarter of 1992. 'The Russian Budget Deficit', by Keith Bush, *RFE/RL Research Report*, 9 October 1992, p. 32.

184 'The Russian State Budget', by Erik Whitlock, *RFE/RL Research Report*, 23 April 1993, p. 34.

185 On 4 February 1993, Boris Yeltsin rebuked his Economics Minister, Andrey Nacheyev, for not putting a single enterprise through bankruptcy. A new law on bankruptcy took effect on 1 March 1993. See *Current Digest of the Post-Soviet Press*, 3 March 1993, and 21 April 1993.

186 Sargent (1982).

187 Lutz (1949) describes the 1948 German reform, and also details the economic conditions that are almost eerily reminiscent of the reforming Russian economy.

188 Nove (1982, pp. 90–92).

189 It is widely feared that privatization will result in high monopoly prices, however. This perceived difficulty is discussed in the chapter on monopoly.

One method to link the currency reform with privatization is as follows. Announce that in a certain amount of time, three months, say, old roubles will be exchanged for new roubles. In the meantime, old currency will be accepted as means of payment for shares of state enterprises sold at auction. People who are nervous about the purchasing power of the new currency will then have a strong incentive to purchase the enterprise shares. Simultaneously, the sale of state-owned firms will both increase current government revenue and remove future government financial obligations. Clifford Gaddy and I proposed a similar currency reform–privatization scheme in 'A Plan to Cool the Hot Rouble', *Journal of Commerce*, 11 May 1990. Official privatization with vouchers is sufficiently underway now (see the chapter on privatization) that the reform described here is no longer relevant for Russia.

190 The IMF programme is not guaranteed to provide a credible disinflationary policy, since the conditions of such agreements can sometimes be broken by the government, without a reduction in aid. Foreign aid itself, however, provides another non-inflationary channel for a government to finance its budget deficit.

191 Wellisz (1991, p. 213).

192 Rodrik (1989) examines the importance of clearly signalling a break with past regimes in reducing the costs of reform.

193 See, for example, the letter by Edgar W. Malkin in the *New York Times* on 8 September 1993, p. A22.

194 There would still be a 'peak-load' problem. The demand for parking is quite variable, with demand high during certain hours of the day (or on special occasions) and relatively lower at other hours. Since prices of parking spaces cannot be continuously adjusted at reasonable cost, there would still be times when it would be difficult to find a parking space. This point was brought to my attention by Dani Rodrik.

195 A check on Nexis in July 1993 yielded 451 newspaper and magazine articles after 1991 that included the words 'rouble' and 'worthless' within 5 words of each other, with 194 of the citations occurring after the 2 January 1992 price liberalization.

196 Grossman (1977, p. 30n).

197 Shlapentokh (1989, p. 212).
198 See, e.g., 'Time and Patience are Running in Short Supply in Moscow', by Francis X. Clines, *New York Times*, 15 January 1992, p. A9.
199 Jones and Moskoff (1991, p. 91).
200 Alexeev (1988a).
201 On the rouble shortage, see, e.g., 'Economic Furor is Growing over Changes by Yeltsin', by Celestine Bohlen, *New York Times*, 3 June 1992, p. A3. In Western reports of the difficulties in the Russian economy, it is not uncommon to find a detail or two that indicate that the situation is not completely dire. In this article on the rouble shortage, for example, then First Deputy Prime Minister Gaidar is reported to be ordering government transportation agencies '. . . to accept credit to cover ticket costs as Russians set out for summer vacations'.
202 Quoted in Smith (1990, p. 185).
203 Quoted in Wren (1990, p. 181).
204 See, for example, Institute of Sociology (1992), cited in the comments of Vladimir Mau following Lipton and Sachs (1992, p. 267).
205 See, e.g., Azariadis (1975).
206 See, e.g., Harrison (1986).
207 Hewett (1988, p. 42) suggests that Soviet unemployment rates in the mid-1980s were under 2%. Porket (1989) puts the figure at closer to 3%, and cites the concurrence of Shmelev (1987). Gregory and Collier (1988, p. 616), relying on interview data collected from émigrés, estimate a lower bound for unemployment in the late 1970s to be 1.2–1.3%.
208 Lane (1986, p. 9).
209 Anti-parasite laws were superseded by the 'Law on the Employment of the Population', which also officially recognized unemployment. The law took effect on 1 July 1991 (Heleniak (1991, pp. 16–17)).
210 Bergson (1991, p. 42).
211 About 85 per cent of able-bodied adult Soviet females worked (Moskoff (1984, p. xii)). The over-representation of women in low-paying occupations and in lower category jobs, familiar in the West, was also a feature of the Soviet labour market. See Nove (1986, p. 220f).
212 Gaddy (1991).
213 Moskoff (1984, p. 34).
214 Over 20 per cent of Soviet pensioners held official, full-time jobs (Marnie (1992, p. 156)).
215 Nove (1986, chapter 8) provides a good account of the traditional Soviet labour sector.
216 In 1976, 68.1 per cent of newly hired industrial workers were employed from the factory gate. Bergson (1984, p. 1080).
217 Anti-parasite laws were not strictly enforced in recent years. See Millar (1990, p. 236).
218 The wage component forms only 60-66 per cent of official monetary compensation, with the remainder being made up of bonuses and other additional payments (Spulber (1991, p. 99)). A Pravda article in 1987, cited by Matthews (1989, p. 10), suggested that wages then formed only 50 per cent of official monetary compensation.
219 Nove (1986, pp. 205–210), offers a thorough examination of evasion of wage controls. In their study of Rezina, Burawoy and Hendley (1992, pp. 375–376) note that the management of one Rezina plant (RTI-3) believed that in order to retain one category of worker, 'they should be paid 1000 roubles per month, which would violate limitations on the wage fund. But as the director of RTI-3 told us with a wink and a nod, there are ways around those restrictions'.

220 See Gaddy (1991) for an empirical examination of informal non-wage compensation.
221 Treml (1992b, p. 37).
222 Gaddy (1991) demonstrates the inverse relationship between official wages and informal compensation.
223 See Holmstrom and Milgrom (1991) for a theoretical analysis of 'multi-task principal agent problems' that leads to these sort of conclusions under Soviet conditions.
224 On labour hoarding, see Nove (1986, p. 224).
225 On soft budget constraints, see Kornai (1980).
226 Hanson (1986, p. 86) argues that full employment is maintained primarily via the systemic incentives, as opposed to the law or direct planning guidelines.
227 Spulber (1991, p. 95) notes that planned labour demands exceeded labour supplies by 2 to 2.5 million workers annually, throughout the 1970s. See also Pietsch (1986, p. 181).
228 Porket (1989, p. 119), endnote omitted.
229 Kotkin (1991, p. 17).
230 In the late 1960s the Soviets originated an experiment whereby enterprises could shed redundant labour, and use part of the savings as incentive pay for the remaining workers. (Enterprises were also supposed to help the displaced workers find new jobs.) Named the Shchekino experiment after the Chemical Combine where it was first implemented, the reform extended to enterprises covering perhaps ten per cent of the industrial labour force by 1980. The Shchekino experiment was generally considered a success in reducing redundant labour and raising labour productivity, though nearly half of the displaced workers were transferred to other jobs within the same enterprise. See, e.g., Dyker (1992, pp. 53–54, 69–71).
231 Kotkin (1991, p. 17) makes this observation with respect to the Magnitogorsk steel mill.
232 An early Gorbachev-era reform aimed at increasing the differential in official pay among job classifications. See Atkinson and Micklewright (1992, p. 89), and the sources mentioned there.
233 Millar (1990, p. 220) notes some of the barriers to the free movement of labour into urban areas. Marrying a resident of large cities was one route out of the provinces, creating an informal market in marriages of mobility.
234 Burawoy and Krotov (1992, p. 22n) note average waits of 12 years (at Polar Furniture) and 20 years (at other local enterprises) for apartments.
235 Grossman (1979) provides a list of legal private economic activities.
236 On turnover rates, which have been falling (from approximately 20 per cent) for twenty years, see Marnie (1992, p. 163, endnote 2), Heleniak (1991, p. 4)), Lane (1987, p. 68), and the comparative bar graph in IMF et al. (1991, vol. 2, p. 217). Complaints about high turnover rates were frequent in the USSR and in other socialist countries (Vodopivec (1991, p. 139)).
237 Absenteeism in the USSR, about 20 days per worker per year in industry, was twice the American rate (see Moskoff (1984, p. x), and Porket (1989, p. 118)).
238 This point is made with respect to absenteeism in China in Jefferson and Rawski (1991, p. 8).
239 Akerlof, et al. (1991, p. 2), estimated that only eight per cent of Eastern German employees were employed in firms that were solvent post-reform. In Eastern Europe (Poland, Hungary, and Czechoslovakia), Jackman, et al. (1992, p. 31) suggested that as many as 50 per cent of workers were in jobs that would not have come into existence without the previous central planning.
240 Most of the open unemployment that arose early in the transition process in

Poland, Hungary, and Czechoslovakia was due to reduced hirings, as opposed to layoffs. See Jackman, *et al.* (1992, p. 16).

241 Jackman, *et al.* (1992, p. 13) provide unemployment statistics for Poland, Hungary, and Czechoslovakia. The Russian labour force consisted of approximately 71 million people in 1993 (OECD (1994, p. 80)).

242 The 25 per cent overstaffing estimate for the former USSR is roughly consistent with Eastern European estimates. Svejnar (1991, pp. 128–129) notes that a generous estimate of Eastern European overstaffing is 30 per cent of employment. The International Labour Organization estimate appeared in a press release dated 30 March 1992. The unemployment figure was an estimate for 1992. Actual measured unemployment in the former Soviet Union in 1992 remained substantially below this figure.

243 The Russian labour force fell by approximately 3 million people between 1991 and 1993 (OECD (1994, p. 80)).

244 Tobin (1957, p. 599).

245 A dramatic fall in absenteeism following the German currency reform of 1948 is chronicled in Lutz (1949, p. 133).

246 The rapid growth of the private sector in Eastern Europe is discussed in Svejnar (1991, pp. 130–131). See also Johnson (1992, p. 34).

247 European Bank for Reconstruction and Development (1994, p. 34).

248 Johnson and Kroll (1991).

249 Kotkin (1991, p. 133).

250 See Braithwaite (1991) and Sheila Marnie, 'The Social Safety Net in Russia', *RFE/RL Research Report*, 23 April 1993.

251 Dornbusch (1991) makes a similar point with respect to Eastern Germany.

251* Sachs (1994, p. 43). The figure of labour costs as a share of total costs is suggested as applying to firms in the military-industrial complex.

252 *RFE/RL Daily Report*, 4 November 1993.

253 Porket (1989, p. 28), footnote omitted.

254 Harrison (1986, p.81).

255 Economists call this the 'Theory of the Second Best'. In the presence of economic distortions, government policies that further 'interfere' with the workings of the market economy may be socially desirable.

256 Akerlof, *et al.* (1991, p. 42).

257 For a good discussion of the possible causes and consequences of fixed wages, see Hall and Taylor (1993, pp.473-502).

258 See, e.g., McKinnon (1990a), who argues that many socialist firms will be illiquid when faced with foreign competition, even if they are solvent in the long run after they adapt their production techniques. Imperfect competition arguments for low employment equilibria are becoming increasing popular in Western macroeconomics. See, e.g., Pagano (1990).

259 Burawoy and Krotov (1992, p. 33).

259* Rostowski (1994, p. 73) notes an insensitivity of reform to credit unavailability in Poland, and suggests that credit may be unimportant in a transitional economy because the emergence of so many highly profitable opportunities implies that self-financing is available.

260 Åslund (1994, p. 63) Ascertaining real interest rates is not straightforward because an estimate of future inflation is required.

260* Rostowski (1994, p. 73) notes how credit was allocated to the wrong firms during the Polish transition.

261 Ickes and Ryterman (1992, p. 331).

262 In early June of 1992, the chairman of Russia's Central Bank offered his resignation rather than submit to Parliament's demand that the Central Bank

loan money to 'commercial' banks at 50 per cent annual interest. At the time, the fixed rate in use by the Central Bank was 80 per cent, though in the high inflation environment, even this was probably too low. 'Russian Backlash is Forcing a Delay in Approval of Aid', by Louis Uchitelle with Steven Erlanger, *New York Times*, 7 June 1992, pp. 1 and 4.

Soft loans to state-owned enterprises in 1992 totalled approximately 20 per cent of Russian gross domestic output (Sachs and Woo (1994, p. 108)).

263 See, e.g., Ickes and Ryterman (1992, pp. 359–360). An enterprise may also be willing to extend credit that is unlikely to be repaid if by doing so it can secure an ownership claim during privatization.

264 This paragraph is based on 'Russian Credit Markets Remain Distorted', by Sergei Aukutsenek and Elena Belyanova, *RFE/RL Research Report*, 22 January 1993, pp. 37-40.

265 'Russian Credit Markets Remain Distorted', by Sergei Aukutsenek and Elena Belyanova, *RFE/RL Research Report*, 22 January 1993, p. 39.

266 'The Soviet Miners Strike', by Clifford Gaddy, *The Brookings Review*, Vol. 9, No. 3, Summer 1991, p. 54.

267 Jones and Moskoff (1991, pp. 25–26), for example, provide some figures for the pay of workers in cooperatives. Koen and Phillips (1993, p. 20), note a wage differential of more than one-third between state and private-sector employees.

268 In Poland, taxes on wage increases in state-sector enterprises were also applied to private firms (Johnson (1992, p. 27)). Wage controls in the state sector are themselves not unambiguously desirable, since they may prevent firms that are successfully reforming from hiring new workers, or even make it more difficult to shed lower-quality labour.

269 Machiavelli (1947 [1532], p. 15).

270 Wage rates in market economies may involve 'rent sharing', where workers in successful industries are better paid than their counterparts in less successful industries. Recent empirical evidence on industry effects on wages appears in Holmlund and Zetterberg (1991). They find that workers in strong industries in the US are better paid than their counterparts in other industries, while industry effects are smaller in Germany and even smaller in Nordic countries.

271 On the perceived unfairness of negative movements away from the status quo, see Isaac, Mathieu, and Zajac (1991).

272 The referendum of 25 April 1993, which resulted in majorities both for Yeltsin and his reform programme – despite the overwhelmingly negative reports on the state of the Russian economy – suggests that such concerns may be overblown.

273 On some 'mafia' millionaires in pre-reform Russia, see Vaksberg (1991).

274 Treml (1992b, p. 20).

275 The training of an average doctor in Russia was also much inferior to the training of an average US doctor.

276 The over-supply of technically-trained people in Russia is nicely illustrated by the comments of an American Peace Corps volunteer working in Saratov, Russia: 'You know in America we say, "It doesn't take a rocket scientist". Well, I'd never met one. Now I've met hundreds, and a lot of them are driving taxis'. 'Volunteers From U.S. in Business in Russia', by Steven Erlanger, *New York Times*, 6 April 1993, p. A6.

277 Lutz (1949) notes how traders were the main early beneficiaries of the German monetary reform of 1948.

278 Hanson (1991, p. 308) notes survey evidence indicating that attitudes towards free markets by younger workers are more favourable than the attitudes of older workers.

279 'A Renewal of Public Confidence in the Russian Economy?', by Mark Rhodes, *RFE/RL Research Report*, 3 September 1993, pp. 59–61.

280 The statistics are drawn from *Economic Report of the President* (1992, p. 346).

281 See, e.g., Aven (1991, p. 184).

282 Perhaps co-incidentally, by mid-1992, official real wage statistics had re-achieved the 1987 levels (Koen and Phillips (1993, p. 16)).

283 'Good for Some, Tough for Others', by Nicholas Denton, *Financial Times*, 30 October 1991.

284 Sachs (1993, p. 73).

285 Alford and Feige (1989) call this the 'observer-subject-policymaker' feedback.

286 OECD (1994, p. 80).

287 Rose (1994, pp. 13–14).

288 Marx and Engels (1964 [1848], p. 82).

289 The survey is cited in Starodubrovskaya (1994, p.9).

290 Pinto, Belka, and Krajewski (1993) details the extent of favourable changes in state-owned enterprises in Poland prior to privatization.

290* Boeva and Dolgopiatova (1994, p. 116).

291 This position echoes that of Weitzman (1991).

292 Grossman (1989, p. 81).

293 Barzel (1989, p. 107).

294 While informal compensation responded to market forces, the bonuses that were supposed to provide incentives for fulfilling the plan were in practice used to iron out horizontal inequities both within and among enterprises. And the plans were regularly revised, in part to reflect the actual output. See, e.g., Hewett (1988, pp. 188–189, 208–210), and Burawoy and Krotov (1992).

295 See, e.g., Dyker (1992, p. 49).

296 Lazear (1991). Housing and energy prices are two examples where internal Soviet prices and world prices differed considerably. It should be kept in mind, however, that prices played different roles under Soviet central planning than they do in market economies.

297 Grossman (1977, p. 31).

298 Grossman (1977, p. 40).

299 See, e.g., Barzel (1989, p. 5).

300 The continuation of subsidies is perfectly sensible as long as continuing price controls, combined with the unknown value of inter-enterprise loans, distort the meaning of profits.

301 See Sutela (1993), and 'You're Privatized. Now What?', by David Brooks, *Wall Street Journal*, 23 April 1993, p. A14.

302 Small enterprises (those with less than 200 employees and a book value of assets as of 1 January 1992, of less than 1 million roubles) must be sold at open or sealed-bid auctions. Medium sized firms and structural subdivisions of larger enterprises (those with 200-1000 employees and a book value between 10 and 50 million roubles) can be privatized into a joint-stock company if their labour collective so chooses.

A good review of the privatization options is provided in *Izvestia*, 28 September 1992, p. 4. (Translated in *Current Digest of the Post-Soviet Press*, Vol. 44, no. 40, November 4, 1992, pp. 7–9.)

303 Sutela (1993). In many privatizations the percentage of shares auctioned off for vouchers was less than 29 per cent, however.

304 Stiglitz (1991) makes this point. To partly offset the perceived disadvantage of voucher-holders who are not employees of large privatizing enterprises, the Russian government is considering the use of vouchers in the privatization of land.

305   See Weitzman (1991) for an alternative view.
306   Weitzman (1991).
307   Sutela (1993).
308   IMF *et al.* (1990, p. 26) and IMF *et al.* (1991, vol. 2, p. 40). Also see Kahn and Peck (1991, pp. 63–67).
309   See, e.g., Uno (1991, p. 152).
310   More precisely, from output prices that exceed marginal costs.
311   This is a paraphrase of a comment by Indiana University economics professor Michael Alexeev.
312   The US figure is for industries at the SIC 4-digit level (Kahn and Peck (1991, p. 65)).
313   Hewett (1988, pp. 170-176). See also Kroll (1991, p. 146n).
314   Hewett (1988, p. 171).
315   Kroll (1991, p. 147).
316   Newberry and Kattuman (1992, pp. 315, 334).
317   This point was brought to my attention in a meeting (June 1991) with Russian anti-monopoly expert V. Tsapelik.
318   IMF *et al.* (1991, pp. 28–31).
319   Actions for breach of contract could be brought against a supplier, but this was not a very potent weapon. See, e.g., Kroll (1987).
320   Of course there were black markets, and the collective farm markets provided competition in the retail market for food.
321   Such wasteful lobbying efforts fall under the general rubric of 'rent seeking'. See Tirole (1988, Chapter 1) for a good discussion of distortions due to monopoly.
322   Enterprise prices were generally set on a 'planned branch average cost plus profit' basis. See Bornstein (1987).
323   Monopoly producers may not have as strong a bargaining position as may at first appear because they may be teamed with monopsonistic customers. The oil extraction industry, by and large, delivers its output only to the oil processing industry. This example was used by Yegor Gaidar in a Moscow meeting, June 1991.
324   Hewett (1988, p. 173).
325   A second concern with according anti-monopoly legislation a low priority in the reforming Russian economy is that even if the resulting competition lowers the social costs of monopoly, there may be undesirable distributional impacts. It is virtually impossible to detail these impacts, however, and any other course is also potentially subject to undesirable effects with respect to the income and wealth distributions. See the following chapter for more discussion of the importance of distributional problems during reform.
326   Tirole (1991, p. 230).
327   This point was brought to my attention by Professor Barry Ickes of Penn State.
328   In a private meeting in Moscow, June 1991.
329   Koen and Phillips (1993, p. 10) note that by mid-1992, 23 areas in Russia had enacted such trade barriers.
330   The 11 August 1992 government resolution was 'On the State Regulation of Prices and Rates for Goods and Services Produced and Rendered by Monopolist Enterprises in 1992–1993'. See Capelik (1994, pp. 22–23).
331   Samuelson (1970, p. 106).
332   Quoted in 'Chaos Looms Over the Soviets, Gates Says', by Elaine Sciolino, *New York Times*, p. A8, 11 December 1991.
333   Goldman (1992, p. 35).
334   'The Yeltsin Revolution', by Martin Malia, *The New Republic*, 10 February 1992, p. 25.

335 'Shock Therapy in Russia: Failure or Partial Success?', by Michael Ellman, RFE/RL Research Report, August 28, 1992, p. 48. The quoted passage is taken from the abstract that precedes the article. Ellman did note some positive developments. The sentence immediately following the quoted passage reads 'Nevertheless, the situation is not entirely black'.

336 'Clinton's Greatest Challenge', by Richard Nixon, *New York Times*, 5 March 1993, p. A17.

337 Litwack (1991b) provides a detailed theoretical model of coordination failure in a centrally-planned environment.

338 Zubova, Kovaleva, and Khakhulina (1992, pp. 94–95).

339 Flakierski (1992) provides some preliminary empirical evidence of the effects of Russian reform on income distribution.

340 Rose (1994, p. 12).

341 The 'gross' in GNP refers to the measure of investment. Every year, new machines are built, but at the same time, old machines wear out. Gross investment counts all the new machines produced, whereas 'net' investment, and hence 'net national product', excludes those new machines which serve to replace the old machines. Net national product, minus sales and excise taxes (and some other minor items) yields an income measure known as 'national income'.

342 The extent of the 'nation' is the basis for the distinction between gross national product and gross domestic product (GDP). GDP includes all income arising within a given geographical area, while GNP includes the worldwide income of a nation's residents. See Kendrick (1972, pp. 33–34). In order to be more in concert with international standards, the United States is beginning to highlight GDP in its economic statistics. *Economic Report of the President* (1992).

343 Another method of calculating the value of all final goods sold is to sum value added at all stages of production.

344 Exports are included in a country's calculation of GNP because they represent goods made in the country, but will not appear as consumption because they are purchased by foreigners. Imports are not produced in the country, but get included in the consumption component of GNP. To avoid counting this consumption as part of a country's product, imports must then be subtracted from GNP.

345 There are many nuances involved in calculating GNP that are omitted from this discussion. For example, investment represents gross private domestic investment (hence 'gross' national product) which includes investments that only offset depreciation. Kendrick (1972) addresses many of these nuances.

346 Dasgupta and Weale (1992, p. 119).

347 From a Robert F. Kennedy address in Detroit, 5 May 1967, as quoted in Ross (1968, p. 351). Sen (1987) explores many non-market facets of the standard of living. The essay by Muellbauer (1987) in Sen (1987) is particularly stimulating.

348 The identification of these issues relies on Eisner (1989).

349 Imputations are made for certain types of non-market output in the USA, such as the rental value of owner-occupied housing.

350 The discussion of investment follows Eisner (1989, p. 5–6) fairly closely.

351 It is possible to avoid some of the problems with government spending and investment by focusing on the consumption component of GNP. Concentrating on consumption, though, is misleading when people are changing the amount of their income that they are willing to invest as opposed to immediately consuming. Economists would say that GNP is 'neutral' with respect to changes in individual decisions to save versus consume, whereas measures of consumption clearly are not neutral in this respect.

352 The separation of quality improvements from price increases is attempted by the compilers of national income statistics in the USA. See *Economic Report of the President* (1992).
353 Two methods of achieving comparable measures of output are to use market exchange rates, or to assess how much it would cost to produce one country's output in another country – the purchasing power parity approach.
354 Because this section looks primarily at historical calculations of Soviet (i.e., Russia plus the other 14 republics) GNP, the old terminology 'Soviet Union' and 'USSR', will generally be employed here.
355 Goskomstat did begin to publish GNP figures in 1988 – see Treml (1988, pp. 80–81, 86–87). Nove (1986, Chapter 12) offers a good introduction to Soviet economic accounting.
356 See, e.g., Birman (1989), Åslund (1990), and Belkin (1991). For discussions of the controversy, see GAO (1991) and Rosefielde (1991).
357 IMF *et al.* (1990, p. 51).
358 Belkin (1991).
359 In calculating growth rates of Soviet GNP, the CIA relies primarily on data expressed in physical units.
360 The CIA methodology is described in Joint Economic Committee (1982).
361 Generally, higher income individuals had access to goods at lower prices. Citing Goskomstat, Aven (1991, p. 184) writes: '. . . in 1984 a family with a monthly income per person of 150 roubles paid an average of 2.96 roubles for a kilo of meat, while a family with an income of less than 50 roubles paid 3.93 roubles'. Housing subsidies also tended to favour wealthier families (Kosareva (1992, p. 40)).
362 Rosefielde (1991).
363 GAO (1991, p. 29).
364 To calculate the geometric mean, the two estimates are multiplied together, and the square root of the result is the final estimate.
365 The CIA does make some correction for waste in agriculture. JEC (1982, pp. 266–269).
366 Belkin (1991, p.19).
367 Rosefielde (1991, p. 598). Forced substitution occurs when shoppers make purchases of items that they would otherwise find undesirable, because the goods that they would prefer to buy are not available in the shops.
368 Rosefielde (1991, p. 609).
369 Feshbach and Friendly (1992).
370 Bergson (1991, p.37), which presents a useful discussion of Soviet living standards, notes the environmental impact on welfare.
371 See Rowen and Wolf (1990).
372 Åslund (1990, p.22–23, and Appendix 1).
373 See, e.g., Belkin (1991, p. 18).
374 Lipton and Sachs (1992, p. 219).
375 Aven (1991, p. 184) and Åslund (1990, p.57–8).
376 Åslund (1990, p. 20).
377 Pitzer and Baukol (1991, p. 59) provide a graph of the investment component of Soviet GNP since 1960.
378 See, e.g., Birman (1989).
379 Belkin (1991, p. 18).
380 The generally low quality of nominally free education and medical care also impacts negatively on Russian living standards.
381 Kosareva (1992, p. 38).
382 Shlapentokh (1989, pp. 82–83).
383 IMF (1992a, p. 60).

384 Alexeev, Gaddy, and Leitzel (1991).
385 OECD (1994, p. 80).
386 Koen and Phillips (1993).
387 Rose (1994, p. 6).
388 Roberts (1993).
389 The relative improvement in the lot of many rural areas and small towns is supported by a good deal of anecdotal evidence. Zubova, Kovaleva, and Khakhulina (1992, p. 87) briefly note this phenomenon.
390 Gaddy (1992, pp. 7–8).
391 Raleigh (1992, p. 604) discusses the Moscow–St.Petersburg focus of the West, and also suggests that the April 1991 coup plotters themselves misunderstood Russian provincial attitudes.
392 Novosibirsk and Nizhny Novgorod (Gorky) are in a near-tie for third, and fifth is Yekaterinberg (Sverdlovsk). Clifford Gaddy first subjected me to this quiz.
393 Cooper (1991b, p. 23–24).
394 Atkinson and Micklewright (1992, pp. 81, 114).
395 Mickiewicz (1992, p. 14).
396 Rodrik (1991) develops the 'political cost-benefit ratio', which measures how many dollars (roubles) must be shuffled in redistribution per dollar of efficiency gain. In the case of trade liberalization, Rodrik demonstrates that this ratio tends to be much lower when liberalization is accompanied by structural reforms.
397 See Atkinson and Micklewright (1992, pp. 87–89) on distributional changes over time in the USSR.
398 See 'Economic Reform and Poverty in Russia', by Shelie Marnie, *RFE/RL Research Report*, 5 February 1993, pp. 31–36.
399 McGee and Feige (1989, p.83).
400 Kosmarskii (1992, p. 27).
401 Jones and Moskoff (1991, p. 125).
402 Zubova *et al.* (1992, p. 85).
403 Zubova *et al.* (1992, p. 87).
404 Shlapentokh (1989, p. 140), reference omitted.
405 Feshbach (1991, p. 49).
406 Peck (1991, p. 3).
407 See, e.g., Smith (1976).
408 Ickes and Ryterman (1992, p. 345n).
409 'Wolf at the Door', by Maggie Mahar, *Barron's*, 19 October 1992, p. 8.
410 Starodubrovskaya (1994, p. 6). This has been confirmed in discussions that I have had with representatives of Russian enterprises.
411 Boeva and Dolgopiatova (1994, p. 116) discuss some motivations for barter, including tax evasion. Goldberg (1993) notes how the transitional arrangements with respect to foreign exchange led to international barter as a means to escape taxation.
412 Smith (1991 [1776], vol. 2, p. 155).
413 Ilin (1931, p. 33). This fascinating book is an English translation of a Soviet book designed to acquaint 12- to 14-year olds with the first 5-Year plan. The 'socialist vice', the over-emphasis on production and intermediate goods, is evident throughout its pages.
414 Wiles (1962, pp. 282–283).
415 The report is cited in 'Half Soviet Potato Crop Wasted', *Financial Times*, 16 October 1991, p. 7.
416 See, e.g., Wiles (1962, chapter 14).
417 The quote and attribution appear in Wiles (1962, p. 283).
418 '. . . statistical results which in a normal market would be signs of much

increased material satisfaction are accepted as such in circumstances where they actually give no increased satisfaction' (Polanyi (1960, p. 96)).

419   Hewett and Gaddy (1992, pp. 8–9), footnotes omitted.
420   Aven (1991, p. 181n). Åslund (1990, p. 22) cites Soviet economist Abel Aganbegyan's claim that the Soviet tractor stock was 4.5 times as large as in the USA.
421   The tractor factory did close for 2 weeks in January of 1993, and again in the late spring of 1994.
422   On early Gorbachev reforms, see Goldman (1992, chapter 4).
423   Treml (1988, p. 71).
424   Goldman (1992, p. 86f).
425   See, e.g., 'Rutskoi Loses Responsibility for Agriculture', by Don Van Atta, *RFE/RL Research Report*, vol. 2, No. 18, April 1993, pp. 11–16. Graham (1993, p. 14) indicates that a regard for technology and a disregard for economics may have predated the Soviet era in Russia.
426   Treml (1992a, p. 130). This sentiment is echoed by two Russian researchers, Faramazian and Borisov (1993, p. 46): 'It is extremely difficult to estimate the real size of our defense complex primarily because of the lack of statistics that are reliable to any degree. The real figures on Soviet military spending have always been a riddle to both foreign and Soviet specialists'.
427   Cooper (1991b, pp. 25–28).
428   See, e.g., Cooper (1992, pp. 281–283).
429   Alexander (1992, pp. 303–304), and Kireyev (1990).
430   See, e.g., Cooper (1991a, pp. 139–140). Hendley (1992) offers a case study of one privatized defence plant.
431   Eighty per cent of the defence industry was scheduled for privatization by the end of 1994. See Keith Bush, 'Aspects of Military Conversion in Russia', RFE/RL Research Report, vol. 3, No. 14, 8 April 1994, pp. 31–34.
432   This quote appears in 'Weapons Industry Faces Pain in New World Order', by David E. Rosenbaum, *The News and Observer*, Raleigh, NC, 4 August 1991, p. 17A. I would like to thank Richard Stubbing for bringing this article to my attention.
433   Crane and Yeh (1991, p. 108) note that by 1989, 60 per cent of the value of defence industry output in China consisted of consumer goods. The extent to which the actual physical conversion of production lines was responsible for the increased civilian goods production in the defence complex is unclear.
434   Aganbegyan, quoted in Åslund (1990, p. 26).
435   RFE/RL Daily Report, 8 June 1994, and 14 June 1994, indicate that there may still be hidden subsidies that cloud the size of the actual defence budget.
436   See, e.g., RFE/RL Daily Report, 21 June 1994.
436* Åslund (1994, p. 66).
437   Hewett and Gaddy (1992, chapter 1) provides a good overview of the prereform Soviet foreign trade situation.
438   Hewett and Gaddy (1992, pp. 10–11).
439   Hewett and Gaddy (1992, pp. 16–17).
440   The value-added tax is applicable to imports, though exports are zero-rated. Following the January 1992 liberalization, some 70 per cent of Russian exports were still subject to export quotas, partly because of the price controls that remained in place for some goods, such as oil. Aven (1994, pp. 84–85).
440* Aven (1994, p. 90) indicates that current account convertibility has been achieved in Russia.
441   The separation between current and capital account convertibility is not complete. Current account convertibility often provides informal access for capital transactions.

442 Fischer (1991, p. 23).

443 See, e.g., RFE/RL Daily Report, 6 May 1994.

444 See, e.g., IMF *et al.* (1990, p.23).

445 The total amount of foreign investment in Russia at the end of 1993 was estimated at $2.7 billion [RFE/RL Daily Report, 28 June 1994]. In contrast, foreign investment in China for the year 1992 alone was reportedly $11.01 billion (Perkins (1994, p. 32)). Investment can occur even without capital account convertibility through bilateral agreements and joint ventures.

446 Rodrik (1992) estimated the cost to Eastern European countries of the collapse of COMECON. For example, the end of Soviet trade subsidies is estimated to have cost Poland $5 billion in 1989.

447 Dornbusch (1992). The relative importance of the foreign trade regime is probably greater in smaller, more open economies such as those in Eastern Europe.

448 Lazear (1991).

449 Incidentally, such arbitrage is taking place. It is estimated that up to 1/3 of Russian oil exports are conducted informally – oil is significantly underpriced in the domestic Russian economy.

450 Hewett and Gaddy (1992, p. 80).

451 This was the approach taken to zloty convertibility in Poland. See, e.g., Lipton and Sachs (1990, pp. 118–119).

452 The level at which the exchange rate is fixed must also be low enough to prevent massive attempts to exchange roubles for foreign currencies.

453 This is particularly true for the trade of goods, so-called current account transactions. As noted, it might be sensible for the government to impose some controls on asset sales during a transition.

    The use of a fixed exchange rate creates one issue that may not be easily resolved, namely, at what price should the exchange rate be fixed? And a fixed exchange rate, as with fixed prices more generally, tends to lead to resource misallocations, and can also create an impetus for more central controls to deal with balance of payments problems.

454 See, e.g., David (1985).

455 See 'U.S., Allies Set $24 Billion in Aid for Ex-Soviet States', by Ann Devroy, *Washington Post*, 2 April 1992, p. A1.

456 'Moscow Stops Paying Debt Principal', by Terrence Roth and Tim Carrington, *Wall Street Journal*, 5 December 1991.

457 In a letter to the *New York Times* (4/7/92), Jeffrey Sachs notes that Russia received $15.6 billion in aid in 1990–91, and paid $13.1 billion of the $15.5 billion on accumulated interest and debt that was due during that period. Sachs writes, 'Overall, almost no resources came to Russia in 1990–91, after taking account of debt payments'.

458 This applies to the aid that actually reaches Russia. A substantial amount of 'foreign' aid tends to go to Western firms and consultants, sometimes with minimal benefit to the foreign country.

459 There is a fundamental and difficult theoretical question as to why foreign aid is necessary to induce a government to take policies that are in its own long-run best interests (see Diwan and Rodrik (1991)). The practical importance of this question in the Soviet case is limited, however, since the former Soviet Union is already receiving substantial Western aid.

460 See 'Entrepreneur of Necessity Runs Afoul of Old Lithuania', by Steven Engelberg, *New York Times*, 25 September 1991.

461 State provision need not mean state production. The state should provide defence, but defence enterprises could be private.

462 The low exchange rate of the rouble enables valuable Russian research to be purchased for relatively small amounts of hard currency. Ninety thousand dollars is being used to hire 116 Russian fusion scientists for a year. 'U.S. Plans to Hire Russian Scientists in Fusion Research', by William J. Broad, *New York Times*, 6 March 1992, pp. A1, A4.

463 COCOM, the Coordinating Committee for Multilateral Export Control, which oversaw restrictions on exports to the Soviet Union, is being reconfigured to fight exports to countries that support terrorism or that are trying to develop weapons of mass destruction, and Russia is expected to join. See RFE/RL Daily Report, 9 November 1993.

464 'Nunn Urges US Help to Convert Soviet War Power', *Washington Post*, 20 June 1991, p. 8.

465 Perkins (1994, pp. 23–24).

466 Perkins (1994, p. 24). The 8.8 per cent figure is for the average growth rate in GDP.

467 Grossman (1963, pp. 118–121). His framework was also employed in examining the Chinese reforms by Nystrom (1994).

468 The figures on the percentage of the Chinese and Russian labour force in agriculture are taken from Sachs and Woo (1994, pp. 105–106).

469 Prosterman, Hanstad, and Rolfes (1993, p. 15).

470 Perkins (1994, p. 27).

471 Koen and Phillips (1993, pp. 10–11).

472 Perkins (1994, p. 26).

473 Reed (1967 [1919], p. 61).

474 Quoted in 'The High Risk Options for Russia's Economics Chief', by Leyla Boulton, *Financial Times*, 21 November 1991.

475 Ilin (1931, p. 161).

476 Gibbon (1985 [1776–1788], p. 81).

477 The 25 April 1993 referendum was particularly telling in this regard. Of the four questions on the ballot, one concerned support for the president, Boris Yeltsin, and a separate question concerned support for his economic reforms. It was thus possible for Yeltsin supporters to express their dismay with reform while still backing their president. As it turned out, Yeltsin and economic reform both enjoyed majority support.

Bibliography

Akerlof, G. A., Rose, A. K, Yellen, J. L. and Hessenius, H. (1991) 'East Germany in from the Cold: The Economic Aftermath of Currency Union', *Brookings Papers on Economic Activity* 1: 1–87.

Alexander, A. J. (1992) 'The Conversion of Soviet Defense Industry', in C. Wolf, Jr and S.W. Popper (eds) *Defense and the Soviet Economy: Military Muscle and Economic Weakness*, a RAND Note.

Alexeev, M. (1988a) 'Are Soviet Consumers Forced to Save?', *Comparative Economic Studies* 30: 17–23.

——(1988b) 'Market vs Rationing: The Case of Soviet Housing', *Review of Economics and Statistics* 70, 3: 414–420.

——(1991) 'The "Storming" Pattern of Enterprise Behavior in a Centrally-Planned Economy', *Journal of Economic Behavior and Organization* 15: 173–185.

Alexeev, M., Gaddy, C. and Leitzel, J. (1991) 'An Economic Analysis of the Rouble Overhang', *Communist Economies and Economic Transformation* 3: 467–479.

Alexeev, M. and Walker, L. (1991) *Estimating the Size of the Soviet Economy. Summary of a Meeting*. Commission on Behavioral and Social Sciences and Education, National Research Council, Washington, DC: National Academy Press.

Alford, R. R. and Feige, E. L. (1989) 'Information Distortions in Social Systems: the Underground Economy and Other Observer-Subject-Policymaker Feedbacks', in E. L. Feige (ed.) *The Underground Economies*, Cambridge: Cambridge University Press.

Åslund, A. (1990) 'How Small is Soviet National Income?', in H. S. Rowen and C. Wolf, Jr (eds) *The Impoverished Superpower*, San Francisco: Institute for Contemporary Studies.

——(1993) 'The Gradual Nature of Economic Change in Russia', in A. Åslund and R. Layard, (eds) *Changing the Economic System in Russia*, New York: St. Martin's Press.

——(1994) 'Russia's Success Story', *Foreign Affairs* 73, Sept.–Oct.: 58–71.

Atkinson, A. B. and Micklewright, J. (1992) *Economic Transformation in Eastern Europe and the Distribution of Income*, Cambridge: Cambridge University Press.

Aven, P. O. (1991) 'Economic Policy and the Reforms of Mikhail Gorbachev: A Short History', in M. Peck and T. Richardson (eds) *What is to be Done?*, New Haven: Yale University Press.

Aven, P. (1994) 'Problems in Foreign Trade Regulation in the Russian Economic Reform', in A. Åslund (ed.) *Economic Transformation in Russia*, New York: St Martin's Press.

Azariadis, C. (1975) 'Implicit Contracts and Underemployment Equilibria', *Journal of Political Economy* 83: 1183–1202.

Ball, L. (1993) 'What Causes Inflation?', *Business Review*, Federal Reserve Bank of Philadelphia, March/April: 3–12.

Barton, P. (1957) 'The Myth of Planning in the U.S.S.R.', *Saturn* 3, Jan.–Feb.: 38–50.

Barzel, Y. (1989) *Economic Analysis of Property Rights*, Cambridge: Cambridge University Press.

Belkin, V. (1991) 'Comparison of Macroeconomic Indicators in Market and Nonmarket Economies', *Matekon* (1990) Fall: 3–23, translated from *Ekonomika i matematicheskie metody* 26: 790–802.

—— (1993) 'On the Reliability of Information', *Russian Social Science Review* 34: 59–72, translated from *Svobodnaia mysl'* (1992) no. 10: 97–104.

Belanovskii, S. A. (1992) 'The Army As It Is', *Studies on Soviet Economic Development* 3: 55–63.

Bergson, A. (1984) 'Income Inequality Under Soviet Socialism', *Journal of Economic Literature* 22, Sept.: 1052–1099.

—— (1991) 'The USSR Before the Fall: How Poor and Why', *Journal of Economic Perspectives* 5, 29–44.

Berliner, J. S. (1952) 'The Informal Organization of the Soviet Firm', *Quarterly Journal of Economics* 66, Aug.: 342–365.

Berliner, J. S. (1956) 'A Problem in Soviet Business Administration', *Administrative Science Quarterly* I, June: 86–101.

—— (1976) *The Innovation Decision in Soviet Industry*, Cambridge, MA: MIT Press.

Birman, I. (1978) 'From the Achieved Level', *Soviet Studies* 30: 153–172.

—— (1989) *Personal Consumption in the USSR and the USA*, London: Macmillan Press Ltd.

—— (1990) 'The Budget Gap, Excess Money, and Reform', *Communist Economies* 2: 25–45.

Boeva, I. and Dolgopiatova, T. (1994) 'State Enterprises During Transition: Forming Strategies for Survival', in A. Åslund (ed.) *Economic Transformation in Russia*, New York: St Martin's Press.

Bornstein, M. (1987) 'Soviet Price Policies', *Soviet Economy* 3: 96–134.

Boyes, R. (1990) *The Hard Road to Market: Gorbachev, the Underworld, and the Free Market*, London: Secker and Warburg.

Braithwaite, J. D. (1991) 'The Social Safety Net in the USSR in the (Sovereign?) Republics', presented at the 23rd AASSS National Conference, Miami, November.

Bronfenbrenner, M. B., Sichel, W. and Gardner, W. (1984) *Macroeconomics*, Boston, MA: Houghton Mifflin.

Burawoy, M. and Hendley, K. (1992) 'Between Perestroika and Privatization: Divided Strategies and Political Crisis in a Soviet Enterprise', *Soviet Studies* 44: 371–402.

Burawoy, M. and Krotov, P. (1992) 'The Soviet Transition From Socialism to Capitalism: Worker Control and Economic Bargaining in the Wood Industry', *American Sociological Review* 57: 16–38.

Capelik [Tsapelik], V. E. (1994) 'Should Monopoly be Regulated in Russia?', *Communist Economies and Economic Transformation* 6: 19–3.

Coase, R. H. (1960) 'The Problem of Social Cost', *Journal of Law and Economics* 3: 1–44.

Conquest, R. (1991) 'Excess Deaths and Camp Numbers: Some Comments', *Soviet Studies* 43: 949–952.

Cooper, J. (1991a) 'Military Cuts and Conversion in the Defense Industry', *Soviet Economy* 7: 121–142.

—— (1991b) *The Soviet Defense Industry. Conversion and Economic Reform*, New York: Council on Foreign Relations Press.

—— (1992) 'The Contradictions of Soviet Defense Industry Civilianization', in C. Wolf, Jr and S.W. Popper (eds) *Defence and the Soviet Economy: Military Muscle and Economic Weakness*, a RAND Note.

Crane, K. and Yeh, K. C. (1991) *Economic Reform and the Military in Poland, Hungary, and China*, Santa Monica: RAND.

Dasgupta, P. and Weale, M. (1992) 'On Measuring the Quality of Life', *World Development* 20: 119–131.

David, W. (1985) *The IMF Policy Paradigm*, New York: Praeger Publishers.

Desai, P. (1992) 'Reforming the Soviet Grain Economy: Performance, Problems, and Solutions', *American Economic Association Papers and Proceedings* 82: 49–54.

de Soto, H. (1989) *The Other Path*, New York: Harper and Row.

Devons, E. (1950) *Planning in Practice*, Cambridge: Cambridge University Press.

Diwan, I. and Rodrik, D. (1991) 'Debt Reduction, Adjustment Lending, and Burden Sharing', mimeo, September.

Dornbusch, R. (1991) 'Comments and Discussion', *Brookings Papers on Economic Activity* 1: 88–92.

—— (1992) 'The Case for Trade Liberalization in Developing Countries', *Journal of Economic Perspectives* 6, Winter: 69–85.

—— (1993) 'Introduction', *Policymaking in the Open Economy*, Oxford: Oxford University Press.

Dornbusch, R. and Fischer, S. (1994) *Macroeconomics*, sixth edition, New York: McGraw-Hill, Inc.

Dyker, D. A. (1992) *Restructuring the Soviet Economy*, London: Routledge.

Economic Report of the President (1992) Washington, DC: US Government Printing Office.

Eisner, R. (1989) *The Total Incomes Systems of Accounts*, Chicago: University of Chicago Press.

Ellman, M. (1983) 'Changing Views on Central Economic Planning: 1958–1983', *ACES Bulletin* Spring: 11–34.

Ericson, R.E. (1990) 'The Soviet Statistical Debate: Khanin versus TsSU', in H. S. Rowen and C. Wolf, Jr (eds) *The Impoverished Superpower*, San Francisco: Institute for Contemporary Studies.

—— (1991) 'The Classical Soviet-Type Economy: Nature of the System and Implications for Reform', *Journal of Economic Perspectives* 5: 11–27.

European Bank for Reconstruction and Development (1994) 'Transition Report', London.

Faramazian, R., and Borisov, V. (1993) 'Two Approaches to Military Economy and Conversion', *Problems of Economic Transition*, Dec.: 42–57, translated from *Mirovaia ekonomika i mezhdunarodnye otnosheniia* (1993) no. 3: 23–34.

Farrell, J. (1987) 'Information and the Coase Theorem', *Journal of Economic Perspectives* 1: 113–129.

Fernandez, R. and Rodrik, D. (1991) 'Resistance to Reform: Status Quo Bias in the Presence of Individual–Specific Uncertainty', *American Economic Review* 81, December: 1146–1155.

Feshbach, M. (1991) 'Untold Story: The Enormity of Soviet Union's Health Disaster', *Cosmos* 1: 44–49.

Feshbach, M. and Friendly, A., Jr, (1992) *Ecocide in the USSR*, New York: Basic Books.

Feurer, L. S. (ed.) (1959) *Marx and Engels Basic Writings on Politics and Philosophy*, Garden City, NY: Doubleday and Co., Inc.

Fischer, S. (1991) 'Issues in International Economic Integration', Working Paper no. 579, MIT Department of Economics, April.

—— (1994) 'Prospects for Russian Stabilization in the Summer of 1993', in A. Åslund (ed.) *Economic Transformation in Russia* New York: St Martin's Press.

Fischer, S. and Frenkel, J. (1992) 'Macroeconomic Issues of Soviet Reform', *American Economic Review Papers and Proceedings* 82, May: 37–42.

Flakierski, H. (1992) 'Changes in Income Inequality in the USSR', in A. Åslund (ed.)

Market Socialism or the Restoration of Capitalism?, Cambridge: Cambridge University Press.

Gaddy, C. G. (1991) 'The Labor Market and the Second Economy in the Soviet Union', Berkeley–Duke Occasional Papers on the Second Economy in the USSR, 24, Jan.

—— (1992) 'Inflation, Living Standards, and Russian Reality', mimeo.

—— (1993) 'Economic Reform and Individual Choice in Russia', paper prepared for the Aspen Strategy Group, The Aspen Institute, Aspen, CO, August 8–13.

General Accounting Office (GAO) (1991) 'Soviet Economy. Assessment of How Well the CIA Has Estimated the Size of the Soviet Economy', Washington, DC, September.

Gibbon, E. (1985 [1776]) *The Decline and Fall of the Roman Empire*, London: Penguin Books.

Gogol, N. (1972 [1842]) *Dead Souls*, Middlesex: Penguin Books.

Goldberg, L. S. (1993) 'Foreign Exchange Markets in Russia', *IMF Staff Papers* 40, Dec.: 852–864.

Goldman, M. I. (1983) *USSR in Crisis*, New York: Norton.

—— (1992 [1991]) *What Went Wrong With Perestroika*, New York: Norton.

Graham, L. R. (1993) *The Ghost of the Executed Engineer*, Cambridge, MA: Harvard University Press.

Gregory, P. R. and Collier, I. L. (1988) 'Unemployment in the Soviet Union: Evidence from the Soviet Interview Project', *American Economic Review* 78, Sept.: 613–632.

Grossman, G. (1963) 'Notes for a Theory of the Command Economy', *Soviet Studies* 15: 101–123.

—— (1977) 'The Second Economy of the USSR', *Problems of Communism*, Sept.–Oct., 25–40.

—— (1979) 'Notes on the Illegal Private Economy and Corruption', in *Soviet Economy in a Time of Change*, Joint Economic Committee, US Congress, Washington DC: US Government Printing Office.

—— (1987) 'Roots of Gorbachev's Problems: Private Income and Outlay in the Late 1970s', in *Gorbachev's Economic Plans*, Joint Economic Committee, US Congress, Washington, DC: US Government Printing Office, vol. 1.

—— (1989) 'The Second Economy: Boon or Bane for the Reform of the First Economy', in S. Gomulka, Y. Ha and C. Kim (eds) *Economic Reforms in the Socialist World*, Armonk, NY: M. E. Sharpe.

Grossman, G. and Treml, V.G. (1987) 'Measuring Hidden Personal Incomes in the USSR', in S. Alessandrini and B. Dallago (eds) *The Unofficial Economy*, Aldershot, England: Gower Publishing Company Limited.

Hall, R. E. and Taylor, J. B. (1993) *Macroeconomics*, fourth edition. New York: Norton.

Hanson, P. (1986) 'The Serendipitous Soviet Achievement of Full Employment: Labour Shortage and Labour Hoarding in the Soviet Economy', in D. Lane (ed.) *Labour and Employment in the USSR*, Sussex: Wheatsheaf Books Ltd.

—— (1991) 'Soviet Economic Reform: Perestroika or "Catastroika"?', *World Policy Journal* 8, Spring: 289–318.

Harrison, M. (1986) 'Lessons of Soviet Planning for Full Employment', in D. Lane (ed.) *Labour and Employment in the USSR*, Sussex: Wheatsheaf Books Ltd.

Hayek, F. A. (1945) 'The Use of Knowledge in Society', *American Economic Review* 35: 519–530.

—— (1972 [1944]) *The Road to Serfdom*, Chicago: University of Chicago Press.

Heleniak, T. (1991) 'Unemployment in the USSR: A Growing Problem for Market Transition', presented at the 23rd AAASS National Conference, Miami, November.

Hendley, K. (1992) 'Legal Development and Privatization in Russia: A Case Study', *Soviet Economy* 8: 130–157.

Hewett, E. A. (1988) *Reforming the Soviet Economy: Equality versus Efficiency*, Washington, DC: The Brookings Institution.

—— (1989a) 'Economic Reform in the USSR, Eastern Europe, and China: The Politics of Economics', *American Economic Review Papers and Proceedings* 79, May: 16–20.

—— (1989b) 'Editorial Perspective', *Soviet Economy* 5: 104–106.

Hewett, E. A. and Gaddy, C. G. (1992) *Open for Business. Russia's Return to the Global Economy*, Washington, DC: Brookings Institution.

Hicks, J.R. (1935) 'Annual Survey of Economic Theory: The Theory of Monopoly', *Econometrica* 3: 1–20.

Holmlund, B. and Zetterberg, J. (1991) 'Insider Effects in Wage Determination. Evidence from Five Countries', *European Economic Review* 35: 1009–1034.

Holmstrom, B. and Milgrom, P. (1991) 'Multitask Principal–Agent Analyses: Incentive Contracts, Asset Ownership, and Job Design', *Journal of Law, Economics, and Organization* 7: 24–52.

Ickes, B. W. and Ryterman, R. (1992) 'The Interenterprise Arrears Crisis in Russia', *Post-Soviet Affairs* 8: 331–361.

Ilin, M. (1931) *New Russia's Primer*, Boston, MA: Houghton Mifflin Company.

Institute of Sociology (1992) 'Mirror of Opinions: The Result of a Sociological Poll of the Population of Russia', Moscow: Russian Academy of Sciences.

International Monetary Fund (1992a) 'Economic Review. The Economy of the Former U.S.S.R. in 1991', Washington, DC: IMF, April.

—— (1992b) 'Economic Review. Russian Federation', Washington, DC: IMF, April.

IMF, International Bank for Reconstruction and Development, Organization for Economic Co-operation and Development, European Bank for Reconstruction and Development (1991) *A Study of the Soviet Economy*, vols. 1,2, and 3, Feb.

IMF, IBRD, OECD, EBRD (1990) 'The Economy of the USSR. Summary and Recommendations', Dec.

Isaac, R. M., Mathieu, D. and Zajac, E.E (1991) 'Institutional Framing and Perceptions of Fairness', mimeo.

Jackman, R., Layard, R. and Scott, A. (1992) 'Unemployment in Eastern Europe', presented at the NBER Conference on Transition in Eastern Europe, Cambridge, MA, February.

Jefferson, G. H. and Rawski, T. G. (1991) 'Unemployment, Underemployment, and Employment Policy in China's Cities', Working Paper, Department of Economics, University of Pittsburgh, Sept.

Johnson, S. (1992) 'Private Business in Eastern Europe', presented at the NBER Conference on Transition in Eastern Europe, Cambridge, MA, February.

Johnson, S. and Kroll, H. (1991) 'Managerial Strategies for Spontaneous Privatization', *Soviet Economy* 7: 281–316.

Joint Economic Committee (JEC) (1982) *USSR: Measures of Economic Growth and Development, 1950–1980*, Washington, DC: US Government Printing Office.

Jones, A. and Moskoff, W. (1991) *Ko-ops*, Bloomington: Indiana University Press.

Kahn, A. E. and Peck, M. J. (1991) 'Price Deregulation, Corporatization, and Competition', in M.J. Peck and T. J. Richardson (eds) *What is to be Done?*, New Haven: Yale University Press.

Kawalec, S. (1992) 'The Dictatorial Supplier', in J. R. Wedel (ed.) *The Unplanned Society*, New York: Columbia University Press.

Kendrick, J. W. (1972) *Economic Accounts and Their Uses*, New York: McGraw-Hill.

Khanin, G. (1992) 'The Soviet Economy–From Crisis to Catastrophe', in A. Åslund (ed.) *The Post Soviet-Economy*, London: Pinter Publishers.

Khrushchev, N. (1974) *Khrushchev Remembers. The Last Testament*, translated and edited by Strobe Talbott, Boston, MA: Little, Brown and Company.

—— (1990) *Khrushchev Remembers. The Glasnost Tapes,* translated and edited by J. L. Schecter with V. V. Luchkov, Boston, MA: Little, Brown and Company.

Kireyev, A. P. (1990) 'Conversion in the Soviet Dimension', *International Affairs,* May.

Koen, V. and Phillips, S. (1993) 'Price Liberalization in Russia', IMF Occasional Paper 104, June.

Kornai, J. (1980) *The Economics of Shortage,* Amsterdam: North-Holland.

—— (1990) *The Road to a Free Economy,* New York: Norton.

—— (1992) *The Socialist System,* Princeton: Princeton University Press.

Kosareva, N. B. (1992) 'The Housing Market and Social Guarantees', *Studies on Soviet Economic Development* 3, Feb.: 38–46.

Kosmarskii, V. (1992) 'Public Attitudes to the Transition', in A. Åslund (ed.) *The Post-Soviet Economy,* London: Pinter Publishers.

Kotkin, S. (1991) *Steeltown, USSR,* Berkeley: University of California Press.

Kroll, H. (1987) 'Breach of Contract in the Soviet Economy', *Journal of Legal Studies* 16: 119–148.

—— (1991) 'Monopoly and Transition to the Market', *Soviet Economy* 7: 143–174.

Lane, D. (1986) 'Marxist-Leninism: An Ideology for Full Employment in Socialist States?', in D. Lane (ed.) *Labour and Employment in the USSR,* Sussex: Wheatsheaf Books Ltd.

—— (1987) *Soviet Labour and the Ethic of Communism,* Boulder, CO: Westview Press.

Lange, O. and Taylor, F. M. (1938) *On the Economic Theory of Socialism,* Minneapolis: University of Minnesota Press.

Lazear, E. P. (1991) 'Prices and Wages in Transition Economies', Hoover Institution Working Paper E-91-13, Nov.

Leitzel, J. (1993a) 'The Choice of What to Procure', in J. Leitzel and J. Tirole (eds) *Incentives in Procurement Contracting,* Boulder, CO: Westview Press.

—— (1993b) 'Goods Diversion and Repressed Inflation', in 'Essays on Second Economy Markets', Berkeley–Duke Occasional Papers on the Second Economy in the USSR, 37, Dec.

Lipman, M. and McGraw, W. R. (1988) 'Employee Theft: A $40 Billion Industry', *Annals of the American Academy of Political and Social Science* 498, July: 51–59.

Lipton, D. and Sachs, J. (1990) 'Creating a Market Economy in Eastern Europe: The Case of Poland', *Brookings Papers on Economic Activity,* 75–147.

—— and —— (1992) 'Prospects for Russia's Economic Reforms', *Brookings Papers on Economic Activity,* 213–283.

Litwack, J. (1991a) 'Discretionary Behaviour and Soviet Economic Reform', *Soviet Studies* 43, March: 255–279.

—— (1991b) 'Hierarchical Coordination Failure and Soviet Economic Decline', mimeo, Stanford University, Nov.

Lutz, F. A. (1949) 'The German Currency Reform and the Revival of the German Economy', *Economica,* May 1949.

Macauley, S. (1963) 'Non-Contractual Relations in Business: A Preliminary Study', *American Sociological Review* 28: 55–67.

McCloskey, D. (1985) *The Rhetoric of Economics,* Madison: University of Wisconsin Press.

McGee, R. T. and Feige, E. L. (1989) 'Policy Illusion, Macroeconomic Instability, and the Unrecorded Economy', in E. L. Feige (ed.) *The Underground Economies,* Cambridge: Cambridge University Press.

Machiavelli, N. (1947 [1532]) *The Prince,* T. G. Bergin (ed.) Northbrook, IL: AHM Publishing Corporation.

McKinnon, R. I. (1990a) 'Liberalizing Foreign Trade in a Socialist Economy: The Problem of Negative Value Added', Mimeo, Stanford University, Oct.
—— (1990b) 'Stabilising the Rouble', *Communist Economies* 2: 131–142.
Malyshev, N. (1987) 'Laundering of Money in the USSR through the Purchase of Winning Bonds and Lottery Tickets', in 'Studies on the Soviet Second Economy', Berkeley–Duke Occasional Papers on the Second Economy in the USSR, 11, Dec.
Marnie, S. (1992) 'Employment and the Reallocation of Labour in the USSR', in A. Åslund (ed.) *Market Socialism or the Restoration of Capitalism?*, Cambridge: Cambridge University Press.
Marx, K. and Engels, F. (1964 [1848]) *The Communist Manifesto*, New York: Washington Square Press.
Matthews, M. (1989) *Patterns of Deprivation in the Soviet Union Under Brezhnev and Gorbachev*, Stanford: Hoover Institution Press.
Mickiewicz, E. (1992) 'Findings of Four Major Surveys in the Former Soviet Union', mimeo.
Millar, J. R. 1987) (ed.) *Politics, Work, and Daily Life in the USSR*, Cambridge: Cambridge University Press.
—— (1990) 'The Soviet Household Sector: The View from the Bottom', in J. R. Millar (ed.) *The Soviet Economic Experiment*, Urbana: University of Illinois Press.
Moskoff, W. (1984) *Labour and Leisure in the Soviet Union*, New York: St. Martin's Press.
Muellbauer, J. (1987) 'Professor Sen on the Standard of Living', in A. Sen (ed.) *The Standard of Living*, Cambridge: Cambridge University Press.
Newberry, D. M. and Kattuman, P. (1992) 'Market Concentration and Competition in Eastern Europe', *The World Economy* 15: 315–334.
Nove, A. (1982) *An Economic History of the USSR*, New York: Pelican.
—— (1986) *The Soviet Economic System*, Third Edition, Boston: Allen and Unwin.
Nutter, G. W. (1969) *The Strange World of Ivan Ivanov*, New York: World Publishing Company.
Nystrom, E. J. (1994) 'Can a Hybrid Economy Survive? The Chinese Experience and Its Lessons for Soviet Central Asia', mimeo, Duke University.
OECD [Organization for Economic Co-operation and Development] (1994) 'Short-Term Economic Indicators. Transition Economies', 2/1994.
Ofer, G. (1987) 'Soviet Economic Growth: 1928–1985', *Journal of Economic Literature* 25: 1767–1833.
Orwell, G. (1983 [1949]) *1984*, New York: The New American Library.
Pagano, M. (1990) 'Imperfect Competition, Underemployment Equilibria and Fiscal Policy', *The Economic Journal* 100: 440–463.
Peck, M. J. (1991) 'Introduction.' in M. J. Peck and T. J. Richardson (eds) *What is to be Done?*, New Haven: Yale University Press.
Perkins, D. (1994) 'Completing China's Move to the Market', *Journal of Economic Perspectives* 8, Spring: 23–46.
Pietsch, A. (1986) 'Shortage of Labour and Motivation Problems of Soviet Workers', in D. Lane (ed.) *Labour and Employment in the USSR*, Sussex: Wheatsheaf Books Ltd.
Pinto, B., Belka, M. and Krajewski, S. (1993) 'Transforming State Enterprises in Poland: Microeconomic Evidence on Adjustment', World Bank Policy Research Working Paper.
Pitzer, J. S. and Baukol, A.P (1991) 'Recent GNP and Productivity Trends', *Soviet Economy* 7: 46–82.
Polanyi, M. (1960) 'Towards a Theory of Conspicuous Production', *Soviet Survey*, Number 34, pp. 90–99.
Porket, J. L. (1989) *Work, Employment and Unemployment in the Soviet Union*, New York: St. Martin's Press.

Powell, R. P. (1977) 'Plan Execution and the Workability of Soviet Planning', *Journal of Comparative Economics* 1: 51–76.

Prosterman, R. L. and Hanstad, T. (1991) 'Trip Report Updating Our Monograph on "The Prospects for Individual Peasant Farming in the USSR",' mimeo, Rural Development Institute, Oct.

Prosterman, R. L., Hanstad, T. and Rolfes, L. J., Jr (1993) 'Agrarian Reform in Russia', RDI Monographs on Foreign Aid and Development 11, May.

Raleigh, D. J. (1992) 'Beyond Moscow and St. Petersburg: Some Reflections on the August Revolution, Provincial Russia, and Novostroika', *South Atlantic Quarterly* 91, Summer: 603–619.

Reed, J. (1967 [1919]) *Ten Days That Shook the World*, New York: New American Library.

Richards, S. (1990) *Epics of Everyday Life*, New York: Penguin Books.

Roberts, B. (1993) 'The Initial Welfare Consequences of Price Liberalization and Stabilization in Russia', mimeo, University of Miami.

Rodrik, D. (1989) 'Promises, Promises: Credible Policy Reform Via Signalling', *Economic Journal* 99, Sept.: 756–772.

—— (1991) 'The Economic Opening of Developing Countries Why So Late? Why Now? Will It Last?', mimeo, Hoover Institution, Nov.

—— (1992) 'Making Sense of the Soviet Trade Shock in Eastern Europe: A Framework and Some Estimates', mimeo, January.

Rose, R. (1994) 'Getting By Without Government: Everyday Life in a Stressful Society', Studies in Public Policy Number 227, Centre for the Study of Public Policy, University of Strathclyde, Glasgow.

Rosefielde, S. (1991) 'The Illusion of Material Progress: The Analytics of Soviet Economic Growth Revisited', *Soviet Studies* 43: 597–611.

Ross, D. (1968) *Robert F. Kennedy: Apostle of Change*, New York: Trident Press.

Rostowski, J. (1994) 'Dilemmas of Monetary and Financial Policy in Post-Stabilization Russia', in A. Åslund (ed.) *Economic Transformation in Russia*, New York: St Martin's Press.

Rowen, H. S. and Wolf, C., Jr (eds) (1990) *The Impoverished Superpower*, San Francisco: Institute for Contemporary Studies.

Rutgaizer, V. M. (1992) 'The Shadow Economy in the USSR', Berkeley–Duke Occasional Papers on the Second Economy in the USSR, No. 34, Feb.

Rutland, P. (1985) *The Myth of the Plan*, La Salle, IL: Open Court.

Sachs, J. (1993a) *Poland's Jump to the Market Economy*, Cambridge, MA: MIT Press.

—— (1993b) 'Western Financial Assistance and Russia's Reforms', in S. Islam and M. Mandelbaum (eds) *Making Markets. Economic Transformation in Eastern Europe and the Post-Soviet States*, New York: Council on Foreign Relations Press.

—— (1994) 'Prospects for Monetary Stabilization in Russia', in A. Åslund (ed.) *Economic Transformation in Russia*, New York: St Martin's Press.

Sachs, J. and Woo, W. T. (1994) 'Reform in China and Russia', *Economic Policy* 18, April: 101–145.

Samuelson, P. A. (1970) *Economics*, eighth edition, New York: McGraw-Hill.

Sargent, T. J. (1982) 'The Ends of Four Big Inflations', in R. E. Hall (ed.) *Inflation: Causes and Effects*, Chicago: University of Chicago Press.

Schelling, T. C. (1984a) 'Economics and Criminal Enterprise', in T. C. Schelling, *Choice and Consequence*, Cambridge, MA: Harvard University Press.

—— (1984b) 'What Is the Business of Organized Crime?', in T.C. Schelling, *Choice and Consequence*, Cambridge, MA: Harvard University Press.

Schroeder, G. E. (1979) 'The Soviet Economy on a Treadmill of "Reforms"', *Soviet Economy in a Time of Change*, Washington, DC: Joint Economic Committee, US Congress: 65–88.

Schultze, C. L. (1992) *Memos to the President*, Washington, DC: The Brookings Institution.

Sedik, D. J. (1991) 'Price Policy and the Demise of the New Economic Policy in the USSR, 1923–29', Paper presented at the Western Economic Association International Meetings, Seattle, July.

Sen, A. (1987) *The Standard of Living*, Cambridge: Cambridge University Press.

Shlapentokh, V. (1989) *Public and Private Life of the Soviet People*, New York: Oxford University Press.

Shleifer, A. and Vishny, R. W. (1991) 'Reversing the Soviet Economic Collapse', mimeo.

—— and —— (1993) 'Corruption', *Quarterly Journal of Economics* 108, 3: 599–617.

Shmelev, N. (1987) 'Avansi i dolgi', *Novy Mir* 6, June: 148–149.

Simis, K. (1982) *USSR: The Corrupt Society*, New York: Simon and Schuster.

Slider, D. (1991) 'Embattled Entrepreneurs: Soviet Cooperatives in an Unreformed Economy', *Soviet Studies* 43: 797–821.

Smith, A. (1991 [1776]) *The Wealth of Nations*, New York: Knopf, Everyman's Library.

Smith, H. (1984 [1976]) *The Russians*, New York: Ballantine Books.

—— (1990) *The New Russians*, New York: Random House.

Spulber, N. (1991) *Restructuring the Soviet Economy*, Ann Arbor: University of Michigan Press.

Starodubrovskaya, I. (1994) 'The Nature of Monopoly and Barriers to Entry in Russia', *Communist Economies and Economic Transformation* 6: 3–18.

Starr, S. F. (1993) 'Year One of Capitalism in Russia', Hudson Briefing Paper, No. 150, Hudson Institute, March.

Stiglitz, J. E. (1991) 'Theoretical Aspects of Privatization: Applications to Eastern Europe', Institute for Policy Reform, September.

Sutela, P. (1993) 'Insider Privatization in Russia: Speculations on Systemic Change', Paper presented at American Association for the Advancement of Slavic Studies, Honolulu, November.

Svejnar, J. (1991) 'Microeconomic Issues in the Transition to a Market Economy', *Journal of Economic Perspectives* 5, Fall: 123–138.

Tirole, J. (1988) *The Theory of Industrial Organization*, Cambridge, MA: MIT Press.

—— (1991) 'Privatization in Eastern Europe: Incentives and the Economics of Transition', *NBER Macroeconomics Annual 1991*, 221–267.

Tobin, J. (1957) 'Comment', in *The Measurement and Behaviour of Unemployment*, Princeton: Princeton University Press.

Treml, V. G. (1988) 'Perestroyka and Soviet Statistics', *Soviet Economy* 4: 65–94.

—— (1992a) 'Soviet Statistics Under Gorbachev: A Western Perspective', in C. Wolf, Jr and S. Popper (eds) *Defense and the Soviet Economy: Military Muscle and Economic Weakness*, a RAND Note.

—— (1992b) 'A Study of Labor Inputs into the Second Economy of the USSR', Berkeley–Duke Occasional Papers on the Second Economy in the USSR, Number 33, Jan.

Treml, V. G. and Alexeev, M.V. (1993) 'The Second Economy and the Destabilizing Effect of its Growth on the State Economy in the Soviet Union: 1965–1989', Berkeley-Duke Occasional Papers on the Second Economy in the USSR, No. 36, December.

Uno, K. (1991) 'Privatization and the Creation of a Commercial Banking System', in M. J. Peck and T. J. Richardson (eds) *What is to be Done?*, New Haven: Yale University Press.

Vaksberg, A. (1991) *The Soviet Mafia*, New York: St Martin's Press.

Vodopivec, M. (1991) 'The Labor Market and the Transition of Socialist Economies', *Comparative Economic Studies* 33: 123–158.

Weitzman, M. L. (1991) 'How Not to Privatize', *Revista di Politica Economica* 12, Dec.: 249–269.

Wellisz, S. (1991) 'Poland Under "Solidarity" Rule', *Journal of Economic Perspectives* 5: 211–217.

Wiles, P. J. D. (1962) *The Political Economy of Communism*, Cambridge, MA: Harvard University Press.

Wilhelm, J. H. (1985) 'The Soviet Union has an Administered, Not a Planned, Economy', *Soviet Studies* 37, Jan.: 118–130.

Wolf, T. A. (1991) 'The Lessons of Limited Market-Oriented Reform', *Journal of Economic Perspectives* 5, Fall: 45–58.

Wren, C. (1990) *The End of the Line*, New York: Simon and Schuster.

Zaleski, E. (1980) *Stalinist Planning for Economic Growth, 1933–1952*, Chapel Hill: University of North Carolina Press.

Zubova, L., Kovaleva, N. and Khakhulina, L. (1992) 'Poverty in the USSR', *Problems of Economics*, Feb: 85–98, translation of (1991) 'Bednost' v SSSR: tochka zreniia naseleniia', *Voprosy Ekonomiki* 6: 60–67.

Index

THE WEST IN RUSSIA AND CHINA

Religious and Secular Thought in Modern Times

DONALD W. TREADGOLD

Institute for Comparative and Foreign Area Studies
University of Washington

VOLUME 1

RUSSIA, 1472–1917

CAMBRIDGE

At the University Press

1973

Published by the Syndics of the Cambridge University Press
Bentley House, 200 Euston Road, London NW1 2DB
American Branch: 32 East 57th Street, New York, N.Y.10022

© Cambridge University Press 1973

Library of Congress Catalogue Card Number: 72-78886

ISBNs

0 521 08552 7 hard cover
0 521 09725 8 paperback

Composed in Great Britain
by Alden & Mowbray Ltd
at the Alden Press, Oxford

Printed in the United States of America

CONTENTS

Volume 1

Volume 2

PREFACE

This book endeavors to trace the development of Western thought in Russia and China through its chief phases. In writing it I have used many secondary works, but in many cases I have gone to the sources – especially in those areas where secondary treatments are inadequate or non-existent, but not only in such areas. The claim that this book might have to the attention of readers rests not mainly in the information that it brings for the first time to the attention of specialists, though it does contain some such information, but rather in the new way that it attempts to interpret material much of which has been previously known. It seeks to achieve a synthesis without being exhaustive; many significant figures or groups are touched on lightly or not at all, and much of the historical significance of some figures and groups discussed may lie outside the discussion of them to be found here.

The book is intended not as history of philosophy (for which one may consult Fung Yu-lan's and V. V. Zenkovsky's works on China and Russia respectively), history of culture (C. P. Fitzgerald and James H. Billington provide introductions), history of science (Joseph Needham and Alexander Vucinich), or history of religion (here there are no one-volume manuals, though there are histories of Churches, which are not the same thing), but as history of thought – of ideas that had some public impact, and specifically ideas of Western origin.

History of religious thought is prominent in the story up to the point where it ceased to be prominent in Russian and Chinese reality. Religious connections with the West are not the subject investigated, before or after that point; for example, the Chinese Roman Catholic community after the eighteenth century, though it was considerably larger than the Chinese Protestant one, receives next to no attention. When matters outside of thought within the field of religion are referred to, the purpose is to explain the limits of the influence or simply the negative effects of religious thought in the given instance. The non-religious thought studied is chiefly of the kind associated with belief in and commitment to a goal (or goals), and in fact much of it was not only chronologically but logically connected with the religious ideas that had been enunciated earlier. Obviously, not all ideas transmitted from the West to Russia and China are examined; obviously, the ideas studied here were important ones.

I have sought to avoid posing the problem as one of the direct causal relation of a given Western work or thinker on a given Russian or Chinese. Limited inquiries of such a kind have produced and will doubtless produce interesting and useful studies. However, here attention is drawn rather to the way certain trends of Western thought took hold in Russia and China and were developed in an institutional context quite different from the one in which they originated.

The reader will not find in this book an evaluation of any thinker or group of thinkers as unequivocally beneficent or pernicious. Christians, liberals, and socialists (including Communists) may all find here ample ground for both praise and blame of themselves or others. However, the objective has been first to understand what happened. There is room for differing evaluations of what happened and how it happened, and my own will be evident before the end of the book.

It is possible that some readers whose interest is confined chiefly to the contemporary world may impute their own feelings to me and accuse me of projecting attitudes of the present into the past. Of course Communist rule in Russia and China is a fact of overwhelming importance, and its recency (despite the difference between 1917 and 1949) makes dispassionate evaluation difficult. If one likes Communism, one may argue that our story is of the indispensable preparation for the victory of the good in two great countries; if one dislikes it, one may hold that the story shows an uninterrupted march toward disaster. The background of Communism in Russia and China today needs to be understood, and if someone wishes to read this book in order to learn more about it, I have no objection. My aim, however, has been to trace the course of Western thought, in Russia and China, distributing attention in a defensible manner among periods and phases, comparing developments in the two countries. Some of the comparison is not explicit; often studying events in one country has affected my approach to events in the other.

The question of the extent to which Russia and China are comparable ought to be distinguished from the question of whether they are similar. Benjamin I. Schwartz has well said, 'the question of whether Russian culture has or has not been part of or "affiliated" with the culture of the West remains un-answered. But there can be no doubt about the separate evolution of Chinese culture.'[1] Equally, it may be added, there can be no doubt that the same major phases of Western thought and many of the same individual ideas and thinkers were influential in both countries, and there thus seems good reason to explore the ways in which the reception of Western thought was similar or different in Russia and China. There exist divergent views on the degree to which state and society in Russia were like state and society in China. My own views on the issue will appear, for what they are worth, but the possible usefulness of a comparison of cultural development does not depend on any particular view of that problem.

One attitude of mine that will be prominent in the exposition to follow is sympathy for solutions of the West–East cultural confrontation that represent what I call 'syncretism'. In using the term I have in mind several men I have known, of whom I shall mention three: the Very Rev. Georges Florovsky,

Hsiao Kung-ch'üan, and the late Hsia Tsi-an. Each of the three – two now living, one dead – was deeply rooted in his own cultural tradition and also found firm footing in that of the West as well. They also taught me something of what heights culture has reached in Russia and China, not so much by their formal instruction (though in two of the three cases that was also helpful) as by their persons and their lives.

I thank the following in particular for assistance: The Far Eastern and Russian Institute (now renamed Institute for Comparative and Foreign Area Studies), its two successive directors, George E. Taylor and George Beckmann, and my colleagues in the Russian and East European Seminar and the Modern Chinese History Project Colloquium at the University of Washington – the members of each group read and criticized every chapter in their field of interest in draft (sometimes more than one) form; Marc Raeff; Fr Francis A. Rouleau, SJ; Oswald P. Backus; Gustave Alef; my colleagues and the staff at Toyo Bunko, Tokyo; my colleagues and the staff at the Institute of History of the USSR Academy of Sciences, Moscow; the staffs of the Lenin State Library, the Central State Archive of Literature and Art (TsGALI), and of the Central State Archives of Old Documents (TsGADA), all in Moscow; Gordon B. Turner and the American Council of Learned Societies; Bryce Wood and the Social Science Research Council; the Guggenheim Foundation; John K. Fairbank and the rest of the SSRC Committee on Exchanges with Asian Institutions. Mr and Mrs Wong Young-tsu assisted me with the translation of numerous Chinese materials, but I take full responsibility for the cases in which I may have overridden their superior judgment. Mrs George Fisher has patiently and flawlessly typed the entire manuscript in several successive versions. More personal indebtedness I shall not attempt to discharge here.

The Wade–Giles system of romanization of Chinese and the Library of Congress systems of transliteration from Russian and Ukrainian have been used, with certain modifications. I have tried not to allow consistency to make usage foolish in any given instance, and I have used more modifications in the text than in the notes. Not everyone will like all the decisions of this kind I have made, but I would be grateful if such decisions could be distinguished from errors.

D.W.T.

January 1972

INTRODUCTION

A product of modern European civilization, studying any problem of universal history, is bound to ask himself to what combination of circumstances the fact should be attributed that in Western civilization, and in Western civilization only, cultural phenomena have appeared which (as we like to think) lie in a line of development having *universal* significance and value.

MAX WEBER

THE PROBLEM

One of the most significant developments of modern history is the Westernization of the non-Western world. Many leading thinkers of non-Western countries have facilitated that process; far from resisting Westernization, they have frequently taken the initiative in adopting features of Western civilization, urging or even forcing them on their own countrymen. Thus even Westerners who do not necessarily 'like to think', as Weber does, that cultural phenomena of universal significance have appeared only in the West are compelled to recognize that the 'fact' to which Weber refers has come to be widely accepted as such in the non-West.

The cultural phenomena Weber has in mind, and discusses successively in the author's introduction to *The Protestant Ethic and the Spirit of Capitalism*,[1] include the following: systematic theology ('the full development' of which 'must be credited to Christianity under the influence of Hellenism'), science (its mathematical foundations, the method of experiment, a rational chemistry) historical scholarship, canon law, music (rational harmony, the orchestra, the system of notation), architecture (the Gothic vault), painting (rational utilization of lines and perspectives), printing (that is, a printed literature 'designed *only* for print and only possible through it'), the State 'in the sense of a political association with a rational, written constitution, rationally ordained law, and an administration bound to rational rules or laws, administered by trained officials', and capitalism – which is the main subject of Weber's book.

Over the whole of modern history (from the fifteenth to the twentieth centuries) the peoples outside the West have wrestled with the question of whether they should adopt such cultural phenomena in whole or in part, in what order, and how fast. In general what seems striking is how weak the resistance to Westernization was among the non-Western cultural elites, how rare the uncompromising nativists and xenophobes were, and how ineffective their efforts proved. Usually the stance of total opposition to Westernization has been but a brief and transitory phenomenon attending the early stages of the process. In our own day the cry 'Yankee, go home!' may not be followed by the facetiously attributed postscript, 'and take me with you', but it is almost always accompanied by the tacit prayer, 'and leave here much of what you have brought us'.

After the resistance of the principled xenophobes was beaten down, the debate in non-Western areas tended to be one among defenders of various competing currents of Westernization, with one category of interesting exceptions. Though almost no informed and intelligent non-Westerner thought his country could do without substantial Western importations, a number sought to combine indigenous cultural themes with Western ideas. I have called such persons 'syncretists'. Those who admit the possibility of a multiplicity of differing values in mankind's cultures ought to study the syncretists with special care. Though their record of success thus far is meager, even in the twentieth century they may still have a future. For as potential supporters they may be able to recruit – if not in the arena of conscious, literary expression, then in action – the inarticulate, at most partly educated masses of the people in their countries, who may cling to their traditions no matter how much compulsion, violence, and terror are employed by their Westernizing rulers.

The whole subject of cultural Westernization of the non-West, since the fifteenth century, might be approached in a single essay.[2] This study is limited in two respects. It deals only with Russia and China, omitting the rest of the non-Western world, and it confines itself chiefly to the thought of intellectuals, omitting any systematic survey of belles-lettres, the fine arts, or the non-intellectual aspects of religion, and attempting no examination of religious, social, or political movements among the uneducated or poorly educated. Scientific, technological, and economic (in the strict sense) ideas are not emphasized; the religious, philosophical, and political ideas mainly studied are those which took precedence over other aspects of Westernization and to a large extent determined the institutional and cultural changes that did occur. (This is intended not as a judgment of relative importance but as an interpretation of what actually took place.)

THE RISE OF THE WEST

Four areas of the world produced what Alfred Weber calls 'primary high cultures' (*die primären Hochkulturen*) in the sense of not being derived from any previously existing civilizations of which we have knowledge: Egypt, Babylonia, China, and India.[3] India and China survived as cultures as well as societies. Egypt and Babylonia perished as cultures, though their institutional patterns persisted in the face of repeated foreign conquest. They were succeeded by 'secondary' cultures, which Weber describes in two stages. The first saw Jewish and Persian cultures appear in Western Asia and the cultures of Greece, Rome, and Christian antiquity in the Eastern Mediterranean basin. In the second stage there may be distinguished an 'East' (*Morgenland*) consisting of Byzantium, Islam, and Russia, and a 'West' (*Abendland*), medieval and modern.

It may be preferable to discard Weber's classification of 'secondary' cultures in favor of one in which, side by side with those of the Jews and Persians, there are distinguished pre-Christian Hellenic and Roman cultures, followed by a single or at least not sharply differentiated Christian Greco-Roman culture throughout the whole Mediterranean, after the conversion of Constantine and especially after orthodox Christianity became obligatory in the Empire with Theodosius in 380. It was a culture strong enough to survive the inundation of the Western Roman Empire by barbarians, so that the latter accepted the culture of the areas they conquered. Islam was culturally related to Christian Greco-Roman culture. It was first considered a Christian heresy akin to Arianism and became a 'post-Christian' religion, 'a product of that process by which Christian theology, formulation of dogma and contention over it grew and developed...from the second to the seventh century A.D.'[4]

As for Weber's other 'secondary cultures', Byzantium, Russia, and the West, one should avoid making sharp distinctions among them at too early a date. It was a single Christian Church which produced the highly rationalized and consistent theology and anthropology to which Max Weber refers, enunciated during the first centuries Anno Domini and approved by the first seven ecumenical councils up to 787. It was a single Christian society that was the ideal of the primitive church and for a time approached reality in the Byzantine Empire, tenuous as the links between Charlemagne's realm or Abyssinia may have been with Constantinople. However, as the Arabs and other invaders reduced Byzantine domains, they overran the territories of three of the patriarchates of the early church: Alexandria, Antioch, and Jerusalem (the last achieved that status only in the fifth century). There remained two: the see of Constantinople, which survived in a Christian state until the city fell in 1453 and thereafter came under Muslim rule, and the see of Rome, whose obedience was Western Europe. In one respect Constantinople fared better than Alexandria, Antioch, and Jerusalem. The lands of the last three were largely converted to Islam; but Greece, Bulgaria, and Serbia remained largely Orthodox after they became subject to the Ottoman Empire, as did Russia, which was regaining its independence of the Mongols at about the time that Mohammed II captured Constantinople. By about 1000, Christianity survived as the religion of only a small minority in Asia and Africa, but it not only remained the religion of Southern Europe but had extended its sway to most of Northern Europe as well. Europe was Christian, the adjacent areas of Asia and Africa were Muslim.

If in the fifth century one can speak of a unified Christian culture in Southern Europe, Western Asia, and Northern Africa, by the fifteenth the Christian culture of Europe had become two: Roman/Latin and Constantinopolitan/Greek, or Roman Catholic and Eastern Orthodox. The differentiation had taken shape over the previous five centuries. The Schism of 1054 has been given exaggerated significance as the moment of division. It was not so much theological dispute as political and social development which sundered East and West within Christendom. As Byzantine energies were consumed by fighting off invader after invader, Christian Western Europe grew from a region of poor barbarians to one of high culture and flourishing economy. Some of the dazzling achievements of the West during the High Middle Ages were the logic of Abelard around 1100, the experimental beginnings of Roger Bacon and the synthetic philosophy of St Thomas Aquinas in the mid-thirteenth century, the Gothic cathedrals which provided both challenge and outlet for new tendencies in painting, sculpture, music, and letters as well as architecture, the renewal of Greek studies and extension of work on Latin in the disciplined literary enterprise of the Humanists, the explosion of Italian creativity in the fine arts, and the growth of mathematics, astronomy, and technology. By the time of what is by convention termed the Renaissance, as if it were a calling into life of what had been dead rather than steadily growing for five centuries, the Western cultural phenomena which Max Weber claims had 'universal significance and value' were all, in varying degrees, in evidence.

By the fifteenth century the boundary extending from the Arctic to the Adriatic that separates Finland, the Baltic regions, and Poland from Great Russia, Belorussia, and the Ukraine, Transylvania from Moldavia–Wallachia, Croatia from Serbia, also divided Western from Eastern Christian culture. There were mixed areas: Polish and most Transylvanian landlords were Roman Catholic, Ukrainian (though in the core of Poland the peasants were Polish like their landlords) and Rumanian peasants Orthodox. But in most places the boundary was remarkably firm.

It had also become a line between adversaries. After the Second Lateran Council (1139), when Christian knights who used the cross-bow *adversus Christianos et Catholicos* were anathematized but were left to do as they pleased against non-Christians and non-Catholics, Eastern Christians could have little doubt about what treatment they might expect. When the Crusaders penetrated the Baltic and especially when they sacked Constantinople in the Fourth Crusade (1204), feelings of deep hostility had taken root. Subsequent discussions of reunion of the churches in return for Roman Catholic aid to the Orthodox beleaguered by the Turks foundered, even when leaders reached agreement, on the popular memory in the East of the fact that Constantinople had been captured only once during its whole history (up to 1453), and on that occasion not by Muslims or pagans but by Western Christians.

The common Christian culture once shared by Spaniards and Russians, Englishmen and Greeks, did not disappear because of mutual hostility. But separation deepened the cultural gulf; Orthodox culture in the post-1204 period ceased to grow as before, and became impoverished under Ottoman rule, while culture was rapidly growing and powerful independent states were forming in the West. By the fifteenth century Eastern Christian culture exhibited few of the features Max Weber enumerates, and it was in general in no condition to undertake any program of triumphant expansion, even in its Greek stronghold, let alone in Russia.

RUSSIA AND CHINA

Ivan III of Muscovy (1462–1505) was the only independent Eastern Christian ruler of consequence in his time. Having successfully repudiated subservience to the succession states of the Mongol Empire, his government turned to the West for support, and thus our Russian story begins with Muscovite relations with Italy in the 1470's.

Western Europe's discovery of Muscovy (which like many other areas that have been 'discovered' was both there all the time and known to some people outside it) coincided approximately with its discovery of the coasts of Africa and Asia. From the passing of Cape Bojador in 1434 to the rounding of the Cape of Good Hope in 1488, Portuguese sailors traversed over sixty degrees of latitude in less than sixty years. Vasco da Gama reached Mozambique and India, both in the year 1498; and other Portuguese settled at Macau in 1577. Thereby the 'Occident' began its contacts with the two of Alfred Weber's 'primary' cultures that had survived: India and China. Such cultural contacts were initially largely based on the religious initiative of Westerners, that is, their effort to convert the non-Christian Indians and Chinese to Roman Catholic Christianity. The Portuguese made a few converts immediately in Goa and Macau. However, serious missionary effort, building on adequate cultural preparation, began only with the arrival of the Jesuits Matteo Ricci in Macau in 1582 and Roberto de' Nobili in Goa in 1605. Our Chinese story begins with Ricci.

The West reached out to the Orthodox East and the ultra-Christian East at about the same time. Russia belongs to the former, China to the latter. No other Orthodox state was comparable to Russia in size. None had a culture shaped through a period of more or less isolated development, like the more than two centuries of Mongol overlordship. As for China, it had a cultural unity and continuity lacking in India, the only other 'primary' culture millennia old. It did not fall under the rule of Westerners, as India did; and its unity was self-generated, not Western-imposed, as India's was.

Russia and China were also, as it happens, the two largest states to come under Communist rule in the twentieth century. Any Communist-ruled state demands and tries to produce a unified culture. The origin of Communist culture cannot be in doubt: it owes its basis to Karl Marx and Friedrich Engels, who were cosmopolitan Germans thinking and writing in terms primarily of Western Europe (even though they produced in passing remarkably well-informed observations about non-Western areas as well). Marx and Engels emerged from the intellectual tradition of the West, and no other.

It has been suggested by Jules Monnerot that Communism may be best regarded as a new Islam,[5] or, in van Leeuwen's phrase, 'the Islam *of the technocratic era*'. The latter warns against understanding Communism as a new religion. It is, he contends,

a counter-church; and its typically heretical character consists in its having fastened, with fanatical single-mindedness...upon a *partial* truth which it exalts into the one complete, exclusive and infallible dogma at the expense of all other aspects and points of view.

Gustav Wetter also uses the phrase, 'counter-church', and illustrates his point in powerful detail.

'It has often been remarked', he writes, 'that communism incorporates a whole series of particular Christian doctrines in secular form.' The 'fall of man' is equivalent to the transition from primitive Communism to slavery; 'original sin' takes the form of the exploitation in all class societies, from which no individual can escape; redemption comes from a 'sinless sacrificial lamb: the proletariat, by its undeserved suffering', emancipates not only itself but all of mankind; redemption is bound up with a sort of revelation, with Marx's discovery of the laws of history that could only have been made when it was, when 'the fullness of time' had come to pass; the Marxist scriptures contain absolute authority, but must be distinguished from commentaries; they are interpreted by the 'infallible authority' of the Central Committee; the Party serves as Church, requiring of its members conscious and overt commitment enabling them to participate in truth only when they stand 'in vital and organic communion with this mighty organism, in which the spirit of truth resides'.[6]

Communism, like Islam, bears the marks of an heretical movement within the Judeo-Christian tradition, broadly speaking. It 'fixes upon a partial truth' and exalts it to universal significance, which is as van Leeuwen correctly points out the *differentia specifica* of heresy. Nevertheless, it does not appear to be a partial truth of *Christianity* which Communism – perhaps unlike Islam – exalts.[7] Christianity has no doctrinal pronouncements to make on the economic and political organization of society, even though the doctrine of the absolute value of the individual (based on the Christian teaching that man is made in the image of God) seems to have been Marx's starting point, as it was for socialism in general. Despite Communism's rejection of Christian theology, clearly it is historically related to Christianity, as Wetter shows, in such a fashion as to preclude coincidental resemblance – even if we did not know the background of Judeo-Christian thought from which Marx and Engels, and indeed Lenin, came. The fact that two thinkers may start with a common point and end with two quite different and even contrary ones has long been familiar to Greek philosophers and Christian theologians. Communism in Russia and China may have turned into something quite different from Marxism or even radically alien to it; but neither that nor the history of change within Marxism generally is germane to this inquiry.

In the period under attention (1472/1582–1917/1949) Russia and China began by enduring Roman Catholic efforts to convert them and ended by conversion to Communism. The changing Western intellectual impact on the two countries over that long period is the subject of this study. The story is often one of the intellectual impact of various religious doctrines and thought patterns associated with them. Many of the Russians, Chinese, and Westerners studied were not primarily religious men, and some were not religious at all – aside from those who accepted the quasi-religion of Communism. Nevertheless it ought to be clear that the religious ingredient of the story was a vital one, and one that scholars (who are seldom fully trained in religion these days) may ignore at their peril.

ORIENTAL AND WESTERN SOCIETIES

Why have Islam and Communism made deeper inroads in the East than Christianity (though we should, to be sure, remember the extent that Nestorianism spread in Central Asia in the early Middle Ages)? Very possibly because Islam and Communism adapted the superb intellectual instruments of Greece, Rome, and Western Europe to the institutional circumstances of the Orient. In the societies of Egypt, Mesopotamia, India, and China (and later in the Aztec, Inca, and other societies far away) the characteristic pattern was one wherein a single ruler and the bureaucracy centered great power in themselves. Karl A. Wittfogel has in our day attributed the growth of despotism in the Orient – a phenomenon countless writers have discussed – to the power conferred by control of the large-scale waterworks upon which the irrigated agriculture of the great river valleys depended.[8] No social classes enjoyed wealth or status which did not depend ultimately on the favor of the central authority. The despot ruled by fiat; if there were laws, they were given by him (or his predecessors) and he could withdraw or ignore them. Private property might exist, even extensively, but it had no security or sanction against interference or seizure by the despotism. Typically the despot acted as high priest (or the priests were closely dependent on him); thus the Chinese emperor alone could make sacrifices to Heaven, on behalf of the whole society. Religious systems other than that of the state were seldom prohibited, and typically no requirement existed of active conformity to the state cult, though often overt challenge of it was punished. Outside the centralized state institutions there might exist local (communal or other) authorities that might deal with many of the everyday affairs of the people, but they were subject to central interference if need be. The individual was at the mercy of the authorities, being protected from injustice only by the character of the magistrates, who were enjoined to be just, or (if they were not so, and sometimes if they were) by bribery; but no laws, no institutions, no religious or philosophical teachings maintained any basis for the notion of individual rights. In fact, van Leeuwen uses the phrase *horror individuationis* (abhorrence of the concept of the individual),[9] to be found in the religious and non-religious concerns of what Weber calls the 'primary' civilizations of the East.[10]

The Oriental pattern may be summed up schematically as follows:

(1) political monism: concentration of significant political authority in a single center;

(2) social monism: dependence of all social groups on the central authority for what limited enjoyment of rights and property is theirs;

(3) weak property: possession of which is conditional and subject to un-limited interference;

(4) arbitrariness: the rule of men rather than of law;

(5) lack of emphasis on the individual, with the Indian *horror individuationis* at the extreme but in any event the absence of any generally accepted doctrine that the individual has absolute value.[11]

In other contexts further refinements and illustrations of such a pattern may be needed. Here it may suffice as a rough characterization of the kind of society that existed in China, some would say from the foundation of the Empire in 221 BC, but at least after the Sung dynasty (ended 1258), and that took form in Russia during the Muscovite period (*c*. 1450–*c*. 1700).

In Western Europe a different pattern emerged after the Dark Ages and the rise of feudalism. In the West there was a plurality of social classes, so that nobles, clergy, townsmen, and peasants not personally enslaved lived side by side under conditions in which no single one of these groups was powerful enough to impose its will unconditionally on the others. Typically the king was in origin the senior feudal lord, and feudalism was pre-eminently a system characterized by poor communication and fragmented power. The king, unlike the later Roman emperors, was unable to make law simply by virtue of his own will. Law grew out of the customs of tribes, contractual arrangements among princes, nobles, towns, and ecclesiastical institutions, the decisions of legal advisers, and finally of courts, based on precedents either of Roman or 'common' legal origin. A law might be infringed by princes or other powerful persons, but the charge of violation might always be pressed to the point of punishment. In the Orient monarchs might be murdered by those who wanted their thrones; in the West they might – infrequently – be deposed or even executed for violating the law. Long before any notions of equality became current, law was regarded as something that bound mighty and lowly alike.

The rule of law in the West grew as social pluralism grew, and the inter-dependence of these two features received institutional embodiment, as early as the medieval period, imitating the form of the ecumenical councils of all Christendom – namely, in the estates or parliaments that mark the initial stage of constitutional government. At least the major social classes, including all freemen, were regularly represented in these assemblies, which were assumed to speak for the whole country to the prince who summoned them. The English Parliament survived and transformed itself into a democratically elected legislative body; the Diets of Poland, Hungary, Transylvania, and Croatia made the transition from medieval to modern times; even the memory of the States-General served to stimulate the revival of constitutionalism in France. The principle that the chief executive rules by consent of the people and in conformity with law is not a modern invention, but an inheritance from what is inaptly called the 'Dark Ages'. Constitutional government changed from aristocratic to democratic, consultative to legislative, but its twin pillars, social pluralism and the rule of law, remained.

The many-centered Western society has been based on recognition that the interests of groups and individuals differ. Clear sanction for individual rights is a relatively new development, but it is based on the ancient Christian doctrine that every man has absolute value, for in Christ there is 'no more Jew or Gentile, no more slave and freeman, no more male and female' (Galatians 3.28, Ronald Knox trans.). Institutions that fostered the domination of one or another ethnic group, slaveholder over slave, man over woman, existed, but the Christian doctrine always threatened and often was used to oppose such domination successfully.

The Western pattern may be summed up in this manner:

(1) political pluralism: that sharing of authority by princes, in law and fact, with central and local governmental institutions, developing into constitutional government;

(2) social pluralism: the existence of social classes whose property and rights were partly secured by contractual and other legal bases independent of princes;

(3) strong property: possession of which is secured by contract or clear title;

(4) the rule of law;

(5) application of the religious doctrine of the absolute value of the individual, unevenly and intermittently but nevertheless persistently, to secular institutions.

From early medieval times such features have persisted in Western Europe and spread to North America, Australia, and New Zealand; and in striking ways Japan (despite differences not needing exploration here) was similar.

THE DIFFICULTY OF 'CROSSING THE INSTITUTIONAL DIVIDE'

As Europeans reached out to every corner of the globe during the Age of Discovery, the likelihood that some cultural traits would be transmitted to the lands they visited was overwhelming, and the possibility arose that individuals or groups would accept entire cultural patterns from Europe. Among such patterns capable of export was Western thought, including thought about institutions – how they had originated, what they were or should be like, and how they could or should be changed. As the men of the East discussed their Western visitors (or invaders or conquerors), the question was posed whether part or all of the Westerners' institutions could be borrowed without part or all of the culture – or vice versa.

In Russia institutional borrowing from the West finally proceeded further than in any other non-Western country. Russia had for centuries possessed the Christian doctrine of the value of the individual, but by the fifteenth century the Oriental pattern was taking firm hold there. Paradoxically, this pattern was fixing itself on Russia precisely during the earliest stages of Western contacts. Western influences were important both in rationalizing the continuing growth in power of the single-centered Russian state and society (for example, in the work of Peter the Great) and in undermining that development, fostering a quite different sort of pattern (in the eighteenth century and after).

Kievan Rus, the geographical ancestor of the Ukraine, the institutional ancestor of Muscovy, was a land with some feudal characteristics. These included an intricate if not fully structured set of relations among princes and nobles providing some security for the tenure of property, a partially dependent peasant population, a dyarchy of authority between church and princedoms, and an economy combining primary agriculture with even more trade than was characteristic of the feudal West.

When Mongol overlordship was ended around 1450, however, the state now centered in Moscow rapidly took on new contours.[12] The earlier tsars were 'autocrats' merely in the sense of being rulers independent of foreign states; but their successors came to control all of society. A new service group (gentry or *dvorianstvo*) was created to replace the old hereditary boyars, and the weakened boyar class was largely massacred or dispersed by Ivan IV. About the same time the peasantry was bound to the soil, partly assigned to the management of the gentry and partly retained on lands belonging directly to the state. Trade changed character, the towns became less commercial and more administrative in character, the merchant and trading class was compelled to discharge state functions. Finally the independence of the Russian Orthodox Church was challenged and broken, and the clergy harnessed to state control. By Peter the Great's time the process was complete.

Peter's ambiguous domestic revolution both strengthened the despotism and gave posterity the means for weakening that despotism. During the eighteenth century and later the gentry used Western ideas to secure its own emancipation from state service, and thereafter some of its members began to consider emancipating the rest of the population. Social and political pluralism, a rule of law, and strong property were beginning to appear by the late nineteenth and early twentieth centuries.[13] Western political ideas, falling on ground made fertile by the Christian conception of individuality and perhaps by some residues from the institutional tradition of medieval Rus, helped institutional change advance rapidly. In 1917 Russia was approaching, if it did not stand squarely astride, the 'institutional divide' that separates the Oriental and Western patterns.[14] War and revolution jeopardized the fragile foundations of a Western pattern in Russia; Communist victory destroyed it. (Communism itself was a product of cultural Westernization, but explaining the paradox must be left till later.)

China's history was full of change, and Sinologists have rightly pointed out that notions to the contrary are founded on myth. Under the Chou 'dynasty', a feudal or semi-feudal society seemed to be forming, then began to weaken. The foundation of the Ch'in Empire in 221 BC dealt the semi-feudal pattern the *coup de grâce*. The separate states with their princes and nobles, the cities, and the peasantry all became subject to the rule of the emperors and their bureaucracy. The Ch'in dynasty was short-lived, but some features of the imperial order they created persisted for 2,100 years. The Confucian literati, after suffering under the Ch'in, were honored by the Han and subsequent dynasties and raised to the status of a kind of secular priesthood. Confucianism itself was transmuted from a doctrine of individual obligations and relations under Heaven, reflecting the looseness of a semi-feudal society, into the ideology of an imperial bureaucracy, which James Legge called 'imperial Confucianism'.

After the Han period Chinese unity crumbled, partly as a result of 'barbarian' invasions, and the growth in property of great local families made restoration of the centralized state impossible throughout the so-called Six Dynasties period (222–589), during which once again a semi-feudal society seemed to be taking form. The Sui and T'ang dynasties unified China once again, reviving a number of Han institutions including the Confucian examination system for recruitment of officialdom, which was now strengthened so that the old aristocracy came to be challenged by a new bureaucracy of talent. The taxation system was effectively reformed, and the very lay-out of the new capital, Ch'ang-an, in unflinchingly rectilinear fashion, reflected the system of rationalized control worked out by the T'ang.

Another interval of disunity followed the T'ang, but only a relatively brief one (907–60, the 'Five Dynasties' in the north and the 'Ten Kingdoms' in the south). The Sung dynasty, though sacrificing the possibility of reconquering all of the north to the security provided by subordination of the military to the civil government, established its rule over much of the country and gave the imperial institutions a kind of rigor that might justify the term 'despotism' for the whole remaining millennium of the Empire. The aristocracy was now clearly eclipsed by the bureaucracy recruited by examination,[15] a development in which the new use of printed books played an important part. After 1127 the Sung were driven out of their capital of Kaifeng, which was in the north, but the dynasty lasted until 1279 in the south. During the Sung social and political institutions became fixed in a pattern which remained sub-

stantially unchanged until the twentieth century, and from the time of the
Mongol conquest (which led to the establishment of the Yüan dynasty in
1271) to the present the whole of China proper (plus varying dependencies)
has been governed as a unit from the same capital, Peking (except for about
forty years under the early Ming and the period of Chiang K'ai-shek's rule of
the mainland). Trade developed but did not come to dominate the economy.
No single social group was able to establish a position from which it could
challenge the state or even protect privileges or rights of its own. Foreigners
ruled in the Yüan (1271–1368) and Ch'ing (1644–1911) periods, Chinese in the
Ming (between them), but the centralized Chinese bureaucratic state, or
despotism, which had taken shape by Sung times though its foundations may
have been laid under the Ch'in a thousand years earlier, persisted.

The question of whether China ought to borrow institutionally from the
West was not seriously posed during the first Western contacts in the time of
the Jesuit mission; it began to be raised by both Chinese and Westerners only
during the nineteenth century, when the Ch'ing dynasty had already clearly
evinced symptoms of decline – symptoms the Chinese had come to recognize
well over the centuries. Western-inspired political change was proposed by
one of the leaders of the T'ai-p'ing rebellion in its later phases. At least two
Western-style agencies had been installed within the Chinese governmental
framework: the customs office under Sir Robert Hart, the salt revenue administration under Sir Richard Dane. The Chinese navy and army were
almost entirely reorganized along Western lines, though the result was not
forces that had Western efficiency. In the very last years of the Manchus
constitutionalist projects were brought forward. Political monism was under
attack; social monism was not very seriously disturbed.

Russia's attempt at full-fledged Western democracy in 1917 proved premature, though there were decades of relevant political and legal experience
behind the leaders of the Provisional Government; China's attempt in 1911
was hopelessly in advance of possible success. The Westernized army, under
Yüan Shih-k'ai and then other generals, took over the little-damaged bureaucratic system with which the new Parliament was impotently struggling. There
was no real Republic and soon no more unity. The old single-centered system
broke into fragments, but only as the magical broom was broken in the legend
by the sorcerer's apprentice; each fragment reconstituted itself in miniature.
The Nationalists under Chiang K'ai-shek managed, after a decade and a half
of warlord regionalism, to restore something approaching effective central
government. Strides were made toward putting finances in order, creating a
genuine court system, and making elective parliamentary institutions opera-
tive. The time was too short. The Sino-Japanese War intervened, exhausting
the Nationalist regime, and the Communists took their opportunity.

The character of the social and political processes under way in Russia after
1700 and in China after 1900, though they were advancing irregularly, is
scarcely in doubt: they constituted institutional Westernization.

Cultural Westernization had some relation to these processes in both countries. In China, a few European missionaries influenced T'ai-p'ing leaders; a few missionaries had an impact on the reformers of the 1890's; John Dewey and Bertrand Russell provided some ideas for the radicals of the 1920's. In Russia a few Westerners were close to Muscovite tsars and Russian emperors; Western political and economic tracts were perused by reforming rulers; Western radical writings inspired Russian radicals at home and Western revolutionaries provided models for Russian revolutionaries in Paris, Zürich, and London.

'Western thought' was many things, successively and alternatively, and there existed no such thing as a full-fledged analysis by Westerners of what the essential institutional characteristics of the West were, let alone any ready-to-hand prescription for non-Westerners who desired to establish a similar social and political system. Western thought, as it was exported to the East, naturally tended to consist not of an explanation of the unarticulated assumptions and assumed prerequisites for the writings of current interest in the West, but simply those writings. The result was something like delivery of a library from each of whose books the initial chapters had been torn, or a series of speeches over a public-address system that works only in the final minutes of an evening. For a long time few Easterners had the time or opportunity needed to supply themselves with the necessary background.

If institutional Westernization was the objective, then most of the *thought about institutions* that was carried eastward was insufficient. Military technology tended to be imitated first, constitutions later, but there were treatises' on such subjects. The question of the kind of status, experience, and habits essential to the exercise by a free man of effective citizenship was rarely discussed in the writings available; the problem of institution-building at a given moment by conscious will instead of gradually by history and tradition was scarcely explored. Equally, in the East, there were few theorists of despotism; many of the defenses of autocracy in Russia, for example, drew on the thought of Western conservatives who opposed the ideas of the French Revolution but who never thought of supporting the unlimited fiat of an Oriental potentate, while Confucianism contained all sorts of avenues for the critique of bad rulership and no very trustworthy philosophical defenses for arbitrary acts of a ruler. Major inroads on the foundations of the single-centered society of Russia were made by the initiative of successive autocrats, who along with their advisers were often deeply influenced by the wish to borrow Western institutions; even Tz'u Hsi in the last imperial years was persuaded to abolish the examination system and set in motion constitutional changes, while Chiang K'ai-shek never questioned that the Western political model was one that he must follow. There was surprisingly little dispute about the need for institutional change in either Russia or China once the question was clearly posed.

Thought about institutions was, then, not in the forefront of debate, either on the part of Westernizing Russia or Chinese or on the part of their opponents

Institutional Westernization advanced – or did not advance – in a curious disjunction from cultural and intellectual Westernization. Russia seemed to come to the brink of the 'institutional divide', and after a few months fell back from it into something quite different from the Western pattern; China nominally hurtled over it, but the Chinese then realized something was wrong, tried to correct it, and after a third of a century had to acknowledge failure. 'Crossing the institutional divide' is a task that several peoples have set themselves; in no large country has it yet clearly occurred in modern times. If the thought had been more carefully attended to, the institutional results might have been more satisfactory; but Westerners who even today prescribe instant parliaments and presidencies as possible, even necessary, remedies for the social ills of the non-West are in no position to find fault with the Russians and Chinese who attempted the colossal task.

PHASES OF INTELLECTUAL WESTERNIZATION

There are some reasons for regarding the process of exporting Western culture as a continuum, but it seems best to distinguish several successive phases, however arbitrary. At the time of the Age of Discovery, and long afterward, the intellectuals of the West were mainly clergy, as they had been almost to a man in the Middle Ages. In this respect the West was unlike Byzantium, for example, where quite a number of distinguished secular intellectuals flourished during the same centuries. Outside their home continent, these clerics were missionaries; they were Roman Catholics almost without exception, since the Protestant mission movement developed only later; and those who had a significant intellectual impact came mainly from the Society of Jesus. Jesuit preparation was literary and scientific as well as religious, and thus this period is termed that of 'Roman Catholic humanism'. The dissolution of the Jesuit order in 1773 brought this period to an end, with the single and curious exception of Russia, where the Society found a haven until it was restored by the papacy.

The period of Protestant influence overlapped with the previous one in Russia, where it rapidly surpassed Catholic tendencies in importance, in the form first of scholastic and then of pietist influences. Protestant scholasticism never reached China, and indeed any kind of Western intellectual impact was nil for much of the eighteenth and the early years of the nineteenth century. The pietists came to China in force, and for decades had some degree of effect, but they were rather rapidly swamped by modernists in the early twentieth century. Protestant modernism had minimal impact in Russia.

Out of Protestant philosophy in Western Europe came, in the nineteenth century, several teachings with a tacitly or aggressively secular orientation, partly reacting against the whole Christian tradition, partly transmuting it into new forms: they were liberalism and socialism – in both anarchist and Marxist varieties. They influenced Russia first, and later China and the rest of

Asia and Africa. In Russia and China Marxism, in its Leninist form, achieved victory.

The phases to be studied may be schematized as follows:

WEST	RUSSIA	CHINA
Roman Catholic humanism	1472–1730 (1773–1815)	1582–1722 (1722–74)
Protestantism		
scholasticism	1717–c. 1840	no significant impact
pietism	c. 1750–1824	1807–c. 1900
modernism	(1890–1925)	c. 1900–c. 1925
Liberalism	c. 1770–1917	c. 1900–c. 1925
Socialism		
anarchism	c. 1840–1917	(1905–22)
pre-Leninist Marxism	c. 1860–1917	no significant impact
Marxism–Leninism	1903–17	c. 1918–49

Such a chart cannot, of course, distinguish the intensity, extent, and significance of the phases enumerated. However, it may serve as a guide to the narrative and analysis that follow.

It has already been argued that currents of thought in Russia and China that stood for total rejection of Western intellectual influence were surprisingly rare and weak, over the whole period. They existed, and will occasionally be mentioned, but they are not the subject of this study. What will be considered is syncretism – here used (in a manner not entirely original, but not precisely as other writers use it) to refer to currents of thought in which there was an effort to combine ideas drawn from the West with ideas coming from the indigenous tradition. The term is not entered in the above chart, because syncretism was not peculiar to any period. In Russia it may be found in the almost unique Juraj Križanić, circles close to the tsarevich Alexis Petrovich including the prelate Stefan Yavorsky, some great writers and thinkers in the later nineteenth century, and in several different strands of the thought of the Silver Age just before the Revolution. In China examples are to be found among both the European Jesuits and Catholic and non-Catholic Chinese influenced by them in the seventeenth century, and then not again until K'ang Yu-wei, Liang Ch'i-ch'ao, and a few others in the twentieth. In our own day cultural syncretism is having a substantial revival in Russia, though it has thus far not often been recognized as such; its exemplars have been closely scrutinized by outsiders for signs of political opposition, and the regime has been all too ready to attach such a stigma to them, despite the fact that their concern with politics may be limited or non-existent. Few traces of such thought have been observed in China since the Hundred Flowers interlude in 1957, but the Chinese intellectuals have had millennia of experience in adopting protective coloration, and if syncretic ideas reappear in the near future no one should be surprised.

The Russians and Chinese who were open to Western influences and often embraced them with enthusiasm were few in number. In this area quantitative measurements may produce more confusion than clarity. For one thing, in such a society as existed in autocratic Russia and China, one man – the ruler, if his position was firm at the moment – might be as good as a heavy majority. It will not do to assume the existence of a kind of free market of ideas akin to that of the West. The ruler could and did intervene time and again to decide the fate, sometimes permanently, of one or another of the currents studied: Peter the Great's ecclesiastical reform and Alexander I's virtual establishment of pietism in 1817 and disestablishment of it in 1824 are Russian examples; in China it was the K'ang-hsi emperor who rendered judgment on the vexed question of the meaning of the Rites, even though the Jesuits obeyed papal authority despite the fact that they thought the emperor right.

Secondly, small groups often exerted a weight out of all proportion to their numbers – a phenomenon not unknown in the West. In the nineteenth century there were many more Chinese Catholics than Chinese Protestants, and yet the latter were clearly more influential in that period. There were but a handful of Communists in Russia in 1917, and yet the much more numerous liberals, non-Communist socialists, and anarchists were defeated by them. Intellectual history, like other history, has had a way of being made not by majorities or in some instances even sizeable minorities, but by the few who are powerful – sometimes in intellect, sometimes in managing the weapons of political control.

Having mainly the West in mind, Alfred North Whitehead makes some telling remarks whose force is only increased by reflection on the intellectual Westernization of Russia, China, and the rest of the non-Western world:

The great conquerors, from Alexander to Caesar, and from Caesar to Napoleon, influenced profoundly the lives of subsequent generations. But the total effect of this influence shrinks to insignificance, if compared to the entire transformation of human habits and human mentality by the long line of men of thought from Thales to the present day, men individually powerless, but ultimately the rulers of the world.[16]

FOREWORD TO VOLUME 1

THE HIGH CULTURE OF PRE-MUSCOVITE RUS

> Now in the manner of Euripides
> I will the Passion tell which saved the world.
> Unknown author of the Byzantine
religious drama, Christus Patiens[1]

In the words of B. H. Sumner: 'Byzantium brought to Russia five gifts: her religion, her law, her view of the world, her art and writing.'[2] That is to say, Russia (or Rus, to use a more precise term for the period) acquired her high culture from Byzantium. Russian historians, for example B. D. Grekov, have noted that there existed in Rus, long before a Slavic alphabet was created and Greek books were translated, a preliterate culture of great interest which 'has often – and completely undeservedly – been ignored', and Grekov compares this culture with that of the Druids before Caesar came to Gaul.[3] The preliterate culture of Rus deserves respect and attention, like that of many other so-called barbarian peoples of Europe and elsewhere before they accepted conversion to world religions and opened up for themselves the possibility of attaining a high culture.

To be sure, world religions and high cultures have not always been inseparable. Greece and Rome, for example, produced high cultures of a kind that gave the Western tradition ever afterwards its standards of what the very phrase 'high culture' means, though their religious pantheons remained provincial and limited, while ancient Judea produced nothing by way of a non-religious high culture but a religion which at least held the potential of a world religion – a potential fully realized later by Christianity and Islam.

Rus had no high culture, religious or non-religious, before the introduction of Christianity. In this respect the Rus were no different from any of the other Indo-European and Uralic barbarians who streamed into Europe after the Roman Empire had become Christian and who acquired their high culture from the Empire.

It has been pointed out that the ancient Eastern Slavs, although they possessed some deities comparable to those of ancient Greece and Rome, such as Yarilo (Apollo) and the Domovye (Penates), lacked any one parallel to Athena or Minerva, the goddess of wisdom.[4] That is no matter for surprise. None of the early medieval barbarians had any such deity. What is of moment is that the Rus acquired no 'goddess of wisdom' from Byzantium after conversion.

In the work from which the verse quoted in the above epigraph comes, some students have seen ridiculous incongruity (perhaps confusing a genuinely comic mixture of styles with a not so obviously ill-matched juxtaposition of ideas).[5] In fact the verse may suggest the fundamental feature of Byzantium's high culture: it married ancient Greek and in part Roman thought to the Christian religion. The resultant marriage was not always without dispute and difficulty. While Aristotle stimulated commentary after commentary from Byzantine scholars over the centuries (with an apparent break between the seventh and eleventh centuries), Plato was suspect from the time of the condemnation of Origen's teachings in the sixth century, and when the great Psellus attempted a Platonic revival in the eleventh century it was attacked and crushed with the help of authority.[6]

Aristotle and Plato have never been a satisfactory basis for creating a culture unifying an intellectual elite with the ordinary people – this was true of Byzantium as of other societies. In the Byzantine Empire, however, a high culture came into existence which did penetrate to the plebs and unify society; it was a Christian culture – Greek Christian, but not specifically Hellenic Greek Christian. Perhaps it can be argued that this was the first high culture in history to penetrate to the level of the ordinary man. Or, perhaps, it is better to suggest that the high culture of the sophisticated theologian, learned monk, and trained schoolman and the low culture of the urban and rural masses were different aspects of the same thing.

The channels through which Christian culture reached the Byzantine masses were chiefly two: the liturgy and monasticism. As Baynes points out, there were two principal Byzantine monastic traditions. One followed the mystical and ascetic line of the solitary, which may be traced from Origen through Maximus the Confessor and St Simeon the New Theologian to the Hesychasm of the Mt Athos monasteries; the other emphasized the communal and active life, after St Basil the Great and St Theodore of Studion. The holy man, writes Baynes, was 'the realization of the Byzantine ideal'.[7] The monk, to whichever of the two traditions he owed more, might not be a cleric at all, and when the layman outside the monastic life turned to him for inspiration or counsel, there was no formal social barrier to cross.

Of course the ordinary layman and the monk did not cross paths every day. For a large proportion of the 'Romaioi' (the Byzantine term which was the Greek word for 'Romans' and meant in practice anyone who adhered to the Imperial Byzantine Church)[8] there was a different channel by which Christian culture reached them regularly and frequently. It was the liturgy, by means of which the written word, painting, music, architecture, and the decorative arts were combined in the service of God. Byzantium's 'five gifts' to Rus were almost all those of the liturgy. Byzantine law, which was Roman law harmonized with a version of the Christian ethic, stood outside the liturgy, but the latter was the medium by which the other gifts were transmitted. The Rus acquired the reflection of Byzantine high culture in Byzantine low culture which came through the liturgy. They did not acquire either the Aristotle, Plato, and Euripides of the Byzantine scholar or the habits of trained exercise of the mind deriving from discussion of Christian theology by Greek writers educated in the philosophical schools; or, more precisely, they acquired very little of the latter and virtually none at all of the former.

Why did they not do so? The essence of the answer comes from the fact that the Eastern Christian (unlike the Western Christian) tradition was to use local vernaculars as liturgical languages. Having accepted Christianity from Byzantium instead of Rome, the Rus were under no compulsion to learn a classical language. Not Greek but Church Slavic was the language of the divine service. There was a long succession of Greek metropolitans and clerics who held office in Rus and a number of South Slavic clergymen who knew Greek visited or emigrated to Rus, and yet few of them, as writers or thinkers, seem to have left any mark on the Rus's high culture.

According to the Russian Primary Chronicle, the decisive element in the conversion of the Rus to Byzantine rather than Roman Christianity (or Islam or Judaism) was aesthetic and not theological. In the churches of Constantinople, reported the envoys of Prince Vladimir,

We knew not whether we were in heaven or in earth. For on earth there is no such splendor or such beauty and we are at a loss to describe it. We only know that God dwells there among men, and their service is fairer than the ceremonies of other nations. For we cannot forget that beauty.

There is reason to believe that this passage from the Chronicle is no very satisfactory account of the reasons for Vladimir's conversion, but as a source for popular conceptions of religion among the ancient Rus (and to an extent modern Russians), it has its place. Russian Christianity from the first sought to reproduce the beauties of the services of the Constantinopolitan churches. Byzantine iconography, ecclesiastical architecture, and liturgical music were imported at once, and became the starting point for brilliant and original achievements by the Russians themselves. Byzantine learning, for the most part, never arrived.

What Byzantine literature was brought to Russia may be summed up in the words of André Mazon:

extracts from the Fathers, homilies, edifying collections with highly poetic names (*The Bee, The Pearl, The Emerald, The Golden River*), lives of saints, the popular Bible or *Paleia*, apocryphas of Bulgarian origin, like that of the Wood of the Holy Cross or that of the Journey of the Virgin Through Torments, chronicles (chiefly those of Malalas, Hamartolos, and Manasses), Josephus' Jewish War, translated very freely in Russia after the Greek text and decorated with interpolations about Jesus which have earned more attention than they deserved, the epic of Digenis Akritas, in which one would like to find the basis for an ancient epic poetry almost no traces of which, however, remain, and, of course, juridical texts depending chiefly on canon law.[9]

As a result, Old Russia's most gifted Christians achieved much in the field of aesthetics and ethics, little in the field of thought. Old Russia was a land where the categories of goodness and beauty were honored, and where the category of truth lagged far behind.[10]

The culture of Old Russia was a silent culture. Father Georges Florovsky begins his basic study of Russian 'theology' (and other aspects of thought) with the remark: 'In the history of Russian thought there is much that is puzzling and incomprehensible. To begin with, what is the significance of the silence of Russia, lasting for ages, too long and too protracted?'[11] Those seeking to write the history of Russian philosophy have found great difficulty in getting around this fundamental obstacle: there existed next to no Russian philosophy, until very recent times. There was, from the early centuries of the Christian era, culture among the Eastern Slavs; from the tenth century at least, there was high culture, including thought – for centuries, almost exclusively religious thought; but there was no philosophy in the Western sense until the nineteenth century was well along. Prince Eugene Trubetskoi argued that Russian icon painting constituted a system of what he called 'speculation in oils', and his point is well taken.[12] But that is not philosophy. Much of Russia's intellectual history is in consequence a striking example of the aphorism: 'He who has no philosophy is condemned to borrow another's.' This is not to argue the value of philosophy or its indispensability to peoples; it is simply to point to the historical record of what occurred.

The conversion of the Rus to Christianity did not occur in an instant. There was a bishopric in Kiev before Oleg captured Kiev about 882, after which Kiev reverted to paganism. Grekov takes seriously the tradition, dating from the fourth century, that the apostle Andrew had preached to the Scythians,[13] but nothing is known about any Christianity among Eastern Slavs before the ninth century. Princess Olga certainly went to Constantinople to be baptized in 957, and doubtless Christianity had followers in princely circles before Vladimir accepted Orthodox baptism in 989 in the Greek city of the Black Sea coast, Kherson.[14] There were other alternatives still. Papal missions appeared at the court of Kiev in 991 and 1000. Vladimir and his successors had close relations with other newly baptized barbarian rulers and their heirs who had accepted Christianity from Rome.

The differences between Byzantine and Rome with regard to religion were not in the tenth century what they subsequently became. The brutality of the West Europeans in the Fourth Crusade (1204) was probably more important than the Schism of 1054 in dividing them and the countries that followed their respective leads. Around the turn of the eleventh century Vladimir's children married into the royal houses of Hungary, Sweden, and Poland, and a few decades later the children of Yaroslav the Wise added France and Germany to this list. Royal marriages went in the same direction as active trading relations. Trade moved through the Baltic Sea, first in the ships of the Rus and after about 1240 by way of the Hansa, and overland to Regensburg and other centers of Central Europe, and commerce with Byzantium also continued.

The Church of Kievan Rus knew men well-versed in Scripture and apparently other learning of the time, such as the Metropolitans Ioann II (d. 1089) and Kliment Smoliatich (twelfth century). The former was Greek, the latter a Rus. Of both the chronicler writes that there had never been such a learned man in the land of Rus.[15] The Kievan Church also had gifted preachers, such as Hilarion of Kiev (mid-eleventh century); laymen deeply imbued with the Christian ethic, such as Prince Vladimir Monomakh (d. 1125); ascetics devoted to Byzantine traditions of monasticism, chiefly to the one which emphasized communal living and good works, such as St Feodosy, a founder of the Monastery of the Caves (Pecherskaia Lavra) in Kiev.

'Probably the most potent channel of Byzantine influences in Russia', write Meyendorff and Baynes, 'was Monasticism.' It was the rule of Theodore of Studion which was introduced in the Monastery of the Caves, and the subsequent monastic foundations followed a similar pattern; some seventy were established in or near towns up to the middle of the thirteenth century. Of 61 Russian saints canonized by 1549, 23 were founders or superiors of monasteries.[16] The Monastery of the Caves became 'the center of Russian national thought, the fountainhead and school of the Russian ecclesiastical leaders'.[17] The monastery was founded in the days of Yaroslav 'the Wise', of whom the chronicler writes:

Great is the fruit of book learning; by books we are shown and taught the ways of repentance, we acquire wisdom and conscience from the words of books; they are rivers watering the universe, they are the fountainhead of wisdom, by them we are comforted in sorrow, they are the bridle of temperance.

All the ingredients seemed to be present for the development of a high literary culture in Kievan Rus. Some of its literary monuments were indeed noteworthy: the Russian Primary Chronicle, the epic poem entitled *Tale of the Host of Igor*,[18] the fragments of orations and essays from such men as Hilarion of Kiev and Vladimir Monomakh. The only thing that can be said is that the potentialities were not fully realized. The Kievan state underwent a process of disintegration in the twelfth century; the nomadic incursions from the southern steppe demanded much of its energies; the shift of trade routes to the south, connected with the Crusades, hampered its economic growth. Probably the single most important obstacle to purely cultural development was the lack of access to any outside tradition of higher learning, since few in Rus of the Kievan period learned Greek and there were insufficient translations from Greek (classical or Byzantine) literature to serve as a substitute. In any event the time allotted Kiev was short. In the eleventh century monasteries were founded; already in the twelfth century Kievan unity was shattered; in the early thirteenth century came the Mongols.

By its sheer destructiveness the Mongol conquest struck a formidable blow at the still young Russian Church and its islands of literacy and learning. But the unexpected happened. The Church revived and enjoyed an heroic period of growth despite Mongol (or Tatar) domination, for the Mongols, in accordance with their law, guaranteed freedom from taxation and recruitment to clergymen of all religions and to learned men generally, from Rus to China. During the period of Mongol rule Novgorod established close relationships with the Baltic trading centers of the Hanseatic League, but for the most part the connections between Rus and both Western Europe and Byzantium were impeded if not severed during the initial phases of Tatar rule. The Russian Church was thrown almost exclusively back on its own resources. Kiev was devastated. The newer monastic centers of the northeast, such as Suzdal, had to serve as the basis of revival.

Before the Mongol conquest there had already been a few efforts at monastic colonization and missionary activity; for example, from 1159 the monk Avraamy had spread Christianity among the Votiaks (Udmurts) and Cheremis (Maris). However, only after the Mongols came did a new type of monastic institution arise, no longer following the pattern of association with urban settlement, but appearing in rural and indeed wild regions, even ahead of peasant migration. As new monasteries were founded, more often on eremitic than on the previous cenobitic lines, so learned clerics appeared anew and important translations were newly made.

The chief inspiration of the eremitic (or *skit*) colonizing monasteries was St Sergius of Radonezh (1319–91). It is doubtful that he or his contemporaries can be credited with much knowledge of the Byzantine movement, contemporary and parallel to that of the hermits of Rus, known as Hesychasm;[19] in Epifany the Wise's *Life* Sergius is portrayed as a boy who had difficulty with his studies, so that comprehension finally came 'not from men but from God'. The Monastery of the Trinity and St Sergius (Troitse-Sergieva Lavra) in present-day Zagorsk, which grew up around the saint, served as the point of departure for two lines of monastic colonization, one northeastward via the Kostroma river toward the Vychegda, the other slightly northwestward via the Sheksna to the White Lake (Beloe Ozero), where the Monastery of St Cyril of the White Lake was founded, by Cyril himself, in 1397. Missionary activity accompanied part of the movement of monastic colonization. The monastery of Valamo on an island in Lake Ladoga, founded by the monks Sergius and German, was a center for a mission to the Karelians; a monastery on an island in Lake Onega, founded by the monk Lazar, sponsored a mission to the Lapps.[20]

The greatest of the medieval Russian missionaries was St Stephen of Perm (1340–96). He was a learned man, inventing a new alphabet for use in converting the Permians or Zyrians of the northeast, even though the Muscovite Church soon adopted a policy contrary to such cultural pluralism in Rus and the Permian Church did not survive as such. Stephen and his contemporary Metropolitan Alexis of Moscow were among the few Rus credited by medieval sources with having some knowledge of Greek. One monastery in Rostov had a library of Greek books which Stephen used as a young man, and in Rostov cathedral one of two choirs sang in Greek.[21] His most important achievements, however, were in the northeastern wilderness, and there also were the most visible traces of the medieval florescence of the Russian Church generally. The movement continued into the fifteenth century, when nineteen new monasteries were founded by the monks of the White Lake region, including one in 1429 on Solovki island in the White Sea which later achieved renown. It was from this great colonizing surge that the group of the so-called Transvolgan Elders emerged in the fifteenth century, chief among whom was St Nil of the Sora. The whole movement seems to have had partly indigenous roots, reflecting the hermit monks' perception of needs prompted by contemporary conditions in Rus, but it also was inspired, at any rate in its later stages, by some knowledge of Byzantine Hesychasm and its literature.

Much of the latter was brought to Rus by South Slavs. Among them were Cyprian, a Bulgarian educated in Greece who became metropolitan in Rus (1389–1406); his nephew Gregory Tsamblak, who also became metropolitan; and Pachomius, a Serb who wrote saints' lives in the Monastery of the Trinity and St Sergius.[22] A number of important translations were executed on the soil of Rus, probably seldom by Russians and much oftener by South Slavs, both translating into Church Slavic.[23]

Among the 'extracts from the Fathers' referred to by Mazon in the passage quoted earlier as being translated in Kievan times were some doctrinal works: by St John of Damascus and St Gregory Nazianzen, with a commentary by Nicetas of Heracleia, which were widely used, St Athanasius's *Contra Arianos*, which apparently was not. In the later fourteenth century were translated several works of Pseudo-Dionysius the Areopagite, with whose obscurity the Rus were ill-prepared to wrestle.

More popular were works of homiletics and ethical uplift. In Kievan times St John Chrysostom became the best loved of the great Greek preachers, along with St Ephraim the Syrian. In the late fourteenth century many more guides to the Christian life became available in translation, in particular materials dealing with mysticism. Earlier mystical works, such as those of St Isaac the Syrian and St Simeon the New Theologian, were translated and in addition contemporary authors expounding the Hesychast movement in Byzantium. It was Metropolitan Cyprian who introduced the veneration of St Gregory Palamas (d. 1359), the central figure of Hesychasm, into Rus. However, the doctrinal basis which Palamas and others gave to the revival of the ascetic tradition of mysticism in the Byzantine Empire remained less familiar to the Rus than its practical consequences for the monastic life.

What the monastery could provide the learned Russian ecclesiastic in the latter fifteenth century is indicated by the sole surviving catalogue of such a library which we have: that of the monastery of St Cyril (d. 1427) of the White Lake (Beloozero).[24] It is known that this monastery was one of the richest in manuscripts. It had 212 volumes, surpassed only by the Holy Trinity Monastery of St Sergius, which had about 300. Liturgical works numbered 110; lives of saints, ascetical works, and miscellaneous collections had 20-odd each; issues of dogma were dealt with in only 4 volumes. Fedotov points out that every single volume was religious in character.

Since the libraries of early Rus were of such a kind, it is easy to appreciate that secular literature was not even an issue. *The Emerald* (*Izmaragd*), a book of devotional readings probably first compiled by a fourteenth-century Russian from Greek materials, in arguing that ignorance was worse than sin and thus advocating the reading of books, assumed that all books were sacred books – and moreover, divinely inspired books, considering neither secular nor heretical[25] works to be any problem. And yet it champions books in tones suggesting they were much in need of defense, vigorously challenging the view that books were only for monks. The contents of the *Izmaragd* were entirely ethical and in fact moralistic in character. Its message is: be good. The message is carried to a clearly non-Christian point in emphasizing the dangers of unworthy participation in the Eucharist. The devotional handbook in question, hundreds of copies of which have survived to the present day, probably had a significant effect. However the fear of unworthy communion, which led to the practice of infrequent communion in the whole Russian Church, clearly is older than *The Emerald*.

The character of the translated literature of Kiev and Mongol times, the distribution of types of works in the medieval monastic libraries, and the case of *The Emerald* help to make clear the reasons for the suggestion that not only was old Russian culture 'silent' rather than conceptual, but also that its values were partly for that reason incomplete. The beauty of the divine service, appealing powerfully to the worshipper through eye and ear, and the emphasis on practical godliness or goodness through the pastoral writings and admonitions which were current, overshadowed the search for intellectual comprehension of God's works, sacred or secular, in Russia or, briefly, the search for beauty and goodness overshadowed the search for truth.

The deficiency might have been remedied by the kind of exposure to the Byzantine heritage which only a much more widespread command of Greek could have permitted. Before the Russians could undertake the task of arming themselves linguistically and in general intellectually for such an advance, the West began to make its presence felt in Russia. The objective of renewal of the Russian Orthodox Church and old Russian culture through closer acquaintanceship with the Byzantine heritage was repeatedly posed after the fifteenth century, and finally was approached in part by the scholar-priests of the nineteenth and twentieth centuries. But after the fifteenth century there was a powerful twofold complication: the growth of the influence of the West on Russia, and also of the influence of the West on Constantinople and the remainder of the Orthodox East[26] – after 1453 subject to Ottoman rule and constantly threatened by organizational corruption and intellectual stagnation. (There was powerful influence by Byzantium on Western Europe during the Middle Ages, and it did not cease with 1453; but soon it came to be the

West which influenced the lands of Eastern Orthodoxy more than the reverse.[27])

In the late fifteenth century, then, the Russian Church could not be regarded as a haven of learning, and the high culture it had developed was not mainly one of literature and thought. Nevertheless there was vigor and strength in Russian Christianity: in the monastic centers, though such spiritual athletes as Sergius of Radonezh and Nil of the Sora regarded them with some ambivalence; in mission movements to the north and east; in devotional concerns, and in particular in the Russian ascetically mystical movement that was developing. During the reign of Ivan III, there began a confrontation of Russian Christian culture, with all its strengths and weaknesses, with two new forces: the culture of the Roman Catholic West, and the absolutism of the Muscovite state. They were formidable forces, and it remained to be seen whether either or both would be, from the standpoint of Russian Orthodoxy, harmonious complements, competitors, or adversaries.

RUSSIA SCALE 1 : 9,000,000

0   100   200   300   400   500
MILES

NORWAY

SWEDEN

FINLAND

1689

WHITE SEA

Solovki

Archangel
Kholmogory

N. Dvina

Pechora

Perm

Stockholm

Helsinki

Viborg

Lake Ladoga

Lake Onega

White Lake

1462

Vologda

Viatka

Kama

BALTIC SEA

Narva

Tsarskoe Selo

St. Petersburg

Reval

ESTONIA

Dorpat

LIVONIA

Pskov

Novgorod

Yaroslavl

Kostroma

Rostov

Nizhni Novgorod

Volga

Kazan

Riga

COURLAND

Memel

LITHUANIA

Königsberg

Danzig

Braniewo

Marienburg

Poznań

Pultusk

POLAND

Warsaw

Lodz

Brest

1914

Lublin

Sandomierz

Kraków

Sambor

Lwów

Dniester

Vilna

Nowogródek

Minsk

Polotsk

Vitebsk

Smolensk

Orsha

Mogilev

BELORUSSIA

Dnieper

Rovno

Goszcza

Ostrog

Kiev

Vinnitsa

Chigirin

Khotin

Kamenets-Podolsk

MOLDAVIA

Volokolamsk

Mon. of Trinity
and St. Sergius

Moscow

Tver

Vladimir

Kaluga

Tula

Yasnaia Poliana

Riazan

Orel

Sevsk

Chernigov

Lubny

Poltava

Kharkov

Samara

Penza

Tambov

Saratov

Voronezh

Don

Volga

Rostov-on-Don

Astrakhan

HUNGARY

Budapest

TRANSYLVANIA

Kishinev

Kherson

Odessa

Taganrog

1689

TRANSCAUCASIA

Belgrade

WALLACHIA

Bucharest

SERBIA

Danube

BULGARIA

Sofia

CRIMEA

Sevastopol

Kerch

Bakhchisarai

BLACK SEA

Tiflis

ALBANIA

GREECE

Mt. Athos

Constantinople

TURKEY

UKRAINE

1*

THE MEETING OF ROME AND MOSCOW (1472–1533)

Offend not, O Tsar, the holy churches of God and the honorable monasteries, which God has given as an inheritance of eternal goods, for the memory of the last generation.   Filofei of Pskov, writing to Vasily III

THE BACKGROUND OF THE IDEOLOGICAL STRUGGLE

In the late fifteenth century the spiritual and cultural strength of Eastern Orthodox Christianity, more or less successfully indigenized from Byzantium, was exemplified in Russia chiefly by the Transvolgan Elders or Hermits (*startsy*), whose leader was St Nil of the Sora (1433–1508).[1] A powerful challenge to Orthodox Christian doctrine was newly presented by the 'Judaizers', an heretical group evidently akin to proto-Protestant or even Antitrinitarian currents in the West, which appeared first in Novgorod and then in Moscow, and which gained support at court and more or less openly from Grand Prince Ivan III (1462–1505) himself. The 'Judaizers' were vigorously combatted by a third faction led by St Joseph Sanin, abbot of Volokolamsk, and Archbishop Gennady of Novgorod, known as the 'Josephites' or later 'Possessors' (*stiazhateli*) as against the 'Non-possessor' (*nestiazhateli*) Transvolgans. The Transvolgans refused to join in the Josephite campaign against the Judaizers, and their obstruction can even be said to have served as a protection for the heretics, though there is no evidence whatever that St Nil or his followers accepted Judaizer doctrines.[2]

As the Josephites' ideological offensive gained momentum, it became directed against not only the Judaizers but the Transvolgans as well. Despite his attraction to the heretics, Ivan III yielded at last to Josephite pressure, and his successor Vasily III appeared to decide the struggle in favor of the Josephites. In order to obtain assistance in the debate, he called for monks from Mt Athos, the intellectual and spiritual center of the Orthodox world. Maxim the Greek, who came to Muscovy as a result, became identified with the Transvolgans rather than the Josephites; he was defeated along with the Transvolgans and he was imprisoned.

Western influences are to be discerned in all three parties to this remarkable ecclesiastical, political, and in general ideological struggle. Doubtless the

---

* Parts of pp. 11–23 of this chapter also appear, in revised form, in the author's article in A. Blane (ed.), *Russia and Orthodoxy: Essays in Honor of Georges Florovsky* (Mouton & Co., S-Gravenhage, 1972).

Judaizers had some debt to the West, though its character is difficult to determine. The Josephites eventually drew heavily on Western sources and argumentation. Even the most gifted of the Transvolgans' spokesmen, Maxim the Greek, proved to be strongly influenced by the years he had spent in the West (of which his Russian contemporaries knew little or nothing) and to have accepted much of what may be called 'Roman Catholic humanism'.[3]

This struggle may be said to mark the close of the Russian Middle Ages, in the sense that it resulted in the gradual submergence of Byzantine influences and the end of princely resistance to Muscovite centralization, and the beginning of modern Russia in the sense that there began to take root the idea of a state that was not only independent but secular and the idea of a high culture whose achievements were to be measured to some extent by Western standards.

THE INTERNATIONAL POSITION OF IVAN III

Relations with three entities conditioned the international position of Muscovy and its grand prince at the time of Ivan III's accession in 1462: the Tatars, the papacy and the Roman Catholic states, and Byzantium – both the real or imagined heritage of Rus's relations with the fallen (1453) Empire and current relations with the patriarchate of Constantinople and other Greek hierarchs under Ottoman rule. Relations with the Tatars need no discussion here; they never had a significant cultural component (though they had important cultural implications, since the Mongols let the Russian Church grow without interference), and the decline of the Golden Horde made even the political importance of the cessation of tribute in 1480 more symbolic than real.

Before 1453 there had been several attempts to adjust relations between the Roman Catholic West and the Greek Orthodox East, profoundly damaged by the Fourth Crusade (1204) and the ensuing period of the Latin Empire in Constantinople (to 1261). Renunion of the Churches had been accepted by two Paleologi emperors: Michael VIII at the Second Council of Lyon in 1274[4] and by John VIII at the Council of Ferrara–Florence in 1439, with the assenting signature of Isidor, the Greek who was metropolitan of Kiev and thus senior prelate of the Russian Church. The 1274 union was fiercely resisted in the East and never put into effect. That of 1439 was implemented for a time in parts of Greece. However, out of 29 Greek prelates who signed the act of union, 21 repudiated it on returning home,[5] and in general it was also a failure.

When Isidor returned to Rus as papal legate and cardinal, he met a hostile reception. Though in Kiev he seems to have achieved acceptance of reunion of the Churches, shortly after his arrival in Moscow in 1441 he was arrested by Grand Prince Vasily II (1425–62).[6] Soon afterward he escaped to Rome. The Muscovite principate repudiated the union.

The actual see of Kiev lay by then within the state of Lithuania, which had entered a dynastic union with Poland in 1385. In 1299 Maxim, metropolitan of 'Kiev and all Rus', had found the city untenable and had gone north to establish himself in the grand princely center of Vladimir. His successor, Peter, moved to Moscow and died there in 1326.[7] In the following decades the Lithuanian princes, in particular Olgerd (Algirdas, 1321–77), expanded their realm southward to include the depopulated Kievan lands right up to the Black Sea. Shortly before his death Olgerd accepted Orthodox Christianity, but when his son Jagiello (Yagailo) married Jadwiga of Poland, the dynasty became Roman Catholic and remained so. The new union, however, proved fragile; Vitovt (Vytautas, 1392–1430) secured from his cousin Jagiello recognition as grand prince of Lithuania. Vitovt chafed at the fact that the ecclesiastical superior of the great majority of his subjects, who were Eastern Slavs, was in Moscow. In 1415 an attempt was made to establish a separate metropolitanate under Gregory Tsamblak, but it lasted only four years. Casimir IV (1446–92) managed to unite the two thrones again and succeeded in obtaining, with the support of the former Kievan metropolitan Isidor, the establishment in 1458 of a Uniat metropolitanate in Kiev. The see was assigned to Gregory the Bulgarian (not to be confused with Gregory Tsamblak, also a Bulgarian). However, in 1470 Gregory was received into Orthodoxy and recognized by the patriarch of Constantinople, Dionysius I, as 'metropolitan of Kiev and all Rus'.[8] After the repudiation of the 1439 union, a council in Moscow had, without Constantinople's approval, elected as metropolitan of 'Kiev and all Rus' Iona, bishop of Riazan, in 1448. He died in 1461, and his successors, in order to assert the importance of the city in which they lived, entitled themselves metropolitan of 'Moscow and all Rus'. From 1470 there were thus two Orthodox metropolitanates for the Eastern Slavs.[9]

The action of the patriarch of Constantinople in recognizing the see of Kiev and not that of Moscow as legitimate angered Ivan III. In an epistle to Iona, archbishop of Novgorod (not to be confused with Metropolitan Iona), Ivan warned him against any relations with the 'false metropolitan of Kiev, Gregory', and declared that since Orthodoxy had been debased among the Greeks what the patriarchs of Constantinople did henceforth was of no concern to him.[10]

Without knowing the tangled background of such a repudiation of the link with Byzantium, one might find it difficult to fathom the meaning of the marriage that Ivan was at that moment engaged in arranging – one with the niece of the last Byzantine emperor, Constantine XI.

Ivan's first wife, a princess from the Russian principality of Tver, had died in 1467, and his opportunity to remarry was also an opportunity to raise Muscovite prestige. Already a few Westerners were in Moscow. One of them, Giambattista della Volpe, a man from Vicenza who had been entrusted with the supervision of Muscovite coinage, sent two agents back to Italy to seek additional skilled assistants. Their arrival prompted someone at the court of

Pope Paul II to consider trying to arrange a marriage. The choice fell on Zoe Paleologa, the late emperor's niece, whose family was Uniat and who herself had converted to Roman Catholicism. In 1472 Zoe proceeded with a retinue headed by a papal legate, Antonio Bonumbre, and including the two Uniat Greek brothers Trakhaniot, through Germany to Lübeck, by boat to Reval, and through Pskov to Moscow. When she reached Pskov Zoe reverted to Orthodoxy. It was an Orthodox ceremony through which she was married to Ivan in Moscow in November 1472, and she received the new name of Sophia.

The significance of Ivan III's marriage to a Byzantine princess has been misunderstood. Arnold Toynbee has depicted it as a Byzantine restoration in Moscow,[11] but the conclusion is clearly unfounded. Despite her family tradition, Sophia had been raised in Rome and had no clear memories of Byzantium. Many in Moscow aptly called her 'the Roman woman'.[12] K. V. Bazilevich, who recently examined the question of Sophia's responsibility for introducing Byzantine influences into Russia, justifiably brands it as simply a 'legend'.[13]

In many ways the marriage may be justifiably termed 'the beginning of Russian Westernism'.[14] It was followed by several Muscovite embassies to Italy, especially Milan and Venice. One such embassy returned in 1475 with the architect Aristotle Fioravanti, who proceeded to build the Cathedral of the Dormition of the Virgin (Uspensky Sobor) in the Kremlin, and other Italians constructed the Hall of Facets (Granovitaia Palata) during the same period. Diplomatic intercourse with other European states followed: with Stephen the Great, hospodar of Moldavia, by 1480, with Matthias Corvinus of Hungary by 1485; the first envoy of the Holy Roman Empire, Nicholas Poppel, visited Moscow in 1488.[15] It was to Poppel that Ivan made a well-known statement (enunciated for him by the official Fedor Kuritsyn) in which he rejected what he regarded as being an offer of kingship, though Poppel had offered only to intercede with the emperor to obtain a crown for Ivan.

The arrival of Italian architects and European diplomats is clear enough. Much more obscure is the contribution of Western thought – or, at this stage, rather documents and intellectual devices – to the intricate struggle that ensued. Nevertheless we must try to disentangle it, for it constitutes the beginning of our story.

THE 'JUDAIZER'–JOSEPHITE–TRANSVOLGAN DISPUTE

Heretics in Novgorod and Moscow

According to Joseph Sanin, the 'Judaizers' appeared in Novgorod in 1470. It is possible that the group had some relation to the sect of Strigolniki (perhaps 'Shearers', though we are not certain to what the term referred), which is first mentioned in the chronicles for 1375/6.[16] We know that they protested against simony among the clergy. They were charged with holding that clergy who owed their positions to simony were *ipso facto* deposed and in effect with rejecting the legitimacy of the entire Russian Orthodox clergy on that ground; avoiding the sacraments of the Eucharist and penance because they were administered by false clergy, and resorting instead to the rite of confession to the Earth (a pagan survival not peculiar to the sect);[17] and rejecting the 'tree of life', that is, the Eucharist, identifying themselves instead with the 'tree of thought' (*drevo razumnoe*), whose basis was Scripture.[18] We have none of their own writings; the latest surviving document of the polemics against them is the epistle of Metropolitan Foty of Pskov of 23 September 1427.[19] They were thus roughly contemporaries of the later Waldensians, to whom they bear some resemblance,[20] but there is no evidence of influence. Fedotov is probably right in concluding that 'the Strigolniks simply repeated on Russian soil the religious experience of the Western sects'.[21]

One piece of evidence suggests that some Strigolniki survived into the late fifteenth century. In an epistle to the council of 1490, Gennady, later archbishop of Novgorod, writing as the abbot of a monastery, attacked one of the monks named Zakhar as a Strigolnik and recorded statements of his accusing the entire clergy of simony and giving this as the reason for abstaining from the Eucharist. Such tenets were Strigolnik and not Judaizer in character.[22] As Klibanov points out, it is unlikely that Gennady would have overlooked any heresy of Zakhar's, and yet he makes no mention of the iconoclasm or anti-trinitarianism of which the Judaizers were accused. Any filiation between the Strigolniki and the Judaizers remains conjectural, but it may cast light on the religious situation in Novgorod, a city deeply involved in trade with the West, to know that sectarians had existed there for a century before the Judaizers made their appearance.

On contrast to the Strigolniki, the Judaizers left behind some of their own writings,[23] though the chief sources are still the works of their opponents, in particular the *Enlightener* (*Prosvetitel'*) of Joseph Sanin.[24] In 1470, he reports, Prince Michael Olel'kovich was summoned from Kiev by the pro-Lithuanian faction in Novgorod and brought with him a Kievan Jew named Skharia. The latter at once began to convert others to his beliefs, which included denial of the Trinity and refusal to venerate saints and ikons. Among his converts were two priests, Denis and Alexis. When Ivan III visited Novgorod in 1480, he took these two men back with him to Moscow, where they began to spread the heresy in the capital. It has been widely assumed that these were the circumstances through which the heresy of the Judaizers was transplanted from Novgorod to Moscow and that a single Judaizer heresy existed throughout the period from 1470 at least to 1504.

However, in a recent study Lur'e has challenged the view that the term 'Judaizer' is appropriate at all and has argued that the Novgorod heresy must be distinguished from the Moscow heresy.[25] Even if the two were more closely related than Lur'e believes, it may be fruitful to start from the fact that the Novgorod heretics were punished by the councils of 1490 and 1503–4, the

Moscow heretics by only the councils of 1503–4, and examine what happened in two stages.

The first stage is more difficult to puzzle out. Although Joseph Sanin had previously attacked the Novgorod heretics,[26] after he resigned the abbacy of Borovsk monastery in 1479 in order to found a new one at Volokolamsk he became bolder in his charges. Borovsk monastery was under the territorial authority of Ivan III; Volokolamsk was 'under the protection of Ivan III's brother and antagonist, Boris'.[27] Thus Joseph identified himself with the patrimonial princes resisting the claims of the grand prince of Moscow.[28] The Novgorod heretics seemed to be identified with the burghers of the city, many of whom were willing to make common cause with Ivan and Moscow against the local boyars.[29] As the campaign against the heretics was intensified, Ivan III and Metropolitan Geronty of Moscow showed reluctance to take any steps against them.

In 1484 the new archbishop of Novgorod, Gennady (Gonzov), took up cudgels in opposition to the heretics, and Joseph reports that many fled the city to escape him.[30] In 1488 Gennady demanded punishment for two Novgorodian priests and two laymen accused of heresy; the grand prince and metropolitan proceeded against three, but they let the fourth off.

Despite the campaign in Novgorod, the heresy was by this time taking root in Moscow. According to Joseph, among the converts were Fedor Kuritsyn, a high-ranking secretary at court who specialized in foreign affairs; Zosima, then archimandrite of the monastery of St Simon; and, most important, the wife of the grand prince's eldest son Ivan, Elena of Moldavia, whose son Dmitry might aspire to succeed as grand prince instead of Sophia's son Vasily if fortune should smile. The heretics seem to have been associated with ideological efforts to buttress the grand prince's power. It is likely that Fedor Kuritsyn was the author of the *Tale of Dracula* (*Povest' o Drakule*), a work dealing with a fearsome but actual ruler of Wallachia; Kuritsyn had gone on an embassy to Moldavia and Hungary in 1482–4. In a fashion somewhat similar to that of Ivan Peresvetov half a century later, the author of the *Tale* 'undoubtedly approved' Dracula's harshness toward the great Rumanian boyars and upheld 'the necessity of even cruel, but just and impartial power'.[31] It was Kuritsyn, as already noted, who in 1486 conveyed to Poppel Ivan's reply concerning the possible grant of a crown from the Holy Roman Emperor, in which Ivan contended that his ancestors had ruled from the beginning in their own right. In 1489 his claims were restated and buttressed, in a missive to the emperor, by references to the friendship and love borne Ivan's ancestors by 'the first Roman emperors, who gave Rome to the pope and themselves ruled in Byzantium'.[32] Lur'e notes that it is 'curious' that the envoy who carried this missive was Sophia's servant Yury Trakhaniot, who was evidently instructed not to refer to the hereditary rights of his own mistress. Lur'e does not mention that Ivan's assertion that Roman emperors gave Rome to the pope is, as Medlin puts it, the 'first known reference by Moscow' to the *Donation of*

Constantine (*Donatio Constantini*),[33] which will appear again in our narrative. This same Western document (which had already been proved a forgery but was accepted by Russians then and later as genuine)[34] was also used by the anti-Ivanite circle of Gennady in a somewhat different manner.

The Gennady circle

In order to deal with the heretics who had become so firmly lodged in the councils of the grand prince, at the end of the 1480's Gennady organized a literary circle which would use the best ideological weapons available against the enemy. Its members included as a sort of director Gerasim Popovka, a deacon and later archdeacon; his brother Dmitry Gerasimov, translator and diplomat educated in Livonia; and a Slavic, probably Croatian, Dominican monk, Veniamin (at least as early as 1491).[35] Some men in Moscow, especially the Uniat brothers Trakhaniot, were also working closely with the Novgorod circle.[36] In 1490 Yury Trakhaniot was evidently an intermediary in arranging talks between Gennady and Georg von Thurn, envoy of the Habsburg emperor, which are recorded in *Conversations with the Imperial Envoy* (*Rechi posla tsesareva*). The work contains an account of the Spanish inquisition, 'with a developed analogy between the Spanish and Russian heretics ("marranos" and Judaizers)'.[37] Its central idea is that of 'unity of the ecclesiastical and secular powers in the spirit of the concordat of the pope with (though he is not mentioned by name) Ferdinand the Catholic'. Obviously the conversations made a deep impression on Gennady. In the same year, 1490, he wrote to Metropolitan Zosima: 'With what tenacity do the Franks [lit. for *friazove*, meaning "West Europeans"] hold to their faith! The envoy of the emperor told me about the Spanish king and how he cleansed his country.'[38] Gennady would do likewise.[39]

In 1492 there was produced a work entitled *Tale of the White Cowl* (*Povest' o belom klobuke*), probably by Dmitry Gerasimov.[40] According to this work, a white cowl, symbolizing purity of faith, was presented to Pope Sylvester I by Constantine the Great. When, however, the Apollinarian heresy[41] had triumphed in Rome, an angel frightened a later pope into returning it to Constantinople. Another vision was needed to make Patriarch Philotheos (1354–5, 1364–76) transmit it to Novgorod to Archbishop Vasily Kalika (in office 1331 to 1352, and therefore too early to receive anything from Philotheos as patriarch): in the vision appeared Constantine and Sylvester, and it was the pope who told him that the third Rome was now in Russia (*Na tretiem zhe Rime, ezhe est' na Ruskoi zemli*) – Malinin points out, the writer does not quite dare to say 'Novgorod', as he might prefer to do, and will not say 'Moscow'. Therefore Russia is to be called 'Holy Russia' (*i strana narechetsia svietlaia Rosiia*). Sedelnikov points out that the work contains a reflection of the *Donation of Constantine*, which mentions the white cowl as the headdress of Sylvester I, and plausibly concludes that the intent of the author was to defend the prestige and inviolability of the domains of the archbishop of Novgorod.[42]

As the year 1492 (7000 by the Orthodox calendar) approached, there was much speculation that the world would end during that year.[43] The heretics were ridiculing such expectations, which many Orthodox clerics took seriously. In 1489 Dmitry Trakhaniot composed an explanation of why the apocalypse would be delayed, and in 1495 Gennady translated a part of the medieval treatise by William Durandus called *Rationale divinorum officiorum* which dealt with calendrical problems.

In 1497 another work was published by the Gennady circle entitled *Brief Discourse Against Those Who Would Violate the Movable and Immovable Property of the Universal Church* (*Slovo kratko protivu tekh, ezhe v veshchi sviashchennye podvizhnye i nepodvizhnye sóbornye tserkvi vstupaiutsia*). Probably composed by the monk Veniamin in Latin and translated by Dmitry Gerasimov, this polemic defended the faith against heresy and the inviolability of monastic properties against any possible plans of the grand prince to secularize them.[44] Recently a new version was brought to light that showed tempering with the original; for the name of Charlemagne, that of Prince Vladimir (under whom Rus was converted) was substituted, and from the phrase 'we Christians, Greeks, Rus, and Latins' (*gretsi rus' i latini*) the words 'and Latins' had been removed.[45] Zimin suggests that Joseph Sanin's advocacy of the primacy of the clergy over the secular power was influenced by the *Brief Discourse*, which upholds it at length; in any event the work furnishes an especially clear case of Roman Catholic influence on the Josephites.[46]

The most impressive achievement of the Gennady circle was the collection of Biblical translations finished in 1499. It contained several books partly or wholly translated from the Latin Vulgate: the Wisdom of Solomon, Paralipomena Jeremiae, Ezra, Nehemiah, Tobit, Judith, Maccabees, Esther, Proverbs, and Sirach.[47] The chief student of this enterprise writes, 'the foreword and explanatory articles in the Gennadian Bible constitute the first contribution of medieval Western scholasticism to Russia...'; Gennady's Biblical collection marked 'the first serious victory of Catholicism on Russian soil'.[48] Other translations were made, including those of two Western treatises against Judaism: in 1501 the work of Nicholas de Lyra, a fourteenth-century Franciscan, called *De Messia eiusque adventu*...and in 1504 a treatise by a certain Samuel.

In 1504 Gennady disappears from history and the work of his circle seems to have ended. In the late 1480's a great effort had been needed simply for Gennady to secure copies of all the books the heretics were using and to distribute them to those clerics who might prepare replies; by 1504 the literary arsenal of the Josephite, anti-heretical camp was a substantial one, owing to the work of the Gennady circle.

The dispute (1490–1504)

In 1490 the pro- and anti-heretical camps engaged in an inconclusive test of strength. The metropolitan, Geronty, died, and was succeeded by Zosima, himself influenced by the heretics. Gennady demanded that a council held in October consider the problem. Several suspected heretics were jailed or excommunicated, though the council refused his demand for capital punishment. Some were returned to Novgorod for action by Gennady. He had them

mounted on horse-back on pack saddles and their clothes...turned back to front, and [he] bade them turn their backs to the horses' heads that they might not look to the west [?] at the fire prepared for them; and on their heads he ordered [to be placed] birch-bark hats, pointed like devils' hats, with bast cockscombs and rims made of straw mixed with hay and with labels written in ink on the hats: 'behold the army of Satan!' And he ordered them to be led through the town...and then he had the hats which were upon their heads burned.[49]

This curious treatment was the precise result of what he had learned about the methods of the Spanish Inquisition from von Thurn.

Present at the council of 1490 were St Nil of the Sora and Paisy of Yaroslavl; judging from their views expressed later, one may speculate that they might have resisted Gennady's zeal for punishing heretics.[50] The council of 1490, argues Lur'e, was the moment of the Josephites' victory over the Novgorod heretics, whom he wishes to distinguish rather sharply from their fellow heretics of Moscow. As evidence that the two groups were different he mentions that Metropolitan Zosima, who was close to the Moscow heretics, took an active part in the condemnation of the Novgorodians, and even after Zosima was forced out of his post in 1494 heretics remained in high positions in Moscow right up to 1502-4.[51] Though the Moscow heretics accepted Scripture, they denied ecclesiastical tradition, and chief among the elements of tradition they attacked was monasticism. There were, to be sure, extreme radicals among them; but the leading strain seems to have been merely a challenge to the Church Fathers, for example to the expectation founded in patristic writings of the end of the world in 7000 (1492). Metropolitan Zosima wrote an *Exposition of the Easter Cycle* (*Izlozhenie paskhalii*) in 1492 in which he referred to Moscow 'and the whole Russian land' as 'a new city of Constantine' in the sense of replacing Constantinople in its universal significance.[52] Such assertions helped to form the official ideology of the autocratic state, and in general Lur'e stresses the link of the Moscow heretics with the grand-princely power.[53]

In the 1490's there seem thus to have taken form two alliances: one among the Moscow heretics, the court party around Elena of Moldavia and her son Dmitry, and perhaps to some extent the Transvolgan Elders; the other between the Josephites and the court party around Sophia and her son Vasily. The attitude of Ivan III was first favorable to the former, and then shifted toward support of the latter apparently against his own preferences.

Despite the fall of Zosima, the heretics' prominence continued in the

1490's. In 1497 there appeared the earliest document extant today that contains the two-headed eagle in the grand-princely seal, a charter written by Fedor Kuritsyn. The party of Elena was behind the exposure of a plot of Sophia against Dmitry in 1497 and the temporary disgrace of Sophia. In 1498 Dmitry was crowned Grand Prince of Vladimir, Moscow, and Novgorod – in effect, Ivan III's heir – and in the coronation ceremony there were used for the first time the regalia of 'Monomakh', which in contemporary writings (for example, the *Tale of the Princes of Vladimir* or *Skazanie o kniaz'iakh Vladimirskikh*) are connected with the alleged descent of Russian tsars from Augustus.[54]

The most prominent heretical official, Fedor Kuritsyn, had been instrumental in arranging the betrothal of Ivan's daughter by Sophia, Elena (not to be confused with his daughter-in-law Elena of Moldavia), to Grand Prince Alexander of Lithuania. The latter was accused of attempting to convert his wife to Roman Catholicism; this alleged offense may have been a reason for the Muscovite war with Poland–Lithuania of 1499. We may surmise that Ivan was reluctant to engage in this war, as he was at odds with Elena's mother Sophia and his relations with the heretics could be used to embarrass him in a war over an ostensibly religious issue.[55] In 1499 Sophia helped to induce harsh measures against the so-called 'old boyar' party, in particular Ivan's aides Prince Ivan Yurievich Patrikeev and his son Vasily and Prince Semën Ivanovich Riapolovsky. Both Patrikeevs were saved from execution only by the intercession of Metropolitan Simon;[56] Riapolovsky was executed. At about the same time Sophia's son Vasily was named Grand Prince of Novgorod and Pskov, leaving Moscow and Vladimir to Dmitry. Soon afterward Fedor Kuritsyn's name ceased to appear in documents. In April 1502 Dmitry and his mother Elena were placed under house arrest, but already since the previous August Vasily had been entitled Grand Prince of All Rus.

When Vasily received this title Ivan III remained the 'greater' sovereign, and from this situation may come the use of the appellation 'the Great' by Westerners. But in fact Ivan had become nearly the captive of his enemies. The Josephites won along with Sophia. At a council in August 1503 the question of the Moscow heretics was raised, along with the question of the justifiability of the monasteries' possession of large landholdings. On the eve of the council Joseph Sanin had had extensive conversations with Ivan, who made a partial confession of error and in effect capitulated to the Josephite party in advance of the council. The council did not take final action, but another council in December 1504 decided to execute a number of heretics. In Lur'e's view, Joseph Sanin's *Enlightener* (in the shorter redaction) must be regarded as documentation for the indictment of the heretics by the council of 1504.[57] Several were burned, including Ivan Volk Kuritsyn, brother of Fedor, and Ivan Maximov, brother-in-law of the priest Alexis (d. 1490) who had been instrumental in leading Elena to embrace heresy. Severe punishments were meted out to others as well. Ivan III died the following October.

By this time the divergencies between the Josephites and the Transvolgan Elders were clear. At the council of 1503 St Nil of the Sora, with Ivan's apparent support, attacked the amassing of large monastic properties, and Joseph Sanin, who had already left the meeting, returned to defend it. On this issue the terms 'Non-possessors' (*nestiazhateli*) and 'Possessors' (*stiazhateli*) came to be used; but the two parties also differed on the treatment of heretics. Joseph and his followers refused to accept the repentance of heretics as genuine once they were apprehended; the Transvolgan Elders, especially Vassian (the monastic name of Vasily) Patrikeev, were quite willing to do so.[58] Shortly before he died Ivan pardoned some repentant heretics, as if to reassert his closeness to the position of the Transvolgan Elders if not to the heretics themselves.

It remains to assess the degree of Western influence to be found in the various parties to the dispute of Ivan III's reign. The Transvolgan Elders exhibited, during this period, no visible Western influences; they represented the main strength of the indigenous Orthodox tradition as well as one tendency at least of Byzantinism. As shown above, their position was deeply rooted in the most significant developments that had taken place in the Russian Church under Mongol rule.

As for their doctrines, the 'Judaizers' or Novgorod–Moscow heretics have points of similarity with such proto-Protestant, anti-clerical, and semi-rationalist groups as the Hussites before them and the Antitrinitarians of Poland and Transylvania after them. No causal connection has yet been shown with either. They were at least willing, however, to go along with and perhaps entered with enthusiasm into the effort to construct a new official ideology of the autocratic state on the basis of pseudo-Western and non- or even anti-Byzantine claims, as shown by the use made of Fedor Kuritsyn by Ivan in his exchanges with Western rulers, Kuritsyn's probable authorship of the *Tale of Dracula*, the calendrical work of Zosima, and so forth.

The clearest Western influence on this dispute was on the Josephites through the Gennady circle and others. Their willingness to draw on the aid of Dominicans, the precepts and practice of the Inquisition,[59] and such Western documents as the *Donation of Constantine* in attacking heretics and defending monastic property is plain enough. Through Yury Trakhaniot, at least, they also participate in setting forth sweeping claims for the grand-princely power. The emphasis on tradition over Scripture in the Josephite *Svodnaia Kormchaia* (*Collection of the Rudder*) has been pointed out by N. P. Popov as a reflection of Roman Catholic influence.[60]

Ya. S. Lur'e sets himself the task of criticizing Popov's views and in general questioning the *extent* of Roman Catholic influences on Gennady's circle – though he does not attempt to deny the *existence* of such influence. However, he approaches the question in a curiously inverted religious form, asserting, 'we have no basis whatever for asserting that any of the Russian "accusers" [i.e., the Josephite leaders] sympathized with these [Roman

Catholic] tendencies'.[61] He refers to the very interesting and curious missive mentioned by Sedel'nikov sent to Pope Sixtus IV (1473–84), probably in 1473, from 'all of us true [*sushchikh*] Russian Slavs', which contains an unconditional recognition of papal supremacy,[62] as the only Russian document which reflects sympathy for the Union of Florence, and asserts that it has nothing to do with Gennady; it is true that no such link has been proven. (Sedel'nikov does hint that the brothers Dmitry and Yury Trakhaniot, who were heavily involved in the negotiations for Ivan III's betrothal to Sophia and who were members of Gennady's circle, may have been behind this missive.) But the issue of whether Gennady and Joseph were animated by a desire to become or to make the Russian Orthodox populace become Roman Catholics or Uniats is irrelevant to our concerns; the question is whether they were influenced by Roman Catholic thought and scholarship. Lur'e further points out that a whole section of the seventh chapter or discourse of Joseph's *Enlightener* is directed against the views of Latinizing heretics. But that is no more conclusive disproof of Roman Catholic influence than the fact that a given Soviet writer attacks 'Western capitalists' shows he is not influenced by the West, or even by persons party officials might consider 'capitalists'.

It is of little use to speculate whether for Gennady and Joseph, Western ideas about the primacy of the ecclesiastical power, the obligation to deal with heresy, and the necessity to use tradition to interpret and understand Scripture, were as attractive as what they were able to learn about the methods of the Spanish Inquisition or other instruments of the power of the Roman Catholic Church. There is evidence that both the ideas and the methods were used, which does not at all require us to suspect that the Josephite leaders were crypto-Catholics or crypto-Uniats.

Joseph was concerned to exterminate heresy, which he saw as a new phenomenon in Russia, not once mentioning the precedent of the Strigolniki. (He wrote that 'never before were there tidings of heresy in our land...'[63]) The Church had the preservation of orthodoxy and other important prerogatives to uphold and defend, and could do so properly only with the support of substantial monastic properties. It must act in close coordination with a single state power, not as part of the whole of Christendom or even of Eastern Orthodox Christendom. Muscovy must reject the Second Rome and become a Rome itself, a Third Rome.[64] The position of the boyars as close advisers to the grand prince was suspect and dubious: perhaps in principle, at any rate in the persons of the Patrikeevs and Riapolovskys, who along with the Transvolgan Elders defended the Second Rome, the Byzantine heritage. The boyars must be replaced by monks. (This view was protested by Vassian Patrikeev even though he had become a monk.[65]) In the last days of Ivan III this, the Josephite position, seemed to have carried the day.

VASILY III AND MAXIM THE GREEK

When Ivan died the persistent if irregular protection he had given the

'Judaizers' disappeared. Indeed the heretics themselves seem to have disappeared not long afterwards. In 1511 Joseph summoned Vasily III to chastise them; a Josephite publicist polemizes with antitrinitarians in the foreword to the *Khronograf* of 1512, and that is nearly all.[66] Fennell points to a certain 'Isaac the Jew, magician, sorcerer and seducer',[67] who was condemned by a council of 1520, as having been 'in all likelihood the last of the Judaisers to be detected and brought to trial'. But such an identification of Isaac is not certain, and has been questioned.[68]

What is certain is that the support Ivan III had shown the Transvolgan Elders before long found an echo in the policy of his son, who in 1505 became Vasily III. In 1509 the monk Vassian Patrikeev, who since St Nil's death the previous year was recognized as the leader of the Transvolgan Elders, was permitted to return to Moscow and to reside in the St Simon monastery. Its archimandrite, Varlaam, who sympathized with the Non-possessors though he was evidently not one himself, replaced Metropolitan Simon of Moscow when he died in 1511.[69] Meanwhile, Joseph of Volokolamsk was biding his time. In 1507, perceiving a danger to his monastery in the ambitions of the prince of Volok, he had placed it under the protection of the grand prince, was chastised by his archbishop, and was saved only by Metropolitan Simon and the Council of bishops, who removed and interned the archbishop, Serapion. Joseph died in 1515 at the age of seventy-six. Before his death there was chosen to succeed him as abbot of Volokolamsk the monk Daniel, who was soon to recoup the Josephite fortunes. Vasily III soon became friendly with him.

It was also in 1515 that Metropolitan Varlaam decided, evidently in agreement with the Transvolgan Elders, to seek out monks from Mount Athos who could correct defective texts and generally assist in raising the intellectual level of the Muscovite Church. Perhaps this decision came in connection with the disputes with the 'Judaizers',[70] but it may be doubted that the anti-heretic campaign was the main consideration in the minds of such men as Varlaam and his ally Vassian Patrikeev. The fact that the Transvolgan Elders had all along condemned the use of capital punishment against the heretics, as indicated above, argues in support of such doubts. It is of course possible that the Transvolgans wished to transfer the debate from the realm of punitive measures to the literary arena. Probably fundamental in their minds was the aim of renewing and strengthening the intellectual and ecclesiastical connection with Byzantium. Since the establishment of *de facto* autocephaly in 1448 and the fall of Constantinople in 1453, the Russian Church had had only the feeblest of relations with the senior Orthodox patriarchate.

The Muscovite embassy reached Constantinople at the end of the summer of 1515. The Turks showed their suspicion of their guests, but also their great interest in the sumptuous gifts the Russians had brought for Mt Athos. Many obstacles were placed in the way. Finally, however, Sultan Selim I, after his preferred candidate had declined and suggested in his own place

Maxim the Greek, chose the latter to go to Moscow. The embassy returned in 1518, accompanied by a number of Greeks hoping for additional Russian aid and support, but its chief cargo was Maxim.

Maxim the Greek has been shown to be the same as Michael Trivolis, a remarkably learned monk who spent more than half his life in the West.[71] Born at Arta in present-day Greece about 1470, he came from one of the great families of Byzantium, members of which had been friends and counselors of emperors and included a patriarch of Constantinople (Callixtus I, 1350–63).

About 1492 he went to Italy, and became immersed in the philosophical currents of Neoplatonism which owed much to Marsilio Ficino. Denissoff writes: 'One may even say that it was Marsilio Ficino and his disciples who, through the interpretation of Maxim the Greek, turned Russian thought in a Neoplatonist direction at the dawn of its philosophical history.'[72] This conclusion may not be easy to substantiate from the history of Russian thought in the decades or even centuries that followed Maxim's stay in Muscovy, but Maxim's own Platonism remained firm enough. In Florence he learned of the discovery of America, which he was to inform the Russians about decades later, studied with John Lascaris, and was powerfully influenced by the preaching of Savonarola. The total result was that he became a humanist with pagan overtones, and this he remained during stays in Bologna, Venice, and Milan and the four years he spent with Giovanni Francisco Pico della Mirandola, nephew of the great humanist (who died in 1494).

Experiencing a religious conversion about 1501, he returned to Florence to enter the Dominican monastery of San Marco. His own long-standing admiration for Savonarola had been stimulated by his stay at Mirandola, 'the last foyer of the defeated Savonarolian revolution',[73] and his choice of Savonarola's own monastery to enter reflected all this, but the conversion was lasting whereas his Dominican monkhood was not. He never revealed his Dominican period to the Muscovites. Nor did he dare cite St Thomas Aquinas, whose works he had studied carefully for a much longer period than his two years in San Marco, though he found a substitute in St John of Damascus, one of Thomas's own Greek sources.

It is unclear why he left San Marco, though the monastery was rent by divisions during his time there and no doubt disappointed his expectations. At any rate in 1505 or 1506 he had returned to Greece to become a monk at the Vatopedi monastery on Mt Athos. His writings there reflect his continuing Platonism in their radical dualism of soul and body and their treatment of the soul.[74] Chosen to go to Moscow, he thus brought (in a fashion doubtless unknown or not fully comprehended by either the Turks or Russians) the best scholarly training in philosophy, theology, and patristics available in his time. As Denissoff wryly puts it, 'a malicious destiny thus brought the ex-Dominican Maxim Trivolis to succeed the Dominican Benjamin'[75] – referring to Gennady's chief translator.

When Maxim arrived in Russia he did not know Church Slavic, and no one he worked with knew Greek; but a system was worked out by which he translated Greek originals into Latin and Russian translators rendered the Latin into Slavic. His gift for languages before long enabled him to translate directly, but under both systems errors were made which his enemies were later to use against him. He promptly became very friendly with both Vassian and Metropolitan Varlaam. The influence he had may be reflected in the charge later levied against Vassian that he followed the teachings of Aristotle and Plato; the name of Aristotle was already known in Russia, but Plato may well have been the more offensive name to his Josephite accusers. The charge of Monophysitism, a heresy in which the primacy of the spiritual is an important ingredient, might also, whether or not justified, mirror Maxim's Platonism. However speculative such observations might be, there is no doubt that Maxim's personality made a tremendous impression on all who knew him in Moscow, and since he was an intellectual of stature, his ideas must have been communicated to some extent to his friends.

Before Denissoff identified Maxim with Trivolis, it was known that Maxim had spent time in the West, and his chief biographer even produced a generally accurate account of where he had been, deducing, for example, that he had not visited Paris but had been only in Italy.[76] Scholars unaware of the identification naturally tended to concentrate on what he actually wrote and did in Muscovy. Nevertheless Ikonnikov manages to identify, as the men who chiefly influenced Maxim, John Lascaris (who Maxim told Prince Andrei Kurbsky had been his mentor in philosophy) and, above all, Savonarola, with whom he compares Maxim at length.[77]

In his writings Maxim took a line critical of the Roman Church. However, it is noteworthy that he also praised several aspects of Roman Catholicism openly and in other respects was silent about what others criticized. Whereas the accepted Muscovite enumeration of Roman heresies ran to thirty-two, Maxim criticized only the Filioque doctrine (of the Procession of the Holy Ghost), belief in purgatory, and the use of unleavened bread.[78] He recognized the Roman Catholic Inquisition as beneficial to religion; he did not hesitate to speak of the popes as the legitimate heirs of St Peter and of the primacy of Peter among the apostles.[79] He held up the morals of the French and Italian monasteries as a model for Russians to follow, though he made a practice of adding phrases like 'although they are Latin by faith' – Ikonnikov suggests, as a concession to those around him.[80] But Maxim went still further:

Thus the Latins, although in many ways they have yielded to temptation and invented certain strange doctrines, having been tempted by their own great learning in the Greek sciences, nevertheless have not finally fallen away from faith, hope, and love for Jesus Christ, and therefore those among them who have dedicated themselves to the monastic life assiduously order their service to God according to His holy commandments, since their harmony of belief, brotherly love, non-possessorship [nestiazhatel'nost'], silence, lack of concern for worldly things, and care for salvation in many ways ought to be imitated by us, so that we would not show ourselves worse than they. This I say in respect of the assiduous fulfillment of the commandments of the Gospels.[81]

Maxim worked in Moscow for seven years. His first task was to translate the *Interpreted Psalter* (*Tolkovaia Psaltyr'*), for which purpose he had assigned to help him Dmitry Gerasimov and one Vlasy. Maxim translated from Greek into Latin and the latter two translated from Latin into Russian. Gerasimov, born perhaps in the 1460's, had learned Latin and German as a child in Livonia, and served on diplomatic missions. Before assisting Maxim he had been, as a youth, one of Gennady's circle in Novgorod,[82] and may have been responsible, as already mentioned, for transmitting the essence of the *Donation of Constantine* to Russia. In 1525, after Maxim's fall, he was to be sent to Rome by the grand prince with a missive in which Vasily III expressed to the pope his willingness to enter into an alliance against the unbelievers. Returning the next year, he continued his translation work, producing another version of the Psalter with commentaries by the Latin Fathers in 1535. Gerasimov thus lived into the reign of Ivan IV.[83]

Outside of his translation work, Maxim polemized with several persons, including the interesting figure, Nikolai 'Nemchin' ('the German', or better, 'the Westerner') or Bulev, the personal physician of Vasily III,[84] and also his admirer, the Russian boyar Fedor Ivanovich Karpov.[85] It was not a very sharp kind of polemics. Karpov favored the union of churches and, being strongly attracted by the notion of an inalterable order of nature, had a strong interest in astronomy and astrology. Maxim cautioned him of the need to separate questions of faith and science. Another participant in these exchanges was the *diak* of Pskov (appointed 1510), Mikhail Grigorievich Misiur-Munekhin, also something of a Westernizer, with whom Dmitry Gerasimov corresponded at the time he was assisting Maxim.[86] It was in these very polemics with overt Westernizers that Maxim showed the restraint already referred to in criticizing Rome.

In the second decade of his reign Vasily III may have begun to weary of Metropolitan Varlaam's intervention in favor of persons he believed unjustly accused, and through the shrewdness of Daniel, the new abbot of Volokolamsk, was again drawing nearer to the Josephites with whom his mother had been allied. In 1521 Varlaam was deposed, and shortly afterward Daniel became metropolitan of Moscow.[87] By sanctioning Vasily's divorce of Solomonia (of the boyar family Saburov) and his subsequent marriage to Elena Glinskaia in 1525–6, Daniel bound Vasily firmly to himself and his party. Early in 1525 Ivan Bersen-Beklemishev, an outspoken courtier and friend of Maxim's, was executed. Soon afterward Maxim himself was condemned and he was incarcerated in none other than the monastery of Volokolamsk. Though forbidden to write, he nevertheless managed to compose a number of works defending himself and attacking abuses in the Russian Church. Thereupon Daniel had Maxim tried again in 1531 and the same council condemned

Vassian for good measure, Maxim was moved to the Otroch monastery in Tver; Vassian was confined in the cell Maxim had just vacated, where he died, probably not of natural causes, about 1532.

Maxim lived until 1556. The last thirty-odd years of the life of this remarkable savant were spent in confinement and largely wasted, as a result of the victory of the Josephites and the customs of doctrinal dispute in the Tsardom of Muscovy. As Sobolevsky points out, however, even during his imprisonment 'his authority did not decrease in the eyes of his contemporaries'. He was widely considered a pillar of Orthodoxy and of orthodoxy; just after his death someone wrote that he was 'a truly pious man and in him there was not a single heretical flaw'.[88] His exceptional spiritual qualities were posthumously recognized as those of a saint. A cult of Maxim as 'blessed' appeared a century (1651) after his death, and both Old Believers' and official Church icons depict him as a saint, even though the official Church, while acknowledging his sanctity, denies he has been formally canonized.[89]

His intellectual qualities, his breadth of outlook and devotion to truth, were not so widely appreciated until modern times. In his preface to the *Psalter*, Maxim wrote that the book 'is instructive for those studying theology and enlightening for those studying nature',[90] thereby making a distinction not widely recognized in sixteenth-century Muscovy. He pleaded against objections that he had been guided 'not by audacity or pride but by zeal for the best of everything and love for the truth'. Translators, he said, must be 'perfectly instructed in grammar, poetics, rhetoric, and philosophy itself'; though he freely confessed that he himself fell short of this ideal.[91] 'Thus,' concludes Ikonnikov, 'Maxim the Greek was the first man in Russia to treat the tasks of literature from all aspects and critically.'[92] Metropolitan Makary (Bulgakov) argued that 'in the person of Maxim the Greek, for the first time, European enlightenment, then already having begun to develop, penetrated to us and cast its rays, although still weak ones, on the dense gloom of ignorance and superstition enveloping Russia'.[93]

A few men in his own day perceived his gifts and, inspired by his example, continued after he was condemned their own contributions to culture begun under his guidance. Among these were the monk Silvan, who learned Greek well enough to act as a translator from it himself; Dmitry Gerasimov, who was to accomplish important translations in Novgorod in the 1530's under Archbishop Makary; Zinovy Otensky, who followed Maxim's teachings in many respects until his death around 1570; Vassian; and, perhaps most important of all, Prince Andrei Kurbsky, who when he fled to Lithuania from Ivan IV had a number of his books sent to him there, Maxim's foremost among them.[94] The result of Maxim's work was chiefly to strengthen the party of the Transvolgan Elders, who were inspired by him despite his condemnation, but his influence was not confined to them; Gerasimov, who had worked with the Josephites earlier and was to do so again, was an example.

In Maxim is to be seen a kind of humanism which owed much to the

Italian Renaissance. Despite Denissoff's suggestion that his neo-Platonism had substantial influence on Russian thought, it does not seem warranted to take such a remark very seriously. In the person of Maxim the Renaissance, in Denissoff's own words, was only 'a light zephyr incapable of melting the layer of ice which covered the land of Moscow'.[95] The depth and subtlety of Maxim's training and thought eluded most, though by no means all, of those about him. Such qualities did not prevent his being condemned, and an air of tragedy surrounds the story of this man who had so much to give to Russian culture and was permitted to give so little.

Maxim was, however, condemned not as a Westernizer but as 'the Greek'; in this respect he somewhat foreshadows Patriarch Nikon of the seventeenth century, whose intellectual antecedents were also somewhat misunderstood by his contemporaries. If the fact that he was Greek was not the real reason for his punishment, it was at least known that the Transvolgan party with which he had become identified was inspired by Byzantine teaching and example. It was not any external taint of the West that doomed Maxim, for he had none recognizable by Russians.

Maxim has been called 'the only learned man of Muscovite Rus'[96] and may be considered one of the earliest precursors of Westernization in Russia,[97] despite his deep roots in the Byzantine heritage. But his persecutors, the Josephites, have also their debt to the West. Their ready resort to Roman Catholic assistance, their willingness to borrow from the methods of the Spanish Inquisition, their use of Roman arguments and legends to buttress the position of the Church and state of Moscow, their eagerness to replace boyar with cleric advisers to the grand prince, their insistence on retaining large monastic properties, all owed much to Western inspiration. If Maxim drew on Italian humanism, the Josephites drew on Spanish and other Roman Catholic super-orthodoxy; if Maxim provides a flicker of reflection of the Renaissance in Russia, the Josephites give more than an inkling of the influence of the same trends from which the Counter-Reformation would develop. By the victory of the Josephites the strongest and most vital elements in the Russian Church – the monastic currents which derived from the great northeastern colonization, were reinforced by Byzantine contact, and found their highest expression in the Transvolgan Elders – were dealt a heavy blow. The way to further Western borrowings was opened, but not necessarily to contacts that would bring into Russia the finest fruits of Western Christian culture.

Vasily III himself was not a prime mover in the events that have been described, but he was by no means averse to the changes that were appearing in Russia's cultural orientation. Florovsky stresses that Sophia raised him 'in the Western manner'.[98] He was willing to have as his personal physician Maxim's friendly antagonist, Nicholas Nemchin, the adept in astrology and astronomy and supporter of the reunion of Eastern and Western Churches.[99] His second marriage, to Elena Glinskaia, which was accompanied by the triumph of the Josephites, strengthened the Western connection. He had welcomed to his court a number of Lithuanians who had been in the West, including the controversial and restless Prince Mikhail Lvovich Glinsky, uncle of his future second wife. Glinsky had spent twelve years in the West, having served in the armed forces of Albrecht of Saxony and the Emperor Maximilian I. In Italy he had converted to Roman Catholicism and learned the major European languages. Returning to Lithuania, he was one of the closest advisers to Grand Prince Alexander, who married Elena Ivanovna, daughter of Ivan III. After Alexander died in 1506 Glinsky fell out with Sigismund, the new ruler, and found it wise to flee to Moscow for protection. Vasily found his Western connections useful, but Glinsky's personal ambition almost undid him. When the Muscovites took Smolensk in 1514, he demanded the governorship of the new area – in vain, and in his chagrin planned to redefect to Lithuania. He was caught, and saved his life by reconverting to Orthodoxy (though it should be noted that as long as he remained loyal to Vasily his Roman Catholicism had been no obstacle to his success). He was imprisoned, but when Vasily chose Glinsky's niece as a second wife, he was released and was again appointed to important governmental posts.[100]

Vernadsky has suggested that the birth of a son in 1530 (the future Ivan the Terrible) strengthened Vasily's confidence that he had chosen the right path, and led him to support the strong measures against the critics Vassian and Maxim the Greek which had been taken in 1531.[101] He shaved his beard to make himself look of an age nearer his young bride, but in sixteenth-century Moscow shaving was also an act with religious and cultural meaning which implied Western leanings. He died when his son Ivan was three, and the immediate result was a dynastic crisis.

THE DOCTRINE OF 'MOSCOW, THE THIRD ROME'

It was near the outset of Vasily III's reign that the doctrine of 'Moscow, the third Rome', was set forth in fully developed form. Although the doctrine has probably received more attention than it deserved, in comparison to its actual official use or even to the seriousness with which its contemporaries took it (difficult as that is to assess), it serves a convenient marker on the path of several complex historical developments: the formation of the official ideology of the Muscovite autocracy; the transformation of the Josephites from critics and even attackers of the power of the grand princes into its defenders, paradoxically replacing the 'Judaizers' of the reign of Ivan III in that position; and the growth of Western influences in Russia.

In a letter to M. G. Misiur-Munekhin,[102] the elder of the Eleazar monastery, Filofei (Philotheus) of Pskov wrote:

All Christian monarchies have come to an end and have been gathered into a single monarchy of our sovereign, according to the books of the prophets, that is to say the Russian monarchy; for two Romes have fallen, the third stands, and a fourth there cannot be.[103]

In a roughly contemporary epistle to Vasily III he repeated the same idea. Along with it Filofei is concerned with two other major points: the desirability of filling the vacancy in the archbishopric of Novgorod and Pskov which the removal of Archbishop Serapion in 1509 (for opposing Joseph's transfer to grand-princely protection) had left,[104] and the inviolability of monastic properties. He is addressing Vasily III's governor in Pskov (1510–28), Misiur-Munekhin, and the grand prince himself. In effect he is pleading with the grand prince not to listen to the Transvolgan Elders – in particular Vassian Patrikeev – who are urging on him measures to secularize monastic properties and at the same time glorifying his power, which Filofei hopes will be used in other ways.[105] He must be regarded, on the basis of both his personal connections and his general argumentation, as a Josephite.

Various sources of the doctrine have been indicated. D. Strémooukhoff concludes that the idea was taken from the Gennady Bible, and was based on the image of the three-headed eagle interpreted as 'three kingdoms' in IV Ezra 11 and 12.1–39. IV Ezra was translated from the Latin Vulgate by the Dominican monk Veniamin assisted by Dmitry Gerasimov, with whom Filofei was in close touch. Lur'e confirms this conclusion with additional evidence, in particular a gloss on IV Ezra in a copy of the 1493 collection of Veniamin which he has located, and which may be taken to have been the work of Veniamin himself.[106] The most exhaustive examination of the work of Filofei is that of V. Malinin, who concludes that one of the chief sources of the doctrine was Dmitry Gerasimov's *Tale of the White Cowl*. Other suggestions have been made. What needs to be done is to analyze the idea of Moscow the Third Rome into its component parts in order to disentangle the evidence about its sources.

The doctrine has five overlapping but distinguishable elements: (1) the idea of a *translatio imperii*, or replacement of one seat of universal empire by another; (2) *translatio* from Constantinople to Moscow; (3) *translatio* from Rome (to Constantinople to Moscow); (4) justification of *translatio* on the basis of the faithlessness of the previous seat of empire; and (5) suitable scriptural basis for regarding the *translatio* as fulfilled prophecy.

The idea of *translatio imperii* was as old as Charlemagne's Holy Roman Empire – it was not needed when the capital of the same empire was simply moved from Rome to Constantinople. The Bulgarians also expressed it on behalf of Trnovo. *Translatio* from Constantinople to Moscow was first expounded, as far as is known, by Metropolitan Zosima in his *Exposition of the Easter Cycle* (1492).[107] The accusation of faithlessness against the Byzantines and explanation of their fall as due to it are made repeatedly and soon after 1453; for example, in 1471 in an epistle of Metropolitan Philip to the citizens of Novgorod: 'The Greeks reigned, the Greeks gloried in piety; they united with Rome, and now they serve the Turks'.[108] But *translatio* is not justified, or even mentioned, in such passages. Justification of *translatio* on the basis of faithlessness is given in Gerasimov's *Tale of the White Cowl* in 1492,[109] but it is *translatio* to 'Russia', not to Moscow, and the author's actual concern is with Novgorod instead.

Filofei combined Zosima's idea of *translatio* from Constantinople to Moscow with Gerasimov's of *translatio* from Rome to Constantinople to 'Russia' and produces a clear 'third Rome' in Moscow. He also provides an adequate scriptural prophecy of this event, in IV Ezra. He states that he composed his argument according to 'the prophetic books'; he refers to IV Ezra by name in another epistle;[110] Križanić later unhesitatingly identified the notion of Moscow the Third Rome with the three-headed eagle of IV Ezra;[111] the book was translated with the participation of Gerasimov, who was close to Filofei. Thus Filofei has combined all five elements.

The idea of *translatio* was current in the West since Charlemagne; the idea of *translatio* to Russia was contained in the *Tale of the White Cowl*, which was brought direct from Rome; in it is a Roman pope who pronounces that Russia is to be the Third Rome; IV Ezra was translated from the Latin Vulgate (it is not in the Septuagint) by a Roman Catholic monk; the notion that Constantinople fell because it betrayed the faith was at any rate reinforced by another Roman Catholic, Bulev. There is thus a basis for holding that the theory of Moscow the Third Rome was inspired by Rome itself – that is to say, by Roman Catholic influences on the Josephites.

Filofei proclaims Moscow the Third Rome, but he also boldly holds that the state guarantees to the clergy its properties (see epigraph to this chapter). This too he does on Roman authority. Medlin points out that the first authority Filofei invokes in support of his position is the *Donation of Constantine*,[112] and several after him were to cite this document as if it were Orthodox canon law. The Byzantine heritage was cast into the shadow; the position of the Byzantine Empire had been forever compromised by the treason of the Council of Florence; the Byzantine tradition, one version of which the Transvolgan Elders were endeavoring to defend and perpetuate, was not something the Josephites cared to glorify. Roman Catholic influences were more acceptable.

The fact that the fully developed idea of Moscow the Third Rome was advanced in Pskov by a Josephite at just the time of Vasily III's annexation of the state (1510) is not surprising. The Josephites were bidding for influence over the rapidly centralizing Muscovite state. The replacement of boyars by monks of their own party[113] was the means of attaining such influence. Moscow was to be glorified; but the Josephites were to retain their ecclesiastical properties, on the basis of which alone the monks might have some firm claim to be taken seriously. Fortified by Roman Catholic learning of a sort they themselves could not provide, the Josephites hoped to gain ascendancy in Church and state. The glorification of the Muscovite principate was a cheap price to pay for such an objective. They made their offer near the beginning of the reign of Vasily III, in the epistles of Filofei of Pskov. By the end of the reign Maxim (1525) and Vassian (1531) had been condemned and sentenced;

the Josephites appeared to be, and doubtless thought they were, victorious. They were wrong; Ivan IV's reign was to witness their disappearance. The final victor was not to be the Josephites, nor their opponents the Transvolgans, but the power of the Muscovite autocracy.

CONCLUSION

The reigns of Ivan III and Vasily III were marked by the progress of Western influence. It would be exaggerated to suggest that the intellectual influence was deep; it was certainly less noticeable than the work of the technicians who had built churches and introduced knowledge of astronomy and pharmacy. The intellectuals from abroad had done little more than translate books, but that was far from being unimportant. It was accepted that the world of Roman Catholicism – identical with the world of the West, for the Reformation made noticeable impact on Russia only after Ivan IV came to the throne – had learning that could be of use to Russians. Despite such xenophobic moments as would come with the ascendancy of Filaret in the early seventeenth century, no intelligent Russian was ever to challenge that proposition again. The question remained, what exactly ought to be borrowed, and how ought it to be put to use?

For Ivan III and Vasily III, for the Gennady circle and Joseph of Volokolamsk, it was primarily a matter of deciding what might serve their interests, what might help tsars rule more effectively or what might enable clerics to achieve greater influence in the state and defeat challenges to their views or to their authority in the Church. For Maxim the Greek it was not quite the same; Maxim had experienced profound influences of the West in Italy, and had the intellectual formation of a humanist derived partly from Byzantium and partly from his Italian experiences. For him it was a question of deciding which aspects of this formation could be safely exposed in his cultural work and which it would be better to conceal, not what ideas or formulas to borrow.

Then and later one may note the differences between those Russians who propagandized for some sort of Westernization without clearly understanding what the West was like and those who had real knowledge and experience of the West; at any rate one may distinguish persons in a continuum of which those were the two extremes. Clearly attempts to discover who in Russia most loved the West will not be of much help to the cultural historian, and those Soviet historians who may tend to equate Western influence during the fifteenth and sixteenth centuries with a favorable attitude toward the Roman Catholic faith risk haring up a blind alley. Maxim was certainly more Westernized than Gennady of Novgorod, but Gennady seemed far more eager than Maxim to borrow from Roman Catholicism. Maxim, the most Westernized man in Russia in the sixteenth century, was identified with the strongest indigenous currents in Russian religion and culture. He wanted nothing to do with the heresy-hunting, wealth-cherishing Josephites, who wanted to turn the Russian Church to a new sort of path and found certain Roman Catholic models useful in so doing.

Similarly, it may be asked whether Western influence during the period was intended and organized and if so to what extent. It appears that the marriage of Zoe Paleologa to Ivan III was the brain child of Cardinal Bessarion, who was charged with the rearing of both Zoe and her brother Andrew,[114] though Ivan III certainly had his own reasons for agreeing to the proposal. There is evidence that some Roman Catholics had plans for a joint Western–Russian crusade against the Turks as the result of a bargain that would be struck recognizing the Muscovite grand princes as heirs to the Byzantine Empire; in 1519 Nikolaus von Schönberg was ordered by the pope to suggest the possibility to Vasily III.[115] Possibly not merely zeal against the infidel but also concern with the fearful threat of Lutheranism and the whole Reformation to Rome impelled such overtures to be made. Baron Herberstein, writing to Pope Clement VII, urged attention to what Muscovy could contribute to a campaign against the Turks, pointing out for the first time the use that the Christian populations of the Balkans might be as auxiliaries, and frankly urging 'direct relations with Moscow, removing [the necessity for] any mediation in this affair by the King of Poland'. The Poles were concerned by such a possibility, and in 1553 Sigismund Augustus even threatened to break off political relations with Rome and conclude a pact with the Sultan if Rome pursued it.[116] But none of these plans matured.

Obviously Rome cannot be credited with planning the education of Maxim the Greek, and it is uncertain whether those at the papal court who assisted Dmitry Gerasimov and others to peruse the *Donation of Constantine* and other such documents did so with the intention of fixing any intellectual mortgages on Russia. There appears no warrant for believing that during the reigns of Ivan III and Vasily III anyone in Rome, let alone in the various European states, conceived the notion that the revival and successful implementation of the Union of Florence might be a reasonable hope, or that anyone drew up any other plan for mass conversion of the Muscovites.

And yet during this seventy-year period the influence of the Roman Catholic culture of Western Europe became perceptible in Muscovy. The meeting of Rome and Moscow was accomplished, beginning a long story with fateful consequences for Russia.

2

ECHOES OF THE REFORMATION AND CATHOLIC REFORM (1533-1613)

I am writing this to you, divinely-appointed lord, not in order to teach and instruct your penetrating mind or your noble wisdom, for it does not behoove us to forget our station and to presume so far, but [I write] as a disciple to a teacher, as a servant to a master.

Archbishop Feodosy of Novgorod to Ivan IV

INTRODUCTION

By the time Vasily III died in 1533, the great religious ferment sweeping Europe had begun to make itself felt among the Eastern Slavs in both Muscovy and Poland-Lithuania.[1] The growing challenge to the Roman Catholic Church took two forms: the Protestant Reformation that followed Martin Luther's theses of 1517 and John Calvin's emergence as a Reformer in 1534, and the Antitrinitarian radicalism for which the Protestants were much too moderate; it developed from the Anabaptists' secession from Zwinglianism in 1525 through the teaching of Michael Servetus to the emergence of organized Unitarianism in Poland by 1565 and in Transylvania by 1568.[2] As Protestantism and Antitrinitarianism expanded in both Western and Eastern Europe, Rome responded with a Catholic Reform whose general lines were shaped by the Council of Trent (1545–63) and also with a large-scale counter-offensive spearheaded by the Society of Jesus, founded in 1540.

The Eastern Slavs who lived in the Polish-Lithuanian state were hard pressed from the first. Lutheranism and Calvinism moved eastward rapidly, and organized Unitarianism actually originated in Poland and Transylvania; Catholic counter-action was not long in coming. The Belorussians and Ukrainians of the *Rzecz Pospolita* were largely peasants, with a sprinkling of nobles and clergy (the hierarchs and parish priests being separated by a deep social gulf). In cultural as well as political movements, leadership was provided only by nobles and the not numerous high clergy until the beginning of the seventeenth century.

In resisting Protestant (chiefly Calvinist), Antitrinitarian, and Catholic pressures, the Orthodox nobles of Poland-Lithuania could in theory look for assistance to their coreligionists across the frontier: those in the only sizeable independent Orthodox state, Muscovy, or to the highest ecclesiastical authority, Constantinople. However, Muscovy was preoccupied with the Livonian War (1558–82) and the Time of Troubles (1598–1613), and could do little to

24

help, while the Patriarchate of Constantinople had little freedom of action under the Ottomans.

In Poland-Lithuania the Counter-Reformation returned most of those who had joined Protestant and Antitrinitarian churches to the Roman fold, and by the Union of Brest in 1596 the reunion of the Orthodox population with Rome was proclaimed. The abortive Union of Florence (1439) was therewith revived with partial effectiveness. Nevertheless, Orthodox resistance continued. The nobility had exhausted its strength; leadership now passed to the Cossacks of the Dnieper valley, but results were not immediately visible. At the end of the sixteenth century it appeared that the Unia might be successfully imposed on almost all Orthodox of the Ukraine, and the temptation to zealous Roman Catholics of Poland, headed by Sigismund III, was to essay a crusade against Muscovy that would extend the Unia to include the Great Russians as well as bring about some kind of union, dynastic or territorial, between the Muscovite and the Polish states.

Muscovy seemed to be in no condition to resist. The state had been weakened and the society ravaged by the policies of Ivan IV; the Riurik dynasty had been extinguished in direct consequence of the tsar's brutality – through murder of his son Ivan. In the cultural field things were no better. At the outset of Ivan IV's reign the Transvolgan Elders and the Josephites were still struggling for ascendancy in the Church and for the leadership of Russian cultural development. While the contest went on, political reform was proposed and religious radicalism contributed to the dialogue. When it ended, the Josephites appeared the victors; heresy ceased (until the eighteenth century) and political reform was discussed no longer. The autocrat embarked on his reign of terror, and soon the Josephites disappeared from the scene as had their defeated antagonists the Transvolgans. While Ivan IV harried his domestic foes, Muscovy's culture ceased to grow.

Ivan's successors tried to do their best. Boris Godunov, as regent and then as tsar, hastily sought to erect ecclesiastical defenses by establishing an independent patriarchate of Moscow, and he had more far-reaching plans to shore up Russian culture. His efforts were abortive. Polish culture, borne by armies of mixed composition, twice swept into Moscow. The Poles were defeated militarily by Russian resistance based on the cooperation of several social groups and by Polish mistakes, including the maladroitness of King Sigismund. By 1613 a Russian ruled again in Moscow. However, soon thereafter it became clear that Russian culture had not been thereby restored to health and strength. The door of Moscow had been successfully closed to Poland and to Roman Catholicism, but during the seventeenth century a side entrance was found in Kiev – though not for conversion, which was ruled out after 1613 as an alternative for Russia.

Through Ivan IV's reign and the Time of Troubles the Roman Catholic religious offensive and the power of the Polish state periodically threatened the Orthodox of both the Ukraine and Muscovy. Cultural influences properly so-called were not always in the foreground, though enormous cultural consequences seemed to impend. An effort will be made to identify the cultural influences within the context of the ecclesiastical and political events.

THE ENTRANCE OF PROTESTANTISM INTO LITHUANIA AND MUSCOVY

The teachings of Martin Luther spread immediately into German-ruled territories from Holland to the Baltic. The Grand Master of the Teutonic Order accepted Lutheranism, secularized his domain, and took the title of Duke of Prussia in 1525. The territory of the Livonian Knights (or Knights of the Sword), to the east of Prussia but separated from it by Lithuania, experienced widespread conversions among both the dominant Germans and the subject Estonians and Latvians, but no secularization on the Prussian model had occurred when Ivan attacked Livonia in 1558. In the subsequent years many Livonians were taken prisoner or exiled to Muscovy, and for those in the city of Moscow Ivan IV allowed a Lutheran church – the first Protestant church in Russia – to be built in 1575–6. However, four years later the *oprichniki* destroyed it, and for the remainder of the reign no open Lutheran worship was tolerated. Thus any direct infusion of Lutheranism from Livonia into Muscovy was insignificant. Protestantism came to be called 'Lutheranism' by the Russians simply because Luther's teachings were the first variant with which they became acquainted.

A single Muscovite work has survived from this period which opposes Lutheranism and has therefore permitted speculations that Lutheran doctrines were by then sufficiently widespread to evoke rebuttal. The work, by a certain Parfeny the Holy Fool (*Urodivyi*), was written about 1560 and later used by Ivan IV as his own answer to an exposition of Protestant views delivered by the Moravian Brother Johann Rokyta, who accompanied a Polish embassy to Moscow in 1570 and was evidently mistaken for a Lutheran by the tsar. However, a recent scholar concludes that Parfeny's original correspondent was not, as some have thought, a Russian but some foreign Lutheran.[3]

Lutheranism never exerted a significant influence either through conversion or otherwise among the Eastern Slavs of either Muscovy or Poland-Lithuania. Calvinism and Antitrinitarianism were another matter.

Since the ecclesiastical separation of Moscow and Kiev in 1470 the Orthodox Church in Lithuania had grown increasingly feeble. The metropolitan 'of Kiev and all Rus' actually had his cathedral seat at Nowogródek. The Ukrainian Orthodox were tolerated by the Roman Catholic rulers of Lithuania and (after 1569) of Poland, but the Orthodox Church suffered much more from the way in which the royal right of patronage was exercised than the Catholic Church did. Little care was used to select capable men as bishops. During the sixteenth century the situation became scandalous. Monks of little or no education and dubious morals were raised to the metropolitanate; in 1589 an especially bad metropolitan, Onisifor, had to be defrocked.[4] The Orthodox hierarchy in Lithuania was too weak to resist the religious incursions of Protestantism and Catholicism.

In the early sixteenth century Protestantism made great gains in both Poland and Lithuania.[5] Most of Polish Prussia and much of Great Poland became Lutheran, and Lutheranism appeared in Lithuania also. Starting later, Calvinism overran Samogitia and Little Poland almost entirely, and from the 1550's largely replaced Lutheranism in Lithuania and continued to spread there. In Great Poland the Moravian Brethren achieved considerable strength. In both Poland and Lithuania Antitrinitarianism was also spreading. By 1552 the Diet (Sejm) had an overwhelming Protestant majority and in effect legalized the continuing defections from the Roman Church. Sigismund II Augustus (1548–72) was a partisan of toleration or even perhaps a concealed sympathizer with the Reformation. In 1570 three of the main Protestant groups, Lutheran, Calvinist, and Moravian Brethren, formed a common front in the Union of Sandomierz (*Consensus Sendomiriensis*), though the Antitrinitarian 'Minor Church' which had split off from the Calvinists in 1562–5 was not included. In 1573 the Confederation of Warsaw, drawn up as a preliminary to a royal election, required the monarch to take an oath to refrain from religious oppression. King Stephen Batory (1575–86), although he showed favor to Roman Catholicism, generally maintained his oath.

Thus from the 1550's to the 1580's at least a generally permissive religious atmosphere prevailed in Poland-Lithuania. Although the Union of Łublin in 1569 was largely motivated by a need to integrate Poland and Lithuania as a measure of common defense against Muscovy in the Livonian War, it took account of the changing situation sufficiently to recognize the different nationalities within the state and thus served as a sanction for claims of religious or ethnic distinctness, especially by the Orthodox Ukrainians.

However, the Union of Łublin also transferred the Ukrainian territories from Lithuanian to Polish administration, in consequence intensifying the thrust of Western influences into the area. Vlasovs'kyi writes that in the Ukraine the Reformation 'undoubtedly had great significance of a *general cultural character*, tending to promote awakening from a situation of cultural decay'.[6] Its impact became noticeable beginning with the conversion to Calvinism of a number of great nobles, including the Lithuanian Catholic Prince Nicholas Radziwiłł the Black in 1533 and Nicholas Radziwiłł the Red, his cousin and brother of Queen Barbara of Poland, in 1564. Several Orthodox nobles followed suit, some of them overtly, such as Jan Chodkiewicz and Prince Simeon Pronsky. Others were more cautious; a certain Ostafy Volovich, while assuring Moscow that only prudence prevented him from taking a public stand against Calvinism, in the 1570's was raising funds to establish a Calvinist chapel in Vilna.[7] In Novgorod–Litovsk province, out of 600

Orthodox *szlachta* families only 16 remained Orthodox, and widespread conversions were also taking place in Volhynia.[8]

Soon the Antitrinitarian Minor Church also entered the scene. Before his death in 1565, Nicholas Radziwiłł the Black moved toward it, though it was just in the process of being organized. Half the Calvinist ministers in Lithuania, headed by Martin Czechowicz, openly affiliated with the Antitrinitarians.[9] Radziwiłł's nephew Jan Kiszka did the same; his protection was important in the career of Simon Budny. Budny, born the son of a poverty-stricken Polish squire in 1533, was appointed by Radziwiłł as minister of a newly-founded Reformed church in Nowogródek, where he made converts from Orthodoxy and published a large catechism in Slavonic. He came to be leader of the radicals within the Minor Church, holding against the then-dominant Unitarian view the position that Christ was purely human and ought not to be worshipped, which led his party to be dubbed 'Judaizer'. In 1584 he was expelled from the church and Kiszka's protection was terminated.[10] Probably he died in the early 1590's.

The question has been raised whether Antitrinitarianism in Poland-Lithuania may have had Muscovite as well as Western roots. Wilbur states that 'Judaizer' doctrines had spread into Lithuania from Northern Russia.[11] It is true that Feodosy Kosoi ('the Squint-Eyed'), who had been branded a heretic in 1554 by a council in Moscow, fled to Vitebsk and Polotsk and there preached Antitrinitarian doctrines. When Muscovite armies took Polotsk in 1563 and the Protestant community there was dispersed, Feodosy and a collaborator named Ignaty were working farther to the west.[12] The question needs further exploration.

By the 1570's the Ukrainian nobles were attempting to mobilize for self-defense against the growth of Protestantism and Antitrinitarianism (and the Catholic counter-offensive), which they saw as threats to the culture as well as the religion of the Ukrainian Orthodox. The chief figure was Prince Konstantin Ostrozhsky (1526–1608), son of a hetman of Lithuania. In a letter he wrote, 'we have weakened in our faith, yet our pastors cannot teach us anything, cannot defend God's church. There are no teachers, no preachers of God's word'.[13] In order to provide a basis for cultural revival, he undertook to sponsor a series of translations and publications. He assembled a circle of translators and in 1575 summoned from Lwów the printer Ivan Fedorov and an assistant. These men were refugees from Muscovy. In 1563–5 in Moscow Fedorov had been responsible for printing the first books in Russia,[14] but his press was burned and he was driven out by a mob incited by scribes fearing for their livelihood. He first found haven in Zabludiv with Hetman Gregory Chodkiewicz and then in Lwów from where Ostrozhsky summoned him.

With difficulty the prince's circle of scholars obtained a copy of the Biblical collection directed by Gennady of Novgorod and used it and other Slavonic translations as references, yet tried to make the original texts the basis of their finished product. The result was the so-called Ostrog Bible, which Fedorov printed in 1581 and was extensively distributed in a sizeable edition. Other works followed.[15] Fedorov returned to Lwów shortly before his death in 1583, but the Ostrog press continued. Around 1600 Prince Ostrozhsky moved a section of the press to the Dermansky monastery, where the learned priest Demian Nalivaiko undertook several additional publications, and a few years later Ostrozhsky founded a third press at the Monastery of the Caves in Kiev.

In 1580 Ostrozhsky founded a school in Ostrog concerning which data are sparse, but there seems no doubt of its significance. A number of Greeks were attracted to it, for example its first rector, Cyril Lucaris, educated in the West and later patriarch of Constantinople. Among its teachers were such distinguished men as Gerasim and Melety Smotritsky, Iov Boretsky, and Nalivaiko. The Ostrog academy seems to have been the model for the school set up in 1586 by the Lwów lay 'brotherhood', which in turn was imitated by other brotherhoods of the Ukraine.

Close relations with Prince Ostrozhsky were established by Prince Andrei Kurbsky after he had fled from Ivan IV to the Kowel region, living there from 1564 until his death in 1583. Endeavoring to correct the paucity of patristic writings available in Slavonic versions, he arranged for translations from St John of Damascus, St John Chrysostom, and other Byzantine Fathers. Some of this work was done by Kurbsky and scholars directly associated with him, some by members of the Ostrog school at his instigation. In his later years Kurbsky himself studied Latin in order to be better prepared for his task, since the available texts were mainly critical editions in Latin prepared by Roman Catholic scholars. He criticized certain Biblical translations that had been carried out on the basis of Protestant or proto-Protestant writings, such as Frantiszek Skorina's translation of part of the Hussite Bible of 1509 and Vasily Tiapinsky's and Valentin Negalevsky's translation of the Antitrinitarian Scriptures produced by Simon Budny and Martin Czechowicz. Kurbsky, who had known Maxim the Greek and wrote a biography of him,[16] strove to be faithful to Orthodoxy and the Byzantine tradition. Like Maxim, however, he did not shrink from acknowledgment of the achievements of Roman Catholic learning, and clearly was more concerned about the threat of Protestantism than that of Rome.

However, Prince Ostrozhsky came to be increasingly committed to Westernization and much more to the Reformers than to the Roman Church; as a result Kurbsky was finally brought to criticize the trend of his thinking. Although Ostrozhsky married a Roman Catholic, he soon developed close relations with Protestants and even more with Antitrinitarians, employing one of the latter, Motovila, to write a tract refuting Jesuit writings. Wilbur writes (with approval) that Ostrozhsky was suspected of being a 'Socinian' at heart,[17] and notes that his daughter married Jan Kiszka, the chief Socinian magnate of Lithuania. Other Orthodox nobles were leaning to Socinianism, and some converted to it.

Thus Protestant and even Antitrinitarian influences were felt for a time among the Orthodox of Poland-Lithuania, even those who at least began as defenders of Orthodoxy against the encroachments of the Reformation. However, under the onslaught of the Counter-Reformation most such influences were soon to disappear.

THE ROMAN CATHOLIC COUNTER-ATTACK AND THE UNION OF BREST

Although Sigismund II Augustus was subjected to some Calvinist influence through the connections of his second wife Barbara Radziwiłł, he permitted the mounting of a serious Roman Catholic effort to regain lost ground. The initiative was taken by Stanislaus Cardinal Hosius, born in Kraków of German parents named Hosen, who in 1564 accompanied a new papal nuncio from the recently adjourned Council of Trent (over which Hosius had twice presided) to the Polish court. In the same year he brought members of the Society of Jesus into Poland, and in 1569 they entered Lithuania. They worked both by contact with individuals and through several educational institutions they founded, in Braniewo in 1564, Pultusk in 1566, Vilna, and other cities.[18]

After the return in 1573 of Peter Skarga, a young Pole who had become a Jesuit in Rome, successes increased not only in reconverting Protestants but also in converting Orthodox. Two sons of Radziwiłł the Black were examples of the former; among the latter were the sons of Prince Konstantin Ostrozhsky and Prince Andrei Kurbsky. In 1576 the Jesuit Antonio Possevino founded a College of St Athanasius in Rome intended for Greeks and Slavs of the Eastern Rite.[19] A few years later Russian translations of Roman Catholic manuals were published in Rome and Vilna. When Stephen Batory recaptured Polotsk in 1579, most Orthodox properties were turned over to the Jesuits.

At this point Rome was given an apparently promising opportunity. In the winter of 1581 there appeared at the papal court a courier of Ivan IV, Leonty Shevrigin, with a letter which proposed an alliance against the Turks, with whom Stephen Batory was accused of allying himself, and which requested that a papal envoy be sent to Moscow. Gregory XIII dispatched Antonio Possevino, who had in papal service proved an accurate observer and able diplomat. His mission was designed not merely to offer the mediation in the Livonian War Ivan had requested but also to inaugurate a Roman Catholic apostolate in Russia. Possevino tried to prepare himself for his mission as best he could, but he knew neither Russian nor any other Slavic language, and his knowledge of the Russian Church never equaled that, for example, of Peter Skarga's.[20]

Possevino succeeded in arranging the Truce of Yam–Zapolsky (1582), which ended the war between Muscovy and Poland. Upon its conclusion Possevino came back to Moscow, where he finally managed to persuade the reluctant tsar to discuss questions of religion with him.[21] Possevino spoke of the affinity between the Greek and the Roman Churches, and the need for the Eastern Church only to renounce the innovations made by the patriarchs Photius and Michael Cerularius. Ivan replied:

The Greek religion is called thus because the prophet David predicted, well before the birth of Jesus Christ, that Ethiopia would have the first fruits of the divine mercy; now, Ethiopia is the same as Byzantium, and Byzantium was the first Christian kingdom: that is why the Christian religion is called the Greek religion. As for us, we profess the true Christian religion, which in many respects is not in accordance with the Roman religion.[22]

Ivan IV was not the utter ninny in matters of history and religion that this statement suggests, but it conveys well enough the impermeability of the tsar to any arguments of Possevino's.

Possevino conceived a plan for the conversion of Russia to Roman Catholicism, which Father Pierling interprets in the following form:

With a sagacity which it would be unjust to fail to recognize, Possevino had discovered the road to follow in order to penetrate to the very heart of the Slavic world. The fact was that there were several Russian provinces under Polish rule: their inhabitants...were kinsmen of the Muscovites; they had the same blood, the same faith, the same language; their political fortunes were identified with the fate of Poland. These compatriots abroad thus had points of contact with the two Slavic centers; the Catholic church could freely expand among them; as soon as they were removed from schism and put in possession of the truth, by the very force of circumstances they would become apostles to the Muscovites and by means of the latter they would reach the Tatars of Kazan and Astrakhan, the mountaineers of the Caucasus, the Moslems of Asia.[23]

In order to accomplish this stupendous task, it was necessary, Possevino believed, to train the men who would do the job – that is, for suitably qualified Roman Catholics (the Jesuits would be logical choices) to train the 'Russians' (that is, Eastern Slavs) of Poland and Lithuania – in seminaries and schools founded with that end in view, with printing presses and libraries close by.

In fact part of Possevino's long-range program of Jesuit education and proselytism was to be put in motion, and was to have perceptible effects on Russian culture for almost 250 years thereafter. The Jesuit intellectual machine, then unequaled in sophistication and effectiveness, made substantial headway in many corners of the earth, but it is doubtful that it ever had a chance of winning in Russia. Whereas in China the Jesuits identified themselves with the local culture and avoided being compromised by association with any foreign power, in Russia the situation was quite different. They never produced any gifted adepts of the Orthodox Eastern Slavic cultural tradition, and they made common cause with the Polish monarchy to such an extent that most Russians came to view them as agents of Russia's enemies. The temptation to draw on the power of the Polish state in converting the Ukraine before making any serious approach to Muscovy was too great to resist. The Union of Brest (1596) was bound to place grave handicaps on any Jesuit efforts to penetrate Muscovy.[24]

Shortly after the truce of Yam–Zapolsky, Stephen Batory died. In 1587 Sigismund III was elected his successor after consideration of several candidates including Fedor, son of Ivan IV and now tsar of Muscovy. Some highly placed Poles were so confident of the power of Poland and Polish culture that they were considering electing Fedor in the hope that the result would be reunion of the Orthodox Church of Russia with the Roman Catholic Church. Possevino secretly but strongly warned against any such step,[25] though it is uncertain how much influence his warning had.

Sigismund III ruled for forty-five years. Reared by the Jesuits, he was proud to be called 'the Jesuit King'.[26] Evidently less interested in politics than in religion and the arts, he bent his energies toward supporting the Catholic Reform. Although he followed his predecessors in swearing to uphold the Confederation of 1573, securing religious liberty, it cannot be said that he was faithful to his oath in spirit. Peter Skarga, the leading Jesuit in Poland, was called to become court preacher soon after Sigismund's accession, and for twenty-three years (he died in 1612) had a strong influence on the monarch's policy. He tried to reclaim 'heretics' throughout the Republic, disapproving the use of force against them and attempting instead to employ reason, but he demanded that they be kept out of public office.

In 1577 Skarga had published a book entitled, *On the Unity of the Church of God Under One Pastor* (*O iedności kościoła Bozego pod iednym pasterzem y o Greckim od tey iedności odstąpieniu*), and dedicated it to Prince Ostrozhsky, whom he had first met a decade earlier. The first edition was almost entirely destroyed, and the second edition, published in 1590, was dedicated not to Ostrozhsky but to Sigismund III.[27] In the book Skarga discussed the prospects of reunion, laid stress on the captivity of the patriarch of Constantinople to the Turks, and ruled out union with Muscovy for the time being because it was fighting the Republic. It is noteworthy that this most important of works thus far by any Westerner to consider the problem of relations between Western Christendom and Russia, and also the chief polemical piece that Skarga wrote, was directed not against Protestants but against the Orthodox. Moreover, therein he declared that theology, philosophy, and other such sciences were taught in no institution of learning in any language other than Latin, that with only Church Slavic no one could ever be learned, and that no one knew if Church Slavic had even a grammar, since there were no books on that subject. (The first Slavic grammars appeared beginning in 1586.[28]) In 1577 such statements were technically accurate; but the contempt for Russian culture shown in Skarga's phrasing goes far to show why many Russians reacted to Roman Catholic influences as they did. Nevertheless there were those among the Ukrainians who were influenced by such arguments, and the book played its part in preparing the way for the Union of Brest.

A number of Orthodox replies to Skarga followed. The chief one was the *Apokrisis*, which appeared first in Vilna in 1597 under the name of Christopher Filalet (Philalethes), but is now believed to have been compiled by a Polish

Calvinist layman and diplomat named Martin Broński, under the commission of Prince Konstantin Ostrozhsky.[29] It was based largely on Calvin's *Institutes* and other Calvinist literature. The theological helplessness of the Orthodox Church among the Eastern Slavs was clear. In any event the fate of the O thodox of Poland-Lithuania could no longer be affected by the theologians; it had been decided in an ecclesiastical–political struggle in which the Orthodox also had to turn to the Protestants for help against the all-out attempt by Rome to revive the abortive Union of Florence.

In 1582 the promulgation of the Gregorian calendar by the papacy raised a side issue that well illustrates how ecclesiastical and other cultural problems were intertwined. Possevino had worked for the adoption of the new calendar in Poland and showed his impatience with the opposition to calendrical reform. Of course the uneducated Ukrainian peasantry could not be expected to deal with the issue on the basis of evidence, but many Orthodox clergy set their face against the change and in consequence made fools of themselves in print. As Halecki notes, 'that in the matter of the calendar the Pope was right...can be proved, of course, scientifically and independently of any religious considerations'. He adds, 'just because it was not a matter of faith and morals, it probably was a tactical mistake to insist upon the immediate acceptance of a change which affected the daily life of the conservative Orthodox people'.[30] In the event the authors of the Union of Brest did not insist on calendrical reform, but the debate may have helped to lead Possevino and others by the late 1580's to decide that rational argument was likely to be of less utility in achieving their goal than resort to the powerful political weapons lying ready to hand.

The crisis which led to the Union of Brest was opened by the unexpected visit of Patriarch Jeremiah II of Constantinople. In 1588 the patriarch, who had been expelled by the Turks from his see after a quarrel, chose to visit Poland-Lithuania and then Muscovy, returning to Lithuania in July 1589. He was the ecclesiastical superior of the metropolitanate of Kiev, which as already noted had fallen into the hands of incompetents or worse. Meeting with a large gathering in Vilna of the Orthodox hierarchy, he dealt severely with clergymen against whom misconduct was alleged, and deposed Metropolitan Onisifor himself. Other measures he took, especially in support of the Orthodox lay brotherhoods, further deepened the insecurity of the clergy. The Jesuits were prepared to take advantage of the situation, though it cannot be said that they created it.

In 1591 four Orthodox bishops were persuaded to write privately to Sigismund III offering to accept union with Rome if the Slavic ritual could be retained. A period of feverish behind-the-scenes activity ensued within the Orthodox fold and also among the Catholics, by whom the offer was regarded as being of the highest importance. Among the Orthodox there was a division between the high clergy and the lay leaders. The chief figure among the high clergy was the monk Ipaty, born Adam Potei, whose character and ability set him apart from most of his colleagues in the hierarchy, and in fact he had been a layman, only becoming a monk and then bishop in 1593. He perceived and lamented the low spiritual and cultural level of the Orthodox Church in the Republic, and became a zealous proponent of union as a means of raising it to what it should be.

The lay leaders took a quite different stand. The foremost among them, Prince Ostrozhsky, declared himself willing to consider union, but only provided that the whole Eastern Church and not merely the metropolitanate of Kiev engaged in the discussions – a condition he well knew was most unlikely to materialize. By this time Ostrozhsky had increasingly fallen under Calvinist and Socinian influences; and he turned for aid to Greeks who themselves were strongly influenced by Calvinism. The patriarchate of Constantinople was by now in deep difficulties, and the most influential figure of Eastern Orthodoxy was Meletius Pigas, patriarch of Alexandria. The latter sent Cyril Lucaris, who had earlier taught at Ostrog, as his representative to oppose the union. Lucaris was an able theologian, who lived to become himself patriarch of Alexandria (1602) and later of Constantinople (1621). Having studied in the West, he knew Latin better than Greek,[31] and introduced Calvinist teachings into the Eastern Church on a broad scale. The Ukrainian Church was too weak to stand alone against the formidable cultural pressures from without; the leadership divided, high clergy turning to Rome, nobles turning to Protestantism for help. At the Synod of Brest Ostrozhsky was accompanied by a number of Protestants and Socinians, and made his headquarters in the house of a prominent Socinian. One of his chief supporters there was Damian Hulewicz, who was accused of being a Protestant if not an 'Anabaptist'.[32] One of Ostrozhsky's demands at the synod was that Protestants be admitted – which was not granted.

The Orthodox hierarchy of Poland-Lithuania had cast their lot with Rome, and the rest was anticlimax. Despite the fervent opposition of Prince Ostrozhsky and others, union was proclaimed by Sigismund in 1595 and ratified by a council of Brest in 1596 – or, more accurately, one of the two parts into which that council split, which boasted the majority of Orthodox bishops. The other part, consisting mainly of Orthodox laymen, supported by the delegates of the Eastern patriarchates, tried its best to resist. The king, however, backed the Uniat council, and the Union of Brest was the term used to describe the arrangement by which the Orthodox of Poland-Lithuania acknowledged papal supremacy and reconciliation with the Roman Catholic Church.

Actually the result was more complicated than that. Prince Ostrozhsky continued to fight, and at the council of Vilna in 1599[33] was instrumental in the conclusion of a pact between Orthodox and Protestants to resist the Counter-Reformation. In 1608, at the age of eighty-two, he died, recognizing that the struggle within the boundaries of the Republic was largely lost. Of his own family, only one son (Alexander) remained Orthodox; the other two sons and a daughter accepted Roman Catholicism. Soon after his death his press and school at Ostrog passed into Catholic hands, and in 1636 his granddaughter ordered his bones to be disinterred, cleansed, and reburied according to Roman rites in a Catholic chapel.[34] A number of other Orthodox nobles accepted conversion to Roman Catholicism directly (seldom the Uniat Church). This was often the result of Jesuit instruction of the young, for where high culture went, in Poland of the seventeenth century, there usually went the Roman faith. A section of the peasantry and townsmen became Uniats; others refused to do so, and when the Cossacks provided the recalcitrant Orthodox with militant leadership a sharp struggle was still to ensue.

The degree of success which the Union of Brest achieved is attributed by Halecki to such factors as the greater interest of Clement VIII in Poland than some of his predecessors, the zeal of Sigismund III, and the stand taken by the 'Ruthenian' hierarchy.[35] It indeed seems doubtful that the union could have had more than nominal significance, whatever the vigor of pope and king, if the high Orthodox clergy had not themselves decided for Rome. The attempt to reinvigorate Orthodox intellectual and spiritual roots had failed. The battle thus came to be one between pro-Catholic and pro-Protestant forces within the Orthodox camp – or, more accurately, those who thought it possible to preserve at least the Slavic rite and revive their church in Poland-Lithuania by union with Rome, and those who had accepted substantial cooperation with Protestants within the Republic and with the Protestant-influenced Eastern patriarchates.

It was rather broadly cultural than specifically religious considerations which underlay this battle. Ipaty Potei, who became Uniat Metropolitan, wrote to Patriarch Meletius Pigas of Alexandria that in Alexandria there was Calvin instead of Athanasius; in Constantinople, there was Luther; in Jerusalem, Zwingli. 'Among the Greeks the Gospels had been distorted, the traditions of the Fathers profaned and shattered, holiness had withered; everything had declined and become disorganized under Turkish despotism.'[36] For Ipaty the Orthodox Churches of the East in their current condition could offer no promise of revival. For him, and for many Uniats, the only possible way was in the opposite direction, not south but west, toward Rome in culture, remaining in Poland as a state where freedom could be said to have considerably greater meaning than in Muscovy or the Ottoman Empire.

Florovsky concludes that the Unia was 'rather an act of cultural–political self-determination than of religious self-determination'.[37] And so, it appears, was the issue primarily regarded by such leaders as Prince Ostrozhsky, despite the Protestant and Socinian religious influences which also seemed to have weight with them. The Unia threatened the ethnic and cultural identity of the 'Ruthenians' or Ukrainians, not with Romanization so much as with Polonization. There was no substantial theological difference between Orthodoxy and Roman Catholicism, as a number of Polish nobles were reminding themselves at the time Tsar Fedor's candidacy for the Polish throne was at issue. No doubt by so saying they were rationalizing their own hopes of imperial expansion at Muscovy's expense in a manner similar to that by which the Union of Łublin had led to Polish annexation of Lithuanian territory; but it was a fact nonetheless. The theological difference remained solely the issue of the *Filioque* phrase in the Nicene Creed; the differences in religious practice could be regarded (and properly so) as secondary. The position of the pope offered a problem not so much in principle (the early councils had recognized his honorary primacy among the five great sees of Christendom) as in fact – fact rooted in the power politics of the Europe of the sixteenth century, the wealth and property of the Holy See and its dependencies secular and ecclesiastical, and the cultural history of Europe, in its turn not unrelated to the economics and politics of the previous half-millennium; but the result of all this was the threat of being culturally submerged or absorbed by the West. The Ukrainian nobles were by this time unable or unwilling to resist in the name merely of the flourishing and rich Orthodox past, which sadly lacked worthy continuation in the present at least partly because of the Ottoman (and, in the view of some, also Muscovite) captivity of the contemporary churches. They had to find effective weapons of cultural resistance somewhere, and the non-Roman faiths of the Reformation period were the only possible source.

For both sides there were less exalted motives than those of cultural uplift or cultural defense. The high clergy were prudentially concerned with the interference of the laity, especially the powerful Ukrainian nobles, in church affairs, and were willing to accept Rome's protection, not to mention the intervention of the Polish monarchy, as an alternative. The lay nobles were, in their eagerness to defend Orthodoxy, willing to accept aid from Greek prelates who were compromised by their readiness to serve the cause of the sultan's ambitions in Eastern Europe.[38] On such matters both sides could and did trade charges which had some foundation – but not for long after the Union of Brest. By the beginning of the seventeenth century the plight of Orthodoxy in Poland was sad indeed. Melety Smotritsky, in commemorating the death of Prince Konstantin, wrote:

Where is the mansion of the Princes Ostrozhsky, from which the old faith radiated? Where are the other jewels of that crown, the priceless sapphires and precious diamonds and all the glory of the great princely Russian houses?[39]

They were gone, for centuries if not forever.

IVAN IV: THE END OF THE TRANSVOLGAN–JOSEPHITE STRUGGLE

By the time of the Union of Brest Roman Catholicism had appeared to mobilize for a crusade to the east, and such a crusade was an aspect of the dynastic crisis and political chaos of the Time of Troubles (1598–1613). Conversely, Muscovy's cultural weakness was one factor that led to and prolonged the crisis. That weakness was to a large extent the result of Ivan IV's reign, in which the Josephites finally defeated the Transvolgans, only to be swept aside themselves in turn; the Church was placed in the shadow of the autocracy, and only defenders of the autocrat's power remained visible.

Ivan acceded to the throne in 1533 at the age of three. For five years his mother, Elena *née* Glinskaia, headed a regency. When she died in 1538 the government fell into the hands of the Boyar Duma, headed by the Shuisky family. He was challenged by a rival boyar faction under Prince I. F. Belsky, who had the cooperation of Metropolitan Daniel, leader of the Josephites at that point. Belsky was imprisoned; Daniel was exiled and succeeded as metropolitan by Ioasaf, hegumen of the Trinity monastery and a dedicated Transvolgan. Ioasaf persuaded the Shuiskys to free Belsky, who seized the leadership himself briefly in 1540 before the Shuiskys got rid of him. Ioasaf was almost killed but finally was in turn exiled and replaced as metropolitan by Makary, archbishop of Novgorod, in 1542. The Shuiskys' regime was, however, doomed. It had treated the young Grand Prince Ivan with scant respect, and in late 1543 Ivan abruptly had the leader, Prince A. M. Shuisky, seized and slain.

The Shuiskys had not, as might have been expected, attempted to restore the old patrimonial principalities at the expense of the central power. The Belskys seem to have admired the looser political order of Poland-Lithuania,[40] but they had no time to emulate it. The two clerical parties seem to have made no clear alliances with the boyar factions. Ioasaf, a Transvolgan, was named metropolitan under a Shuisky but fell through intervening on behalf of a Belsky. The Josephites suffered, in the person of Daniel, at the hands of one Shuisky, but regained the metropolitanate, in the person of Makary, with the help of another. The political and ecclesiastical issues of the previous two reigns were not solved, but did not come to the fore.

From 1543 to 1547 the government was again in the hands of the Glinskys, the family of Ivan's mother. In 1547 Ivan was crowned 'tsar' – a title that Ivan III and Vasily III had used from time to time but that only now became unequivocally official. A few weeks later he married Anastasia Romanovna, and thus a famous family entered Russian history. Ivan now took up the reins of government, but leaned on the advice of the so-called Select Council (*izbrannaia rada*),[41] consisting of Sylvester, priest of the Cathedral of the Annunciation in the Kremlin; A. F. Adashev, who came from a noble family of Kostroma; and others including Prince Andrei Kurbsky.

Sylvester was a Transvolgan, though he might be described as a moderate Non-possessor.[42] Coming from a rich merchant family of Novgorod, he worked there for a time producing icons and manuscripts for sale. There seems reason to link his rise with that of the Shuiskys. By 1545–6 he had come to Moscow to take up his post in the Annunciation cathedral. It was probably at Sylvester's urging that Ivan, at the council of February 1549, proclaimed the end of the persecution of the boyars and the beginning of reforms in Church and state.

In his works Sylvester echoed several favorite themes of Maxim the Greek and other Transvolgans. In a letter to Ivan of 1550, he sets forth his conception of the duties of the tsar, regarding him first of all as the defender of the Orthodox faith, calling on him to pursue his objective of 'justice', as exemplified in his introduction of a 'just court', by giving it the coloration of 'gentleness', and urging him to rid himself of 'favorites', which probably meant (as Zimin says) Josephite monks. In a letter of 1553 to A. B. Shuisky-Gorbaty, who was about to take up duties as an official in the Volga valley, he recurred to his earlier-expressed conception of justice and advised the creation of a 'just court' for the local population (as well as Christianization of the Tatars around Kazan).[43] This letter leads Budovnits to suggest that in it Sylvester, 'it is true, in a somewhat veiled form, *develops the idea of limitation of the tsar's power*'; he points to expressions that indeed suggest factual limits on what the tsar can do,[44] but to none that propose any legal limitations.

One need not try to make Sylvester into some kind of early constitutionalist in order to show that he, like his Transvolgan predecessors, urged 'justice' in the sense of restraint and 'humility' as the proper principles by which the ruler should be guided and contended that the proper persons to advise him were the boyars rather than the monks (as the Josephites argued).

Sylvester as a Transvolgan had, however, a competitor in the Josephite Makary, who achieved prominence before he did. Makary was born in 1481 or 1482, became a monk at the Pafnuty monastery of Borovsk, as Joseph Sanin had done, and in 1506 became archimandrite of the Luzhitsky monastery at Mozhaisk. At the instance of Vasily III he was named archbishop of Novgorod in 1526. In 1542 he succeeded Ioasaf as metropolitan, owing to his friendship with A. M. Shuisky rather than to any Josephite preponderance on the council that chose him.[45] However, his elevation was followed by several important appointments of Josephite bishops or archbishops, at Novgorod, Krutitsy, Kolomna, Suzdal, and elsewhere. By 1550 a 'complete seizure by the Josephites of the Russian church hierarchy' had been carried out.[46] There followed a whole series of measures to glorify the Moscow tsar, to raise the prestige of the Russian Church, and to identify the one with the other – but at the same time there was an effort to warn the tsar away from any attempted seizure of monastic lands.

Even before he became metropolitan, Makary secured (in 1538) the insertion of Joseph Sanin's *Enlightener*[47] in the *Great Reading Compendium* or *Menologos* (*Velikie chet'i minei*). This gigantic religious encyclopedia, much of whose compilation was supervised by Makary, embraced every kind of material from Scriptural apocrypha to contemporary tracts in over 13,000 large folios. In 1546, by Makary's order, the new bishop of Krutitsy, Savva Cherny, wrote an official life of Joseph Sanin. In 1547 and 1549 church councils canonized several new Russian saints. In 1547 Makary composed the rite of coronation, including extensive quotes from Joseph.

In 1550 Makary composed a letter to Ivan on the problem of monastic landholding which set forth the Josephite position with full documentation. Its first part consisted of an epistle by Archbishop Feodosy of Novgorod (Makary's successor in that see), which included as its 'fundamental part' the *Donation of Constantine*, along with other materials, as evidence that the position of church lands was inalienable. This repeated the use of the *Donation* in the Josephite polemics of previous reigns, earlier analyzed as a case of Roman Catholic influence. When the protocols of the Council of a Hundred Chapters (*Stoglav*) were drawn up, the *Donation* was included as Chapter 60.[48]

The Hundred Chapters Council, however, did not mark complete victory for the Josephites. Sylvester had also been active. Some of what he had in mind is contained in the *Ordering of the House* or *Domostroi*, which was probably composed after 1547,[49] and at least a portion of it before 1556. Whether or not it mirrored the reality of the time to some extent, there seems no possibility of denying that the work incorporated someone's views of how things ought to be, and since, according to Zimin, many ideas are to be found repeated in Sylvester's *Instruction* (*Nakazanie*) to his son Anfim, they may well be Sylvester's. At any rate Sylvester prepared for the Council a program of church reforms, including some degree of secularization of church lands. But the Council (January–February 1551) had a Josephite majority, and the leading roles in it were taken by Makary and Nikander, archbishop of Rostov, a favorite of the tsar, who christened Ivan's infant son Dmitry in 1552. Bakhrushin and Zimin speak of the outcome as a compromise. In May 1551 princely estates which had been illegally given to monasteries were redeemed and given out as service lands or *pomestiia*;[50] monasteries were prohibited from buying land without special permission, and there were other measures.[51] At the same time some of the most implacable opponents of secularization were removed; Archbishop Feodosy of Novgorod was stripped of his see and replaced by a Non-possessor, Pimen. Artemy, one of the most prominent Non-possessors, was named hegumen of the Trinity monastery, and proceeded to obtain the transferral of the imprisoned Maxim the Greek to his new base. The Josephite bishop of Suzdal, Trifon, was also replaced by a Transvolgan.

And yet Sylvester's days were numbered. The Hundred Chapters Council achieved part of Makary's objectives. The core of the monastic lands was left untouched. The Council evidently was designed to serve as a climax to Makary's efforts to renovate the church, and in so doing to match the contemporary Roman model of how such a thing was to be done: the Council of Trent, which had begun in 1545.[52] But like his predecessors, Ivan IV could not let either the Josephites or the Transvolgans win completely. The Transvolgans espoused secularization, but emphasized the restraints, moral and theological at least, on autocratic power; the Josephites were not troubled by scruples about exercise of the tsar's authority, but they opposed secularization.

In 1553 Ivan fell seriously ill and found great difficulty in compelling the boyars to swear allegiance to his son Dmitry. Although Adashev did support Dmitry, Sylvester did not, and made common cause with the boyar opposition supporting Vladimir Staritsky as heir. When Ivan recovered, he wished to undertake a pilgrimage to St Cyril's monastery. Kurbsky tells us that Ivan first consulted Maxim the Greek in the nearby Trinity Monastery, and Maxim advised him not to go; he then asked the advice of Vassian Toporkov, who counselled Ivan to make the pilgrimage, at the same time saying: 'Keep not counsellors wiser than yourself.'[53] Kurbsky clearly implies that it was the Josephites who urged him to go,

for those wealth-loving monks do not consider that which of pleasing to God... But they are always zealously on the watch for what might be pleasing to the tsar and to the powers, in other words how they might wheedle out of them estates or great wealth for the monasteries...[54]

Sylvester, like Maxim, was opposed to the trip, but Ivan went anyway. On the journey his young son Dmitry died. This did nothing to revive Sylvester's fortunes, and he now faced serious dangers. In October 1553, shortly after the return of Ivan from his pilgrimage, a council was summoned to condemn a certain Matvei Bashkin. In his teachings and in those of Feodosy Kosoi an aspect of the history of the previous two reigns seems to be repeated. Again a group of radical heretics appeared; the Josephites raced enthusiastically to condemn them, while the Transvolgans resisted such condemnation and were alleged to be protecting them.

Bashkin, who came from a family of junior boyars (*deti boiarskie*), by 1550 occupied a service estate (*pomestie*) in Borovsk. By 1553 there was a circle of theological radicals around him. He was often enough in Moscow to have as his confessor a priest of the Annunciation cathedral; and he seems to have been close to Vladimir Staritsky, the boyars' candidate for the succession. Bashkin put difficult questions to his confessor, and after the decision of Ivan to go on his pilgrimage Bashkin was sent to Sylvester, who in turn reported to the tsar. Two Josephites, Gerasim Lenkov and Filofei Polev, were assigned to investigate. Apparently the chance to strike at Sylvester was tempting; in October Ivan Viskovaty, chief of the Foreign Office (Posol'skii prikaz), accused Bashkin's confessor, Sylvester, and the abbot Artemy of links with Bashkin. Smirnov declares this to have been a plot of the Romanovs to overthrow Sylvester.[55] However, the accusation went too far; Viskovaty also attacked the new icons that had been placed in the Annunciation cathedral, which embarrassed the whole Josephite leadership of the church. Viskovaty had to do penance. But a council of December 1553 condemned Bashkin, and he was sentenced to confinement in the Volokolamsk monastery. He escaped. His subsequent fate is not clear; it is possible he was burned by decree of a second council in the summer of 1554. Bashkin was condemned for teaching that Jesus was not equal to God the Father, that the eucharist consisted merely of bread and wine, that the church is simply the community of faithful, and that confession was unnecessary, and for iconoclasm. Sylvester and Simeon testified that the charge about the Trinity was unfounded; we have no way of evaluating the others.

Bashkin, doubtless under torture, implicated Artemy, declaring that he rejected the authority of the Church Fathers and accepted only the Bible, and uttered 'many blasphemous things' about the eucharist and icons. Artemy was confined in the monastery of Andronicus, but after he simply walked out he was brought before a council where several new charges were added: while he had earlier been at the Pskov–Pechery monastery, he had visited the Livonian border town of Neuhausen, and was alleged to have praised the 'Latins' and the faith of Neuhausen (apparently not yet Protestant at that time) and to have failed to curse the Novgorod heretics (Judaizers), presumably posthumously.[56] He took the tack of simply denying that any heretics were presently in existence in Russia, which was a mistake. Artemy was sent to the Solovki monastery, but a year or two later fled to Lithuania. He was for a time in Vitebsk with Feodosy Kosoi, who had earlier been a pupil of his, then lived at the court of the prince of Slutsk, dying about 1570. Unlike Feodosy, in Lithuania he defended Orthodoxy in a series of writings against Roman Catholicism and Protestantism, which faithfully repeated some of the teachings of Nil Sorsky.[57]

Immediately after the charges against Artemy were disposed of in January 1554, the Josephites turned to Feodosy Kosoi. He was originally a slave (kholop) of one of the tsar's servitors in Moscow. Fleeing to Beloozero, he became a monk and a pupil of Artemy when he was an elder at Porfiry hermitage, along with other comrades of his, perhaps also in flight from bondage in Moscow. In 1554 he was seized at a monastery just south of Beloozero and jailed in Moscow along with his supporters Ignaty, Vassian, and Porfiry. He and his confrères escaped, however, from the monastery where they were confined, and fled to Lithuania. There he and some of his fellows joined the Antitrinitarians, and apparently Feodosy and Ignaty married as a sign of their views. We know nothing of Feodosy's ideas at first hand but only through his opponents, chiefly Zinovy, a Non-possessor monk of Otensky hermitage who wrote about him. It appears that Feodosy believed that Christ was simply a man, objected to icons as idols and to ritual in general, attacked the clergy, denied the necessity of monasticism, and attacked monastic property – on the last score referring to Maxim the Greek and Vassian Patrikeev in support of his own views.[58] Obviously he, like Bashkin, had something in common with the Judaizers; certainly he became one of the Antitrinitarians of Lithuania, and may well have been close to Simon Budny.[59] The available evidence shows no influence of the Antitrinitarianism of the West upon him; there seems to have been instead convergence – that is, independent formulation of positions as old as heresy itself in Christendom.

Feodosy was no closet theologian, and preached vigorously wherever he went. Zinovy speaks of him as being influential in Lithuania in the 1560's. In

Vitebsk his followers became Calvinists, but about his own position there can be little doubt: he remained an Antitrinitarian. What is of greatest interest about Feodosy Kosoi is that he was the last Russian heretic until the eighteenth century.[60] At the time that the struggle between the Transvolgans and Josephites finally came to an end, heresy disappeared too.

After the affairs of Bashkin and Feodosy, Sylvester's fortunes declined. The Josephites were active; in 1553 the tsar, with the approval of Makary, erected the first printing press in Muscovy. The deacon Ivan Fedorov, P. Mstislavets, and M. Nefediev were found to operate it. They did not manage to publish the first book (the Acts of the Apostles) until 1564; shortly afterward the press was destroyed and they escaped to Lithuania, as already described. However, a new press was founded, and printing was resumed. In the 1560's a reworking of the chronicles produced a *Book of Degrees* (*Stepennaia kniga*) which constituted a sort of Josephite history of Rus. In the work 'the whole of Russian history is depicted...as the history of "Holy Russia" and is identified with the history of the Tsar's dynasty';[61] its purpose was to glorify Ivan IV as the culmination of those annals.

By this time Sylvester had fallen. It seems that the tsar's increasing alienation from Sylvester and his circle became final over the issue of foreign policy. Despite the conquest of Kazan in 1552 and Astrakhan in 1556, there remained a third remnant of Tatar power on Russian borders: the Crimea. Sylvester's concern with the Christianization of the Tatars of the Volga has already been noted; he now wished to settle with the Crimean khan, and keep peace with Lithuania. But in 1558 Ivan invaded Livonia, when Sylvester's influence was already fast waning. When a truce with Lithuania of many years' standing expired in 1562, the Muscovites were fighting Sigismund Augustus as grand prince of Lithuania. When Ivan returned from his first victory at Polotsk, it was Makary who welcomed him and lauded him in that he had 'cleansed the holy churches from the Lutheran iconoclasts'[62] (which must have referred to Livonia, as it could have had little relevance to Polotsk).

In 1560 the Tsaritsa Anastasia died. Relations between Sylvester's circle and the Romanovs had been cool at best; the Romanovs' probable connection with Viskovaty's charges has been mentioned. Ivan now broke with the Transvolgans. The Boyar Duma and a church council, meeting jointly, exiled Sylvester to Solovki monastery, where he died probably within a few years. Adashev died mysteriously, and several relatives of his were executed. Other executions followed. They were the first in fifteen or sixteen years. Kurbsky deserted to Lithuania in 1564,[63] and five or six other notables did the same within a few months.

The relation of two other publicists of the period to the Josephites deserves notice. One was Ermolai, who took the monastic name of Erasmus (Erazm) and is often called Ermolai-Erazm. Zimin characterizes him as a moderate Josephite, and suggests that as in Sylvester the Non-possessors' views appear in a less militant and consistent form, so in Ermolai-Erazm the Josephites' views are in some respects shaded; he 'criticizes possessions only because they contradict his conception of the norms of the ascetic life of monasticism'.[64]

Ermolai-Erazm evidently was writing from the 1540's, lived in Pskov for a time before coming to Moscow, and around 1560 became a monk. Probably he was forced to do so and to leave Moscow as punishment, but we know next to nothing about him personally. His writings of interest include *The Governor* (*Pravitel'nitsa*: the noun is feminine), which proposes regularization of peasant obligations, tax reforms, and the abolition of the *kormlenie* system of tax-farming.[65] In this work, which Zimin dates to 1549, and others he writes with a sympathy for the peasantry unusual among Josephites, proposing that their dues be limited to one-fifth of the harvest.[66] *The Governor* has been called the first 'specialized economico-political treatise' in Russian history.[67] Ermolai's link with earlier Josephites is clear in his *Great Trilogy* or *Book on the Trinity* (*Bol'shaia trilogiia* or *Kniga o troitse*), in which he defends Orthodox doctrine against heretics. His arguments include such naive ones as that all natural phenomena are triune: the sun, moon, and stars correspond to the Three Persons; so do wind, thunder, and lightning. Zimin notes that Nicholas Bulev earlier advanced the same kind of arithmetical notions. Ermolai's chief target was the Lutherans, though he also devotes attention to Muslims and Jews (neither of whom were of course Christian heretics at all).

Ermolai's Josephism emerges in his contention that 'the power of the priest was higher than the Tsar's'. He simultaneously attacks the boyars and supports the tsar's power against them. He stresses that the rich man is more pure before God, and that to become perfect one must give one's property to the poor. Filofei of Pskov earlier argued in the same vein, not with the purpose of suggesting that the Josephite monasteries impoverish themselves but rather to give the boyars food for thought and to restrain any tsar from casting greedy eyes at monastic holdings.[68] But Ermolai goes further, attacking the ambitions (if not the properties directly) of his monastic brethren; 'now we see false monks not only in thought but deed puffing themselves up and seeking greatness'.[69] He was no ordinary Josephite.

The other publicist to be considered is Ivan Peresvetov.[70] Peresvetov was an émigré from Lithuania, whose Russian contains slight traces of Polish influence. He evidently served under Sigismund I of Poland and the Emperor Ferdinand (about 1532), and he came to Russia in 1538 or 1539. He was an ideologist of autocracy whose ideas were not complicated by concern about monastic landholding and the influence of the clergy as the Josephites' were. His chief works were three: *The Tale of Peter the Wallachian* (*Skazanie o Petre Voloshskom*), *The Tale of the Turkish Tsar Mohammed* (*Skazanie...o tsare Turskom Magmete*). and *The Great Petition* (*Bol'shaia chelobitnaia*), his last work, whose final version Zimin dates to 1549.[71] His starting point is to call for justice, lamenting through the mouth of the Wallachian voevoda Peter that although the Christian faith was perfect in Moscow, 'there is no justice there'. In practice, however, the prerequisite of 'justice' turns out to be the ruler's *groza* or awesomeness. His model is the Turkish sultan, or what he imagines the sultan to be like; he praises the ferocity of the sultan's measures against offenders, including flaying alive, the appointment of officials irrespective of heredity or property, and the like. The solution he advocates is the union of 'the true Christian faith' of Moscow with 'Turkish justice'.[72]

Rzhiga and Philipp have pointed to contemporary Turcophilia in Western Europe as a probable source of Peresvetov's views; certainly Peresvetov came from Lithuania and doubtless had access to such interpretations.[73] However, there is also a possible relationship with Peresvetov's Russian predecessors that ought not to be overlooked. There is a logical relationship between the ideology of Moscow the Third Rome, advanced by the Josephites (using Roman Catholic models) half a century earlier, and the conclusions drawn by Peresvetov, on the face of them rather startling, about the desirability of using the Ottoman Empire for a political model. If the Byzantines perished because they were wrong, why then should not one conclude that their conquerors, the Turks, were right? Peresvetov was not a Muslim, and so, following some of his Western contemporaries, put into the mouth of Mohammed II the wish to be converted to Christianity; but the significant conclusions he draws are not religious but political. The Russian tsar ought to imitate the Ottoman despot, crush the aristocracy, and use 'fearfulness' as his means of securing 'justice'.[74]

It is impossible to say how much Peresvetov influenced Ivan; one may presume that Ivan read some of his works, since they were addressed to the tsar personally. What is known is that at the end of 1564, after the chief crisis of Ivan's life and reign, there ensued a change of policy resulting in a reign of terror 'fearful' enough to satisfy any Turcophile of the day.

At the end of 1564 Ivan withdrew from Moscow, returning with the understanding that he would have free rein to deal with what he regarded as the theft, malfeasance, and betrayal of the boyars, the clergy having been accused of at least concealing the boyars' crimes. This was the beginning of the creation of a state within a state, the *oprichnina*, by means of which Ivan set out to destroy his enemies – and this meant chiefly the boyars. He had already threatened the clergy; and the meaning of the threats soon became clear. Makary died in 1563, a few months after welcoming Ivan home from Polotsk. In 1564 a monk of the Chudov monastery, Afanasy, was chosen to succeed him; the council that chose him decided that the metropolitan and the archbishop of Novgorod were to wear a white cowl, a symbol by now linked with the Josephite camp.[75] Afanasy, however, renounced the office in 1566, and his successor was Filipp, hegumen of the Solovki monastery. Filipp first insisted on the abolition of the *oprichnina*, but was prevailed upon to withdraw this demand. Nevertheless after he was consecrated he renewed it. In a little over a year Ivan lost his patience and compelled a council to condemn and depose Filipp. In 1569 the former head of the church was strangled in his monastery cell by Maliuta Skuratov, one of Ivan's chief oprichniks. The succeeding metropolitans had little power to restrain the tsar from his bloody massacres of his 'enemies'.

When Sigismund II Augustus died, Ivan supported the candidacy of his son Fedor for the Polish throne, and also made other proposals, including partition of the Republic between the Holy Roman Empire and Muscovy. Stephen Batory, emerging as the new king, vigorously prosecuted the war. In 1579 he retook Polotsk; by 1581 he was besieging Pskov. The Swedes, whom Ivan had tried in vain to obtain as allies, took Narva the same year. In 1580 Ivan turned to the papacy for mediation, and Possevino helped arrange the truce of Yam–Zapolsky in January 1582. Ivan had to renounce Livonia and Polotsk, and by a treaty of 1583 with Sweden had to give up Narva and other cities. The westward offensive, having lasted twenty-five years, was a failure. In 1581 Ivan had fatally injured his eldest remaining son, Ivan. When Ivan died in 1584, there was no one to succeed him but the weak-minded Fedor and the latter's younger half-brother Dmitry. Dmitry died in 1591, and the direct line of the House of Riurik therefore became extinct when Fedor died in 1598. The Time of Troubles that followed seemed to contemporaries like God's judgment on Ivan's personal life and public policy.

The contest between the Transvolgan Elders and the Josephites appears to be the central thread of ideological tension for the first thirty years of Ivan IV's fifty-year reign. By 1549 Sylvester was in an important position, and maintained it for several years; but from Makary's election as metropolitan of Moscow in 1542, and in certain respects as early as his elevation to the archbishopric of Novgorod in 1526, he was working methodically and quietly to buttress the Josephite position by means of a many-sided and systematic ideological campaign. Already in 1550 the Josephites occupied the crucial positions in the Church hierarchy, and used them to head off the challenge to monastic landholding which Ivan IV and Sylvester intended to press in the Hundred Chapters Council of 1551. The Josephites knew how to use the succession crisis of 1553 to their own advantage; how to turn the trials of the heretics Bashkin (1553 and perhaps also 1554) and Feodosy Kosoi (1554) to account by striking at Artemy and other Transvolgans, even if Viskovaty's attack (which they disowned) on Sylvester proved premature and abortive; how to identify themselves with the Livonian War; how to profit from Ivan's break with the Transvolgans in 1560. However, Makary died in 1563, and the Josephites were unable to solve the problem of linking themselves with the great anti-boyar purges that followed the crisis of 1564, even though their ideological position should have meant that there were few obstacles to their doing so. Although Metropolitan Afanasy was inaugurated under Josephite auspices, he withdrew from his see in 1566. The brutal treatment of his successor, Filipp, who was strangled in 1569, may have deterred the Josephites from attempting any open moves to recoup their fortunes. (Filipp, apparently, cannot be identified with the Transvolgans, though his involvement in schemes of the Staritskys in 1537 and the fact that both Artemy [1554] and Sylvester

[1560] were confined in the Solovki monastery where he was abbot may suggest the possibility that he had something in common with them.[76])

While the Josephites enjoyed ascendancy, their effort to marry themselves to the autocratic state as security of their monastic properties seemed to have succeeded. Metropolitan Makary glorified the tsar and sought to give the church pre-eminence by compiling religious writings, canonizing saints, and persecuting heretics. In these respects he seems to have been influenced by Roman Catholic examples of his own day as were Gennady of Novgorod and Filofei of Pskov before him, though in none of these cases is any sympathy for Roman Catholicism to be found, and indeed Makary's enthusiasm for the Livonian War suggests the reverse. Evidently the Josephites wedded themselves to the notion of a centralized autocracy in the deluded belief that they could themselves become the tsar's chief advisers and guide the state in the direction of supporting the Church and crushing dissent.

However, the crisis of 1564 and its consequences soon made clear that 'he who rides a tiger' takes grave risks. Ivan IV's treatment of Metropolitan Filipp constituted a lasting warning against any serious attempt by high clergy to restrain the tsar's ferocious brutality and arbitrariness. The terror of the *oprichnina* affected all who served the autocrat; to see its effect it is enough to compare Ivan's failure to bring the boyars to swear allegiance to his son Dmitry in 1553 with their reaction to his fervently expressed wish to abdicate in 1581 after he had killed his son Ivan – many feared he was simply testing them, and all insisted that he remain on the throne.[77]

After Ivan IV and his *oprichnina*, the question was no longer whether Josephites or Transvolgans would win the upper hand in a basically ecclesiastical and cultural debate. The autocrat was not going to allow any outcome of which he disapproved. Muscovy had traveled some distance in a dubious direction from the time when Ivan III was outmaneuvered by the Josephite clergy. Ivan IV's undoubted wish to strengthen Russian Orthodoxy in scholarship and prestige was frustrated, for a few stealthy borrowings from Roman learning were quite insufficient to achieve the objective. When pressure from the West was mounting, the international cultural encounter was bound to threaten the Muscovite Church. But the power of the tsardom to decide any cultural contests domestically was clearly established. For three centuries the state was to be arbiter of the fate of Russian culture.

ROME ENTERS MOSCOW: THE REIGN OF FEDOR AND THE TIME OF TROUBLES

Fedor (1584–98) was not competent to rule. For a few months his uncle Nikita Romanovich Yuriev was in effective charge, but the uncle fell ill, and for the remainder of Fedor's reign state affairs were directed by Boris Godunov. Boris had been the favorite of Ivan IV in his later years and was the brother of Irina, whom Fedor had married in 1580.

The most important event of his reign was the creation of a patriarchate of Moscow. The propaganda of the Jesuits in Poland-Lithuania had been making much of the subjection of the Orthodox Church to the 'Sultan' and contrasted the chaotic condition of the see of Constantinople with the stability of the see of Rome. It seemed to Boris Godunov that the way to fend off such taunts was to establish an independent see in Moscow.

In 1586 Patriarch Joachim of Antioch had visited Moscow, and it was secretly proposed to him that he consecrate Metropolitan Dionisy as patriarch, but he agreed only to consult the other Eastern patriarchs. In 1588 Jeremiah II of Constantinople, having just taken a hand in the affairs of the Church in Poland-Lithuania, abruptly appeared in Smolensk. The Muscovites were embarrassed; they wondered what had happened to Theoleptus II, who had held the see of Constantinople when Joachim assembled his credentials. Jeremiah was, if the Muscovites knew it, a prime example of the condition of the Ecumenical Patriarchate that evoked Jesuit taunts. He had been twice deposed by the Turks; his second deposition, in 1584, has been followed by exile to Rhodes. The French ambassador had secured his release but not his restoration to his see. Four other prelates held it in rapid succession; he was restored only in 1589, *in absentia*, after he had left Muscovy to re-enter Poland. If he is to be regarded as rightful patriarch of Constantinople during his journey to Muscovy, he was the first and last holder of that office to undertake such a visit.[78]

In 1587 Fedor had for the third time been a candidate for the elective Polish throne, and this time he actually had a majority of electors, but the Muscovites threw away his chances by maladroit treatment of the commissioners sent to arrange details.[79] As a result Boris was all the more eager to clarify Moscow's ecclesiastical status, in case other chances arose for a Muscovite tsar to become king of Poland. The regent made a pretense at a solution by inviting Jeremiah to remain in Muscovy, thus providing the country with a patriarch. However, he set unacceptable conditions, and when Jeremiah declined Boris promptly proposed that he consecrate Metropolitan Iov as Patriarch of Moscow. Jeremiah's financial need and the virtual confinement in which he was held induced him to agree, and Iov was consecrated in 1589. At the same time four new metropolitanates were created for Krutitsy, Novgorod, Kazan, and Rostov. At length Jeremiah was permitted to depart, and he eventually dispatched to Moscow evidence of the approval of the other Eastern patriarchs.

Superficially Boris had achieved his aim, though it was soon to be plain that cultural self-defense was not to be obtained so easily. A taste of the danger to come was provided by a war with Sweden in the 1590's. Sigismund III of Poland, elected after Fedor's advisers had mishandled their opportunity, in 1592 became king of Sweden also. For a time it looked as if the armies of both countries would be directed against Moscow. The threat did not materialize. When in 1595–7 the Croatian priest Komulović visited Moscow as envoy of Pope Clement VIII with another proposal for a crusade against the Turks,[80] the threat of war with Poland and Sweden nevertheless must have made Boris's response even cooler than it might otherwise have been (though nothing is known of what he said).

In 1598 Fedor died; his only child, Feodosiia, had died four years earlier. Boris Godunov (1598–1605) was crowned tsar. Although his enemies suspected him of the murder of Dmitry Ivanovich, Feodosiia, and Fedor himself, modern historians have found, despite Karamzin, Pushkin, and Mussorgsky, that there is no reliable evidence to support the charges.[81] Boris had considerable skill in statecraft, and also a vision of the need to raise the cultural level of Muscovy. He wished to found a higher school in Moscow, in which foreigners would be the teachers, and he sent several young men to study in the West (who vanished during the next turbulent decades, with the exception of one who became an Anglican priest in England; none returned to Muscovy).

Boris was undone by domestic problems. As a former boyar he knew well what might be feared from the boyars, and from 1600 he took harsh measures against them, in particular the Romanov family; he forced Fedor Nikitich to become a monk and his wife to become a nun and exiled the children, including the future tsar Michael. The boyars awaited their opportunity to get rid of Godunov. In 1601 famine and plague struck, and armed gangs penetrated Moscow itself. In early 1604 it became known in Moscow that a young man had appeared in Poland claiming to be the Tsarevich Dmitry.

His real identity remains obscure, though it seems certain that he was a Russian by origin.[82] He appeared first as a monk at the seat of Prince Konstantin Ostrozhsky; he went from there to the Socinian school at Goszcza, where he formed close ties with the renowned preacher Tvardokhleb. Some time later he declared himself to be Dmitry to Prince Adam Wiśniowiecki. The latter promptly took him to a relative by marriage, the palatine George Mniszech of Sandomierz. He was soon betrothed to Mniszech's daughter Marina. King Sigismund recognized him as Dmitry but declined to promise direct support. The Jesuits took him up, and in April 1604 he underwent conversion to Roman Catholicism. In August he set out at the head of an army for Russia. Many towns welcomed him, and troops sent to oppose him defected. In April 1605 Boris Godunov suddenly died and was succeeded by his son Fedor. Fedor Godunov was dispatched by agents of the First False Dmitry, as subsequent events require him to be called, and in June the pretender entered Moscow.

It seems clear that a significant group of boyars, fearing Boris might become a new Ivan IV, were decisive in this curious episode. However 'Dmitry', intelligent, energetic, and committed to reform, soon gained great popularity with the common people of Muscovy also. He was interested in cultural improvement, and spoke of the desirability of an education abroad, from which he himself had benefited at least to some extent.

His religious attitudes are uncertain. In Poland he had had ties with Roman Catholics including Jesuits and the papal nuncio, Bishop Claudio Rangoni; but in Muscovy he refused to honor promises to introduce Roman Catholicism there. He maintained ties with Antitrinitarians; Tvardokhleb even headed the staff of a mission of theirs in Moscow while he was tsar.[83] The Calvinist brothers Buczynski enjoyed 'Dmitry's' confidence more than any other Poles, and he sent one of them to Poland as envoy. Miakotin declares that he was 'rather indifferent to the distinctions between the religions, in which may be reflected the influence of Polish Arianism [i.e., Antitrinitarianism]'.[84] 'Dmitry's' apparent indifferentism, however, cannot be ascribed to the influence of the Antitrinitarians, for such people cared very much about the differences. It must rather be assimilated to the *politique* attitude (not suggesting that he knew of it) of some of his contemporaries in France, who sought to overcome religious quarrels by ignoring them. Moscow was worth a mass. Doubtless he wanted power; the evidence suggests that he also wanted to be a good ruler and might have made a better one than many who ruled Muscovy for long periods.

However, his power lasted a little less than a year. Within weeks after entering Moscow, he deposed the patriarch, Iov. 'Dmitry' chose as Iov's successor Archbishop Ignaty of Riazan, a Greek who had spent some years in Rome. It was Ignaty who crowned him tsar in July 1605. Though Ignaty repeatedly attacked 'Latins', he was willing to acknowledge the at least nominally Roman Catholic 'Dmitry' as ruler and later to accept the Union of Brest – after he was deposed (under Vasily Shuisky) and exiled to Poland.[85] 'Dmitry' refrained from taking harsh measures against his enemies; for example, he commuted the death sentence of Prince Vasily Shuisky, his chief opponent, to exile. From there Shuisky returned to organize a successful conspiracy. On 8 May (O.S.) 1606, he married Marina Mniszech, who was crowned a few minutes before the wedding. Eight days later the conspirators broke into the Kremlin, shot 'Dmitry', burned the body, and fired the ashes from a cannon pointed westward, whence he came.

One curious personage who attained prominence during 'Dmitry's' brief reign deserves mention: the eccentric Prince Ivan Khvorostinin. Kliuchevsky comes close to identifying him as the first Russian Westernizer,[86] while Platonov calls him 'the first swallow of the spring of Muscovite culture'.[87] He was only eighteen when he became a favorite of 'Dmitry's' at the tsar's court. He had studied Latin, signing himself 'Duks [dux] Ivan', and seems to have had a number of pro-Western religious views, such as holding Roman and Greek icons to be equally worthy of veneration.[88] Later he was incarcerated for his allegedly heretical opinions, once under Vasily Shuisky and again in 1623–4 under Michael. He may be called the first 'internal *émigré*' in Russian history, complaining bitterly that 'in Moscow of men there are none, but all are gross and not to be consorted with'. The nature of his religious views is difficult to establish. Platonov suggests that at least on one issue Khvorostinin's position comes from Socinianism. Commenting on a manuscript that proves he was required to swear strictly to adhere to the Orthodox doctrine concerning the resurrection of the dead, which suggests that he was at least suspected of believing differently, Platonov points out that Socinians taught that the dead would be resurrected only spiritually.[89] On the basis of this conclusion, Pascal calls Kliuchevsky to task for suggesting that Roman Catholicism was the chief foreign influence on Khvorostinin.[90] The young prince was certainly fond of Latin books and ways. However, the known evidence fails to support any clear answer to the question of whether Protestant, Socinian, or Catholic ideas carried more weight with him – much as in the case of 'Dmitry'. Both saw enlightenment to be derived from the West, and Khvorostinin (not 'Dmitry', who was more adroit) voiced his scorn for those who disagreed. In personality Khvorostinin seems indeed to have been, as Kliuchevsky suggests, a 'remote spiritual ancestor of Chaadaev',[91] who was not one to suffer fools gladly.

Immediately following the murder of 'Dmitry', Vasily Shuisky was proclaimed tsar. However, he was soon faced by unrest among both the new serving-class (dvorianstvo) and the Cossacks. Armies of sorts from both groups joined and marched on Moscow, but at Kolomenskoe, just south of the city, they quarreled and the dvorianstvo made peace with Vasily. The Cossacks under Ivan Bolotnikov fled to Tula. There they rallied to a new pretender, a Cossack known as the False Peter,[92] who had appeared among the Terek Cossacks while the First False Dmitry was in power. By the summer of 1607 Vasily Shuisky had defeated these challengers.

However, by then a Second False Dmitry had made his appearance. Setting up his camp in Tushino, he was joined by many Cossacks, Poles including Marina Mniszech (who publicly 'recognized' him as her husband, although a secret marriage was performed to legalize the union), and several Russian boyars including Fedor Romanov, who had been raised to the rank of metropolitan of Rostov by the First False Dmitry as 'Filaret'. This curious coalition, which treated the new 'Dmitry' with scant ceremony, was strong enough so that Vasily was unable to defeat it. When he tried to obtain help from the Swedes, Sigismund III reversed his hitherto non-interventionist policy and declared war. He summoned the Poles who were in the entourage of the Second False Dmitry to join him; some did, others hesitated. Filaret, who was named patriarch by the new 'Dmitry' in 1609, and others now approached Sigismund to discuss the possibility of naming his son Władysław tsar, and in February 1610 an agreement was signed whereby Władysław had to share power with the boyars and the so-called zemsky sobor.

As two different armies approached Moscow from two directions, one a Polish force under Hetman Żółkiewski and the other under the Second False Dmitry, a court cabal deposed Vasily. Fearing the second 'Dmitry', the cabal admitted the Poles to Moscow and in August 1610 Władysław was proclaimed tsar; it was now stipulated that he would have to convert to Russian Orthodoxy. By this time, however, Sigismund had decided that he wanted the Muscovite throne for himself, and a party in Moscow was willing to accept him as tsar. Abruptly the Second False Dmitry died, and it appeared that Sigismund might succeed.

However, Patriarch Hermogen appealed for resistance to the Poles, and although he was imprisoned for doing so his appeal was heeded. Again a *dvorianstvo* militia and a Cossack force approached Moscow; the Poles shut themselves up in the Kremlin and awaited Sigismund. Again the *dvorianstvo* and the Cossacks fell out, and the Cossacks proclaimed the son of Marina (now living with a hetman) and the Second False Dmitry as tsar. In early 1612 another militia was assembled, and it was at last successful. Led by the butcher Kuzma Minin and Prince Dmitry Pozharsky, it moved from Nizhny Novgorod toward Moscow and in October took the Kremlin. Sigismund found it prudent to retreat, and in February 1613 a zemsky sobor chose Filaret's son Michael Romanov as tsar. It had first determined that no foreigner or adherent of a non-Orthodox faith was eligible for the throne. Hermogen, before his martyrdom (1612) at the hands of pro-Władysław Muscovites for his blessing of Pozharsky's army, had declared that only one who had been baptized (or rebaptized) as Orthodox could rule in Moscow. What was not true in 1605 had become true by 1613; the tsar must be Orthodox. No Russian monarch tried openly to violate the rule again before the Revolution.

For Sigismund, deciding for Władysław, Moscow was not worth a mass; or perhaps a mass was worth even more than Moscow. In a letter to Pope Paul V in October 1610 Sigismund gave as his first objective in his campaign against Moscow 'the propagation of the orthodox [i.e., Roman Catholic] Christian religion...' Indeed, the pope had already blessed his cause as a crusade.[93] The election of Michael by no means persuaded the Poles to abandon their efforts. Władysław, now bent on the conquest and annexation of Muscovy, advanced again on the capital but was repulsed by Pozharsky. In 1618 a truce was concluded at Deulino, ceding to Poland Smolensk and other lands, but marking the end of any Polish king's chance to convert Muscovy by force to Roman Catholicism. (It was, however, only in 1634 that Władysław, by then king of Poland, renounced his claims to the Muscovite throne.)

THE SITUATION IN 1613

In Poland-Lithuania the Orthodox Eastern Slavs had witnessed great gains by the Protestants and Antitrinitarians within the country and some inroads among themselves, followed by a recapture of the lost ground by the Roman Catholics and a subjection of their own Orthodox Church to Rome in the Union of Brest. The counter-attack of Rome was poised on the Polish–Muscovite frontier. At that point the religious and cultural strength of Muscovy was at a low ebb. The Transvolgans' defense of the indigenous tradition, coupled with willingness to borrow (as in the cases of Maxim the

Greek, Andrei Kurbsky, and others) from the learning of the Roman Catholics, was at an end. In retrospect it may be regarded as an early faint, unconscious or only partly conscious form of Russian syncretism. The best of the Transvolgans did not fear or anathematize everything coming from the West; they showed little disposition to persecute heretics, from the Judaizers to Bashkin and Feodosy, whether or not any influence of the West on such persons could be proven; what they feared was too great an involvement in worldly and secular affairs of the sort defended by the Josephites. We shall meet again their combination of cultural traits and beliefs rooted in the native soil with some degree of openness to what was good of foreign origin.

The Josephites were a less gentle breed; despite their love for their Church and their culture, they were willing to borrow from Roman Catholic militancy and its intellectual weapons in rooting out heretics and in glorifying the Muscovite autocracy in the hope that they would be left the properties they believed essential to maintain the faith. Their claims for an exalted role for the clergy in society and state were not successful; their properties were in time infringed; though the heretics were rooted out, they themselves did not survive either, and disappeared with puzzling rapidity. There remained the strengthened autocracy that was the legacy of Ivan IV. After the tsar demonstrated in the case of Filipp what he was capable of doing to troublesome priests, the obscure prelates that followed, even after they were given the title of patriarch, were in no position to shore up the cultural defenses of Muscovy. Credit should be given to the moral courage of Patriarch Hermogen, but that is all.

Thus far Western thought had made only a minor and marginal contribution to the ecclesiastical and political struggles in Muscovy, though the uses made of it by the Muscovites are of interest in their own right and throw light on the character of the participants. When the Roman counter-attack crossed the Muscovite frontier during the Time of Troubles, the possibility seemed real of implanting Western cultural orientations in Moscow in a decisive manner. A glimpse of such possibilities when not closely linked with Polish power is provided by the year-long reign of the First False Dmitry; such possibilities when harnessed to Polish state interests are shown by the crusade of Sigismund III, the prospects of his or his son Władysław's becoming tsar of Muscovy, the march and counter-march of Polish troops in the heart of Russia.

The Roman Catholic offensive toward Muscovy in the late sixteenth and early seventeenth century had weak intellectual and moral foundations. Such zealots as King Sigismund might be concerned for the Russians' immortal souls but not much for their mortal coils. Such clergymen as Possevino and Skarga might value Russians as human beings but had a condescending or even contemptuous attitude toward their culture; even adequate knowledge of Russian culture was lacking, Skarga being almost the sole exception. The Roman Catholic approach to Russia was conspicuously deficient in what the

Jesuit mission to China possessed: deep respect for, indeed devotion to the indigenous culture. A single lonely man, Juraj Križanić, though not a Jesuit, was to attempt such an approach in the later seventeenth century. After the Poles had occupied Moscow, however, the possibility of widespread Russian acceptance of either the Unia or Catholicism was as firmly excluded as the possibility of a Roman Catholic tsar on the Russian throne. Nevertheless there remained open the possibility of substantial Roman Catholic influence without conversion, and the possibility was to be tested in the seventeenth century.

3

MOSCOW AND KIEV (1613–1689)

They paint the image of Emmanuel the Saviour with the face plump, the lips red, the hair curly, arms and muscles thick, the fingers dimpled, and likewise the legs with thick hips, and altogether make him look like a German, big-bellied and fat, except that no sword is painted at the hip.

The Archpriest Avvakum, *Life*, written 1672–5

INTRODUCTION

When the Time of Troubles ended in 1613, a Russian and Orthodox tsar, Michael, sat on the Muscovite throne. The Poles had been expelled from Moscow, even if peace had not yet been concluded, and the danger that Roman Catholicism or the Unia might engulf Muscovy seemed to have passed. The immediate result was something of a xenophobic reaction which went beyond anything to be found earlier, but neither Michael nor his mentor and father, Patriarch Filaret, was able to get any further in erecting cultural defenses against Western penetration than Ivan IV or Metropolitan Makary.

The Cossacks of the Dnieper valley assumed the leadership of the Orthodox in Poland-Lithuania, and the man who showed the greatest understanding of their cultural needs, Peter Mogila,[1] succeeded in making Kiev the most advanced center of Orthodoxy. In doing so, however, he borrowed so liberally from Roman Catholicism that it may be questioned whether he did more to advance or to retard Rome's cultural expansion. The Cossacks, in any event, succumbed to the problems of their difficult geographical position. They were compelled to try to deal with Poland, the Ottoman Empire, and Muscovy all at once. They could not hold all three at bay, and finally yielded their independence to Muscovy. The passage of Kiev into Muscovite hands in 1667 was followed by powerful though indirect pressure of the Catholic Reform on Muscovy.

For the time being, to be sure, the foreground of religious and cultural controversy was held by the reforms carried out in the Russian Orthodox Church by Patriarch Nikon and the resistance to them by the 'Old Believers'. The latter were utterly defeated and became 'schismatics' outside the fold of the official Church. That did not mean, however, that Nikon was victorious. He aimed at a renovation of the Church that approached the magnitude of a revolution, one which nominally relied on the authority of Constantinople, though his ostensible 'Greek' orientation deserves close scrutiny. Whatever

54

his own aims, he lost control of that revolution, which passed into the hands of men amenable to closer cultural ties with Rome. Russia felt the influence of the Catholic Reform most strongly during the regency of Sophia (1682–9). An isolated episode of some interest is found in the career of Juraj Križanić, who envisaged the possibility of weaning the Russians away from the Greeks toward reunion with Rome; but, perhaps partly because he advanced his plans a few years prematurely, he met with complete failure.

When Peter I overthrew Sophia in 1689 Roman Catholic influences on Muscovy via Kiev were mounting in intensity. Peter was, however, to replace them with Protestant influences. Thus in Russia (as in China) the greatest successes of the Reformation came after the greatest impact of the Catholic Reform, reversing the order of what happened in Western Europe.

THE ZAPOROZHIAN COSSACKS AND PETER MOGILA

In the fifteenth century the tightening of peasant bondage, both in Poland-Lithuania and Muscovy, helped to lead to the emergence of a social group whose origins are obscure: the Cossacks. In the southern territories tributary to both Poland-Lithuania (after 1569, to Poland directly instead of Lithuania) and Muscovy there arose free, self-governing communities of frontiersmen who might with justice be described either as freebooters or pirates. Earlier the term 'Cossacks' had been used to refer to a group of Tatar auxiliaries in Lithuania, but it came to mean Eastern Slavs, either non-taxable and non-serf men in both Poland-Lithuania and Muscovy or the fishers, hunters, and farmers of the steppe outside the effective control of both states.[2]

Although the Cossacks thus may be seen as originating in aspirations of the lower classes for a free life, from fairly early some of the Orthodox nobles of Poland-Lithuania identified with them and furnished them leadership. In the middle of the sixteenth century a certain Dmitry Vyshnevetsky became a leader of the Cossacks on the Dnieper and tried to organize them, with the help of either Muscovy or Lithuania, against the Tatars. By the latter sixteenth century a Cossack stronghold or *Sich* existed beyond the Dnieper rapids in the so-called *Zaporozh'e*, and the Zaporozhian Cossacks developed a clear organizational pattern. The Polish-Lithuanian Government tried to bring them and the other Cossacks of the Ukraine under effective control, but they maintained their autonomy, by their activities against the Tatars and in Moldavia bringing the Sultans into frequent conflict with Poland-Lithuania. When Poland took over the Ukraine directly in 1569, however, the process of 'registering' Cossacks made progress, and some Cossack detachments were used in the Polish armed forces. The nobles of the Ukraine sometimes antagonized the Cossacks, and armed fighting resulted. The Poles were not interested in protecting the Orthodox nobles, but when the Zaporozhian Cossacks, having made an alliance with the Habsburg emperor, looted Moldavia, the Poles sent forces to subdue them. They were defeated at

Lubny in 1596, and their leader was executed. At the same time the Sejm made the decision to eliminate the Cossacks for good.

This decision was, however, ignored by Sigismund III and the Polish-Lithuanian hetmans who intervened in Moldavia and in Muscovy during the Time of Troubles. Many Cossacks, registered and not, were enlisted in the Polish armies that accompanied the First False Dmitry, and under Hetman Peter Sagaidachny the Zaporozhian Cossacks allied themselves with Władysław in his last effort to take Moscow in 1618, just before the truce of Deulino. In the meantime Cossacks were raiding Tatar and Turkish territory, and their prestige abroad grew. Sagaidachny was for the first time recognized by the Poles as chief of all registered Cossacks.

The Cossacks were now in a strong enough position to make it possible to think of educational and cultural revival. Already there had been significant literary efforts in the Ukraine to defend Orthodoxy – which now had no legal sanction in Poland-Lithuania – and to combat the Unia, whose spokesmen included Peter Skarga, Ipaty Potei, and others. The monk Ivan Vyshensky, who returned from Mt Athos in 1605, was an early contributor to the Orthodox side.[3] Other more erudite men produced substantial works of Greek inspiration, notably the *Lamentation for the One Ecumenical Apostolic Eastern Church* (*Threnos*) (1610) of Melety Smotritsky and the *Book of Defense of the Holy Catholic Apostolic Ecumenical Church* (*Palinodiia*) of Zakhariia Kopystensky. Kopystensky, whose book was composed in the first quarter of the century but not published until the second half of the century, was familiar with the Greek Fathers and Byzantine literature generally. Smotritsky, archbishop of Polotsk and son of the rector of the Ostrog school Gerasim Smotritsky, as time passed became more deeply concerned by the Protestant influences he discerned in his Greek contemporaries such as Cyril Lucaris, and finally accepted, first secretly (1627) the Unia and then Roman Catholicism.[4] In 1628 a newly produced volume of Smotritsky's was burned by the Orthodox.

Despite the gifts of such men as Kopystensky, the fundamental Orthodox predicament remained what it had been earlier: the Greeks themselves had entered a period of cultural impoverishment, and could provide little assistance; therefore the Orthodox Eastern Slavs were driven, as before, to try to draw on the intellectual arsenal of the Western Church for defense against Rome. Although some had sought Protestant aid, the growing tendency was in the direction of borrowing from Rome itself to defend against Rome. However, as shown by the case of Melety Smotritsky, some of those who did so ended up in Uniat or Roman Catholic ranks themselves.

During the early years of the seventeenth century the center of Orthodox cultural activity shifted from Vilna and Lwów to Kiev; the crucial institutions in this shift were the schools of the Orthodox 'brotherhoods'. Such schools had been founded in Lwów and Vilna in 1586. In 1615 a brotherhood was founded in Kiev; by this time a group of learned monks, mainly from Lwów, had been assembled in the Monastery of the Caves by Abbot Elisei Pletenetsky and a printing press set up whose first work appeared in 1617. Soon a brotherhood school opened in the city with Iov Boretsky as rector. Iov had been rector of the Lwów brotherhood school from 1604, and taught for a time in the household of Prince K. K. Ostrozhsky before coming to Kiev.

In 1620 Patriarch Theophanes of Jerusalem was passing through the city of Kiev. Hetman Sagaidachny, understanding the importance of restoring the Orthodox hierarchy in the Ukraine, persuaded him to ordain secretly Iov Boretsky as metropolitan of Kiev and to consecrate seven new bishops (one of whom was Melety Smotritsky) as well. Sagaidachny did not long survive this significant achievement. He maintained harmony with the Poles, and in fact his death resulted from a wound received at Khotin (1621), where a Cossack force relieved a besieged Polish army and drove the Turks to retreat.

Another soldier at Khotin was Peter Mogila, who was to achieve recognition of the restored Orthodox hierarchy by the Poles. By this time pro-Catholic and pro-Uniat trends were running strongly among the Orthodox. In 1618 Kirill Trankvillion-Stavrovetsky had written a book entitled *The Mirror of Theology* (*Zertsalo bogosloviia*), the first dogmatic treatise of the Orthodox Eastern Slavs; a 'completely Thomist' tract, as Florovsky describes it, was produced by another writer, Kasian Sacowicz.[5] Both works were condemned in Kiev as well as Moscow, which echoes of the Orthodox revival were beginning to reach. Both men went over to the Uniats, and Sacowicz finally became a Roman Catholic outright. Metropolitan Iov, who leaned to harmony with the Unia but nothing more, was compelled to deal with the open conversion to it of Melety Smotritsky in 1628; appalled by the threat that the Union of Brest would undermine the newly revived Orthodox hierarchy, Iov died in 1631 without reaching any solution.[6]

The man to hold the line against conversion to the Unia was found in Peter Mogila.[7] This gifted man was the son of the man who was hospodar of Wallachia (1601–7) and then of Moldavia (1607–9),[8] the family having close relations with the Lwów brotherhood, since the city at the end of the sixteenth century was a cultural center not only for the Ukraine but for the Rumanian principalities, which were also Orthodox, as well.[9] He was born in 1596 and as a boy came to Poland with his family, which had to take refuge from a victorious rival. Receiving the rudiments of an Orthodox education from members of the Lwów brotherhood school, he finished by hearing lectures at foreign universities – exactly which are unknown. After he took part in the battle of Khotin, we know nothing of him until he was named successor to Kopystensky as archimandrite of the Monastery of the Caves in Kiev in 1627.[10] Probably the support of Metropolitan Iov Boretsky and of Polish magnates friendly to his family helped overcome the reluctance of the local clergy to accept a thirty-one-year-old, who was evidently still then a layman,[11] in the post. Evidently he was close to Melety Smotritsky, whose defection to the Unia was the great scandal of this period, and this may have prevented Mogila's succession to the metropolitanate when Iov died in 1631,[12] despite

Iov's preference for him. Wishing not to be obligated to the new metropolitan, Isaiah Kopinsky, Mogila established a school of his own at the Monastery of the Caves, distinct from that of the Kiev brotherhood, but when the brotherhood teachers declared their submission to the patriarchate of Constantinople, he proceeded to unite his school to that of the brotherhood. This was achieved by the beginning of the academic year 1632-3. In his own school before and after it was joined to the other, Latin was the chief language of instruction, in contrast to the Greek that had taken first place in the previous institutions of the Ukraine.[13]

In 1632 the crusading Catholic King Sigismund III died and was succeeded by Władysław IV, the man who had almost become tsar of Russia two decades earlier. He was from the first eager to achieve religious peace among his subjects, and Mogila, who was in agreement with his policy, was promptly named metropolitan – Isaiah Kopinsky was abruptly deposed. Mogila was consecrated in 1633, and remained metropolitan until his death in 1647.

Mogila's aim, along with Władysław's, was to establish a separate Ukrainian patriarchate uniting the Orthodox and the Uniats, with himself as patriarch, which would be in communion with both Rome and Constantinople.[14] Since he modeled the Kievan college (to be raised in 1701 to the level of 'academy' by Peter I) on the Jesuit schools of Poland and other Roman Catholic institutions, and borrowed liberally from Catholic learning, there were many charges in his own time that he was pro-Roman. Florovsky concludes that Mogila raised the Orthodox Church in the Ukraine out of its state of collapse, but only at the price of adopting 'crypto-Romanism'. He declares: 'It was a case of a sharp Romanization of Orthodoxy, a Latin pseudomorphosis of Orthodoxy.'[15] Hrushevsky makes similar allegations from a viewpoint relatively more sympathetic to Protestantism: Mogila, he contends, turned Ukrainian culture back 'from Reformational tendencies to obscurantist Latin medieval scholasticism'.[16] Golubev defends Mogila against insinuations of pro-Uniat leanings, but does not try to deny that extensive use of Latin learning was made by Mogila and his associates. Golubev writes:

In the period under consideration the West had far outdistanced the East from the standpoint of learning...Among the Orthodox South Russians [*iuzhno-russy*], where the sciences had only begun to grow, it was natural to make use of the scholarly results achieved by neighboring peoples even though they were of a different faith.[17]

Utilizing Golubev's analysis of the Orthodox polemical literature of the period, it is possible to see what using Catholic 'scholarly results' meant. Golubev examines five works produced by Mogila's circle, all in Polish though the initial words of the titles are all Greek or Latin, from 1635 to 1644. The first, called *Exegesis*, is a reply to a lost anti-Mogilian work probably written by the Uniat Metropolitan Veliamin Rutsky. The charge was that the Mogilian schools were teaching Protestant heresy. In answer, the author of the *Exegesis*, Sylvester Kossov (later to succeed Mogila as Orthodox metropolitan, 1647–57), expounds the doctrines of the Socinians, Calvinists, and Lutherans in turn, shows how they differ from Orthodoxy, and finally resorts to irony: the teachers of Kiev and Vinnitsa, his opponent contends, 'studied in the academies of Rome, Poland, Lithuania, and the Empire; they teach in Latin, in no way violating the ancient Greek religion: therefore they are Calvinists. Truly I did not know that you, calumniator, were such a first-rate Peripatetic [i.e., Aristotelian and logician]'.[18] In a bold and frank admission in which Mogila's conscious policy of imitation of Rome is set forth, Kossov wrote:

Whence come your magnificent preachers? From the schools. Whence your confessors who lift their thoughts up to God? From the schools. Whence your angelic theologians? From the schools. In a word, whatever ornaments you have may be entirely ascribed to schools.[19]

What Mogila was trying to do was to raise the cultural level of Orthodoxy and the Ukraine by borrowing the superior techniques of Roman Catholic education and learning. Golubev is frank to avow the result; the *Exegesis*, he writes, is a 'monument giving evidence of the content of theology at that time and, apparently, on a strictly Orthodox foundation utilizing Catholic systems to a substantial extent, in certain cases not without damage to the foundation mentioned'.[20]

Golubev has analyzed the sources of another polemical work, apparently composed by the Mogilian circle (not, he thinks, by Mogila himself) in 1644, called the *Lithos* (*Rock*). This work was in reply to a book by Kasian Sacowicz, the son of an Orthodox priest who had been (1620–4) rector of the Kievan brotherhood school, converted to the Unia in 1625, and in 1641 had accepted Roman Catholicism. The *Lithos* showed much greater erudition than Sacowicz's book, which itself was a testimony to the cultural gains Mogila's policies had made. Its sources are revealing. Golubev lists seven categories: Orthodox service books in Ukrainian, and partly in Greek, Muscovite, and Roman editions; Roman Catholic service books; decisions of ecumenical and other councils; Fathers of the Church, mostly Eastern but including Augustine, Hilary of Poitiers, and Ambrose; historical works including Caesar Baronius and Jan Długosz; Roman Catholic theological works, including Alcuin, Thomas Aquinas, Duns Scotus, Durandus of St Pourçain, Bernard of Clairvaux, Bonaventura, and Bellarmine; and 'miscellaneous' contemporary works.[21] Of the seven categories, it is obvious that the Western Church accounts for part of at least six.

Much of the polemic of the *Lithos* is sharp and even repugnant to the taste of a later day. Sacowicz as an infant had been so unfortunate as to have his ear destroyed by a hog that attacked him in his cradle. The *Lithos* makes a number of gibes occasioned by this accident: 'It would be better for you to discuss the pigs which ate your ear than to fix new forms of the sacraments.'[22] Yet in responding to Sacowicz's attacks on Eastern rites, the *Lithos* refrains from criticizing Western rites and even praises them; dogma and ritual must be distinguished, it declares, and as dogma is immutable ritual is mutable and must be in turn divided into 'essentials' (dating from apostolic times) and 'accidentals', the latter obviously being negotiable. In the schools Mogila created, in which Latin was the language of instruction and in which the dogmatic system of Aquinas was the basis of theological training,[23] there was preparation taking place not only for further progress on the cultural front of the Ukraine, but also for possible later moves toward church reunion.

The works produced by Mogila alone and without assistance were not numerous. One was the *Evkhologion* or *Trebnik* (Prayer-book) of 1646, based on the Roman Ritual of Pope Paul V, a Croatian translation of which, prepared by the Jesuit Kasić and published in Rome in 1637, was used.[24] A *Katekhizis* (*Catechism*) was prepared, possibly with others' assistance, and presented to a council in Kiev in 1640; its occasion seems to have been the need to counter the Calvinist-influenced Orthodox Confession (1633) of Cyril Lucaris, condemned by a council in Constantinople in 1638. In turn Mogila's *Catechism* evoked much controversy and was published only in 1667 (in Greek translation) in Holland, in Leipzig in 1695 in Latin. From the latter (and original) language came the Slavic translation issued in Moscow in 1696. But although Mogila did not publish the whole of it in Kiev, he issued a short version there in Polish, and it was republished in Moscow in 1649. Its debt to Rome was no less clear than Lucaris's Confession's to Geneva.

Mogila's efforts to raise the level of Orthodox culture in the Ukraine at the cost of the extensive reception of Roman Catholic learning were partly abortive, for they depended for their ultimate success on at least the maintenance of order and unity in the Polish state and perhaps also on the continuation of a policy of religious and cultural harmony such as Władysław IV advanced. However, Władysław died in 1648, a year after Mogila, and the consequence was the so-called 'Deluge', lasting until 1667, which was comparable in some ways to Muscovy's Time of Troubles of half a century before. The difference was that Muscovy recovered; Poland did not.

A rising of the Cossacks in 1637–8 had both alarmed the Poles and reassured them, since the 'registered' Cossacks had remained loyal to the throne and helped put down the peasant rebels who had joined the Zaporozhians. The 'registered' Cossack leadership was, like Mogila, willing to cooperate with Władysław, who had a bold dream of restoring royal power in Poland by means of a popular war with the Crimea and the Ottoman Turks in which he would have massive Cossack aid. The plan was exposed and enraged the Diet before the king died. In 1648 the ablest Cossack leader since Sagaidachny, Bogdan Khmelnitsky, raised the flag of rebellion. Crushing a large Polish army, Khmelnitsky captured Lwów and Kiev and was urged to march on Warsaw. He contented himself with deciding the election of the king, John II Casimir, and withdrew. Soon, however, he found himself in the midst of an immensely complicated series of negotiations and then wars, involving the

Crimean Tatars, the Ottoman Turks, Moldavia, and Muscovy. Khmelnitsky, for whom at the start 'the only important question was that of religious freedom',[25] came to take a broader view of the Ukraine's future and aspired to be, in his own words, 'the independent ruler of Rus [the Ukraine]'.[26]

In 1654 the Cossack chieftain consented to the signing of the Pereiaslavl Agreement with Muscovy, by which the Cossacks accepted Tsar Alexis as their ruler. Exactly what the agreement meant has been the subject of dispute even since.[27] In 1657 Khmelnitsky died. A lengthy Polish–Muscovite war ensued, but the Poles were no longer able to defeat the Muscovites. The peace of Andrusovo in 1667 recognized Moscow's annexation of Smolensk and Chernigov. Although Kiev was not ceded by the treaty, the chief city of the Ukraine was to be occupied two years longer by the Muscovites, and in fact the continued turbulence led to prolongation of their control.[28] In 1686 Kiev was to become formally a Muscovite possession.

The conclusion of the Polish–Muscovite peace of 1667 had been prompted by the revival of the Ottoman Empire under the Köprülü viziers, which was soon to lead to a last offensive to the gates of Vienna (1683), and by the deepening of the fear both powers felt of the Ottoman Empire and its Crimean Tatar allies. In 1669 the Cossacks, now led by Peter Doroshenko, concluded an agreement with the Ottoman Turks, and it was only when the Polish King John III Sobieski was about to make peace with Turkey in 1676 that Doroshenko surrendered to the Muscovite tsar Alexis. Doroshenko was, astonishingly though perhaps wisely, treated with favor during his remaining years. In 1681 Moscow and the Turks made peace at Bakhchisarai, and a year later a new leader of the Ukraine, Ivan Mazepa, acquired the favor of Moscow; in 1687 he became Hetman. The devastation on the west bank of the Dnieper had led to a very sizeable migration eastward. By this time Kiev was no longer an eastern outpost of a Ukraine largely in Poland, but the western outpost of a Ukraine largely in Muscovy, and not merely because the political frontier had been shifted, but because such a substantial number of people had moved.

During the 1670's the Kievan college had been revived, under the rectorship of Varlaam Yasinsky, later metropolitan of Kiev. He had studied in Elbing, Olomouc, and Kraków; a number of the teachers had studied at the Jesuit academy in Ingolstadt and in the Greek College of St Athanasius in Rome. Some had experienced Protestant influence; Innokenty Gizel and Adam Zernikav had studied in Königsberg.[29] During this period in order to study in Jesuit schools it was necessary to accept at least the Unia, and some Ukrainians accepted Roman Catholicism outright; such, for example, was the case of Stefan Yavorsky, who studied with the Jesuits in Lublin, Poznań, and Vilna as a Roman Catholic. Ioasaf Krokovsky, who had studied at the College of St Athanasius in Rome and became rector of the Kievan college, taught theology according to St Thomas Aquinas and under his rectorship a student Marian Sodality was formed which aggressively propagated the doctrine of the Immaculate Conception of the Virgin Mary.

Thus for decades the increasing Roman Catholic influence on the Ukraine had been putting down institutional roots. The days when the strength of the Polish state had been great enough to carry Western culture eastward into the midst of the Orthodox Eastern Slavs were past. The change in the political balance was reflected in the annexation of the left bank of the Dnieper by Muscovy in 1667. However, the balance of cultural forces did not shift accordingly. Though the Muscovites grew strong enough to annex much of the Ukraine, their intellectual strength had not increased. When Kiev became a Muscovite city, from the cultural standpoint it was Kiev which increasingly was influencing Moscow, not the reverse. Kiev was from the formal point of view a bastion of Orthodoxy, a center which had in the half-century following 1630 lifted the Ukraine out of religious and cultural disorder and revived the Orthodox Church, in sad disarray since the time of the Union of Brest in 1596. The content of the teachings of the Kievan college and the literature of its circle, however, show that the incorporation of Kiev did not result in a strengthening of Orthodox intellectual traditions in Moscow. On the contrary, to a considerable extent Kiev was a Trojan horse which the Roman Catholic Poles had left for the Orthodox Muscovites to drag inside their gates. Roman Catholic influence in Muscovy was finally checked; but what checked it was not Orthodoxy, but rather Protestantism.

THE COMING OF THE SCHISM

In 1613 Michael Romanov was elected tsar; six years later, after the truce of Deulino, his father Fedor Nikitich, as a monk known as Filaret, returned from Polish captivity. He was at once installed as patriarch, replacing a *locum tenens* who had served since Michael's accession. From 1619 to 1633 Russia was 'formally a diarchy', though in fact Filaret was ruler; he 'filled the vacuum left by his son's incapacity'.[30] The prolonged detention Filaret had experienced had not increased his sympathies for the Poles, Polish or European culture, or Roman Catholicism. No doubt considerations of state also carried weight with him. During the Time of Troubles Muscovy had been invaded and partly occupied by her Western neighbors, and the invasion and occupation had been facilitated by the willingness of many Russians, high and low, to collaborate with the intruders. At any rate, as Keep writes, he 'had nothing but disdain for western culture', and attempted to isolate Muscovy as no previous Russian prince had ever done.

Filaret subjected all incoming books to careful scrutiny. Conscious of increasing immigration from Poland-Lithuania (especially the Ukraine), he paid special attention to works originating there or written by Ukrainians after arrival. In 1627 L. Z. Tustanevsky, a monk from the Ukraine who had been commissioned to write a catechism, was charged with various errors, including the explanation of the movements of heavenly bodies in scientific terms, and his book was withheld from circulation. Filaret's caution was such that when he died, 124 manuscripts were found in his charge which had been approved by censors but which he had not sent on to be printed.[31] He required re-baptism for any conversion to Orthodoxy. In 1620 he attacked his predecessor, Iona, for allowing two Roman Catholic converts to be admitted to the Ortho-dox Church without rebaptism, and in 1624 Iona was dismissed from the metropolitanate of Krutitsy and exiled to a monastery. The same year a regula-tion was issued requiring even Ukrainian Orthodox immigrants to be re-baptized.[32]

The purely obscurantist policy of Filaret died with him, but the fourteen years it had prevailed had done damage. Conversion to Roman Catholicism had been successfully prevented; but the result was a false sense of security. The Orthodox Church was not prepared to defend itself either culturally or institutionally. It was ill-equipped to ward off the doctrinal influences of the Roman Catholic West that resulted from such policies as those of Peter Mogila – nor was it in a position to protect itself against the Russian state. Filaret's efforts to deal with the Western intellectual challenge by simple repression and his position as head of both Church and state weakened the Church in both respects. The circumstances that the patriarch was also in fact tsar was accidental and never to be repeated; the death of Filaret suddenly threw the Church on its own resources, which were meager both culturally and institutionally.

The attraction of Kiev, based on superior scholarship and command of languages, could not help but make itself felt. Shortly before he died, even Filaret felt constrained to speak of the desirability of organizing a school in Moscow that would in some degree imitate the model of the Kievan college. Nothing came of the scheme. However, under Michael and even before Filaret's death were appearing men in whom were germinating the seeds of intellectual discontent and ferment which were to make the succeeding reign so stormy.

Among such men were Ivan Nasedka. Born in 1570 in a village near the Monastery of Trinity and St Sergius, he had become a deacon in 1594 and a priest in 1608. He was sent to Moscow in 1615 and worked on the correction of sacred books, but soon fell under attack for his work. When Filaret returned he was restored to favor and sent on an embassy to Denmark (1621). His experience there gave him the basis for his *Exposition against the Lutherans* (*Izlozhenie na liutory*), finished in 1623.[33] Evidently as a result he was named sacristan of the Cathedral of the Assumption, Moscow's first church. As the foremost authority, he was in 1644 called in to polemize with a Lutheran pastor concerning the question of whether Count Waldemar of Schleswig-Holstein, son of Christian IV of Denmark and his morganatic wife, had to be rebaptized in order to marry the Tsarevna Irina. Nasedka did poorly; a Kievan monk, Isaaky, had to be summoned to aid him, and another confronta-tion was somewhat more successful. All this effort went for naught when the Tsar Michael died and the negotiations for the Danish marriage collapsed.

From 1638 to 1652 he acted as editor in the Press Office, assisting one Michael Rogov, with whom he had compiled *The Book of Cyril* (*Kirillova Kniga*) in 1644, which was based on his earlier *Exposition*. At the end of 1652 he was removed from the Press Office, as a result of his criticism of some of the reforms of the new patriarch, Nikon, and exiled; probably he died soon afterward.[34]

During his last years Nasedka was summoned from the monastery of his exile to testify about friends of his who had fallen afoul of Nikon. Those friends were a group of remarkable young men who made up the 'Friends of Piety' (*kruzhok revnitelei blagochestiia*). Its geographical source was Nizhny Novgorod, from which had arisen the resistance movement that ended the Time of Troubles. In 1636 a group of nine priests from the region presented a petition to Patriarch Ioasaf (1634–40) in which they begged him to take measures to correct the abuses from which the Church suffered.[35] The initiative belonged to Ivan Neronov, born probably just before 1600[36] of a simple peasant family in the Vologda region. Around 1620 he spent a few years at the Monastery of the Trinity and St Sergius, then went on to Nizhny Novgorod. Neronov there installed himself in an old abandoned church which he soon made into a religious center attracting many followers, and was one of the leaders of the movement for moral reform that gave rise to the petition to Ioasaf. In 1649 he came to Moscow and joined the circle.

Another of the group was Avvakum, who was born in the Nizhny Novgorod region in 1620. He was ordained deacon at twenty-one and priest at twenty-three, probably at Suzdal.[37] In 1647 a dispute with the authorities led him to flee to Moscow. Still another figure of the circle was Nikon, born in 1605, who had first become a priest, then after his wife died, a monk in 1634. About 1640 he became abbot of a monastery on Lake Kozhe. In 1646 he visited Moscow and remained there as archimandrite of the monastery of the Romanov family, Novospassky. The most notable intellectual cleric of the group was Stefan Vonifatiev; we know nothing of him before the accession of Alexis in 1645, but soon afterward he became confessor to the tsar and remained so until his death. One distinguished layman connected with the group was Fedor Rtishchev, a boyar enthusiastic about education and culture. His uncle, Spyridon Potemkin, had, while living in Smolensk, learned Latin, Polish, and Greek, and wrote theological polemics against the Uniats. He himself was eager to discuss matters with foreigners, preferring the Orthodox of the Ukraine; and as gentleman of the bedchamber (*postel'nichii*) to Alexis, he had the most intimate access to the throne.

The first few years of Alexis's reign may be compared with the opening of the reign of his descendant Alexander I. Both were young and idealistic; Alexis acceded at sixteen, Alexander at twenty-three. Like Alexander, Alexis, himself well educated for the day, surrounded himself with young zealots who had in view a thoroughgoing reform. Alexis's advisers wanted to renovate the Church, and sympathized with the men in the Press Office who wished to raise the cultural level of Muscovy. There were major differences; in order to reform the country Alexander sought to improve the machinery of state, Alexis to purify and elevate the intellectual level of the Church; Alexander was from the start ready to borrow outright from the West (chiefly France and England), at the outset Alexis was ready only to draw on the support of the West indirectly through Kiev, though in his later years Westernism became almost a passion with him. There was, in any case, much that was similar in the atmosphere of fervor and hope that permeated the entourages of the two tsars a century and half apart.

Alexis was spurred on in the direction of reform from two directions: the circle of rather puritanical clerics who belonged to the Friends of Piety (with whom Patriarch Iosif, elected in 1642, sympathized) and the scholars who staffed the Press Office.[38] The cleric Vonifatiev and the boyar Rtishchev had concerns about both moral and intellectual reform; Nikon was soon to show that he regarded the relationship of Church and state as the primary problem and that he considered regulation of it as fundamental to the necessary improvement. Thus all the major figures in the religious dispute leading to the great Schism in the Russian Orthodox Church came out of the same nucleus of friends. However, the potential for disagreement among them was present from the start.

The young reformers had their eye on Kiev as the proper model in achieving reform. From the 1620's the scholarly publications of the Kievan college had seized the attention of some Muscovites. After the accession of Alexis the learned men of the Press Office were better able to pursue their objective: 'to intellectualize the [Orthodox] faith with the assistance of the books of the South and West'.[39] In 1648 they published a *Book of the One, True, and Orthodox Faith* (*Kniga o vierie edinoi istinnoi pravoslavnoi*),[40] a compilation of different polemical tracts which had been assembled in 1644 in Kiev and translated under the supervision of Stefan Vonifatiev. It presented 'an opinion of the Greeks new to Moscow', as Belokurov puts it, contended that the Greeks did not betray the faith at the Council of Florence, and declared that the Russians ought to listen respectfully to the patriarchate of Constantinople. In 1649 the *Little Catechism* of Peter Mogila[41] was published in translation, providing Muscovites with their first popular manual of religious instruction. The *Kormchaia Kniga* (*Book of the Rudder*, from *korma*, stern of a boat and by extension rudder; a book of ecclesiastical and in part civil laws), existent for centuries in various versions, was published in 1650, including additions direct from Mogila, among them a chapter on marriage which he himself had translated from the Roman *Ritual* of Pope Paul V.

In some of these publications the Grecophilia of such members of the circle of Friends of Piety as Stefan Vonifatiev showed itself. However, the chief foreign influence displayed was Roman Catholic. As Pascal writes,

The distinctions between form, matter, and the administration of sacraments came from scholastic teaching; the convenient presentation of the catechism in questions and answers, which required reformulation of dogmas in precise form, was borrowed from the Council of Trent; the doctrines of the Immaculate Conception of the Virgin and of the operation of transubstantiation through the words of Christ and not by the invocation of the Holy Spirit, incorporated in the Little Catechism of 1649 as in the Great Catechism of 1627, then in the Missal of 1651 – all belonged to the Catholic tradition.[42]

He adds that Nasedka and Vonifatiev 'did not suspect that, in spite of everything, by way of Kiev and Mogila, it was Latin influences which were creeping into the old faith and threatened to contaminate it'. This was doubtless true, but in the 1640's there existed in Moscow a possible conflict between the wish to recapture the pristine Greek tradition and the willingness to accept Latin influences via Kiev in the effort to raise the intellectual level of Russian Orthodoxy.

In 1648 Alexis sought abroad for scholars who could translate from Greek into Church Slavic, as Vasily III had done well over a century before – the complete disappearance during the interval of the traces of Maxim the Greek's work and of the endeavor of the Transvolgans to renew links with the Greek Church could scarcely be more clearly shown. In 1649 Mogila's successor (the old man had died in 1647) sent to Moscow two elders: Arseny Satanovsky and Epifany Slavinetsky.[43] Satanovsky did not know Greek, and had to translate from Latin, but Slavinetsky, the generally more learned of the two, knew Greek, and soon found in Nikon someone who was willing to make use of his services.

When the two Kievans arrived in Moscow, an important visitor had just left; he was Patriarch Paisios of Jerusalem. He had brought with him a Greek named Arseny (not to be confused with Satanovsky). Arseny was soon involved in a scandal and arrested. He deposed that he had as a youth gone to Venice, abjured Orthodoxy, studied five years in Rome and then three years in Padua, finally returning to Constantinople to abjure Roman Catholicism and to wander north via Wallachia, Moldavia, and Poland to Kiev. He was sent to the monastery of Solovki, but Nikon, among others, did not forget him. For Paisios by this time had done much through private conversations quite abruptly to change Nikon's mind about the Greeks and to persuade him that reform in the Russian Church ought to hinge on cooperation with them.[44] The patriarch of Jerusalem thereupon connived in Nikon's being named archbishop of Novgorod and the removal of the hapless tenant of that see to a monastery. The tsar, Stefan Vonifatiev, and Rtishchev were all concerned with reform, and reform that would proceed in harmony with the Greeks.

The arrival of the Kievans signaled the ascendancy of the Friends of Piety in their campaign for moral and cultural reform. Taverns were closed, morality was preached, canonization of new saints (including Cyril of the White Lake), correction of books and church ritual proceeded with the enthusiastic support of the circle. Rtishchev patronized the establishment of the monastery of St Andrew as a scholarly institution especially hospitable to monks from the Ukraine, many more of whom appeared in Moscow. The reformers sought to introduce the use of one voice at a time in services (*edinoglasie*), replacing the older many-voiced usage. Obviously the people could not understand anything when one cleric was singing, another reading, and a third praying simultaneously; but the older clergy defended the practice because it shortened services[45] and thus produced results less onerous for the indifferent variety of parishioner. Each side could cite authority; the Council of a Hundred Chapters (1551) had sanctioned the many-voiced usage in Russia long before. The issue became much more important than it deserved when Patriarch Iosif opposed *edinoglasie* and the tsar, urged by Vonifatiev, Rtishchev, Nikon, Neronov, and others, championed it. By the help of the patriarch of Constantinople the reformers secured the reversal of a conciliar decision taken not long before by a council which acted in 1651. Their basic motive seems to have been a quasi-Protestant one, although no Protestant influences can be discerned; they sought a church service, if not a language, 'understanded of the people'.[46]

Patriarch Iosif died in April 1652. The candidate of the Friends of Piety and of the tsar to succeed Iosif was Nikon, who was at the moment, in a symbolic coincidence, on a journey to bring back the relics of the Metropolitan Filipp – who had died in a struggle with his tsar, as Nikon was to be ruined in a struggle with his – to Moscow.

In July Nikon assumed the patriarchate, and almost immediately began to introduce reforms into Church practice – beginning with ordering the sign of the cross to be made with three and not two fingers and reducing the number of prostrations during the prayer of St Ephraim the Syrian in the liturgy. Many of his old friends understood that a rupture was taking place with them, and that he was going to pursue his own vision of reform alone,[47] though Stefan Vonifatiev maintained his friendship with Nikon until Stefan died, and the tsar continued resolutely to support the new patriarch.[48] What happened was that the circle of the Friends of Piety disintegrated. Vonifatiev, without breaking with Nikon, was to die as a monk in 1656; Neronov, who like Nikon would weep on Stefan's tomb, was exiled; Avvakum was arrested in 1653 and exiled to Siberia. Avvakum would still play a part, but the circle as such no longer existed.

In the meantime Nikon proceeded to lay firm hands on the Press Office. He got Arseny the Greek back from Solovki and brought him into service. A young pupil of Epifany Slavinetsky's named Evfimy was named an editor in the Press Office. Soon afterwards Nasedka and his colleagues were removed, and Nikon's men were in charge.

At a council in 1654 Nikon announced his determination to make changes in the Church ritual to conform to contemporary Greek practice, condemning Russian 'innovations'. He could not have been surprised at the consternation produced by a Russian patriarch who questioned the foundations of Russian piety; nor can he have been unaware that he himself had dispersed the very group that might have been his firmest supporters in reforming the Church. He rested his whole case on authority, and outside (Greek) authority at that. After the Greeks were to desert him he was utterly isolated, and what was intended as the beginning of a great Reform became instead a great Schism.

Immediately after the Council of 1654 Nikon consulted Patriarch Paisios of Constantinople concerning the questions of crossings and prostrations. However, before any answer could arrive Patriarch Makarios of Antioch appeared in Moscow seeking alms.[49] Shortly afterward Nikon publicly put out the eyes of a number of new 'Frankish' and Polish icons brought to him for the purpose,[50] deeply shocking Muscovites, and ordered three-fingered crossing with the backing of Makarios.[51] At a council in March 1655 Makarios renewed this injunction and added others, including a prohibition of the recent Russian practice of rebaptizing Polish Roman Catholics who had converted to Orthodoxy;[52] this decision reversed the council of 1620. Nikon on this occasion uttered the renowned phrase: 'I am a Russian and the son of a Russian, but my faith and religion are Greek.'

A month after the council Paisios's letter arrived, not lending his support to Nikon's zeal concerning matters of fingers and knees, but gently trying to distinguish between essentials and accidentals.[53] Nikon's Greeks had begun to fail him, but he was not to be deterred. In February 1656 Nikon, in the presence of the tsar, the boyars, and the clergy, anathematized all those who crossed themselves with two fingers. He also pressed on with the puritanical campaign for the suppression of games and amusements and of Western-influenced icons. By now the uproar was nationwide; Iona, metropolitan of Rostov, had raised popular murmur by enforcing Nikonian alterations in the rites, and the monastery of Solovki had met with defiance the arrival of Nikonian revisions of service books. Already Nikon was identified with 'Latinizing' in the popular mind.[54] By early 1658 the tsar had had enough, and made clear his disapproval of Nikon's course. Nikon replied by laying down the duties (though not the office) of the patriarchate and withdrawing to a monastery forty miles from Moscow. Apparently he thought he could achieve his aims by imitating Ivan IV's departure from Moscow, which had been followed by a penitent recalling of the tsar to the capital by a delegation which approved the establishment of the oprichnina. If so, he was wrong; it was the end of his influence and, Pascal concludes, also the end of effective leadership in the Russian Orthodox Church.[55]

The council of 1660 declared the patriarchal seat vacant, and elected a replacement for Nikon named Pitirim. But Alexis did not dare enforce the decision, and was at a loss what to do. The solution was found for him by the appearance in Moscow of Paisios Ligarides. A Greek by origin, he was, Palmer asserts, 'a Latin in his own belief (if he had any belief) rather than Greek' but was ready to argue either side. He had studied at the College of

St Athanasius (1625–36) in Rome, been ordained (Roman Catholic) deacon and priest, in 1651 had been accepted into the Orthodox Church by Paisios of Jerusalem, ordained priest and deacon and consecrated bishop or metropolitan of Gaza by him, anathematized in 1660 by that very prelate, reverted to Roman Catholicism as a priest in Poland, and then in 1662 arrived in Moscow, resuming his profession of Orthodoxy and his title Metropolitan of Gaza.[56] This Romanized Greek of dubious character was used by the tsar in disposing of the recalcitrant patriarch. In a series of answers by which Nikon commented on an exchange between the boyar Simeon Streshnev and Ligarides it is possible to assess the contention that Nikon was inspired by Roman Catholic influence.[57] That contention was not only the substance of popular rumor. The Polish envoys in Moscow in 1667 reported that they had been credibly informed that the patriarchs of Alexandria and Antioch had been brought to Moscow to accomplish the deposition of Nikon 'chiefly for this reason, that he was favourable to the Roman church'.[58] Moreover, certain relatives of the Tsar had commented concerning the *Donation of Constantine*, which Nikon had ordered to be added to the *Kormchaia Kniga*, that Alexis had no choice but to defeat Nikon or to cede to him Moscow as Constantine had ceded Rome to Pope Sylvester.

In his reply to the 24th question and answer, Nikon challenges an assertion by Paisios that Alexis had given him everything Constantine gave Sylvester. What the tsar had 'given' was expropriation of Church property and expulsion of the patriarch, Nikon retorted ironically.

But what is the good that the Tsar does? Is it this, to take feloniously to himself the order of priesthood? For the order of priesthood is one thing, and that of empire is another...Priesthood is from God; and it is from the priesthood that kings receive the unction of royalty...God can acquit him whom the Tsar has condemned. And over the Tsar himself the judgment of God is impending... But if the priest bind any one on earth, not even God himself will absolve that man, as he testifies, saying, 'He shall be bound in heaven'...In spiritual things which belong to the glory of God, the bishop is higher than the Tsar: for so only can he hold or maintain the spiritual jurisdiction. But in those things which belong to the province of this world the Tsar is higher. And so they will be in no opposition the one against another.[59]

Having said this, Nikon at once adds a qualification: the bishop has a certain interest in things secular, but the tsar has none whatever in things spiritual. The power and authority of the Church, he continues, was most highly developed in the time of Constantine, who made a grant to Sylvester. The relation between ecclesiastical and state authority is that between the sun and the moon.[60] Here Nikon unequivocally asserts the primacy of the patriarchate over the tsardom.

One of his chief complaints against Alexis was the creation of the Office of Monasteries (*Monastyrsky Prikaz*), an 'unlawful tribunal' by which certain ecclesiastical cases were to be handled by lay judges, in violation of ecclesiastical immunity. He attacks the Office, the Code (*Ulozhenie*) of 1649 which created it, and Prince Nikita Odoevsky, who was the man chiefly responsible for compiling the Code, especially for the implication in the Code that judgment was not God's but the tsar's, but also for unequal punishments prescribed in it, such as milder penalties for insulting a patriarch than for insulting a bishop, etc. In citing from the lives of various Church Fathers, Nikon points out 'how they not only did not submit themselves to the jurisdiction of the emperors, but further corrected and rebuked the unrighteous judgments of emperors, though they many times threatened them with tortures and death'.[61]

Thus Nikon cannot be called a 'Romanizer'[62] in the sense of a person sympathetic to Roman Catholic usages or doctrines or interested in borrowing from the cultural achievements of Roman Catholics – as Peter Mogila was. He used arguments and documents of Roman origin and assistants of Roman training in quest of the supremacy of the sacred over the secular, the chief prince of the Church over the ruler of the state, a position for which there was only one contemporary model available: not the patriarchate of Constantinople, not the office of any Protestant cleric, but only the papacy. He cannot be called an intellectual or a well-educated man even by the standards of his time and place. It is doubtful that he deserves the name of 'Grecophile' in any sense that implies an understanding of what the Greek tradition was. Florovsky declares: 'Imitation of the contemporary Greeks did not in the least lead to a return to the lost tradition. Nikon's Grecophilia was not a return to the Greek foundations and was not even a revival of Byzantinism.'[63] Palmer writes of him as if he were something like a Protestant, or at least deserving of the sympathy of English Protestants: Palmer's dedication reads,

> The Patriarch Against the Tsar,
> The Church Against the World;
> Smyrna and Philadelphia Against Pergamus and Laodicea,
> Patience and Charity Against Violence and Iniquity;
> The Resurrection (Voskresensk)
> And the New Jerusalem (Novi Ierusalim)
> Against Babylon and Antichrist

Nikon, was, however, not mainly inspired by Rome, or Constantinople, or Wittenberg or Canterbury or Geneva; he knew only Russia. He fought against the growing power of Muscovite absolutism in the name of his God and his Church. He did so awkwardly, alienating the mass of the people, his fellow-reformers who might have supported him in seeking the very objectives he sought, and the tsar himself, who had great personal regard for Nikon. One scholar writes,

In the personal fate of Nikon the chief role was played by his view of the significance of the patriarchal power. As Iu. F. Samarin said, Nikon wished 'to establish in Russia a private national papism'. 'The priesthood is higher than the tsardom', said Nikon, supporting his opinion by reference to various sources including the Donation of Constantine...The patriarch, in the opinion of Nikon, was the image of Christ himself, the head of the church, and therefore he could not recognize another 'lawgiver'.[64]

Doubtless Nikon sought power for himself and his office; but he also had other aims in mind that might deserve sympathy: the moral and intellectual reform of the Russian people and the autonomy of the Church.

In any event the Schism was consummated without the participation of Nikon. Before Paisios arrived, Alexis had recalled Avvakum from Daurian exile in 1660; he removed Arseny the Greek from the Press Office in 1663 and sent him back to Solovki. Avvakum reached Moscow early in 1664, was received with joy by Rtishchev, and found haven in the household of the *boyarynia* Morozova,[65] widow of Gleb Morozov and an impassioned adherent of the unreformed faith. But there were others newly arrived in Moscow, especially Simeon of Polotsk. Born Samuel Sitnianovich, he received his education at the Kiev-Mogila college and at various Jesuit schools subsequently, and was tonsured monk in 1656 under the name of Simeon. The same year the tsar visited Polotsk, and Simeon presented him with verses of his own composition on the occasion, delighting Alexis. In the summer of 1663 he came to Moscow to stay,[66] promptly becoming interpreter for Paisios Ligarides as well as Latin instructor to young undersecretaries (*pod'iachie*) of the Privy Chancery (*Tainyi prikaz*) in a special new school founded for the purpose in the Spassky monastery. Borozdin states: 'With this school there was laid in Moscow the foundation of the party of Latinizers, that is, the adherents of Latin education.'[67]

It was in August 1664 that Alexis reached a decision: against Nikon, for his reforms.[68] Metropolitan Pitirim, *locum tenens* of the patriarchal throne, was abruptly retired without being replaced. The archimandrite Paul of the Chudov monastery, adept of Latin and Polish, admirer of Simeon of Polotsk, amateur of the sciences and arts of the West, became metropolitan of the influential see of Krutitsy. Avvakum, who had reached Moscow only a few months earlier, was seized and again sent into exile, this time to Pustozersk on the Pechora river in the far North. He was excommunicated by the council soon to be held. In exile he composed his own *Life*, one of the first prose monuments of vernacular Russian. He had no further part in events.

Alexis now advanced to the task of condemning Nikon. Paisios advised him to obtain the help of the Eastern patriarchs. There were defects in the procedure, but Paisios of Alexandria (not to be confused with Paisios of Constantinople, Paisios of Jerusalem, or Ligarides) and Makarios of Antioch came to Moscow, the latter for the second time. A council was summoned, and with the participation of the Greek prelates Nikon was condemned in 1666. Two bishops protested; the council suspended them, declaring, 'they truly *niconise*, or rather *papisticise, who try to lessen the empire, and are zealous to extol on high the episcopate*'.[69]

The 'Old Belief' (*starover'e*) or 'Old Ritual' (*staroobriadchestvo*) was condemned; the only Schism ever to divide the Russian Orthodox Church was an accomplished fact. Simultaneously the traditional practice of election of priests by parishes was terminated; priests were to be named by bishops. Actually and potentially the power of the state over the Church was significantly increased by the decisions of the Council of 1666–7.

Discussion of these events has tended to center on the personalities of Nikon on the one hand and Avvakum and his fellow puritans on the other; the sharp and uncompromising character of Nikon's reforms of ritual, the pious and heroic but shortsighted and ignorant resistance of Avvakum and others. Actually Nikon and Avvakum had much in common: in the zeal each had for his own position, in the refusal of both to bow or recant in the face of harsh punitive measures, in the fundamental weakness which hamstrung both – lack of education. Nikon staked everything on bringing the Russian Church into line with contemporary Greek practice, yet knew no Greek at all himself. As for Avvakum, in the words of Pascal he 'without books, without direct knowledge of the Greek and Latin theological tradition, without precise terminology, without even aspiring to be able to attain to precision, was condemned in advance to expound errors which were not in his mind at all'.[70]

Both had aspirations which deserve the respect of later generations: Nikon contested the supremacy of the state and sought the autonomy of things spiritual and cultural; Avvakum defended the authentic integral tradition of a unified Muscovite culture and the Muscovite religious tradition which had nothing schismatic in it, as Paisios of Constantinople had recognized in trying to cool down Nikon's zeal before it was too late.[71] What is more, it is inaccurate to suppose that all Old Believers then or later suffered from Avvakum's educational disabilities: Rtishchev's uncle, Spyridon Potemkin, was an example of a well-educated man who resisted Nikonianism; the first leader of a functioning Old Believer community, Andrei Denisov, was a learned man who later knew Peter the Great and Feofan Prokopovich and whose textual criticisms, according to Zenkovsky, constitute the 'first Russian linguistic and archeographic researches'.[72] Zenkovsky goes so far as to call the Old Believers 'the last representatives of Great Russian Muscovite culture'.[73] It would be better to be more cautious. Muscovite culture before the Schism had already experienced Western influences, and the increase in the latter during the decades that followed 1667 did not destroy the Muscovite cultural heritage. Perhaps more important is a different point. The Schism cut off a substantial section of the most pious believers, most of them Great Russian, from the Orthodox Church and thereby from continuing contact with the interaction of Russia and the West in the realm of high culture. The result was cultural impoverishment and a kind of fossilization of the cultural life of the Old Believers.[74] By the same token, however, the official Church suffered impoverishment by losing many of the most faithful laity and some clergy.

The Old Believers' piety and devotion became fixated on one notion: not that Nikon's reforms were in themselves fatal to true religion, but that they were external signs of the advent of Antichrist in the world and therefore of the imminence of the Last Judgment. They remained imprisoned in this single belief, and could only escape from it by leaving the Old Believer communities.

It requires emphasis, however, that the historical importance of the Schism lies chiefly neither in Nikon and his Grecophilism nor Avvakum and his old-Muscovite orientation. Both were defeated. What was victorious was the scholarship and the influence of the West; and their victory was secured by the decision of the authorities of the Russian state.

Kapterev convincingly writes:

Nikon attracted to Russia that force which it hitherto had lacked: the force of science and education, which alone could create for Russia and establish for her an effective leading role in the whole Orthodox world, since for this the external and material prosperity alone of church and state was insufficient. For such a role what was chiefly necessary was cultural capital, richness of spiritual life which would show itself, among other things, in a broad development of education...From just this point in Russia for the first time it was recognized that scholarship and education had the right to have decisive significance in ecclesiastical questions, and anyone who, like the opponents of the church reform of Nikon, boasted of the fact that he had studied nothing and even did not consider it necessary to study anything could no longer pretend to an influential or leading role in the Russian church.[75]

And yet the Greeks who acted as arbiters of the fate of the Russian Church by virtue of their superior knowledge at the Council of 1666–7 had only a fleeting triumph. It appeared that Russia had finally accepted the Greeks as a model; 'in reality, however, something completely different occurred'. The Russians discovered that 'all the learning of the Greeks and all their scholarly knowledge had been borrowed by them from the Western Latin schools... would it not [thus] be better for the Russians, bypassing the Greek intermediaries, to turn for scholarship and education directly to the source, to the West itself?'[76]

Therein lay the chief significance of the Schism. The tsar had decided against Nikon, and for his reforms; for scholarship and the West, more specifically for the Roman Catholic-influenced learning of the Ukraine; but it was the tsar who had made the decision. Many of the high clerics who wished Nikon deposed thoroughly sympathized with his struggle to make the Church independent of the state and even its judge,[77] but there was no easy way out for them. The two bishops who, according to the charge, wished to 'niconise, or rather papisticise', not in the name of Rome but in the name of the autonomy of the Russian Church, were quickly shown that Nikon's real cause was lost, though his changes in ritual might be approved.

The Schism offers several paradoxes. The most prominent antagonists, Nikon and Avvakum, were both defeated. The authority of the Greeks, with which Nikon sought to justify his reforms, was also the device the tsar used to rid himself of Nikon. Although the Greek-approved changes were confirmed at the time Nikon himself was condemned, it was not Greek learning but Latin learning which emerged as the most important foreign influence on the Russian Church and culture. Although Latin learning was the victor in the dispute, the Roman Catholic position on Church–state relations, which was to assert the independence or even the supremacy of the Church, was decisively rebuffed; and it was the Roman Catholic position which had been sustained most uncompromisingly by the Grecophile Nikon, using some Roman Catholic arguments.

Out of the Schism came the first serious cultural division in Russian history. The Old Belief had several different aspects. One was ethnic, leading to tension and estrangement between different groups of Great Russians and between some Great Russians and some Ukrainians: Ukrainian influences grew stronger in Moscow, while in the view of some scholars Great Russian culture became the object of official harassment.[78] It fell back on its most ancient strongholds, the monasteries of the north, and then when Solovki, which had offered armed resistance, fell (1676) and other monasteries were safely in Orthodox hands, the Old Belief still survived outside them. It was no accident that the strongest of the Priestless (*Bezpopovtsy*) Old Believer sects was known as the *Pomortsy* or Shore Dwellers, referring to the shores of the White Sea. Another aspect of the Old Belief was social; the faithful were largely peasants, though the communities turned to trade in order to survive and by the nineteenth century Old Believer merchants were well known and well off. Another aspect was cultural: although Old Believer villagers might often be literate or at any rate able to recite Scriptural passages from memory, whereas Orthodox villagers were not, the Old Belief was unavoidably a form of self-abnegation of high culture. Despite the fact that such learned men as Spyridon Potemkin and Andrei Denisov adopted the Old Belief at the time of the Schism, it was able to establish no educational institutions and remained generally cut off from the further progress of enlightenment in Russia, a fragment of Old Muscovy petrified forever. Nevertheless it may well be, as many historians, Russian and other, have believed, that the most authentic religious impulses in Russia were the property of those driven out of the Church by the decisions of 1666–7, not of those who conducted the expulsions.[79]

Despite the Potemkins and Denisovs, the Old Believers were soon back at the position of their greatest leader and martyr, Avvakum – that is, devout ignorance. It is perfectly true that from the doctrinal standpoint there was no need for a schism, and that the Old Believers were as orthodox as the Orthodox, so that when after 1917 émigré bishops proclaimed the Schism to be at an end (in the USSR, however, it still continues), there was no single doctrinal position that had to be altered to permit the announcement of reunion. The cultural differences that soon came to distinguish the two groups and the cultural consequences for both were nonetheless significant and indeed momentous for the later fate of Russian culture.

Those consequences must be seen as ultimately owing to the cultural developments in the Ukraine of the latter sixteenth century. The weakening of Ukrainian Orthodoxy, the triumphal progress of Roman Catholic culture eastward, the adoption of much of it by Orthodox clergymen, especially Peter Mogila, in order to preserve their ecclesiastical independence, and the inability of the Muscovite Church to compete with the Ukrainian immigrant culture, decided the outcome. The Old Belief fought for Old Muscovy, the patriarch fought for Greece, but neither won; the outcome was a more rapid reception of Latinism in the Russian Church and Russian culture – now beginning to reflect the contemporary cultural currents of Poland and Germany in secular genres, such as the drama, rhetorical verse, and even painting.

Immediately after the Council of 1666–7 the influence of Simeon of Polotsk increased. He was made tutor of the tsar's children, Alexis, Fedor, and Sophia. He wrote instructional manuals based on Latin sources in which, 'if he did not fall into Latinism [i.e., Roman Catholicism], at any rate he raised no objections against it'.[80] He composed poems as well as plays for presentation at the palace at Kolomenskoe, propagandized for enlightenment and against rudeness and ignorance, composed official statements on behalf of the tsar and the ecclesiastical hierarchs, and conducted official polemics against the Old Believers.

The Council of 1666–7 elected a patriarch, Ioasaf II, who lived only five years longer. One of his significant actions was to forbid the practice of rebaptizing Roman Catholic converts to Orthodoxy, which dated from 1620.[81] He was succeeded in 1672 by Metropolitan Pitirim of Novgorod, who lasted only a few months. In 1674 Ioakim became patriarch, a man who in his own words was 'ready to obey' his superiors in everything.[82]

In Alexis's last years, Pascal writes, 'he had no longer eyes for anything but the West'.[83] He summoned musicians and comedians from Courland, ordered the translation of all sorts of secular books in German, Latin, and Polish, sent abroad embassies including Roman Catholics (for example, the Scot Menesius to the Holy Roman Emperor) and received Dominicans and Jesuits from abroad.

KRIŽANIĆ AND ALEXIS

While Nikon was in sullen retirement and Alexis had not decided what to do next, there appeared the first serious Roman Catholic missionary to Moscow, the Croat Juraj Križanić. He failed not only to make conversions but even to establish communication with the Muscovites, but his career nevertheless has its interest and significance.

Križanić was born near Karlovać, Croatia, in 1618. He was educated in the Jesuit schools of Zagreb, Graz, and Bologna, and at the age of twenty-two came to Rome, where he obtained admission to the College of St Athanasius in order to prepare himself for a mission to Moscow. In a document entitled 'Della Missione in Moscovia', written probably in 1641, Križanić expounded his analysis of the religious problem that he saw as underlying his missionary aim.[84] The Muscovites were 'neither heretics nor schismatics', he contended, but only simple people misled by the Greeks. Unlike Possevino, who had refused to kiss the hands of Russian bishops and regarded the miracles of Russian saints as spurious, but respected the Greeks for their great cultural tradition, Križanić distrusted the Greeks but approached Russian Orthodoxy – or perhaps it would be more accurate to say, the Russian people – with great respect. He envisaged writing a general history of all Slavs which would show that no prince among them in his day compared with the Muscovite tsar, and then present the tsar with the book as explanation of why he wished to serve him. After four or five years of careful preparation, encouraging virtue and the arts among the Muscovites, Križanić would ask the tsar to declare war on the Turks. In order to wage war Muscovy would need Western aid, which would be given only if the reunion of the Churches were accomplished, and thus Križanić might hope to achieve his mission in his own lifetime. The naive timetable ought not to be allowed to obscure the respect and love with which he approached Russia.

Ordained priest in Rome in 1642, he failed to obtain from the Holy Office permission to celebrate in Church Slavic, and instead of going directly to Muscovy as he wished he was sent to work among the Serb and Orthodox minority in Croatia. He managed to get Rome's authorization to go to Moscow only after years of impatient waiting, and then, in a mission whose object seems unclear, spent only two months there at the end of 1647. From Moscow he wrote to the man who had been his mentor in the *Propaganda Fide*, Rafael Levaković, and was now bishop of Ohrid, confirming his original aims and approach to the Muscovites.[85]

Križanić was able to visit Constantinople briefly in 1651, but when he returned to Rome the following year he was drawn into South Slav problems. Apparently Olearius's new edition of his travels (1656), reporting the opening of new schools at which Greek and Latin were taught – the reference must have been to Rtishchev's school – was important in reawakening his never-forgotten interest in Muscovy. But he was unable to gain support for his desire to go to Moscow for a prolonged period, for Pope Alexander VII declared he should wait until peace was concluded between Poland and Muscovy. In 1658 he simply went without permission, arriving in Moscow in September 1659. He offered Alexis his services as grammarian, and was promptly given a house and allowance. But after only a little more than a year, in 1661, he was exiled to Tobolsk. His antipathy toward the Greeks, whom he blamed for what he regarded as Russia's religious shortcomings, was apparently such that he might be willing to postpone correction of texts rather than accept the ascendancy that might come to Greek clerics if they were important in making the corrections.[86] Thus Avvakum, the Russian traditionalist and theological incompetent, and Križanić, the Roman Catholic and perhaps the most learned man in Russia, were both punished for their opposition to the Church reform that Nikon had begun and that Alexis had taken over.

During his fifteen years of Siberia exile Križanić wrote nine major works.[87] Among them was the first treatise on politics written in Russia, the so-called *Politika*, or more properly *Razgowóri ob wladátelystwu* (*Discourses on Government*).[88] Although Križanić identifies himself with the Russians in writing the *Politika*, he finds fault with the Slavs – Russians and Poles are specified – for a number of things, notably their exaggerated fondness for foreigners or xenomania and their submission to foreign rule (here he has the Poles in mind).[89] He criticizes two peoples sharply: Germans and Greeks. The Germans' main weakness is passion for novelty; the Greeks', condemnation of learning. To be sure, the Greeks first taught Russians the Orthodox faith, and deserve gratitude for that, but the Germans should be shunned as disseminators of heresy.[90] Plainly he is less concerned with the Germans as a people than with Protestantism as a religion. His method of criticism is noteworthy: the Greeks or Germans say thus-and-so; but '*reason dictates*' (*ratio suadet*) such-and-such. At the outset he announces two mottoes: 'Know thyself' and 'Do not believe foreigners'.[91] His real message is more accurately stated toward the close of his work: 'Knowledge of oneself and good legislation.'[92] He advises the tsar to legislate wisely and for the benefit of the people, sharply attacks some of Alexis's predecessors, in particular Ivan IV, and states flatly, 'Unlimited tyrannical power is contrary to [God's law] and to the law of nature, for nature teaches us that kingdoms are not created for kings, but kings for kingdoms.'[93] Defending monarchy as the best form of government, he makes his book a plea for the tsar to legislate in favor of prosperity, power, and wisdom, and to give the country what he thinks 'we Russians' need.

Križanić was released from Siberian exile when Fedor came to the throne in 1676 and left Moscow for Poland in October 1677. Legend has it that he died under the walls of Vienna in 1683, acting as chaplain to the Polish troops under John Sobieski who were relieving the city from Turkish siege and thus serving a more grateful Slavic monarch than Alexis had proved.

The scholarly literature on Križanić has tended to concentrate on the national issue. Was he an early pan-Slavist? Could he truly have been a Slavic patriot and a Roman Catholic at the same time? Sergei Soloviev said he was both, but that this was a 'contradiction' in his character that he could not resolve.[94] M. N. Tikhomirov implies that his Catholicism pertained somehow to his early West European period and not to Russia, and writes that his observations in Russia were produced by his 'great love' for that country as well as his Slavic patriotism.[95]

No doubt he was a kind of early pan-Slavist; the curious artificial language in which he composed the *Politika*, in a common Slavic vocabulary sprinkled with Russian, Church Slavic, and Serbo-Croatian terms,[96] is the best evidence of the fact. His epigraph stated boldly: 'I wish to expel all foreigners...to stand for all people of the Dnieper (*omnes Boristenitas*), Poles, Lithuanians, Serbs, and every warrior of the Slavic race...'[97]

The bulk of his work, however, is devoted to proposals for the reform and indeed transformation of Russia, especially its cultural transformation by means of Western thought. There are three sections of the book: On Wealth, On Power, and On Wisdom; the third has over five times the number of sub-chapters as the first two. In the third section he explains Aristotle's different varieties of cause, the method of electing the Polish kings and Holy Roman Emperors, the virtues of philosophy, and much else, quoting extensively from Western writers ancient and contemporary.

He was the first Westerner to envisage the transformation of Russia by means of Western thought; moreover, he was willing to throw his own life into the effort through becoming a Russian himself by adoption and outlook. He approached Russian civilization with an attitude of realism combined with respect; he neither minimized its vices nor exaggerated its virtues, but made his starting point the kind of persons the Russians actually were at the time.

Unlike Matteo Ricci, the first Westerner to envisage the transformation of China by means of Western thought, Križanić was not a missionary to a given religious organization who was assigned to perform a task. More than one writer seems to have forgotten that he went to Russia against the wishes of his superiors and was even frustrated in his natural desire to report to Rome the results of his mission after he left Russia. But missionary he was, even if an unauthorized one – a missionary not merely of his Church but of the West. Unlike Ricci, he was entirely alone; unlike Ricci, he did not possess a superior mind – much of the *Politika* consists of fragments and snippets of information, unorganized and unrelated to other things. At any rate he remained an isolated figure, making no conversions and perhaps seeking to make none, leaving no traces of his mission when he departed, having to be rediscovered much later. Witsen mentioned Križanić in his book on Siberia in 1692 and a few years later in Holland told Peter I, who had never heard his name, about him. Novikov mentioned him in 1772. However, his works were published only after the middle of the nineteenth century.

In one respect Križanić's aims were achieved, though he had nothing to do with their achievement as far as is known. At the beginning of Fedor III's reign, in 1676, the remaining Greeks were expelled from Moscow. Paisios Ligarides was summarily returned to Palestine. In 1682 the government of Tsar Fedor approved a plan for an academy, or institution of higher learning, to be established in Moscow; the plan had been worked out by Simeon of Polotsk (who had died in 1680) and his pupils, chiefly Sylvester Medvedev.[98] There was to be one more challenge to the cultural ascendancy of the Kievans that would try to use Greeks as a counterweight to them; it was to come under Sophia.

THE REGENCY OF SOPHIA: DEEPENING OF ROMAN INFLUENCES (1682–1689)

The death of Fedor in 1682 left two half-brothers eligible for the throne, Alexis's sons Ivan and Peter. At first Peter was chosen to rule alone. The decision was engineered by the patriarch Ioakim. He had been involved in the condemnation of the Old Believers, and whatever his real motives were for supporting Peter, the Old Believers evidently interpreted Peter's enthronement as an ill omen for themselves. Only a couple of weeks later, the arquebusiers of Moscow or Streltsy, who included a strong Old Believer contingent, revolted and killed several members of the family of Peter's mother, the Naryshkins. The crisis was temporarily solved by the proclamation of a dyarchy of Ivan and Peter, with Sophia, Ivan's sister, as regent.

Born in 1657, baptized by Nikon himself, Sophia had of course remained in the Orthodox Church, but she had early been subjected to Western influences. In order to teach her, males were allowed for the first time to enter the terem in which Muscovite women were secluded. Her instructors included Simeon of Polotsk, Sylvester Medvedev, and Karion Istomin. The pro-Catholic leanings of such teachers were shared by certain nobles Sophia had come to know during Fedor's reign, notably Prince V. V. Golitsyn. Since she owed her elevation to the regency at least in part to Old Believers, however, she had to be cautious about exhibiting her partiality to the West. In July 1682 she permitted a public debate on the religious issue between Old Believer spokesmen and the official hierarchy. Keeping her head despite audacious provocation by some of the Old Believers, she probably prevented the Streltsy from taking a position openly in their favor at the debate or afterwards. Tension still ran high; in August the court found it prudent to remove to Kolomenskoe, outside Moscow. But within a few weeks Sophia engineered the seizure and execution of Prince Ivan Khovansky, the commander of the Streltsy and the potential replacement of Avvakum (burned with the other prisoners of Pustozersk only two weeks before Fedor died) as the leader of the Old Believers. Her action brought about the submission of the Streltsy, and Sophia returned to Moscow triumphant.

Sophia's regime was one in which Prince Golitsyn was chief minister (as well as her lover) and Sylvester Medvedev was her cultural counsellor. Stern measures were taken against the Old Believers, especially after 1684, partly on the urging of Patriarch Ioakim. Ioakim continued, like his predecessor Nikon, to lean on Greek authority; Medvedev wished to broaden connections with Kiev and Latin culture. In 1685 came a clash. Medvedev petitioned Sophia for confirmation of the charter of an academy granted by Fedor in 1682[99] but never implemented; Ioakim wished the academy to be Greek in orientation. Unfortunately for Medvedev, about the same time there was published his book *Khleb Zhivotnyi* (*On the Bread of Life*), which held that transubstantiation during the mass was achieved by the repetition of

Christ's words ('Take, eat...') uttered at the Last Supper. This was a doctrine of Roman origin transmitted through Peter Mogila.[100] A substantial public debate ensued. According to Miliukov,

This was perhaps the first attempt at an independent theological discussion of a purely Russian religious problem. No wonder that 'not only men, but women and children', everywhere and upon all occasions, 'at feasts, in the market-place, at all times' discussed the 'Holy Sacrament... at what words and moment do the bread and wine transubstantiate'.[101]

Ioakim and the Grecophile party brought charges of 'bread worship' against Medvedev, and in 1686–7 he was forced out of his positions in the Press Office and the Zaikonospassky School (that is, 'in the Spassky Monastery behind the icon wall'), founded in 1665 by his master Simeon of Polotsk. Sophia either felt unable to protect Medvedev or was reluctant to involve herself in Church affairs. In 1690, after her overthrow, a council condemned 'bread worship' as heresy. The Jesuits who had become established in Moscow were expelled, and suspicion was cast on all Ukrainians; but not for long.

The first Muscovite institution of higher education was nominally established in 1685 as the 'Helleno-Greek' (*Ellino-Grecheskaia*, despite the apparent redundancy of the phrase) Academy,[102] which name it bore until 1700. Ioakim was, however, unable to provide instructors, and had to request the Patriarch Dositheos of Jerusalem to send to Moscow theologians to combat Latinism. He sent the brothers Ioanniky and Sofrony Likhud, who reached Moscow in March 1685.[103] In the autumn of 1687 they were allowed to begin instruction in a new building in the Spassky monastery, and the date may therefore be taken as the effective beginning of Moscow's first institution of higher learning, modest as the beginning was. However, the brothers Likhud proved very feeble reeds for Grecophiles to lean on; they proved to have studied at Venice and were doctors of Padua University, and thus their credentials as Latinophobes were not convincing. They also got into other difficulties, attempted to flee Moscow, were captured, returned, and converted into teachers of Italian – as a result of a perhaps sounder identification of their true intellectual affiliations than had been made earlier. This happened in 1694. By this time Sophia's regency was over and Patriarch Ioakim was dead (1690). He had accomplished Medvedev's fall, secured the transfer of the ecclesiastical allegiance of the metropolitanate of Kiev from the patriarchate of Constantinople to that of Moscow (1686), and proscribed fifteen Kievan books.[104] It was Patriarch Adrian, also Grecophile, who had had the embarrassing task of getting rid of the Likhud brothers. Soon afterward, as will be seen, the Kievans took over the Academy.[105]

The episode of the Likhud brothers brought about no interruption in the process of the increase of Western and in particular Roman Catholic influence in circles concerned with learning and the arts. In foreign affairs similar tendencies mounted in strength. Sophia came to power at a moment when the powers of Southern Europe were concerned with the Ottoman offensive and the need to counter it and drive it back. In September 1683 a Roman Catholic archbishop, Sebastian Knabe, who had been preaching in Armenia, reached Moscow with a proposal that Muscovy join Poland and the Holy Roman Empire in an anti-Turkish alliance,[106] and a Polish envoy arrived soon after to urge a similar proposal. An alliance with the Roman Catholic powers appealed to Sophia and Golitsyn, and they considered how simultaneously relations with Poland might be regulated and the danger from the Sultan's Crimean vassals might be ended. In 1686 Sophia's diplomats helped to convert the Peace of Andrusovo (1667) into a treaty of permanent peace between Muscovy and Poland. As part of what in effect was an alliance with Poland, Prince Golitsyn embarked on two campaigns against the Crimean Tatars, in 1687 and 1689. Both were failures, despite Sophia's desperate attempts to portray them as victories. Golitsyn tried to blame the Cossack hetman, Samoilovich, for the first defeat, and replaced him with the shrewd, ambitious and Westernizing Ivan Mazepa. The second failure brought down both Golitsyn and Sophia. Since 1687 the young co-tsar, Peter, had been taking more interest in state affairs, and his marriage to Evdokia Lopukhina in January 1689 had in effect announced his coming of age (he was seventeen). He refused to participate in welcoming Golitsyn back from the second Crimean campaign; this precipitated a crisis. Believing or pretending to believe that he was in danger, Peter fled to the Monastery of the Trinity and St Sergius, where he gathered such strength that finally Sophia risked everything on a pilgrimage to talk to him. He declined to see her. Shortly afterward she was sent to Novodevichi monastery to finish her days.

The regency of Sophia was a period of marked increase in translations from Western literature, the importation of Western technical novelties, and of greater prominence for foreigners. General Patrick Gordon, a Scottish Roman Catholic, was an important army commander and became an intimate of Golitsyn. Golitsyn himself, like Ordin-Nashchokin, spoke Latin and Polish fluently and possessed an impressive library of Western books. He urged boyars either to send their children to Polish schools or to hire Polish tutors for them. In his Moscow mansion, fitted out in European style, he kept perhaps the first salon in Russia, opening it to all sorts of foreign visitors including Jesuits.[107] In this and other ways Golitsyn and Sophia showed an interest in Roman Catholics and their cultural attainments and a concern for bringing the latter to Russia. It was not that the regency showed some kind of predilections for the interests of the papacy; on the contrary, Sophia offered the French Huguenots asylum in Russia in 1689, after the revocation of the Edict of Nantes.

THE SITUATION IN 1689

The last years of Alexis's reign, Fedor's, and the regency of Sophia, that is, the interval roughly from 1667 to 1689, together have many features of a Russian Baroque period, and in important respects the Baroque continued into the eighteenth century.[108] Čiževskij in using the term 'Baroque' has in mind chiefly ornateness, obscurity, grotesqueness, and exaggeration of all kinds in literary style, the appearance of new genres such as poetry, belles-lettres 'in the proper sense of the word', drama, and the like, and the revival of such genres as the sermon. He also mentions 'ideological influence' and 'external forms of life', but has very little to say about what might be meant by Baroque in such connections except to refer to notions of changeability and transitoriness.

The cause of the development of Baroque literature and to some extent art is to be found in the immigration of Ukrainians to Moscow. In addition to the Ukrainian persons and ideas already mentioned, there are significant figures such as Metropolitan Dmitry Tuptalo (called 'Rostovsky' after the northern town where he began). Dmitry began to compile a new, *Small Menologos* (*Malyia Chet'ii Minei*) in Kiev in 1684 and it was later reprinted in Moscow.[109] Influenced by Peter Skarga's work on Polish saints, he drew on Latin and Greek sources to produce in it hagiographical material which retained scholarly value as well as popularity long afterward. He also wrote sermons, poems, and plays. He was outstanding, but not unique, in his breadth of interests and exemplified the influence of Roman Catholic culture that went beyond theological ideas and writings.

The latter half of the seventeenth century also witnessed the beginning of translation of Western works in the natural sciences. Epifany Slavinetsky translated the 1641 edition of Vesalius's *De humani corporis fabrica* (1543) in 1657–8 and the 1645 edition of Johan Blaeu's *Theatrum orbis terrarum, sive Atlas novus* in 1661, the first work to be given the Russian reader in which the writer expounded the Copernican heliocentric view and did so with favor,[110] even though avoiding the direct question of whether it or the Ptolemaic system was nearer the truth. Arseny Satanovsky translated the Latin work of Johann Meffret of Meissen (fifteenth century), *Hortulus reginae*, a kind of encyclopedia of all sorts of knowledge ranging from theology to medicine. The brothers Likhud taught some elementary physics for a time in the new Academy.[111]

There were on the face of things Greek and Latin influences at work in Moscow in 1689 to an extent that represented a very extensive change, almost a cultural revolution, since the time when Filaret tried to enforce a regime of cultural exclusion and xenophobia as 'co-ruler' with Michael. In reality, however, the Greek influence was shallow, virtually non-existent. The Greeks who had made an impact in Moscow – Arseny, Paisios Ligarides, the Likhud brothers – had all been trained in the West in Roman Catholic institutions. The dispute that occurred between Medvedev and Patriarch Ioakim in the 1680's was decided by the same kind of ostensibly 'Greek' victory that the Council of 1666–7 had been, followed by further progress of

Roman Catholicizing tendencies and continuation of importation of the culture of Roman Catholic countries.[112]

The Council of 1666–7 and the outcome of the Schism had been characterized, as Pascal puts it, by an acceptance of the 'predominance of the political spirit over the religious spirit...secularization of the Church itself and next a withering of the faith...'[113] Secularization in the sense of an acknowledgment of the primacy of state over Church did not begin in 1667. An important milestone on this path had been 1569, when Ivan IV had had Metropolitan Filipp strangled. The process would not be complete until 1721, when Peter placed the Church under direct state administration. Nevertheless 1667 may be regarded as the decisive step in secularization, and of the Westernization which, now creeping, now hurrying, had been becoming increasingly familiar to the few Muscovites who counted in the realm of culture since the last decade of the fifteenth century. From 1667 to 1689 the cultural impact of the Catholic Reform, even though distant in time and space, made itself felt to a significant extent. The opportunity for serious religious penetration existed during the 1680's to a much greater extent than a century before when Possevino had dreamed of conversion without being able to do more. But there was only one Križanić, who had appeared prematurely on the scene, was no longer in Russia, and followed his utterly isolated and lonely path to his grave. Whoever the few Jesuits in Moscow during the 1680's were, we can assume that none had Križanić's gifts, modest as they may have been, or his love or respect for Russian culture.

During Peter's reign the muted and veiled impact of the Catholic Reform was cut short. That should not prevent understanding of what it was that Kiev's influence, before and after the city was annexed in 1667, brought even if only temporarily to Russia.

4

RUSSIA'S QUASI-REFORMATION
(1689–1761)

Once one has gone to the Germans, leaving them is very difficult.

Alexander Herzen

INTRODUCTION

When Peter drove out Sophia he did not immediately take over the reins of government, and did not immediately alter Sophia's cultural policy. For the moment he followed her willingness to accept the Ukrainian orientation which had been spearheaded by the monks of Kiev and continued with the importation of literary styles and elementary scientific manuals via this route. His later visits to the West and his own instincts and perceptions of the needs of the state he ruled led him to inaugurate a pronounced shift in the direction of the Western orientation of the regime – not so much to increase the tempo of Westernization, though he did that, as to alter the character of the Westernization under way, to turn his attention from Catholic Poland and the Catholic German states to the Protestant part of Germany, Protestant Sweden, Holland, and England. His 'establishment' of the Russian Church (that is, subjection of it to state control) was the clearest sign of his change in cultural policy; it came quite late in his reign. The change in Russia's sources of cultural importation was marked. The change was the result of a growing resolution by Peter himself, which reached its climax only in 1715–18; it was carried out in opposition to the chief intellectual currents and groupings of the time, with the support of only a very few learned clerics.

After a brief reign by Peter's widow Catherine I, the government of his grandson Peter II undertook to reverse Peter's policies in a number of respects, including cultural: there was a brief pro-Catholic reaction along with the effort to assert the claims of the aristocracy. This reaction was halted by Anna Ivanovna (1730–40), who returned to Peter I's vision of change. The Empress Elizabeth (1741–61), after she had overthrown the fleeting regency for Ivan VI, partly continued the cultural policies of Peter and Anna, partly countenanced an indigenous reaction to them. The pro-Protestant orientation of the autocracy was not fundamentally altered again, and in some ways lasted until 1917; but the borrowings from Protestantism that were important for Russian culture tended to center in the early eighteenth century, and after that time they experienced several different kinds of sharp challenge.

Peter's early years

On the overthrow of the Regent Sophia, Peter's mother Natalia (born Naryshkin) became regent until her death in 1694. Ivan V died in 1696, but his disappearance had no important consequences. Peter's family was in control from the moment of Sophia's fall, and when his mother died he had fully to assume the reins of government himself. From a roistering life as amateur soldier, sailor, and man-about-town in Moscow's German Suburb (Nemetskaia Sloboda), he found himself in a new kind of position. He surrounded himself with foreigners and Russians of low as well as high social origin. His whole experience up to then had prepared him to break with many Muscovite traditions, but at first he had no clear objectives concerning the direction of change.

He plunged first into a war with Turkey, and after one failure succeeded in taking the fortress of Azov at the mouth of the Don river in 1696. His initial concern as ruler was in holding Azov and prosecuting further the war with Turkey, and for these ends he sought diplomatic, military, and technical assistance by way of his first visit to Western Europe in the 'Great Embassy' of 1697. It was the first time in recorded history that a ruler of Russia had visited foreign countries on a peaceful mission, and not since Sviatoslav (d. 972) had a ruler been abroad even in war.

From his journey he returned without any promises of support against Turkey, but he had new diplomatic commitments and new (or at any rate greatly reinforced) cultural orientations. He had joined an alliance with Denmark and Poland–Saxony (both ruled by Augustus II) against Sweden. Thus he had become deeply and, as it proved, permanently involved in the affairs of the northern and Protestant part of Western Europe. During his visit to the German states, Holland, and England he found the sort of technical achievements and industriousness that formed his life-long image of Europe. The part of Europe which spoke Germanic languages, and which was Protestant in religion, was rising to world power on a foundation of shipbuilding, navies, and commerce. This made a powerful and instant impression on him and through him on Russia. The fact that his new alliance was brought into play soon after his return was of significance. In 1700 he entered the Great Northern War against Charles XII, seeking a lodgment on the Baltic, whose sea routes gave access to the Europe of his journey. The war was to last twenty-one years. Despite the crushing defeat the Russian army suffered at Narva (1700), he did not delay in trying to secure the Baltic outlet. In 1703 he began the construction of St Petersburg and the establishment of the fortress of Kronstadt on an island nearby in the Gulf of Finland. During the same period he began the reconstruction of Russia's educational system along Western lines and in general a revolution in Russian culture.

On his West European trip (his first, since he was to make another later) he had encountered savants already interested in Russia or willing to serve the cause of science in the country. Nicolas Witsen, explorer and map-maker who had dedicated works to Peter and Ivan V several years earlier, served as interpreter to Peter in Amsterdam and arranged for lessons for the tsar in navigation and ship designing.[1] Peter met skilled engravers, anatomists, and other specialists. He commissioned the printer Jan Thessing to start a Russian press in Amsterdam specially for scientific and technical works, not for 'ecclesiastical books' which, it was noted, were printed already in Moscow. There was an attempt to move this press to Russia in 1708, but the Swedes seized it in Danzig while it was *en route*. In England he obtained the services of a Scottish mathematician, Henry Farquharson, and two young colleagues. In the West he was far from indifferent to problems of Church and state, and his talks in England with Bishop Burnet gave him a knowledge of the control the English state exercised over the Anglican Church which was an important step toward adopting a similar system for Russia. As he passed through Germany one of the greatest men of his day and perhaps the last universal genius in history, Gottfried Wilhelm Leibniz (1646–1716), was aware of his progress but did not then meet him. Leibniz was one of the few Westerners to whom Peter's appearance among them was not a puzzle and an embarrassment, for the German scholar was already preoccupied with the question of cultural relations between Europe and both Russia and China, was endeavoring to learn the relations between the languages spoken in the East, and had some idea of the 'heroic designs which he [Peter] has formed for the good of Christianity and his own peoples'.[2]

In 1701, not long after his return from the West, Peter established one of the first – if not the very first – non-ecclesiastical schools in Russia,[3] the School of Mathematics and Navigation in Moscow, under the Scot, Farquharson. He was responsible for the plan to translate into Russian a number of volumes on mathematics of a high order of sophistication, but he could not provide many Russian consumers of such material. Very rare were such men as Leonty Magnitsky (1669–1739), a Russian who had studied in the Helleno-Greek Academy of Moscow, learned mathematics and Western languages, and became a teacher in the School of Mathematics and Navigation in the year of its founding. In 1703 his two-volume *Arithmetic* (*Arifmetika*) appeared, a textbook consisting mainly of translations from Western works on several of the natural sciences, which was used for many decades afterward. When the School of Mathematics moved to St Petersburg in 1715 (and renamed the Naval Academy), Magnitsky was not taken with it.

Stefan and Feofan, Peter and Alexis

What was perhaps Peter's most important action in the field of cultural policy during this early period was precipitated by the death of the patriarch, Adrian, in October 1700. Adrian had at least verbally repeated the claims of

Nikon for the supremacy in its own field of ecclesiastical authority. In the circular letter he distributed at his accession as patriarch, Adrian developed the argument of two authorities, the priesthood and tsardom, the tsardom having full power on earth, the priesthood having power both on earth and in heaven since it had the power to bind and loose which Christ had promised would be recognized in the hereafter.[4] This line of argument repeated almost verbatim the position Nikon had set forth in his answers to Paisios Ligarides.[5] The difference was that Adrian did not appear to take the argument very seriously, or at any rate was unable to implement it during his tenure as patriarch. His willingness to set forth such claims, at least, constituted a possible nuisance to Peter. Therefore instead of arranging for a successor to Adrian, Peter in December 1700 appointed a *locum tenens* to take charge of the patriarchal office, Stefan Yavorsky. In fact there was to be no patriarch elected again until after the February Revolution of 1917.

Stefan Yavorsky was born in 1658 in an Orthodox family which moved across the Dnieper after the 1667 Treaty of Andrusovo to be in Muscovite territory.[6] He was educated in the Kievan college; he was a student especially of the famous scholastic Ioasaf Krokovsky, and found favor in the eyes of Varlaam Yasinsky, later metropolitan of Kiev. In 1684 he left Kiev, accepting conversion to Roman Catholicism in order to study in Polish schools as was frequently done by Ukrainians of the period. He was a pupil in the schools of Lwów, Łublin, Poznań, and Vilna. Three years later he returned to Kiev, reverted to Orthodoxy, and was tonsured monk. He taught in the Kievan college and served as chief assistant to Metropolitan Yasinsky in the affairs of church administration. By chance Peter heard Stefan preach while he was on an errand in Moscow in 1700. Impressed, the tsar ordered that he be appointed to some post nearby, and he became metropolitan of Riazan and Murom, although he would have preferred to remain in Kiev. The death of Adrian came only a few months later, and Stefan became *locum tenens* of the patriarchate.

Stefan's schooling had given him views sympathetic to Roman Catholicism which doubtless were visible at this stage to those who were discerning, and those views were later to cause Peter no little difficulty. Why, then, did Peter's choice for *locum tenens* fall on Stefan? The answer may be that Peter's concerns in 1700 were more narrowly educational, only later broadening to focus on the religious and cultural principles he came to regard as fundamental to the kind of state he tried to build in Russia; he certainly had returned from Western Europe full of the belief that Latin must be more widely used in Russian schooling, and Stefan was eager to use it. The new *locum tenens* was immediately entrusted with the supervision of the Helleno-Greek Academy, which was then the only Russian institution of higher education except for the Kievan college (from 1701 also called 'Academy'), and ordered to 'introduce into the [Moscow] Academy Latin learning'.[7] Stefan needed no persuasion. He employed as teachers mostly Kievans, notably his lifelong collaborator and posthumous disciple, Feofilakt Lopatinsky, later archbishop of Tver – and indeed most of the students were from the Ukraine.⁸ To be head of the Slavo-Latin Academy, as it was called from 1700 to 1775, Stefan chose Pallady Rogovsky. Like many other Orthodox Pallady had accepted the obedience of Rome to study in the West, and had renounced it on his return in 1698. However, we now know that he along with the deacon Peter Artemev was converted to Roman Catholicism by the Bohemian Jesuit mission that was in Moscow from 1685/6 to 1689,⁹ and there is reason to think that both kept the faith until death.¹⁰ With Rogovsky as rector and Lopatinsky, who followed Aquinas in his lectures,¹¹ as teacher, the Academy was for some time to serve as a significant pro-Roman influence.

As *locum tenens* of the patriarchate, Stefan might, given his evident leaning toward a tradition in which the Church yields to no other power, have preferred to put forward claims for patriarchal or in general ecclesiastical supremacy of the sort Nikon had advanced and Adrian had repeated. As things were he could hope to do no more than take up the defense of the rather tenuous position the Church occupied after 1700. Thus it came about that Stefan, 'although he based his theology on [the ideas of the Roman Catholic, Cardinal] Bellarmine, in reality was defending the Russian Church against the Reformation which was being introduced into it',¹² and many of the Orthodox higher clergy rallied to his support.¹³ In his capacity as the last even temporarily effective defender of the independence of the Russian Church, Stefan found himself in the role of Nikon. The difference was that Stefan was an educated man, not inclined to give offense needlessly, and prepared to wage covert struggle as long as the battle had not gone clearly against him.

The cause and genesis of Peter's successful effort to bring the Church under state control are easy to describe in general terms, difficult to trace with precision. One recent investigator has studied the influence of Samuel Pufendorf (1632–94), the German Protestant jurist who was successively professor at Heidelberg and Lund and then served the royal courts of Sweden and Prussia, on Peter's ecclesiastical policy. Pufendorf's advice concerning the relations between Church and state was unequivocal. The state must be supreme, in religious matters as in others; otherwise

[there] must be perpetual feuds between civil magistrates and Church governors, which would never end but in the ruin of one or the other . . . it is incumbent upon those who contend for the necessity of depriving the civil magistrates of the supreme power in religious matters, to show a positive command for this in the New Testament . . . [It is] absolutely necessary for the peace and security of every state that they [i.e., the clergy] be kept under; nor can there be a single instance produced from history, where a power independent of the civil magistrate has been long exercised by churchmen without producing infinite mischief.¹⁴

In so arguing, Pufendorf might be considered merely to be upholding the position common to the ideologists of a significant part of the Protestant world

(Lutheran and Anglican, though not Calvinist) that the state should be supreme over the Church as well as other institutions within its borders. Still, in some respects his special position was noteworthy. Some Protestant thinkers might only be willing to tolerate as a necessary evil what he advocated as an unequivocally desirable principle of social organization. Moreover, whatever his views, Pufendorf was respected as one of the foremost jurists of the time, and anything he said was likely to be taken seriously in European courts.

The state which Peter inherited was not very much like the Protestant kingdoms of Northern Europe. His predecessors had already liquidated most of the major institutions and social groups outside the sphere of state control. The competing principalities had fallen to Moscow under Ivan III and Vasily III; the boyars' powers had been curtailed by Ivan IV; the peasants had been reduced to a codified form of serfdom by Alexis. By Peter's time there remained outside the firm control of the state only one institution: the Russian Orthodox Church. It was a likely target whatever ideological justification might have been adduced for subjugating it to state control. Peter did not begin the process of undermining its independence; since Ivan IV it had not been able to protect itself fully from state encroachment, and Alexis's handling of the Schism had left it in a debilitated condition. And yet the Petrine Church reform was a decisive event in modern Russian cultural history.

It cannot be determined exactly when Peter decided to place the Church under state administration, but it is clear that he was acquainted with Pufendorf and specifically the *Einleitung zu der Historie* before 1703. Moreover, he evaluated it positively, as in that year he ordered his son Alexis, then twelve years of age, to read from the book each day and to translate another work of Pufendorf's.[15] In 1714 a finished translation into Russian of the *Einleitung* was produced in manuscript, and in 1718 it was published with a foreword by Gabriel Buzhinsky, who noted that Peter used to speak of himself as the 'Russian Pufendorf'. In the text of the law that actually carried out the Church reform, its author, Feofan Prokopovich, prescribed one of Pufendorf's works, *De officio* (in turn a summary Pufendorf himself had prepared of his treatise *De jure naturae et gentium*) as the text for the sixth year of seminary training for Russian Orthodox priests. This prescription was apparently somewhat premature, since Peter gave the order that it be translated into Russian only in 1721, the same year as the law was promulgated. In any case there can be no doubt that Peter knew of Pufendorf before he met Feofan Prokopovich (1706), that Feofan himself was favorably disposed toward Pufendorf's ideas, and that Feofan was instrumental in applying them in Russia.

The Petrine Church reform undoubtedly owed something to Pufendorf's ideas, and the policy underlying it was zealously supported and defended by Feofan Prokopovich; its chief clerical opponent was certainly Stefan Yavorsky. The talented Slavophile writer, Yury Samarin, in the nineteenth century structured a master's thesis around the notion that Stefan and Feofan, standing respectively for the Roman Catholic and Protestant influences within the Russian Church, were the chief antagonists and the men who best symbolized the polar positions in the ideological struggle. The same issues have been treated in the form of a historical novel by Dmitry Merezhkovsky with the chief antagonists as Peter and his son Alexis;[16] and his symbolism is carried to the point of assimilating the two men to Antichrist and Christ respectively. Both the Slavophile publicist and the novelist (despite his extravagant symbolism) have pointed to part of the truth. Qualification of Samarin's scheme is needed; actually not Feofan but Feodosy Yanovsky, who will be discussed shortly, was given primacy in ecclesiastical affairs at an early stage and his position was not seriously challenged until Peter's death. However, it is true, as Samarin implies, that Feofan was used in the ideological struggle more extensively during Peter's reign, even though Feodosy was the more powerful man in the philo-Protestant clerical camp and among the clergy as a whole.[17]

Concerning Peter himself, Merezhkovsky's fundamental point is sound, and goes to the heart of the great historiographical and ideological controversy about Peter which has probably been the most pervasive single one in modern Russian history. Peter's reforms were not mainly concerned with technique, despite the technological revolution he began, or with science, despite the important steps he took to introduce scientific studies, or with statecraft, despite the national and partly local governmental reorganization he carried out, or with the economy, despite the growth in manufacturing and shift in trade which he did much to bring about. The Petrine reforms were ultimately concerned with the cultural question: was the Russian tradition to be supplanted as extensively and swiftly as possible by Western importations, or was it to be the basis from which the reform of Russian life was to proceed? Peter stood for the former answer, his son Alexis for the latter. It is quite unjust to impute to Alexis the stance of a bland reactionary. One scholar writes that he was

not stupid and in any case inquisitive, perhaps even in a certain sense a progressive, but only not of the new generation but of the old one, of the epoch of Alexei Mikhailovich and Fedor Alexeevich, which also was not deficient in men well educated for their time...Neither was the tsarevich a man unfit for practical work; all that is known concerning his carrying out of tasks allotted him by Peter provides no basis for any such allegation; but he was only an obedient executor and was unqualifiedly unsympathetic to that work which Peter demanded of him.[18]

The story of Peter and Alexis is perhaps one of the most dramatic in history, in the sense that individual psychological factors and fundamental historical issues were intertwined in the tortuous and finally fatal confrontation between father and son. Alexis spent much of his childhood with his mother, and all his life resented Peter's forcing of her to become a nun (when he was eight years old) and Peter's refusal to give him permission even to communicate with her after that, though he secretly did so. He loved his father and yet stood in mortal terror of him; his fear overshadowed any feelings of resentment toward Peter's new and plebeian wife, Catherine. Despite his hatred of Menshikov, Catherine's protector, he sought and obtained her intercession with Peter on his own behalf on more than one occasion.

Alexis received a good enough education for the time; it was often interrupted by Peter's orders to join him on campaign, but royal education even in Western Europe in that day was often somewhat sporadic. He learned German and Polish, studied some French, read on politics according to Pufendorf, as already mentioned, and occupied himself with other subjects. At the age of twenty he was reading six or seven hours a day, taking part in disputations at the University of Kraków, avid to learn more about foreign lands. Partly because Peter took away his tutor, Baron van Huyssen, when he was fifteen, he came to spend much time with clergymen. Peter seems quite early to have sensed that he was not fond of the soldier's life – which was the chief fault the father found with his son. The same was true of Frederick the Great's father, and yet the son lived to be an effective monarch and war chief.

In October 1715, when within two weeks sons were born to Alexis and then Peter, the father chose to stake the future on his newborn son (who actually died in 1719) and began the series of ultimatums to Alexis which led to the latter's flight to Vienna. He was tricked into returning home to torture and death (1718) at Peter's order if not partly by his own hand. It is the only known case in modern European history in which a father who was a monarch killed his own son.

In Merezhkovsky's evocation of the funeral, Stefan Yavorsky has first to kiss the corpse. Merezhkovsky writes: 'Stefan buried with him [Alexis] all that he loved – the whole Muscovite tradition, the Patriarchate, the freedom and greatness of the ancient church, his last hope – "the hope of Russia".'[19] Stefan had used this phrase of Alexis in 1712, and in consequence had been forbidden to preach any more. He had recognized in Alexis not an obscurantist or a traitor, but a prince devoted to the welfare of the people and the Russian cultural tradition, who grieved for the economic burdens and physical agonies Peter had imposed on Russia and had no love for the all-powerful state that Peter was building. Neither Stefan nor Alexis was opposed to Russia's drawing nearer the West; both had had considerable education which was based on Western learning. If Peter had died ten years earlier than he did, there is no reason to suppose that Russia under Alexis would have ceased to import Western techniques, knowledge, and ideas.

Stefan Yavorsky produced a great many sermons, in which he cited numerous ancient Greeks and Roman authors and, among early modern Roman Catholic writers, such as Cesare Baronius and Philippe de Commynes.[20] But he wrote a single major work, *The Rock of Faith* (*Kamen' very*).[21] He was led to write the book by the affair of the heretic Dmitry Tveritinov, to be discussed below. He completed it in 1718. It was published only in 1728, after his death, on the authority of his loyal aide Feofilakt Lopatinsky, who survived both Peter I and Catherine I as a member of the Synod – thus during the reign of Alexis's son, the baby born in 1715, Peter II (1727–30) – and new editions followed in 1729 and 1730.[22]

Stefan's book had two sections, the first expounding the dogmas of Orthodoxy with supporting arguments from the Bible, the decisions of the Ecumenical Councils, and the works of the Fathers; the second was directed against Protestant doctrine. He drew heavily on the writings of Roman Catholic writers including Jesuits, especially Becan, Bellarmine, and again Baronius.[23] In the first section he made a strong defense of 'tradition' (*predanie*), regarding it as having two aspects: it was part of the divine revelation, the part existing outside Scripture, authentic as Scripture itself; and it was an everlasting prerogative of the Church, by virtue of which it determined the meaning of Scripture and decided other questions. All this of course was a fundamental challenge to Protestant views. He also discoursed at length on the problems of good works and divine grace, using a series of syllogisms in the process.[24] Samarin concludes: 'Thus a Catholic element was drawn in to the book of Stefan Yavorsky in the form of proofs. Attempting to give a logical justification to the dogmas of our [i.e., the Orthodox] church, he borrowed from the Catholics [their] system as a ready-made mould and inserted into it Orthodox dogmas.'[25] In his last chapter, Stefan discusses the punishment of heretics, again on the basis of Roman Catholic writers; he declares that the Church has two swords, 'spiritual and material', and if the first does not achieve its object the second must be used.[26]

Stefan's *Rock of Faith* was not his first tract against heretics. A certain Old Believer preaching the imminence of the Apocalypse (there were also others, then and later) named Talitsky appeared in Moscow near the beginning of Stefan's tenure as exarch. Stefan wrote against him a work largely based on the Spanish theologian Malvenda's book on the same subject.[27] But it was the case of Dmitry Evdokimovich Tveritinov which occasioned the writing of the *Rock of Faith*. Tveritinov was a man from Tver who had no distinction of birth or education but an active intelligence. Coming to Moscow about 1692, he acted as a servant in foreigners' homes and as an apprentice pharmacist. By the early 1700's he was actively preaching doctrines of Lutheran origin and going further to advance some of his own ideas. He rejected the hierarchy – 'I myself am the Church'[28] – and relied on Scripture alone as authority. In 1713 Stefan had him and several followers of his charged with heresy. Under examination they ostensibly renounced their heresies, and Peter ordered Stefan to restore them to the Church without further ado. Flouting the tsar's wishes, Stefan continued the investigation and imprisoned the accused men in a monastery. In 1714 the ecclesiastical council in Moscow anathematized the heretics and turned them over to a civil court. One of the accused, Foma

Ivanov, was burned in Red Square; however, Tveritinov himself was finally freed in 1718 and in 1723 the Most Holy Synod restored him at last to the Church.

The Tveritinov case was the climax of Stefan's struggle with Peter. Tveritinov's views had been widely known years before he was accused. Stefan's timing of the case may have been influenced by Peter's introduction of 'fiskals' or state inspectors into Church courts in 1711, which Stefan sharply criticized the following year (and on the same occasion spoke of Alexis as the 'hope of Russia'). In pressing charges against a pro-Protestant heretic, Stefan was striking at the tsar himself. While the case was in progress Peter took the decisive steps to remove Stefan in fact, though not in name, from his position as chief ecclesiastic. The tsar managed to find two other men to assist him in dealing with the Church and who were willing to defend his own Protestant leanings: Feodosy Yanovsky and Feofan Prokopovich. The crucial stage in the Petrine revolution in the Church, which entailed a revolution in Russian culture, can be dated 1715–18.

Feofan and Feodosy

From about 1700 Peter had begun to evince his own religious leanings in a curious and even incredible manner through an ecclesiastical parody, apparently of his own invention, which he called 'The Most Licentious Council of Buffoons and Drunkards'.[29] Over the years he devoted an enormous amount of time to this mock institution. At first, Samarin points out, one figure (Zotov, Peter's old tutor) was designated 'Prince-Pope'; he was dressed in papal vestments, and Roman Catholic rites were the ones parodied. Little by little, however, the vestments and rites were altered, and came to approximate those of the Orthodox Church. In 1715 a grotesque ceremony was staged in which a man playing the role of 'Patriarch' in a mock wedding took a bride – Zotov was now the 'bride' and no longer the chief cleric.[30] Samarin declares that Peter was teaching a lesson: that the patriarchate – there had been no patriarch, after all, for fifteen years – was the 'specter' of papism. In any event he moved from public ridicule of Roman Catholicism to burlesques of the hierarchy and the ceremonies of Orthodoxy, but he did not mock Protestantism; on the contrary the extraordinary proceedings of the 'Council' had as their target many objects of Protestant criticism of both Catholicism and Orthodoxy. Ivanov had been burned the previous year; but there would be no more burnings of Protestant sympathizers, and the Church would be brought under the control of the state, where Pufendorf and other Protestants said it belonged and where Peter himself and his successors (not Alexis and his offspring) would be able to guide it.

Peter's two chief aides in pursuing such a policy came to be Feodosy Yanovsky and Feofan Prokopovich. Feodosy, probably born in the 1650's, came from the Polish szlachta. Like Stefan, he studied in the Kievan college.

Despite the shadow of scandal from his early years as a monk, he rose rapidly.[31] By 1704 he was, as archimandrite of the Khutyn monastery, already in close relations with the tsar. In 1708 Peter sent him to St Petersburg and entrusted him with supervision of the churches and clergy of the newly conquered territory in the vicinity. He presided over several important ceremonial occasions, including the marriage of Anna Ivanovna to the Duke of Courland in 1710. In 1712 he became archimandrite of the newly-founded monastery of Alexander Nevsky, which was given primacy among all Russian monasteries. Soon he became the tsar's closest adviser on religious affairs generally; on Peter's second journey to the West in 1716–18 Feodosy traveled with him constantly. Friedrich Wilhelm von Bergholz, the noted diarist of Peter's reign, mentioned several times in his diary that Feodosy was 'the first ecclesiastic of the realm, who enjoyed the Tsar's confidence'.[32] By this time Feofan Prokopovich was very much part of the picture, but he was careful publicly to acknowledge the primacy of Feodosy. Feodosy had his views – Stefan was worried by them and Alexis and his friends simply considered him a Lutheran – but his literary and rhetorical gifts seem to have been meager; however, Feofan made up for that.

Feofan Prokopovich was born in 1681 into a Kiev merchant family.[33] His father died when he was a boy; his mother turned beggar to keep the two of them alive, and then died in turn. He was taken by his uncle, who was rector of the Kievan college, and the uncle enrolled his nephew in the school. In 1692 the uncle died; someone else took him and kept him in school until 1698. He then attended Polish schools – it is not certain where – as a Uniat, and as such was tonsured monk. The provincial of the Basilian order sent him to the College of St Athanasius in Rome. The Jesuit who was head of the college was much taken by him, and thought he had traits similar to Pope Urban VIII. In 1702 he returned to the Ukraine and in 1704 became a teacher of poetry at the Kievan Academy. The kindness shown him in the Roman Catholic world did not leave him grateful. He later wrote that 'the great Paul long ago told us that the dark angel as well as his servitors usually clothe themselves in light; in actuality the very sham-piety of the Latin monks serves for me as the chief proof of their impiety'.[34] Like Stefan, he carried a Roman Catholic education away from the West; unlike Stefan, he emerged such a dedicated foe of Catholic influences that he developed strong Protestant leanings. In the Kievan Academy he was an enemy of Roman Catholic scholasticism, but not of scholasticism in general. Florovsky declares that 'he belongs to the Protestant scholasticism of the seventeenth century'; if there had not been the name of a Russian bishop on his tracts, 'it would have been the most natural thing in the world to suppose that he was a professor in some Protestant theological faculty'.[35]

In 1706 Peter first heard Feofan preach on a visit to Kiev; in 1709, after the decisive victory at Poltava over the Swedes, the tsar heard him again. In 1711 Peter took him on the campaign against the Turks, and on his return he was made hegumen of the Brotherhood monastery in Kiev, rector of the Academy, and professor of theology. In 1715 he was summoned to St Petersburg,[36] but illness delayed his departure and when he arrived in the capital in the autumn of 1716 Peter, accompanied by Feodosy, was in Western Europe. Peter was welcomed on his return in October 1717 by three orations of Feofan's: one in the name of the baby tsarevich, Peter (although only in February 1718 would the manifesto be issued substituting Peter Petrovich for Alexis as heir), the second in the name of the Tsarevna Anna, and the third in the name of the Russian people.[37] The occasion foreshadowed Feofan's close identification with the new, Petrine Russia during the last seven years of Peter's life, and marked as clearly as any other the ascendancy of Protestant sympathies in the life of the Russian state.

In 1718 Feofan was, despite charges of heresy against him by two of Stefan's collaborators, Gedeon Vishnevsky and Feofilakt Lopatinsky, made bishop of Pskov and Narva. Peter entrusted him with the task of drawing up the new law placing the church under one of the new state bureaus, or 'colleges', to which Peter was entrusting the whole administration. It was not purely accident that the condemnation and death of Alexis took place during the same year.

On 23 February 1720, the so-called *Ecclesiastical Regulation* (*Dukhovnyi Reglament*) was approved and signed by the tsar, and on 25 January 1721 a manifesto formally created an Ecclesiastical College, within a few months to be renamed the Most Holy Governing Synod.[38] Stefan was named president; Feodosy, on the last day of 1720 named archbishop of Novgorod, first vice-president; Feofan second vice-president. After 1718 Stefan was virtually powerless, and his health declined rapidly, but Peter would not let him resign. Though president of the Synod, he refused to sign its protocols since he did not take part in its sessions; he was actually under police surveillance. In November 1722 he died in Moscow, defeated and overshadowed by his Protestant-leaning rivals.

Formidable support is given by the text of the *Regulation* to those who believe Peter's military reforms were both the beginning and the model for everything else he did:

It is known to the whole world how inadequate and weak was the Russian army when it did not have proper training and...how it became great and formidable beyond expectation when Our Most Powerful Monarch, His Tsarist Majesty, Peter I, instructed it with most excellent regulations...Especially is this to be appreciated as regards the administration of the Church...[39]

Peter certainly believed that as autocrat he had to adjust all aspects of life to the needs of the day as he conceived them, and among the foremost of those aspects left unsettled by 1721 was the Church. In our story, of greatest interest is the ideological inspiration for the settlement or, as it has been called, the 'establishment' (by analogy with the Established Church of

England) of the Church. The Synod, as Alexander Muller has pointed out, was really a kind of Lutheran consistory, which Webster's International (third edition) defines as 'an administrative body of clerical and lay officers appointed by civil authority to administer ecclesiastical affairs...' In fact, the *Regulation* was a rather close imitation of the *Kirchenordnungen* of the Lutheran states and in particular of the 1686–7 statutes of Charles XI of Sweden. The text of the *Regulation* itself mentions precedents, but only pre-Christian ones from ancient Jerusalem and Athens; it must have been too embarrassing to mention its contemporary models.[40] There were theological as well as institutional borrowings in the *Regulation*. In a boldly Protestant manner, the law states: 'Holy Scripture itself contains all the laws and commandments needed for our salvation...'[41] Page after page calls for combating 'superstition' – false saints' lives, relics, holiday observances of pagan origin, and the like. Nothing here explicitly calls into question any Orthodox rituals or practices; the tone, however, is that of the sermon originating in Wittenberg or Geneva. The flat assertion is made that learning was at a low ebb throughout Europe during the Middle Ages (fifth to fourteenth centuries);[42] obviously the writer is thinking more of Western Europe, however accurately, than of the Byzantium which an Orthodox cleric might be expected to consider as fundamental to his own church history.

The author of the *Regulation*, Feofan, wrote a number of books which bear his own name. They are carefully examined by Yury Samarin. Of course in them he criticizes Protestants, but his gentleness with them may be illustrated by the following passage:

Calvinists and Lutherans, although they do not overlook true and sound evidence [in support of the authority of Scripture], are at fault in that they introduce along with such evidence other proofs that are unsuitable, and give them out as primary, and prefer the less true to the more true. For some of them as evidence for Scripture advance the inner action of the Holy Spirit, and others the inner signs of the same Scripture or the very infallibility of the Holy Scripture. Both points are valid: that is, that we are led to believe Scripture by the Holy Spirit, and that the Holy Scripture is infallible. And the faithful will believe both. But to the infidel God and only God can vouchsafe the first, and through the first instill the second.[43]

No Protestant could take much offense at such 'criticism'. In fact Feofan was as deeply committed to the notion that Scripture was sufficient and tradition unnecessary to salvation as any Protestant. He himself wrote that even before he had heard the name of Cardinal Bellarmine (that is, when he was in Jesuit school, presumably), he had held Bellarmine's opinion to be correct that in Scripture 'there were things that were vague, ambiguous, obscure, and unnecessary'; but he abandoned that 'error'.[44] Making an exception for the first seven ecumenical councils, he treated the decisions of local councils as if their validity was to be judged by the *individual* on the basis of whether they harmonize with Scripture, and thus he made the same transition as in Protestantism between the doctrine of sufficiency of Scripture and the right of private judgment. As for the salvation of the private individual, he discussed both works and faith but tended to reduce works to faith. When he was denounced in 1718, he wrote quite accurately about one of his accusers: 'What most of all displeases him is justification through Christ without works [tunie, that is, justification by faith].'[45] Samarin attributes his position on the doctrine of justification by faith to the Lutherans, in particular Melanchthon, Chemnitz, and Gerhard.[46] Certainly the first two, at least, were known for their uncompromising advocacy of that doctrine.

If the individual is to be exalted in religious doctrine, at a certain point the position of the Church as an institution may be endangered. Samarin declares that Feofan accepts the Protestant principle of private judgment, in which the individual takes upon himself that of which only the Church is capable; 'in the system of Feofan the fact of the Church occupies a subordinate place'.[47] This was true not only in theory but in practice; not the actual subordination of the Church to the state, which was Peter's doing, but its justification and defense, owed more to Feofan than to anyone else. Chistovich declares that he did the tsar's bidding, 'sometimes forgetting holy truth and sacrificing truth for sake of obsequiousness to the tsar'.[48] It is always difficult to judge motives. No doubt Feofan had his own theological and more broadly intellectual convictions, and after his return to Kiev in 1702 there seems to be no indication that his position changed significantly.

That there was a prudential streak in Feofan, however, seems clear; it is illustrated by his attitude to Feodosy. For a long time Feofan had deferred to him. Finally, however, Feodosy was brought to condemn Peter's invasion of ecclesiastical prerogatives – to be sure, after Peter was dead, and after he himself had become deeply embroiled in difficulties; he may have spoken up out of weariness of repressing his real convictions, or perhaps out of fury at his critics, unrestrained any longer by fear of Peter. At any rate Feodosy declared that Peter's death was God's punishment for the fact that the tsar 'interfered with ecclesiastical affairs and properties',[49] and proceeded to be so blatantly rude to Catherine I as to compromise himself. Once he had clearly done so, Feofan hastened to denounce his long-time collaborator and superior. Feodosy was exiled in May 1725 and died in February 1726 in confinement.

As for Feofan, he successfully survived the first post-Petrine dynastic crisis. At the crucial moment he had intervened, in the meeting of the self-constituted council of notables which decided the succession, by throwing his weight behind Menshikov's effort to enthrone Catherine. His tract entitled *The Justice of the Monarch's Will*, which he had composed in 1722 to justify Peter's succession law (Peter had died without using it), was reprinted and distributed to justify the accession of Catherine I as if Peter had designated her his successor by the 1722 law[50] – which he had not done.

Feofan triumphed, despite the unhappy interlude for him of the reign of Peter II (1727–30), though the full measure of his success was not visible until after his own death in 1736. What triumphed was not merely the influence of his own views and writings, which became strong, nor pro-Protestant doctrines in Russian Orthodox thinking and writing, although they became influential, nor the idea that the state should be higher than the Church, which Pufendorf and other Lutherans as well as Anglicans had been willing to accept in theory and practice. It was also the idea that the state should organize, supervise, and control culture. Feofan need not be charged with holding the idea. He was not responsible for the fact that Russia had become a completely single-centered society over an extended period as a result of a complex evolution or for the fact that Peter was not merely a dynamic and forceful ruler but wielded autocratic powers unknown to an English or German monarch. Nevertheless it was the Russian state, whether Feofan wished it or not – and thus the power of the state even after Peter's death, when the rulers were infants or women not interested in ruling – which directly subordinated the church to its own direct administration and henceforward claimed that teachers, scholars, and men of learning should serve its needs.

Pososhkov

It has been shown that the opposition to Peter was far from being monolithic. Jurij Šerech has, following Ternovsky, distinguished three parties among the high Orthodox clerics of the day:[51] (1) conservative Muscovites, following Patriarch Adrian and later such men as Metropolitan Iov of Novgorod; (2) Ukrainian scholastics, following Stefan Yavorsky, Feofilakt Lopatinsky, and Dmitry Rostovsky;[52] and (3) pro-Protestants following Feofan and Feodosy. (We shall soon see that laymen as well as clerics were to be found in these ideological groupings.) Peter's *coup* of 1689 was supported by conservative Muscovites, then headed by Patriarch Ioakim, and partly directed against both the Ukrainians and the Old Believers (the latter were not, of course, a group of 'Orthodox clerics'). As the tsar's policies took form, he had to create his own faction in the pro-Protestant circle led by Feodosy and Feofan. The Ukrainians, led by Stefan, and the conservative Muscovites including some of the clerics around Alexis, made common cause against the Petrine policies, supported by the Old Believers to the extent they had any weight even indirectly in this struggle.

It will not do simply to label this bloc as 'reactionary'. The Ukrainians had for close to a century, at least, been identified with reform; even the so-called 'conservative Muscovites' were clerics who supported the Nikonian reforms of the Church; the Old Believers, as above discussed, had at least an aspect which opposed absolutism, combated personal licentiousness, and produced creative innovation in forms of communal living. As for Alexis himself, he was doubtless closer to the 'conservative Muscovites' than to any other single group, but Stefan's willingness to support him, which has been mentioned, obviously went beyond mere hostility to Peter, and there were qualities in

Alexis's character and education which could commend themselves to the Ukrainians.

However, there was a fourth group whose make-up may be indicated by reference to an apparently lonely and certainly self-taught figure, Ivan Tikhonovich Pososhkov.[53] Pososhkov was born about 1652, the son of an ordinary dues(*obrok*)-paying, non-farming serf of a village then near Moscow, now absorbed into the city. The village belonged to the Armory (Oruzheinaia Palata), and many of its peasants were also craftsmen, whence came Pososhkov's array of technical skills. To begin with he ran a distillery; he minted coins; he proposed to manufacture playing cards that would avoid giving religious offense – changing the design of the clubs so as not to resemble the cross, for example. Already his deepest concerns showed themselves here. Pavlov-Silvansky points out that 'the greater part of Pososhkov's works were devoted to questions of an ecclesiastical and religious-moral kind'.[54] He wrote against the Old Belief and Protestantism in *The Clear Mirror* (*Zerkalo ochevidnoe*) of 1708, which delighted Dmitry Rostovsky, and in several letters to Metropolitan Stefan and other works advocated concrete measures to raise the spiritual level of the Orthodox Church.

His best-known work, *On Poverty and Wealth* (*Kniga o skudosti i bogatstve*, 1724), proposed a series of measures for 'the total reform, the renovation of Russia', in Pavlov-Silvansky's words; if those measures were put into effect, Pososhkov claimed, 'our entire great Russia will be renovated in the realm of things both ecclesiastical and civil (*kak v dukhovnosti, tako i vo grazhdanstve*) ...'[55] His first chapter deals with the Church; only then does he go on to discuss war, law, and the economy. Until now there has been no evidence produced that any of Pososhkov's views, including the economic views which have attracted attention in recent times, were derivative; he was an independent and even original thinker. He urged an active role of the state in the economy, and thus has been compared with the Western ideologists of 'mercantilism' or even called a 'mercantilist', but his views are about as different from those of Montchrétien and Boisguillebert as the Russian state was different from the French state of the time. One might as well say that he was a Physiocrat because he writes that 'if the peasant is rich, so is the ruler; but the poverty of the peasant is the impoverishment of the ruler (*krest'ianskoe bogatstvo – tsarstvennoe, a nishcheta krest'ianskaia – oskudenie tsarstvennoe*)'.[56] But he was neither particularly concerned with the balance of trade on the one hand nor with freedom of trade on the other, and as far as his economic views are concerned he is most sensibly to be regarded as a rather modest kind of reformer within the institutional limits of the Russia in which he lived.

The same is true of his views on the military, law, and so forth. For him there was no question of limiting the power of the autocrat, for he found good words to say of the Turkish system; but he did envisage a new code of laws, to be considered by a national council. It is exaggerated to impute to Pososhkov, as some have done, a commitment to the emancipation of the serfs;[57] but he did speak of the power of the landlords over the serfs as 'temporary' (*vladeiut imi vremianno*),[58] and such expressions were enough to cause the censorship to hesitate to pass the book in 1842, over a hundred years after it was written. In summing up Pososhkov's views, Pavlov-Silvansky writes: 'In contrast with the *Westerners*, that is, Peter and his closest collaborators, Pososhkov was a typical *Muscovite progressive*.'[59] The same may be said of certain contemporaries of his: the unknown author of 'the twelve articles', Ivan Filippov, Vice-Governor V. Ershov, the manufacturer Daniel Voronov, and others. Accepting Pavlov-Silvansky's formulation, Kafengauz goes on to say that the Muscovite progressives 'often showed themselves to be in complete agreement with the "Westerners"....'[60]

Consideration of Pososhkov's view may make it necessary to modify the formulation of Šerech's (or Ternovsky's) alluded to above. There were doubtless 'conservative Muscovites' who wanted no change and no effort to learn from abroad; but at least several 'Muscovites', deeply committed to the Orthodox religious outlook of old Muscovy, not only were willing to consider change but were eager advocates of reform. Thus to Šerech's list of three anti-Petrine Orthodox groups there deserves to be added a fourth, the 'progressive Muscovites'. They were willing to make common cause with other reformers, notably the Ukrainians, and in certain respects were in agreement also with such 'Westerners' as F. S. Saltykov, a dvorianin who collaborated with Peter.[61]

Pososhkov presented *On Poverty and Wealth* to Peter in August 1724. He was arrested just a year later, after Peter was already dead, and after several months in confinement died in January 1726. The reason for his arrest is uncertain, but scholars have generally believed that it related to the contents of the book.[62] We can only speculate what parts of it offended the authorities most. Perhaps it is enough to point out that like the Tsarevich Alexis and Stefan, Pososhkov was known to be out of sympathy with Peter's fundamental cultural orientation. It was ironic that Archbishop Feodosy, who had been Peter's willing instrument all along but renounced him after his death, perished at the same time as Pososhkov, and there are even mysterious links between the 'criminal' dossiers on the two men.[63] Perhaps Peter was right to scent enemies everywhere, but he seemed unable or unwilling to distinguish between lack of sympathy for his views and active disobedience or obstruction of his orders (let alone treason).

The 'Protestant' reconstruction of Russian education

If Russia's chief apostle of Protestantization was an Orthodox clergyman, Feofan, the chief person to inspire educational and cultural change during Peter's reign was a foreign Protestant layman, Leibniz.[64] Though Peter corresponded with the great polymath earlier, the two men met only at Torgau in 1711 (to be the scene of another famous meeting of Russians and Westerners in 1945); the meeting was arranged by Alexis's tutor, Baron van

Huyssen. A document found in the Moscow archives and ascribed to Leibniz, advising creation of administrative 'Colleges', traces a detailed plan for the introduction of Western-style education and research as a function of a College of Learning (*Gelehrt-Collegium*).[65] Guerrier believes it to date to 1716; Richter thinks it may have been composed in 1711 at the time of the Torgau meeting.[66] Certainly the first 'College' was actually created in 1712, others followed. No College of Learning was ever created, but an Academy of Sciences, owing much to Leibniz's conception of the Berlin Academy of Sciences which he was instrumental in founding in 1700, eventually came into existence.

Leibniz devoted a great deal of time to matters Russian, and not least of his concerns was Russia's position in a grandiose vision of Christian missionary expansion to all corners of Asia which he cherished, and which he related to the progress of the Jesuit mission in China which he was also following with great interest.[67] He died in 1716, before some of Peter's most important reforms were carried out. Probably never before had a Westerner who had not actually spent time in Russia come to know so much about Russia as Leibniz did. And yet, as Benz points out, he knew next to nothing about Russian culture or about the fear and hatred Peter's policies had evoked in all walks of life; the figure of Peter himself, the creator of St Petersburg, the victor over Sweden, had hypnotized him. Leibniz, writes Benz, 'gained the impression that this people was really a *tabula rasa* that felt itself destined to be given shape by a ruler of genius'.[68]

Leibniz's vision of learning in the new Russia was one in which theology, by implication Protestant theology,[69] would have a very prominent role. Peter was finally to actualize part of that vision, but he began with attempts at creating chiefly secular schools to supplement the rather modest system of ecclesiastical schools, leading to and including the Moscow and Kiev Academies, which were the only ones in pre-Petrine Russia. The schools Peter created were all state schools, not private ones; and in this respect also they followed the Leibnizian principle that the state should take the lead in organizing education and harnessing the sciences.

Such schools included the Moscow School of Navigation already mentioned,[70] the gymnasium founded by Ernst Glück, a Lutheran pastor from Marienburg, which opened in 1705 and collapsed in 1715; and the 'ciphering' (*tsifirnyia*) schools, to be established according to a decree of 1714 in each of the new (from 1707) provinces to furnish mathematically trained young men to the new navy. There came nominally to be 27 of these by 1722, after the closing of 14 of them in that year. The reason for the closings was that Peter had created a new system of seminaries in accordance with the provisions of the Ecclesiastical Regulation of 1721;[71] simultaneously the clergy were permitted to shift to the seminaries and did so – leaving 14 of the ciphering schools without pupils. All the ecclesiastical schools, hitherto private, thereupon became state schools.

Both kinds of schools, lay and ecclesiastical, were merely forms of state service; compulsion and harsh disciplinary measures were used to obtain pupils and to force the pupils to work – a law threatened to forbid marriage to students who once in the ciphering schools did not complete them success-fully, for example – though all Peter's decrees of this sort led to precious little. Out of some 2,000 students brought either voluntarily or by compulsion into the ciphering schools before 1727, over a third were town-dwellers or clergy-men's sons who had left when they had the chance (1720 and 1721 respec-tively); a fifth escaped; 15% had been found to be 'illiterates, idiots, or unfit'; 6% had been taken for official appointments before finishing the course; less than a fifth had been graduated. (It may be safely doubted that all of the other four-fifths were successfully prevented from marrying subsequently.) A total of 500 were left. Twice the Admiralty proposed that the remaining ciphering schools be combined with the ecclesiastical schools, but the Synod refused. The ciphering schools thus languished a while longer, and collapsed entirely in 1744.

In 1727 there were 46 ecclesiastical schools; out of over 3,000 pupils, only some 200 had dropped out.[72] The number of pupils in the latter climbed steadily through the century, and furnished instructors to all sorts of lay schools well into the nineteenth century. Florinsky notes that the ecclesiastical schools had greater vitality, 'perhaps because they had behind them a certain tradition which the lay schools lacked'.[73] Despite Peter's zeal in supporting his Protestantizing clerics, these schools continued to be patterned on the Roman-scholastic model of the Kievan Academy until about the middle of the century, for Ukrainians were still almost the only teachers available. Theology continued to be taught according to St Thomas Aquinas and his Kievan commentators, and philosophy according to Aristotle in Roman-scholastic interpretation, with texts written by Polish Jesuits.[74] Only around 1750 did Aquinas yield to Feofan Prokopovich, along with Calvin, Polanus von Polans-dorf, and Johann Gerhard in the study of theology, while in philosophy Aristotle and the Roman scholastics yielded to Christian Wolff, especially through the textbook of Baumeister used in Kiev from 1752 and published in Moscow in 1777.

Whatever his intentions, what Peter did to Russian education was thus not to secularize it. The number of pupils in Russian schools greatly increased, but most of them were in the new ecclesiastical schools. Neither did he Protestan-tize the schools instantly, as just observed; but the change from an emphasis on Roman Catholic learning to a Protestant tendency could take place the more easily because of the remarkable fact that the new schools were con-ducted for the most part in Latin. Latin was the language of Protestant as well as Roman scholasticism throughout Europe and America. (Those who associate Protestantism with the spread of the vernacular would do well to ponder the case of Russia.) The increase in Protestant influences led to the use not of less Latin but of more – much more, since the school system itself greatly expanded. In the eighteenth century the priests who did have any education learned their Scripture in Latin and wrote in Latin, even though they had to conduct services in Church Slavic. No wonder the Eastern Slavic vernaculars were slow to produce a modern literature.

State compulsion was the hallmark of Peter's educational reforms, as of his other reforms. Sons of the gentry were ordered to attend school, abroad and in Russia; Peter's hostility to monasticism, which he shared with Protestants, led to a variety of measures to make the black clergy do 'useful' things – at least by his standards; the ukase of 1723, which ordered all monks younger than thirty to assemble in the Zaikonospassky school for compulsory Latin training, is an example of what he thought to be useful. There are those who regret all such measures of compulsion, and yet are apt to assert that they were unavoidable if Russia was to be modernized or Westernized. The least that can be said in reply is that compulsion might have been partly avoided if the schools to which young Russians were being driven had had a less remote relationship to their own language, culture, and tradition; moreover, it has been shown that the compulsion used actually led to very little real education.

Peter's intention was to crown his educational reforms by the foundation of a national academy of sciences comparable to that of England, France, or Prussia. His visit to the Paris Académie des Sciences in 1717, when he himself was elected a member of that body,[75] led him to serious efforts to create a Russian academy. In this endeavor the pupil of the dead Leibniz and professor at Halle University, Christian Wolff (1679–1754) was instrumental.[76] Peter's German physicians, Johann Schumacher and Lavrenty Blumentrost (he was the son of a German but was born in Russia), attempted to enlist Wolff's assistance and even invited him to come to Russia to take part. Wolff was at that moment in the process of being driven out of Halle because of the charges leveled at him by his theological enemies, the pietists led by August Hermann Francke; he found refuge in Hesse at Marburg University, where he was later to become the chief mentor of the Russian student and future savant, Lomonosov. He was cautious, however, about exposing himself to possible theological calumnies in Russia. Despite Blumentrost's assurance that he need not worry, for 'in Russia the Emperor himself is *supremus pontifex*',[77] Wolff did not go to Russia. He did help to arrange for a number of foreign savants to come to be among the first members of the Academy, among them Daniel and Nicolaus Bernoulli, mathematicians, and Georg Bilfinger and Christian Martini, physicists.

By the end of 1725 sixteen scholars, of which thirteen were Germans and the others Swiss and French, were in St Petersburg. In December Peter's widow formally founded the Academy of Sciences. As Florinsky writes, 'it was not, perhaps, inappropriate that the Russian Academy of Science should have been inaugurated by Empress Catherine I, a former Lithuanian peasant girl, who never mastered the mysteries of reading and writing'.[78]

The Academy's first president was Blumentrost, who had also been instrumental in starting in the capital a museum called the Kunstkamera, at first mainly noted for its collection of various pickled monsters, and a library. Western science (mainly but not entirely physical science), no doubt, had come to Russia, but thus far Russia was only a geographical location for it; the scientists had little to do with their surroundings. No Russians were involved in the Academy; the foreigners knew no Russian and published their proceedings in Latin. The plan was to have the academicians teach in a university and a gymnasium attached to the Academy, as well as do research. When the gymnasium was opened in 1727, there were few Russian students; the university had none at all, and resorted to importing eight German students in order to pretend to function. Until the reign of Catherine II the Academy was the scene of constant scandals and disputes, the preserve of foreigners whose studies were of little interest or use to the Russians, and altogether, in the view of foreign observers, a waste of a good deal of money. The university never did become a functioning institution, and perished altogether before the end of the century. The story is very similar to that of Peter's ciphering schools.

Russia's 'Reformation'

From the cultural point of view the crisis of 1715-18 and the triumph of Feofan marked the reversal of the growth of Roman Catholic tendencies and influences which had begun in the sixteenth century, had had temporary victories in the enthronement of False Dmitry I and Władysław during the Time of Troubles, had renewed their pressure in the seventeenth century and emerged strengthened from the struggle climaxed by the Schism, and had seemed to be climaxed again by the ascendancy of Stefan Yavorsky. By the time of Peter there were outright Russian conversions to Roman Catholicism, as already mentioned, and at least one or two even became Jesuits.[79] The Roman Catholic initiatives from Poland had not been characterized by sympathy for Russia's culture or its people; but the Catholic-influenced Ukrainians of the early eighteenth century played an honorable role in a fateful struggle.

In opposition to the main thrust of Peter's policies there stood a loose coalition consisting of Stefan and the Ukrainians, Pososhkov and the 'Muscovite progressives', and Iov of Novgorod and the more conservative Muscovites defending the reformed (1667) Orthodox Church; as long as Alexis remained alive, they placed their hopes in him. The coalition stood for independence of the Church from the state and for lightening the burdens of the common people; they opposed Peter's reliance on force and compulsion and his policy of Westernization of Russia by state fiat, though they were willing (the Ukrainians very actively so) to accept much Western learning. To an extent their aims and interests coincided with those of the Old Believers, though all three groups in the coalition adhered to the post-1667 Church. Taken as a whole this bloc, which deserves more thorough and objective study than it has received, can thus be seen to have elements of syncretism in its cultural out-look. Despite the debt of Yavorsky and Alexis to the West and at least the convergence of Pososhkov's views with Western ideas, the coalition defended the indigenous tradition against the arbitrary measures by which Peter, in their eyes, threatened to destroy it. They were defeated.

Culturally, Protestant influences were victorious. Institutionally, their success was accompanied by the apotheosis of Russian autocracy. Herein lies the great paradox of Peter's reign. Culturally he was a great innovator, turning Russia sharply and with virtually no preparation in the direction of North-western, Protestant Europe; but institutionally he made Russia less like England or Holland and more like China. He carried to the most extreme point the evolution of Russian society in the direction of single-centeredness, whereby society became completely dependent on state power, which had been under way at least since the fifteenth century. The fact that his institutional changes were superficially patterned on Western political organization meant little or nothing to his subjects.

And yet there is a second paradox to be mentioned; though the institutions of Petrine Russia were only the old Muscovite institutions painted over and hung with Western placards, the Western placards themselves eventually had their effect. Russia was to go to school to the West – this was Peter's demand. In fact some Russians had for a considerable period been going to school to the West, through the educational institutions of Poland or otherwise. It was a different West that Peter had in mind, but it was the West. And as Russians increasingly went to school, the Western placards hung on the old Muscovite organs of state control and oppression threatened to become reality.

From the crisis of 1715–18 Russia emerged with a kind of Reformation. The Church was subjected to state control, and the direction of educational importations and other foreign borrowings was pointed toward Protestant Europe. Russia's chief Reformer, Feofan Prokopovich, lived to see much of it happen; Russia's chief reformer, Peter, was dead before much of the educational change he had in mind could be carried out. But the word 'reform', whether upper or lower case, is misleading in this connection. The preconceptions which underlay all Peter's policies and the measures he enacted, in every realm of life, amounted not so much to reform as to revolution – a revolution which threatened to destroy, not modify, Russian traditions; a revolution which ostensibly rested on the latest Western models and ideas but in fact depended on the non-Western model and idea of the all-powerful state. For one of the first times in history the world was able to observe the phenomenon in which the intention to borrow from the West, far from assuring Westerniza-tion, might lead in fact to the deepening of the hold of non-Western institutions on non-Western peoples. Pre-Petrine Russia was far from being a free society, but it was a society in which vestiges of institutions and thought still existed outside state control. When Peter died those vestiges had been virtually exterminated. Whatever the limitations of the outlook of such men as Stefan

Yavorsky, Ivan Pososhkov, and the Tsarevich Alexis, they defended those vestiges against state domination as long as they could, and perished honorably in the struggle to do so.

By the end of Peter's reign or perhaps better of Catherine I's, since the 1725–7 period was but a kind of coda to the preceding one, the Westernization of Russia was, as nearly every historian has observed, indeed proceeding at a pace far greater than when Peter began to rule. However, that formulation is too crude to serve as more than an initial generalization. The modest beginnings of cultural Westernization from Roman Catholic sources, gathering momentum slowly and sporadically from the late fifteenth century, had been very roughly handled; the basis for the substantial spread of Protestant influences had been laid. At least as important for Russian culture was the fact that the state had assumed greater powers than ever, and had specifically undertaken to place all cultural institutions under its own control and organize them for its own direct benefit. The submission of Western Protestant Churches to state authority had had deleterious consequences, no doubt, but it was a quite different sort of state to which they submitted, which placed far less sweeping demands on them. The Petrine Church 'establishment', then, originated in Western ideas, but its institutional features cannot be blamed on Protestantism.

Peter and Feofan Prokopovich warred on 'superstition' and crusaded for enlightenment. The term 'superstition', however, as used by them, must be understood to refer not simply to any form of religious belief (as many atheists use it today) nor to actual credence in magical results obtained through ecclesiastical (or other) means (as the term is best defined), but to commitment to the hierarchical ordering of the Church, the power of the sacraments, the divinely-ordained function of the clergy, and the use of various material adjuncts to worship, such as icons. Although Peter and Feofan never explicitly condemned any of these practices, the tendencies they encouraged threw them all into question.[80] The clergy remained the only learned class in Russia, or at any rate the only class in which any sizeable number of learned men were to be found. It has been argued that they were simply obscurantist, and had to be dragged into the realm of enlightenment by force. The enrollment in the new seminaries, especially as compared with the attitude shown toward the lay schools, disproves such assertions. However, the seminaries, with their Latin as the medium of instruction and Western textbooks, served not so much to educate the clergy and broaden their horizons as to disorient them and to divide their minds into two compartments, Russian and foreign in form and substance.

After Peter and Catherine I, then, there ensued a strange cultural silence, broken only by the labors of a handful of German academicians, the work of a very few Orthodox who were capable of inner-directed thought and action (such as St Tikhon Zadonsky, despite his debt to German mysticism), and the efforts of a small number who were willing to follow Feofan Prokopovich in going to school to German Protestantism.

THE COMING OF PIETISM (1727–41)

It appeared, with the death of Catherine I, that the way of Alexis might still posthumously triumph over the way of Peter. The candidacy for the throne of Peter Alexeevich, the eleven-year old son of Alexis, attracted the support of a coalition similar to that which had seemed to be possible behind his father, consisting of the old aristocracy and a section of the clergy, including those sympathetic to Roman Catholic influences. Because his candidacy as the sole remaining male Romanov had been so obvious, indeed unavoidable, Peter I's surviving aides had attempted to insure their continued pre-eminence by betrothing the boy to Menshikov's daughter Maria. This plan seemed to work – for four months only. In September 1727 Menshikov was arrested and exiled. The aristocratic families led by the Dolgorukis and Golitsyns had the confidence of the young emperor, and after a time a new betrothal was proclaimed, this time to a young Dolgoruki princess.

In the short period of Peter II's reign a cultural counter-revolution seemed to impend. Moscow was the scene of his coronation and was on the way to becoming the capital once again. There was discussion of restoring the patriarchate which Peter I had abolished, and Stefan Yavorsky's disciple Feofilakt Lopatinsky might have succeeded if he had had any ambition to obtain the post.[81] Stefan's book *The Rock of Faith* was approved for publication and appeared in 1728. It was promptly and sharply attacked, first in a review that appeared in the Leipzig *Acta Eruditorum* in May, then in the summer in a tract that appeared in Jena entitled *Defense of the Lutheran Church Against the Calumnies of Stefan Yavorsky* (*Epistola apologetica pro ecclesia Lutherana contra calumnias et obtrectationes Stephani Javorscii ad amicum Mosquae degentem scripta*), signed by Johann Franz Buddeus, a renowned professor of Jena University. In November Buddeus died. Some, including Russians of that day, have suspected that the real author of either or both tracts was not Buddeus but a Russian, perhaps Feofan Prokopovich himself. Robert Stupperich sees no evidence for the suspicion,[82] and believes Feofan was not even the man who sent Buddeus the book he set about to demolish; he identifies the intermediary as a former student of Buddeus who was in Moscow, Peter Müller. Buddeus had earlier been favored by some unidentified friend with a copy of the proposal of the Sorbonne divines whom Peter I had met in 1717, in which they invited the Russian clergy to consider reunion of the Roman Catholic and Orthodox Churches;[83] this proposal Buddeus had denounced in 1719 in a tract called *Ecclesia Romana cum Ruthenica irreconciliabilis* published in Jena. Stupperich believes Müller, not Feofan, was also the intermediary in this instance.

The polemic did not end with Buddeus's death, and at this point Roman Catholics entered it directly. In 1728 the Abbé Jacques Jubé, who had converted Princess Irina Petrovna Dolgoruki in Holland,[84] came to Russia with his returning convert. He formed close liaison with the Spanish envoy in

Russia, Jacobo Francisco, duke de Liria, and his household priest, the Dominican Father Bernardo de Ribera. Ribera wrote a counterattack to Buddeus's book called *Responsum antapologeticum*, but when it appeared Peter II was dead and the atmosphere in Russia had markedly changed. A substantial party of Russian clerics appeared responsive to the effort to unite the Churches: Feofilakt Lopatinsky, Archimandrite Feofil Krolik of the Chudov monastery, Archimandrite Evfimy Coletti of the Novospassky monastery. Coletti, a Greek, had been the Tsarevich Alexis Petrovich's chaplain, and in 1718 was exiled. After eight years Peter II had freed him. It was the closest former collaborator of Stefan Yavorsky, Feofilakt, who was chosen to write another response to Buddeus; apparently Prince Dmitry Mikhailovich Golitsyn persuaded him to do so.[85] This work was the *Apokrisis*; it also appeared after the end of Peter II's reign, and led to the author's arrest and imprisonment. (He was to be released only after the end of the reign of Anna, by the government of Ivan VI; but by then his health was impaired and he died a few months later, in 1741.[86]) There were still other books which went into the polemic over *The Rock of Faith*, such as the *Hammer on the Rock of Faith* (*Molotok na Kamen' very*), which was written in the 1730's, and the *Rebuttal to the Hammer* (*Vozrazhenie na molotok*), which appeared under Elizabeth (1741–61). However, after the reign of Peter II the victory of pro-Protestant tendencies in the Russian Church was no longer seriously contested, and when a certain amount of pro-Catholic sentiment and interest reappeared near the end of the eighteenth century they were outside the Church.

Peter II died of smallpox on what was planned as his wedding day in 1730. The nascent coalition of aristocracy, pro-Roman Catholic feeling, and a segment of the Russian clergy attached to the Muscovite tradition, which had tended to grow up around Alexis and reappeared under his son, was doomed by the son's unexpected and premature death. Prince D. M. Golitsyn refused to acknowledge Peter I's children by Catherine as legitimate, and the ruling agency of the coalition, the Supreme Privy Council, turned to Anna, duchess of Courland, daughter of Ivan V (Peter's half-brother) as an alternative. The Supreme Privy Council undertook to compel her to accept a series of Conditions (*Konditsii*) which would have limited her power. It was a hazardous undertaking, for some of Peter I's aides were still alive and influential, such as Paul Yaguzhinsky, former procurator-general, and Count A. I. Ostermann, still a major figure in foreign affairs, who had managed to protect Feofan Prokopovich. They were able to influence a sizeable number of gentry. As a result, Anna came to Moscow, tore up the Conditions with the support of the anti-Golitsyn faction, and assumed the throne as an autocrat.[87] From the Synod, once again in the grip of Feofan, his clerical enemies were ejected.

Anna Ivanovna identified herself with Peter's policies by returning to St Petersburg in 1731 and by filling high offices with Germans brought from Courland and elsewhere. From 1732 on her commander-in-chief was Burkhard Münnich; her lover and chief adviser, Ernst-Johann Bühren or Biron, became the symbol of the reign. *Bironovshchina* ('the wicked deeds of Biron') was a term used to refer not merely to Germanism but also to the regime of terror, execution, and exile over which Anna presided. Feofan, the sympathizer of German Protestantism, was restored to his former position of influence. He died in 1736. It is said that on his deathbed he murmured, 'O, head, head of mine, having drunk deep of reason, where will you now rest?'[88] (*O, glavo, glavo; razuma upivshis', kuda sia priklonish'*?) Aside from the overtones of regret and repentance in this utterance, Feofan could properly claim to have had much to do with furthering the fortunes of 'reason' or at any rate rationalism in Russia. He had promoted theological scholasticism; if it was different in content in its Protestant leanings from the Catholic-leaning scholasticism of his also-Ukrainian predecessors, it was not so different in form. It helped train generations of Russians in the habits of precision in reading, understanding, and criticizing texts and ideas. As to whether his influence was to strengthen the Russian Church spiritually (in any event it did much to weaken the Church institutionally), that is another matter.

The reign of Anna, as has recently been pointed out,[89] was by no means an unequivocally 'dark' period, as some have considered it. The Academy of Sciences began to produce some results. Daniel Bernoulli completed a treatise on hydrodynamics, even though he left Russia immediately thereafter. The great mathematician Leonhard Euler and the historian Gerhard Müller, both of whom came to Russia at the age of twenty, and the naturalist Johann Georg Gmelin, who was seventeen at his arrival, all made much of their careers in Russia. Though Euler was tempted into moving to the Prussian Academy in 1741, he returned to St Petersburg in 1766 and remained there until his death in 1783. Müller and Gmelin undertook an extensive expedition to Siberia in 1733–43, and Müller was the first to undertake systematic publication of Russian historical documents in the *Sammlung russischer Geschichte*, beginning in 1735. The first Russian to become a member of the Academy, V. E. Adadurov, was named adjunct in mathematics in 1733, though his main achievement was to produce, in 1731, a grammar of Russian based on Melety Smotritsky's Slavic grammar.[90]

The most important foreign influence on Russian thought of the period continued to be Protestant, as it had become under Peter I; but it was a new current in Protestantism which came to be significant in Russia of the 1730's rather than the Protestant scholasticism of Feofan Prokopovich. The current was German pietism, and its chief fruit was the so-called Elizabeth Bible a few years later. The pietists' stronghold was the University of Halle, in the city which was the capital of the duchy of Magdeburg. The university was officially founded in 1694 on the urging of Pufendorf. On his advice there came to the new institution his pupil Thomasius, the young Lutheran theologian August Hermann Francke (1663–1727), and others. Francke, a disciple of the father of German pietism, Philipp Jakob Spener (1635–1705), was seeking to transform Lutheranism by means of pietist tenets in opposition to the prevailing scholasticism.

Pietism was a revival in a new guise of the ancient mystical and personal-devotional tradition within Western Christianity, which reached back to St Bernard of Clairvaux and St Thomas à Kempis. The works of such men had been drawn on by Johann Arndt (1555–1621) in writing his major work, *Wahres Christentum* (1606–9), which in turn, along with English Puritan and Swiss Calvinist works, had inspired Spener to produce his *Pia Desideria* (1675). Spener regarded Christianity as more a matter of the heart than the mind, of love rather than of doctrine. His followers, concentrated in the Halle school, produced little scholarly research, but like him they strongly emphasized Scripture,[91] and in a country such as Russia which as yet had no vernacular Bible, the latter tendency was to produce results. The struggle against scholasticism which they undertook in Germany was not quite reproduced in Russia. It is true that the Halle pietists, not content with bringing about Christian Wolff's expulsion from Prussia,[92] tried to neutralize his influence in Russia by writing there in order to charge him with atheism. Evidently Feofan Prokopovich supported Blumentrost and Schumacher in reassuring Wolff in 1724 that the pietists could not damage his standing in Russia, since in that country the clergy was engaged in 'putting religion into a rational condition and liberating it from every kind of superstition'.[93] The pietists had a number of contacts with Russian clerics and laymen, as for example with Baron I. A. Korff, president of the Academy of Sciences from 1734 to 1740, but their friends did not seem to wish to polemize with the Russians influenced by Protestant scholasticism. In any event a man appeared in Russia, Simon Todorsky, who was strongly influenced by pietism and attempted to implement its tenets. If Feofan had lived any longer he might have been constrained to urge caution, but as mentioned he died in 1736.

Simon Todorsky was the son of a converted Jew of the Ukraine, born in 1699; he entered the Kievan Academy at eighteen and spent ten years there.[94] Coming to St Petersburg, he became tutor to the children of a Russian general who took him to Reval with the family in 1724. There he encountered pietism among the Lutherans, who persuaded him to go to Halle to study. He studied in Halle from 1729 to 1735, where he mastered German and learned Greek, Hebrew, Arabic, and Syrian. He translated into Church Slavic a number of pietist works. Most important of all, he translated Arndt's *Wahres Christentum* into contemporary Russian. The book was published in Halle in 1735 and distributed in Russia with the support of Baron Korff and Feofan. It was later reprinted many times and was widely used in the Russian Church until the beginning of the twentieth century. Other books were also published in Russian in Halle. But Todorsky left the city and appeared again in Kiev in 1738, where he became professor at the Academy. Once again in Russia, he interested himself in the project for the translation of the Bible into Church Slavic which had been begun in 1713 by order of Peter I. The translation had been mainly completed by a group appointed by Stefan Yavorsky and after the latter's fall Feofilakt Lopatinsky had carried it forward for a time. Under Catherine I he had been cautious, and the project had languished until Todorsky took it up. Then Anna died, and the situation threatened to change.

In the later 1730's the base of Russian exposure to Western culture had broadened. Russia's first newspaper, *The St Petersburg Record* (*Sanktpeter-burgskiia Viedomosti*), which had been founded under another name by Peter I in 1703, and issued by the Academy of Sciences in German after 1727 (and later also in Russian), included in its supplements accounts of various things Western, ranging from Malta to Mme de Maintenon, and extracts from contemporary Western literature, for example from Brockes's *Irdisches Vergnügen in Gott*.[95] The work of Barthold Heinrich Brockes (1680–1747) consisted of nine books of poetry in which he expressed his religious interpretation of nature, derived from the mystical pietism he had imbibed from studying at Halle and reading Arndt.[96] Münnich had been the moving spirit in establishing the Kadetskii korpus, a training school for not merely military service on the Petrine model but also for civil and court service. Its curriculum including riding, fencing, dancing, and etiquette, and its pupils formed a literary circle where French and German works were studied and where the poet Sumarokov read his first odes.[97] At court Italian theater and music, owing to the tastes of the court chamberlain, Count Reinhold von Löwenwolde, were much in evidence.

ELIZABETH AND THE TWO PROTESTANT INFLUENCES (1741–1762)

Biron had tried to prepare his own survival after the death of his empress-protectress, as Menshikov had striven to do in 1727. Biron prevailed on Anna to appoint as successor the baby son of Anna Leopoldovna, Ivan V's granddaughter and duchess of Brunswick-Bevern-Lüneburg, he himself to be regent. The infant Ivan VI had scarcely acceded to the throne, however, when his mother overthrew Biron through the help of Münnich. Her ascendancy lasted only a year. Another *coup* placed Peter I's daughter Elizabeth in power (1741–61), and both Ostermann and Münnich lost their influence.

Ostermann's anti-French and pro-Austrian foreign policy was not abandoned at once; it was continued by Alexis Bestuzhev-Riumin. However, the rise of Prussia under Frederick the Great upset the balance of power in Europe, and Bestuzhev's influence did not survive the diplomatic revolution of 1756 from which Russia emerged as an ally of Austria's astonishing new friend, France. These developments had an impact on Russia's cultural history, but did not determine its course. The French alliance aided French influence, but the Germanic connection could continue whether the friendly state was Austria or Prussia.

Being unmarried, Elizabeth designated Peter, son of her sister Anna[98] and duke of Holstein, as her heir. Since he was a Lutheran, the proper person had to be found to preside over his necessary conversion to Orthodoxy. The choice fell on Simon Todorsky. In 1745 he received the title of bishop of Pskov – in 1748 archbishop of the same see[99] – and also was named to the Holy Synod. He was now able to press the project of translating the Bible on to completion. In 1751 the so-called 'Elizabeth Bible' was published.[100] The project that had begun with the Russian Church in the pro-Catholic hands of Yavorsky was finished with the Church under the influence of Protestant pietism in the person of Todorsky and others.

Pietism left its imprint on two other major figures of the culture of the time, one clerical and one lay. The cleric was St Tikhon Zadonsky (1724–83), son of a poor sacristan of Novgorod.[101] He studied in Novgorod, first in the ecclesiastical school and then (from 1740) in the seminary there, remaining as a teacher of Greek, then rhetoric, and finally philosophy as well. In 1758 he became a monk; the next year he moved to Tver to become rector of its seminary; in 1761 he became bishop of Kexholm and Ladoga, in 1763 bishop of Voronezh. In 1767 he obtained consent to his retirement, and from 1769 until his death remained at the Zadonsk monastery of the Virgin. The influence on him of pietism and in particular of Arndt's *Wahres Christentum* was strong; his own book, *Ob istinnom khristianstve* (6 parts; St Petersburg, 1785 and 1803), bore the same title. Florovsky calls his book 'the first attempt at a living theology' in contrast to the scholastic erudition which had been prevalent in the Russian Church.[102] He was far from being mainly a Westernizer; his love for the peasantry and common people from which he himself sprang was proverbial; he was recognized as the most saintly man of eighteenth-century Russia. But in his academic and intellectual side he owed much to Germany.

The layman was Gregory Savvich Skovoroda, son of a Ukrainian Cossack, born in 1722 and taken into the court choir of the Empress Elizabeth in 1741. He accompanied a general on a service tour in Central Europe, and on returning after various adventures became teacher of Greek at a school in Kharkov. He published his first book in 1766, *The Door to Christian Morality* (*Nachal'naia dver' k khristianskomu dobronraviiu*); in a few years came *Narcissus or Know Thyself* (*Narkis ili poznai samogo sebia*). He spent his last years as a hermit, dying in 1794.[103] A number of writers, notably Zenkovsky, have considered Skovoroda 'the first Russian philosopher in the strict sense of the word'.[104] He was actually not a Russian, but a Ukrainian, like the distinguished Kievans who by now had almost dominated Russia's intellectual life for a full century. Was he a philosopher? Shpet writes, 'Skovoroda was from beginning to end a *moralist*. Not scholarship and not philosophy as such dominate his thoughts, but rather he is seeking the way to happiness and blessedness for himself and showing it to other.'[105] In his search he was influenced by a number of Greek writers, but his Latin and German were better than his Greek;[106] he also was under the spell of German mystical and pietistic writers of the preceding decades. The Bible was for him a hunting-ground for mystical symbols, and it was the Elizabeth Bible which he used and used constantly. In Skovoroda we find much that is original, and does credit to a powerful religious insight; we also find something that represents one of the chief signs of the times: the transition from pietism, which comes from the Church, to Freemasonry, which comes from outside it, as the chief Western influence on Russian thought of the day. Skovoroda was probably not a Mason himself, but he was close to the lodges, and his penchant for allegory and symbolical exegesis was close to theirs.

Side by side with pietism as a seminal influence there remained Protestant scholasticism. If in Russia pietist impulses were to be secularized in Freemasonry, then scholasticism was to prepare the way for Voltairianism. Before this was to occur, however, scholasticism contributed to systematic studies in the sciences and humanities.

The outstanding example of this phenomenon was Michael Lomonosov (1711–65). Born in a well-to-do fisherman's family in Archangel province near the White Sea, he wished to attend the Slavo-Latin school opened in Kholmogory in 1723 but as a poll tax-paying peasant could not do so; he succeeded, however, in entering the Slavo-Latin Academy in Moscow to prepare for the priesthood in 1730.[107] When Baron Korff ordered compulsory recruitment of suitable students from the monasteries and ecclesiastical schools for the Academy of Sciences' gymnasium and university in 1735, Lomonosov was among those sent to St Petersburg. In Moscow he had learned his Latin and his scholastic philosophy well, and he was prepared for his assignment of studying German, philosophy, and the natural sciences at the University of Marburg with Christian Wolff, the leader of Protestant scholasticism, from 1736 to 1739. After a few months in Freiburg, he returned to St Petersburg in 1741. In 1745 he became professor of chemistry[108] and full member of the Academy – the first Russian to do so.

Here is not the place to attempt another re-evaluation of Lomonosov's work. He was a naturalist who produced perceptive anticipations of later discoveries, such as the law of conservation of matter and the falsity of the phlogiston hypothesis; he was a philologist who tried to analyze the difference between Church Slavic and Russian and advance principles for the proper use of words; he made pioneer efforts at writing history, and much else. He is more suitably to be compared with Benjamin Franklin than with Leonardo da Vinci or Newton – as some Soviet writers have allowed themselves to do. He was vain and quarrelsome, believing (quite rightly) that most of his contemporaries did not appreciate his achievements, but he was not a nationalist, as some have alleged; his incessant squabbles were directed 'not against foreigners in general or against the Germans, many of whom were his friends'.[109] Indeed his closest friend in later years was the German Jacob Stählin, while his chief rival was the Russian Sumarokov. He was in many respects a typical eighteenth-century cosmopolitan, but not a Voltairian or freethinker. Following the greatest Protestant scholastics, Leibniz and Wolff, he acknowledged the obligation 'to search for methods...to explain and avert all so-called conflict between science and religion';[110] in so doing, he drew on precepts of Fathers of the Church, and appropriately so, but his intellectual formation was closest to the scholastics who were his teachers both in Russia and Germany, in childhood and adulthood. He had much to do with the founding of Russia's first university, that of Moscow, in 1755. Like its predecessors, that institution used Latin and German, and it was not until 1767 that the rector, M. M. Kheraskov, ordered that Russian be the language of instruction in all subjects. By now there was a Russian vocabulary to convey the ideas of Western scholars. As for Lomonosov, who had done so much to create that vocabulary, he had died in 1765.

Protestantism had had its victory in Russia, but the two faces it had in contemporary Germany soon enough showed themselves there as well. The scholasticism of Leibniz, Wolff, and Feofan Prokopovich, warring on 'superstition', emphasizing the individual critical faculties, leaning on the predominant or exclusive use of reason, prepared the way for Lomonosov – and with the shedding of the supernaturalist commitment, for the Voltairianism of the reign of Catherine II. The pietism of Francke, the Halle school, and Simon Todorsky, emphasizing 'true Christianity' and the inner light, prepared the way for the mystical Freemasonry of the Catherinian period, the moralistic and sentimentalist currents of Alexander I's reign, and the missionary fervor of the Russian Bible Society.

After the accession of Anna, the cultural forces sympathetic to Roman Catholicism appeared to have suffered irreversible defeat. With the accession of Elizabeth, the 'German' regime seemed to have been overthrown, and nativistic overtones were prominent in the atmosphere surrounding the Elizabethan *coup* of 1741. Such overtones lay to a large extent in the realm of official myth, a myth which had to be retrospectively extended to Elizabeth's father, Peter. A folksong of the period ran:

Arise from your grave, oh [*sic*] noble Russian Tsar. Look on your guards, your regiments in ranks, how sorrowfully they hang their heads; for now they have no Tsar to rule them, no Russian prince gives command...but our commander is Biron, the evil tyrant from German lands. Arise, awake, our Tsar, our sun.[111]

Peter I, the forcible Germanizer, became in memory (if not in the memory of all or most Russians, notably the Old Believers) a 'Russian prince' replaced by a German bureaucrat, and his daughter became the restorer of Russian pride. However, when guards regiments in Viborg mutinied and demanded that their foreign officers be put to death, Elizabeth made clear by her severity of punishment that not all foreigners were going to be dispensed with; and she did not hesitate to make Biron's brother chief court chamberlain.

In fact foreign influences continued to flood into Russia, as Russians continued in increasing numbers to go abroad. These phenomena of the realm of high culture affected chiefly the gentry and the clergy, and had little if any impact on the townsmen and peasantry; but there was also German influence on the latter in the appearance of non-Orthodox, Protestantomorphic sects such as the Stundists and even the Khlysty, who lived distant both intellectually and geographically from the Latin and scholastic schools and the largely German Academy of Science in eighteenth-century Russia. For the Old Believers and for most Orthodox peasants, Latin, German, and French were equally alien, Roman and Protestant equally anathema, Voltairian and Freemason equally incomprehensible. But for the court and the gentry and the clergy, at the end of Elizabeth's reign Latin was taken for granted as the gateway to education, Western science accepted as *the* science, and Protestant influences, scholastic and pietist, tended to set the limits within which thought was formed and expressed. Russia's quasi-Reformation had made great headway. It had been introduced by the state under Peter. However, as the century advanced and as the educated class began to feel more at home with Western cultural importations, the state began to lose the tight grip on cultural life that it had in Peter I's last years. The natural result was the formation of an intelligentsia, whose beginnings can be discerned in the last decades of the eighteenth century.

5

RATIONALISM
AND SENTIMENTALISM (1761–1825)

My body was born in Russia, but my spirit belongs to the French crown.
Ivanushka, in Fonvizin's The Brigadier

Is the way of enlightenment not one and the same for all nations?...The main
thing is to be men, not Slavs. Karamzin

INTRODUCTION

The last third of the eighteenth century and the first quarter of the nineteenth
constituted the golden age of the Russian gentry. Newly freed from compulsory state service, they set about to learn through trial and error how a group
of free men should act in Russia. Some suggested that they ought to concentrate on organizing themselves as a class for political and social action. In fact
they did not do so until 1905, despite the corporate organization given them by
Catherine II. Some settled for the court life of St Petersburg, which was
familiar; many went to live on their provincial estates; altogether the majority
lived off their income, which was derived from the labor of the enserfed masses
and which they did little to earn, and devoted little thought to economic,
political, or cultural self-improvement. A minority yielded to a series of new
moral and intellectual enthusiasms: Freemasonry, Voltairianism, the way of
the Society of Jesus, Protestant-oriented pietism, Decembrism.

The thinking minority, by now educated in the languages and thought of
France, the German states, and Great Britain, moved along lines similar to the
rulers of the period. Peter III (1761–2) was apparently a Mason; Catherine II
(1762–96) flirted with the West European Enlightenment and tolerated the
Masons for a time and the Jesuits throughout her reign because of the cultural
uses of both groups; Paul (1796–1801) started as a Mason and ended by falling
under strong Roman Catholic influence; Alexander I (1801–25) combined the
main tendencies of the period in an uneasy and turbulent juxtaposition. He
began as a rationalist adept of the Enlightenment, and never entirely lost his
fondness for constitutional charters and systematic projects of reform; but
from an early age he was also attracted by the sentimentalist, pietist, and
mystical currents of the day, and in the last decade of his reign raised pietism
to the status of a virtual state ideology. Time after time quite abrupt changes in
the ruler's enthusiasms meant more or less severe repression of intellectuals
from the gentry and other groups[1] whose interests had not long before been
shared by that very monarch. Such cases included Catherine's dispersion of

the Masons (1792), Alexander's expulsion of the Jesuits (1815), banning of secret societies (1822), and abolition of the 'combined ministry' (1824). The cultural evolution of Russia, following in the lines of West European influence laid down by Peter, was still subject to the fiat of the crown.

As in Western Europe, so in Russia a long step toward secularization of thought took place during the period. Atheism, exemplified by such men as Holbach and Helvétius in the West, found little echo in Russia, but the skeptical deism of Voltaire and others acquired a widespread if superficial following, and, still more important, moral and religious searchings tended to migrate outside the Russian Church and its clergy into the Masonic lodges; their offshoots, the Decembrist secret societies; the Bible societies; and circles interested in the Jesuits' learning. In the 1770's Novikov, tiring of satirical attacks on those of the educated class who had received inadequate moral training, turned to preaching the necessity of such instruction. 'The clergy', he thought, 'could have assumed the burden [of such training], but it had itself departed a great distance from the idea of Christ; retaining the appearance of the educator class, it least of all provided examples of moral living. It was a burden that had to be assumed by society itself...'[2] Not rejection of religion but a diminution in the role of the Church and clergy was a keynote of the period. There was an attempt to remake the Church from without through what will be called the 'pietist revolution', but it was a failure, like some other 'revolts' and 'revolutions' of Russian history. One ecclesiastical reform succeeded: it was the revision of the ecclesiastical schools' curriculum, in 1814. It was of great importance, since such schools remained the backbone of whatever educational system Russia could be said to have. Young men were introduced to contemporary philosophy; the results appear in the reign of Nicholas I, when many of the other temporarily influential intellectual currents of the period 1761–1825 are forgotten.

PETER III, CATHERINE II, AND THE ENLIGHTENMENT

The German Protestant orientation of the regime seemed to be dramatically confirmed by the accession of Peter III. His aunt Elizabeth had him proclaimed heir in 1742. He was then, at fourteen, duke of Holstein; since he was heir presumptive of the Swedish crown as grandnephew of Charles XII, the great antagonist of his grandfather Peter I, his early education was based on the assumption that he was to be prepared for the Swedish throne. In 1742 he was a stranger to Russia, and in an important sense he remained so, since his intellectual outlook had been largely formed by the Lutheran education he had received in Kiel, and his deepest attachments continued to be to Holstein and the Germanic environment where he had spent his childhood. The attempt to start his education over in preparation for the throne of Russia did not succeed. Peter's fondness for the military, partly owing to his admiration for Frederick the Great, reached such eccentric excesses that several courtiers were urging Elizabeth in her last days to reconsider, substituting as heir either Peter's son Paul or Peter's wife, the former princess of Anhalt-Zerbst and now Grand Duchess Catherine. She hesitated to do so, and died without making any change.

After Peter acceded to the throne (25 December 1761/5 January 1762), he at once exhibited his Protestant leanings by closing the churches attached to the imperial household; he did not conceal his contempt for Orthodoxy. Lutheran motives doubtless made him embrace with enthusiasm the idea of a 'college of economy', which by an early decree of his was entrusted with the management of all ecclesiastical properties.[3] Finding Russia embroiled in the Seven Years' War (1756–63), he abruptly withdrew from the alliance that was on the point of overwhelming Frederick II's Prussia, thus saving his hero from ruin. Instead Peter planned a war against Denmark in order to conquer Schleswig and reunite it with Holstein. He hoped to bring Frederick into that war as an ally. Such policies created consternation. Peter's organization of new Guards units, using Prussian drill, and other challenges to the privileges of the military elite created by his grandfather finally precipitated his removal. He was deposed and then murdered by Guards officers acting in conjunction with his wife Catherine. There was irony in the fact that it was guardsmen who overthrew him, for his most important decree had been to end compulsory state service for the gentry, the class of which the guardsmen were the leading element.

Peter's wife, summoned to Russia in 1745 from her little German principality to marry him, was one of the most remarkable women of the century or perhaps of modern times. Her morals were openly scandalous, but by no means uniquely so in the Europe of her day, and for most of her reign she distinguished between those men on whom she bestowed her favors and those she considered worthy to have a say in state affairs. Her education, founded on French works, notably those of the *philosophes*, was irregular and incomplete, yet she managed to give the appearance of a person fully cognizant of the philosophical and literary issues of her day. Her possession of the throne rested upon its illegal seizure and the murder of its occupant, yet she never allowed the uncertainties she felt or the dangers she courted to show on the surface. At her death she left a Russia greatly expanded in territory of immense strategic and economic value, for the first time effectively administered on the local level, and confirmed the emergence of the first non-clerical class in Russia for centuries to have won independence of state obligations – the gentry. At the same time she left a people who were suffering perhaps more than ever before, since under her rule serfdom was extended to new areas and the power of the serf-owner over the serf became so great as in practice to approximate serfdom to slavery.

Catherine's intellectual commitments were, through most of her reign, to the West European Enlightenment. Such commitments were limited in practice and contained much that was meretricious or fraudulent; however, it would be a mistake to brush them aside as merely sham. The precepts of the Enlightenment were shown in many actions she took. Her Instruction (*Nakaz*) of 1767 for the Legislative Commission, based largely on Montesquieu and Beccaria, led to no codification of laws, but the Commission produced much thought and some legislation. When she established new provinces, she scorned tradition and drew boundaries in the spirit of pure rationalism, thus anticipating the Revolutionary revision of the French administrative map. In enacting measures of *Gleichschaltung* for the Ukraine, the Baltic regions, and the Russian part of Finland, she insisted on Russification much as Joseph II insisted on Germanization in Austria, because it was more orderly to think in terms of a single language and culture. Her cosmopolitanism was shown in her encouragement of foreign immigration, especially that of Germans. The use of 'enlightened despotism' to remove restrictions on the economy was shown in her measures to carry out an effective land survey, to establish some degree of competitive enterprise, and to stimulate economic growth. She was willing to encourage the Rousseauian ambition of Ivan Betsky to create a new kind of humanity through the training of children in boarding schools, even though only the Smolny and the Novodevichi Institutes (1764–5) were actually founded and lasted, like other fragments of sweeping reform schemes which dot Russian history. She sponsored the imitation of the Austrian school reform of 1774, in turn based on the Prussian model, with the aid of the Vojvodina Serb Yankovich-de-Mirievo, who came to St Petersburg in 1782 for that purpose; the result was the creation of one pedagogical school in St Petersburg, 41 'major' (five-year), and over 200 'minor' (two-year) schools in the towns of Russia by the end of the century.[4] These lay institutions formed a significant competing system to the ecclesiastical schools, and the latter by governmental order had time and again to give up sizeable numbers of their best teachers to staff the new lay system.[5] The empress courted the admiration of the Paris intellectuals by her creation of the Imperial Free Economic Society in 1765, which promptly began to consider all sorts of questions concerning free enterprise, and of the Russian Academy in 1783, under Princess Dashkova, to deal with the arts – which were neglected in the Academy of Sciences.

Not only did Catherine's policies show the influence of Enlightenment ideas, but she entered into direct personal relations with the major *philosophes*. We have 153 letters between her and Voltaire, exchanged over the period from 1763 to 1778.[6] She commissioned him to write the history of Peter the Great. She invited Diderot to transfer the publication of the *Encyclopédie*, banned in France, to Russia; since it was the bookseller's property, Diderot could not accept. Thereupon the empress bought Diderot's library for 15,000 livres and paid him 1,000 livres a year as librarian of his own collection, soon decreeing that he be paid fifty years in advance. In 1773 Diderot came to Russia, and Catherine praised him immoderately without, however, taking much of his freely proffered advice – she told him, 'as for your exalted ideas, it is good to fill books with them, bad to act on them'.[7] She proposed to d'Alembert that he come to Russia to serve as tutor to Grand Duke Paul; he declined. She offered Beaumarchais the chance to settle in St Petersburg in order to publish Voltaire's works, and she had *Le mariage de Figaro*, banned in France, staged in Russia. She summoned Mercier de la Rivière to consult on legislation; she personally supervised the translation of Marmontel's *Bélisaire*, which contained a chapter on religious toleration censured by the Sorbonne; she offered Beccaria asylum.

What did she hope to gain from all this? There were some noteworthy public rewards; Voltaire approved the First Partition of Poland in 1772 as exemplifying the triumph of tolerance over fanaticism, and Diderot declared she combined 'the soul of Brutus with the charms of Cleopatra', thus helping to situate her image where she wished it to be, back of the Middle Ages in the classical antiquity which was the preferred model for the eighteenth-century *philosophes*. Ternovsky implies that her attachment to Voltaire and other writers, gained in her lonely younger years just after coming to Russia, may have been genuine enough, but he concludes that her motives in seeming to espouse the Enlightenment as empress were to influence Western public opinion, becoming a real force only in the eighteenth century, in her own favor and in Russia's.[8]

Certainly Catherine could falsify if it served her purpose, as in the well-known assertion that the Russian peasant could always eat chicken but sometimes preferred turkey. She could also be honest, if at the same time circumspect and adroit. When Voltaire begged her to forbid the kissing of priests, hands, she replied that it was an old custom with the Russians, and if Voltaire should come to Russia and become a priest, she would willingly kiss the hand 'that had written so much that was good, so many useful truths'. Doubtless the Instruction of 1767 had its hypocritical parts, but it also expressed some genuine aspirations of hers, as for example her desire to see law take a greater role in Russian life than before, to have the gentry function as a class no longer entirely dependent on the state, to define the relationship between lord and serf, and to assure the serf some minimal rights of life and occupation of land.

Moreover, she was at one with the *philosophes* in desiring to reduce the importance of the Orthodox Church still further; it was she who carried out the expropriation of most Church property – a measure which was comparable in significance to Peter's *Ecclesiastical Regulation* and which marked a kind of completion of his quasi-Reformation. In this respect, as in respect to the emancipation of the gentry, Catherine followed her late husband. Peter III had promulgated legislation to expropriate Church land; Catherine repealed it within a few weeks of her accession, and then in 1764 in effect reenacted the same laws. Church lands were placed under a college of economy, and the government subsequently decided how much should be appropriated for the administration of the Church and the monasteries. Arseny, archbishop of

Rostov, tried to oppose this measure; the empress used the Synod as an instrument to have him officially proclaimed 'the liar' (*vral'*) and thrown into prison, where he died in 1772.

Frequently Catherine's detractors have dismissed her attachment to the Enlightenment as hypocrisy; in contrast, such writers as Ternovsky, out of a wish to exculpate her from the suspicion of religious deviation, ascribe it to *raison d'état*. Neither view is persuasive. Her devotion to certain aspects of the outlook of the *philosophes* was real, even though in practice it was prudently limited, in view of her responsibilities as ruler and of fears provoked by events in Russia – chiefly the Pugachev rebellion – and abroad – the successive phases of the French Revolution.

The chief charge that can with justification be leveled at Catherine is that under her rule the lot of the enserfed masses grew substantially worse – which is true. It has also been easy to link that fact with the favors she showed the gentry, beginning with its emancipation from state service, and to suggest that therefore she merely strengthened the oppressor at the expense of the oppressed. To a large extent that charge is also justified. However, she had in mind to lighten the burden of the serf, and was deterred from doing so probably more because of the Pugachev rebellion, which seemed to threaten the foundations of the state, than of solicitude for gentry feelings. In the long run, moreover, Catherine has to be regarded as the ruler who began the emancipation of the Russian people from state domination, precisely because she implemented the emancipation of the gentry.

One should neither exaggerate nor underestimate the immediate spiritual effect of creating a class of freemen within an autocratic state. Freedom of person did not mean, for the gentry, escape from the exercise of arbitrary state power. Their heritage of servitude did not prepare many of them to use their freedom creatively either in the cultural or social sphere. And yet a few – such as Novikov and Radishchev – had the capacity to use it immediately; moreover, it existed as an example of what liberation might mean to the masses. The question of emancipation of the serfs could scarcely be raised while their owners were themselves in servitude; someone had to be free to suggest that the rest might become so too. In the Orient, Hegel wrote, only one is free. Catherine's merit was to increase the number one by thousands. She did it in emulation of the West, its pluralistic society, and the ideas of its writers on legal and political problems.

The spiritual consequences of the emancipation of the gentry are not to be found in Catherine's reign. There was a brilliant court life in St Petersburg, into whose ballrooms some of the gentry came, as Lord Macaulay wrote, 'dripping jewels and vermin'. But the more significant aspects of the new life the gentry was able to lead must be sought in small circles and partly in secret – to begin with, in the Masonic lodges. There were persons outside the gentry who contributed to the process of cultural and moral reform, but it was mainly the gentry that turned its attention to the regeneration of Russia with significant effect – or, more precisely, its creative minority, for much of the freed class was sunk in lethargy and corruption.

FREEMASONRY AND VOLTAIRIANISM

Masonic ritual honors a variety of ancient and medieval organizations as lineal ancestors of the modern fraternity, but scholarly consensus holds the modern lodges to be quite different. They began with the founding of the Grand Lodge of England in 1717. By 1725 Freemasonry appeared in France, by 1728 in Ireland, by 1731 in the British colonies in America, by 1737 in the German lands. The first lodges in Russia seem to date to the 1730's and 1740's, though their members were mainly foreigners, above all Britishers and Frenchmen. In the middle 1750's a lodge existed in St Petersburg that included a number of young Russian officers of the Guards regiments, among them such literary luminaries as A. P. Sumarokov, Prince M. M. Shcherbatov, and I. N. Boltin.[9] But only from 1770 did Freemasonry become a real force in Russia, beginning with the election of I. P. Elagin as grand master of the St Petersburg lodge.

What was modern Freemasonry? At root it was an effort to find outside the Christian Church values that were earlier assumed to be accessible only in the Church. Major elements included the direct search for God, growing out of the mysticism which for centuries had hovered on the border between what the Christian Church forbade and what it tolerated; the quest for true brotherly love accompanied by a cosmopolitan willingness to coexist with any kind of genuine religious belief and rejection of the exclusiveness that had contributed to the religious wars of early modern times; and the pursuit of truth, especially that part of it presumed to be hidden and to promise mastery over matter. There were different branches of Freemasonry, ranging from the matter-of-fact and sedately ceremonial British lodges to the gnostic and zealously esoteric Swedish ones. Elements of both what we may call 'knightly' and 'mystical' Masonry appeared in Russia and lasted for decades; but the former was dominant from the beginning, becoming significant by about 1770, while the latter overshadowed it from about 1780. Though mystical Masonry was dispersed and driven underground in 1792 with the arrest of Novikov and others, it revived later. During the reign of Alexander I, both types existed again; it was the mystical type which was most influential in official circles, and the knightly type which led to the Decembrist secret societies.[10] After Alexander I's death Freemasonry ceased to play a significant role in the history of Russian thought; in fact the lodges seem to have ceased to exist until around the turn of the twentieth century.[11]

On the eve of Catherine's accession circumstances were already propitious to the growth of Masonry. Peter III was, as Vernadsky puts it, 'evidently' himself a Mason,[12] and widespread rumors to that effect had assisted recruitment to the lodges while Elizabeth was alive. As tsar he gathered a circle of

Masons around him at Oranienbaum. Perhaps the foremost Masonic figure from among the gentry, Count Roman Larionovich Vorontsov, who had been the most influential member of Elizabeth's commission to compose a new code of laws, seems to have been one of the chief figures behind the manifesto of 18 February 1762, liberating the gentry.[13] The manifesto was greeted enthusiastically by the Masonic gentry; it 'corresponded to the program of the economic liberalism' prevalent among the British-style Masons, as did the ukaz of 28 March on the freedom of the grain trade. Peter's murder did not injure Masonic fortunes, for the leader in the *coup* (and Catherine's lover), G. G. Orlov, was also a Mason.[14] For a time the new empress showed Masonry some favor. In such measures as the founding of the Free Economic Society in 1765, her willingness to countenance at least discussion of economic liberalism was exhibited, some of the chief discussants being Masons – for example, Count R. L. Vorontsov and Count G. G. Orlov. However, Catherine was not and could not be a Mason, because of her sex, even if she had wished, and the fortunes of Masonry under Catherine were bound to be quite different from what they might have been like if Peter had lived.

During the 1770's Masonry swept the Russian gentry, so that there came to be few families who did not boast a member of the lodges.[15] The British system which dominated the decade offered, to the less intellectually inclined, rites and honors attractive to a class which had been wholly state serving men and now felt aspirations to become a real aristocracy; to the more serious-minded, it provided a kind of non-denominational religion of rationalism, with overtones of political and economic liberalism, which had the authority of the West behind it. Imperial officials, mostly of gentry origin, flocked into the lodges. In 1777 4 out of 11 members of the Imperial Council were Masons; 11 out of 31 gentlemen-in-waiting; 13 out of 60 members of the Russian Academy; about one-fifth of the Senators (ten years later, about one-third); from one-sixth to one-third of the entire bureaucracy.[16] The lodges to which the gentry and officials of the 1770's belonged were of the British variety, as noted, following the leadership of Ivan Perfilievich Elagin – himself Privy Councilor and Senator – or of the somewhat less ritualistic and more philosophical Swedish–Berlinian type, following Baron Reichel. In 1776 the two groups united.

In this period many Masons were also adepts of the fashionable French *philosophes*, especially Voltaire, and thus at the outset Freemasonry and Voltairianism greatly overlapped,[17] though they came in the next decade to diverge sharply. In the 1770's 'Freemason' and 'Voltairian' were often used as synonyms. If Catherine tolerated Freemasonry for most of her reign, she personally presided over the growth of Voltairianism. Already in the reign of Elizabeth Voltaire had used influence (1745) to get himself elected honorary member of Russia's Academy of Sciences; chief among his Russian admirers was the empress's lover I. I. Shuvalov; from 1756 translations of his writings were appearing in Russian periodicals.[18] But it was only in 1768 when *Candide* was among the first choices made by Catherine's Commission for Publication in the Russian Language of Worthy (*khoroshie*) Foreign Books that his works in the original covers, in translation, and in manuscript deluged the Russian reading public and affected all of Russian literature and theater.

Whatever Catherine's motives and inner feelings toward the *philosophes* may have been, publicly she gave the lead to discussion of their ideas, enthusiasm for their principles and reading of their books. Naturally many nobles followed that lead without necessarily understanding the intellectual issues at stake. Catherine had a habit of telling noblemen that she had heard this or that one had a fine library and that she would like to come to inspect it. Immediately a handsome room would be set aside and quantities of books, especially by the empress's favorite authors beginning with Voltaire, were purchased to fill it, whether or not the promised imperial visit ever materialized.[19] The noblemen might even read some of the books they had been tricked into buying, or at least talk about their authors without reading them. The empress corresponded with the *philosophes*, so many gentry tried to do so as well. She was never in France to visit them, but a number of nobles often were and did. Prince D. A. Golitsyn, ambassador to Paris, Princess Dashkova, Count Gregory Orlov, and others paid calls on Voltaire. Dashkova also visited Diderot; Orlov befriended Dr Zimmermann of Hanover. The fever was not limited to gentry, and included even priests who read *Candide* and other works of Voltaire with freethinking enthusiasm.[20]

There was not only passing acquaintance, but more substantial influence of the Encyclopedists on some Russian writers. The *philosophes* did not recognize miracles, so Boltin and Shcherbatov[21] in their historical works did not. Freethinking was the hallmark of the advanced thinkers of France, and so it became fashionable among the Russian gentry, not only in the capitals – F. F. Vigel reported hearing slurs on religion in Penza.[22] He wrote in his memoirs that atheism (*neverie*) was considered the 'indispensable condition of enlightenment' in the circles in which he moved. If Diderot and Holbach went beyond Voltaire in denying the existence of God, and Voltaire, though accepting the existence of God, went beyond what Catherine found suitable in the skeptical and satirical treatment of organized religion, many of the Russian gentry during the 1770's probably did not make these distinctions.

About 1780, however, the winds were changing rapidly. If the quasi-rationalist Masonry of the 1770's could easily coexist with 'Voltairianism' (ranging from adherence to Voltaire's views to simple freethinking), the mystical Masonry of the 1780's could not, and even made the *philosophes* its chief target of attack. The old quasi-rationalism continued to influence individuals for some time afterward; for example, Prince Michael M. Shcherbatov produced his attempt (in Vernadsky's words) to 'apply the new rationalist religion to the life of the whole state', *Voyage to the Land of Ophir* (*Puteshestvie v zemliu Ofirskuiu*) in 1784, the Utopia of the Masonry of the 70's.[23]

Perhaps the beginning of the change can be dated to the appearance of one of the chief mystical manuals of the day, Claude de St-Martin's *Des Erreurs et de la Vérité*, published in 1775, in Russia about 1777.[24] It was 1785 before a Russian translation appeared, but many of the gentry could read it in French. The Elaginist lodges were too prosaic for the consumers of this kind of literature. In 1776 Nicholas Novikov, who was to become the leader of mystical Masonry, transferred his affiliation from an Elaginist lodge to one under the Berlin Grand Lodge, which was under some Swedish influence. In 1777 the Swedish king, Gustavus III, visited Russia and is said to have personally initiated the Grand Duke Paul himself into the new kind of Masonry.[25] There were other channels of Martinist influence on Russia. Paul's new fiancée, a princess of Württemberg who was to take the name Maria Fedorovna, had been born in Étupe near Montbéliard, today in France, then in possession of Württemberg; St-Martin had spent a good deal of time there, and the new grand duchess was much interested in his views, along with the sentimentalist side of Rousseau's works.

In 1779 Novikov moved from St Petersburg to Moscow, and set up in effect the center of the new mystical Masonry. He was born in 1744 in Avdot'ino near Moscow, the son of a well-to-do member of the gentry. After teaching in the Moscow University gymnasium for a few years he was dismissed for absence from duty, and shortly afterward, in 1762, joined the Izmailovsky regiment of the Guard. In 1767–8 he served in the bureaucracy, retiring in 1768. He began in 1769 to publish a series of four satirical journals, and in 1773 launched the important historical publication *Old Russian Library* (*Drevniaia russkaia vivliofika*), which earned him international attention. His interest in Masonry, begun in St Petersburg, became a dominating passion. Through his close relations with Michael Kheraskov, curator of Moscow University, poet, and Mason, Novikov rented the university press, and began to print works designed to advance the new current in Masonry.

His mentor in Moscow came to be Johann Georg Schwarz. Born in Transylvania in 1751, he became interested in Masonry in his youth in Germany, and came to Russia on the invitation of a fellow Mason, Prince N. S. Gagarin, in 1776. He first served as a tutor in the home of a relative of Gagarin in Mogilev; when the relative died, Schwarz came to Moscow in 1779. Through Kheraskov's influence he was appointed reader in German in the university; in 1780 he was named professor ordinarius of philosophy.[26] In 1781–2 Schwarz went abroad, visited Prussia, and brought back from the Rosicrucian, Johann Christof Wöllner (1732–1800), authority to establish an Order of the Golden Rosicrucians in Russia. In addition to Novikov and Kheraskov, the new group admitted I. V. Lopukhin, who had just undergone a religious conversion, I. P. Turgenev, A. M. Kutuzov, and others. Rosicrucianism meant for them the spread of scientific and philosophical knowledge but also and chiefly the endeavor at moral self-perfection by Rosicrucian arts, the aim being 'to make oneself sinless like Adam before the fall'.

Schwarz died in 1784, but for nearly a decade the Rosicrucian, mystical current was predominant. It was from the first connected with Prussia, where Wöllner was influential, and with the Grand Duke Paul. Catherine had earlier pursued a pro-Prussian policy, based on the alliance of 1764 which continued officially until 1788, but in fact became a dead letter from about 1780, as Panin's influence declined and Potemkin's rose. Meanwhile Maria Theresa of Austria died and was succeeded by Joseph II, who was interested in closer ties with Russia. The result was a Russo-Austrian alliance in 1781. Thereupon the Russian Rosicrucians' ties with Prussia and Paul's close relations with both evoked increasing concern in Catherine. Many Masons regarded Paul as future Master of their order and thought of ways of hastening his accession as tsar.[27] A number of diplomats were drawn into intrigues in Paul's favor. After Frederick William II acceded in Prussia in 1786, Wöllner and the Rosicrucians almost dominated the court of Berlin, and the days of the Novikov circle were numbered.

For the time being, however, books poured from the presses of the Typographical Company, including mystical and alchemical tracts of all sorts; Schwarz offered a prestigious course divided into three parts each reflecting, as he conceived it, one of the modes of human cognition: reason, feeling, and revelation; the circle exerted effort in educational and charitable activities. New literature was in circulation among the Rosicrucians: Count Haugwitz' *Pastoral Letter* (*Pastyrskoe poslanie* in its Russian version), which appeared in German in 1785 and was promptly translated, had a great influence on them. It revived the pietism of Elizabeth's day in a sharp form; one contemporary wrote that Haugwitz 'wants to make all Masons into Herrnhuters'.[28] In it the pietist themes of the 'inner church' and 'true Christianity' reappeared; I. V. Lopukhin developed them further in his book *Some Sketches on the Inner Church* (*Nekotoryia cherty o vnutrennei Tserkvi*) in 1798. In the same vein were a manifesto translated by Prince N. N. Trubetskoi addressed to all bishops of the world called *New Outline of True Theology* (*Novoe nachertanie istinnoi teologii*) and a book called *The Truth of Religion* (*Istina religii*); they envisaged a society of true believers as a means for achieving a new kind of earthly state and an international order foreshadowing the Holy Alliance.[29]

Catherine had already in 1785 ordered that Metropolitan Platon of Moscow investigate Novikov, and the metropolitan had reported that he prayed that 'the whole world would be filled with such Christians as Novikov'. Florovsky comments dryly that Platon's standards in this respect were not very strict.[30] In fact Platon himself was strongly influenced by the pietist and sentimentalist currents of the day. Once after hearing a sermon of his, the empress remarked: 'Father Platon does with us what he wants. If he wants us to weep, we weep; if he wants us to laugh, we laugh.'[31] On examining the volumes Novikov had published, Platon reported that they fall into three categories: the first useful, the second mystical – which he 'did not understand', the third the works of the French Encyclopedists, which he considered harmful.[32]

No doubt some of the mystical works were hard enough to understand, even for most of the Moscow Rosicrucians, but it is noteworthy that Platon evaluated the other two categories just as the Masons did. They combated the *philosophes* and after the French Revolution had begun attacked them as 'anti-Christian freethinkers' who had contributed to the coming of the Revolution. For the time being Novikov was left alone.

The empress's suspicions, however, were mounting. The Rosicrucians' assaults on freethinking and the French Revolution did not save them. In 1786 Catherine had staged three of her own comedies directed against the Rosicrucians: *The Deceiver* (*Obmanshchik*), *The Deluded One* (*Obol'shchennyi*), and *The Siberian Shaman* (*Shaman Sibirskii*). In 1787 the Typographical Company had to close as the result of an edict forbidding the publication of religious books by any press but that of the Synod.[33] In April 1792 Novikov was arrested, and the Rosicrucians were dispersed. What precipitated this step was Catherine's alarm at Novikov's 'relations with the Tsarevich and his [Paul's] Berlin friends'.[34] Prince N. N. Trubetskoi and I. P. Turgenev were sent to their estates; Prince N. P. Repnin was sent to a kind of honorary exile as Governor-General of Riga. Novikov was the only person severely punished. When in 1796 he was released by Paul, he was a broken man who was to take no further part in public activity.

The effects of the Masonic enthusiasms of the 1780's persisted after the lodges of that period had been closed. Young Nicholas Karamzin, who had been accepted into a Moscow lodge in 1785, was under strong Masonic influence since he arrived in Moscow at the age of eighteen and roomed with the young disciple of the now dead Schwarz, Alexander Petrov. When Karamzin traveled to Western Europe in 1789 he was especially eager to visit such mystics as Lavater and Bonnet in Switzerland, and they obviously made an impression on him at least as strong as that made by Kant in Königsberg, Herder and Wieland in Weimar (he saw Goethe only once, through the window of his home), and a performance of *The Messiah* in London attended by George III and William Pitt.[35] When he returned to Russia he broke with the Masons, but emerging as 'the leader, if not the initiator' of the sentimentalist movement in Russian literature,[36] he retained his debt to the 'inner light' as well as to the Rousseau who had also fascinated the Rosicrucians.

Freemasonry was still to have its greatest successes under Alexander I; as for 'Voltairianism', it was dead, though rationalism and skepticism would reappear in new and powerful forms.

RADISHCHEV

'Never in our history', wrote Kliuchevsky, 'has there been seen such civilized barbarism as prevailed during the second half of the eighteenth century.'[37] As the gentry worked its way up to a point where the autocracy found it possible to emancipate it, the plight of the serfs, miserable before, became unspeakable. The gentrywoman who took sadistic delight in torturing and murdering her own serfs, Daria Saltykova ('Saltychikha'), and was only very belatedly brought to justice, was the most extreme example of the abuses perpetrated by some of the newly freed serf-owners. Her case was exceptional, but it was usual to sell serfs exactly like slaves, apart from the land they had occupied, and to advertise them for inspection and sale in the growing periodical press. One such advertisement Novikov satirized, at the expense of the advertisers rather than the merchandise they offered:

Young Russian pig, who has traveled in foreign countries for the enlightenment of his mind and who, having completed his travels with profit, has returned a complete swine; those wishing to inspect him may see him daily in many streets of this city.[38]

The miseries of the peasantry, many of whom expected that the emancipation of the gentry would be followed by their own liberation, were the dry tinder which the Cossack Emelian Pugachev set afire in the last great serf rebellion of Russian history, 1773–4. The rebellion put a damper on the enlightened aspirations of the empress and stirred the consciences of the educated portion of the gentry. From contemplation of the wretchedness of the Russian people came some of the impulses toward liberalism of the Masons and of the Masonic and non-Masonic Voltairians of the 1770's, and the *cri de coeur* which was the book of Alexander Radishchev, *A Journey from St Petersburg to Moscow* (*Puteshestvie iz Peterburga v Moskvu*). In fact Radishchev may be seen as himself coming from the Masonic–Voltairian milieu of the 70's, and his book in some respects deserved to be classified as one of the Masonic Utopias, along with Shcherbatov's *Ophir*; but because of its subsequent influence and also because of the lengths Radishchev went in condemning the abuses of serfdom, it may merit brief separate treatment.

Radishchev was a nobleman, born in Moscow in 1749.[39] Until he was seven he lived on the family estate in Saratov province; he was then sent to Moscow to live in the home of a relative, A. M. Argamakov. At thirteen he was chosen to join the Imperial Corps des Pages, and after some delay went in 1764 to St Petersburg to serve in the new Winter Palace. Six of the pages, along with six other young men, were selected to study at the University of Leipzig; they included Radishchev, his closest friend throughout life, A. M. Kutuzov, and A. K. Rubanovsky, two of whose nieces Radishchev later successively married (though the second niece could not be married legally by Church law). At Leipzig Radishchev heard professors, notably P. E. Platner and C. F. Gellert, who introduced him and his fellow students to a gentle version of Enlightenment teachings, with emphasis on humaneness and individual morality. Radishchev studied there from 1767 to 1771, returning to serve as a clerk in the Senate along with both Kutuzov and Rubanovsky. He held other bureaucratic posts until 1790, except for two years of voluntary retirement from 1775 to 1777. The *Journey from St Petersburg to*

Moscow, mainly completed before the end of 1788, had the misfortune to appear in May 1790, anonymously, but it was not hard to learn who the author was. The empress read part of it, ordered an investigation, read more of it, and ordered his arrest. He was first sentenced to death; the penalty was commuted twice and became ten years' exile in Ilimsk, Siberia. Released by Paul in 1797, he was permitted to settle on an estate not far from Moscow; in 1801 Alexander I granted him a full pardon and he was appointed to the codification commission. For reasons that are unclear, he committed suicide in September 1802; the emperor sent his personal physician, who was too late to save him from the effects of poison he had taken.

In the dedication of the *Journey* to his friend Kutuzov, Radishchev begins his story: 'I looked about me – my heart was troubled by the sufferings of humanity. I turned my eyes inward – I saw that man's woes arise in man himself, and frequently only because he does not look straight at the objects around him.'[40] The book is certainly not travel literature; there are no more than a few lines which refer to places on the route, and many of the 'encounters' described are palpable inventions.[41] It is an outcry against serfdom on the one hand; on the other, it is a Utopia. In the chapters 'Khotilov' and 'Vydropusk' occur essays each entitled, 'A Project for the Future'. The work owes its form to Laurence Sterne's *A Sentimental Journey through France and Italy by Mr Yorick* (1785), which Radishchev read in German translation (1769); its literary sources are more fundamentally Goethe's *Sorrows of Young Werther*, Rousseau's works, and Raynal's *Histoire des deux Indes*.[42] The sentimentalism of young Goethe and above all Rousseau and the burning indignation of Raynal against human bondage are perhaps the foreign influences to which he is most indebted. However, Western influence on Radishchev ought to be construed more broadly. He was, as McConnell's title rightly has it, 'a Russian *philosophe*'. He belonged to an international and cosmopolitan movement, which provided him with the fundamentals of an outlook which he applied to Russian reality, in a manner often imitative – but not necessarily more so than that of a number of eighteenth-century Western writers, in an age when one's indebtedness was far less often acknowledged than today – and yet creative.[43]

Radishchev indicted serfdom, and called for a new and consistent humaneness in relations among men. For the intellectual milieu from which his message was generated, one must look to the decade of the 1770's, when British-style Masonry and Voltairianism, coexisting and overlapping, had such a powerful influence in Russia. Radishchev's closest friend was Kutuzov, who joined a lodge in 1775 and became an ardent Mason; his superior from 1777 until his arrest and even afterward his supporter, interceding many times on his behalf, was Count A. R. Vorontsov, a Mason whose father had been Grand Master; Radishchev himself visited lodges and had other Masonic contacts in St Petersburg during the 70's. V. P. Semennikov concludes that Radishchev 'was a Mason'.[44] He denied at his trial that he was a Martinist, and indeed criticized the mystics in the *Journey*. But that simply showed that he was not a sympathizer of the Rosicrucian type of Masonry, important in Moscow in the 1780's.[45] The literary society in St Petersburg to which he belonged when writing the *Journey*, the Society of Friends of Literature, was founded and led by Masons. Radishchev was apparently not attracted by the ritual and ranks of the lodges, as perhaps befitted one who wanted to abolish the Table of Ranks of Peter the Great (in the chapter 'Vydropusk'). However, the ideas of natural law,[46] Stoicism, and humanitarianism, prevalent among the Masons and Voltairians of the 70's, were also the ideas that underlay the *Journey's* attack on serfdom. Radishchev marshaled them for his assault on Russia's fundamental social institution, and in doing so went further than any of his contemporaries.

Soviet scholars have argued that he was a revolutionary, pointing to such passages as that in the chapter 'Mednoe' of the *Journey*: 'But all those who might be the champions of freedom are great landed proprietors, and freedom is not to be expected from their counsels, but from the heavy burden of slavery itself.'[47] They paradoxically summon to testify in their behalf Catherine II, who commented on the passage just quoted: 'That is, he puts his hopes in a peasant rebellion.'[48] McConnell is more judicious; Radishchev, he writes, was 'not a revolutionary except in the last resort'.[49] The word 'revolutionary' is probably best reserved for those who desired revolution and worked, however effectually, to further its chances. There is no evidence that Radishchev desired revolution, let alone worked for it in any way; he desired the end of serfdom. In the chapter 'Khotilov', he begs his fellow gentry to go to the serfs, proclaim the end of serfdom, and ask forgiveness. Only if emancipation was withheld did he even predict revolution, and that 'across a whole century'; but a few references to the Pugachev rebellion were enough to convey to the reader that the author's fears were not based on fantasy.

Radishchev was above all a humanitarian; less learned than Lomonosov, whom he eulogized in the last chapter of the *Journey*, and also less vain and self-centered, he was more concerned with the moral foundations of society, and the long duration of peasant bondage did not for a moment blind him to its violation of the dignity of man. The extent to which he was willing to boast of his achievement is shown by the part of the *Ode* to liberty which he omitted from the chapter 'Tver'; he voiced the wish that some young man might 'come to my deserted grave and feelingly may say: "He who was born here under the yoke of tyranny and bore gilded fetters was the first to proclaim liberty to us"'.[50] He was a prophet, not of revolution, but of freedom. In his prophecy he appealed to the Christian tradition of Russia which had prompted Ermolai-Erazm, Pososhkov, and others to deprecate the moral degradation that serfdom inflicted on both lord and serf, but it was only contemporary Western writers who gave him the intellectual courage to say flatly, 'Every man is born into the world equal to all others' ('Zaitsovo'), and 'the bestial custom of enslaving one's fellow men, which originated in the hot regions of Asia' ('Khotilov'), and which has been adopted in Russia, must be utterly abolished.

Radishchev did not found a school. He had a few continuators, who have been assiduously studied by Soviet scholars: Ivan Pnin, who began to publish in 1798, natural son of Prince Repnin, an enthusiast of the Moscow brand of Masonry and a man so powerful that the empress chose to punish him only by making him Governor-General of Riga; V. V. Popugaev, and a few others.[51] But for the most part Radishchev was forgotten; Pushkin had practically to rediscover him, and he only partly succeeded, for the *Journey* was not republished until Herzen's edition of 1857 and in Russia only much later.

THE JESUITS UNDER CATHERINE II

In 1784 the empress ordered to be confiscated a hostile account of the Jesuits, prepared by Novikov's printing company.[52] A few decades before such a work probably would have excited little interest. However, by 1784 the fate of the Society of Jesus had, through a curious series of events, become a matter of significance to Russian cultural life.[53]

After the First Partition of Poland in 1772, a sizeable Roman Catholic population and several Jesuit institutional centers passed into the Russian Empire. The very next year the papacy, finally yielding to the Enlightenment furor against the Jesuits, dissolved the order. However, Catherine II found it expedient to refuse to allow the publication of the papal brief *Dominus ac redemptor* (1773) in Russia. Why did the Protestant-born, Orthodox-convert empress take such a step, which not only had noteworthy consequences for Russia but which alone enabled the Society to survive into our day?

The fact that the skeptical Frederick II also allowed the Jesuits to continue for a time in his Prussian domains (though he expelled them in 1781) might offer a clue. For both sovereigns the services of qualified teachers, no matter what their religious or other commitments might be, were urgently needed, and no organization excelled the Jesuits in its capacity to supply well-educated men eager to instruct the young. A letter of Catherine's to Count Stackelberg in 1780 makes this clear; it was 'useful and most convenient for the education of the youth of the region, in which respect no one could yet replace' the Jesuits, she wrote, to retain the order in the newly annexed territories.[54]

A second factor was the need to assure the transfer of loyalty, especially on the part of the nobility, from the Polish to the Russian state. Such alternative instruments as the Piarist order were ruled out because its members were mostly Polish. The Jesuits, in contrast, were not tied to any state; as Popov puts it, 'the concept of nationality never had any particular importance in the eyes of the Jesuits'.[55] The Jesuits in Belorussia understood what the empress required of them, and helped to persuade the local population to cooperate with the new Russian rulers. There was a third consideration. Catherine feared the papacy as the most influential opponent of the partitions of Poland. She hesitated to aid in the destruction of any possible instrument she might hope to use against Rome; knowing that the Jesuits had sometimes been critical of papal power, and would certainly feel no increased warmth toward it as a result of the order of dissolution of the Society, she chose to preserve it. Perhaps something akin to French Gallicanism might arise or be created among the now sizeable Roman Catholic population of the Russian Empire. Popov holds that Jesuit criticism of the papacy was the 'chief cause' of Catherine's decision to protect the Society.[56]

The Jesuits in the two Russian provinces which incorporated the new territory, Pskov and Mogilev, found themselves in an awkward position with respect to their new superior. Catherine had raised the bishop coadjutor of Vilna, Stanisław Siestrzencewicz-Bohusz, to be bishop of all Roman Catholics in the empire; he had commended himself to her by his own critical attitude toward the papacy and subservience to the secular power, but he was far from friendly to the Jesuits. The latter attempted to ingratiate themselves with personages close to the throne, and had some success with Prince Potemkin and Count Chernyshev, Governor-General of the two Belorussian provinces. It was Potemkin who arranged the suppression in 1784 of Novikov's anti-Jesuit work already mentioned. In order to circumvent Siestrzencewicz, as well as to legitimize the surviving fragment as the center of what they hoped soon would again be the worldwide Society, the Jesuits tried to secure the appointment of a new general. They were partly successful; in 1782 Catherine permitted them to elect a 'vicar-general', and they chose Stanisław Czernie-wicz, who was able to act as general despite his more modest title. However, the empress showed her continued favor to Siestrzencewicz by successfully demanding that the pope promote him to archbishop.

The French Revolution began something of a reversal of opinion on the value of the Jesuits, first in monarchical quarters. In 1793 the duke of Parma requested that some of them be dispatched from Belorussia to his realm, and other princes followed suit. Many French émigrés were welcomed to St Petersburg by the empress, and they included numerous Roman Catholic priests and monks among whom were 'ex-Jesuits', so called because they had belonged to the order elsewhere than Belorussia before 1773. By now firmly established and growing in Belorussia, the Society was able to establish contacts in the imperial capital. French tutors had been the rage for some time, and one observer declares that it now became difficult to find a noble household in St Petersburg which did not boast a Roman cleric as mentor of the children.[57] Father Moroshkin, the chief Russian historian of the Jesuits in Russia, refers also to the large number of atheist tutors who, he asserts, Frenchified their pupils so thoroughly that if they did experience religious awakening later it was apt to be the Roman Catholic Church that they joined.

Thus far the Jesuits in Belorussia had worked at establishing good relations with some of the empress's most highly placed advisers in the capital, including Governor-General Chernyshev who spent most of his time there rather than in his Belorussian provinces. However, for the rest they had concentrated on building up their base in Polotsk and other cities of the region. In 1777 they petitioned the empress to permit them to establish a novitiate – which would mean not merely survival but perpetuation of the order – and in 1780 they were allowed to do so. A few months later Catherine visited Polotsk and the new novices were presented to her by Count Chernyshev. On this occasion the Jesuits went to great pains to illuminate the local church with prisms and transparencies portraying the empress herself, in exercise of minor skills at which they were particularly adept. In 1787 she was greeted in Mstislavl, on her way to visit the Ukraine, by the Orthodox, Uniat, and Roman Catholic bishops and Gabriel Lienkiewicz, who had succeeded Czerniewicz as vicar-general two years before. Lienkiewicz presented her with verses in Latin, Polish, German, and Italian, after delivering a welcoming speech in French, and presented her with a picture painted by Gabriel Gruber, an Austrian who shortly before had resumed active membership in the order on arriving in Belorussia. The Jesuits well knew how to put their best foot forward in the realm of culture. But though Catherine never showed signs of regretting her preservation of the order, it was only with her death that the Jesuits acquired the opportunity to advance from their Belorussian base to positions of influence on an empire-wide scale.

PAUL AND ROME

Catherine II managed to show favor to diverse intellectual groups and currents without committing herself passionately or decisively to any of them; perhaps it can be said that she handled her intellectual enthusiasms with a relative detachment comparable to the way she treated most of her succession of lovers. Paul, in contrast, took his ideological entanglements rather more seriously, although they changed during his short reign. He certainly bore marks of the emotional damage he suffered by having to countenance through subsequent inaction his father's murder (he was only eight when it occurred) and to accept deprivation of the throne for a third of a century thereafter. At the same time, the passion he showed toward ideas marks him a son of the time when sentimentality, phony, real, or both, swept an educated generation.

Paul's enthusiasms shifted from Protestantism in the direction of Catholism. He began with some of the same leanings toward Protestant northern Europe that his father had shown; he had Peter III's delight for Prussian drill, for example. From the age of six his chief tutor had been N. I. Panin, who continued to direct his education until his marriage in 1773. Panin supported the notion of a 'Northern Accord' in diplomacy, bringing Russia closer to Prussia, Sweden, England, Denmark, Saxony, and Poland (all Protestant states except the last) in counterpoise to Roman Catholic France, Austria, and Spain. It was Panin who introduced Paul to some of the mysteries of Freemasonry in its Swedish and Prussian forms. Evidently by the time of his accession in 1796 his interest in Masonry had waned. Though he soon released Novikov from the imprisonment which Catherine had ordered at least partly because of Novikov's efforts to establish contacts with him, he made no move to revive the lodges, and his interests centered more and more on the French émigrés and Roman Catholicism. As grand duke he had met Pius VI in Rome, and on his accession the Romans, in particular the Jesuits, had high hopes.

At the start of Paul's reign, it has been suggested, the only exception he made to his rule of reversing everything his mother had done was to continue her policy as regards administration of the Roman Catholic Church in the Russian Empire.[58] He began by showering marks of favor on Archbishop Siestrzencewicz. In 1798 the latter received the title of metropolitan and the award of commander of the Order of St John of Jerusalem ('the Knights of Malta'), an honor especially important in showing Paul's approval. But he soon went beyond Catherine's cautious policy. He received as a regular envoy a papal nuncio (Cardinal Count Litta, archbishop of Thebes) in Russia, which his mother had refused to do. French émigrés abounded: the Count of Provence (the future Louis XVIII) was established in Courland, the Count of Artois (the future Charles X) in St Petersburg. Paul was sympathetic to the French Bourbons, and to a number of Roman Catholic Poles, especially Ilinski and Czartoryski, who were in Russia, but toward the Orthodox hierarchy he was cold and distant, and on his accession promptly quarreled with his old religious tutor Metropolitan Platon.

Immediately after his coronation he made the journey from Moscow back to St Petersburg by way of Orsha, accompanied by Siestrzencewicz and his Martinist favorite, Neledinsky, and there he was met by Vicar-General Lienkiewicz of the Jesuits and Father Gabriel Gruber. At that point Paul was close to the metropolitan, and not very close to the Jesuits or the nuncio, who supported the latter. Within a year the situation would be the opposite. Litta's brother appeared in St Petersburg to request that the revenues of the Ostrog priory be returned to the Maltese order. Paul granted this request and tripled the sums involved, at the same time guaranteeing the existence of the Maltese order in Russia for ever and founding a Russian grand priory of it. In June 1798 Malta was betrayed by a handful of knights to Napoleon, returning from Egypt. By this time Paul had already accepted the title of protector of the Maltese order; a few months after Napoleonic conquest of the island he became Grand Master of the order with papal consent. The antiquity and the paraphernalia of the order evidently made the same sort of appeal to him that Freemasonry had once done, but he was not merely diverting himself; he imagined himself a new Godfrey of Bouillon, leading a new crusade of the European aristocracy against the French Revolution. The papacy, the brothers Litta, and the Jesuits saw their opportunity – not so much for the recovery of Malta, which Paul had vowed, or even an anti-French crusade, but for reunion of the Churches and perhaps even the Romanizati 1 of Russia.

Early in 1799 the new vicar-general of the Jesuits (Lienkiewicz had died), Franciscus Xavier Kareu, dispatched Gabriel Gruber to the capital. Born in Vienna in 1740, Gruber had become a Jesuit in 1755, and had been the last Austrian Jesuit to lay aside his habit and vows. In 1787 he had come from Austria to Polotsk and resumed his membership in the Society of Jesus. He was a mathematician, historian, chemist, musician, painter, and philologist; he knew Latin, Italian, French, German, Polish, and Russian. Equipped with numerous inventions to present to dignitaries and letters of introduction, he arrived in St Petersburg. He did not have to wait long for an unexpected opportunity. The Empress Maria Fedorovna developed a bad toothache. He offered to treat her, and was successful. Delighted, Paul offered him high honors, which he refused, replying that his service was only to the greater glory of God. The reply was almost as efficacious in winning Paul's admiration as the cure he had accomplished. He abruptly became a confidant of the emperor, and Paul had the habit of greeting him with the words (they were actually the motto of the Society), 'Ad majorem gloriam Dei!'[59]

The influence of the Jesuits mounted rapidly. A church and a school in St Petersburg were assigned to them. Siestrzencewicz's influence diminished; he was forbidden to appear at court, the Maltese decoration was taken from him, and in November 1800 he was put 'on leave' from his position and was soon under effective house arrest. According to Moroshkin, Napoleon himself, hearing of Paul's increasing distrust of Austria and Great Britain and the emperor's apparent willingness to change Russia's attitude toward him – especially after he became First Consul in November 1799 and rather more kingly than revolutionary in consequence – entrusted to Gruber personally the task of bringing about a shift in Russia's alliances.[60] Whatever Gruber's role may have been in Paul's actual abandonment of the Second Coalition, *rapprochement* with Napoleon, and campaign against British India, what is noteworthy is that the Jesuits were not tied to the pro-Bourbon party in Russia or any other European power, and were prepared to go along with any diplomatic shift provided they could carry on their work successfully.

The results they achieved in Paul's reign were meager, but identifiable. Two Great Russian names appear on the list of men belonging to the Society in 1800–1.[61] Conversions of the gentry around the turn of the century included Princess Alexandra Petrovna Golitsyna,[62] a Countess Rostopchina, Countess Protasova, Princess Vasilchikova, Countess Tolstaia, Shuvalov, Countess Golovina, and others. Roman influence was certainly making itself felt among the Russian nobility, but it was only the groundwork for real intellectual influence. A final triumph was achieved: Paul was induced to request the pope to re-establish the Society of Jesus in the Russian Empire alone, but officially; the pope consented, in a missive that arrived after the emperor's death.

Gruber had acquired a position with Paul comparable to that which Schall or Verbiest had won with Chinese emperors a century or so before.[63] He certainly hoped that the Jesuits might be instrumental in bringing about the religious victory of Rome in Russia. According to Moroshkin, Gruber worked out, with the help of the now ex-nuncio Litta and after correspondence with Rome, a draft of a proclamation for the reunion of the Orthodox and Roman Catholic Churches, and appeared at the door of Paul's study on the fateful morning of 11 March 1801, as usual to see the emperor and present the draft for his signature. However, Count Pahlen blocked his way and detained the emperor until he was about to be late for an inspection ceremony, deliberately putting him into a bad temper. Paul dismissed Gruber with his draft.[64] By the next day Paul was dead.[65]

After the Time of Troubles no Russian ruler ever showed Roman Catholicism such favor as Paul. His death was a blow that the Jesuits and Catholics, foreign and Russian converts, felt very severely. The Westernization of the Russian gentry was proceeding rapidly, as the Westernization of the court was already largely achieved. The Jesuits' ability to act as teachers of the nobles' children, demonstrators and defenders of Western technical and scientific achievement in St Petersburg drawing rooms and at least potentially on provincial estates, and exemplars of educated clergy in a nation which suffered from severe deficiencies in that respect, was unmatched by any other group. Chance may have given them their opportunity in Russia, but they knew well how to exploit it. They perhaps wagered too heavily on Paul, who reigned only five years, of which they had only three to show what they could do.

ALEXANDER I AND THE JESUITS

The accession of Alexander did not mean an immediate end to the Jesuits' opportunity, but his own ideological commitments were not congenial to them, and their best efforts were not enough to change him.

Though he was not reared a Protestant as his grandfather had been, Alexander I had an only partially successful indoctrination in Orthodoxy. Moroshkin describes his religious tutor, Archpriest Andrei Samborsky, as 'rather a good agronomist than a theologian; an Englishman rather than a Russian Orthodox priest'.[66] More influential were his secular tutors, especially César Laharpe, whom Catherine twitted as 'monsieur le jacobin', and who did much to produce in Alexander the mixture of intellectual enthusiasms that were to war within his breast during his whole reign. Florovsky writes that Alexander was 'reared in the influences of sentimental humanism. From there the step to the mystical religion of the heart was neither long nor difficult.'[67]

During Alexander's first years as emperor he was closest to a group of young liberal and rationalist friends: Prince Adam Czartoryski, Count Paul Stroganov, Count Victor Kochubey, and Nicholas Novosiltsev, who formed an Unofficial Committee (*Neglasnyi Komitet*) to meet with the emperor to discuss reforms. It was agreed among them that autocracy should be replaced by constitutional government and serfdom abolished, but out of their actual deliberations came little more than the creation of ministries (1802) to replace the eighteenth-century colleges. That Alexander's constitutionalism and reformism were genuine, despite the fact that only modest results were achieved in Russia proper, is shown by his peace aims conveyed to William Pitt in 1804, promising constitutional changes for Europe once Napoleon was overthrown; his retention of the existing constitution of Finland in 1809, his granting of a constitution to Poland in 1815, and his successful insistence on a constitution for the restored French monarchy and other European states; and his support of the constitutionalist schemes of Michael (later Count) Speransky,[68] whom he dismissed in 1812 not because he had changed his views but because he thought the political situation required him to sacrifice his most valued adviser.[69]

The contest among differing Western influences was, however, one which involved much more than individual advisers of the emperor. One of the contending parties that remained in the picture despite the loss of its protector Paul was the Society of Jesus. There were still persons close to the emperor who were prepared to support the Jesuits to a greater or lesser degree: such Polish families as the Czartoryskis and Ilinskis, Russian ones such as the Zavadovskys and Razumovskys, a few West Europeans such as Richelieu, Paulucci, and Maistre. Moreover, some having no particular fondness for the Jesuits did value their possible contribution to the Westernization of Russia, such as the pro-English Novosiltsev (educated in England), Kochubey, and Stroganov.[70]

In China in the seventeenth century the Jesuits had been to a certain extent agents of cultural Westernization, but they had started with a deep respect for Chinese traditional culture which they never abandoned as a basis for their work.

In Russia they appeared, in contrast, to be a serious threat to the traditional religious culture. What explains the difference? Partly the reason may have been that chance had made the survival of the whole Society dependent on what happened to its fragment remaining in Russia, and any undue identification of the Jesuits with Russian traditions might prejudice their capability of later worldwide restoration. But perhaps there was also another reason: as a result of Peter's policy and that of his successors, among educated Russians themselves by the early nineteenth century there was no longer much respect for or interest in national traditions, even when lip service was paid to them, and the Jesuits therefore did not feel compelled to pay much attention to Russian culture.

Thus the Jesuits in Alexander's reign appeared to be a sort of reformist cosmopolitan group, and until English-oriented pietism arose as a serious competitor, they continued to increase their influence. There seemed in particular to remain an opportunity to convert the Russian gentry, or at least its metropolitan segment. The non-Jesuit abbé Nicole had arrived in St Petersburg and established an aristocratic *pension* about 1794. It lasted ten years, for the first time provided a place where noble children were educated together and not by individual tutors, and numbered among its pupils he children of Prince Yusupov, Orlovs, Golitsyns, Naryshkins, Menshikovs, Gagarins, Pleshcheevs, Benkendorfs, Volkonskys, and others.[71] After an epidemic in 1805 the pupils were dispersed, and perhaps Jesuit competition also had effect in leading Nicole to migrate to Odessa, where he founded a *lycée* Richelieu which operated until 1820.[72] For in 1803 a Jesuit pension was founded on a plan drawn up by Father Gruber. The pupils included a young Count Kochubey, Prince Viazemsky, Dmitry Severin (later envoy to Munich), Count Alexander Tolstoy, and others. By 1805 the *pension* had 60 enrolled and a connected parochial school had more than 400. But in March 1805 Gruber died tragically in a fire, and his successor as general, Thaddeus Brzozowski, could not match his ability. It is possible that Gruber might have avoided the mistakes that led to the expulsion of the Jesuits.

Some outstanding Roman Catholics, clerics and laymen, were now in St Petersburg, winning friends and admirers for their co-religionists belonging to the various orders and for their religion. First in time and not least in importance had been the Chevalier Jean Dominique Bassinet d'Augard, who had reached St Petersburg in 1796, and until his death in 1808 captivated the ladies in many salons. The ablest cleric in this sort of situation was Jean-Louis de Leïssègues Rozaven, a Breton by birth, who left France before the Revolution and reached Russia in 1804 to join the Jesuits. But the man who gained most attention was Joseph de Maistre.

Maistre[73] came to St Petersburg in 1803 at the age of fifty as envoy of the Kingdom of Sardinia. Born in Chambéry, he came from a family of the senatorial bourgeoisie of Savoy. On his appointment to Russia he had been ten years in exile from his Savoyard homeland. Though his diplomatic post was not of great importance, his personal abilities made him an influential figure in Russia and his writings, most of which were composed in St Petersburg, entitle him to a significant place in the history of thought. He came to Russia with two clear aims in mind which went beyond his instructions. One was to obtain Russia's help in recreating Sardinia not merely as a state independent of French occupation but as a power dominating northern Italy; the other was to make Russia an instrument of God's judgment in destroying the French Revolution as the international movement it had become.[74] He neither wholly succeeded nor wholly failed in either aim, though he ended his days in a mood of deep pessimism.

'Enchanting Petersburg society with his intelligence, earning universal respect by the uprightness of his character, Count de Maistre for a time enjoyed the personal confidence of the emperor Alexander I', writes Bartenev.[75] Maistre regarded Alexander as 'a *philosophe* through and through', but he acted as if it were possible to influence the emperor in another direction even though he feared that what he regarded as the fancies of Alexander's youth might recur. If he was to achieve his aims, he had to influence the emperor and the elite of Russia. All his major works, as Berti points out, were chiefly written for Russia: *Soirées de St-Pétersbourg, Du Pape, L'essai sur le principe générateur des constitutions politiques.* He believed the problems of Russia (and of Europe in general) to be at root religious. Liberation of the serfs might be desirable, indeed required by Christian teaching, but it was dangerous in a country where the clergy was as weak as it was in Russia. The clergy's weakness derived partly from its inclination to Protestantism (an inclination whose historical roots have been traced above, and about which Maistre was right and Berti is wrong).[76] As for the government, its leaders had their eyes closed to the evil of Protestantism, taking the 'serpent' to be at most an 'eel'.[77] Thus ran, in brief, Maistre's view of Russia.

It was certainly the case that the Orthodox clergy regarded Maistre with suspicion, while liberals valued his works and referred to them repeatedly. Feoktistov remarks that 'the manner in which de Maistre defended his convictions, the spirit of disturbing analysis with which he was imbued, seemed always suspicious to parties who relied foremost on authority and who feared the paths of reason'.[78] Berti, although a leftist writer, declares that Maistre understood the French Revolution better than anyone else in Europe;[79] though he regarded it as 'Satanic' in character, he recognized a number of positive aspects in the political order emerging from post-1789 events and the necessity of coming to terms with the latter. Maistre[80] and the ablest Jesuits earned admiration not so much for their religious convictions as for their trained minds and advanced education.

For a time Maistre achieved a unique position in Russia. He was in the imperial anteroom when Speransky emerged after the emperor dismissed him in 1812; he was in the Kazan Cathedral when an official arrived with a special message, whose contents soon swept through those attending the service: 'he has been captured' – meaning Napoleon. He did not achieve any of his more grandiose aims. However, to his credit must be placed imperial action in recognizing the Polotsk college as an academy with rights equal to Russian universities,[81] and he had a share in the responsibility for the growing fashionableness of Roman Catholicism in and around court and among the high gentry. Unfortunately for his cause, its very success brought disaster upon it. Maistre and the Jesuits had powerful opponents whose star was rising sharply. Their opportunity came when the nephew of Prince Alexander Golitsyn, by now the emperor's chief counselor, declared his desire to become a Roman Catholic. When the emperor learned of it, Maistre wrote: 'The fire darted out of his nostrils.' Alexander first ordered the young man to be entrusted to an archbishop for reindoctrination; after consulting with the uncle the latter was dispatched at 5 a.m. to the old metropolitan, Siestrzencewicz, ordering that masses be said two hours later without the

Jesuits and that they be expelled from the capital that day.[82] It was December 1815.

In the previous year, 1814, the pope had reestablished the Society of Jesus for the whole world, under the head of the Russian fragment, Brzozowski, as general. Two months after the restoration of the order, Brzozowski wrote Prince Golitsyn: 'It is to the Russian government that we are indebted for the resurrection of our Society.'[83] He was quite right. Catherine II had preserved the Society in Russia as soon as the pope abandoned it globally; but Alexander I banned it in Russia as soon as the pope had restored it globally.[84] Maistre stayed about a year longer, and was recalled at Russian request to Turin in May 1817. He had no successors approaching his stature or influence. As Moroshkin points out, after the reign of Alexander I a number of notable conversions of Russians to Rome were made, but they occurred mainly abroad. The irony that attended the expulsion of the Jesuits was that a large share of the conversions were made with no participation by them, and during Gruber's lifetime only one is known.[85] However, in the succeeding decade Gruber's caution had been discarded.

The dazzling even if brief and limited successes of the Jesuits in Russia are explained by the sharply hostile critic Yury Samarin as follows, 'all their strength consisted in the spiritual weakness of that milieu in which they were operating. In the highest strata of St Petersburg society, and of course only there, everything was favorable to them.' Although, he continues, the dogma that all faiths were equal had widely spread, many Russians found the conversion of an Orthodox to Roman Catholicism more justifiable than the contrary; the reason lay 'in the attractions of a higher civilization and in the sincerity of conviction proclaimed by the daring of such a deed. This view was transferred from the sphere of society to the governmental sphere and passed for toleration.'[86]

THE PIETIST REVOLUTION:
HOLY ALLIANCE AND 'COMBINED MINISTRY'

In Russia of 1800 'the dogma that all faiths are equal' may well have served the Roman Catholics in good stead, but it cannot be said to be either Roman Catholic or Eastern Orthodox doctrine; it was rather characteristic of certain tendencies in Protestantism as the Reformation progressed. It indeed was Maistre's 'serpent', Protestantism, that was making its influence felt in Alexander's reign – Protestantism of the evangelical and pietist variety that had been given new vigor by late eighteenth-century movements in England, and not only religious pietism, but secular as well.

There were differences of style, of manners, and of social origin in the groups to which the pietists and the Jesuits appealed. In general the Jesuit influence was, as Samarin writes, strong among the gentry and especially the titled nobility. The pietists were more apt to be found among the clergy, who had received educations that included pietist elements, and the lower gentry. The social lines were not clearly drawn, however, and among the pietists were to be found nobles and even, in an important sense, the emperor himself. The pietism and the mysticism of the educated classes did not reach into the common people any more than Roman Catholic tendencies did; but there was nevertheless a pronounced growth of mystical sects among those of little education, the middle and lower classes, among Russians, such as the Khlysty, Skoptsy, Dukhobors, and Molokane, and a simultaneous spread of mystical German or Central European sects in Russia, such as the Mennonites and Moravian Brethren. Such movements had gathered momentum as early as Catherine's time, but by the turn of the century they had become more evident. Florovsky suggests that under Alexander the mysticism of lower and higher classes in many ways converged.[87]

There was, in any event, a convergence of another kind that affected the educated class alone: that of the mysticism of the Masonic lodges with the pietism of the evangelical Protestant revival. A number of 'conversions' occurred, not in the sense of a change of religious faith, but in the specific evangelical sense of a religious experience transforming one's outlook and life. The principal 'conversions' were of Prince Alexander Golitsyn and of Alexander I himself. The results were an attempt at what has been called 'theocratic Utopianism', in which the emperor and his advisers attempted to make pietism the foundation for state policy at home and abroad. In foreign policy the instrument was to be the Holy Alliance; in the cultural affairs of the Russian Empire, it was the formation of a combined Ministry of Spiritual Affairs and Public Enlightenment (1817).

Prince Golitsyn has recounted how he unwillingly assumed the office of procurator of the Most Holy Synod in 1805, which he entered with the appalled and sarcastic reactions of the deist he then was.[88] He did not want, he wrote, 'this Gothic office', and indirectly confessed to the emperor that he was not religious at all; but Alexander made him accept, conferring on him the new right of seeing the emperor personally on Synod business.[89] 'The unbelieving school of the eighteenth century', Golitsyn continued, 'had put down deep roots in my heart.' But in order to learn his job he set about to inform himself on the necessary problems, and among other things he read the New Testament for the first time. 'Conversion' followed – to be sure, not automatically or entirely accidentally. A. F. Labzin, who had been a follower of Schwarz in 1782 at the age of sixteen and had become historiographer of the Maltese order, by order of Paul, was a personal friend of Golitsyn's. For several months in 1806 he published a mystical organ called *Messenger of Zion* (*Sionskii Viestnik*). He wrote a good deal about the value of 'awakening' and 'conversion'.[90] The old mystic Rodion Koshelev, personally linked with Johann Kaspar Lavater, Claude de Saint-Martin, and Karl von Eckhartshausen, renowned mystics of the day, was finding a hearing for similar views.

In a short time Golitsyn acquired a new reputation for sanctity. He conducted extensive private charities, and people began to bring their children to him to be blessed. In 1810 he became chief administrator for foreign faiths. When the St Petersburg Bible Society (renamed Russian Bible Society in 1814) was formed in January 1813,[91] he became its first president. A number of Masons and former Masons, such as Koshelev and Labzin, either entered the Bible Society or published their works and distributed them through Bible Society channels. The Bible Society thus became the institutional center of Christian mystics and Masonic pietists, and distributed Rosicrucian mystifications along with Bibles. The Bibles themselves, however, had no notes at all, since it was accepted that any kind of dogmatic intrusion would prevent each reader from making his own interpretation, and it was assumed that the Bible spoke entirely for itself. In this and other respects the Bible Society followed the ideology of the British pietists. A number of English Quakers visited Russia during the period, though English Nonconformism in general, which had its own outlet in the British and Foreign Bible Society, had the most powerful influence on the group. Beginning with the aim of spreading the Bible among non-Orthodox only, the Society annexed from the Synod the task of distributing Slavonic Bibles, and finally decided on publishing a new translation of the Bible into Russian. The New Testament was published in 1821, but the Bible Society was broken up before the Old Testament was complete.

It was through reading the Bible (in French translation, before and after the New Testament was translated into Russian) that the emperor himself, in 1812, under the impact of the Napoleonic invasion, underwent his own 'conversion'. Koshelev and especially Golitsyn had prepared the ground. The consequences were first exhibited in the Holy Alliance, understandably since the emperor's first need was to put an end to the affair of Napoleon and define Russia's position in international affairs. The character of the Holy Alliance is well enough known. What seems not to be properly understood is that it represented not a casual fantasy of Alexander's based on chance meetings with such eccentrics as Baroness Krüdener, but an attempt to translate the sentimentalist and pietist tendencies of a powerful segment of the Russian educated class of the time into political action on a worldwide scale. The effort of historians to ask what political consequences the Holy Alliance had – and correctly answer, none of any significance – is understandable; but, judging from most of the general histories, understanding that the idea was conceived not for political reasons but on the basis of religious and cultural principles seems far from easy. Actually the problem of making pietism the foundation of the concert of Europe was not an easy one to solve, since pietism emphasized the individual so strongly. Alexander's solution was to ask each individual sovereign to make a pietist commitment and sign his name to it – even including the pope as temporal sovereign. Naturally, since his fellow rulers of Europe were not pietists, they did not take it seriously as he did, and the affairs of the continent were managed on the basis not of the pietist covenant, but of the

Quadruple Alliance, an instrument more congenial to anyone experienced in eighteenth-century diplomacy.

Two years after Waterloo and the final act of the Congress of Vienna, Alexander got around to applying his new commitments to domestic affairs. The result was the foundation in October 1817 of a new combined Ministry of Spiritual Affairs and Public Enlightenment, with Prince Alexander Golitsyn as minister. Michael Speransky, himself strongly influenced by the mystical currents of the day, said that the law creating this ministry was 'the greatest state act since the very introduction of the Christian faith'.[92] It was founded in the hope of 'combining forever science [i.e., secular knowledge] and religion'.[93] How to accomplish that end was not obvious. The ministry had two departments; the first, for spiritual affairs, was entrusted to A. I. Turgenev, who was not a strong believer, while the second, for education, was given to V. M. Popov, who was none too well educated. The affairs of all religions, including Islam and paganism, were under the same department. Thus nominally all faiths, including Russian Orthodoxy itself, were placed on the same level – which in itself meant the elimination of the religious monopoly granted, or assumed to exist, by Peter's establishment of the Orthodox Church in 1721. In fact Orthodoxy received something less than equal treatment. The views of the Protestant-oriented pietists were in the clear ascendant, and repressive measures were used against those Orthodox who questioned the mystics and their ideology. The best-known case was that in 1818 involving the book by Evstafy Stanevich, *A Conversation on the Immortality of the Soul on the Grave of an Infant* (*Razgovor o bezsmertii dushi nad grobom mladentsa*), in which he condemned Labzin's mystical journal, *Messenger of Zion* (which he had been allowed to revive in April 1817), and criticized the assumptions underlying the new ministry. Stanevich was exiled from St Petersburg on 24 hours' notice, and the distinguished archimandrite and rector of the St Petersburg Academy, Innokenty Smirnov, who as clerical censor had passed the book, was ordered to be sent to Orenburg as punishment. Friends got the destination changed to Penza, but Smirnov died a few months after arriving there.

The mystics and pietists, with their organizational center in the Bible Society, their primacy in state policy guaranteed by Golitsyn's new ministry, the universal scope of their aspirations signaled by the Holy Alliance, embodied something close to a new religion established by the state. The staunchly Orthodox writer and diplomat, Alexander Sturdza, called it 'the Anglo-Russian sect'.[94] Sturdza concluded that the Bible Society 'drew each and every man by the shortest route to the side of Protestantism'.[95] The contradictions produced by state establishment of a kind of Protestant evangelicalism in a nominally Orthodox country were striking and occasionally a trifle absurd. For example, the staunchly Orthodox Sturdza, as a member of the emperor's cabinet, was ordered to write to Rome defending the active membership of the Roman Catholic Bishop Siestrzencewicz (whom the Jesuits had not without some justification called 'that Calvinist') in the

Protestant-oriented Bible Society. About the same time, Sturdza wrote a theological treatise in French directed against the Jesuits. He had no enmity toward the Jesuits; he was later to be living near Orsha when the Jesuits were expelled, and found the expulsion 'painful' to witness; he was merely theologically opposed to them, as were the pietists and mystics. Nevertheless Labzin, the Masonic mystic, was furious with Sturdza's book and said that any old peasant woman (*baba*) could refute it. The reason, of course, was that Labzin had no patience with traditional Christian theology of any kind, though he was certainly not less hostile to the Jesuits than Sturdza was. Curiously Count de Maistre, the friend and advocate of the Jesuits, was not notably hostile toward the Masons, having been one himself, and believed Masonry not dangerous in non-Roman Catholic countries, but he regarded the Bible Society with great suspicion (he left Russia several months before the 'combined ministry' was set up). At this point it can be understood that the expulsion of the Jesuits and the termination of significant Roman Catholic influence was prompted not merely by Orthodox resentment at conversions of Russians to Rome; it was more fundamentally the result of the ascendancy of Protestant-oriented mystics – both the expulsion from the capital in 1815 and the final ban in 1820, which was decided on by Golitsyn and justified to the emperor by a memorandum written by A. I. Turgenev.[96]

The period of 'theocratic Utopianism' had its positive aspects. The importation of Englishmen and English Nonconformist ideas which had given rise to the Bible Society had other results. There were several attempts to create Lancaster schools, after the model of the English schools sponsored by that gentleman on the principle of each-one-teach-one.[97] A society was formed to work in prisons, imitating English groups of the same kind. Many approved the idea of translating the Bible into Russian and distributing it in various languages, although they might disagree with the theology that underlay the assumption that the Bible needed no interpretation to be understood by every believer (or non-believer), and were alarmed at the ending of the preface to the Russian New Testament: 'read, make yourself wise, and save yourself'. The phenomenon was increasingly noted of provincial governors who made their speeches sound like pietist sermons; in many cases the Orthodox must have acknowledged that for such gentlemen, woolly theology may have been preferred to none. The excitement was undeniable, the confusion obvious, the excesses unavoidable: some of the most ardent mystics, including V. M. Popov, head of the education section of the new ministry and secretary of the Bible Society, participated in the ecstasies organized by Ekaterina Tatarinova, a lady who had formerly been an admirer of the Skoptsy leader Kondraty Selivanov.[98]

The Orthodox clergy were often swept into local Bible Societies as they proliferated throughout the country. Some of them had read certain of the mystics currently popular in the West in their seminaries, and it has already been noted that such prominent clerics as Metropolitan Platon of Moscow were strongly influenced by pietism long before the ascendancy of Golitsyn was established. Other clergymen who found all the religious excitement irresistible, being none too sophisticated religiously or philosophically, were nevertheless troubled by a nagging feeling that something was rotten in Denmark.

One of these was the Archimandrite Foty; and it was he who was the active agent, encouraged by the powerful Count Arakcheev, in pushing the whole pietist establishment over. Through his protectress Countess A. A. Orlova, Foty met Golitsyn, and for a time seems to have hoped to make him see the error of his ways. In March 1824 matters came to a head over the scheduled publication of a Russian translation of Fr Johann Gossner's *Geist des Lebens und der Lehre Jesu Christi*. Gossner was a Roman Catholic priest who had become an enthusiast of pietism and, having had to flee his German parish, came to Russia in 1820.[99] An opportunistic official, M. L. Magnitsky, who had earlier proclaimed himself a zealous pietist and had carried out a kind of pietist reign of terror at Kazan University as curator beginning in 1819, now sensed that the winds were changing. He used the Gossner book as the basis of charges against Golitsyn. Foty wrote to the emperor in the same vein and then after an audience with him felt secure enough to curse Golitsyn to his face in a remarkable scene. Alexander ordered the burning of the Gossner book and the trial of those involved in the affair; in May 1824 he dissolved the combined ministry and dismissed Golitsyn. Golitsyn was succeeded by Admiral Shishkov as minister of education ('public enlightenment') alone, at the insistance of Arakcheev, who had regarded Golitsyn not so much as a religious heretic as a political rival. Golitsyn also resigned as president of the Bible Society; it lingered until 1826, when Nicholas I ended its existence.

DECEMBRISM

On the death of Alexander I his successor was expected to be his brother Grand Duke Constantine, viceroy of Poland; but secret arrangements occasioned by Constantine's morganatic marriage had been made for the second brother, Grand Duke Nicholas, to become emperor instead. It took over two weeks for the situation to be clarified, and when the time came on 14 December 1825 for a new oath (reversing the one taken earlier) to Nicholas I to be taken in St Petersburg, members of a secret organization within the Guards regiments had prepared to refuse it and stand fast for Constantine. The vague hope was that this gesture would enable them, under the rule of Constantine, to achieve broader political aims. The demonstration was crushed, as was an accompanying and initially successful mutiny in the Ukraine, and these events became known as the Decembrist revolt.[100] The secret societies which existed from 1816 to 1825 with the object of achieving political reform have thus become known as 'Decembrist' from the date of their unsuccessful uprising.

The Decembrist revolt was in form similar to the eighteenth-century coups of the Guards regiments which several times had determined the succession, but the aims of the Decembrist leaders were very different from those of their predecessors. The Decembrist secret societies were in form derived from the Masonic lodges (as were also the contemporary West European radical secret societies). The impetus for the formation of such societies in Russia was given by the experience of young officers, especially those of the Guards, before and during the Napoleonic Wars in Germany and France, or, as Miakotin puts it, by 'the intellectual impressions made during the years of their more or less early youth by the works of French Enlightenment literature of the eighteenth century, heightened patriotic feeling, [and] both direct and literary acquaintanceship with the constitutional life of the European West...'[101] Several of the future Decembrists had been Masons, including the ideological leaders P. I. Pestel and Nikita Muraviev, in sum about one-fifth of those later tried for conspiracy, but this meant that the other four-fifths had not been lodge members.[102] They moved from reading Western writers directly into the secret societies. M. P. Bestuzhev-Riumin read Voltaire; Paul Pestel, Destutt de Tracy; A. N. Muraviev, Rousseau; A. A. Bestuzhev-Marlinsky, Bentham; K. F. Ryleev, Benjamin Constant.[103] The Masons of the 1770's had read several of these writers (others, of course, had not yet published their works), but frequently had gone on from such liberal treatises on social organization to the only practical avenue that seemed to be open: individual self-improvement and attempts at moral self-perfection. This tendency, pietist and often mystical, had been wrecked in the 1790's, but had revived in the earlier years of Alexander I's reign and had been an important ingredient of what was called above 'the pietist revolution' of 1817 and after. The generation of the Decembrists, for the most part, had stood aside from the attempt to make pietism the state religion over which Count Golitsyn had presided. During his tenure of office they were entering new secret societies which were in spirit not like the lodges that had been dominant since the 1780's but harked back to the quasi-rationalist lodges of the 1770's.

The new societies were founded by men who had been Masons or close to the lodges, had imitated much of their ritual and organization. Even the name of the first group had Masonic overtones: it was the Order of Russian Knights (*Orden russkikh rytsarei*), founded in 1816 by M. F. Orlov and Count M. A. Dmitriev-Mamonov. It was not a success, but at the end of the same year in St Petersburg a new group did better. It was the Union of Salvation, or Society of True and Faithful Sons of the Fatherland (*Soiuz spaseniia*, or *Obshchestvo istinnykh i viernykh synov otechestva*); formed on the initiative of Alexander Muraviev, it included Nikita Muraviev, Prince S. P. Trubetskoi, Prince I. A. Dolgorukov, Sergei and Matvei Muraviev-Apostol, Colonel F. N. Glinka, Captain I. Yakushkin, Colonel Paul Pestel, and others. The majority were officers of the guards, and were scions of the gentry from the central provinces. Its aims were set forth in a charter drawn up by Pestel in

1817, which read like a Masonic document: they were to 'work with all one's powers for the general good, support all beneficial measures of the government and useful private undertakings, oppose all evil and to that end expose abuses of officials and dishonorable actions of private parties'.[104] In 1818 it was renamed the Union of Welfare (*Soiuz blagodenstviia*), and the charter was reworked as the so-called 'Green Book'. The emperor was informed of all this, and gave a copy of the 'Green Book' to the Grand Duke Constantine to read. N. Shilder writes, 'at first the Tsar did not recognize in this society a political conspiracy', and indeed, despite the political radicalism of Pestel and others, it is doubtful that it originally *was* one. The 'Green Book' was virtually a copy of the charter of the German Tugendbund.

Following the mutiny of the Semenovsky guards regiment in 1820, a meeting was held in Moscow of the Union of Welfare which ended by proclaiming the dissolution of the group. This appears to have been chiefly a stratagem to get rid of untrustworthy members. The leaders did not know that Alexander was keeping abreast of developments, but when confronted in May 1821 with a report on them, answered Adjutant-General Vasilchikov, 'vous savez que j'ai partagé et encouragé ces illusions et ces erreurs', and then after long silence concluded, 'ce n'est pas à moi à sévir'. On 1 August 1822 he issued an edict closing all Masonic lodges and secret societies in general, but made no real attempt to enforce it. Immediately after the Moscow meeting two new societies were formed, called simply the Northern and Southern. The more active was the Southern, under the leadership of Pestel; the Northern Society showed more activity after the poet Ryleev joined it in 1823. In the same year there was formed still another group, called the Society of United Slavs (*Obshchestvo Soedinennykh Slavian*),[105] which soon fused with the Southern Society.

The aims of the societies soon came to be political. Nikita Muraviev drew up for use of the members of the Northern Society a draft constitution for Russia, strongly influenced by the French Constitution of 1791, the Constitution of the USA, and the Spanish Constitution of 1812, which envisaged the country as a constitutional and federal monarchy, with serfdom abolished and equality guaranteed to all citizens before the law. The Southern Society followed the lead given by Pestel in his Russian Justice (*Russkaia pravda*) and State Testament (*Gosudarstvennyi Zavet*). He planned for a centralized republic on the Jacobin model. Muraviev's final solution was to free the serfs with about five-acre allotments; Pestel wished to expropriate large tracts of land with only partial compensation and convert half the land of the localities into 'social property', which each citizen might use to the extent necessary for subsistence. The two societies generally shared the view that a revolt should be carried out by the military to which so many of the members belonged and if possible (even the constitutional monarchists thought) remove the ruling dynasty. How this should be done and what should follow were, however, the subject of endless and inconclusive discussion. The unexpected death of the emperor at Taganrog on 19 November 1825 found the members of the societies as perplexed about what to do as the ruling circles of the state. As the weeks passed the rumor (based on fact) spread that arrest of some of the conspirators was imminent, and on 14 December there occurred the tragi-comic events on Senate Square in St Petersburg which formed the central part of what became known as the Decembrist revolt. Arrest of the Decem-brists followed. In July 1826 five, including Pestel and Ryleev, were hanged; several dozen were exiled.

The Decembrists owed their ideology to the West, from the sedate constitu-tionalism of the Philadelphia Convention to the Jacobinism of Robespierre, though the question of emancipation of the serfs and what should follow they had to work out for themselves. They owed the form of their organization to Western political secret societies but also through them and directly to Freemasonry. The Muravievs and others had in fact been Masons earlier, and one of the draft constitutions (a republican one) was prepared by Nicholas Novikov, nephew of the great Freemason. Their aspirations for 'self-perfec-tion', central to Masonic doctrine, had been transferred from the sphere of the individual to that of the state.

The alliance of mystical Masonry and Protestant pietism that had been fundamental to the ruling ideas of Alexander and Golitsyn for so much of the reign was also to be found in Decembrism. Pestel was a Lutheran of German origin, educated in Dresden. Masaryk writes:

The governmental centralisation to which he aspired would have been no less absolutist than was the 'enlightened' tsarism of the preceding epoch. This is especially plain in his views upon religion and the church. Here Pestel is wholly at one with Peter the Great. The clergy are not to form a distinct order, being merely entitled to the exercise of a specific profession; and they must do their work as constituents of the governmental machine...no member of the clergy ought to be subject to any foreign authority, seeing that the clergy are state servants. Foreign monastic orders...could not be tolerated in Russia. Of course the proposals were mainly directed against the pope and the Catholics. Pestel's attitude toward the church serves also to explain why he desired that Poland and the Polish provinces should be separated from Russia.[106]

As for the Jews, in Pestel's plan they were to be assisted to migrate *en masse* to Asia Minor, in a premature vision of Zionism – except that it was to be imposed on the Jews regardless of their wishes.

Many of the Decembrists were constitutionalist, some, such as Pestel, were quasi-socialist, all were in some degree liberal in their political views; the shape of their ideal state was sketched with precision in their proposed constitutions.[107] Nevertheless there was a degree of utopianism in their politi-cal plans, for although the desired end was depicted in some detail (as is characteristic of all utopias), there was no clear indication of how the end might be attained. There are indications that the Grand Duke Constantine might have entertained some reform proposals, at any rate more readily than his brother Nicholas (even before the latter was frightened by the Decembrist revolt); there are none that he was ready to enact a Decembrist constitution. Those who came after the Decembrists understood this sufficiently so that there were no constitutional projects circulating again until the reign of Alexander II, when there seemed to be hope that the autocrat might actually enact some sort of constitutional law.

CONCLUSION

Decembrism, then, harked back to the eighteenth century, but only formally to the guardist *coups*. Its substance had a kinship with the constitution-making of the American and French Revolutions in the West; but it also drew on the rationalist tradition which had obtained a toehold in Russia.[108] From the time of its introduction in the seventeenth century, Roman Catholic and then later Protestant scholasticism had helped to prepare the ground for the reception of the Enlightenment doctrines of the *philosophes* in mid-eighteenth-century Russia, the rationalist and liberal side in the Freemasonry of the 1770's, and even the systematic education of the Jesuits as it became increasingly popular in the reigns of Paul and Alexander I.[109] All these currents affected only small numbers of people and had shallow roots in Russia; but the same was of course true of Decembrism itself.

The competing tradition was one of individual morality, inner feeling, mysticism, and sentimentalism; it stemmed from German pietism, was reinvigorated by the Rosicrucians of the 1780's, and saw a revival in the pietism of British origin and the renewed mystical Freemasonry which together produced the 'combined ministry' and the endeavor to establish pietism as a state cult. The sentimentalist tradition, implemented by the autocracy, was wrecked in 1824; the rationalist tradition, in the hands of the advanced young gentry, was defeated in 1825: 1824–5 was thus the first great testing point of Western influence on Russian intellectual history. Having gathered momentum for two centuries or more, the waves of Western ideas seemed to shatter on the rocks of the single-centered Russian society.

For it was the state that still determined the cultural outcome, even though the individual rulers of Russia and their advisers were in turn deeply influenced by the cultural currents originating in the West. The passions and debates of Alexander's reign were not decided by the plausibility of the arguments, the attractiveness of forms of expression, or the ability of the contenders. No one could compete successfully with the Jesuits, for example, so the pietists, having obtained temporary ascendancy over the emperor, secured their expulsion. Having enthroned pietism, he was compelled to dethrone it a few years later. Since his own pietist enthusiasms were genuine, he did so with a heavy heart, and maintained his personal friendship with Golitsyn to the last. His own death, coming only a year after the cultural *coup d'état* of 1824, found him in a state of confusion and unhappiness which helped to give rise to rumors that he was about to be converted to Roman Catholicism, that he had not died but had fled to become a monk in Siberia, and so forth.[110] The personal story of Alexander I, who himself had both rationalist and senti-mentalist sides, has elements of tragedy.

The story of Russian culture during his reign ranges from tragic to farcical, but only because the state still controlled its growth. In the Russia of 1800 there was incomparably more civilization in the Western style than there had been in 1500. But with all the barbarousness and bloodiness of Ivan III's time, he was not yet in a position to decide cultural questions by a stroke of the pen; problems were set by men in the Russian Church as well as in the state, considering both Byzantine and Western models, and the grand prince was by no means the unquestioned arbiter. In the Russia of 1700 problems were still set by clergy as well as by officials and the ruler himself; the models were almost entirely Western; the ruler determined the outcome, often brutally. In the Russia of 1800 the models were Western, the problems set by gentry, clergy, and officials; Alexander I did not usually act with brutality in his capacity as arbiter of them, but he was, like Peter I, the arbiter, since he was an autocrat.

A new beginning was required. Neither the theocratic utopianism of the 'combined ministry' nor the political reformism, which proved utopian, of the Decembrists offered a way out. The new directions were provided by philoso-phy, and more particularly German idealist philosophy.

Alexander I's reign, as Florovsky writes, marked 'the awakening of the heart...but not the awakening of thought' in Russia.[111] And yet the founda-tions for the latter were laid before Alexander died. The cause was to a large extent the reform of ecclesiastical schools carried out by the ukaz of 30 August 1814 and also the expansion of the (secular) university system.[112] In conse-quence the training of the seminarians was directed more extensively into philosophy and in particular into post-Kantian German philosophy. As the expulsion of the Jesuits, the ousting of the pietists and mystics, and the banning of the secret societies removed important contenders from the cultural scene, a void was created into which there moved the Russian lovers of German philosophy, more or less determined to avoid the direct connection with the imperial court which had helped to make the Jesuits and pietists vulnerable.

Florovsky sums up the position in the early nineteenth century thus:

Philosophy was studied in the Russo-Latin schools already from the seventeenth century, first out of [Roman Catholic] scholastic textbooks, later out of the books of Wolff and Baumeister. In the libraries that had then been assembled, we find a good many philosophical books – in the library of Feofan Prokopovich, or the renowned Archangel library of Prince D. M. Golitsyn, who also had a collection of manuscript translations. Teachers and pupils read a good deal, especially in Kiev, sometimes including recent philosophers in what they read. However, taken as a whole this academic instruction, still reflecting no genuine philosophical life, was to a relatively minor extent expressed in the inner forma-tion of the Russian spirit. More important were literary-philosophical enthusiasms, Voltairianism and Masonry...[but] only in the period of Alexander, in the reformed ecclesiastical schools, there began to be felt in the teaching of philosophy a more organic and responsible treatment of problems.[113]

Out of the *coup* of 1824, in the words of Metropolitan Filaret of Moscow, there came a 'return to the times of scholasticism'.[114] That is, with the defeat of pietism came a revival of scholasticism, if one thinks of the two competing currents of eighteenth-century Church education. Filaret himself came out of a largely scholastic tradition in the seminary of the Trinity-St Sergius monastery, even though he sought later to accommodate himself to pietism in certain respects and, argues Florovsky, his sense of history separates him from both positions.[115] Filaret did his best to implement the injunction of the new charter of 1814 that the differences among the chief philosophers be explained to students. In the Moscow Academy Feodor Golubinsky began to teach philosophy, and continued in the post from 1818 to 1854. Rector Innokenty of the Kiev Academy declared that 'philosophy is the demand of the century and without it the teacher of the Church will have no importance in the eyes of his pupils'.

The 'return to scholasticism' was thus not merely that but also and significantly a development of modern and contemporary philosophy; and it was an event that affected not merely the ecclesiastical schools, but also the whole of Russian education and thus the thought of the next generation. From among the students at the ecclesiastical academies came, as had been the case earlier, many of the professors in the universities. N. I. Nadezhdin was a student at the Moscow Academy before he became professor at Moscow University; the first exponents of philosophical idealism came out of the ecclesiastical schools: Vellansky from the Kiev Academy, Galich from the Sevsky seminary, Pavlov from the Voronezh seminary; and the professors of philosophy in the major universities (F. Sidonsky and M. I. Vladislavtsev in St Petersburg, P. D. Yurkevich and M. M. Troitsky in Moscow) came from the seminaries. Philosophy became so firmly established in the ecclesiastical schools that even when Nicholas I banned philosophy from the universities in 1850, he allowed it still to be taught there – often by the very teachers of the university teachers he had silenced. But by that time even in the universities philosophy had done much to suggest new directions for Russia.

6

GERMAN IDEALISM AND FRENCH
ANARCHISM (1825–1855)

Yes, Madam, the time has come simply to speak the language of reason. It is
no longer a matter of blind faith, of the beliefs of the heart; we must address
ourselves directly to thought.

Peter Chaadaev, the eighth *Philosophical Letter* (1831)
(Zeldin trans.)

'OFFICIAL NATIONALITY' IN THE REIGN OF NICHOLAS I

Nicholas I was reputed to be the handsomest man in Europe, and the power
of his presence was such as to send howling mobs instantly to their knees
and to strike awe into the hearts of foreigners and Russians alike. He drove
himself relentlessly and furiously, attempting to take in hand all significant
affairs of state and many insignificant ones. Aside from the Decembrist revolt,
he repressed a revolution in the Kingdom of Poland and a good deal of sporadic
disorder in Russia proper, and his impact abroad, especially in 1848, was
such as to earn him the sobriquet 'the gendarme of Europe'. His power was
envied by fellow monarchs, feared by fighters for liberty. The might of his
regime, however, was proven by Russia's defeat in the Crimean War to be in
great part façade, and one writer summed up in the words: 'The main failing
of the reign of Nicholas consisted in the fact that it was all a mistake.'[1]

Nicholas I was in many ways a reactionary, and yet he inaugurated a series
of changes in Russian life which helped to prepare the way for the Great
Reforms of his son Alexander II and to a certain extent were even prerequisites to the latter. The first codification of Russian law since the *Ulozhenie*
of Alexis was carried out (1832 to take effect in 1835) under the direction of
Count Speransky, without which the legal reform of 1864 would have been
nearly impossible. The municipal statute of St Petersburg (1846) pointed in
the direction of the establishment of municipal dumas in 1870. New provincial
commissions (1833, 1834, 1851), in which local representatives sat side by
side with bureaucrats, may have paved the way for the establishment of zemstvos in 1864.[2] Unwilling as Nicholas was to undertake emancipation (at the
same time as he recognized the evil of serfdom), a number of measures,
notably the reforms affecting the state peasants (1838, 1855) carried out under
the leadership of Count P. D. Kiselev and the 'inventories' defining the
obligations of master and serf in the Western provinces during the very last
(and generally very un-reformist) years of the reign, played a not insignificant

role in preparing the way for the Emancipation of 1861. The aspect of Nicholas's reign that was reformist has not been sufficiently understood.

There was no contradiction, of course, between Nicholas's unswerving devotion to autocracy and his execution of reforms; the examples of Peter I and Catherine II, not to mention Alexander I, may suffice. But Nicholas, unlike Alexander, did not flirt with constitutionalism; it is true that he was willing to countenance Kiselev's 'organic statute' for the Rumanian principalities, accepted by the Sultan in 1834, but that was never intended as the precursor of any such action in Russia. In many ways his policy and his attitude toward his throne partook of the ideology of enlightened despotism of a half-century before. Like his Prussian relatives, he was happiest amid the rationalism of the barracks: in the army, he said, 'there is order...no contradiction, all things flow logically one from the other...'[3] Another motif in his thinking had been prominent in that of such men as Frederick II and Joseph II: it was the notion of duty and service. However, he gave it a Protestant sort of coloration which they did not. On one occasion he said: 'I consider the entire human life to be merely service, because everybody serves.'[4] On another, he pointed out that he was far from being able to do as he pleased, and gave the explanation:

Duty! Yes, this is no empty word for those who have become accustomed from youth to understand it as I have. This word has a *sacred meaning* which makes all personal considerations retreat, everything must keep silent in front of this one feeling, everything must step back, until one, together with this feeling, disappears into the grave. That is my key word. It is hard, I admit it, I suffer more from it than I can tell...[5]

The words could have been written by a Puritan divine or an evangelical missionary in Asia, but never by an Ivan III or an Alexis. The Protestant strain in his attitude has been noted by such German writers as Schiemann, who points out that the tsar habitually read the Bible in the evening, at a time when it was usual among neither Catholic nor Orthodox to do so.[6] His Prussian relatives were Lutheran, as were the Baltic Germans who were so important among the officials of his government, so that there were ample opportunities for him to perceive such attitudes, and it was natural to imitate them.

Altogether Nicholas was a ruler to whom dynastic ties were foremost, for whom the cosmopolitan royal and aristocratic milieu of eighteenth-century Europe remained a reality, for whom Russia was not a nation but an empire, and an empire of the European, particularly Germanic, variety. He was not a thinker or searcher (as his brother Alexander I had been) for a truth always proving elusive; he knew where he stood, and that was on the ground of the Petrine empire, the Westernized and especially Germanized state that had taken shape in the previous century, the state that led his German-born finance minister, Count Egor Kankrin, once to remark: 'If we consider the matter thoroughly, then, in justice, we must be called not *Russians*, but *Petrovians*.'[7]

Around Nicholas gathered a number of officials and publicists, ranging from those who were sincerely devoted to the monarch and regime to unattractive sycophants the genuineness of whose convictions is open to question, who jointly for the first time in Russian history attempted to put together some kind of positive doctrine favoring the *status quo* which at the same time might have pretensions to intellectual respectability. This doctrine was called 'official nationality' (*ofitsial'naia narodnost'*); the originator of the phrase was Count S. S. Uvarov. Uvarov, who had as a youth attracted the attention of Goethe and Napoleon, was a classical scholar of some ability and had been president of the Academy of Sciences since 1818. In 1833 he became minister of education, and in that capacity began to use the three-fold slogan of 'Orthodoxy, Autocracy, and Nationality' which he had already advanced some months earlier. The historian Sergei Soloviev aptly satirized the new ideology and its author:

He [Uvarov] instilled in him [Nicholas] the thought that he, Nicholas, was the creator of some new enlightenment, based on new principles, and he devised these principles, that is the words: Orthodoxy, autocracy and nationality; Orthodoxy – while he was an atheist not believing in Christ even in the Protestant manner, autocracy – while he was a liberal, nationality – although he had not read a single Russian book in his life and wrote constantly in French or in German.[8]

Uvarov, at any rate, was a Russian. The chief of the gendarmerie, General Count Alexander Benckendorff, was ethnically a German, but that did not stop him from rebuking 'official nationality's' most renowned critic, Peter Chaadaev, with the words, 'Russia's past is admirable; her present more than magnificent; as to her future, it is beyond the grasp of the most daring imagination...' The sardonic Florinsky comments: 'This statement of the Baltic-German nobleman was appropriately delivered in French.'[9]

Benckendorff made his chief contribution to the stability of the Nicolaitan regime through police work, not ideological precept. But the background of some of the chief journalists who echoed Uvarov's 'trinity' was comparable to his. Nicholas Grech was a Protestant like his grandfather, Johann Ernst Gretsch, a German who had come to serve in Russia at the time of Biron.[10] Faddei Bulgarin was a Pole who had actually fought against Russia in the Napoleonic invasion and other campaigns of the French Emperor before being pardoned by Alexander I, and a Roman Catholic. Osip Senkovsky ('Baron Brambeus') was also a Pole, of whom one writer says that 'he could not love Russia for he did not know it. He was perfectly cosmopolitan, with only a certain special attachment for the East [he occupied the chair of Oriental languages at the University of St Petersburg] which he liked because of its bright and original colors.'[11] In a word, the identity of the defenders of 'official nationality' rendered highly suspect its purported aim of defending

'Orthodoxy' and Russian 'nationality'. 'Autocracy' these men took more seriously, but to many of them it meant chiefly serfdom, and Nicholas I himself did not quite share their view. 'Autocracy' was given a conditional meaning; the tsar was to have unlimited power so long as he did not use it to abrogate the landlord's power over the serf. German aristocrats at home, it had been said, maintained a similar position: *Hoch der König absolut, | Wenn er unser Willen tut*. As Florinsky points out, serfdom was 'the real issue between the Crown and the nobility';[12] it would be more accurate to say, between the Crown and the conservative nobility or gentry. The tsar was, as already noted, no fervid emancipator, and yet he was clearly attempting to lay the foundations for curbing the evils of serfdom and ultimately doing away with it. His officials and subsidized journalists, among whom French-speaking Germans and Poles were so prominent, wanted no such thing.

There was, however, as Riasanovsky indicates, another wing of the propagators of 'official nationality', led by the historian Michael Pogodin and his collaborator Stefan Shevyrev. Riasanovsky distinguishes this nationalist, plebeian, and intellectual group, centering in Moscow, from the dynastic, aristocratic, and official group already discussed, centering in St Petersburg.[13] Adhering to the same formulas, what may be called the Pogodin wing of the school of 'official nationality' gave them a somewhat different content. The incongruous spectacle of Protestant Germans preaching Orthodoxy and of aristocrats instructing the autocrat in the meaning of Autocracy was not present in the work of Pogodin. In his writings on Russian history he attempted to make the nation's past meaningful to his contemporaries. His socially (though not politically) democratic views led him to frequent use of the aphorism *Vox populi vox Dei*; his real concern for the peasants impelled him to polemize with Uvarov on the question of serfdom and to welcome the Emancipation when it came. He supported autocracy partly as a past and possibly future agent of reform; despite his glorification of the Russian people, he once wrote that the peasants 'will not become human beings until they are forced into it'.[14] He, like Uvarov and the dynastic wing of 'official nationality', extolled Peter the Great (though not wholly uncritically) and the direction Peter had given Russian history. Pogodin went so far as to defend Peter's execution of Alexis, in a versified tragedy entitled *Peter I*; in this respect he found a kindred spirit in Nicholas I, who once threatened to emulate Peter's treatment of Alexis in respect of his own son Alexander.[15]

The ideologists of 'official nationality', whether they belonged to the 'dynastic' or 'nationalist' wing, had little use for the indigenous traditions of Russian culture. Pogodin had more than most of his fellows, and yet his primary allegiance was to the Petrine empire, to 'Petrovia' rather than to 'Russia'. 'Orthodoxy' was reduced by Pogodin to a naive and crude manual of religious or pseudo-religious aphorisms,[16] but even that was more than several of his fellows did with it; in their writings it appeared as little more than an injunction to go to church and behave oneself, offered in a spirit which partook of Protestantism. 'Autocracy' was insistence on obedience to the substantially Germanized regime of bureaucrats, with certain clear if unspoken reservations about the necessity of the tsar's keeping away from serfdom. 'Nationality' was the requirement of loyalty from all who lived in the Russian Empire, though the Pogodin wing of the school incorporated the beginnings of genuine nationalism.

As far as the 'dynastic' ideologists were concerned, one scarcely need speak of Western influence, for many of them were simply Westerners; as for the 'nationalist' group, they were familiar with the West and reflected substantial Western influences – in their whole allegiance to the Petrine orientation of Russia, in their effort to emulate Western political, literary, and other forms, in their mode of life; and in their stated views, adherence in many respects to current Western doctrines of nationalism.[17] Uvarov, who combines some features of both wings of the school, knew Maistre personally and corresponded at length with him; he read Chateaubriand; he was himself a classical scholar of the European type. He liked to lecture, as he himself reported, on 'the necessity of being a Russian in spirit before trying to become a European in education, the possibility of combining the unshakable loyalty of a subject with higher learning, with the enlightenment that belongs to all people and all centuries'.[18] To him, being a 'Russian' meant first and foremost loyalty and acceptance of the existing order, and to some of the other ideologists of 'official nationality' it meant that and nothing more. Loyalty to the existing order included support of the arrangements by which Nicholas and the governments of his German relatives and fellow monarchs tried to maintain the post-1815 European system without substantial change, and indeed 'official nationality' was in that respect quite as international and cosmopolitan as the bureaucracy of Nicholas I itself. It was a Russian variant of the Metternich international dynastic system, with overtones of the new nationalism which was already in the West being put to radical as well as conservative uses. As a purportedly indigenous phenomenon, it was largely sham.

Toward the end of Nicholas's reign, the revolutionary threat abroad led to a still greater emphasis on the dynastic theme and a condemnation of the nationalist one; after 1848 the Baltic Germans' position was strengthened still further in the Baltic regions and in the Empire as a whole. To the end, in the eyes of Nicholas, being a Russian, let alone a Slav, in the ethnic sense connoted no higher value. When he was urged to consider arousing Slav rebellion against the Turks on the eve of the Crimean War, he refused; the furthest he would go was to consider the idea of fostering a religious, anti-Muslim kind of uprising, and he abandoned that in the face of protests by his German foreign minister, Nesselrode. There were nationalists, or persons influenced by contemporary nationalist doctrines, in Russia during the reign of Nicholas I, but the regime was far from being a nationalist one; General Ermolov, who thought of begging Nicholas: 'Your Majesty, make me a German!' divined the character of the regime better than those historians who have interpreted the reign as one of indigenous reaction against all foreign influences. The ideas of 'official nationality' belong only partly to the realm of intellectual history, and for the rest to the realm of subsidized publicistics. In both realms, those ideas exemplified Russia's debt to the West.

'THE *LOVERS OF WISDOM*'

Outside of the ideologists of 'official nationality', it is possible to observe a development of Western-influenced Russian thought during the reign of Nicholas I along three main lines, all owing much to German philosophy and in particular to the idealist doctrines of Schelling and Hegel. They were (1) Slavophilism, (2) Westernism, and (3) the stirring of philosophy among the Orthodox clergy. Taken together, they signify an important step in Russian intellectual history, for all three developed outside official circles and to a large extent in a position of estrangement from officialdom and hostility to it. The estrangement was not complete: some of the ideologists of 'official nationality', such as Pogodin and Shevyrev, had certain views in common with the Slavophiles;[19] some of the Slavophiles, notably Samarin, lived to have a note-worthy part in the actual working out of the Great Reforms of Alexander II; and even Westerners, such as Herzen and Bakunin, had an impact, though mostly distant and indirect, on official policies. What was perhaps of greatest significance was that for the first time schools of thought developed apart from the monarch and officialdom, whereas our history up to this point has been almost exclusively concerned with thinkers who had connections with the rulers and their entourage, were influential mainly through those connec-tions, and when they became inacceptable to the government were silenced or punished by it.

Russian owes this service, if as such it be regarded, largely to the emergence of an educated gentry, which had itself for over half a century been free from total dependence on the state; the intellectual basis for the new phenomenon was, as already noted, German idealist philosophy.

The nucleus of young men from which the philosophical debates of the 1830's and 1840's developed was known as 'the Lovers of Wisdom' (*liubo-mudry*: a Russian translation of the Greek *philosophoi*).[20] A number of youths who had been members of a circle around the teacher and poet S. Raich which was devoted to the study of Schelling formed in 1823 a society for the study of German idealistic philosophy generally. The president of the Lovers of Wisdom was Prince V. F. Odoevsky, its secretary the young poet D. V. Venevitinov; its participants included the future Slavophiles A. I. Koshelev, the brothers Ivan and Peter Kireevsky, and F. S. Khomiakov, brother of the foremost Slavophile of all; the future ideologists of 'official nationality', Pogodin and Shevyrev; and others.

Schelling[21] had been discovered in Russia by such men as Professor D. M. Vellansky, who had been a student of Schelling's in Germany and propagated his ideas in the St Petersburg Medical–Surgical Academy; Professor A. I. Galich, of the University of St Petersburg; and such professors at the University of Moscow as N. I. Nadezhdin and M. G. Pavlov. All, as already noted, were former seminary students.[22] In the seminaries and elsewhere German had been increasingly studied in order to read Kant, Fichte, Schelling, and other contemporary philosophers.[23] When one of the young men of the 30's plunged into the reading of Kant, he found it difficult and declared that he had to find a seminarist to help him.[24]

In the 1820's, however, philosophy had begun to spread from the ecclesiastical schools into the secular schools, and the Lovers of Wisdom were mainly young men who had been students of Pavlov's and Nadezhdin's at the University of Moscow. They worked in the Archives of the College of Foreign Affairs, and thus were nicknamed 'the archive youth'. In 1824–5 they published an almanac called *Mnemosyne* (*Mnemozina*), mirroring the Schellingian views or at any rate enthusiasms that Pavlov had given them. Prince Odoevsky in his *Russian Nights* (*Russkiia nochi*) wrote: 'In the beginning of the nineteenth century Schelling was the same as Christopher Columbus in the fifteenth; he revealed to man an unknown part of his world, about which there existed only fabulistic traditions: his soul.'[25] What Schelling revealed about man's soul, in the view of his followers, was the identity of mind and nature in the Absolute, but the progressive self-revelation of the Absolute occurred only when the consciousness to be found in the human mind triumphs over the unconsciousness of nature and, passing beyond the understanding of nature, comes to understand itself. The locus of what is most important in this process is the ego. Thus Schellingianism, despite the complexities of its doctrines at any given moment and the permutations through which they went in time, may be perceived to have been an especially attractive instrument for the young gentry to pose the question, 'Who am I?' Or, collectively – and for all of Schelling's egocentrism the collective was never forgotten for a moment by him or his followers – 'What are we?'; in Moscow in in the 1820's, 'What is Russia?'

The Lovers of Wisdom disappeared as did the Decembrists, and at the same moment, for the circle was dissolved by its own members as a result of fears the revolt provoked.[26] Following the advice of the poet Pushkin, a distant relative (although Pushkin did not share most of the circle's enthusiasms), Venevitinov undertook to publish a monthly magazine, *Moscow Messenger*. Its purpose was to create 'a scientific aesthetic criticism on the basis of German speculative philosophy and to implant in the consciousness of society the conviction that it is necessary to apply philosophical principles (*nachala*) to the study of the sciences and arts of all periods'. Venevitinov died in March 1827, however, at the age of twenty-two. 'Born more for philosophy than for poetry', as Kireevsky wrote of him, Venevitinov might if he had lived have developed into a major figure of Russian intellectual history. But though the circle was short-lived and its most gifted member died in his youth, the Lovers of Wisdom pointed the way for the following decades much more than their infinitely more famous Decembrist brethren.

THE CIRCLES OF THE 1830'S

Sir Isaiah Berlin in his sparkling lectures called 'A Marvellous Decade' has suggested that the increase in study by Russians in German universities after the Napoleonic Wars led to a rapid diffusion eastward of the Romantic ideas current there; the Russian students 'rightly judged that if youth, barbarism, and lack of education were criteria of a glorious future, they had an even more powerful hope of it than the Germans'.[27] It was necessary to grasp the essence of the universe and act according to one's proper place in it. It was not sufficient to draw up constitutions, as the Decembrists did, or divulge 'secrets' to one another, like the Rosicrucians, and certainly not to confine oneself to the intellectual resources made available by the contemporary Orthodox Church. It was necessary to get to the root, to plunge into philosophy – which then meant to some extent Kant and Fichte, but above all Schelling, and a bit later Hegel.

The philosophy, however, was embraced in a largely religious spirit, with passion and faith; not entirely unlike the way in which the German youth of the time approached it, but with a kind of fervor and indeed fever which exceeded theirs, and without the burden of previous intellectual tempering which limited German flights of fancy or at any rate provided a surrounding tissue of skepticism toward the greatest philosophical excesses. Stankevich, writes Berlin, 'preached a secular, metaphysical religion which for him had taken the place of the doctrines of the Orthodox Church in which neither he nor his friends any longer believed'.[28] Berlin is not quite accurate in regard to Stankevich himself,[29] but the statement applies very well to the process observable from the 1830's on in Russia. Note that Berlin does not speak of the replacement of religion by atheism or materialism, but of Orthodoxy by 'secular, metaphysical religion'. (The atheism and materialism came later.)

Stankevich, born in 1813 in Voronezh province, attended a *pension* for young nobles from the age of twelve, and in 1830 entered Moscow University, living in the home of the Schellingian Professor M. G. Pavlov and attending Professor Nadezhdin's lectures. The circle that soon began to meet in Stankevich's apartment to discuss German idealist philosophy had a membership of now mostly forgotten young men, such as Stankevich's close friend Yanuary Neverov. When the latter departed for St Petersburg in 1833 there were new recruits, however, who became better known: Vissarion Belinsky, Konstantin Aksakov, and a bit later Michael Bakunin, Timofei Granovsky, and Michael Katkov. Stankevich was in Moscow only part of each year after he took his degree in 1834 and left for Berlin in 1837, but Bakunin and Belinsky held the circle together until they too departed, in 1839 and 1840 respectively. In its last stages the circle acquired one more notable-to-be: Ivan Turgenev.

The intensity of feelings which bound the members of the circle to each other as well as to their new philosophy and the extent to which it approached a religion in function is illustrated by Stankevich's tortured love life. Driven into an attachment to Bakunin's sister Liuba by his own romantic fancies, he was also by the same impulses driven out of it and into the circle's campaign to 'liberate Varvara', another sister of Bakunin, from her conventional marriage. Stankevich was finally joined by Varvara in Italy, just before he died of tuberculosis in 1840.

A similar series of infatuations affected the philosophical commitments of some members of the circle. The best example is Belinsky, who was converted to Schelling's views, then to Fichte's, then to Hegel's (or more accurately to extreme Right Hegelianism), and finally rejected Hegel in favor of a passion for Schiller, all within half a decade. Belinsky, exceptionally mercurial and unable to read foreign languages himself, depended on others, such as Nadezhdin (for his infatuation with Schelling) and Bakunin (for his Hegelian conversion),[30] as intermediaries for the ideas he thought he believed in. Both he and Bakunin owed much to Stankevich, but no individual dominated the 'Stankevich circle' – or the Westerner and Slavophile groups which partly grew out of it.[31] For the young men of the 1830's, ideas came before people – ideas which might be accepted with religious fervor, no matter for how brief a time, no matter how dimly understood, but ideas nonetheless.

Side by side with the circle of Stankevich there was another called the 'circle of Herzen'. Alexander Herzen was the illegitimate son of an old-style member of the gentry named Yakovlev by a German girl casually encountered in Kassel and taken home. Herzen was born shortly after their arrival in Moscow in 1812, and lived in a curious atmosphere compounded of paternal solicitude and nastiness, with almost no chance to get outside the house, until he was seventeen. He was raised in the Orthodox Church but went much oftener to Lutheran services with his mother. He had various tutors, perhaps most important a seminarist named Protopopov who helped to instill in him liberal views.[32] In literature his youthful tastes progressed from Rousseau to Schiller, under whose aegis occurred the formation of his lasting friendship with a cousin, N. P. Ogarev, whom he met at fifteen, and with whom he took the famous 'Hannibalic' oath on the Sparrow Hills to devote their lives to liberty for Russia, as the Decembrists had done – but the device of the oath was straight out of Schiller's *Don Carlos*, modeled on that of Carlos and Posa.[33]

In 1829 he enrolled in the University of Moscow, entering a totally new life in which he spent the next five years. He soon showed his capacities to lead by forming a circle which, unlike Stankevich's, boasted no names that would later win fame – except for Ogarev, whose renown was chiefly based on being Herzen's friend. Herzen had already learned something of Schelling. A cousin who had a bent for natural science tried to talk him out of his leanings toward *Naturphilosophie*, and persuaded him to enroll in the Faculty of Physics and Mathematics – where the professor was, unfortunately for the cousin, Pavlov, Russia's foremost Schellingian. The circle that Herzen put together has been thought to be 'almost exclusively political' as against the 'almost exclusively speculative' Stankevich circle, one of '*frondeurs* and Frenchmen' as contrasted with the latter, composed of 'sentimentalists and Germans' (in the words of Herzen himself, writing many years later in *My Past and Thoughts*). This is highly doubtful. All were Schellingians at this point, though Malia is willing to call Herzen a 'Left Schellingian',[34] in token of his greater eagerness to consider the practical and political implications of philosophy. Like his contemporaries, he was reading widely: he was impressed by Speransky's *Historical Study of the Code* (*Istoricheskoe izsliedovanie o Svodie*) in 1833;[35] in the same year he and Ogarev discovered the St Simonians (rather than St Simon himself) and their 'social Christianity'. Herzen, Ogarev, and others were arrested in 1834 on the vague suspicion that their ideas or actions were somehow connected with a series of fires in Moscow, and during five years of exile in Viatka and then Vladimir Herzen continued in a state of mind perhaps best described as Romantic in the contemporary European sense. Contemporary Western influences were reinforced by voices out of the Alexandrine past as he fell under the spell of A. L. Witberg, his friend and mentor at Viatka, a Freemason who had been a protégé of Labzin and an acquaintance of Novikov. Herzen wrote to him soon after leaving Viatka that the question of the day was to 'reconcile religion with life, revelation with thought'.[36] It was such an endeavor which precisely first attracted him to Hegel while he was in exile. For the members of both circles, that of Stankevich and that of Herzen, the ideas of German idealist philosophy, which came out of German Protestant Christianity, were the basis of their view of the world.

German idealism was acceptable, the Russian tradition was not. Around 1830 three or four separate articles sought to establish that point, perhaps not fully consciously, but definitely. In 1834 Belinsky, echoing an article of Nadezhdin's published in 1828, declared that Russia had 'no literature'.[37] In the article called 'The Nineteenth Century' which he published in his journal *The European* (*Evropeets*) in 1832, Ivan Kireevsky pointed to Russia's lack of classical (Greek and Roman) heritage as responsible for her lack of any philosophy worthy of the name, which the Eastern Church and its Fathers had been unable to provide.[38] Finally, in 1836 Nadezhdin published in his *Telescope* (*Teleskop*) Chaadaev's first *Philosophical Letter*, which declared Russia to be culturally nothing but a dead place (Necropolis). The trio was oddly assorted: Belinsky, who was to become an uncompromisingly non-religious Westerner; Kireevsky, to become a religious Slavophile; Chaadaev, religious, a Westerner, to become a member of neither camp. At that point, however, there was largely agreement on the direction Russia had to follow in the intellectual realm. *Ex occidente lux* – light was to come from the West *and nowhere else*. The dissenters were few, and to be found only among a small group of educated Orthodox clergymen, whose weight in Russian culture had diminished so sharply, in comparison to the new gentry intelligentsia, that generations of Western historians as well as Russians of all sorts have managed to ignore them almost entirely, along with the centuries of Russian cultural history during which the clergy had been dominant.

PUSHKIN AND CHAADAEV

It was Belinsky's misfortune that the year he chose to write his youthful pronouncement about Russia's lacking a literature saw the greatest of all Russia's poets at the height of his powers, just having published the last of his masterpiece *Eugene Onegin*: Alexander Pushkin (1799–1837). (Belinsky was later to correct his mistake by giving Pushkin a critical appraisal that did full justice to his genius.) Pushkin only marginally belongs to our story; his supreme gifts were those of an artist and not a thinker. Nevertheless his literary achievements constituted one of the decisive milestones in Russian culture, one that had important implications for Russian thought, and his views on culture and politics, such as they were, are illustrative of some of the basic tensions of his epoch.

Pushkin was the great-great-grandson of an Ethiopian, Abram Gannibal, bought or stolen from his captor the Ottoman sultan for Peter the Great. Pushkin himself, and others, were wont to attribute the sensuality of his private life to his black ancestry; a more interesting (and unanswerable) question is where he came by the flawless discipline he showed as a poet. Every step in his literary career, in Weidlé's words, 'was also a step in the formation of the Russian language, its prose and even more its verse'. Of his poetry, Weidlé writes that 'the delicate perfection of their verbal fabric – their rhythm, sonority, syntax and shades of meaning' almost defies translation.[39] His great debts to a series of modern European authors – Voltaire, Byron, Ariosto, Shakespeare, Scott, Goethe, and others – (despite the fact that he never got farther west than Kishinev) is obvious, and yet no critic would call Pushkin derivative. In his art he represents a kind of premature leap to a position few but him reached, in other branches of cultural life, till the end of the century: that of being simultaneously and fully European and Russian, not hesitating to borrow from abroad because he had no feeling that his cultural identity had anything to fear from doing so. An important qualification is needed: Pushkin did not quite manage to recapture the link with old Russian culture (which had to await the syncretists' halting, painful search beginning with the Slavophiles and culminating in the Silver Age); he transformed with his magic the *skazki* of his old nurse on the Mikhailovskoe estate near Pskov, but what the icons, the saints, the esthetics and ethics of the pre-Muscovite or even Muscovite Orthodox heritage might have meant eluded him. Of course it could not have been otherwise in his day. He tried to seek out his own roots (for example, in *The Moor of Peter the Great* [*Arap Petra Velikogo*], 1827), and though he knew that his paternal ancestors were nobles centuries before Peter, his search did not really get farther back than that monarch. In a fundamental sense he belonged to Petrine Russia, which he both embraced and rejected in the masterpiece of his maturity, *The Bronze Horseman* (*Mednyi Vsadnik*, 1833). Petrine Russia both produced him – his education, his life-style, his vision of the world and of his vocation – and killed him, for he died as the result of a duel that was the all too foreseeable outcome of the life of aristocratic meaninglessness he was forced to lead, not knowing how to lead any other.

Pushkin's views are of much less importance than his art. In summary, he became known as a radical of sorts already at the Tsarskoe Selo *lycée* (1811–17); he did not like Alexander I, but tried his best to like Nicholas I – who was in effect his personal probation officer from 1826 until his death; he was close to the Decembrists without being one. He had no political program or commitments; but he loved freedom and hated tyranny, as did many in the circles in which he moved. Count Benckendorff, the Javert to his Valjean, wrote on his death: 'Pushkin had a double personality: he was a great poet and a great liberal, the enemy of all authority.' Soviets tend to agree with the Tsarist policeman; but it is an overstatement. Pushkin was a great poet with a clear vision of the human spirit and what conditions it required to flourish, but he did his best to come to terms with authority. The fact that Nicholas and his toadies could never stop hounding him in the most picayune and philistine manner (or the view that it was in the nature of autocracy to act thus) ought not to be confused with the facts about Pushkin's attitude.

Not in the field of thought but personally, Pushkin provides an interesting link between the Lovers of Wisdom, who welcomed him to Moscow in 1826 (of whose Schellingian ideas only the conception of the poet interested him very much), and Chaadaev, a close personal friend from 1817, when Pushkin was eighteen and Chaadaev twenty-three. The publication of the latter's first *Philosophical Letter* (Pushkin had read it earlier) in 1836 led Pushkin to write, in a friendly and sympathetic note, that Chaadaev was right to indict society. but that 'the government is still the only European in Russia, and that as brutal and cynical as it is, it could have been a hundred times worse .[40] A few weeks later Pushkin was dead; he was a 'Petrovian' (to use Kankrin's expression) to the last. So was Chaadaev (though in a more limited way than Pushkin), for his position was that although Russia was a cultural desert, what little in it was positive derived from Peter. But what Pushkin and Chaadaev had in common was that both were Russian Europeans in personality and outlook, as they saw themselves and as they were perceived by others – Pushkin without ceasing to be a Russian (despite his inability to rediscover the fullness of the Russian tradition), Chaadaev boldly saying that to be a Russian was, culturally speaking, nothing at all.

Born about 1794 in Nizhny Novgorod province in a gentry family,[41] Chaadaev had tutors including an Englishman who taught him to speak English, a rare accomplishment among Russians; he was said to be the best dancer in the vicinity; after 1817 his social graces earned him repute as 'incomparably the most distinguished, remarkable, and brilliant young man in St. Petersburg'.[42] During the Napoleonic wars he had fought at Borodino and Leipzig, and later was sent to Alexander I at Troppau (Opava) as courier with news of the mutiny of the Semenovsky regiment (1820). In what remain puzzling circumstances Chaadaev soon thereafter requested retirement.[43] After staying abroad for five years, he returned to Moscow in 1826 and soon was back in the thick of society. The first *Philosophical Letter* was written in 1829 but only published in Nadezhdin's *Telescope* in 1836. Chaadaev wrote:

We have never marched alongside other peoples; we belong to none of the great families of the human race; we are neither of the West nor of the East, and we do not have the traditions of either one. Placed as it were outside of time, we have not been touched by the universal education of the human race.

Russia had stood aside from Western civilization, which had achieved heights unmatched by others; she had been alone in the world, and had given it nothing – not a single idea. What had reached Russia from foreign countries had made little impact. Peter I had attempted to give Russia civilization and Alexander I had marched Russians across Europe and back, and yet there had been no significant result. 'You will consequently find that a certain aplomb, a certain intellectual method, a certain logic, is lacking to all of us. The syllogism of the West is unknown to us.'[44] Chaadaev recognized that Russia had Christianity, but so had the Abyssinians; it had a culture, but so had the Japanese. Abyssinian Christianity and Japanese culture could not produce an order of things comparable to that of Western Europe.

Chaadaev's letter provoked a storm of controversy previously unparalleled in Russian history.[45] It is well known that the emperor had him declared mad for what he had said, perhaps less well known that as a result he had only to stay home for a few months and be visited by first a rather bibulous doctor, then, at Chaadaev's own demand that he be replaced, by another, for a total of about a month. The doctors never mentioned why they were supposed to be visiting him. During this period he wrote an ironically titled and unfinished essay, *Apology of a Madman* (*Apologie d'un fou*). Therein he enumerates among his 'exaggerations' in the first offending letter a failure to give its due to 'that Church [i.e., the Orthodox Church] so humble, sometimes so heroic, which alone consoles us for the emptiness of our annals, upon which falls the honor of each act of courage, each noble commitment of our forefathers, of every luminous page of our history...'[46] But he follows this with a word of dismissal of what he has just said, which suggests that he might, if pressed, say as much for Abyssinian Christianity. The allegation that Chaadaev recanted his views under tsarist pressure is therefore quite unfair.[47]

The shocking story of Nicholas I's judgment on Chaadaev has been allowed to obscure the fact that the reaction of Chaadaev's fellow intellectuals was almost wholly negative. Not a single person, writes Zhikharev, agreed with the letter entirely, and only a small minority was willing to concede that it had any positive aspects.[48] A whole series of luminaries were readying blasts against it when the tsar acted and made it psychologically impossible for intellectuals to consider publishing their attacks.

Attacks have since been made on Chaadaev, to be sure; what is lamentable is not that, but that he has been somewhat misconstrued as simply providing an apologia for the Roman Catholic faith. In fact he was not at all, as Florovsky points out, a *tserkovnik* (that is, a person who took the standpoint of the clergy or church of any variety).[49] A Soviet writer has correctly pointed out that Chaadaev was not so much attracted by Roman Catholic religion or philosophy as by something else: he calls the latter a 'definite political system' which exhibited an 'incompatibility, however mistakenly he assumed such to be the case, with a system "of the use of force by one part of the people on another" ', and above all what concerned him was 'the progress of enlightenment, reason, and morality'.[50]

Chaadaev states his religious views clearly in a letter of 1835 to Alexander Turgenev. If he had found a ready-made religion, he writes, he would have taken it; finding none, he was compelled to embrace 'the communion of the Fénelons, the Pascals, the Leibnizes and the Bacons. That being so, you are wrong to characterize me as a true Roman Catholic.'[51] Two Roman Catholics and two Protestants are mentioned. He speaks of intellectual method, logic, the syllogism; of England, whose revolution he cites, with justice, as an event in which the Christian religion figured strongly, and one to which the English owe their liberty and prosperity.[52] He finds favorable and unfavorable things to say about the Reformation, and reproaches the Protestants for one thing: their inability to perceive any Christianity in history from the second or third century to the Reformation, and therefore their partial responsibility for the failure of many Europeans – not only Protestants – to appreciate the full effect that Christianity in Europe had had on society and on modern civilization in general.[53] Chaadaev's message was in essence simple. It was: Western Europe has a high culture which Russia thus far does not share to any extent; that culture was developed on the basis of Roman Catholicism before the Reformation and since then the two branches into which it split; the way of Russia, if it was in the future to ascend to a comparable cultural level, could only be the way of assimilating the tradition of the West – not merely the latest fashionable Western ideas. The converse was equally important: the Russian tradition offers literally nothing on which to build a culture with a significant intellectual dimension, and though it has provided a few moments of moral uplift, has no intellectual content. Thus from the cultural standpoint Russia is a *tabula rasa*.

Chaadaev's emphasis on the whole tradition of the West in reality might have broadened the perspective of a Russian educated class that thus far had been nourished chiefly on German Protestant religion and philosophy. For people who had begun to take the Protestant background for granted (including its anti-Catholic elements), it was the Catholic component of the whole Western tradition to which Chaadaev uncompromisingly appealed which they found jarring and offensive. For people who were beginning to seek for Russia's cultural roots outside the West, his argument ran directly counter to their searchings. For people who were by now oriented to following the latest intellectual developments in the West, chiefly in Protestant German lands, Chaadaev's letter was especially annoying, because although it (in their view rightly) held that Russian culture was nothing, it suggested a much more far-reaching, difficult, and time-consuming path than they believed either necessary or desirable, and moreover seemed to sympathize with a Roman Catholic Church which after the Revolution had become identified in their minds with reaction, oppression, and indirectly with such regimes as that of Nicholas I.

Chaadaev's views had no influential adherents in 1836 or later, but one segment of them became the very touchstone of the intelligentsia's credo, whether they always recognized it or not: *ex occidente lux*. Isaiah Berlin writes, 'scarcely one single political and social idea to be found in Russia in the 19th century was born on native soil'.[54] What Chaadaev said was that no idea of any importance should or could be found in Russia; the Westernizing camp accepted the proposition completely, and others were influenced by it. Chaadaev spent the rest of his life in Moscow, a living example of the Westernization he advocated; Count Pozzo di Borgo said that if he could do so he would send Chaadaev to tour the West as an example of a Russian 'parfaitement comme il faut'. He died in 1856.

WESTERNERS AND SLAVOPHILES

When Herzen returned from Vladimir to the two capitals in 1839–40 he found in full swing the ferment in thought from which the Westerner–Slavophile controversy developed. The very phrase, 'Westerner–Slavophile controversy' may be somewhat misleading; it suggests two tidy circles gathered in the same place contesting the issues regularly over some definite period of time. The situation was not quite like that. The 'Westerner' camp was only irregularly represented in Moscow, where most Slavophiles were. Herzen went to St Petersburg in May 1840, was exiled again to Novgorod in November, was allowed to return to Moscow in 1842, and left Russia forever in January 1847. Vissarion Belinsky, born in 1811 in Sveaborg, the son of a ship's doctor and grandson of a village priest from Penza, spent from 1829 to 1832 as a student at Moscow University before being expelled, moved to St Petersburg in 1839, where he chiefly remained until his death in May 1848.[55] Michael Bakunin, born on his gentry family estate at Premukhino in Tver province in 1814, became an ensign in the artillery, resigned the service in 1835, and went to Moscow; by 1840 he had left Russia, to return only as a prisoner extradited from Saxony by way of Austria and then an exile (1851–61) before escaping from the country forever across the Pacific.[56] These were the three chief figures of the Westerner camp; the others were either weaker in personality or intellect, such as Nicholas Ogarev, or moved into the universities and became professors rather than ideologists, such as Timofei Granovsky.

There were, of course, differences among them, but they recognized their ideological ties with one another even when personal differences and quarrels separated them for a time. Those ties can be summarized as belief that Russia ought to take a radically new cultural path, whose outlines could be delineated only on the basis of Western thought; that Peter the Great had begun the task of setting Russia on such a path, but that his successors had stopped halfway with establishing what Bakunin called 'l'empire knouto-germanique'; that Russia's and indeed Europe's Christian tradition must be replaced by a new set of ideas deriving from the most advanced thought of the day in the West, which was recognized as being first German idealist philosophy and then French and German social radicalism, so that the path led from Hegel (for Belinsky and Bakunin, the most uncompromising Right Hegelianism, justifying all aspects of contemporary 'reality' and thus politically conservative, in 1838–9) to Proudhon (for Herzen and Bakunin) – not, it is interesting to note, to Marx.

Belinsky was by profession a literary critic, and his sensitivity to esthetic quality went beyond the bounds of the doctrine he was passionately embracing at the moment. He was notorious for his series of intellectual infatuations: he went from Schelling (1834) to Fichte (1836) to Hegel (interpreted as a defender of what exists, 1838–9), to the French radicals (St Simon, Cabet, Fourier, Louis Blanc, and George Sand, 1841). Unfortunately his confession of 1834 retained a good deal of truth: 'I have a love for truth and a desire for the general good but perhaps no basic knowledge.' His great service to his country and the world was that he could claim to have discovered for the benefit of the Russian reading public Gogol, Lermontov, Turgenev, Goncharov, and Dostoevsky, and to have become the 'chief interpreter of Pushkin'.[57] His great disservice was to leave behind him as widely accepted the demand that literature 'should have a moral effect upon society. If it achieves that goal even entirely without poetry and artistry, for me it is *none the less* interesting... the important thing with me is the substance and not the decoration. Let a story be ever so artistic, if it has nothing to say...*je m'en fous*.'[58] That is to say, art was of value only in so far as it served ends outside of art – morality, which in turn was interpreted as politics and specifically the politics of revolution. Such was by no means all or most of what Belinsky actually said in his critical essays or the basis for what he did in his criticism; but it was the explicit message of his letter to Botkin, and it was what he was taken to mean by most of those who followed him, even if they had not read that letter.

Bakunin, after he broke with his father and refused further government service, decided in Moscow in 1836 to study philosophy and teach mathematics. He was responsible for at least a couple of Belinsky's successive 'conversions' – to Fichte and to Hegel, but that was not any indication of mastery of those authors or of any real command of the philosophy he had set out to study. His psychological instability was too great for him to settle long on any course of study. At the time he was leaving Russia for Germany, in 1840, he was moving from a Right Hegelian to a Left Hegelian position. By the time he wrote 'Reaction in Germany' for Arnold Ruge's *Deutsche Jahrbücher* in 1842, he was committed to revolution. This article ended with the famous sentence, 'The passion for destruction is also a creative passion!', which foreshadowed his later anarchism, though it should be noted that what was to do the destroying, in that passage, was not any revolutionaries but 'the eternal spirit'.

Thereafter Bakunin rapidly came to belong not to any discernible arena of Russian thought, but rather to the European democratic and revolutionary milieu, in which Russia usually received only marginal attention. In 1848 he decided that the bourgeoisie was not a reliable base for revolution and that the lower classes would be crucial; moreover, that the Slavic peoples of the Habsburg monarchy would and ought to seek their independence – for this he was denounced by Marx and Engels. But he did not commit himself to wipe out monarchy; on the contrary, he suggested at various times that Nicholas I, his second cousin General Nicholas Muraviev (Governor-General of Eastern Siberia when he was in exile there), and Alexander II assume the role of ruler of some future pan-Slavic federation. He became an atheist, but only in 1864. In 1866 he developed a largely anarchist vision in his *Revolutionary Catechism*, but still did not entirely reject the national framework. The fact is that his doctrines, in his own day, were less important to others and perhaps even to himself than his incessant and feverish attempts at organization, which led to such a proliferation of interlocking secret groupings that it is difficult even now to tell which, if any, had an existence outside his mind. Some Italian and Spanish anarchists, and a few Russian ones, remembered him after his death in 1876, but his impact depended too much on his personality to produce a continuous Bakunist tradition thereafter.

Herzen, unlike Bakunin, was primarily a thinker, and the changes in his thought are therefore easier to trace. Before 1842, when he was allowed to settle again in Moscow, what mattered most to him was the dignity of the individual. His chief complaint against the autocracy and bureaucracy, as he saw it operate in Viatka and Vladimir and St Petersburg and Novgorod, was its systematic violation of that dignity. At about the same time as Bakunin, he rejected Right Hegelian recognition of reality for Left Hegelian criticism of it, thought he had never indulged in the excesses of Right Hegelian 'acceptance' of what exists that Belinsky and Bakunin had had to be ashamed of. His essay *Dilettantism in Science* (1843) attacked, under the rubric 'dilettante', Slavophiles, ivory-tower Germans, and 'Buddhists' of learning (Right Hegelians), and upheld 'the philosophy of the deed'. In his diary he approvingly quoted the *Deutsche Jahrbücher*'s dichotomy: either Christianity and monarchy or science and republicanism.[59] He had become an atheist, though he remained an Hegelian, an idealist, and a liberal.

This was the period when identifiable 'Westerners' and 'Slavophiles' confronted one another regularly in Moscow, in the press and in the salon. The former used *Annals of the Fatherland* (*Otechestvennye Zapiski*), a journal of St Petersburg whose publisher sought profit rather than radical change and published radical essays because they sold and helped raise circulation to the unprecedented level of 4,000. The latter used *The Muscovite* (*Moskvitianin*) which was run by Pogodin and Shevyrev rather than real Slavophiles but gave them some literary refuge. They had much in common: the privileges and education of the gentry, knowledge of foreign languages, acquaintanceship with German philosophy and especially Schelling and Hegel, a passionate concern for the future of Russia, a deep dissatisfaction with its present, a conviction that right ideas had to precede right action. The Westerners tended to laud Peter the Great, as did the ideologists of 'official nationality', but rejected the monarchy of his heirs, as did the Slavophiles; like the Slavophiles, they emphasized the advantages of Russia's 'youthfulness'; unlike the Slavophiles, they built their vision of the future on the ground of contemporary Western thinkers, either atheist or secular in orientation.

Their common bonds broke down, however, in 1844. While the Slavophiles differed from one another in emphasis, the Westerners had more radical disagreements. If Belinsky had lived and Bakunin had stayed in Russia longer, the split in their ranks might appear one between a sizeable Left and a sizeable Right; as it was, it was mainly Herzen who split from the rest. He fell out with Granovsky in 1846 over the issues of atheism and socialism, while Granovsky supported God and the July Monarchy. In 1847 Herzen left Russia for good, alienated intellectually as well as by distance from his former fellow Westerners for life.

Herzen thought of the position which he reached in the early 1840's, clearly by 1843–4, as socialist; it would be more accurate to call it anarchist. The French radical writers, attachment to which he projected backward to the 1830's in his later memory, came to determine his intellectual course once he had set himself on the Left Hegelian path. He drew on Fourier and Louis Blanc, but above all on Proudhon, whom, as Malia puts it, he interpreted as a 'fellow revolutionary Hegelian', whose 'terrible strength' lay in negation, annihilation of the social structure, and not in his economic ideas.[60] What attracted Herzen was Proudhon's willingness to shatter all institutions, leaving the individual unfettered by them, bound to other individuals only by 'mutualism'. On the basis of Fourier's and Proudhon's ideal visions of a harmonious village, he constructed his own notion of the Russian commune.

Herzen disliked France, despite his fondness for French radicals; it was in Italy, which lacked any centralized institutions, that he found himself at home, and it was, Malia suggests, the Italian peasant which in fact gave him most of

his image of the Russian peasant.[61] But the events of 1848 did much to dis-
illusion him in Europe, in which he found the burden of 'feudalism' to be too
heavy to make revolutionary change easy. Russia, he finally decided in his
writings of 1849-56, had no such burden; it was free from the dead weight of
the past; the state and the institution of property were alien transplantations
from outside; 'young' Russia could surpass 'old' Europe by building a Proud-
honist commune out of the single Russian institution in which he acknowledged hope for the future. And yet he had to start somewhere; and he started
with the Westernized Russian gentry like himself, idealizing them from afar
as he did the Russian peasantry, hoping that they would serve as the agent for
Russia's transformation: that was the burden of his article addressed to the
Russian gentry called 'St. George's Day', written in 1853. Even the autocracy
might, as Bakunin and even Belinsky had at least occasionally thought, help.
But the goal remained a social setting in which the individual might enjoy
true freedom and dignity, in voluntary association with his fellows. There was
in the future to be no authority at all.[62]

Many have suggested that Herzen and even Bakunin converged to some
degree with their purported Slavophile antagonists in respect of their political
views and aims, and the suggestion deserves investigation.

There were six leading Slavophiles:[63] Alexei Khomiakov (born in 1804),
Ivan and Peter Kireevsky (born 1806 and 1808), Konstantin and Ivan
Aksakov (born 1817 and 1823), and Yury Samarin (born 1819). They were all
of gentry origin and had been born in or lived in Moscow, but all had studied
or traveled in the West and knew several West European languages. Ivan
Kireevsky, for example, knew both Schelling and Hegel personally and had
also heard Schleiermacher and Oken lecture in Germany. The dominant
mind was Khomiakov's. Ivan Aksakov was at first closer to the Westerners
than the Slavophiles, Konstantin Aksakov went through a period of enthusiastic Hegelianism, Yury Samarin had the idea that Hegelianism was the only
proper philosophy to support the Orthodox faith; all three yielded in somewhat different ways to the influence of Khomiakov. Samarin's intellectual
crisis of 1843-4 is illustrative. He came to regard his guiding idea as a problem
to be resolved, wavered between Hegelianism and Orthodoxy, and finally
followed Khomiakov to Orthodoxy.

It was Khomiakov who stated Slavophile views most authoritatively. In his
History he traced the operation of two 'principles' in humanity's past, the
'Iranian' principle of freedom and the 'Kushite' principle of necessity. They
were not, however, mutually exclusive. Kushitism had penetrated Iranianism,
in the shape of formalism, legalism, and other ways that hampered free
creativity and life. Such influences through the Kushite Roman state had
entered into the Roman Catholic Church and been transmitted to Protestantism as well. In his own day, Khomiakov wrote, the 'religion of necessity,
material or logical' as most clearly embodied in the 'newest philosophical
schools of Germany' stood opposed to the 'religion of moral freedom' as best

realized in the Orthodox Church. However, Orthodox Russia was by no means free from the taint of Kushitism, introduced from the West especially by Peter the Great. Konstantin Aksakov was the most extreme in praising pre-Petrine Russia, but even he had to acknowledge the historical justifiability of much at least that Peter had done.

What Peter had introduced into Russia that was pernicious, however, was bureaucracy, and he had given a cast to Russian society in which such alien notions as property rights and legalism in general had gained a hold. Samarin especially developed a critique of the state and emphasized the family and above all the village commune as the sound institutions for a rebuilding of Russia.

Riasanovsky has stressed the Romantic spirit and approach in Slavophilism. Hegel's one-sided rationalism needed to be broadened and extended, the Slavophiles believed; Schelling had made the same criticism of Hegel, Hegel of Fichte, Fichte of Kant.[64] The Romantics juxtaposed the good age of Romanticism to the bad Enlightenment; the Slavophiles, facing the passing of Romanticism in the West, transmuted this into regional form: the bad Roman Catholic and Protestant West, the good Orthodox East. They began with the Western Romantics, as Riasanovsky would put it, or (perhaps better) with the German idealist philosophers, and ended with patristics. Koshelev noted that when Ivan Kireevsky made this transition, 'it was annoying to him to recognize that actually there was much in the Holy Fathers that he had been delighted to find in Schelling'.[65] Jacobi, Baader, Möhler, and others among the Germans, and Pascal among the French had an impact on various aspects of Slavophile thought.[66] The fundamental notion of two opposing principles which underlay all Slavophilism probably came from Schlegel's *Philosophy of History*. Riasanovsky declares that Slavophile social, political, and historical views were purely Romantic, and that patristic literature had no appreciable influence on them.

The Slavophiles, writes Florovsky, tried, necessarily in vain, to synthesize the Church and Romanticism.[67] The secular notion of 'society' (*obshchestvennost'*) and the sacred notion of the 'church' (*tserkovnost'*) were, he argues, despite all their similarity not commensurable. In the social teachings of the Slavophiles, the Church was replaced by the commune. Slavophile traditionalism, in Florovsky's view, unexpectedly developed into social radicalism, as the theocratic school and Utopian socialism in France showed kinship. Riasanovsky calls the Slavophiles a 'sort of anarchists'; they were hostile to the state, but saw no way of doing away with it and thus wished to limit it and to keep it as far away as possible from the people – which had been the historical service of St Petersburg, leaving Moscow free to develop Russia's organic national life.

The convergence of the Slavophile and the Westerner programs for Russia was quite striking. For both, the discovery of the commune provided a useful Russian peg on which to hang their Western-derived doctrines; they criticized the state, and set forth the ideal of a future social harmony based on moral imperatives derived from Christian or secularized-from-Christian teachings, whose fundamental unit would be the commune and not the state or any agencies dependent on the state. Such a vision, the Westerners believed, was supported by the best contemporary thought of the West, which had only radical criticism to provide of the existing Western social order; the Slavophiles tried to believe that it represented the wisdom of the Fathers of the Eastern Church, but also knew that it owed much to German idealist philosophy, which they acknowledged as the highest achievement of the human mind to date.

In general, the Westerners thought that leaving behind the state meant, in Hegel's words, a leap from the realm of necessity to the realm of freedom, a natural and culminating stage in human progress from the days of the Oriental despotism when one man was free to the classical era when some were free to the Germanic (the Westerners thought in terms of Europe, and sometimes of Russia as the leader on the way for the whole continent) era-in-becoming when all would be free. The Slavophiles thought it meant rejecting the Germanic and generally West European heritage of legalism, stifling formalism, bureaucratism, and restoring the pristine Orthodox or at any rate Russian virtues, giving the natural feeling of the Orthodox Russian collective (*sobornost'*) full scope, Russia leading the way to the redemption of Europe and mankind.

Of course it was not that simple. Belinsky, Bakunin, and Herzen had moments when they thought not only of reconciliation with the state but also of the tsars' leading the way to their utopian objectives. Samarin, whose own influence on the significant role given the commune in Emancipation was great, welcomed not only the act of 1861 but also the judicial reform (1864) of Alexander II and other such measures. The few remaining Slavophiles in 1905 became 'constitutionalists by imperial decree' in accepting the October manifesto. The state was too powerful in Europe, but especially Russia, to ignore consistently. Nevertheless the Westerners and Slavophiles joined in wishing to end the state, at least to transform it, and in many ways the progress of both was basically to be seen as one from Hegel to Proudhon, from German idealism to French anarchism.

The Slavophiles tried to go beyond Western thinkers and to recapture the badly battered Russian national tradition – in a conscious effort of will begotten by reading Schelling and the German idealists generally. Khomiakov died in 1860, having drawn up a detailed plan for emancipation of the serfs the year before; both Kireevskys died in 1856, Konstantin Aksakov in 1860. Ivan Aksakov lived to become the chief spokesman of a doctrine of another generation, Pan-Slavism, before dying in 1886; Samarin lived to 1876, but his last years were disturbed by illness. By the time Nicholas I died the Westerner–Slavophile controversy was mostly past and new issues and alignments came to dominate the intellectual scene. Herzen outlived many of his contemporaries, and passed harsh judgment on the young radicals of the 1860's: 'They are our fault. We begat them, by our idle talk in the forties.' His prophecies were dire: 'Who will finish us off? The senile barbarism of the sceptre or the wild barbarism of communism; the bloody sabre, or the red flag?...Communism will sweep across the world in a violent tempest – dreadful, bloody, unjust, swift.' Despite his seeming willingness to stake all on revolution, and to embrace a beautiful vision of the distant future, he never forgot his devotion to the dignity of the individual, and refused to sacrifice the real present to a hypothetical goal: 'The end of each generation must be itself.' Herzen, along with other Westerners, the Slavophiles, and many other men, was better than his doctrines, or at any rate than the unadorned logical conclusions of any of the various doctrines he professed.

THE PETRASHEVTSY AND THE BROTHERHOOD OF CYRIL AND METHODIUS

Herzen and Bakunin suffered imprisonment and exile in Nicholas I's Russia; the Slavophiles many times suffered the prohibition of their publications and penalties against individuals concerned with them. Not since the Decembrists, however, had a group been punished for their ideas until the affairs of the Petrashevtsy and the Brotherhood of Cyril and Methodius.[68]

The Petrashevtsy were the first socialist circle in Russia. Its guiding spirit was Mikhail Vasil'evich Butashevich-Petrashevsky. His father was a seminarist in Poltava who transferred to a medical academy and became a doctor, who was summoned to attend the dying Count Miloradovich on the Senate Square in St Petersburg in the Decembrist rising of 1825.[69] His son Mikhail was born in 1821, attended the Tsarskoe Selo *lycée*, and was reputed as a student there already to be a 'freethinker'. He finished with phenomenally low marks in 1839, and the next year entered service in the Foreign Ministry. There he was able to attend lectures in the school of law of St Petersburg University, and Professor V. S. Poroshin influenced him as well as several other later members of his circle in the direction of socialism and particularly Fourierism;[70] they studied the works of Fourier, Proudhon, Louis Blanc, Lorenz Stein, and Haxthausen. In 1844 he tried to become a teacher in his old *lycée*, which had just moved to the capital; he failed, but he became friends with a number of the students, notably A. M. Unkovsky, later a leading zemstvo liberal, N. A. Speshnev, M. E. Saltykov (Shchedrin), the novelist, and N. Ya. Danilevsky, the Pan-Slav ideologist and philosopher of history.[71] The *lycée* (along with St Petersburg University) was the progenitor of the Petrashevtsy in much the same way as Moscow University was of the Westerners.

In 1844 or 1845 at a series of 'Fridays' at Petrashevsky's the young radicals began to gather regularly. To Saltykov, Speshnev, and Danilevsky were added young Fedor Dostoevsky, the poet A. N. Pleshcheev, the writer Apollon Maikov, and others. In 1848 Danilevsky was asked to give a full exposition of

Fourierism and did so. Petrashevsky took his Fourier seriously: he constructed a communal building for the serfs on his rather unprofitable estate near the capital as an approximation to a phalanstery of the kind Fourier advocated; it was burned, probably by the serfs for whom it had been built. By way of Haxthausen he, like other members of the circle, decided that the Russian village commune (*obshchina*) was the vehicle through which socialism could come to Russia,[72] thus recapitulating an ideological journey of Herzen's about which he probably knew nothing.

The Petrashevtsy were not necessarily all of one view. Speshnev, later celebrated as the model for Dostoevsky's character Stavrogin in *The Possessed* (literally, *The Demons – Besy*), was exceptional in several ways. He was wealthy, whereas most of the rest were on the edge of poverty; he had had experience with the West European radical movement, from 1839 to 1847; he called himself a communist on the model of the Babouvists of the past and the followers of Marx and Engels in the present, and he was certainly a revolutionary. 'Socialism', he declared, using the term in a broad sense, 'is not a new form of political economy but a new form of politics'[73] – and so it was for him. He wanted disciplined political action and a dictatorship, hoping to make a revolution that would be spearheaded by peasant revolts of the Pugachev kind. The circle was apprehended in April 1849, a few days after they had held a banquet honoring Fourier's memory. Fifteen were sentenced to death and reprieved only at the very last moment; Dostoevsky was one of those who suffered this barbaric kind of treatment. With a number of others he was sent to Siberia. Petrashevsky died in Yeniseisk in 1866; the circle was dispersed, and socialism in Russia disappeared for several more years.

If the Decembrist societies had a non-Russian Slavic analogue in the Society of United Slavs, the Petrashevtsy had one in the Brotherhood of Cyril and Methodius. The Brotherhood developed from a group organized by Nikolai Ivanovich Kostomarov, son of a Russian landlord and an Ukrainian peasant woman.[74] Born in Voronezh province in 1817, he studied in Moscow University and then transferred to Kharkov where he wrote a dissertation on the Unia, published in 1842. It was, however, rejected; Kostomarov was permitted to write another, on folk poetry, and he received his master's degree. After teaching in Rovno for a time, he became professor of history at Kiev University in 1846. The Brotherhood, which existed from January 1846 to March 1847, subscribed to a programmatic statement called *Zakon bozhii* (literally, 'God's law', a term used to refer to the Christian religion as a school subject), probably written by Kostomarov himself. It drew heavily on Mickiewicz's *Book of the Polish People and Its Pilgrimage* (Paris, 1832), which helped to inspire Lamennais's Christian social ideas of the period as expressed in *Paroles d'un croyant* (1834). The role of earthly Messiah that would bring justice to mankind was assigned by Mickiewicz to the Poles, by Kostomarov to the Ukrainians.[75] A free federation of Slavic peoples was envisaged in which Russia would be divided into several substates and Belorussia, Poland,

Czecho-Moravia, Serbia, and Bulgaria would also be members: Ukrainian Kiev would belong to no state but would be the federal capital. Emancipation of the serfs and a generally equalitarian and democratic social order were advocated. For such hopes Kostomarov was arrested in March 1847, along with other members of the group. After a brief time in jail and some years in exile in Saratov, he was allowed to return to the capital and in 1859 was chosen to succeed, as professor of history in St Petersburg University, Ustrialov, the man who had recommended rejection of his master's thesis. He was before long in trouble again, resigned in 1862, and devoted himself to writing thereafter. The Brotherhood, like the Petrashevtsy, had a few more impatient spirits than the mild leader, notably Taras Shevchenko (1812–61), who had been born a serf, studied art in St Petersburg, and became the foremost Ukrainian poet. For his advocacy of revolution he spent ten years as an army private unable to write or paint, being freed in 1858 through the efforts of powerful friends from his St Petersburg days.

THE REVIVAL OF ORTHODOX THEOLOGY

The reign of Nicholas I was a turning point in Russian intellectual history. The appearance of the first consistent Westerner (Chaadaev) in the sense of one who wished to reject the Russian tradition entirely was followed by that of others who, along with some Westerners, rejected religion entirely, and thus Herzen, Bakunin, and Belinsky may be deemed the first Russian writers who were atheists. The Slavophiles and the moderate Westerners retained their faith, and the Slavophiles tried to work out a syncretist position combining German philosophical method and Orthodox Christian belief. But philosophy now assumed the foreground; if in Alexander's reign came Russia's 'awakening of the heart', in Nicholas's came – not necessarily the awakening of the mind, but a swift spread of the conviction that human reason provided the only sound basis for a better future,[76] and specifically that philosophy provided not merely the best and most fundamental guide to man's affairs but the way to salvation.

Those who did not fit into this massive shift had an uneasy time of it. The most striking example was the unhappy Nicholas Gogol (1809–52), like Pushkin (whom he knew from 1831 though they were not intimates) a great artist first and foremost. Unlike Pushkin, however, he had a deeply troubled personality which made human relations often agonizing and unsatisfying for him; and a religious crisis of 1842–3 threw him into a compulsion to ideologize from which Pushkin never suffered. In *Selected Passages from Correspondence with Friends* (*Vybrannye mesta iz perepiski s druz'iami*, 1847), he called down on his own head attacks from all sides, including perhaps the most celebrated single polemic in the history of Russian literature, Belinsky's *Letter to Gogol*. Belinsky, who had recognized the greatness of his art, now charged him with being a 'preacher of the knout, apostle of ignorance, defender of obscurantism and darkest oppression' for opportunist reasons. Aside from the charge of opportunism, which was simply wrong, what Belinsky said was in a way true, but, much more important, it was beside the point.[77] In the ideas of the *Correspondence* Gogol showed some influence of Catholics he had met or read, such as Mickiewicz and Lamennais, who like him espoused a social Christianity. But his specific message was that Russia and the world must be transformed by each person's acting in the spirit of the true Christian faith; it was the moralist call to self-perfection that had sounded so often in Alexander I's reign. Gogol in his last years had become an epigon of Protestant pietism.[78] However, the atmosphere had changed so much that few understood him, let alone agreed with him. The *Correspondence* was intended as an aid (the immodesty of which Gogol seems not to have recognized) to others' self-perfection (indeed that of all Russians) and testimony to his own efforts in that direction, as a clearing of the decks so that he could turn from the *Inferno* that was Part I of *Dead Souls* (*Mertvye dushi*) to the *Purgatorio* that Part II was to be. But, as Erlich writes, 'to Christianize serfdom was as hopeless a project as to redeem Chichikov'. The unfortunate man made two attempts at Part II, and burned both of them. He decided he was going to die, ceased to eat, weakened, and died. His genius was recognized, but ever since he has suffered the posthumous distortions of commentators who (deciding to overlook the *Correspondence*) acclaimed him as a realist and social critic.[79] Some of those critics might not have been sure what 'pietism' was. However, pietism did not furnish the content or even the motive (whatever the author said in the *Correspondence*) of Gogol's art, which was no more ideological than Pushkin's.

As the German scholastic tradition in the Russian schools begat idealist philosophy, as German–English pietism led to Freemasonry, and as both led further into socialism and anarchism, the role of the Russian clergy, so crucial in the history of Russian thought thus far, became problematical. Clergymen might and did teach philosophy in universities, but their more advanced students were beginning to forsake philosophy for politics. The second quarter of the nineteenth century saw, along with these better-known phenomena, Russian theology strive to establish itself as an area of thought capable of self-direction, dependent neither on the institutional needs of the regime nor the political imperatives of the radical youth. The conflicting tendencies of the previous eras remained at work. The pietist aim was put at the very foundation of the ecclesiastical schools as reorganized by the ukaz of 30 August 1814: 'The inner education of youth in the direction of real Christianity will be the sole aim of these schools.'[80] But the scholastic tendency persisted as before.

What was happening to bring about the emergence of a Russian theology can be seen in the career of Filaret, metropolitan of Moscow (born V. M. Drozdov; 1782–1867, often referred to as 'Filaret Moskovskii' to distinguish him from other clerics of the same name).[81] He was graduated from the seminary of the Monastery of the Trinity and St Sergius, in which both scholastic and pietist tendencies were present, but at any rate Protestant influences prevailed. Filaret was summoned to St Petersburg as a young monk in 1809 and in 1812 became rector of the Academy there. He produced a number of textbooks on the lines of Buddeus; they were his first writings (1816), but reflected less his own leanings than the need to provide students with manuals. In these years he read such Western mystics as Jung-Stilling and Eckhartshausen, and there remained with him traces of such interests. However, writes Florovsky, his sense of history separated him 'both from epigonous scholastics, with their logical pedantry, and from the mystics to whom the Bible too often was reduced to a parable or symbol...'[82] He was replaced as rector in 1819 to become archbishop of Tver, then Yaroslavl (1820), and finally Moscow (1821; he was made metropolitan in 1826).[83] He was forty-six years in the see of Moscow, living to welcome the Great Reforms and himself to write the proclamation of Emancipation in 1861. Filaret represents the best of which the Russian Orthodox clergy was capable under the Petrine Establishment. Amidst the confused and contradictory intellectual currents which combined to make the ecclesiastical schools of the first half of the nineteenth century, Filaret succumbed to none of them exclusively. He was a respected and effective pastor in his see; he was a scholar a list of whose works fills many pages, Academician in the Imperial Academy of Sciences and moving spirit in several learned societies; he was, writes Florovsky, 'the first in modern times for whom theology again became a task of life, the necessary threshold of ecclesiastical deeds and actions'.[84]

As the Russian clergy began to recover some of their intellectual equanimity, even the language changed: Latin gradually passed out of use in the seminaries, and by the 1840's instruction was mainly in Russian. Learned or semi-learned journals in Russian appeared in the field of theology, beginning with *Christian Reading* (*Kristianskoe chtenie*), founded in 1821 by Filaret's successor as rector of the St Petersburg Academy, Grigory Postnikov. Distinguished scholars worked at the task of 'archeography' (that is, searching out and collecting manuscripts and documents of early history), such as Evgeny (born Evfimy Bolkhovitinov, 1767–1837), who was metropolitan of Kiev from 1822.

The way was far from easy and straight, especially as regards relations with the state. The Procurator of the Synod from 1833 to 1836, S. D. Nechaev, was a Mason who was suspicious of the clergy as a class, often ignored the clerical members of the Synod, and used much police supervision. He was replaced by Count N. A. Protasov (held office 1836–55), who had been reared by a Jesuit tutor and surrounded by men from the Polotsk Uniat college, and evidently carried from his early years a taste for 'bureaucratic Latinism'. He wished to renounce the intention of giving clerical education a broad base in general culture that underlay the reform of 1814 and return to the straight state-service conceptions of the eighteenth century. Filaret opposed him with some effect; though Protasov found compliant clergymen willing to follow his lead in his 'wager on simplicity (*stavka na oproshchenie*)', to use the phrase of Florovsky,[85] the ecclesiastical schools continued to grow.

Florovsky concludes that the great merit of these schools was their creative love of learning, their weakness a 'careless maximalism' that was a heritage of their past[86] – in which the pietist search for perfection had played so large a part. Until the 1840's it was the ecclesiastical schools and not the universities that were the strongest institutions, which partly accounts for the fact that the so-called mixed-rank intelligentsia (*raznochintsy*; that is to say, from classes other than the gentry) of the 1860's and later so often had been seminarians. The seminaries made their great contribution to Russian culture as a whole before the middle of the nineteenth century. As the abyss between Christians and atheists in the Russian intelligentsia became deeper, these schools kept the Russian Orthodox Christian tradition alive.

CONCLUSION

The reign of Nicholas I was an extremely vital one in Russian cultural history. The secular universities assumed a crucial role; just at the moment when the Russian Orthodox intellectual milieu gave signs of recovering its equilibrium after the battering given it by Peter I and his followers, the advanced youth abandoned it. They did so not merely or mainly because of what the situation was in Russia, but in imitation of the contemporary West. The intellectual giant of all Europe around 1830 was Hegel, who was Protestant to be sure but was mainly a speculative philosopher with politics at least at the fringes of his world-view, a politics which easily could be placed nearer the center of 'Hegelianism'; for the advanced intellectual of 1850, the French so-called Utopian, non-state socialists and Proudhon the anarchist became more interesting. What Herzen sought to become, when he arrived in Europe, was a Russian lion in a pride of European revolutionary democrats; it was in such circles that he expected to find instantly his spiritual home. Bakunin was more successful than he in doing so. But there was no question where they thought they belonged – not in the West in some vague geographical sense, but among the alienated radical intellectuals of the West, the most advanced of the time. The path from Chaadaev's espousal of the Western heritage and absolute rejection of the Russian present to Herzen's and Bakunin's rejection of the Western present along with that of Russia was quickly traversed – from the publication of Chaadaev's *Philosophical Letter* (1836) to Herzen's *From the Other Shore* (1849) was an interval of only thirteen years. It was no longer possible to follow the advanced thought of the West and remain in Russia – at least without serious risk of exile or imprisonment – and so Herzen and Bakunin began the first of several generations of émigrés. As the Petrashevtsy and the Brotherhood of Cyril and Methodius show, even rather mild radicalism henceforth became dangerous in Russia. The crusading Westerners were driven abroad, where they completed the passage from German philosophical idealism to French Utopian socialism and anarchism.

Those who did not reject the Russian tradition and sought to work out a cultural solution combining Western and Russian elements in some kind of syncretism were not usually arrested and exiled, but any independent thought risked collision with the Germanic bureaucracy that was the nineteenth-century Imperial government. This was true of Pushkin, who foreshadowed rather than exemplified syncretism. The Slavophiles, whose ideas marked a somewhat abortive attempt to combine German philosophical idealism and Orthodoxy, repeatedly ran afoul of authority. Some of the foremost Russian learned clergy had often to exchange blows at close range with the governmental apparatus, a severe distraction when they were still struggling to recover their own intellectual and spiritual moorings. And yet with all their failures, setbacks, and disappointments, it was the syncretists who, in Nicholas I's reign and the following one, proved to lay the foundations and provide the buttresses for the greatest achievements of Russian culture in the last century before the Revolution or, perhaps, up till today.

7

SOCIALISM AND SYNCRETISM
(1855–1890)

Could you please explain to me why belief in God is ridiculous and belief in humanity is not; why belief in the kingdom of heaven is silly, but belief in all utopias on earth is clever? Having discarded positive religion, we have retained all the habits of religion, and having lost paradise in heaven we believe in the coming paradise on earth, and boast about it.

Alexander Herzen, 'Consolatio', *From the Other Shore*

NIHILISM AND POPULISM

The weaknesses of the Nicolaitan system were exposed by the Crimean War for all the world to see, and it was thus not for any ideological reasons but because of recognition of Russia's real needs, so dramatically and unavoidably illuminated, that Alexander II (1855–81) launched the Great Reforms, beginning with the Emancipation of the serfs (1861) continuing with the judicial and zemstvo reforms (1864), the municipal duma reform (1870), and the law on military service (1874) which provided for a citizen army rather than simple transfer of young serfs from civil to military servitude.

Herzen, in London founded the *Polar Star* (*Poliarnaia Zvezda*) at the beginning of the new reign, and in 1857 added the *Bell* (*Kolokol*). In its pages he summoned Russian intellectuals to do as he was doing: to call the state to reform society, beginning with the freeing of the serfs. When Alexander seemed to respond, Herzen used the cry of Julian the Apostate: 'Thou has conquered, O Galilean!' But he no more accepted tsarism in so saying than Julian accepted Christianity; he acknowledged temporary defeat, recognizing that not he and his kind but the tsar had taken the necessary changes in Russian society in hand. Far from accepting Alexander II as an ally, he quarreled even with the liberal heirs of the Westerners who had remained in Russia when he and Bakunin had left, and were some of them actual pupils of Granovsky and friends of *confrères* of his: such men as Boris Chicherin, Kavelin, and others. He believed them too ready to accept not merely the reforms the tsardom was preparing to carry out, but the institutions of tsardom itself. On the other hand, in an article called 'Very Dangerous!!!'[1] he attacked (though not by name) the young radical critics who had replaced Belinsky as the self-appointed social conscience of Russian literature, Nicholas Chernyshevsky and Nicholas Dobroliubov, writers on the poet Nekrasov's journal *The Contemporary* (*Sovremennik*).

In the middle of the nineteenth century, writes Florovsky, although philosophical questions were really shaking everyone, it was usual to propose to satisfy this thirst not by creative work but by '"enlightenment", that is, dilettantism'.[2] As he reminds us, this phenomenon was not peculiar to Russia, but was found to some degree in all of Europe. Some have spoken as if the change that affected European thought so strongly in the middle of the nineteenth century was one from 'romanticism' to 'realism'– in literature, but in other fields as well. Others have pointed to the shift of interest from one major figure to another – from Hegel to Darwin. In an important sense there was a shift from philosophy to natural science, biology in particular. Interest in philosophy as a discipline continued after 1850, and biology did not begin in 1850 or thereabouts. It was rather that the semi-intellectuals and especially those thinkers who desired to solve simultaneously all questions altered their chosen pan-discipline. It was assumed that the key to the understanding of the world lay in biology instead of philosophy as previously thought. The decades after 1850 were quite comparable to those after 1750 in their prevalent 'scientism'– that is, the wish to derive answers to the fundamental problems of mankind from biology, as a century earlier the *philosophes* had wished to derive them from physics.

In many ways the period can be understood as a second wave of the Enlightenment, but in a new guise; in both Western Europe and Russia atheism rather than deism usually constituted its religious side. The 'scientistic' fever in Russia produced first the radical critics of the 60's and then the revolutionaries of the 70's. There was one difference: in Russia the religious element was much less sublimated than in the West, and sometimes was explicitly in the foreground. Vladimir Soloviev later satirized the viewpoint of the anti-religious strain in the radical thought of the period: 'man is descended from the monkey: therefore let us love one another.' The taunt was not far off the mark in application to such men as Chernyshevsky and Dobroliubov.

Chernyshevsky was born in 1828 in Saratov, the scion of generations of parish priests in the Volga valley; his father taught him the Latin he used to read Feofan Prokopovich and other such writers as a boy, adding some Hebrew and Greek and then modern European languages and some Persian and Tatar.[3] He attended ecclesiastical schools, and then was sent to the University of St Petersburg in 1846. He had read omnivorously in Saratov, and in the capital he plunged into the German idealists and historians, especially Hegel, with whom he lacked patience, and Feuerbach (1849), whose work was a revelation driving him to renounce his Christian belief and to adopt an uneasy deism. He had already rejected the Russian tradition in Chaadaevian words: 'What have the Russians given to learning? Alas, nothing. What has learning contributed to Russian life? Again, nothing' (1846). In 1848 he had become convinced that 'we Russians count for nothing' compared to the West.[4] At that time he still believed, like Herzen and Bakunin at various times, in the monarchy as an agency that could achieve social justice; but he was becoming a socialist, having been introduced to the ideas of Fourier and the Petrashevtsy and attending meetings on the periphery of their circle. Two years later his belief in monarchy was gone.

After returning to Saratov to teach for a time, he was back in St Petersburg in 1853. Soon he was writing literary criticism for two warring journals, *The Contemporary* (*Sovremennik*) and *Notes of the Fatherland* (*Otechestvennye Zapiski*), and though he finished his master's thesis he abandoned thought of an academic career for one of journalism. That career made a great impression on Russian public opinion, above all the youth, though it lasted less than a decade. He published his thesis, 'The Aesthetic Relations of Art to Reality' ('Esteticheskie otnosheniia iskusstva k deistvitel'nosti')[5] which aimed at overthrowing Hegelian esthetics (he was forced to remove the name of Hegel, which made it awkward for him) in favor of commonsense, indeed belligerently naive, realism: 'our art to this day has been unable to create anything like an orange or an apple'. The purpose of art, he concluded, was 'to reproduce the phenomena of life that are of interest to man'. In a series of essays on the 'Gogol period of Russian literature', he showed that he meant it by brushing aside Pushkin as obsolete because, though a master of form, the poet lacked content, and by resolutely misinterpreting Gogol as a social critic worthy of emulation. Invoking Belinsky's name and ideas, he announced that art must serve a social purpose, which broadly speaking meant the cause of revolution.

In early 1858 he hailed Alexander II's rescript to Nazimov (making public the tsar's aim to emancipate the serfs) as portending a change in Russian life equal in importance to the Petrine reforms, but as the outlines of the probable emancipation legislation became clearer, he rapidly soured on the prospects. In an essay published in August 1859, he distinguished three political camps, radicals, moderates, and reactionaries, and, though he transparently claimed to be a reactionary, his disavowal of the moderates placed him clearly in the radical camp. He now broke with Herzen and all Herzen stood for, in polemics that began in 1859 and ended in 1862.[6] Chernyshevsky criticized Herzen-style 'accusatory' writings that pointed out abuses but did not come to grips with the socio-political structure; Herzen warned against the revolutionary elitism that Chernyshevsky had come to preach. Ironically, Herzen was unintentionally responsible for Chernyshevsky's arrest, which occurred in July 1862 as the result of the police's intercepting a letter of Herzen's in which he offered to help publish *The Contemporary*, which had just been suspended, in London.

The elitism of Chernyshevsky received its most influential expression in his 'great bad novel', as Lampert calls it,[7] *What Is To Be Done* (*Chto delat'?*), written in the Fortress of Sts Peter and Paul at the turn of the year in 1862–3. It depicted the emergence of the young *raznochintsy* intelligentsia, men like himself (and women), sexually and intellectually liberated and ready to lead the people – toward what, remained cloudy. In a letter published in 1860 under a pseudonym by its target, Herzen, in *The Bell*, he wrote, 'An ax alone can save us, nothing but an ax.' In the 1861 proclamation, 'To the Landlords' Peasants', he issued a summons to mass revolutionary action; however, he praised the freedom he saw as present in England and France and said nothing about socialism[8] – perhaps for tactical reasons.

What he was against is clear enough, however. Feuerbach was and remained his chief inspiration into the years of exile. In his 1860 essay, 'The Anthropological Principle in Philosophy' ('Antropologicheskii printsip v filosofii'), he declared that the sciences 'prove that no dualism is evident in man' and that 'the deduction that fantastic prejudices are totally unfounded' was beyond doubt. As Randall suggests, such 'prejudices' plainly included 'Christianity, Tsarism, and bourgeois liberalism'.[9] In 1877 he wrote from Siberia to his sons: 'If you wish to know what my views on the nature of man are, you can find them in the only thinker of our time who, I think, had a true understanding of things. This is Ludwig Feuerbach...I remain his faithful follower.'[10] Feuerbach had taught him to break idols, but not precisely what to erect in their place. The exact extent of his revolutionary activity remains in doubt. He was certainly close to the radical youth of the 60's and specifically to the first revolutionary organization to take the name Land and Liberty (*Zemlia i Volia*), led by the brothers Serno-Solovevich, though he regarded the young revolutionaries with some ambivalence.[11] Although his trial had elements of judicial farce, he was probably guilty of the charges.[12]

His exile in effect ended his career. It lasted twenty-five years, of which nineteen were in Siberia and six in Astrakhan. There were several plots to effect an escape for him, but they merely led the authorities to tighten the restrictions on him. In 1889 he was finally allowed to return to Saratov, but he died a few months after arrival.

Chernyshevsky's first disciple was Nicholas Dobroliubov.[13] Born in 1836 in Nizhny Novgorod, he was like Chernyshevsky the son of a priest and attended seminary. In 1853 he entered the Pedagogical School at St Petersburg; again like Chernyshevsky, there he lost his Christian faith through reading Feuerbach. Two years later he was a socialist, ardently following Herzen's path as he understood it. In 1856 he and Chernyshevsky became close friends and he joined the staff of *The Contemporary*. His career lasted five years; after an unsuccessful journey to the West to improve his tubercular condition, he died in 1861 at the age of twenty-five. His articles on Ostrovsky's plays and Goncharov's novel *Oblomov* are particularly remembered, but not mainly as literary criticism; he used the works cited to indict contemporary society and to call for action.

In the writings of Chernyshevsky and Dobroliubov the ethical maximalism characteristic of the eighteenth-century pietism which had so much affected the seminaries received full exposition. Turgenev accused them of 'trying to wipe out from the face of the earth, poetry, the fine arts, all aesthetic pleasures, and to impose in their place mere seminarist principles. These men are literary Robespierres; they wouldn't for a moment hesitate to cut off the poet Chénier's head.'[14] The broader perspective which the critics of *The Contemporary* charted were shared by many of the young radical students of the universities of St Petersburg and Moscow (and Kazan, of which something later), but they soon translated them into calls for immediate political action. There were student populist groups in Moscow, following P. N. Rybnikov, in 1854–5 and in Kharkov about the same time.

However, the 'era of manifestoes', as it came to be called, began only in the year of Emancipation itself, 1861. In July 1861 appeared three numbers of a journal called Great Russia (*Velikorus*), advocating in somewhat vague terms a constitutional monarchy; in August a manifesto entitled *To the Young Generation* demanded that the monarchy be replaced by an elective republic in which the communed would be the fundamental unit of society. In 1862 a nineteen-year-old student named P. G. Zaichnevsky while actually in jail wrote and managed to have published a manifesto called *Young Russia* (*Molodaia Rossiia*) in which he attacked *Great Russia*, called for a social-democratic republic, whose supreme authority would be a national assembly elected after the revolution had triumphed, and, echoing Chernyshevsky's letter of 1860, summoned his readers: 'to your axes!' Zaichnevsky (the exploit of the manifesto remained unknown to the government) was sent to Siberia in 1863, allowed to return to European Russia in 1869, sent back to Siberia in 1880, allowed again to return in 1885, sent back to Siberia once again in 1891, and allowed to return once again in 1896, dying in Smolensk in the same year. His Jacobin propensities led him to play some role during the mid-1870's as one of P. N. Tkachev's few followers inside Russia, but he was not typical of his era. The more characteristic tendency was that of Chernyshevsky (despite the 1860 letter), uncompromisingly and puritanically democratic in vision, more cautious in his plans and hopes for the immediate future.

After the death of Dobroliubov and the arrest of Chernyshevsky, it became clear that they were not two isolated individuals but rather the inaugurators of important changes in both the social and intellectual aspects of Russian thought. In the 1860's the term 'intelligentsia' (*intelligentsiia*) came into use and by the end of the decade 'came to be applied to people rather than to an abstraction'.[15] It referred not so much to the entire educated class as to that section of it that had marked socio-political interests, and the word came to connote a definite coloration of such interests – those opposed to the existing structure of government and to the old order in various respects.

The term *raznochintsy*, literally meaning 'men of mixed ranks', but denoting in particular those whose social background was non-gentry, emerged a little later[16] but referred above all to the 'men of the 60's' of the Chernyshevsky–Dobroliubov sort. The assumption was that the pre-*raznochintsy* intelligentsia came from the gentry. As has been indicated, however, before Peter I the social group from which the most influential Russian (and Ukrainian) intellectuals (even those to some extent concerned with socio-political problems) came was the clergy, and the clergy-staffed ecclesiastical schools maintained an important role in Russian thought well into the nineteenth century. The ascendancy of the gentry intellectual was in fact rather short-lived. But in the 1860's the sons of the clergy reasserted themselves dramatically – often as atheists; but even some of the atheists were still very much affected by their earlier religious outlook, as will soon be clear.

The young of the 60's were bequeathed, by Chernyshevsky's departure to intellectual oblivion in Siberia, the foundations of two new currents: nihilism and populism. The first was an attitude centering in literature and thought, the second in preparation for social action of some kind and in such action itself. 'Nihilism' (not to be equated with terrorism, despite many ignorant or wilful misconstructions to that effect) was a term used as early as 1840, by Michael Katkov, to mean someone who had lost faith in everything but science.[17] However, it came into general use in Russia only in the 1860's as a result of its role in Turgenev's *Fathers and Sons* (*Ottsy i deti*), in which the character Arkady defined nihilists as those who 'bow before no authority of any kind, and accept no faith, no principle, whatever veneration surrounds it'. In 1868 Herzen wrote,

Nihilism...is logic without restraint; it is science without dogmas; it is unconditional submission to experience and acceptance without a murmur of all consequences, whatever they may be, if they flow from observation and are demanded by reason. Nihilism does not turn *something* into nothing, but reveals that *nothing*, which has been taken for *something*, is an optical illusion...[18]

The 'Maccabeus of Petersburg nihilism', as Herzen recognized him to be, was Dmitry Pisarev. He was born in 1840 in Orel province, the son of a member of the gentry (not of a priest, unlike many of the other radical critics of the 60's). He was sent to St Petersburg to school at eleven. In his teens he aspired to scholarly distinction, worked hard on a biography of Humboldt, and despised the plebeian writers of *The Contemporary*. However, in 1858 he found employment on a magazine for young women called *Dawn* (*Rassvet*) and soon underwent a personality transformation into a confident, scintillating conversationalist. He also became an atheist and a radical, and at the end of 1859 fell into insanity, attempted suicide, and was confined in an institution for several months.

In 1860, despite an offer of a post from *The Contemporary*, Pisarev began to write for *Russian Word* (*Russkoe Slovo*), its competitor. Nevertheless he soon aligned himself with Chernyshevsky's materialism,[19] and enthusiatically defended the then modish apostles of scientism, Moleschott, Büchner, and Vogt. What 'logic without restraint' meant to the young convert to nihilism was shown in his celebrated 'ultimatum': 'What can be smashed, must be smashed. What stands the blow is good; what flies into smithereens is rubbish. In any case, hit out right and left: no harm will or can come of it.'[20]

Though many of the *Contemporary* staff were angry at *Fathers and Sons*, Pisarev welcomed Turgenev's novelized portrait of the nihilists in his essay 'Bazarov' in the spring of 1862.

A few weeks later Pisarev was in prison, curiously for writing an (unpublished) article against a young man who in turn had attacked a government propagandist (Baron Firks) using the pseudonym D. K. Shedo-Ferroti. Pisarev's manuscript was a defense not of Firks but of Herzen, whom the young radical had calumniated; but it was also an attack on the regime – in fact, it was his 'only explicit political statement'.[21] He was in prison four years, during part of which he was able to write and even publish. He polemized with writers on *The Contemporary*, and in so doing evinced a distaste for populism and hope for industrialism (an outgrowth, after all, of his beloved sciences) which distinguished him from most of his contemporaries. His essay, 'The Destruction of Aesthetics' ('Razrushenie estetiki'), was his swan song. It is only fair to note that Pisarev was enough (and more) of an esthete to be quite familiar with what it was for which he wished destruction. In this respect, among others, he has been defensibly compared with Tolstoy.[22] But in his essay he announced that he 'would rather be a Russian shoemaker than a Russian Raphael', and he proclaimed the coming disappearance of culture, to be replaced by a 'non-cultural' and scientific something, and verbally spat upon 'our nice, pretty-pretty Pushkin' (thereby outdoing Chernyshevsky's cautious dismissal of the great poet) by way of assurance that he really meant it.

Released from prison in November 1866, he found difficulty in knowing what to do as a free man. He worked unenthusiastically on *Annals of the Fatherland*, successor to *The Contemporary*; he fell into a one-sided love affair, in the midst of which he drowned while swimming in the Baltic, July 1868. The weight of evidence seems to indicate suicide.[23]

Four years later, an official censor wrote that 'of all the Russian socialist writers, Pisarev seems to be the most popular among the younger generation...'[24] He was popular in part because he was an effective popularizer, as he himself boasted, of the scientific and pseudo-scientific enthusiasms of the 60's; he acquainted Russian youth with Darwin, and to a lesser extent Comte and Buckle. 'In the dissected frog', he wrote, apropos of Bazarov, 'lies the salvation and the renovation of the Russian people.' This message – that culture, history, and art are useless and that only science can point the way to the future – was the message of nihilism. It became caught up in the journalism and the nocturnal dormitory conversations of students, and was diffused into the atmosphere, needing no organized center to disseminate it and having none.

There was, however, a second and more cohesively lasting inheritance from Chernyshevsky and Dobroliubov. *The Contemporary* and then *Annals of the Fatherland*, under the editorship of the poet Nekrasov, continued their work and developed the school of thought which was later given the name populism (*narodnichestvo*).[25] Despite the controversy this term has aroused, it seems best to use it to refer to the various currents of socialism that arose in Russia in the 1860's[26] and lasted until the organization of socialist political parties of some durability at the end of the 1890's, when the imperatives of political action reduced considerably the number of varieties.

Socialism has had two chief variants: anarchism and state socialism. Anarchism seeks to 'establish justice. . . in all human relations by the complete elimination of the state (or by the greatest possible minimization of its activity) and its replacement by an entirely free and spontaneous cooperation. . .'[27] In fact, many 'populist' individuals and groups were partly or wholly anarchist (Bakunin) in their orientation, whereas a number were partly or wholly state socialist or Marxist (Danielson). Nevertheless all or almost all 'populists' shared one basic tenet: Russia could avoid the Western form of capitalism in passing directly to socialism. Their desire to do so had nothing whatever to do with the Russian cultural or institutional tradition (to which socialism was quite as alien as capitalism). It was the natural reflection of the Russian intelligentsia's discovery that the most advanced Western intellectuals had become socialists; no socialists in the West advocated capitalism (never mind that many of them did not need to; it was already upon them); for socialists to advocate capitalism would have produced not only paradox but tragedy, as Walicki puts it.[28] Marx told Russian socialists repeatedly that they could reach socialism without passing through capitalism; Lenin led Russia into doing so in fact. Why does the opinion persist that it was not 'Marxist' to believe in such a possibility?

For Chernyshevsky, capitalism was not the main enemy – though he was a socialist – but 'Asiatic conditions of life, Asiatic social structure, Asiatic order'.[29] For Mikhailovsky and a number of other populists, capitalism was the great danger: not because they had seen Manchester or the Ruhr, but very possibly because they had read Marx's great indictments of it[30] as Chernyshevsky had not. It was Russian reality that they ignored – the strength of tsarism and the direction of its policy, which had much more to do with the crucial social and economic changes of the late nineteenth century than the endlessly discussed village commune – and Western ideas that they embraced.[31]

This is not to say, any more than Walicki does, that the main intellectual influence on the populists was Marx or that most of the populists were in fact basically Marxists; their other intellectual debts will be mentioned. In its first widespread manifestation, the 'going to the people' movement which gave populism its very name, populism was based on no clear intellectual position at all and plainly reflected its social origin in the newly atheist section of the clergy.[32] The earliest populist preaching in the countryside of which we know was in 1863, led by a priest's son named Orlov starting from Kazan. 'The students called this [movement] "the apostolate",' writes Venturi, 'and the word well expresses the atmosphere of religious enthusiasm which inspired them.'[33] It was a missionary movement, which had something like a board of missions in the editorship of *The Contemporary*, consisting mostly of priests' sons: G. Z. Eliseev, M. A. Antonovich, A. N. Pypin (Chernyshevsky's cousin). (The writer Saltykov-Shchedrin, an epigon of the 40's, whose father was of the gentry of Tver, was a notable exception.) Nekrasov called the group his 'consistory'. In the 60's and 70's the religious character of the movement was scarcely concealed. In his *Alphabet of the Social Sciences* (*Azbuka sotsial'nykh nauk*) (1871), an influential tract composed in the form of a catechism, V. V. Bervi-Flerovsky wrote, 'I strove to create a religion of brotherhood!' In the great wave of 'going to the people' in 1873–4, these themes were no weaker. O. V. Aptekman notes of his fellow 'missionaries' that 'almost all of them had copies of the Gospels',[34] and though a Jew he accepted Orthodox baptism to identify himself more fully with the movement.

A significant early group that 'went to the people' was the Chaikovtsy circle, founded in 1869 among students in the St Petersburg medical school by M. A. Natanson, replaced as leader after his arrest in 1871 by N. V. Chaikovsky. The oldest member was Prince Peter Kropotkin, born in 1842, who had been a member of Nicholas I's Corps of Pages but had broken with high society to spend the period 1862–7 mainly in Siberia on scientific expeditions. Having visited the West, he had fallen under the influence of Bakunin and become an anarchist, though he was the mildest of the lot, emphasizing 'mutual aid' – which he found operating even among the wild animals of Siberia – and harmony among men. The intellectual focus of the Chaikovtsy circle was around Bervi-Flerovsky, who has just been quoted; other members later noteworthy included Sophia Perovskaia, prominent in the conspiracy that assassinated Alexander II, and S. M. Kravchinsky, who wrote under the pseudonym 'Stepniak'. The Chaikovtsy began by an effort to spread socialist propaganda in Russia; when this was thwarted, they undertook direct propaganda among the workers, which led to arrests and dispersal by 1873. (It is quite inaccurate to suggest that the populists then or later were not interested in workers.)

Only in 1873–4 came a spontaneous movement of thousands of young populists 'to the people' in the form of the peasantry. It was organized by no single group; it was the product of a decade of feverish discussion and attempts at organized activity in Russia and it was triggered by the debates of the early 1870's abroad, especially in Zürich. There were several assumptions shared by all those who could verbalize what they were trying to do: a new social order must be worked for and not merely waited for (populists of all stripes shared an unabashed voluntarism); the key to change lay in understanding between the few intelligentsia and the mass of the peasantry; the intellectual foundation for change lay in the most recent philosophical and political ideas of Western Europe. To the extent that the climactic phase of the 'missionary' movement sought conversion, it was to socialism. Like many groups which shared common assumptions, the populists differed sharply about some things, at that point generally following either Bakunin (who has already been discussed) or Lavrov, though Tkachev tried to steer the youth away from both. All three of these men came from the gentry.

Peter Tkachev (1844-86) had come from Velikie Luki to attend school in St Petersburg and entered the university there in 1861.[35] He was arrested almost immediately and four subsequent times before escaping abroad in 1873. In essays from 1862 on he expounded two basic principles: economic materialism and equality (not merely legal but absolute physiological equality, assured by society) among men. The former he discussed with reference to Marx, Adam Smith, and John Stuart Mill; his inspiration for the latter came probably from Babeuf and Buonarrotti.[36] Like Zaichnevsky, he was a Jacobin above all, and after emigrating joined the Western epigons of Jacobinism, the Blanquists. He was willing to cooperate with Bakunin's unruly protégé, Nechaev, and worked out a program along with the latter in Russia in 1869; but he was not in agreement with Bakunin and broke with him in 1876 as he had done with Lavrov two years earlier. Tkachev's disagreements with Lavrov, however, were more serious.

Peter Lavrov (1823-1900) was an army colonel who taught mathematics in the Artillery Academy in St Petersburg until the end of the 50's. He was on the outer fringes of the first Land and Liberty (1862) group. In the atmosphere of fear prevailing in 1866, as a result of Karakozov's attempt on the tsar's life, he was arrested and exiled; in 1870 he escaped to the West. Until the Paris Commune of 1871 he was a reformist; thereafter he became a revolutionary socialist.[37] His first sizeable essay, composed in 1859-60, was dedicated to Herzen and Proudhon; his *magnum opus* was *Historical Letters* (*Istoricheskie pis'ma*), first published serially in 1868-9.[38] It sounded the moral imperative that characterized the whole populist movement: the 'conscience-stricken noblemen' (*kaiushchiesia dvoriane*) and indeed the whole of the intelligentsia were called on to discharge their debt to the peasantry. Progress was not inevitable, but had to be striven for, Lavrov argued, drawing on Kant, the Left Hegelian Bruno Bauer, and Feuerbach;[39] he later qualified his voluntarism considerably, but the theme never vanished from the populists' song. The 'critically-thinking individual', Lavrov argued, was the motive force of history, and through the proper 'preparation' would achieve the understanding with the people necessary to reorganize the state and society.

After Lavrov escaped abroad he joined the First International and became fully preoccupied with Western radical debates, though he remained in contact with a whole series of Russian populist organizations, including the terrorists, all of which acknowledged him as a major prophet.

The Russian youth who 'went to the people' in 1873-4 and tried thereafter to decide why they had failed were, then, partly inspired by the ideas of Bakunin and Lavrov, ideas which were wholly Western.[40] They also were experiencing a religious crisis rooted in the ethical maximalism and the epigonal pietism rife in the early nineteenth-century Russian seminaries from which the characteristic 'men of the 60's' came, which reflected not any indigenous Russian influences but rather an earlier stratum of Western borrowings. Johann Arndt's shade would doubtless have been surprised to hear that his ideas had an indirect effect on the fever of 1873; they did nonetheless. But the goal of self-perfection had, in Western socialism, been transmuted into the goal of an 'earthly utopia', as Herzen noted.

The peasants turned the young populist 'missionaries' over to the police, and a series of notorious trials resulted; nevertheless there was another attempt, in 1877–8. Only in one isolated instance, the Chigirin affair, was any success achieved, and the fact that there the revolutionaries forged manifestos of Alexander II ordering an uprising (purportedly to frustrate his reactionary advisers) outraged a number of high-minded radicals. 'Going to the people' was an utter failure.

In 1878 one of the populists, Vera Zasulich, wounded a police official responsible for harsh treatment of some of the arrested 'missionaries', and in emulation of her deed the movement passed quickly from propaganda to terrorism. The second group bearing the name Land and Liberty (*Zemlia i Volia*), founded in 1876,[41] was riven in 1879 by debate; the anti-terrorists, led by George Plekhanov, formed The Black Partition (*Chernyi Peredel*) and in 1880 emigrated. The terrorists, calling their group The People's Will (*Narodnaia Volia*),[42] went on to kill the emperor in March 1881. A month later almost all the leaders had been hanged, and terrorism was almost wholly extinguished in Russia for a generation.

The resulting 'crisis of populism' was prolonged.[43] Engel'gardt, clinging despite a series of failures to his rural location in the Smolensk region, influenced a number of peasants but transformed no *intelligenty* and by the early 80's finally saw the remaining populists on his estate turn to religion. Uspensky in his *Power of the Soil* (*Vlast' zemli*, 1882) despaired of both peasants and *intelligenty* in the present but called for a new wave of Russia's ancient missionary saints (*bozhie ugodniki*) and promised that, 'though not in the near future, God, without fail, will speak the truth'. Zlatovratsky, having sought frantically for evidence that the commune would survive, found instead that it was collapsing (as did Engel'gardt and Uspensky) and after 1884 ceased almost entirely to write about the peasantry, consoling himself that the future must be better. A few, such as Iosef Kablits (Yuzov) in his *Foundations of Populism* (*Osnovy narodnichestva*, 1882), obstinately reiterated a Bakunist view that the peasantry was the repository of virtue and castigated the intelligentsia for not recognizing it, but in practice he could think of nothing better to do than to drive dynamite into the walls of the Winter Palace.[44] By 1881 N. Minsky lamented that whereas in the 60's students jammed lectures on physiology, in the 70's on political economy, by the early 80's 'almost all the university youth rushes to a lecture [by Vladimir Soloviev] – on Christianity!'[45]

In 1885 a book was published (though it was serialized earlier) that pointed in a somewhat new direction. It was N. Ziber's *David Ricardo and Karl Marx*: it reasserted the view that progress was inevitable (challenged by Lavrov and others fifteen years earlier) and argued that the form of the state would yield to economic change and that the Russian peasant must be 'boiled in the industrial boiler'[46] – boiled by history, not by populists directly or indirectly.

Christianity, recognition of the decay of the commune, Marxism – several indications of the new directions of the 1890's were appearing; but the 1880's were a dark and cheerless decade for most of the Russian intelligentsia.

TOLSTOY

In the 1860's the second wave of the Enlightenment produced the radical critics who helped to spawn populism and also nihilism. The root-and-branch negation by the 'sons' of the 'fathers' ' views startled and shocked many in addition to those fathers. The 'sons' rejected the political and social system under which they (and those in other countries) lived, governments, churches, science, art, and other aspects of modern civilization. Some did so with reservations; Pisarev, as noted, cherished science, and the radical critics placed their faith in certain social doctrines as well. There was one genius who did not exclude science or the revolutionary movement from the category of things he denied – that was Leo Tolstoy. In 1903 he wrote to a French critic that 'the existence of churches, science, art, and especially governments... contradict the truth of a religious conscience'. In the letter he complained that many, his correspondent included, did not accord him 'the simple com- monsense of seeing that the churches, science, art, and governments are indispensable for societies in their present state', and he denied being 'a reformer or a philosopher or an apostle'.[47] The fact that he was unwilling to take any action against existing institutions and even denied that there was such a thing as 'Tolstoyism' or any doctrine that could be properly ascribed to him has misled a number of people and prevented them from perceiving the extent to which Tolstoy was a man of the 60's and carried further than his contemporaries their nihilist enthusiasms.[48] In so doing he was a thinker who owed everything to the West and virtually nothing to the Russian tradition.

Tolstoy was a count who was the great-great-great grandson of a favorite of Peter the Great. Born in 1828 at Yasnaia Poliana, the estate that remained home to him to the moment of his last tragic flight a few days before his death, he lost both parents by the time he was nine, and was raised by aunts.[49] At thirteen he was taken to Kazan by one of them, and there he studied in two schools of the university, Oriental languages and law. He flunked out of the first and left the second by his own wish in 1847. By this time he had already read widely on his own, and in particular had fallen under the spell of Rous- seau, whose fundamental doctrines lay at the root of Tolstoy's views, especially after his 'conversion' of 1880, but also before: in 1862 he wrote, 'man is born perfect – that is the great word spoken by Rousseau, and it will, like a rock, remain strong and true'.[50] In those days he wore a medallion portrait of Rousseau around his neck in place of a cross, and whatever happened to the medallion later, he never rejected the inspiration of the French–Swiss writer. His ideas of education, his attitude toward the peasantry, manual labor, Yasnaia Poliana, and much else, as they developed later, owed much to Rousseau.

In the spring of 1847 he returned from Kazan to Yasnaia Poliana, which he had inherited, with the thought in mind of improving the lot of the serfs. At this point he did not stay; he was off to Moscow, to St Petersburg. In 1851 he accompanied his brother to the Caucasus, applied his Rousseauian admiration for the natural man to the Cossacks there, and entered military service. While there he submitted his first publication to Nekrasov, editor of *The Contemporary*; it was the story 'Childhood' ('Detstvo'), accepted in the fall of 1852. It was an immediate success. Early in 1854 he was transferred to the Danube and got his first glimpse of the outside world in the city of Bucharest. When the Crimean War broke out, he obtained transfer to Sevastopol. As a result of his observation of the fighting he wrote 'Sevastopol in December', which exuded patriotic feelings; then sharp disillusionment overtook him, and 'Sevastopol in May' could only be published after extensive reworking, which he refused to accept, so that it appeared without his name. However, when he appeared in St Petersburg near the close of 1855 (shortly thereafter retiring from the service), he was lionized by Turgenev and the literary circles of the capital as a gifted young writer. He did not find such circles congenial; he criticized the liberal writers and critics, and took pleasure in disagreeing with accepted opinions. After hearing him denounce Shakespeare, Panaev, the co-editor of *The Contemporary*, wrote, 'the man simply does not wish to know any traditions, either theoretical or historical'.[51] It was not merely a youthful foible; in 1903 he wrote an essay on Shakespeare in which it was asserted that the Bard was not 'even an average' writer. This shocked George Bernard Shaw, who first welcomed the report that Tolstoy had challenged Shakespeare's ideas but was scandalized to receive the article and learn that he had also rejected Shakespeare's artistry.[52]

In 1856 Tolstoy visited Western Europe for the first time, seeing something of France, Switzerland, and the German states. On this tour he was reading, among other writers, Proudhon, and associated himself with Proudhon's anarchist ideal. Tolstoy contrasted the barbarism of Russian life with the civilization of Europe;[53] he was one Russian traveler who did not reject the West and sigh with relief at returning home.

Enthusiasm for new directions in education seized him in 1859, when he opened a school for village children in Yasnaia Poliana and himself acted as teacher. He took a second trip to the West in 1860 to familiarize himself with educational theory and practice, especially in the German states, and there he talked to Berthold Auerbach (whose novel *Ein neues Leben* had inspired him

to open his school in the first place) and probably Julius Froebel, nephew of
the originator of kindergartens. He made a pilgrimage to see Proudhon in
Brussels, and declared that 'he was the only man who understood in our time
the significance of public education and of the printing press'.[54] In the spring
of 1861 Tolstoy returned to Russia, and he never left it again. He was discon-
tented, and gave offense in all directions. Appointed a local mediator (*mirovoi
posrednik*) after Emancipation of the serfs, he infuriated his fellow gentry and
had to resign. He visited Turgenev on his estate, and fell asleep over the
manuscript of *Fathers and Sons*.

In September 1862 he married Sophia Bers, the daughter of a girl with
whom he had played as a child; he was thirty-four and she was eighteen. It is
difficult to characterize the marriage. It led to forty-eight years of life together
and many children and grandchildren, and man and wife remained devoted to
each other. The aftermath of his 'conversion' annoyed the wife. A multitude
of large and small disagreements finally drove her into a state of hysteria
approaching madness and led him, in despair, to flee the house forever. And
yet for years, and at many moments after the troubles began, the Tolstoys
were a model family. Twelve months after marriage he was well launched into
War and Peace. The plot and the title took a considerable time before settling
down, and for the title Tolstoy may have been indebted to the reception
Proudhon's *La guerre et la paix* was having in Russia.[55] The book was finished
in 1869, and Turgenev proclaimed him the foremost writer of Russia. One
favorable reviewer, N. N. Strakhov, soon became close friends with the
author, and, if he had not died in 1896, he would have been Tolstoy's literary
co-executor.

War and Peace was, as Sir Isaiah Berlin has brilliantly shown,[56] an attack
on history, that is, on historicism. Napoleon and Alexander I strut through the
grandiose scenes of war, but they have nothing to do with what happens. This
is not to say that Fate or the Mode of Production holds mankind in its grip.
The deeds of the past are bloody and blind, because men do not know the
truth; if they did, they would act on it and there would be no wars or other
man-made calamities. The past teaches nothing, except how not to behave.

Tolstoy's second great novel, *Anna Karenina*, followed quite soon. He
began it in 1873, and it was finished in 1877. He was diverted from it by a
renewal of his educational passions; he wrote a primer, and organized a
training school for peasant teachers, which was scheduled for opening in 1877.
The appearance of only twelve applicants led him to abandon the school and
any further serious efforts to influence education – whose current embodi-
ment he regarded as stupid compulsion and a crime against the natural man. In
1862 he had written an article entitled, 'Who Should Teach Whom to Write:
We the Peasant Children or the Peasant Children Us?' The answer he regarded
as self-evident. At any rate, with the completion of *Anna Karenina* his position in world literature was secure. Anna's natural feelings led to her being
crushed by society. The dilemma of nature versus convention arose again to

plague him. Out of it developed his great religious crisis, which began in 1874[57] and whose first phase thus was contemporaneous with the writing of *Anna Karenina*. In 1877 Strakhov and he paid a visit to Optina Pustyn and the Elder Amvrosy – as Dostoevsky was to do along with Vladimir Soloviev in 1878, just before plunging into *The Brothers Karamazov*. But Tolstoy was not preparing another novel. He was trying to find out what religious position he should adopt – or, perhaps, what position he had already occupied for some time.

Three works marked the turning-point: *Confession, A Study of Dogmatic Theology*, and *Union and Translation of the Four Gospels*. He came to identify himself with the teachings of Christ, in particular Matthew 5.39: 'But I say unto you, Resist not him that is evil: but whosoever smiteth thee on thy right cheek, turn to him the other also.' He rejected the doctrines of Orthodox Christianity, including the divinity of Christ, and the Church itself. What that meant in practice he was to take the next thirty years in attempting to discover, and he never gained any kind of inner tranquillity from his answers. His friends were mostly (except for Strakhov) puzzled and unsympathetic to the spiritual experience he was passing through; his interest in Dostoevsky was aroused only in the last months of the latter's life, too late for them even to meet. He found solace in talking to the Molokane near Samara, the peasant prophet V. K. Siutaev in Tver province, the retired officer V. G. Chertkov, whom he met in late 1883 and who became his lifelong disciple and *alter ego* – and eventually a powerful factor in the disruption of his marriage, owing to the growing jealousy of his wife.

A series of essays poured forth expounding his new understanding of life: 'What I Believe' (1882), 'What Then Must We Do?' (1886), 'The Kingdom of God is Within You' (1893), 'What is Art?' (1898). In the meantime his artistic work did not stop entirely, though some of it directly embodied his moralistic message, such as *The Kreutzer Sonata* (1890), which showed the direct influence of Dr Alice B. Stockham's *Tocology: A Book for Every Woman*. In it he argued the desirability of chastity in marriage as well as outside it, and his detractors declared that he preached the end of the human race. Tolstoy did not claim to be able to practice the ideal himself, but the contrast between his ideals and his life bothered him increasingly. In 1890 he decided to divide his property among his family, and in 1891 he renounced the copyrights of all his works written since 1881.

Increasing numbers of pilgrims came to him, annoying his wife; along with nameless peasants, distinguished foreign visitors, such as Thomas G. Masaryk, journalists, people who simply wanted to brag they had talked to the great prophet. The leader of one of two quarreling Dukhobor sects, Peter Verigin, discovered his teachings and proclaimed adherence to them, and he labored mightily to protect the Veriginists from persecution and to assist them to migrate – finally to Canada (1898). He intervened on behalf of a group of Molokane whose children were being taken away from their parents to be put under Russian Orthodox care – for once successfully; the powerful Procurator of the Holy Synod, Constantine Pobedonostsev, reversed this practice. However, despite some imperial marks of favor (Alexander III himself after an interview with Sophia granted permission to publish *The Kreutzer Sonata* in an edition of Tolstoy's works, and Nicholas II allowed the staging of *The Power of Darkness*), many government officials increasingly feared and hated Tolstoy's teachings and his influence. They struck at him repeatedly through his followers, and though he begged to be punished instead of the latter, the government carefully refrained from touching him directly. He was too popular in Russia, and he had become an international synonym for saintliness.

In 1899 he finished his third and last great novel, *Resurrection*; he had hastened to finish it for the financial benefit of the Dukhobors' migration – he was taking no money himself from his post-1881 works, but devoting the proceeds to charity. Based on a case A. F. Koni told him about, the plot dealt with a man who marries a woman he has ruined years before; he intended to write a sequel about the 'resurrected' sinner, who would live as he thought man should live, but he never did. The novel evidently hastened the action of the Holy Synod in February 1901, approving a document drawn up by Pobedonostsev which declared him to be a heretic. The document is often referred to as an act of excommunication; canonically it was not, but Tolstoy treated it as such. That Tolstoy denied not just this or that doctrine but the whole of Christianity as an organized and historical religion was not in question; the issue was rather whether the government department controlling the Russian Orthodox Church, whose best men were just then engaging in discussions about how to end captivity to the state and revitalize the ecclesiastical body, could not have found more urgent tasks than that of condemning Tolstoy. The reaction was mainly in his favor, and the government found it had made a tactical error of some magnitude. Tolstoy replied to the Synod, but his real reply was to the government, in which he set forth as a minimum program of reform equality of the peasantry, uniformity of law, and the elimination of educational and religious restrictions. It was not at all a recipe for the kind of society he wished; it was merely a sound practical suggestion for the self-preservation of the existing government, which its leaders were unwise not to take.

Tolstoy, as an anarchist, abominated the violence and compulsion of both the government and the revolutionaries. The difference between the killing of the one and the killing of the other was, he wrote, that between the excreta of cats and that of dogs – he hated the smell of both.[58] Though his preaching seemed to the government mainly directed against it, he could be savage with the revolutionaries: to three who visited him he said sharply: 'You sit on your parents' neck, read books, emancipate snub-nosed girl students, think yourselves better than all, and that you have the right to direct not only people, but a whole government.'[59] In a draft of 1906 that he was persuaded

by Chertkov to modify, he attributed to the revolutionaries motives that
were 'either the most insignificant, trifling, vain, almost physiological – an
idle life demands some display of activity – or they are the most low, dis-
gusting motives: vanity, self-love, envy, even cupidity...You do not know
and do not love [the common people].'[60] But in 1908 he returned to denounce
the governmental repressions following the Revolution of 1905 in 'I Cannot
Be Silent'.

His last years were increasingly troubled and lonely. Those who praised or
professed to follow his teachings often repelled him; of one he declared,
'he is a Tolstoyan, that is, a man with convictions utterly opposed to mine'.[61]
Most of his large family could not follow his manner of life, consisting of
manual labor, vegetarianism, and teetotalism. One son denounced him in
print as the bane of Russia. His wife complained with ever-mounting passion
that he was impoverishing his descendants with his renunciation of royalties,
and he was finally driven to draw up in secret from her a will leaving the rights
to all his works (including those written before 1881) to his daughter Alexandra, who alone of his children had fully accepted his position, with the understanding that she would give them away. Yet even that did not assuage his
conscience; he remained a 'conscience-stricken nobleman', benefiting from the
toil of others no matter how much he himself might work in the fields, unable
to practice what he preached without injuring his family, which he would not
do, and he was thus vulnerable to his wife's taunts on this score. When to his
own self-laceration was added the now-hysterical attacks of his wife against
Chertkov, against his disposition of his properties, against him, he finally
fled in despair. In a little house on the railway siding at Astapovo death
quieted his tortured spirit in November 1910.

Tolstoy's towering literary stature, universally acknowledged, is not the
object of our study. He wished to be judged not as a writer, not as a thinker
or prophet, but as a man; yet his teachings had an enormous effect, on
Gandhi, on many groups who tried to found ideal communities, but most of
all on Russians, educated and uneducated, who without becoming 'Tol-
stoyans' felt the force of his moral judgments. Ovsianiko-Kulikovsky has
correctly said that his doctrine was not a religion but a surrogate for religion,
perhaps suitable 'for a group of educated sectarians'. He declared that Tolstoy's
teaching was 'dry, rational, rationalist. It was a religion not of the spirit,
but of syllogisms.'[62] Florovsky points out that Tolstoy did not take his view
from the Gospels; for him the Gospels were written centuries earlier by
'ill-educated and superstitious men', and the way to use them was for each to
take pencils and underline what appealed to him, red pencil for the words of
Christ and blue for other passages. 'First of all,' Tolstoy wrote, 'one must
believe in reason, and then choose from all writings, Jewish, Christian, Muslim,
Buddhist, Chinese, and contemporary secular ones, everything that is *in
accordance with reason*' and throw out everything that is not.[63] Tolstoy was a
kind of epigon of eighteenth-century Western Europe, returning to the epoch

of Alexander I for the scene of his greatest work and for the pietism he secularized, emerging as a moralistic rationalist who saw evil in man, didn't
know where it came from, didn't know what to do about it. Florovsky declares
that Tolstoy rejected the Church because he rejected man, and wished to be
alone with common sense.[64]

Tolstoy rejected the civilization of the West forcefully, and in his words of
encouragement to Ku Hung-ming, prophesying a great future for Asia and
especially China (1906), he excepted the Japanese who had already sowed the
seeds of their undoing through Westernization. But he did so not as a Russian
nationalist but as a complete cosmopolitan and adept of Western thought. In
many ways he carried themes of the 1860's into the first decade of the twentieth century. He had no part of the syncretist effort, for he had no use for
Russian culture. He gave his country a voice crying in the wilderness for
humanity and mercy and love, in the decades when violence opposed violence
and the scene was being laid for a bloody confrontation of the two. He did not
contribute by his teaching to any kind of high culture, for he rejected it;
he was Russia's most thoroughgoing nihilist, though he was also its gentlest
and most humane spirit.

THE REPENTANT REFORMERS: NATIONALISM

By the mid-1870's the mood of exultation which pervaded the 60's had
passed. Into the passionate discussions that enveloped the Great Reforms
there had entered Westerners and Slavophiles, enlightened and retrograde
bureaucrats, the young radicals, everyone. Those who pooh-poohed the
Reforms nevertheless had confidence that change of a different, more sweeping
kind was possible and even perhaps imminent; those who thought they did
not go far enough still hoped soon to push on; those who opposed them
nevertheless had to hold on to their seats as the chariot of history galloped
forward, leaving behind it forever the world of serfdom. Russian *institutions*
were irreversibly being brought closer to those of the West.

What would happen, then, to Russian *culture*? The question was not in
the forefront of men's minds when institutional change was going forward so
dramatically. In the 1870's some Westerners and some Slavophiles felt
the importance of the question, but the issues of the 1840's had plainly
come to need reformulation, and the 70's were not a decade for fundamental
questions. They witnessed a process of transformation and in part degenera-
tion of the original Westerner and Slavophile views, and a posing of political
problems instead of philosophical ones. Examples of this process in the Slavophiles were the appearance of Pan-Slavism and the work of Danilevsky;
in the Westerners, the change of heart of Katkov and Pobedonostsev. Some
Slavophiles and some Westerners had supported and even taken part in the
implementation of the Great Reforms. Ivan Aksakov and Danilevsky did not
precisely repent of having done so, but they lost interest and turned their

attention elsewhere; Katkov and Pobedonostsev repented of their youthful liberalism and tried to find other answers. In both camps the result was nationalism – an authentic Western borrowing, but one which arrived fairly late in Russia.

Pan-Slavism was not the same as Slavophilism, and it was far from being identical or even compatible with the official stance of the regime. In 1849 Nicholas I had put the point with clarity in writing on the margin of depositions given by the arrested Ivan Aksakov and Yury Samarin:

Under the guise of compassion for the supposed oppression of the Slavic peoples, there is concealed the idea of rebellion against the legitimate authority of neighbouring and, in part, allied states, as well as the idea of a general unification which they expect to gain not through God's will but through disorder, which would be ruinous for Russia.[65]

The contradiction between the dynastic and national orientations could scarcely be more succinctly set forth. Pan-Slavism was not a part of official ideology, and it did not represent any widespread concern among the Russian people about their Slavic brothers, for there no such concern existed. It was a rather ephemeral part of the history of Russian thought, which meant that it was a product of a small group of intellectuals.

The transition from Slavophilism to Pan-Slavism may be observed most easily in Ivan Aksakov. Always 'having paid less attention to the theological side of Slavophilism than any of the others', as Miliukov accurately noted,[66] by 1856 Aksakov showed signs of shifting his attention still further from the religious philosophy which was the Slavophile hallmark in the direction of secular technology, science, and problems of state which were to become distinguishing features of the Pan-Slavs. He wrote, 'we do not know of any other weapons for the eradication of evil than those designed for us by European civilization: railroads, emancipation of the serfs, periodicals, newspapers, freedom of expression'.[67] It was the death of the two Kireevskys (1856) and of his brother Constantine and Khomiakov (1860) that thrust him to the fore. As editor of *Day* (*Den'*) from 1861 to 1865, he denounced the Polish rebellion, became preoccupied with the 'Jewish question',[68] and further developed his notions of Russia's mission to liberate and unite the Slavs – in particular the Orthodox Slavs, among whom he placed special trust in the Serbs. He became the moving spirit of the Moscow Slavic Benevolent Committee, founded in his absence in 1858 and lasting until 1878, which spawned corresponding groups in St Petersburg (1867), Kiev (1869), and Odessa (1870).[69]

The Russian Pan-Slavs enjoyed one public moment of splendor in 1867, at the Slavic Congress in Moscow which they (and not the government) hosted, despite the lack of any concrete result; and one heroic moment of identification with great events, during the Russo-Turkish War of 1877–8, when it seemed as if the liberation of the Balkan Slavs and Constantinople was virtually accomplished fact. The moment was fleeting. Aksakov's favorites, the Serbs, turned to Austria in 1882; Bulgaria followed in 1885.

His biographer writes that Aksakov's Slavdom 'was virtually reduced to Montenegro'.[70] Aksakov died in 1886.

The chief manifesto of the Pan-Slavs was written in 1865, and published in *Dawn* (*Zaria*) in 1869, though it had very few readers until the edition of 1888. It was Nicholas Danilevsky's *Russia and Europe* (*Rossiia i Evropa*). Born in 1822, Danilevsky was the son of a gentry officer who had fought Napoleon. He had been educated in the Tsarskoe Selo lyceum (1837–42) and the University of St Petersburg (1843–9). His involvement in the Petrashevtsy affair has already been mentioned; for it he was exiled to Vologda and then Samara. Released in 1853, he participated in several expeditions in the eastern part of the country, and after 1857 was an official in the Ministry of State Domains. He spent much time on biological research; history was his hobby, not science, but it was from science that his thought derived. He was not a Darwinist, and devoted a two-volume work (1885) about Darwinism to criticizing it; but he founded his 'historical naturalism', as Ivask calls it, on the zoological work of Cuvier.[71] For Danilevsky, it was not a question of climbing an evolutionary ladder of superiority for any of the different 'civilizations' he discerned in the world; rather each, like Cuvier's animal types, had its own peculiarities and its own values. In the 1860's he was an admirer of the Great Reforms, an apostle of freedom of expression, progress, and science like so many others. In *Russia and Europe* he began by asking why the West came to the aid of Turkey in 1854 (against Russia) and not Denmark in 1864, and answered that it was because Russia was the opponent in the Crimean War, and Russia was different from Europe. He enumerated ten 'cultural-historical types or distinctive (*samobytnye*) civilizations', of which one was 'Germano-Romanic or European';[72] curiously among the others does not appear any 'Slavic' civilization.[73] The Germano-Romanic civilization had passed its peak, and the time of a Slavic civilization had come. He summoned 'every Slav: Russian, Czech, Serb, Croat, Slovene, Slovak, Bulgar (I should like to add also, Pole)' to place the 'idea of Slavdom' as the highest idea of all, higher than freedom, science, enlightenment, and every other earthly blessing.[74] Slavophilism had been finally secularized, and became Pan-Slavism. Catholic and Orthodox Slavs were summoned to act together, on the basis of a human biology of Danilevsky's invention; their linguistic kinship, and no recovery of a common Eastern Orthodox cultural heritage, was the basis of his summons. (Danilevsky himself was not at all hostile to the Church;[75] it was not a question of personal religious belief.)

Actually when it came to concrete plans, neither Danilevsky nor a number of other Pan-Slavs were very fastidious about limiting their purview to Slavs. His Pan-Slavic Union (*Vseslavianskii soiuz*) was to Rumanians, Greeks, Magyars, and the Turks of part of Asia Minor.[76] Pan-Slavism developed into Russian imperialism; it was not the only case in the nineteenth century in which liberal nationalism became transmuted into a doctrine justifying foreign conquests. In the case of Pan-Slavism, the foreign conquests justified by the doctrine never took place. Instead, as already pointed out, at the point when something like real nationalism did take over the Russian government, under Alexander III, Russia's Slavic brothers (and the total of Russia's allies, until 1891) were reduced to the pinpoint of Montenegro, and not a single Slav was incorporated into any federation.

Another who supported the Great Reforms during the 1860's was Michael Katkov. Born in Moscow in 1818, he was the scion of a family of ecclesiastical officials.[77] In his youth he was an ardent Schellingian, going from the pension of Professor M. G. Pavlov into the Stankevich circle. He studied philology at Moscow University, defending a thesis in 1845, but soon moved into journalism, where he was to make his mark on Russia. As editor of *Russian Messenger* (*Russkii Vestnik*) from 1856 to 1887 (though only rather inactively so from 1862 to 1882) and *Moscow Record* (*Moskovskie Vedomosti*) from 1863 to 1887, he rose to wield an influence unprecedented in Russian journalism. From a defender of free trade he became an apostle of economic self-sufficiency; from an advocate of the zemstvos and the new court system he became a critic of both; and nevertheless he retained a number of liberal traits. For example, he opposed plans to deal with student unrest by repression in the aftermath of Karakozov's attempt on Alexander II, and instead formulated the views that underlay the statute of 1871 on secondary education, to the effect that classical training would wean youth away from nihilism.[78] And he became a nationalist, thundering against the Poles in 1863 but shocking his dynastically-minded bureaucrat friends by proposing to arm the Belorussian and Ukrainian (he considered them Russian) peasants of the Western provinces.[79]

More powerful than Katkov, and often exaggeratedly described as the power behind the throne in the reigns of both Alexander III and Nicholas II, was Constantine Pobedonostsev. He was born in Moscow in 1827; his father was a rather conventional professor of literature in Moscow University, though Peter Pobedonostsev had trained to become a priest like his own father. Constantine studied law at the university from 1841 to 1846, and on graduation entered the bureaucracy of the Senate. He remained an official until the last months of his long life, but for the first ten years or so of his government service he also did a good deal of scholarly publishing. He was a genuinely learned man in the field of law (in the broader, European sense), as shown especially in his masterly three-volume *Course of Civil Law* (*Kurs grazhdanskogo prava*, 1868–80), but in the late 60's he virtually ceased to be a practicing scholar.[80] During the 60's he was an enthusiastic supporter of the Great Reforms, in particular the legal reform of 1864, and frequented liberal salons such as that of the Grand Duchess Elena Pavlovna. He married (1866) a girl named Engelhardt from a Russified German family, traveled to the West frequently, and was especially fond of Salzburg and of England. During the next decade his views changed, and he became a conservative and even reactionary.

Pobedonostsev was selected to be tutor to the heir, Grand Duke Nicholas, in 1861, and then after he died in 1865 to act in the same capacity with the new heir, who became Alexander III. However, his significant influence on the government dates only from 1880, when Loris-Melikov, hoping to conciliate the conservatives so that he could proceed with his reform program, got Pobedonostsev named Procurator of the Holy Synod[81] though Alexander II was extremely reluctant to make the appointment. His chief and certainly crucial moment of impact on the action of the regime and indeed modern Russian history came not long afterward. Following the assassination of Alexander II, when debate was still open and undecided in the highest councils about whether to proceed with the Loris-Melikov reform program, with a majority favoring continuation, Pobedonostsev privately prevailed on his former pupil, Alexander III, to issue an unexpected manifesto proclaiming a quite different policy. However, that incident has led to the mistaken impression that Pobedonostsev dictated policy throughout the reigns of the last two emperors. He did not always get his way even under Alexander III, who especially on one occasion became furious with Pobedonostsev for deceiving him regarding state policy *vis-à-vis* the Baltic Lutherans,[82] and sometimes Nicholas II simply ignored him. To be sure, his influence was considerable, and he exerted it generally on behalf of a conservative nationalist policy. He stood for Russification of the borderlands, resistance to any kind of further liberal reform, and resolute commitment to the state, the Russian Orthodox Church as an army of the state, and the family as a bulwark of the state.

The Western character and origin of Pobedonostsev's conservative nationalism have not been well understood. He translated Thiersch's *Christian Origins of Family Life* (1861), Le Play, and Thomas à Kempis, and he admired and was influenced by Taine, Savigny, Carlyle, and especially the medieval nostalgia of William Morris, whom he called 'the finest of all contemporary writers' and whose photograph stood on his desk.[83] Like many other nationalists, he placed his faith in the common people as they actually were; he distrusted education, including religious education. As Florovsky remarks: 'With all his heart he accepted the Petrine reforms. And despite all his antipathy to contemporary Western liberal and democratic civilization, he remained a Westerner...He was a typical Erastian in his [official] activity.'[84] Far from encouraging any kind of religious revival, he feared it; his ecclesiastical horizons may be illustrated by his wish to correct the Russian New Testament by use of the 'Slavonic original' (*sic*!). He disrupted organizations for the development of religious culture, prohibited promising new ecclesiastical journals, and censored theological scholarship. The Orthodox Church, which was his only direct official responsibility, suffered under this repression more than any other institution.

After 1896 Pobedonostsev was consulted by Nicholas II only on Church affairs, and not always on those. In 1904–5 Witte's recommendations for changes in the Orthodox Church prevailed over his opposition, and immediately after the October Manifesto he was dismissed. He was already ill, and died in 1907.

DOSTOEVSKY

If religion had its part, open and concealed, in the nihilist and populist wings of Russian thought, it also had a role in the other currents of the time. The nihilists and populists (and Tolstoy) owed all their fundamental ideas to the West. The men who sought to advance other currents did not, despite their debt to Western influence. In one way or another they sought to continue, as the Slavophiles had begun to do, to recover living links with not only the pre-Petrine culture of Russia but even with the Byzantine tradition. There was no longer any serious thought of an uncompromising nativism, to the extent that the Slavophiles preached such a thing in spite of their own heavy mortgages to German idealist philosophy. Too many Western borrowings had lodged firmly in the training and background of every Russian intellectual, no matter what his ideals and commitments. Too much of obvious value and utility was to be found in the thought of the West. As a result, the aim of the great figures of literature and thought who belong to what Florovsky calls the 'creative main line' of Russian culture during the later nineteenth and early twentieth centuries was neither nativism nor Westernism, but syncretism (though they did not use the term): that is, the attempt intelligently and creatively to achieve a combination, a symbiosis, of Western and Russian ideas and traditions. There was no school of syncretists; in the latter nineteenth century, until the 1890's, they were mainly individuals, often isolated and in any case independent, often original and sometimes downright cranks. Dostoevsky (and for a brief time the group calling itself *pochvenniki* around Apollon Grigoriev), Vladimir Soloviev, Leontiev, and Fedorov might merit such a classification.

Fedor Mikhailovich Dostoevsky has fascinated several generations of simple readers and sophisticated critics, but it cannot be said that his thought has usually received adequate treatment at the hands of those who wrote books about him. Partly the cause is the contemporary separation of the disciplines; the professional students of literature are seldom eager to discuss a novelist's or a poet's thought. (Tolstoy escaped being considered solely a literary figure partly because he renounced such a position so categorically thirty years before his death.) Some of those who have discussed Dostoevsky's thought, such as Berdiaev and Masaryk, have themselves had such strong views that at the very least the fine edges of Dostoevsky's own position get sandpapered by their own philosophical commitments.

Masaryk is an especially odd case. He claims that the whole of the three-volume *The Spirit of Russia* was founded on his interpretation of Dostoevsky, and much of the recently translated third volume is devoted to the latter.

He declares that Dostoevsky appears to him as 'the greatest of Russian social philosophers',[85] but he plainly finds Dostoevsky emotionally repulsive. Alyosha flees to a monk's cell. 'How preposterously misguided!' Somewhat later he writes that Dostoevsky 'should have been preaching industriousness and prudence instead of monkish asceticism'.[86] He misinterprets Dostoevsky: the novelist is an 'aristocrat'; he is preoccupied with faith 'precisely because he himself can no longer believe'.[87] Both statements are about as flatly wrong as any characterization can be. Masaryk's antipathy to religion of any kind is not concealed, but within the religious sphere his Protestant prejudices are amazing. Protestants are said flatly to tell fewer lies than Roman Catholics or Orthodox, to have a healthier attitude toward sex, and so forth.[88]

Fortunately the best literary work, by general consent, on Dostoevsky also does justice to his thought. Its author, Konstantin Mochulsky, declares, 'Dostoevsky was not merely a *littérateur*; he was one of the world's greatest religio-philosophical thinkers. His ideas cannot be artificially separated from his creative work, for they are categorically fundamental to his writing and to any real understanding of it.'[89]

Dostoevsky was the grandson of a priest and the son of a self-made physician and of the daughter of a merchant family (so much for Masaryk's 'aristocrat'). His preoccupation with acceptance by society and his vulnerability to it or its lack may be traced to his background. He was born in Moscow in 1821. In his lonely youth he and his brother Michael turned to romantic fiction, and passions for Schiller, Homer, Victor Hugo, Shakespeare, Corneille, and Balzac[90] replaced one another with a rapidity reminiscent of Belinsky's liaisons and ruptures with a succession of German philosophers. He was in boarding school from 1833, from 1838 to 1843 in the St Petersburg University School of Engineering. After two years as an officer he retired to try being a professional writer. His personal life, finances, and plans were in constant disorder, fatally compounded by his gambling monomania which afflicted him from 1863 to 1871. After his second marriage at the age of forty-five, he did come to know happy family life, and became a lasting inspiration to men who marry their stenographers, but he never was long at peace with himself – which is perhaps the good fortune of thousands or millions of his readers.

Dostoevsky began to write, naturally, within the world of literature of the 1840's as a young man experienced it. His first publication was a translation of *Eugénie Grandet*, whose sale profited from a brief visit Balzac had just made to St Petersburg. In 1846 his first two short novels were published: *Poor Folk* (*Bednye liudi*) and *The Double* (*Dvoinik*). The ecstatic reception given *Poor Folk* by Nekrasov and Belinsky ('Do you yourself understand what you have written?') carried him instantly to the point of comprehending that he might achieve greatness, and though he had many moments of self-doubt and also bitter reproach for those who scorned or mocked him throughout his life, he never lost that comprehension. Both of the early tales owed much to

Gogol – *The Overcoat, The Diary of a Madman, The Nose* – and yet cannot be called derivative. He sought to depict reality, but he regarded this as a problem and not a technique. Mochulsky justifiably singles out the passage in a letter of 1839 to his brother Michael as embodying his conception of his vocation: 'Man is a mystery. One must solve it...I occupy myself with this mystery because I want to be a man.'

He missed the passionate attachment to Schelling and Hegel characteristic of the advanced youth of the 1820's, 30's, and early 1840's, and the cloudy formulations of German idealist philosophy and its Russian adepts never seemed to appeal to him. He moved from reading the French novelists to the French socialists, and did so before he met Petrashevsky[91] in the spring of 1846. First he borrowed Christian-social tracts from his new friend: St Simon's *Le nouveau Christianisme*, Cabet's *Le vrai Christianisme suivant Jésus-Christ*, Proudhon's *De la célébration du dimanche*. Only then did he begin to take part in the Petrashevtsy circle, and found kindred spirits in A. P. Miliukov, K. I. Timkovsky, A. N. Pleshcheev, and others who highly valued Lamennais and the other writers he himself had been reading.[92] It is now clear, however, that he became involved not merely in harmless literary discussion, but also in a revolutionary group – centered on Durov, but whose leading spirit was Speshnev. The latter seems to have been responsible for the group's withdrawing from the Petrashevsky circle. The objective of the Durov group was to prepare the people for an uprising, starting with the activity of an underground press. Dostoevsky had been converted to atheism by Belinsky in 1846, and in 1848 he was spellbound by Speshnev, who wished to use primitive Christianity as a partial model in constructing a secret revolutionary society. Dostoevsky called Speshnev 'my own Mephistopheles'.[93] Fortunately the police did not scent out the Durov group, and Dostoevsky was therefore tried only for his Petrashevtsy affiliations. The trauma of the last-minute reprieve from execution in St Petersburg and the experience of the Omsk penal colony were no doubt at least powerful contributors to illness and precipitated his first epileptic attacks, which came in Omsk. That they produced a life-long repentance in thought of his presumed revolutionary misdeeds, as some have suspected, is highly unlikely. Despite his later flirtations with imperialism (no Russian who would like the sympathy of the West ought ever to say 'Constantinople'; fortunately Dostoevsky said it only once or twice), and the odd friendship with Pobedonostsev, he never came to defend the tsarist regime as it was. He was not really interested in politics or in forms of government; he had a few good words to say in later life for a zemsky sobor, as a means of sounding peasant wisdom, but that was virtually all.

In the post-exile (he was released in 1854) novels, he sought reconciliation – his own with his people, that of Westerners with Slavophiles, that of Russia with the world. The announcement of his and his brother's new journal, *Time* (*Vremia*) in 1860 partly set forth this aim, though the contention was that the

'Russian idea' *did* reconcile all Western ideas and at the same time was broader than the West, and universal to mankind. Two gifted young critics, Apollon Grigoriev and N. N. Strakhov, were recruited to the staff of *Time*. The result was the formation of the circle of *pochvenniki*, literally 'soil–ers', meaning those who took the 'soil' of Russia as their starting point in thought.

Grigoriev, who was born in 1822, was graduated from Moscow University at twenty and for several years thereafter associated mainly with such Westerners as Granovsky, the Korsh brothers, and Petrashevsky.[94] In the early 1850's Pogodin had tried to broaden the editorship of his journal *The Muscovite* (*Moskvitianin*), bringing in Grigoriev along with the playwright A. N. Ostrovsky, T. I. Filippov, and A. F. Pisemsky. Grigoriev left the journal in 1855, and it came to an end in 1857. In 1860 he proposed that Pogodin allow him to edit it on the basis of a program of emphasis on nationality, anti-materialism, and the espousal of freedom 'against despotism on the one hand and against Tushino Fourierism on the other'.[95] Grigoriev was an interesting critic, who advocated a rounded, 'organic' approach to literary criticism; he emphasized what a proper understanding of the historical background of a given work could yield, insisting at the same time on the application of universal esthetic criteria. In such views his early enthusiasm for Hegel and his later devotion to Schelling may be reflected.

Strakhov was a little younger than Grigoriev. Born in 1828 in an ecclesiastical family, he was educated by an uncle who was the rector of seminaries at Kamenets-Podolsk and Kostroma. His university education was in the natural sciences, which he taught during the 1850's in schools in Odessa and St Petersburg. However, he was seriously and systematically interested in philosophy, and he was critical of anyone, including his ideological allies, who neglected philosophical foundations. More sympathetic to the Slavophiles than Grigoriev, he was less close to the Orthodox Church than they were and kept enough distance from their views so that when Nicholas Danilevsky's book *Russia and Europe* appeared, he took Danilevsky's side against them.

The *pochvenniki* aimed at creating a 'Christian philosophy' on the basis of their concept of *sobornost'* and the immediate relation of man to the native soil.[96] A number of articles Dostoevsky and his friends wrote in 1861 had this aim in view. The reconciliation motif was strong at first. It was by no means a question of identifying with the Slavophiles and trying to bridge the gap to the Westerners; Dostoevsky had too positive an attitude toward the Petrine reforms, and leaned toward the Westerners' side for a time. Pushkin was regarded as a symbolic justification of Peter's work; already the ideas of Dostoevsky's Pushkin speech of 1880 were being worked out. However, reconciliation was soon superseded by polemics with both sides, and the closing of the gap between intelligentsia and common people was relegated to the background while Dostoevsky expressed alarm at the mounting revolutionary movement. He now attacked the line of *The Contemporary*, organ of the radicals.[97]

In 1862 Dostoevsky first visited the West, and his disillusionment was expressed in *Winter Notes on Summer Impressions* (*Zimnie zametki o letnikh vpechatleniiakh*), rather a philosophical essay than a travel diary. He had many negative reactions; the capitalist system bred 'anthills'; the socialists with their attempts to achieve brotherhood by reason and calculation would breed – other anthills. But brotherhood must be sought, brotherhood between the West and Russia: 'We are brothers, we are all your brothers, and we are many and strong; be at ease and of good cheer, fear nothing and rely on us.'

Winter Notes was published in *Time* in 1863, but soon afterward the magazine was banned for a piece of Strakhov's on Poland that was taken to be oppositional. Dostoevsky now went a second time to the West, and after a two-month stay returned to start, with his brother, another journal called *Epoch* (*Epokha*). *Notes from Underground* (*Zapiski iz podpol'ia*) graced its pages; in it Dostoevsky developed some themes from *Winter Notes*, and Mochulsky calls it the 'philosophical preface to the cycle of the great novels'.[98] He expatiated on the problem of evil, which surpasses the power of socialism to cure, and polemized with the positivist reader of *The Contemporary* and *Russian Word*.

After a third trip to the West in 1865, following the failure of *Epoch*, Dostoevsky conceived and wrote the first of the great novels, *Crime and Punishment* (*Prestuplenie i nakazanie*). It has been interpreted, together with *The Idiot*, *The Possessed*, *A Raw Youth*, and *The Brothers Karamazov*, as a great tragedy in five acts, to which *Notes from Underground* serves as prologue.[99] The tragedy of Raskolnikov is a classical one: he is defeated only by Fate, to which he has enslaved himself by his estrangement from Christ – in Christ alone is there freedom.[100]

His growing antipathy to the Westerners was shown in his dramatic breach of 1867 with Turgenev, who for decades seemed to epitomize for him the 'Russian European' whom he had first satirized in *Uncle's Dream* in 1859. Hearing Bakunin at the 1867 congress of the First International, he heard in it merely Turgenev's Westernism writ large. The passion carried him into monarchism and imperialism, or at least so he thought. However, the temper of the times was against him, and doomed *The Idiot* (1868) and *The Possessed* (*Besy*, 1872) to failure. *The Possessed* contained in the character Stavrogin an attack on Speshnev of 1848, in Piotr Verkhovensky one on Nechaev of 1869, centering on the actual murder of the student Ivanov in that year, and in Stepan Verkhovensky an attack on Granovsky; again Westernism is regarded as leading to nihilism. But like the other novels, *The Possessed* was no mere current commentary. The following exchange sounds topical a century later:

PIOTR V.   We believe that our program is right and that everyone, upon accepting it, will be happy. Here is why we are resolved on blood, because happiness will be bought with blood.

STEPAN V.   And what if it will not be bought, what then?

PIOTR V.   We are certain that it will be bought, and this is enough for us.

The radicals anathematized the author of *The Possessed*, and the reactionaries took him up. He served in 1873-4 as editor of *The Citizen* (*Grazhdanin*) at the invitation of the notorious Prince Meshchersky, taking Maikov and Strakhov along as participants. He was befriended by Pobedonostsev, and Strakhov grew distant towards him. To Tolstoy's saga of the nobility in *War and Peace* he replied with *A Raw Youth* (*Podrostok*, 1875); to Turgenev's *Fathers and Children* he replied with *The Brothers Karamazov* (*Brat'ia Karamazovy*).[101]

In the late 1870's, while Dostoevsky was working on the *Brothers Karamazov*, he fell strongly under the influence of Vladimir Soloviev and Nicholas Fedorov. Just before plunging into the last novel and just after the death of his favorite son Alyosha, he visited Optina Pustyn in the company of Soloviev. In the Christ of the 'Legend of the Grand Inquisitor', who is totally silent, and Alyosha of the body of the novel, Dostoevsky's conception of Orthodox Christianity reaches its culmination. It led him back in the direction of his theme of 1863: reconciliation. That was the theme of the speech he made in Moscow in June 1880 eulogizing Pushkin and his capacity for universal sympathy, and it was a triumphant success. Turgenev shook hands with him; for a few weeks polemics among the intellectuals were muted. *The Brothers Karamazov* was completed in November 1880, and in January 1881 Dostoevsky died after three days of illness. The stormy career ended in relative peacefulness and unwonted popularity.

Recognition of his literary greatness, however, was by no means achieved for decades. Foreign critics handled him in a gingerly fashion for years. If Merezhkovsky and Shestov found inspiration in him, Mikhailovsky's 'cruel talent' and Gorky's 'Russia's evil genius' were the phrases that the Russian intelligentsia found apt.[102] Wellek emphasizes the wrongheadedness of trying to find a consistent system of thought in the great novelist. Zenkovsky rightly declares that his 'indications of the positive paths of "Orthodox culture" are as vague as his critique of the "Catholic idea" and of historiosophical rationalism, generally, is powerful'.[103] In the words of Chizhevsky, 'the Russian Enlightenment of the nineteenth century, with its universal rationalism, its conviction that reason is able to grasp all of reality and also to create a new and better reality, was the main thing in Russian life against which Dostoevsky fought all his life'.[104] In a rough draft of *The Brothers Karamazov* appears the following exchange:

ALYOSHA   And this the people will not allow.
RAKITIN   Well, then, eliminate the people, curtail them, force them to be silent. Because the European enlightenment is more important than the people.[105]

It might be accurate to say that what Dostoevsky opposed was less the 'European enlightenment' than those Russians who seemed to believe it more important than the values of their own people.

There was, to be sure, a powerful element of negation in Dostoevsky's thinking. He bitterly attacked the radicals of the 60's, the revolutionaries of the 70's, the Westerners who shared some of the views of both. Such groups opposed the existing order, but that was not what Dostoevsky held against them. He himself was profoundly dissatisfied with much of contemporary Russia as he was with the contemporary West, though he directed his attention to the realm of culture and not primarily or even significantly to the realm of politics. The West, despite its greatness, its 'holiness', was sick, and its disease was spreading to Russia. As Simmons puts it, he identified 'the European radical movement, designed to cure these ills, with the ills themselves. The revolutionary movement of the proletariat he regarded as a moral sickness which presaged the last convulsion of the bourgeois world.'[106] Westernism, despite its earlier great contribution to Russian culture, was seizing on his contemporaries like a demon. It closed the ears of Russians to the wisdom and piety of the common people and crippled the efforts of men like himself to recapture that lost part of the Russian tradition which would enable Russians to reach out to all of humanity.

Dostoevsky was no philosopher and no theologian – few great belletrists are. He sounded a tocsin for a syncretist effort, for a way to amalgamate the gifts of the West with the true, obscured, genius of Russia, but he himself was unable to carry it out. Neither the radicals nor ultimately the reactionaries could be happy with him. (As Simmons observes, 'the temperament of the conservative was essentially foreign to his nature'.)[107] His personal torment was profound, his own consciousness of weakness and sin agonizing. But he still was attracted by a vision of a saved humanity on earth, a 'universal union in the name of Christ', as he wrote at the very last, a vision for whose basis he was willing to use the phrase 'Russian socialism'.[108] Florovsky declares that he remained a utopian, having taken his problematics from Utopian socialism, believing in the historical resolution of the contradictions of life.[109] There was much fantasy in such a belief, and in Dostoevsky generally; but he was by no means alienated from reality. He hoped that he himself had contributed to reconciling Russia and the West as he declared Pushkin had done. As a man and a writer he achieved much toward that end; for his literary greatness came to be recognized as not clearly surpassed by anyone else in modern world literature. If Russian culture contributed something to such a titan, then it indeed had something to give both Russia and the West. Dostoevsky made a notch on the measuring rod of greatness which every man since has had to reckon with.

THE OTHER SYNCRETISTS

Chernyshevsky (to mention the only prominent radical of the 1860's to live for decades thereafter) remained a nihilist as well as revolutionary; Tolstoy remained a nihilist though he was never a revolutionary; Dostoevsky was for a brief time a revolutionary without becoming a nihilist; Vladimir Soloviev was never a revolutionary, though he was for a brief period a nihilist. More than anyone else, he charted a syncretist path for Russian thought and culture.

Soloviev (1853–1900) was the son of Russia's first historian of unquestioned scholarly stature, but the family was of the clergy. His grandfather was a priest, and his mother was descended from Skovoroda. Vladimir was a precocious child who had the first of three visions of Sophia[110] at the age of nine and entered a period of renunciation of religion at thirteen. His friend L. M. Lopatin later wrote of him at this period: 'I never thereafter met such a passionately convinced materialist. He was a typical nihilist of the 60's.'[111] At seventeen he entered the faculty of philosophy and history at Moscow University, but soon transferred to mathematics and physics, under the influence of an article by Pisarev on science.[112] After three years he went back to philosophy and history. At that point he was a socialist or even a communist. In 1873–4 he attended lectures at the Moscow Ecclesiastical Academy. From his youth he was interested in spiritualism and sometimes acted as a medium himself. He defended his master's thesis, 'The Crisis of Western Philosophy: Against the Positivists' (*Krizis zapadnoi filosofii: protiv pozitivistov*), at the age of twenty-one; he had already published an article the year previously. At the base of it, he wrote, lay the 'conviction that philosophy in the sense of abstract, *exclusively* theoretical knowledge has finished its development and passed irreversibly into the world of the past'.[113] The thought came almost verbatim out of Ivan Kireevsky, and the influence of the Slavophiles on the early Soloviev was certainly strong, but his argument came out differently. Under the influence of Schopenhauer and Hartmann, he spoke of the need to 'unite with the logical perfection of *Western form* the *fullness of content of the spiritual contemplation (sozertsanii) of the East*'. Thus, as Mochulsky says, he 'excluded all Russian Messianic motifs and counterposed to Western thought not Russian Orthodoxy but the nebulous "speculation (*umozreniia*) of the East" '.[114] Soloviev's defense of the thesis was a great success and immediately made him famous.

The following year, 1875, Soloviev went to England to study. In the reading room of the British Museum, that sacred place of Russian Westernizers, he had a second vision of Sophia, which sent him abruptly to Egypt; there he had a third (and final) encounter with 'her'. Returning to Russia, he divided his time between Moscow and St Petersburg. In 1877 his acquaintanceship with Dostoevsky ripened into close friendship, whose effects appear in Soloviev's lecture 'Three Forces' ('Tri sily'). The first force, the 'Muslim East', creates a manless God; the second, the West, gives rise to a Godless man; the third, unifying and synthesizing force will come from the Slavs and in particular the Russian people. The lecture had echoes of Tiutchev (the contention that revolution in the West had developed as a reaction to the secularization of the Roman Catholic Church) and Leontiev, but the assertion of the profound

Christianity of the Russian people and of its universal mission owed much to Dostoevsky.

In *The Philosophical Principles of Integral Knowledge* (*Filosofskie nachala tsel'nogo znaniia*), also published in 1877, he rejected the sufficiency of both empiricism and rationalism as modes of cognition and argued the necessity of a third mode, mysticism (as Spinoza and Pascal had done). In 1878 his lectures on theanthropy (*Bogochelovechestvo*) attracted much attention and gave rise to a 'religio-philosophical movement'. In 1880 he defended his doctoral dissertation, *A Critique of Abstract Principles* (*Kritika otvlechennykh nachal*). Herein he reduced all modern Western philosophy ultimately to two syllogisms, whose conclusions were: rationalism (Hegel) holds that the forms of human thought are true being, empiricism (Mill) that the states of human consciousness are true being. The nature or content of true being, however, remains in the shadows. Eastern philosophy, however, leads to recognition of an Absolute; being is an emanation of God. The tinge of pantheism and the influence of Spinoza, who fascinated Soloviev from the age of sixteen, are apparent.

In 1881 came a crisis in Soloviev's life almost as fateful for him as 'conversion' for Tolstoy. Externally it was occasioned by his lecture calling for clemency for the assassins of Alexander II, which led to his being told to be quiet for a while – not to dismissal; he nevertheless resigned his position. But much else was involved. He broke with Slavophilism, and his increasing distance from Orthodoxy led him toward Roman Catholicism; he abandoned philosophy; former friends became enemies.[115] After 1881, he wrote six years later, he concentrated on two questions, the reunion of the churches and reconciliation of Christianity with Judaism. On the latter, he proclaimed that 'the Jewish question is a Christian question'; as Mochulsky says, he made ideological anti-Semitism much more difficult in Russia by his utterances of 1884 and after on the subject.[116] Judaism was not a passing fancy of his; his concern with the cabala dated back to the 1870's, and his obscure notions about androgyny seem to derive from cabalistic doctrines.

During the 1880's Soloviev became friends with both Constantine Leontiev and Nicholas Fedorov, both of whom made an impact on his ideas. But his main concern of the decade was theocracy: the search for a way to Christianize the world, to create a unified church under one senior priest (the Pope) side by side with a politically unified Christendom under one king (Alexander III), both aided by 'prophets' (such as himself?). *La Russie et l'Eglise universelle* (1889), written in French, was the chief expression of this search. He recognized the primacy of the see of Peter, the Immaculate Conception as a doctrine close both to the Russian cult of the Mother of God and to his notions of Sophia, and accepted the *filioque* addition to the Creed. It was, if one likes, the Newman period of his life.[117] He visited Strossmayer, the great Croatian bishop, who had opposed the doctrine of papal infallibility in 1870, in Zagreb, and Paris, where he made Jesuit friends; he evidently did not get to Rome, though Strossmayer arranged an audience with Leo XIII. Contrary to fairly widespread opinion, he never became a Roman Catholic. The contention that he did hinges on the fact that he took communion once from a Uniat priest in 1896; there is, however, no evidence to show that he regarded this as a token of conversion or of anything other than his recognition of the unity of the whole Church.

Once again he shifted his attention. Theocracy proved a chimera. In October 1891 he lectured on 'The Collapse of the Medieval World View' ('Ob upadke srednevekovogo mirosozertsaniia'), indicting the historic church for its failure to concern itself with the salvation of society. It was the first Christian-modernist manifesto in Russia. In these years Soloviev underwent a *rapprochement* with the St Petersburg liberals of *Messenger of Europe* (*Vestnik Evropy*) and the like. He shared their political views and opposed the reactionary atmosphere of the time as they did. His life ended in a prophetic mood. He expected Antichrist, the end of the world, and his own death, which came in July 1900. Only months earlier he finished his last significant work, *Three Conversations* (*Tri razgovora*) in which appears an insertion, somewhat like 'The Legend of the Grand Inquisitor', entitled 'A Tale of Antichrist'. In it a totalitarian ruler splits the churches, promising an earthly paradise to each; a tiny minority of faithful Catholics, Orthodox, and Protestants reunify the Church in Israel; the Second Coming occurs, and Jews and Christians killed by Antichrist are resurrected.

And so Russia's foremost philosopher, who attempted a Christian philosophy and yet strewed it with non-Christian and even anti-Christian ideas,[118] who baffled friends and enemies, was gathered to his ancestors. There was a sizeable flaw in Soloviev. On the one hand there was the erudite, logical, and moderate philosopher; on the other the esthete and amateur mystic, devotee of automatic writing and the cabala, pantheist and erotomane, suitor in a 'romance with God'. He tried to combine the two sides of himself in the realm of religion and at the same time reconcile the truths of the three parts of the sundered church with each other, with the Jews, with the religious insights of the Muslims and the Far East. He not only abjured the nationalism that tempted him but helped to shake Leontiev in his fascination for the primitive Russian culture of his imagination and to lead him towards the real Greek roots of Orthodoxy and of Europe.[119] He was a Christian who became a political liberal. In the field of general culture, he had his important debts to the West in Spinoza, Schopenhauer, Hegel, Schelling, and others.

But he was not merely a member of a school – of philosophy or of enthusiasm. He saw, as Chaadaev did, what the lack of Western philosophical tradition had meant to Russia; like Chaadaev, he desired reunion of the churches as a way of giving Russia a fuller and sounder culture – and, unlike Chaadaev, he believed this would also give something important to the West which it lacked. He did his best to recover the Orthodox roots of old Russian culture, without giving much attention to old Russia itself. He had much to do in a short time, and could not do it all.

One of Soloviev's close friends, Nicholas Fedorov was an illegitimate son of Prince P. I. Gagarin, born in 1828, and took the name of his godfather. He attended a gymnasium in Tambov and studied law for a time in the Lycée Richelieu in Odessa. From 1858 to 1868 he moved constantly, earning a living as a schoolteacher; from 1868 to 1893 he held a post in the Rumiantsev Museum (today part of Lenin Library) in Moscow, and after retiring there held a librarian's job in the Foreign Affairs Ministry's archives. He died in 1903. In Fedorov's thought one may find a kind of voluntarism carried close to madness. Man is not merely to study history and reality, but to take part in it, indeed to mold it; he is to create 'a better world', not in the usual reformist sense but by taking some very dramatic steps. He must end injustice, not resigning himself to it, and injustice he located in two areas: poverty and death, the latter being its ultimate core. Fedorov summons man to the work of resurrection instead of mere belief in a doctrine of resurrection; beginning with securing control of the weather on earth and of the movements of the other planets, man must finally collect the 'scattered particles' of the bodies of his ancestors and resurrect them. A number of important nineteenth-century themes underlie his thought: unrestricted faith in what science may accomplish for man, unlimited confidence in human reason, trust in the salutary effects of social endeavor for the individual and the community. Zenkovsky prefers to de-emphasize the fantastic elements in Fedorov and stress that his 'basic inspiration concerning the struggle with death is so radiant with the light of the Christian gospel of resurrection that its radiance cannot be lessened by his naive formulations...'[120] Florovsky more accurately states that his view was shaped on the basis of French thought – Comtian positivism and Fourieran utopianism – and points out that Soloviev in the 90's took up Comte again under the influence of Fedorov. Florovsky concludes that Fedorov's world view 'was not Christian at all, and is at sharp variance with Christian revelation and experience'.[121] He was a kind of philo-syncretist Westernizer.

Like Fedorov, Leontiev was quite different from Soloviev in his ideas. Constantine Leontiev was born in 1831 in Kaluga province, the youngest child of seven who was almost a textbook case of attachment to the mother. He was in gymnasium at Smolensk in 1841-2, a military school in St Petersburg in 1843-4, the Kaluga gymnasium 1844-9, and then after a false start at a school in Yaroslavl entered the Moscow University School of Medicine, which he hated. His first writings were belles-lettres and date from 1851. He took them to Turgenev, who kindly encouraged him in his work, gave advice on his love life, and urged him to volunteer (which he did) as a doctor in the Crimean War in 1854. After it was over he worked on his writing and published a novel, *Under the Lindens* (*Podlipki*), in 1861. By this time he had abandoned medicine for good. He was then close to the Slavophile camp,[122] but by the time of the Polish revolt of 1863 had lost his confidence in the Russian *narod* and became a frank reactionary. He now entered the diplomatic service and spent the decade 1864–74 in Crete and the Balkans. In 1871, during a severe illness, he underwent a religious crisis.

Before returning to Russia he wrote his main ideological work, *Byzantinism and Slavdom* (*Vizantizm i slavianstvo*), in which, according to Lukashevich, all the main themes of his later thought were expounded. Like many other nineteenth-century thinkers, he had three stages of history (and evolution of forms of life other than man): primeval simplicity (*pervichnaia prostota*), complex flowering (*slozhnoe tsvetenie*), and resimplification (*vtorichnoe uproshchenie*).[123] It was in essence still another Hegelian triad, but one in which the second term was the apogee; before 'complex flowering', individuation occurs, while after it the inequality, discipline, and self-expression characteristic of individuation are destroyed. What Leontiev was really interested in was the 'individuated' person. The values he cherished were to be found in esthetics and religion – but it was a rather unusual sort of religion. Fear was its starting point (as in Proverbs 1.7); fear led to faith in God and obedience to the Church, and only then to the love of God. Esthetics and religion could not be reconciled, but they could fruitfully struggle and thereby enrich individual personality.

Leontiev had little use for the Slavs, and only a little more for the Greeks of his day; what was positive in Russian life came from the old Byzantine tradition, he thought, but that meant to him mainly the Byzantine political and social system. Despite his principled renunciation of the bourgeois West of his day, he had his debts to pay to the West: the greatest age of true individuality he found in the Italian Renaissance, and he also highly valued Germany of the turn of the nineteenth century. Moreover, as a conservative he held out his hand to the socialists: 'the essential aspects of conservative teachings will, nevertheless, be useful to them. They will need to make use of fear and discipline; they will need a tradition of submissiveness and a habit of obedience.' And he foresaw a new 'slavery that would express itself in the most cruel form of submission of individuals to small and large collective institutions, which in turn would submit to the power of the state'.[124] Even the presumed goal of socialism repelled him: 'to believe...in something impossible, in the final kingdom of truth and happiness upon earth, in a bourgeois and workers' paradise, in a drab and impersonal earthly paradise...is stupid and shameful ...' (Would he have declared the USSR of a century later to be 'impossible'?)[125] He was no nationalist; he valued Catholicism in Poland as a barrier to atheism, he opposed Russification of the minorities, not only of Poles but of Asiatics; he despised nationalism as 'nothing but the process of liberal democratization which has already started for some time to destroy the great cultures of the Occident'; he opposed Pan-Slavism. At one point his ideal was to combine the 'Chinese sense of statesmanship with Indian religiosity and by subjecting European Socialism to these two Oriental principles...[create] new and socially stable groups and a new horizontal social stratification'.[126] Berdiaev sums up: 'before Nietzsche's time he was that rare phenomenon, a Nietz-schean Christian'.[127] It is perhaps a formulation that does as little violence as any other to this strange, complex, original man.

In 1874, on returning to Russia, he tried monastic life and other things before becoming a censor in Moscow from 1880 to 1887. From 1887 on his friendship with Soloviev developed, founded in part on Soloviev's sympathetic attitude toward Rome, which he viewed as 'an excellent counterpoise to the ethical-protestant sympathies of the Slavophiles'.[128] In his last months he was tonsured monk, taking leave of the Elder Amvrosy of Optina Pustyn, who, himself on the verge of death, told Leontiev that they would soon meet again. A few weeks after hearing of Amvrosy's death, Leontiev died, in November 1891.

CONCLUSION

The period 1855–90 was an extraordinarily rich and diverse period in the history of Russian thought and in particular the history of the reception of Western thought in Russia. It witnessed the beginning of the revolutionary movement, which owed much to the nihilist rejection of history and culture, though nihilism as an attitude was held by many who did not become revolu-tionaries, such as Pisarev, or were even positively anti-revolutionary, such as Tolstoy. The intellectual and social starting point of the revolutionary move-ment, however, was inextricably bound up with religion. The first revolu-tionaries in thought and action were mainly seminarists and sons of priests, deeply imbued with religious attitudes even when they inverted them into atheist passion, who naturally adopted missionary methods in seeking to spread the revolutionary gospel, whose first large-scale effort, the 'going to the people' movement, was entirely evangelical in form. The century-old heritage of Protestant pietism in Russia had not gone for nothing. When the movement failed, and then the desperate resort to terrorism produced not revolution but the reaction of Alexander III, the revolutionaries passed on to closer imitation of Western socialist theory and practice.

The revolutionaries never sympathized with the middle way or its embodi-ment in the Great Reforms. There were, to be sure, liberals who clung to it even after the Reforms faltered and awaited their chance to go forward on the same road, but they made little impact on Russian thought at least after the 1860's (until the early years of the twentieth century). A number of the men who had ardently supported the Reforms slid over, out of repugnance and fear of the revolutionaries, into conservative nationalism:[129] the Pan-Slavs, Katkov, and Pobedonostsev, among others. Both revolutionaries and con-servative nationalists were Westernizers through and through.

Side by side with them, however, emerged the beginnings of a syncretist camp – 'school' is not the right word, since the divergences among the men involved were substantial and sometimes sharp. Dostoevsky was the best-known because of his novels, but the more serious thinkers included Soloviev and Leontiev. They all sought, despite differences from each other and their individual eccentricities, to recover part of Russia's cultural heritage and to combine it with the influences from the West that Russia had already begun to assimilate and transform. Those who survived into the reign of Alexander III suffered from its atmosphere of political reaction and in particular the oppressive pall laid on the religious sphere by Pobedonostsev. Soloviev's last years were filled with foreboding, only part of which may be explained by any prophetic gifts one may wish to credit him with having; he saw much potentiality, little achievement in the task of harmonizing the Eastern and Western churches and their cultures. From the vantage point of 1917 his forecasts may seem warranted; but already by the time of his death in 1900 a palpable syncretist tide was beginning to run, and within a few years it was to be visible to all.

8

THE PARTIAL RECONCILIATION
WITH THE WEST (1890–1917)

I am not teaching, I am learning; I am not preaching, I am seeking to be
preached to.   Dmitry Merezhkovsky

INTRODUCTION

During most of Alexander III's reign gloom deepened among those who
awaited further movement along the road of reform from above that Alexander
II had entered, while the revolutionaries were dispersed and disheartened. The
liberals winced as law after law sponsored by Count Dmitry Tolstoy's
interior ministry sought to limit or reverse the policy of the Great Reforms.
After the forlorn attempt on Alexander III's life in 1887, the remnants of the
People's Will were mopped up and the revolutionary movement reached a
dead stop. Even the accession of Nicholas II in 1894 soon dashed hopes that it
had fleetingly raised; he did not hesitate to rebuff mild reformist expressions,
uttered by zemstvo liberals, as 'senseless dreams'. The same policies would be
followed as under Alexander III but they would be implemented by a much
less consistent and strong ruler. The despair of the liberals and revolutionaries
was redoubled; even the reactionaries feared that the young new emperor
could never match the strength of his father. The period of the Great Reforms
was clearly at an end; the policy of the regime appeared frozen in immo-
bility.

   The decade or so following 1881 seemed also in the cultural field to mark
the end of an era. A series of deaths signaled some kind of shift: Dostoevsky
in 1881, Turgenev and Mussorgsky in 1883, a promising writer named
Garshin in 1888, Chernyshevsky in 1889, Leontiev in 1891, Tchaikovsky in
1893. The possibility of new directions in politics depended on the monarch;
but new directions in the field of thought and culture did not – not any more,
for gradually during the nineteenth century Russian culture had built substantial foundations of its own outside of court circles. New trends were in
fact forthcoming. Mainly they came out of three developments: the reception
of Marxism, which swept the Russian intelligentsia in the 1890's and transformed the area of radical and revolutionary debate; the esthetic revival in
literature and the fine arts, begun by Merezhkovsky, the symbolists, and the
World of Art group; and the aspirations toward cultural renewal and liberation from state control to be observed in the Orthodox Church. In each of the
three intellectual environments were to be found diehards who abominated

one or both of the others, and yet some interesting links came to exist among all three. Within a few years the result was a cultural renaissance that can be credited to no single trend, group, or person but was marked by a significantly new kind of cultural pluralism in Russia. It created a mood of excitement in all of the Russian public that could boast of education going beyond mere literacy, surprised and dazzled Western Europe, and left behind it traces that are clear and vital even in the USSR of the 1970's – of which the Soviet government approves some, is neutral toward others, combats still others with all its might – thus far without success.

THE RECEPTION OF MARXISM

Foremost during the 90's among the epigons of the populism of the 70's was Nicholas Mikhailovsky. During the 70's, writes one contemporary, he was 'the idol of the youth, of the entire intelligentsia',[1] and he retained his (somewhat diminished) authority long after that. Born in the town of Meshchevsk, southwest of Moscow, in 1842, he was expelled in 1861 from the St Petersburg Mining Institute where he had been studying the sciences. Since the University of St Petersburg was at that moment disrupted, he abandoned plans to study law and instead became a journalist. His chief inspiration came from French radical thought: Proudhon, Comte, and Louis Blanc,[2] as it had become for Herzen and others. In 1869 he joined the staff of Nekrasov's *Notes of the Fatherland* (*Otechestvennye Zapiski*) and in that capacity rapidly acquired the position of chief populist sage residing in Russia, as distinguished from the émigrés Lavrov, Bakunin, and Tkachev. Like Danilevsky, he inveighed against Social Darwinism, especially Herbert Spencer's version of it. Nature showed him no mercy; he would show nature none 'and with bloody labors will subjugate her, force her to serve me, expunge evil and create good'.[3] He thus assumed the typical populist stance of resistance to historicist theories of inevitability. On *Notes of the Fatherland* (until it was closed in 1884), *Northern Messenger* (*Severnyi Vestnik*, from 1885), and *Russian Wealth* (*Russkoe Bogatstvo*, from 1892) he kept the anarcho-socialist views of the populists alive in Russia during a difficult period.[4] In 1893 he took part in the abortive attempt to found a Party of People's Right (*Narodnoe pravo*), which aimed at both political democracy and socialism, but the following spring the police dispersed it – without arresting him. He lived until 1904, having enjoyed a great public tribute in 1900.

In the 1890's the staff of *Russian Wealth* came to include other socialists better able than Mikhailovsky to assess the economic side of the changes Russia was undergoing. One was V. P. Vorontsov ('V.V.'), who in his book *The Fate of Capitalism in Russia* (*Sud'by kapitalizma v Rossii*) (1882) had argued that industrialization had come to Russia to stay, but not capitalism; the more backward the country, the more difficult it was to industrialize via capitalism; the tsarist state, however, could and ought to move by stages to organize both large- and small-scale industry along lines determined not by profit but by the welfare of the people (and thereby spare the peasant from being 'boiled' *à la* Ziber). Russia would thus realize equality and fraternity but not liberty (for which he was dubbed a 'police populist' by his critics).[5] The other was N. F. Danielson ('Nikolai-on'), who helped translate *Das Kapital* and regarded himself as a Marxist. At the suggestion of Marx himself he had written a book called *Outlines of Our Post-Emancipation Social Economy* (*Ocherki nashego poreformennogo obshchestvennogo khoziaistva*) (1893), the first part of which Marx had read and praised (1881). By the time the book was near completion, Marx was dead, and Engels was not so sure about it. At any rate the volume ended with the demand that agriculture and industry be unified in the hands of the direct producers but in the form of large-scale production.[6] The state's precise role in all this, however, was left in obscurity.[7]

Walicki, as has already been pointed out, contends that the populists were led to conceive of capitalism as 'enemy number one' by reading *Das Kapital*, but he fails to mention that Plekhanov, who knew other works of Marx as well, was led by him to regard as the main enemy the 'Asiatic' tsarist state, and therefore he and the other 'Marxists' were not transfixed by fear of capitalism.[8] In the last years of Marx's life and even of Engels's, however, the populists dominated the scene of Russian socialism. They knew very well that industry was growing and railways were being built, and that the state (under the ministers of finance Vyshnegradsky, 1887-92, and Witte, 1892-1903) was staking much on the sponsorship of industrialization.[9] They could cite the authority of Marx's own pronouncements to the effect that he had not meant his feudalism–capitalism–socialism sequence to be applied to the past or future of all countries at all, that Russia might pass directly to socialism, that the commune might be preserved in altered form, and that Russia might even lead an international revolution. The Russian populists wrote to Marx as an oracle of international socialism who would pronounce definitively on the course of history, as the Chinese students of the 1920's wrote to the Sorbonne professors to find out if Christianity and God were beliefs with any merit. It is amazing how often the clear reply of the oracle has been disregarded: Marx replied to the populists, over and over, yes, you are right. Whether that was a 'Marxist' answer is another matter. The determinism and historicism of Marx were still there in his works, despite his vote for voluntarism in Russia. Plekhanov in his chief 'populist' work, 'The Law of the Economic Development of Society and the Tasks of Socialism in Russia' (1879) came out at exactly the same point as Marx himself; Plekhanov declared that Marx did not want 'to stretch the whole human race on a Procrustean bed of "universal laws"', and Marx expressed the same idea in his letter of 1884 declaring Mikhailovsky wrong to convert his scheme in *Das Kapital* into 'an historico-philosophical theory of the *marche générale* imposed by fate upon every people, whatever the historic circumstances...' No wonder several investigators have failed in their effort to find exactly at what point Plekhanov, in an intellectual transformation constantly referred to by many authors, converted from 'populism' to 'Marxism'. In the 1880's there were no such tidy, mutually exclusive categories.[10]

The evolution of Plekhanov's thought, to be sure, was crucial in the formation of socialism in Russia. Born in 1856 in a gentry family of Tambov province, he attended the Voronezh Military Academy from 1866 to 1873.[11] There he became acquainted with radical literature and espoused atheism. Soon he shifted to scientific studies at the St Petersburg Mining Institute. As a student there he joined the Land and Liberty group, was the speaker for the December 1875 demonstration at Kazan Cathedral, and as a result had to flee abroad. Returning to Russia, he opposed the terrorists within Land and Liberty, as already mentioned. Again he emigrated, with a small group of followers; he was not to come home to Russia until 1917.

During the 1880's Plekhanov became a Social Democrat and led a number of other Russian exiles to do so. He and his friends of the Black Partition, Vera Zasulich and Lev Deich, were joined by Paul Axelrod and V. I. Ignatov in the formation of a new Group for the Emancipation of Labor (Gruppa 'Osvobozhdenie Truda'). It was the first Russian Social Democratic organization, and Plekhanov in his writings – especially *Our Differences* (*Nashi raznoglasiia*, 1884), laid down the gauntlet to other Russian socialists. However, only in the early 1890's erupted the debates in Russia that created the widespread opinion that a socialist must be either a 'populist' or a 'Marxist'.

What accounts for the particular time at which 'Marxism' came into being in Russia? A fundamental part of the answer is to be found in the emergence of German Social Democracy. Founded in 1875 by the merger of followers of Marx and Lassalle and adopting a program at Gotha which Marx attacked in a *Critique* that remained unpublished, the German Social Democratic party had soon fallen afoul of Bismarck's anti-socialist laws. But by 1890 the party had polled almost a million and a half votes, and the law was allowed to expire as a failure. The party adopted a new program at Erfurt (1891), dropping several Lassallean features of the Gotha document. The new program was composed chiefly by Kautsky under the guiding hand of Engels (who now felt it safe to publish Marx's *Critique of the Gotha Program* – which was, however, even more radical than the Erfurt language). In 1889 the Second International had been formed. Social Democracy triumphantly proclaimed its new doctrinal purity. In the summer of 1890 Peter Struve visited Germany, and returned to found the first Social Democratic study circle in Russia, at the University of St Petersburg.[12]

Young Struve, then twenty, was the grandson of a German who had settled in Russia to become a famed astronomer and the son of an undistinguished provincial governor. From his teens he read widely and stored what he learned in a photographic memory. By the end of the 1880's he had accepted much of Marx, especially believing that in Russia he was witnessing the recapitulation of the rise of capitalism in the West described by Marx. In 1892–3 he sharply criticized Vorontsov's and Danielson's works in several reviews that he had to publish in German periodicals for lack of Russian acceptances. Mikhailovsky finally replied, and by the spring of 1894 the great debate of the decade was under way. Struve used the term 'populism' to apply to his opponents,[13] thereby lumping together (despite their loud protests) everyone who wished to preserve the commune and on that basis to take Russia on its own non-capitalist path to socialism. To be sure, Marx and Engels themselves had approved the latter alternative, but Engels, in the last year or two of his life, was now uneasy about it again (which heartened Struve) and was also troubled by the squabble among the Russian socialists (for which he blamed Struve). 'Legal Marxism' – a term which ought to be limited simply to Marxist works that were legally published in Russia, for their authors had substantial disagreements among themselves – was one consequence. The first Marxist work published legally in Russia was a series of pamphlets called *What the 'Friends of the People' Are* (*Chto takoe 'Druz'ia naroda'*) (1894) written by a young man from Samara named Vladimir Lenin, who had been born the son of an automatically ennobled official in Simbirsk in 1870. Within a few months there followed Struve's *Critical Notes on the Question of Russian Economic Development* (*Kriticheskie zametki po voprosu ob ekonomicheskom razvitii Rossii*) and Plekhanov's *On the Question of the Development of the Monistic View of History* (*K voprosu o razvitii monisticheskogo vzgliada na istoriiu*). Plekhanov's book, brought in from abroad and published under a pseudonym, was a selective and critical history of eighteenth- and nineteenth-century Western thought, culminating in Marxism.

The proposition that Marxism was the culmination of the best modern Western thought carried all before it among the young Russian intelligentsia of the 1890's. A spirited debate went forward in the halls of the major universities, in the Imperial Free Economic Society – where Struve spoke to great audiences including mainly youth, recalling to some the spell earlier cast by Pisarev[14] – and in the columns of popular journals. Kizevetter found the closest precedent in the 1840's, in the Westerner–Slavophile controversy;[15] but he notes that in the earlier period the intelligentsia was so much smaller, the press so much weaker, that the two debates had quite different impacts on the country. To be sure, there was another difference; the Slavophiles, despite their German Romantic derivation, sought to recover traditional roots as against the flatly xenophile Westerners, while neither faction of Russian socialists, Marxists or 'populists', had any significant debt whatever to Russian thought nor wished to have any.

Marxism's sources of appeal to young Russians were chiefly three. First it had, Berdiaev writes, 'a distinctly higher intellectual and cultural standard than most of the preceding movements'.[16] It is quite true that Struve and his young St Petersburg friends exhibited subtle and critical intellects and a very high level of education (Lenin as a young provincial was both awed by his new friends in the capital and apt to scent in them overrefined failure to grasp the real issues in the political war he wanted to fight). Second and psychologically more fundamental, it brought 'a purpose and a new conception of man'; or, as Sergei Bulgakov puts it: 'I said to myself, men will be gods, and so, it seems, did others.'[17] It secularized the religious vision that remained a vital part of the Russian heritage even for those who, like Berdiaev, were generations away from meaningful Orthodox belief; in contrast, Bulgakov's ancestors had been priests for six generations, and he underwent such secularization as an almost instantaneous personal experience. Third, it was the very latest thing out of the West, in particular out of the advanced German intellectuals' armory of thought. This both validated its soundness as a doctrine and promised – as a gift of history rather than of man's voluntary efforts – the completion of Russia's Westernization. Young Russians had been exposed to Western-style education long enough so that they could now hope not merely to follow the currently popular Western ideas but also to contribute their share to their development. Berdiaev with more than a touch of pride recalls that his first article was published in the German Social Democratic organ *Die Neue Zeit*, edited by Kautsky, and that as a result Kautsky wrote him 'of his [Kautsky's] great hopes that the Russian Marxists would contribute to the future theoretical development of Marxism'.[18] The Russian Marxists, by identifying themselves with the clearly 'European' ideas of Marxism, would merely be the advance point for the general 'Europeanization' of Russia by way of the development of capitalism and socialism.

For many of the Russian Marxists of the 90's, 'Europeanization' was necessary precisely because Russia's social heritage was Asiatic. Plekhanov was a student of Marx, and it was Marx who, building on the work of his predecessors, had worked out a concept of an 'Asiatic mode of production' quite different from the sequence of slavery–feudalism–capitalism he discerned in the West, which provides the basis for an all-powerful state that can bend to its will social classes and any individual under its rule. Such a pattern became established in Russia with the Muscovite period, when the country had a 'completely Asiatic character...alien to Europe and very closely related to China, Persia, and ancient Egypt'. Peter the Great began the long process of Europeanization of Russia, but it was far from being complete. Thus Plekhanov assessed the obstacles to the growth of capitalism and socialism in Russia;[19] he did so on the basis of the concepts of Marx. But the theme of 'Europeanization' had a strong appeal to those who studied the societies of the world much less carefully than Plekhanov. Bulgakov warned that if 'our Easterners, thundering *ex oriente lux* at us...Westerners', oppose European economic formations, they must go on to reject 'all the benefits of European culture which alone give beauty to our lives'.[20] The combination of the sanction of the authority of the advanced thought of the West, the veiled religious appeal of Marxian eschatology and deification of man, and the promise of transforming Russia into Europe together explain the chief motives that swept a generation of Russian intelligentsia into Marxism.

More prosaic causes are often adduced for the victory of Marxism in the 1890's: disillusionment in the revolutionary potential of the peasantry (which had come to many as early as 1873), enthusiam for industrialization, hope for a movement founded on the growing numbers of industrial workers. It is of course true that industrial development was increasingly visible in the 90's; it is also true that, first, none of the prominent Marxists had any significant experience with industry before their conversion to Marxism, and second, that genuine contact with the workers' movement in the late 90's, as it erupted in substantial strikes, produced not orthodox Marxism but deviation from it into 'economism'.[21] Lenin was quite right when he lamented that only 'trade-union consciousness' could be looked for from the workers; he might have added that experience with the workers' movement tended to drive intellectuals in the same direction.

The same causes have since the 90's driven many intellectuals (but few workers) into the Marxist camp in the so-called developing countries – that is, outside the West. The young Russians were the pathfinders, because their country had had an earlier and more thorough exposure to the intellectual roots of Marxism than any other non-Western nation.

In the 1890's Marxism captured the allegiance of a galaxy of gifted young thinkers in Russia: Struve, Michael Tugan-Baranovsky, Nicholas Berdiaev, Sergei Bulgakov, S. L. Frank,[22] and the less sophisticated but yet hard-working and thoughtful Vladimir Lenin, all of whom joined forces with George Plekhanov, their exiled senior. There were also many lesser lights in the field of thought who were dedicated activists, such as Julius Martov, Alexander Potresov, and Paul Axelrod. By 1896–7 the Marxist–populist debate had reached its height, and in 1898, with the abortive First Congress (whose manifesto was composed by Struve) of the Russian Social Democratic Labor Party in Minsk, the Marxists advanced to the task of organizing a party. At this point debates invaded the ranks of the Marxists. In 1899 Struve, who had sounded revisionist notes earlier, aligned himself with Eduard Bernstein's critique of Marxist notions of impoverishment of the worker and cataclysmic revolution. The mass German party was able to hold a Bernstein; the tiny Russian underground nucleus insisted on expelling a Struve, who thereafter cooperated with the Marxists for a time as a radical liberal. Soon the other major figures of the 90's also abandoned Marxism for various other positions. Plekhanov never found a comfortable place in the Russian Social Democratic party, and in his final years followed his old German mentors into the heresy of 'defensism' – that is, patriotism, of course not German but Russian. Lenin was deserted by the other leaders of his generation, who plunged on into philosophical and even religious waters that he could not understand and also despised as dangerous to the revolution.

THE 'SILVER AGE'[23]

Prince Dmitry Sviatopolk-Mirsky writes,

Between atheism and progress, on the one hand, and religion and political reaction, on the other, the alliance was complete. To dissolve these alliances, and to undermine the supremacy of political over cultural and individual values, was the task of the generation of intellectuals who came of age in the last decade of the nineteenth century.[24]

It is too sweeping to assert that in the 1890's the alliances of atheism-progress and religion-reaction were 'complete'. We have observed the wide spectrum of cultural views across the whole of which supporters of the 'progress' that was expected from the Great Reforms of the 60's were to be found; the liberal position of Soloviev was only the most prominent of examples thus far cited of views in which religion did not go along with reaction. Nevertheless the last years of Alexander III's reign were ones in which such alliances seemed powerful indeed, and the disruption of them was, as Mirsky says, an important development of the early years of the reign of Nicholas II.

The esthetic revival of the 90's had various sources. One of them was the Mamontov circle at Abramtsevo, an estate outside Moscow bought by the wealthy industrialist Savva Mamontov in 1870; the circle which took form from 1874 included painters and art historians.[25] In 1882 its members built a church at Abramtsevo in medieval Novgorodian style, and the result was to give powerful impetus to the revival of historical themes and styles in Russian art in the work of such painters as Victor Vasnetsov, Vasily Surikov, and Mikhail Vrubel. However, the circle was also interested in French impressionism, and the later teacher of several Futurist painter-poets, Konstantin Korovin, owed much to Abramtsevo.

Another source of the revival may be found in the essays of two Jewish critics, N. Minsky (pseudonym of N. M. Vilenkin) and A. Volynsky (pseudonym of A. L. Flekser). Minsky's *By the Light of Conscience* (*Pri svete sovesti*) (1890) and Volynsky's critical articles in *Northern Messenger* from 1889 onward broke new ground. Minsky was one of the first to use Nietzsche's ideas as a means of attacking the 'social command' (*sotsial'nyi zakaz*) of the radical critics. The significant manifestoes of the esthetic revolutionaries were those of Dmitry S. Merezhkovsky. Born in 1866 in St Petersburg, son of a palace steward, he attended university there and soon was publishing not overly distinguished poetry. In 1892 and 1893 two works of his appeared: a book of poems called *Symbols* (*Simvoly*) and a series of essays entitled *On the Causes of the Decline and on the New Tendencies of Contemporary Russian Literature*. He concluded in the title essay:

In the symbols of Goncharov; in the artistic sensitivity, impressionism, and craving for the fantastic and wondrous to be found in Turgenev, the disillusioned skeptic, believing in nothing; and, chiefly, in the deep psychology of Dostoevsky [and] in the unflagging quest for a new truth, a new faith, of Leo Tolstoy – everywhere there is to be felt a rebirth of eternal ideal art, only for the moment obscured in Russia by the utilitarian–populist pedantry of criticism, in the West by the crude materialism of the experimental novel...*We must move forward from the period of creative, immediate, and spontaneous poetry to a critical, conscious, and cultured period.*[26]

Here and elsewhere Merezhkovsky's positive ideas were rather murky, but as a battering ram against the citadel of the radical critics, his message was effective. As Mirsky writes, 'this new world of his, with its mysterious connecting-strings and mutually reflected poles, attracted the tastes of a public which had been for generations fed on the small beer of idealistically coloured positivism'.[27] With his wife Zinaida Hippius, whom he married in 1889,[28] he soon became the standard-bearer of the new 'symbolism', but although Hippius was a poet whose gifts exceeded her husband's, the poets who effectively launched the new school were Valery Briusov and Konstantin Balmont, both of whom created a sensation by their publications of 1894.[29]

Their literary debt to the West was openly acknowledged; the Briusov-edited volumes entitled *Russian Symbolists* (*Russkie simvolisty*) contained a number of translations of the French symbolist poets, and their chief slogans were drawn from the West – for example, '*des forêts de symboles*' (Baudelaire). However, the symbolists were among the first people in the history of Russian thought (to which they do belong, though their place in history of Russian literature is more important) who passed from a radically Westernizing phase into a phase of sympathetic re-evaluation of the national tradition without repudiating the former or suggesting that it had any incompatibility with the latter. Despite the ridiculous excesses of symbolism, especially in its early phase,[30] in the respect just mentioned the movement was a significant milestone in the syncretist direction, or if one likes in the maturation of Russian culture. The symbolists soon came under the influence of Russians whose thought was itself not merely derivative from the West: Dostoevsky, Tiutchev, and above all Vladimir Soloviev. Their impact became clearly perceptible only with the so-called second generation of symbolists in the early 1900's, who included Andrei Bely (pseudonym of Boris Bugaev), Alexander Blok, and Viacheslav Ivanov. Bely from childhood knew Soloviev personally; Blok wrote a cycle of poems on the Beautiful Lady and other incarnations of Soloviev's elusive Sophia, without, incidentally, markedly sharing Soloviev's religious interests. Ivanov, whose esthetic theory was 'the most fully elaborated' of any of the symbolists', regarded art as a representation of the world that not only revealed the fundamental nature of things but in turn acted on reality transforming or transfiguring it in what Soloviev called a 'theurgic' manner.[31]

Symbolism's self-consciously ideological stance also had points of contact with science. Bely, a student of the sciences at Moscow University, sought to apply scientific method in esthetics and in 1909 founded a circle in order to study Russian poetry statistically. Blok married Liubov Mendeleeva, daughter of the great chemist who was the author of the periodic table of elements; not only Blok but also his close friend Bely regarded her more than half seriously as an incarnation of Sophia and a complex triangle, partly sexual and partly mystical, resulted.

In 1905 Viacheslav Ivanov rented an apartment in St Petersburg across from the Taurida Palace which became known as the 'Tower'. There he inaugurated the 'Wednesdays' that became the gathering place of the intellectual elite until 1912, when Ivanov went abroad. In the Ivanov circle symbolism fell into fragments, one of which was mystical anarchism following Georgy Chulkov and Ivanov himself. It advocated absolute individualism and spoke of Eros as the means of creating a society 'based on a free *anarchical* union'.[32] Bely, with his companion Anna (Asia) Turgeneva, niece of the novelist, went abroad in 1912 and two years later joined Rudolf Steiner's colony of devotees of 'anthroposophy' in Switzerland.

A direct challenge to symbolism was mounted by a group of former adherents, led by Nicholas Gumilev and including Innokenty Annensky and Sergei Gorodetsky. Gumilev, his new wife Anna Akhmatova (born Gorenko), and Gorodetsky in 1911 founded the Guild of Poets which became the organizing center of Acmeism.[33] It soon recruited the extraordinarily gifted young poet, Osip Mandelshtam, who was of Jewish origin.[34] The Acmeists claimed inspiration in Shakespeare, Rabelais, Villon, and Théophile Gautier; they renounced the obscurities of symbolist thought and sought to write the best possible poetry irrespective of other considerations – Gumilev was loyal to the existing government, he and his wife were Orthodox believers, Mandelshtam as a young man was a Socialist Revolutionary propagandist.

Another school of poets, the Futurists, owed their origin partly to the crisis of symbolism and partly to developments in painting and other arts to be mentioned shortly (though symbolism was also linked with the arts, in the case of futurism painting often preceded the poetry). The Futurist manifestoes appeared in early 1910, partly in response to the 'futurism' of Filippo Marinetti.[35] The center of the Futurist movement was the Hylaea group (which took its name from the ancient Greek name of the region of the Burliuks' home, an estate near Kherson), whose leaders were David Burliuk and his two brothers and Benedict Livshits. They were close to the painters Mikhail Larionov and his wife Natalia Goncharova (great-granddaughter of Pushkin) and to the poets Vladimir Mayakovsky, Velimir (pseudonym of Victor) Khlebnikov, and Alexei (pseudonym of Alexander) Kruchenykh. Larionov and especially Goncharova were for a time primitivists who were interested in the rediscovery of Russian folklore and in particular the icon, but also in the Western *avant-garde*. After about two years the Hylaea group, in 1913, started calling themselves Futurists and then Cubo-Futurists. By this time the use of neologisms, concentration on the theme of the modern city, and graphomania (the use of odd type faces and arrangements of words or letters on the printed page) had become more prominent in the group's concerns. There was a quite separate group, formed in 1911, around I. V. Lotarev (who used the pseudonym Igor-Severianin), which called itself Ego-Futurist; another, organized in 1913, called itself Centrifuge, including Boris Pasternak and Nicholas Aseev in its membership. Pasternak entered the circle not as a poet but as a musician. Members of these groups underwent innumerable crises in personal relations and ideological conflicts, distinguished themselves by deliberately puzzling or shocking behavior, and stirred up enormous interest in the arts all over Russia. Markov wryly comments that George Shengeli was doubtless the only person ever to have proclaimed the phallus a vessel of truth in the city of Kerch.[36] Despite such assertions as one that an American shoe was superior to the Venus de Milo, reminiscent of the 1860's, the artistic *enfants terribles* both rejected the notion that art should be subservient to politics[37] and refused to abjure history and culture – indeed their own debts to both Russian and Western traditions, from the remote past to the present, precluded any possibility of their doing so. Blok wrote that the Futurists might teach his generation 'how to *love* Pushkin *in a new way*... [The Futurists] scold him in a new way and he becomes dearer in a new way'.[38] They also forged new links among all the arts, and though their manifestoes could neither keep up with their works in various genres nor successfully verbalize the significance or implications of those works,[39] they were both genuinely concerned with their cultural heritage and genuinely creative, both cosmopolitan and Russian, both proud to create art that needed no justification and eager to contribute to public thinking and even to serious thought about the path of Russian cultural development.

Another series of developments came in the wake of Merezhkovsky's essay of 1893, though it had many points of contact with the circles of poets and painters just surveyed. It began with The World of Art group, which has been called 'the single instrument'[40] of the revival of fine arts at the turn of the century and also played an important part in the early stages of the literary revival. Merezhkovsky himself was a prominent member. The group grew out of a schoolboy society called the 'Nevsky Pickwickians' at May College in St Petersburg, formed in the late 1880's, of which Alexander Benua (Benois), Dmitry Filosofov, and Walter Nuvel were members. Filosofov became acquainted with the Merezhkovskys and was soon swept into Dmitry's enthusiasms, dreaming of spreading and developing them in an appropriate publication. The group was soon joined by Sergei Diagilev, who had just arrived from the provinces. Filosofov's philosophical and social interests, Benua's skill in painting and writing and his immense knowledge of art, and Diagilev's passion and flair for carrying art to the public were effectively combined. A magazine was planned which would simultaneously reestablish direct contact with old art and promote modern art.[41] Securing support from the Princess Tenisheva and Savva Mamontov, the circle issued the first number of *The World of Art* (*Mir Iskusstva*) in October 1898. Even in its form the journal broke new ground; its staff had to find or create the type, the paper, the style suitable for it, and it took them until 1901 to satisfy themselves in such respects. The members of the circle were united in their view of the supreme value of art, but they were less interested in ideologizing about it than in promoting and indeed creating it. However, they opened their pages to the symbolists and others with a philosophical bent, including Blok, Balmont, Merezhkovsky, and Rozanov. A storm of abuse greeted the first appearance of the journal, but within a few years it had won all its battles. From 1899 to 1903 Diagilev organized annual international art exhibitions; the third was held in the Academy of Fine Arts itself, the citadel of stale academism. In the spring of 1900 the Paris Exposition awarded the gold medal to Valentine Serov and also decorated Korovin, Vrubel, and other members of The World of Art group. Nuvel and others held evenings of contemporary music in St Petersburg from 1902, where young Prokofiev and Stravinsky appeared and Diagilev was moved on the spot to commission Stravinsky to write *The Firebird*. By 1904 the magazine came to an end, not in acknowledgment of failure but in the belief that the task of propaganda was largely accomplished. 'Seldom', writes Diagilev's biographer, 'has any periodical with a circulation of under four thousand exerted so powerful an influence on the whole culture of a period...'[42] Other magazines continued the work of rediscovery, such as *Ancient Times* (*Starye Gody*, founded 1907) and *Apollon*, from 1909, and *The Golden Fleece* (*Zolotoe Runo*, 1906–9) carried the banner of the *avant-garde* painters: Larionov and Goncharova, soon joined by Casimir Malevich and Vladimir Tatlin, who went on to proclaim the non-representative schools of Suprematism and Constructivism.

Diagilev proceeded to carry the great revival of the arts in Russia to the attention of Western Europe. In Paris in 1906 he arranged an exhibition of Russian art that included icons (though since at that time few had been cleaned, their full rediscovery had to await the Moscow exhibition of 1913);[43] he presented concerts of Russian music which gave Chaliapin[44] his fame and made Mussorgsky's and Borodin's works popular in the West, produced *Boris Godunov* at the Opéra, and finally in 1909 offered something new: the combination of dancing, painting, and music that made up the Ballets Russes. *The Firebird*, the first ballet commissioned for production by Diagilev, came in 1910. The dancing, including the unbelievable feats of Nijinsky, produced sensations. When Nijinsky was asked how he managed his dazzling leaps, he replied, according to legend: 'I simply rise into the air and pause a moment.' But it was not acrobatic skill but artistic quality and originality that assured success to the Diagilev productions. There were innovations too great even for Western audiences: after the scandalous opening night of *The Rite of Spring* in 1913, Cocteau, Stravinsky, Nijinsky, and Diagilev rode a cab in silence to the Bois de Boulogne. Was the distinguished array of fares (leaving aside Cocteau) or the ballet they had produced Russian or European? There is no longer any possible answer but 'both'.

THOUGHT AND LEARNING IN THE ORTHODOX CHURCH

In the 1940's Berdiaev wrote that there was a 'cultural renaissance' in Russia at the turn of the century but 'there was not the necessary strength and concentration of will for a religious renaissance'.[45] He then enumerates three sources of the cultural renaissance: Marxism, literature (especially Merezhkovsky), and poetry. As an autobiographical remark, it is sound enough; as an analysis of cultural events, it is inadequate. Development in the Orthodox Church played an important role in the cultural renaissance – whether there was a religious renaissance in all possible senses of the phrase is not a question to which we need address ourselves, though there were certainly indications of a renewal of popular piety in the response given such men as Fr John Sergiev (1828–1908), dean of the cathedral at Kronstadt; the elders of Optina Pustyn, Amvrosy (1812–91), Iosif (d. 1911), Anatoly (d. 1922), and Nektary (d. 1928); and Fr Alexei Mechov – who influenced both Bulgakov and Berdiaev.[46]

The development of culture within the Church for some time largely remained unknown not only to the peasantry but also to the intelligentsia, which undoubtedly goes far to explain why virtually nothing about it has been written to this day by Western historians, many of whom are apt to follow the interests of their pre-revolutionary Russian (as well as Soviet) confrères.[47]

There were several trends observable in the Church at the outset of the reign of Alexander II. One was a continuation and sharpening of earlier Protestant influences already discussed. Examples may be found in the attacks on the Church hierarchy and monasticism published anonymously in Germany by D. I. Rostislavov and I. S. Belliustin in 1858 and later. Florovsky writes that such essays illustrate what might be termed 'Protestantism of the Eastern Rite',[48] employing a phrase current at the time but having partial applicability to the whole period of the subjection of the Church to the Empire through the Holy Synod. The Church experienced a sort of second 'combined ministry' comparable to that of Golitsyn's from 1817 to 1824, under Count Dmitry Tolstoy from 1866 to 1880.[49] To be sure, the Holy Synod and the Ministry of Education were not merged, but Tolstoy himself held the ministerial positions in both. Like other procurators before and after him, Tolstoy was scarcely a believer at all, and used his positions not, as Golitsyn did, for the sake of any religious enthusiasms of his own but rather in curbing or even opposing any serious religious conviction. But Tolstoy only made a bad situation worse; the organizational problem of the Church was simply the Synod – that is, the Church's subjection to the state. In the early years of the reign Constantine Aksakov, A. N. Muraviev, and others criticized the synodal structure and in various ways urged reform. Such advocacy proved premature. Perhaps the cultural revival that occurred in subsequent decades was a prerequisite for pressing demands for structural change.

Signs of the revival appeared in different areas. One was the foundation of academic journals. The Moscow *Orthodox Review* (*Pravoslavnoe obozrenie*) was the most important and one of the earliest (1860). N. A. Sergievsky and A. M. Ivantsov-Platonov, who were close to the Slavophiles, helped develop an historical sense in the clergy by means of that journal. Another Moscow journal was *Spiritually Edifying Reading* (*Dushepoleznoe Chtenie*, from 1860); in Kazan there was the *Orthodox Interlocutor* (*Pravoslavnyi Sobesednik*, from 1855); in Kiev the *Works of the Kievan Ecclesiastical Academy* (*Trudy Kievskoi dukhovnoi akademii*, from 1860). The Christian modernists and liberals used the *Social Messenger of the Church* (*Tserkovno-obshchestvennyi Vestnik*, from 1875) and *The Spirit of the Christian* (*Dukh khristianina*). All of these contributed a wealth of new knowledge and fostered new standards in Orthodox learning. Another area was Biblical scholarship and the beginnings of higher criticism. A new Russian translation of the Bible was proposed by Metropolitan Filaret of Moscow, and it was finished during Alexander II's reign (New Testament, 1862; Old Testament, 1875). The higher criticism dealt largely with the Old Testament – for example, in Filaret Filaretov's work on Job in 1872 and N. S. Yakimov's on Jeremiah in 1874. Church history developed for the first time: Filaret Gumilevsky produced a five-volume history of the Russian Church as early as 1847–9. Makary (Bulgakov), from 1879 metropolitan of Moscow, wrote a longer, thirteen-volume history published over several decades, beginning in 1846, but it left ecclesiastical history still in the chronicle stage. It was from Gumilevsky and the Moscow Academy that an improvement came by way of his student A. V. Gorsky (1812–75) and E. E. Golubinsky (1834–1912), who benefited from Gorsky's work. At the St Petersburg Academy there were I. E. Troitsky and V. V. Bolotov, who returned to Byzantine origins for themes, at the Kievan Academy S. Malevansky and others. An important force in reviving patristic viewpoints was Feofan Govorov (1815–94), bishop of Tambov and later Vladimir, who worked alone for almost thirty years. There was a response to developments in the West when the Old Catholic break-off from Rome occurred as a result of the papal infallibility doctrine (1870); the rector of the St Petersburg Academy, I. L. Yanyshev, was especially sympathetic, and in connection with it the Moscow Society of Friends of Ecclesiastical Enlightenment (Obshchestvo liubitelei dukhovnogo prosveshcheniia) was formed, with a St Petersburg section following in 1872.

After the coming of Pobedonostsev as procurator of the Synod, however, the development of ecclesiastical learning suffered greatly.[50] Although he himself was a learned man (in his field of law), he distrusted and feared culture in the Church. The Friends of Ecclesiastical Enlightenment had to cease to meet; the *Orthodox Review* (in 1891) and other of the best journals had to cease publication. Some new periodicals, such as *Theological Messenger* (*Bogoslovskii Vestnik*, from 1892), were begun, but the level of the material in them was not as high as their predecessors. The seminaries also suffered. State stipends were slashed in 1887, and the total of pupils was cut in half. The ecclesiastical censorship over which Pobedonostsev presided interfered constantly. The gifted cleric E. P. Akvilionov suffered rejection of his M.A. thesis in 1894 and was compelled to rewrite it to suit the Synod's stipulations. The paradox was that Pobedonostsev, the enemy of Tolstoy, did much to blight the development of ecclesiastical learning in a belief quite similar to the latter's that the peasant's level of culture was the proper one to use as the touchstone for religion. The difference was that Tolstoy never wished to have the power of the state applied to stifle anything, no matter how useless he thought it to be.

But Pobedonostsev did not manage to prevent individual clerics from speaking out and from working to resume some of the trends that antedated his procuratorship. In the later 1880's, after a lapse of a decade or two, able youths were again seeking to enter the monastic life. One of them, Mikhail Gribanovsky, later bishop of Taurida, wrote in 1884, 'To think out Christianity philosophically – this is the greatest task of the present moment', and added, 'as Schelling indicates' – this reference to a philosopher who died in 1854 suggests that the task of the learned cleric in Russia in the 1880's was a lonely one, unassisted by many contemporaries either at home or abroad. Others with philosophical interests became prominent, such as Antony Khrapovitsky, rector of Moscow Academy and later metropolitan, but several of them, above all M. M. Tareev (1866–1934), professor of moral theology in the same academy, moved in the direction of a moralism that resurrected pietist themes of the early years of the century.

Florovsky credits Marxism with contributing a renewed interest in ontology and reality to Russian theology and with leading it away again from an emotional moralism. He writes that 'the question of freedom and necessity in the social process...inevitably led to metaphysics...From Marx there was a "return" to Kant and to Hegel, from *Marxism* a passage to *idealism*.' And he quotes with approval G. P. Fedotov's suggestion that 'Marxism influenced the turn of religious searchings in the direction of Orthodoxy'.[51] The predominance of moralism in the theological field – despite important trends of other sorts – corresponded to the moralism of the radical critics. Thus symbolism, asserting esthetics in contrast to ethics, also helped to overcome the moralist pall that Pobedonostsev and the latter-day 'philosophers of the heart' together laid on the Church. It was art – as Florovsky notes, a 'new path' – that led Merezhkovsky back to the Church; it had earlier been philosophy (the Slavophiles) or politics (a few of the populists) that had done so. But it was also Christian thinkers outside the Church who had a great influence on Merezhkovsky, on the symbolists, and finally on the men who had been the leading Marxists of the 1890's: and foremost among such lay thinkers was Vladimir Soloviev. In the summer of 1896 he wrote that what was necessary above all was 'a universal restoration of Christian philosophy', echoing Gribanovsky's statement of the previous decade. It was time for clerics and non-clerics to meet on common cultural ground.

The result was the Religio-Philosophical Meetings which were held from

November 1901–March 1903. Presiding was Sergii Stragorodsky, rector of the St Petersburg Ecclesiastical Academy, and future Patriarch (1943–4). On the one hand were the intelligentsia: Merezhkovsky, Hippius, Filosofov, Rozanov, and others; on the other, the clerics and religious laymen: Professor P. I. Leporsky, Father I. Slobodskoy, and others. A few, such as V. Ternavtsev, had entry to both groups.[52] There were some surprises; Hippius noted with amazement that apparently 'the most important section of Church leaders... are predominantly positivists...' The word 'positivist' may not be the most accurate, but the heritage of German Protestant influence in the Russian seminaries, partly scholastic, partly pietist, had produced some curious phenomena. Actually the St Petersburg Academy numbered some notable professors and pupils and the Moscow Academy even more: Fr P. A. Florensky (1882–1952), a polymath whose knowledge bridged the sciences and arts; V. F. Ern (1881–1915), a philosopher of German descent who turned savagely on the West; and Fr A. V. Elchaninov (1881–1934).

The St Petersburg meetings were banned in 1903 and publication of their minutes stopped by government order, though before they began Pobedonostsev had claimed to support them. In 1905 a 'Soloviev Religio-Philosophical Society' was founded in Moscow, and Elchaninov became its secretary; a similar group was established in Kiev; in 1907 Berdiaev was instrumental in founding such a society in St Petersburg. All these meetings had consequences in publishing. The Merezhkovskys established *The New Way* (*Novyi Put'*) in 1903, and promptly lost interest in *The World of Art*. In 1909 the circle of M. K. Morozova, who was connected with two of the greatest fortunes of rising Russian industry, began the publishing house The Way (*Put'*), which reissued many nineteenth-century essays and published some notable new ones.

The renewed intellectual ferment in the Orthodox Church gave courage to a number of clerics, notably Metropolitan Anthony (Vadkovsky) of St Petersburg, to demand ecclesiastical independence from the state, and to persuade a number of statesmen, notably Witte, that the Church should have it. The ukase of 12 December (O.S.) 1904 announced a policy of greater religious tolerance. Restrictions on the Old Believers and other Christian and non-Christian groups were lifted a few months later, and Witte, by now prime minister, believed it necessary to end state control of the Orthodox Church. Pobedonostsev tried in vain to block Witte's efforts and had to resign. Discussion of proposed Church reforms now became widespread among clergy, laymen, and non-believers. It was assumed that the Holy Synod would be swept away, and the controversies were mainly between those who favored election of bishops and lower clergy and those who did not. While the country as a whole debated the merits of a Duma or Constituent Assembly, the Church (and others) considered the desirability of a national Council. The Synod announced in January 1906 that a Pre-Conciliar Commission (Predsobornoe Prisutstvie) would be convened to prepare for a Council, and such a commission met from March to December of that year. The ebb of the Revolution of 1905, however, delayed the Council as it limited the suffrage and power of the Duma. A Pre-Conciliar Conference (Predsobornoe Soveshchanie) resumed planning for a Council in 1912, but a Council was convened only after the monarchy fell in 1917. The Bolshevik Revolution overtook the process of Church reform; the Orthodox Church was thereafter confronted with the question not of freedom, but of survival.

THE REVOLUTION OF 1905 AND ITS AFTERMATH: *SIGNPOSTS*

By the first years of the twentieth century the formation of oppositional political parties – or more accurately circles of intellectuals calling themselves by that name but realizing that Russia had as yet no political life that would permit real parties – had proceeded far enough so that Social Democrats, Socialist Revolutionaries, and members of the Union of Liberation had an émigré press, a nucleus of organizations inside Russia, and party programs more or less regularly adopted. The Social Democrats, after an abortive attempt at organizing at their so-called First Congress in Minsk in 1898, succeeded in constituting a party, or more accurately two hostile and continuing factions of one, at their Second Congress at Brussels and London in 1903.[53] The defection of the intellectuals of the 90's had left Lenin as leader of a Bolshevik faction; the Mensheviks had no single leader, though Julius Martov was for a number of years probably the foremost figure, but instead followed several men and women – Paul Axelrod, Vera Zasulich, and others – who had been active in the Marxist underground for a number of years. The nearest thing to a party theorist the Socialist Revolutionaries had was Victor Chernov. The Union of Liberation had Paul Miliukov, a prominent historian, and Peter Struve, a former Marxist and author of the manifesto of the Minsk Congress.

The parties did not bring about the Revolution of 1905, nor did they claim to do so. It was the shock of defeat in the Russo-Japanese War of 1904–5, felt in wide circles of public opinion already encouraged or alarmed by the growth of the student movement, the workers' movement, and even a revival of peasant unrest, which led to the revolutionary events. Out of them came a nationally elected representative assembly, the Duma (1906–17), supplemented by a State Council converted from a bureaucratic committee into an 'upper house', a promise of civil liberties, certain other reforms, and a political system based on elections and national representation in legislation that some have called 'constitutional'. There was a constitutional document, issued as the Fundamental Laws of April 1906. It had some structural shortcomings, judged from the viewpoint of liberals or radicals on the one hand and reactionaries on the other. From the viewpoint of the moderate Octobrists and later Nationalists in the Duma, once the latter became a more or less continuously functioning institution (1907), the shortcomings of the Fundamental

Laws were less important than the ways in which the monarchy failed to implement them.

The Revolution of 1905 and the period immediately preceding and following it did not give rise to much that could be termed political thought. The reams of literature issued by the parties, either as material for discussion of party positions by their leaders or as propaganda for citizens they wished to induce to vote for or otherwise support them, consisted in large part of reportage and denunciation of the abuses of the monarchy, argument about what strategy and tactics should be used in overthrowing or limiting it, and enumeration of short-term political goals, to be gained either by mass violence or the electoral process or both. The assumptions of all the revolutionary and liberal groups were drawn directly from the Western political experience, chiefly that of England and France as far as parliamentary institutions were concerned and that of France and Germany with respect to revolutionary action. What the opposition leaders did, in effect, was to attempt to take over wholesale the political results of long and painful trial and error in Western theory and practice and adopt them at once in Russia. There was scarcely any opportunity, in the crisis of 1904–7, to consider first principles; many of the opposition leaders would have thought such activity wasted effort in any case. Russia ought to have a system like England's, said the liberals; Russia should have a bourgeois revolution such as France had had, said the radicals; Russia should have a bourgeois revolution very soon followed by a socialist one, said Lenin and Trotsky (though in 1905 few understood their viewpoint very clearly), as Marx had said Germany ought to have. Any suggestion that Russia was not England, France, or Germany was apt to be branded as counterrevolutionary or reactionary.

In retrospect it can be seen that the trouble with the oppositional assumptions was not necessarily that Russia was not 'ready' for a West European political order of parliamentary democracy or democratic socialism – a contention that especially infuriated the opposition leaders – in the sense that leaders were unprepared or that popular support was lacking. The trouble was that Russia's institutional heritage was quite different from Western Europe's. For one thing, the monarchy, supported by bureaucracy, army, and police, was too strong, and was never as close to collapsing in 1905 as the opposition hoped and some officials feared. That meant failure for the revolution. But, ultimately more important, alternative political institutions and the habits of managing and using them remained embryonic. The opposition leaders wanted too much; the monarchy was willing to concede too little, and the result was that the dynasty destroyed the possibility of its own survival under modified institutional arrangements. In 1907, when the Revolution of 1905 can be said to have ended, this was not clear, to be sure, though it was foreseen by a number of prescient people. What was clear was that both government and opposition had miscalculated the situation. Prime Ministers Witte (October 1905–April 1906) and Stolypin (June 1906–11) attempted to remedy the miscalculation as best they could from the side of the government; both failed partly because of their own shortcomings, of a sort to be found in even the best officials trained under an autocratic regime, but even more because of the unwillingness of the autocrat to trust them, support them, or even understand what they were trying to do. Again, neither Witte and Stolypin nor anyone close to them was a political theorist, and political thought played no serious role in forming government policy.

When the Revolution of 1905 was over, the revolutionary leaders scattered abroad or went into hiding, the liberal leaders tried to do what they could in the Duma. The cultural revival continued in all its major forms. Many of the artistic figures had welcomed the revolutionary events, not as members of this or that political party or as adherent of this or that ten- or fifteen-point program, but as a means of increasing freedom in Russia. Once the revolution was over, they did not necessarily abandon hope that something of the sort would happen again.

A substantial group, though clearly a minority (even a small minority) of Russia's intellectuals, drew from the Revolution of 1905 conclusions different from those of officials, opposition leaders, or *avant-garde* artists. Those conclusions were embodied in the symposium called *Signposts* (*Vekhi*), published in the spring of 1909, which went through five editions in a year. There were seven authors; all but one (Gershenzon) had been Marxists, all but two (Gershenzon and Izgoev) had contributed to a symposium published in 1902 called *Problems of Idealism* (*Problemy idealizma*) in which they had discussed their evolution from Marxism to neo-Kantianism. *Signposts* indicated a further stage in their development. It was Russia's great syncretist manifesto in the field of culture. It did *not* renounce political liberation or even revolution. Berdiaev wrote, however, 'political liberation is possible only in conjunction with, and on the basis of, a spiritual and cultural renaissance'.[54]

Berdiaev attacked the moralism and utilitarianism of the intelligentsia. Its basic premise, he wrote, was 'let truth perish, if by its death the people will live better and men will be happier; down with truth, if it stands in the way of the sacred cry "down with autocracy"'. Russia had to build a 'national philosophical tradition', and there was a basis for doing so in Chaadaev, who had not been understood, Soloviev, who had been ignored, and Dostoevsky; in Khomiakov, to some extent Chicherin, Prince Sergei Trubetskoy, Nicholas Lossky, V. I. Nesmelov. Berdiaev wanted nothing to do with the mystics: their chief representatives, such as Rozanov, Merezhkovsky, and V. Ivanov, scorned real philosophy as much as the intelligentsia. The philosophical tradition 'that we need so much' could be founded on 'concrete idealism'; but in any event it had to be 'both universal and national – only then is it culturally fruitful'. Escape from external oppression was necessary, but its prerequisite was escape from internal bondage and acceptance of responsibility.[55]

Bulgakov's indictment of the intelligentsia went further, provoked by his opinion that 1905 had been a revolution of the intelligentsia.[56] Its antibourgeois attitude was compounded of the feelings of the hereditary aristocrat, plain lack of self-discipline, and unconsciously religious aversion to 'spiritual philistinism'. Its purported worship of the people had led in fact to an arrogant view of them as an object of salvation. The relation between intelligentsia and people was 'basically a clash of two faiths, two religions'. The atheist faith of the intelligentsia represented a misguided borrowing from the West.

From the many-branched tree of Western civilization, with its roots that go deep into history, we chose only one branch, without knowing and without wanting to know all the others, fully confident that we were grafting onto ourselves the most authentic European civilization. But European civilization has not only a variety of fruits and a number of branches, but also roots which feed the tree and with their healthy sap render harmless, to some extent, the many poisonous fruits.[57]

Out of the Middle Ages and Reformation came 'at least half' of Western culture. 'In the struggle for Russian culture, we must fight, among other things, for a more profound, historically conscious Westernism.' Bulgakov independently repeated Berdiaev's charge that the intelligentsia had ignored the Russians who had fought their way toward a sound syncretist position: he mentioned A. M. Bukharev (Archimandrite Fedor, 1822–71, who had left the Church as a result of opposition to his advocacy of the acceptance of secular culture), as well as Soloviev, Prince S. Trubetskoy, Dostoevsky, and even, although there had been a superficial cult of the man, Tolstoy.

Bulgakov added as an obvious commentary on the contemporary scene a specific condemnation of 'spiritual pedocracy' (rule by children). 'Anyone concerned with the future is most anxious about the younger generation. But to be spiritually dependent on it, to flatter it, to truckle to its opinions and take it as a standard, testifies to a society's spiritual weakness.' The ideal of the Christian saint, he wrote, had been replaced by the image of the revolutionary student. Maximalist goals had led to the acceptance of maximalist means, the notion that everything is permitted, nihilism, suicide. He concluded that the intelligentsia's 'abnormal maximalism with its practical uselessness is the result of a religious perversion, but it can be overcome by religious healing'.

The indictment of the intelligentsia by Michael Gershenzon was no less severe than Bulgakov's. However, his criticism was based not on religion but on a non-believer's regard for the individual personality.[58] The intelligentsia had neglected the truth that Russia's best minds – Chaadaev, the Slavophiles, Dostoevsky – had discovered, because consciousness had become disjoined from will. Think about the people, society, the state – this was the demand; thinking about one's own personality was indecent. It was of no use to say, believe, love, to the intelligentsia – here Gershenzon was doubtless on psychologically sound ground. He went on to say that the Russian *intelligent* must be told to become a man and not a cripple. It is doubtful, however, that sort of advice was any more welcome than the other. He ended by declaring that the beginnings of 'creative personal self-consciousness' were visible in Russia.

Gershenzon, like two other contributors to *Signposts* – Izgoev (A. S. Lande) and S. L. Frank – was a Jew. He was an able critic, a discerning historian of culture, and a skilled writer; but he was not a religious believer, and indeed on Rousseauist grounds he came to question the whole concept of culture as he did religion. In *A Correspondence Between Two Corners* (*Perepiska s dvukh uglov*) with V. Ivanov, in 1920, actually written by the two men in the same room they shared in a sanitarium, he confessed that though he had been in contact with European culture since childhood and continued to love it, a voice from the depths of consciousness kept repeating to him, 'this is not it, not it!'[59]

The only essay in *Signposts* that was to any extent political was Struve's, and it reflected no attachment to any particular political party, but rather called for the subordination of all politics to 'the idea of education (*vospitanie*)'. The intelligentsia, he argued, had replaced the Cossack revolutionaries of the seventeenth and eighteenth centuries – this was a realization, Struve might have said (but did not), of Maistre's prophecy of a 'Pougatchev de l'université'. He drew a sharp distinction between the earlier critical intellectuals, such as Novikov, Radishchev, and Chaadaev, and the great nineteenth-century writers on the one hand, and the intelligentsia on the other. The first *intelligent*, he wrote, was Bakunin, 'whose central role in the development of Russian social thought is yet far from having been accurately appraised'. The crucial point was Bakunin's atheism, in which Belinsky, Chernyshevsky, and Mikhailovsky followed him. The result was a group that had 'credulity without faith, militance without creativeness, fanaticism without enthusiasm and intolerance without reverence; in a word, it had and still has, complete, the form of religiosity without its content'.[60] The intelligentsia had placed its wager on revolution from below; in response to the threat of the mob, the government had resorted to despotism. Struve foresaw reduction of the alienation of the *intelligenty* partly as a result of economic growth (as in Germany, perhaps), partly of the likely familiarization with the crisis of socialism in the West. But his main message, and that of *Signposts*, was of moral responsibility.

The impact of *Signposts* on public opinion was tremendous, comparable only to Chaadaev's first *Philosophical Letter*.[61] The Socialist Revolutionaries replied in '*Signposts*' *As A Sign of the Times* ('*Vekhi*' *kak znamenie vremeni* 1910), the Kadets in *The Intelligentsia in Russia* (*Intelligentsiia v Rossii*, 1910). In the latter Miliukov, whose article was about half of the book, declared: 'Just imagine such words as "purification" or "repentance" on the lips of a European intellectual'[62] – for he was committed to being a 'European intellectual', as he understood the phrase, at almost any cost. R. V. Ivanov (Ivanov-Razumnik) facetiously attributed to the authors of *Signposts* the maxim, *pereat mundus fiat iustitia*. It appears that he understood them quite well.

Lenin declared that *Signposts* epitomized the Kadet outlook; it is to be hoped that he nevertheless knew that to the extent the book had a political content it included an attack on the Kadets. One perceptive Kadet, I. V. Gessen, later wrote:

The success of *Vekhi* was astounding. There was no single periodical which did not react against that book [but the main replies made little impression]. I was deeply perturbed by *Vekhi*. For the first time I realized that our epoch was coming to an end; I saw that *Vekhi* had coined the slogans of the future, which were supported by modern knowledge; even science was moving towards metaphysics.[63]

The best study of *Signposts*, which is Leonard Schapiro's, undertakes to explore the political significance of the book, and finds it in its illumination of the fact that the Russian Kadet was not a liberal but a radical or revolutionary. However, the essays themselves are not mainly or even to any noticeable extent concerned with politics. They indict the intelligentsia, not merely or chiefly the Kadet party or even all the left parties together. They take the indictment of tsarism almost for granted, though it is not omitted – Struve's essay speaks of 'the detestable triumph of [post-1905] reaction'. But what the essays are about is Russian culture in its broadest sense. They look back into the history of Russian thought and find antecedents of the negative aspects they attack, and also positive features, which in the last two centuries are said to be the more important. The essays summon the leaders of Russian culture to look simultaneously to their own nation, to its people and their values, and to the great tradition of the West – as did The World of Art group and the best of the poets, following Soloviev and others.

According to Mirsky, *Signposts* 'laid the foundation of a new National Liberalism which rapidly spread among the more cultured strata of the intelligentsia and contributed very much towards the kindling of a patriotic war-spirit in 1914 and towards the success of the White Army movement in 1918'.[64] As for the White movement, it is true that Struve joined the Denikin and then the Wrangel camp, but there is little more to be said; one of the important things that the Whites lacked was precisely any widespread support among serious Russian thinkers. The rest of the statement is more plausible. *Signposts* was intended to mark a crossroads and to bring a turn of major proportions in the progress of Russian thought. One should not overstate what it achieved; nevertheless the trends which it exemplified did have a broader impact than the limited public which found the book persuasive. Plekhanov and other radicals did not accept philosophical idealism or Christianity, but in 1914 even some of them rallied to the national cause – one of the themes of *Signposts*. The quest for a religious philosophy became so pervasive that it invaded the ranks of the Bolsheviks themselves, and Lenin's attempt at a book in philosophy, *Materialism and Empirio-Criticism* (1909), was a counter-attack against the only other Bolsheviks who could claim a position in the field of thought, chiefly Bogdanov (A. A. Malinovsky, 1873–1928) and A. V.

Lunacharsky, who sought for a 'religion of socialism' and thereby left themselves open to the charge of being 'God-seekers' or 'God-builders' like so many others outside party ranks during the same period. The fixed determination to say nothing a 'European intellectual' would not say was fast eroding.

The cultural developments which were at least relevant to the evolution of thought in the last years before the Revolution were manifold, and deserve brief mention. The expansion of education converted Russia from an illiterate country to a half-literate one, and given Russia's size that was no mean achievement. The number of periodicals of all kinds greatly increased. The contents of the 'fat journals' mirrored the breakdown of the traditional political and artistic alliances referred to by D. S. Mirsky. The populist *Russian Wealth* and the liberal *Messenger of Europe* remained hostile to the new currents in arts, literature, and religion; but some radical journals, such as (to some degree) *Contemporary World* (*Sovremennyi Mir*), which was pro-Marxist, the pro-S.R. *Legacy* (*Zavety*), and the non-party radical *Northern Notes* (*Severnye Zapiski*), opened their pages to the moderns, as did the conservative–liberal *Russian Thought*.[65] The universities, disrupted by the Revolution of 1905, returned to normal; 'stimulating philosophical and sociological debates in circles of various ideological orientations became much more common than the shouting of slogans and mob actions'.[66] A crisis of broad proportions overtook Moscow University at the turn of 1910–11, in which learning was crushed for a time between forces of the extreme Right and the extreme Left, but peace, if only a partial recovery, again followed in the Russian universities. Some 7,000 or 8,000 Russians were studying in West European universities in 1912, many of them excluded by discrimination against Jews and other ethnic groups or for political reasons. A number of distinguished scientific organizations flourished: of naturalists, broad (as in Moscow) or differentiated in a modern manner (as in St Petersburg); of scientists in particular disciplines; of experts seeking practical applications of knowledge. The Academy of Sciences showed that it had long since become a national institution. Individual scientists in a wide variety of fields made Russians a force in the world of learning; the physiologists Ivan Pavlov (1904) and Ilia Mechnikov (1908) won Nobel Prizes. What all these scientific developments meant to the world of thought was suggested by the geochemist V. I. Vernadsky, who praised the achievements of modern science at the same time as he outlined its limitations and the need of considering the modes of inquiry peculiar to religion and philosophy. 'It is difficult', he declared, 'to say at the present time which is larger: the field occupied by science in the areas previously dominated by religion and philosophy, or the field acquired by religion and philosophy thanks to the growth of the scientific world view'.[67]

The exclusivist and elitist character of the intelligentsia, which Bulgakov explained partly by the police regime under which it had had to live, was also changing. Little original political theory was being advanced on behalf of democracy, but some little-noticed habits were being preached and practiced in the field of the arts. Chekhov, who was generally non-political in his outlook, wrote plays and stories in which the characters 'are all alike, all made of the same material – "the common stuff of humanity" – and in this sense Chekhov is the most "democratic", the most "unanimist", of all writers'.[68] His first significant play, *The Seagull* (*Chaika*), failed on its first production in 1896, and yet as the drama that opened the Moscow Art Theater in 1898 it was a dazzling success. Stanislavsky and Nemirovich-Danchenko had an approach to their new venture which found Chekhov's plays congenial: the members of the cast were equal, there was no star system, each had his important role to play. Gorky was another playwright whom they produced with success; *The Lower Depths* (*Na dne*) was a sensation in 1902 and went on to an unprecedented run in Berlin. Gorky's popularity derived not from the fact that he was a Bolshevik – which he was – but from his exploration, not only in the play mentioned, of the lives of the outcast and formerly undepicted urban masses. (It should be noted that Gorky, like his fellow Bolsheviks Bogdanov and Lunacharsky with whom he led the Capri party school in 1909, was affected by the currents exemplified by *Signposts*; his own religious searchings were termed 'God-building' [*bogostroitel'stvo*].) Diagilev's ballets were constructed on a basis similar to that of the Moscow Art Theater. The star system, of which Pavlova was a brilliant example, was displaced by a system of 'cooperation' in which no *premier danseur* was encouraged or allowed to overshadow the other performers. Even the world of *avant-garde* poetry felt the force of such ideas; Viacheslav Ivanov, for example, insisted on contact with the common people as a vital objective for the new poetic theoreticians.

CONCLUSION

World War I did not put an end to the new movements in the arts, religion, and thought, but it focused attention on other issues. The destruction, suffering, and disruption of the lives of millions that it brought helped to create a somber mood. A moment of rejoicing at the time of the February Revolution of 1917 was soon followed by a feeling of growing impotence and despair, exemplified by Alexis M. Remizov's *Lament for the Ruin of Russia* (*Slovo o pogibeli Zemli Russkoi*), for example, written in August. The coming of the October Revolution did not convert to Bolshevism any large number of the individuals who have been mentioned; Briusov was one of the few who became party members. Merezhkovsky had hailed the Revolution of 1905; that of 1917 horrified him. Balmont had been a Marxist in his youth, but rejected the October Revolution.

Many, however, accepted the Revolution as a logical outcome of previously existing forces or as a divinely-authored event, either punishing Russia for its sins or offering religious salvation in hidden guise. The poets Blok and Bely followed Ivanov-Razumnik in his 'Scythian' interpretation of the revolutionary cataclysm, alleging the purifying power of destruction in a rather Bakuninian vein. (Ivanov-Razumnik was a Left Socialist Revolutionary; that wing of the party was close to anarchism.) Blok and Gershenzon welcomed the Revolution as a way of casting off the useless baggage of civilization and beginning anew. Berdiaev eventually came to accept the Soviet regime, though he criticized certain aspects of its policy and practice. For nationalist reasons a number of ex-Kadets proclaimed their support of Bolshevism in 1921 in a symposium called *Change of Signposts* (*Smena vekh*), in which none of the original contributors to *Signposts* took part, and which Izgoev had the courage to denounce as a betrayal of the orientation of *Signposts*.[69] The real reaction of the *Signposts* group to the Revolution was contained in the symposium *De Profundis* (*Iz glubiny*) (1921), in which Struve, Berdiaev, Bulgakov, Frank, Izgoev, Viacheslav Ivanov, and others reminded their readers that what they foresaw in *Signposts* had taken place. But the authors were not then or later unanimous in their conclusions about the Revolution, as subsequent polemics indicate. Struve, like Vasily Maklakov (also a former Kadet), saw the catastrophe as a result of the failure of the government on the one hand and the Kadets on the other to cooperate after the Revolution of 1905. Frank regarded it as a lamentable but understandable result of the advance of the peasant masses and the disintegration of the old order, and still believed that the people would produce a new order different from the tyranny that was victorious in October.

Many of the prominent figures of the Silver Age became émigrés, most of them in the ordinary sense, though a few (such as Akhmatova and Pasternak) remained in Russia and became 'internal émigrés'; a few attempted to remain and accept Bolshevism, but most sooner or later failed in their efforts, and a series of suicides and premature deaths resulted.

The Silver Age survived in the emigration for years or decades. Berdiaev took *The Way* to Paris; Struve took *Russian Thought* to Sofia. 'Fat journals' appeared in several European countries and in America. The Ballets Russes and their offspring continued in the West. Writers, painters, and musicians went on with their work abroad. Russian clerics found homes in Orthodox seminaries in Paris and elsewhere. The Silver Age did not at once pass away in Russia either; until the First Five-Year Plan, until Stalin was more or less firmly entrenched in power, the culture of Russia can be said to have been at least as much a continuation of what it was under Nicholas II as a new, Soviet beginning. Thought, to be sure, took a different direction at the summit of power; the questions were, how to make the Soviet regime and its policies acceptable to one or another social group, and how to implement policies that would appear to make 'socialism' a reality in the economy and society of the country. The political parties, except for the Communists, were swept away; the Church again debated, to the extent it was permitted to do so, the question of 1721 as well as 1917 – what should be its position in relation to the all-powerful state, and a new question, could it survive under an atheistic regime?

And still the nagging questions, what was Russia? was its past still alive? whither was it bound? remained to plague Russians, in one form or another, even if not by way of the printed word or public discussion.

In one respect those intellectuals who were pro-Soviet in the years just following the Revolution represented a negation of the previous age and a reversion to the era of Alexander II; they returned to the intelligentsia outlook in a new form. What was good was art and thought that served the people, specifically the proletarian dictatorship; anything else was pernicious, bourgeois, decadent, and so forth. Some of the literary circles, such as Proletkult, LEF ('Left Front of Literature'), and the On Guardists (Napostovtsy), sought to assume the position of officially approved collective dictator over literature, and there were comparable attempts in the other arts. The regime refused to delegate authority in such a manner, and gradually itself assumed the role of interpreting and enforcing the 'social command'. It was applied sometimes gently, sometimes fiercely, with mass execution of those who were found to have disobeyed the 'command' even despite their own effort to comply with it; it is applied in the USSR to this day. Turgenev had once called the radical critics 'literary Robespierres'; invoking the name of those same critics, Stalin removed the phrase from the figurative to the literal realm and went far beyond anything the Jacobin leader had attempted. Culture and thought seemed to die, and yet after Stalin's death they threatened to rise again. It was the metaphor of resurrection that Pasternak used in the Poems of Yuri Zhivago which concluded his great novel, and every passing day of Soviet cultural history adds plausibility to his choice of figure.

The period 1890–1917 thus influenced the years since; however, it deserves consideration in itself as well. The era of Marxist conversions came in the 90's. The decade also witnessed the birth of modernism in the arts, which was closely linked with Western esthetic modernism and individualist ideas (for example, those of Nietzsche and Ibsen) on the one hand, and with Soloviev, Dostoevsky, and the rest of the 'creative main-line' of Russian culture (or what has been called here the syncretists) on the other. Both a proud rediscovery of the Russian past and an unhesitating meeting with the West characterized the period. The reviving intellectual current in Orthodoxy made tentative contacts with the new trends in the arts and secular thought. The early Marxist converts passed beyond Marxism to appeal simultaneously to the national tradition and to the core of Western values – from both Christian and non-Christian standpoints.

The disgruntled intelligentsia chose among several paths: a few followed the authors of *Vekhi* in repudiating the old pattern of alienation; some withdrew in chagrin and despair from political life, or silently (even in hiding) awaited some other chance for the party platforms or policies they had supported; some were acquiring new habits of participation in the life of the professions that were sinking roots in Russia. Reconciliation of the intelligentsia with the monarchy may have had fleeting and frail opportunities during the ministry of Stolypin, at moments during the Third Duma's existence, and again in 1914. In any case the sectarian characteristics of the intelligentsia were being eroded; cosmopolitanism and nationalism were advancing together. The Russian patriots of 1914 were also the most pro-English and pro-French, and some of them were even pro-German to the extent that they distinguished the German people and cultural heritage from the regime of Wilhelm II.

As reconciliation with the West proceeded simultaneously with adumbration or revival of the national heritage, syncretism as a separate current and syncretists as a distinguishable group or congeries of thinkers seemed to disappear. Many of the leading figures in the arts, in secular thought, even in the part of the clergy concerned with culture, were interested in the past of both Russia (and often also Byzantium and the East generally) and the West. Perhaps the situation was something like what Dostoevsky had in mind in his Pushkin oration, with his messianism absent or severely muted.

It is noteworthy that this remarkable period in the history of Russian thought and culture had features strongly reminiscent of old Russian culture: the prominence of the visual arts and their linkage with other branches of art and thought, the defense of esthetics as an independent source of values, the substitution (at least in *Vekhi*) for the discussion of serious questions of moral responsibility for the mindless moralism that had influenced Russian thought for more than a century. Goodness and beauty were rescued again as values and truth set firmly beside them – or at least, there were some who sought such objectives and with greater or lesser success, in an imperfect world, groped toward their realization.

In modern times, however, culture in Russia never entirely freed itself from the restrictions imposed by the state and from the pressures generated in society, especially among intellectuals by concentration on political issues. The crisis in the state, visible in 1905, fatal in 1917, led to a renewed subjection of thought and culture to governmental policies, decisions, and even whims. This occurred just at the moment when it appeared that the emancipation of Russian culture was nearly achieved. The reconciliation with the West and the simultaneous reconciliation between some intellectuals and the mass of the people were making headway. One ought not to imagine the possibility of perfect earthly reconciliation in these or any other respects. Thought and culture in the reign of Nicholas II were by no means of uniform quality. Their achievements were great, their failures far from negligible. But even fifty years after the end of the Civil War, they cast their shadow, both on Russia and the West.

9

THE WEST AND THE RUSSIAN TRADITION

Truly, an historian would not be mistaken if he were to undertake the study of Russian society along two distinct lines, life and thought, for the two had almost nothing in common.   Mikhail Gershenzon in *Vekhi*, 1909

Whatever validity Gershenzon's contention has, it is much less applicable in the early phases of the modern period, beginning with Ivan III. Russian thought of the late fifteenth and early sixteenth centuries was related to the chief concerns of the grand-princely court, both the theological beliefs of the monarch and the political and economic prerogatives he had or sought; it was also related to the position of the Orthodox Church, which contained Russia's educated men almost in their entirety and at the same time the usually ill-educated parish priesthood which provided cultural leadership for the common people. The end of the Tatar yoke and the newly gained independence of the Muscovite state led to the opening of relations with the European states of the day (as well as some in Asia) and to an opportunity for intellectual intercourse with the West denied to the Rus since the days of the Kievan state.

Probably in the sixteenth century Western thought did not impel any of the major contending parties at court and around it to do anything different from what they wished to do anyway. Nevertheless, the fact that Roman Catholic writings and argumentation were borrowed inaugurated certain habits that had fateful implications for succeeding generations. Such imported intellectual tools contributed to the victory that the Josephites won over the Moscow heretics in the councils of 1503–4, at the end of Ivan III's reign, and to the comeback that they made by 1521 in Vasily III's at the expense of the Trans-volgan Elders. Some Western ideas, gained as the result of genuine training abroad rather than seized upon from afar as weapons, animated the work of the intellectually most distinguished of the Josephites' opponents, Maxim the Greek; the Italian Renaissance, rather than the ideational armory of the super-orthodox among the Western Roman Catholic hierarchy, made its modest contribution here. Maxim was silenced, and the notion of 'Moscow the Third Rome' replaced the combination of the Byzantine tradition and contemporary Renaissance influences that he exemplified. In that notion the Josephites, however, helped to sow the seeds of their own eventual destruction; they glorified the Moscow state and principate in return for being allowed to keep their properties and to surround the ruler with monkish advisers, but it was the power of the state that lasted and not the rest of the bargain.

After the 1550's the Reformation seemed almost to inundate the Orthodox Slavs of the Ukraine, then chiefly within the Polish-Lithuanian state, and in the mid-1560's the Counter-Reformation became a formidable threat. An Orthodox self-defense of sorts was mounted by the Ukrainian nobles led by Prince K. K. Ostrozhsky from the 1570's, but despite Prince Andrei Kurbsky's preference for a different strategy the chief nobles resorted more and more to the use of Protestant aid against a Roman Catholicism regarded as the chief enemy. The opportunity for Roman Catholic conversion of the Eastern Slavs seemed great: but Rome opted for a bird in the hand in pushing through the Union of Brest (1596), thereby religiously annexing the Ukraine, but diminishing its chances for success in Muscovy later on. Rome was able to accomplish the Union by way of the cooperation of much of the Ukrainian clergy, who were attracted by the superior culture of the Roman Catholics and repelled by the weakness of Orthodoxy under Ottoman or Muscovite rule.

Meanwhile in the Muscovy of Ivan IV another series of social and cultural struggles was taking place. As in Vasily III's reign, the Transvolgans started with the advantage; again the Josephites, led by Metropolitan Makary, became well-established, around 1550. The Josephites condemned a series of antitrinitarian heretics, and seemed to triumph when Ivan IV broke with Sylvester and other Transvolgans in 1560. But their ascendancy was cut short; after 1564 Ivan's reign of terror left no room for their influence and the murder of Metropolitan Filipp in 1569 made it clear that the tsar would countenance no ecclesiastical curbs. Weakened by Ivan's domestic bloodbath and profitless foreign adventure in Livonia, after his death Muscovy was open to the Polish and Roman Catholic offensives which constituted one aspect of the Time of Troubles. Twice Roman Catholic tsars (though the First False Dmitry may not have been very zealous in his Roman allegiance, Władysław was) were crowned in Moscow, but a combination of bad Polish strategy and a surge of Muscovite patriotism led to failure of the Eastward offensive and a restoration of Russian and Orthodox rule in the person of Michael Romanov.

Cultural weakness had been part of the reason for the prolongation of the Time of Troubles, and the early Romanovs endeavored to reduce it. Filaret did little to build strength, but sought simply to prohibit the importation of dangerous ideas from the West. Such ideas now centered in Kiev. In the early 1600's leadership of the Orthodox cause in the Ukraine had passed from the old nobles to the Cossack leaders, who among other things sponsored the new 'brotherhood' schools. The best of them developed into the Kievan College, which became a center of learning under Metropolitan Peter Mogila in the 1630's and 1640's, languished during the Ukrainian wars of the mid-century, then in the 1670's revived – now newly under Muscovite rule. Learning in

Kiev and other Ukrainian centers was Orthodox in form, but came close to being Roman Catholic in content.

After 1645 the new tsar Alexis and the young Friends of Piety attempted widespread reform in Muscovite culture and life, and turned to the Kievan College for help. The less educated and xenophobic elements in Muscovy were dubious. The man who became patriarch in 1652, Nikon, was soon persuaded that a progressive in the Russian Church ought to be pro-Greek; he thought he was Hellenizing, was accused of Latinizing, and cannot in fact be said to have done much of either. By his maladroitness in introducing ecclesiastical reforms, he alienated the tsar and was removed from office, but his reforms were retained. The new dispensation in the Church was, however, presided over by genuinely Latinizing clergy who came from Kiev or were influenced by its dominant currents, led by Simeon of Polotsk. Roman Catholic influences came to be in the ascendant in the Moscow Academy, founded in 1685, in the entourage of Sophia as regent 1682–9, and in the thinking of the leader of the Church after the death of the last patriarch in 1700 – the *locum tenens*, Stefan Yavorsky.

From the time of Ivan III, and especially after the Time of Troubles, there was little question in the minds of educated men that intellectual and cultural weakness in Muscovy was a problem and that remedies could be found only abroad. By the seventeenth century 'abroad' came clearly to mean Roman Catholic countries.

When Peter, the first Russian ruler to visit the West, reflected on his travels, however, he set about to change the chief source of cultural importation to the Protestant countries. A coalition of reformers and reactionaries, pro-Roman Catholic and indigenously oriented groups placed their hope in Peter's son Alexis. But Alexis was killed, and the coalition's intellectual spokesman, Stefan Yavorsky, was defeated by 1717 and replaced by two frankly Protestantizing clerics as Peter's assistants for cultural affairs: Feodosy Yanovsky and Feofan Prokopovich. Feodosy made missteps but Feofan survived, attempting to make Peter's cultural legacy the teachings of Protestant scholasticism. After two short years of the rule of Peter's widow, Alexis's young son Peter II seemed about to reverse the work of his grandfather, who had done away with his father. A cultural counter-revolution in the cause of the old Alexis–Yavorsky coalition seemed to impend; but Peter II's death in 1730 cut it off. Under Anna, Feofan Prokopovich was restored to honor and influence. Not Protestantism in general, but its scholastic version was given some competition from the reception of Halle pietism by one group of clergy, headed by Simon Todorsky, which was responsible for the 'Elizabeth Bible' (1751). Scholastic currents are observable in Lomonosov and others, and remained institutionally preserved in the ecclesiastical schools that Peter had begun to organize. A quasi-Reformation had been carried out in Russia: the patriarchate had been ended; the Church was ruled by a kind of Lutheran consistory; the clergy learned nominally Orthodox but substantially Protestant theology in the Latin language. The Russian Church became to a considerable extent separated from Russian life.

In the reign of Catherine II the first extra-ecclesiastical influences from the West appear in Russian thought: Freemasonry and Voltairianism, in the 1770's often not clearly distinguishable from each other. The liberal and rationalist Masonry of the 70's was exemplified by Shcherbatov's *Ophir* and (though published later) Radishchev's *Journey*; the mystical Masonry of the 80's showed itself in Novikov. Catherine's son Paul, starting as a Mason, rapidly fell under the influence of the Jesuit order, which Catherine had given asylum in Russia, in particular Fr Gruber. Paul's murder prevented the monarch from developing the implications of this enthusiasm in full.

The Jesuits were closer to Paul than to any other Russian ruler before or since, but they made more impact on the upper ranks of society during the reign of Alexander I. Their discipline, culture, and learning acted as a powerful magnet on the Russian nobility, and their ally, Joseph de Maistre, for a time carried great weight in court circles. But Alexander I, affected throughout his reign by both the rationalism and the sentimentalism of his grandmother's time, kept the Jesuits at arm's length and finally expelled them. His conversion to pietism, demonstrated by the Holy Alliance and the 'combined ministry' headed by Prince Alexander Golitsyn, signaled an effort of his government to lead to similar conversion not only Russia but all Europe. The Masons benefited by the 'pietist revolution', and the revival of their lodges led to the formation of Decembrist secret societies, whose aspirations and programs resuscitated the liberal Masonic ideas of the 1770's, and contributed to the organization of the Society of United Slavs. However, Alexander's pietism led him to disillusionment, and in 1824 he put an end to the 'combined ministry'.

A revival of Protestant scholasticism ensued in the ecclesiastical schools and produced a generation of clergy-teachers committed to German idealist philosophy who staffed the crucial posts in the new universities. Their student adepts formed circles: the Lovers of Wisdom in the 1820's, the circles of Stankevich and Herzen in the 1830's, the Westerners and Slavophiles in the 1840's. Nicholas I worried about the disaffection within the upper ranks of society shown in the Decembrist revolt that inaugurated his reign and in the activities of the Schellingian and Hegelian student circles, little as he may have understood them. His entourage baked him a curious ideological cake in the doctrine of 'official nationality', in which the virtues of 'Russia' were extolled in French and German. Chaadaev denied the existence of such virtues – also in French – and called for Russia to go to school to Western Christian culture. Bakunin and then Herzen went abroad, abandoning German idealism for French anarchism, and founding the Russian emigration. In the West Bakunin went over unequivocally to the revolutionary camp; Herzen shared his anarchism but not his single-minded readiness to resort to force. The Petrashevtsy circle tranquilly read French socialist tracts, and was severely punished for so doing; the Durov circle, which planned revolution, was not discovered. Russian Orthodox theology showed signs of revival and passage from Schelling and Hegel – which clergymen had taught the university students – to the roots of Orthodox Christianity in the primitive church and Byzantium. However, the clergy was now finding itself isolated. By the mid-century an abyss had opened between religious men and atheists within the Russian educated class, and for nearly half a century few tried to span it – except, indeed, some of Russia's greatest writers of all time.

The intelligentsia took form in the reign of Alexander II. Their ideas were wholly Western: what bound them together was generally atheism and socialism in theory and revolutionism in practice. The leaders were Chernyshevsky and Dobroliubov. They began by negation: of religion, of art, of monarchism, of private property, and much else. In all of this they went too far – even for Herzen, atheist and anarchist socialist as he by then had become, and during the 1860's also for a number of epigons of Westernism and Slavophilism who worked in or close to the government in implementing the Great Reforms or merely supported the Reforms and looked hopefully for results. Out of Chernyshevsky's and Dobroliubov's teachings came two rather different sorts of developments. One was nihilism, sweeping away not only tradition but respect for all existing institutions, as exemplified in Pisarev – though in most cases not respect for science; indeed respect became transmuted into religious faith in science, especially in misunderstood biology. The other was socialism, or what it is doubtless too late to call anything else than 'populism'. Starting with isolated manifestoes and circles in the 1860's, it became embodied in the movement 'to the people' and more prestigious if not much larger organizations in the 1870's. The émigré prophets of populism, such as Lavrov, Bakunin, and Tkachev, made their ideological contribution from afar; at home enough of the religious background survived to color deeply the teachings and actions of the youth, at least until the 'going to the people' movement failed, frequently despite their own professions of atheism.

Side by side with the growth of the intelligentsia and its revolutionary movement, there appeared quite different sorts of phenomena. Dostoevsky, fresh from his punishment for involvement with the Petrashevtsy, attempted to bridge the ideological gaps that separated Russia from the West, the intelligentsia from the rest of the educated class. Tolstoy pursued his own lonely path to a nihilism more sweeping than Pisarev's (since he rejected, as Pisarev did not, both science and revolutionism), religious anarchism, and a private faith of his own; the faith won few converts, the man earned almost universal respect and reverence in Russia and abroad. The great writers were read by everyone, but their thought was far less soundly based or influential than their art.

The revolutionary intelligentsia alarmed many by their ideas and horrified more by their violent deeds. A number of those who supported the Great Reforms in the 1860's, and may be with caution described as liberals, reacted by moving to the Right. This was true of the Slavophile epigon who became a

Pan-Slav, Ivan Aksakov; the herald of the new secular Pan-Slavism, Danilevsky; the ex-Westerner, Katkov; and the man who became (not very justifiably) a popular symbol of the repressive regime following the assassination of the Tsar-Reformer, Pobedonostsev. None of these men, however, provided any serious intellectual competition for the attitudes of the revolutionary intelligentsia. The first to do so was Vladimir Soloviev. Something of a radical in his youth, he later took an active liberal stance, exemplifying the (slight) impact of Protestant modernism in Russia, and demonstrating the inaccuracy of the Western habit of classifying everyone outside the revolutionary intelligentsia as a 'conservative'. But he was mainly concerned not with politics but with culture, seeking to bring about a meeting of the ideas of East and West that had some sound philosophical buttressing. No one could question his intellectual standing; he gave courage to such original and even odd thinkers as Leontiev and Fedorov, and bequeathed ideas to the next generation from which a whole new development was to come.

The sectarian character of the intelligentsia became quite marked in the 1855–90 period, but there were shadings that ought to be noted. Mikhailovsky, Danielson, and Vorontsov contributed serious ideas and analysis to the discussion of Russia's social and economic development, and Plekhanov, who did much to set up a new 'Marxist' camp within the Russian socialist orbit, was a thinker of imposing caliber.

Around 1890 the straitjacket of atheism, socialism, and utilitarianism was loosened. The reception of Marxism served as valuable philosophical training for a generation of young Russians. For most of the outstanding Marxists of the 90's Marxism was not a religious dogma but a way station on the road that led to posing anew the fundamental questions about life, history, and Russia's relation to the world. Several of them went from Marxism to neo-Kantianism, and from there some went back to Orthodoxy intellectually and organizationally, others to a politically moderate sociology, still others to esthetically-oriented individualism – and none of those descriptions is exhaustive. In the meantime a sensational series of developments took place in the arts. Merezhkovsky led off a kind of esthetic revolution in the interests of the independent value of esthetics generally and of poetry in particular. The symbolists, some of whom were influenced by Soloviev, sampled new philosophical and quasi-philosophical ideas as they wrote a new type of poetry. One may distinguish two generations of symbolists and then find in the multitude of new poetic schools that followed 1905 – Acmeism, Futurism, and several others – sharp disagreements with symbolism but concurrence with the symbolists in the rejection of the 'social command' of the radical critics. There was much excess, some deliberate 'decadence', some political disillusionment and despair in the so-called Silver Age, but its positive aspects were more important, including a sense of continuing excitement, a creative exchange of differing views, a series of experiments that gained real and lasting popularity – as in the Moscow Art Theater and the Ballets Russes. Within Orthodoxy, some clergy and laity tried to build on the nineteenth-century revival to make religion a force once again among the educated class and to meet with secular intellectuals in fruitful dialogue, in the religio-philosophical movement beginning in 1901 and continuing intermittently for several years. The rediscovery of the Russian cultural heritage proceeded hand in hand with a new and more confident approach to the modernist currents in Western culture; The World of Art group pioneered this fruitful symbiosis of objectives and others continued it. As for the intelligentsia, they seemed, in the years just before and during the Revolution of 1905, to reach out effectively to large sections of the common people in harmonious quest for social reform and constitutional government, but the end of the Revolution called such appearances into question. When the revolutionary tide receded it left a new kind of regime, in which the autocratic power was nominally limited and actually circumscribed in important ways, but one in which few of the liberals could place much hope and which the radicals thought hopeless. The masses, however, showed little concern with the intelligentsia's plight.

In 1909 the former Marxists of the 90's summoned the intelligentsia not necessarily to identify with the Duma which most of them found uncongenial, but rather to engage in serious cultural work and to recognize that trying to carry the troubles of 1905 to the point of overthrow of the monarchy had provoked not only failure but repression and executions – in a word, that the apparent union of intelligentsia and people had lacked foundation. The misplaced religiosity of the atheist socialism which was the creed of the intelligentsia was at fault – the fanatical pursuit of party programs, indifferent to the values of the Russian people.

During the last years before the Revolution Marxism made no further visible headway whatever in the Russian educated class, nor any other class. Culturally there was substantial progress; the scope of popular education, popular interests in the arts, the attainments of science and learning broadened and deepened. The political scene was, however, not equally promising. It is not necessary to contend that, if there had been no World War or no revolution, all would have been well. The mistakes of the government and the blindness of the monarch were of grave importance; the autocracy gave no sign of adaptability and many indications of failure to come to grips with the problems of the country.

The shadows on the political scene, unfortunately, obscured the cultural picture. It is a fact too little understood to this day that the Russian effort to reach a reconciliation with Western thought and culture – which had been knocking at Russia's door since Ivan III, had been thrust forcibly on the state and people by Peter I, had seemed a parlor game for the spoiled and rich during the reign of Nicholas I, and had been converted into a radical cult under Alexander II – in the early years of the twentieth century gave promise of achieving success. Science and religion, the traditional and the innovative, the arts and politics, and what was Russian and what was Western in all of these could in each case be distinguished from each other, the proper place of each discussed sensibly; the claims of each could be heard, and a creative tension pervaded much of Russian cultural life.

Through the whole of modern Russian history a single-centered society was the prevailing form. Until the sixteenth century the boyars and the Church resisted the growing demands of the central power, until 1721 the Church continued to struggle. The model despotism created by Peter began before long to be undermined, by the emancipation of the gentry, by the new ideas from the West that lodged in the minds of a section of the liberated gentry, by the emancipation of the serfs, by the habits of citizenship which began to be acquired in all sectors of the population thereafter. And yet the centralized state and the decisive power of the autocrat lasted until a few days before abdication in 1917.

What this meant for the history of thought in Russia has been made clear. Under Ivan III and Vasily III, and even for the early part of Ivan IV's reign, ideas could exist outside the tsar's entourage – in the Church and among the boyars – and even in part be directed against the tsar's power or his exercise thereof. The contests were still settled by the tsar, but they could take shape in other quarters. In the seventeenth century there was a religious and cultural schism of great dimensions, but the tsar kept the upper hand. In the eighteenth and early nineteenth centuries many of the new ideas flourished in and around the court, and the monarchs – Catherine II, Paul, and Alexander I – took personal part in the cultural conflicts as their eighteenth-century predecessors did not. Under Nicholas I most of the educated class abandoned hope that either cultural growth or political change would be approved by the monarch, and under Alexander II the intelligentsia abjured loyalty altogether while a few other thinkers and writers tried in the cultural realm to keep Russia from flying apart. The monarchy remained aloof from and suspicious of culture of any kind throughout the last two reigns.

Since the state was the arbiter of culture and thought (in a manner not true of the West), the history of thought in Russia must be written in close conjunction with the history of the central power, which time after time determined the outcome of struggle in the realm of ideas. Therefore there was a natural tendency for educated men to consider political changes as necessary prerequisites to anything else; but there was also a countervailing tendency to exclude political changes from discussion because they were either forbidden or regarded as impossible, or both. To a certain extent these contrary pressures cancelled each other out.

Political thought in Russia played a role in all stages of the modern period, in fact it was usually derivative from religious or philosophical ideas. There can be no worse distortion of Russia's history than to write the history of ideas as if those ideas had been mainly and at root political over the last five centuries. Ideas could not be derived from political experience, for there were no political institutions in which people participated as citizens; they could not, over a long period, be easily derived from ecclesiastical experience, for the Church itself was subjected to the state power, its administration was part of the state machinery, its clergy was in danger of being converted into a section of the bureaucracy. That is the significance of the disjunction between life and thought in Russia to which Gershenzon points in the epigraph to this chapter. He may have exaggerated it somewhat, but it was of great significance. It has become customary – in the USSR and sometimes also outside it – to preface works in the history of thought by remarks about grain prices, the growth of cities or railroads, and the state of the economy generally in whatever period the work deals with, but economic changes had precious little to do with changes in thought. If someone wishes to argue that they ought to have, and that it would have been healthier for Russia if they had, he will find no disagreement here, but that does not alter what happened.

During the whole of Russia's modern history thought owed much to the West. Ideas might be borrowed – as the Josephites borrowed them – simply as weapons, but they then might come to be taken seriously; intellectual fashions might be picked up only for the sake of following the mode, as was done by some Russian Voltairians, but after a time they might take root.

The West took little initiative in attempting to bring its thought and culture to Russia. Roman Catholic influence, from the arrival of Zoe Paleologa to the time of Stefan Yavorsky, was mainly the result of Russian endeavors to raise the quality of their intellectual armory. It is true that in the sixteenth century an attempted conversion of Russia was discussed in Rome, and that Sigismund III of Poland not only took the possibility seriously but for a time seemed to have the power and opportunity to make it real. However, the learned Westerners whom the Gennady circle used and the foreign texts they drew upon were the result of Russian debates and not Roman plans; the Jesuit schools which Russian and Ukrainian churchmen went off to attend in Poland in the seventeenth century and the Catholic learning they brought back with them were not the result of missionary strategy for Russia, and the single serious missionary to Muscovy for most of that century, Križanić, was given no support by Rome in his efforts. The Jesuits who appeared briefly and with only modest effect in Moscow in the last years of the seventeenth century and successfully sought refuge after 1773 in the Russian Empire, to be sure, exhibited many of the best talents of their order, and they were certainly bent on converting Russia in the long run if they could. But the little Moscow mission of the 1680's was far less important during the whole period when Roman Catholic influence was the dominant one from the West (1472–1717) than a series of other factors, and the efforts of the Jesuits under Catherine II and her son and grandson never had a serious chance to succeed despite their fleeting, spectacular impact on the Emperor Paul. The most astonishing thing about the Roman Catholic period of our story is that Rome for the most part seemed indifferent to the chance of capitalizing on the inroads its intellectual influence had made. Probably part of the explanation is that Rome did not realize what impact it was having on Russia.

There was no single center of Protestantism. Leibniz had many ideas on the subject of Russia (and Peter borrowed some of them). He was, however, less concerned with whether Russia became Protestant than whether as a Christian nation it could develop a high culture to take its place with others. In the mid-eighteenth century Halle's pietists tried to influence Russia, but they had neither the resources nor the will to launch a major missionary effort. The evangelicals of the turn of the nineteenth century were zealous about the outreach of the Bible Societies, to Russia as to other countries, and indeed helped to fix a certain cast to Russian cultural life for most of a century that partly drew on indigenous non-intellectual or anti-intellectual tendencies in the country but also owed much to the fundamentalist revival that occurred in Great Britain. The single Western influence that before 1917 may be said to have gone deeper than any other in Russia, both among the upper and lower social groupings, was Protestantism (1717–1917) and, within Protestantism, pietism. The taunt, 'Protestantism of the Eastern Rite', that was flung at the Russian Orthodox Church both from within and without by those resentful of Protestant influences, had in it enough truth to hurt.

It was from the clergymen who studied German philosophers in Protestantized schools that the youth of the early nineteenth century learned about Schelling and Hegel. However, as the doctrines of the German idealists were secularized in the West, via Feuerbach, so were they in Russia. Among the educated class atheism led to socialism, which by 1860 had come to be the dominant current. It did not do so instantly. A fair amount of Christian socialism figured in the thinking of the Petrashevtsy, the Herzen of mid-passage, and the Brotherhood of Cyril and Methodius. But by the time the *raznochintsy* emerged to act as the leaders of university youth, in the 1860's, atheism and socialism were firmly linked. Socialism probably claimed the allegiance of the majority of educated men in Russia for most of the period from 1860 to 1917. No longer is it necessary to distinguish professed belief from actual belief, as it was when some Orthodox clergy disseminated Roman Catholic and Protestant ideas without its ever occurring to them, or to others, that they were doing so. The socialists said they were socialists, if not always in print, and in fact were. It has been noted that they carried over much religious zeal (with a pronounced pietist tinge) into their efforts in the 1860's and 1870's. Partly that phenomenon merely reproduced one in the West: modern socialism at root is an attempt to secularize the notion of the Kingdom of Heaven and apply it on earth.

The socialists, however, placed between themselves and the mass of the Russian people a cultural gulf that was so embarrassing it could not be acknowledged. The paradox was that the people who called themselves 'populists' were actually more alien in their values to the peasantry, the real *populus*, and to the uneducated poor of all kinds than the elite had ever been before. Wide as had become the separation between at least part of the clergy from the common people as a result of the Petrine reform in the Church – a separation which even extended to the realm of language – the village clergy had retained a commonalty of attitudes with their parishioners even when subjection to the state had helped to drive them to a sadly depressed intellectual and moral level.

The Slavophiles had begun to perceive the problem of alienation of the elite, and had sought to bridge the gap to the people, but it was only a beginning they made. Some of the great writers went further with such explorations, and Vladimir Soloviev went far to establish a basis. The Slavophiles were still uncomfortable in the knowledge of how deeply they had drunk from German philosophy and of how little they knew the Eastern Church Fathers they had come to hail as authorities. Soloviev could build on a reasonably secure double foundation of Western and Russian-and-Orthodox learning. Thereby he became the leading figure of the syncretism that developed under Alexander II and III and then yielded to an epoch of reconciliation with the West and of transcendence of the categories of Eastern and Western that is observable under Nicholas II.

From the fifteenth to the nineteenth centuries, Russians took from the West the ideas that were acknowledged in the West as currently most advanced. That might mean that they were the ideas prevalent in the incontrovertibly most advanced educational institutions – Roman Catholic ones, before the Reformation – of the West; or that they were the ideas current in the most advanced and powerful countries – Protestant ones, in the eighteenth century – of the West; or that they were the ideas accepted by the writers popular with the most sophisticated intellectuals – Voltaire, Hegel, Comte, Proudhon, Marx – of the West. (Sometimes, of course, two or three of these criteria were met by the same ideas at the same time.)

In the early twentieth century, there was rather abruptly a change. It was not that any xenophobic reaction overtook educated Russians; it was quite the contrary. A new period began in which Russians, building on the example of Soloviev, demonstrated an initiative of their own in the realm of thought, a confident ability to discriminate among currents of ideas, a propensity to test them against the ancient and well-established categories of Western and Mediterranean thought: not only the goodness which had never left Russian consciousness though it had suffered a variety of distortions, the beauty which was deeply revered in Old Russia but had been rejected by the radicals and was now revived, but also truth. When the writers of the early 1900's calmly deny the validity of the radical protest that such-and-such a proposition cannot be true because it endangers the proper political outcome, and demand that truth be honored in its own right, Russia may be regarded as standing at a crucial point of its cultural development.

Svetlana Allilueva has recently said that 'the years just before the Revolution of 1917 were the freest, the most creative the country had ever had. There was an explosion in the arts. There was a profusion of contrary political theories and activities. Russia was boiling with free thought, dissent and challenge.'[1] She does not remember the period, of course; she recalls to her Western hearers its characteristics as one of her generation of Soviet (or ex-Soviet, if she or the Soviet authorities prefer) intellectuals who are seeking to discover, like all thinking men and women in all other times and places, who they are. That question can never be answered until the persons in question koow the past from which they emerged.

ABBREVIATIONS

AHR	American Historical Review
ASEER	American Slavic and East European Review
B-E	Brokgauz-Efron, Entsiklopedicheskii Slovar'
BSE	Bol'shaia Sovetskaia Entsiklopediia
Chteniia OIDR	Chteniia v Imperatorskom Obshchestve Istorii i Drevnostei Rossiiskikh pri Moskovskom Universitete
IORIaS	Izvestiia, Otdelenie Russkogo Iazyka i Slovesnosti, Akademiia Nauk SSSR
PDPI	Pamiatniki Drevne-russkoi Pis'mennosti i Iskusstva
RBS	Russkii Biograficheskii Slovar'
RES	Revue des études slaves
RIB	Russkaia Istoricheskaia Biblioteka
SEEJ	Slavic and East European Journal
SEER	Slavonic and East European Review
TKDA	Trudy Kievskoi Dukhovnoi Akademii
TODRL	Trudy, Otdel Drevne-russkoi Literatury, Institut Russkoi Literatury, Akademiia Nauk SSSR
ZMNP	Zhurnal Ministerstva Narodnogo Prosveshcheniia

NOTES

Preface

1. Benjamin I. Schwartz, *Communism and China* (Harvard, 1968), 39.

Introduction

1. Trans. Talcott Parsons (New York, 1958). (The epigraph comes from p. 13.) Weber goes on to discuss apparent duplications of these phenomena outside the 'Occident'.

2. Rough approximations, none of which sets itself precisely that theme, include: William H. McNeill, *The Rise of the West* (Chicago, 1963); F. S. C. Northrop, *The Meeting of East and West* (New York, 1946); and Arend Th. van Leeuwen, *Christianity in World History* (London, 1964).

3. Alfred Weber, *Kulturgeschichte als Kultursoziologie* (Leiden, 1953), Ch. 2.

4. Van Leeuwen, *Christianity in World History*, 343.

5. Jules Monnerot, *Sociologie du Communisme* (Paris, 1949); an English translation is *Sociology and Psychology of Communism* (Boston, 1953). Van Leeuwen takes up the suggestion in *Christianity in World History*, 342–8.

6. Gustav A. Wetter, *Dialectical Materialism* (trans., New York, 1958), 559–60. Fr Wetter, evidently seeking an analogy with the papacy, cites the Central Committee of a Communist Party as its 'infallible authority'; but it might be more apposite to cite the periodic Party Congress as an equivalent of the ecumenical councils of the Christian Church in the capacity of *vox Dei*. A number of acts of Stalin, clothed in the garb of the Central Committee or its Politburo, have been challenged, as well as acts of Khrushchev, but no Soviet Party Congresses have been retrospectively illegitimized, not even those Stalin controlled most completely.

7. When Arnold Toynbee declares to the contrary, he seems to be speaking loosely. He writes in *A Study of History* (London, 1961), XII, 545: 'The Communist ideology was a Christian heresy in the sense that it had singled out several of the elements in Christianity and had concentrated on these to the exclusion of the rest. It had taken from Christianity its social ideals, its intolerance, and its fervour.' That is, he speaks of attitudes rather than doctrines.

8. Karl A. Wittfogel, *Oriental Despotism* (reprint, New Haven, 1963), esp. Chs 2 and 3. Not all specialists on Chinese history accept his thesis as applied to China. See, for example, F. W. Mote, 'The Growth of Chinese Despotism: A Critique of Wittfogel's Theory of Oriental Despotism As Applied to China', *Oriens Extremus*, Jahrgang 8, Heft 1 (August 1961), 1–41. But Professor Mote does not contend that Imperial China was not a despotism; the main thrust of his essay is that after the Sung Chinese despotism underwent significant change and development, becoming 'heightened' in the Yüan and early Ming periods in a way that persisted in the Ch'ing.

9. Van Leeuwen, *Christianity in World History*, 183.

10. It is worth noting that Wittfogel's starting point is institutions, and China; van Leeuwen's is cultures, and India; and yet the descriptions of the phenomena converge at most crucial points.

11. In China some doctrines (aside from the element of stress on the self-cultivation of the individual found in Confucianism) emphasizing the individual were advanced – Chuang-tzu's notion of freedom (*hsiao-yao*), the *Lü-shih ch'un-ch'iu's* discussion of 'valuing life and attaching importance to self')

(*kuei sheng chung chi*) and its reiteration in the *Huai-nan-wang shu* – as Hu Shih pointed out in *Chung-kuo chung-ku ssu-hsiang shih ch'ang-pien* (Taipei, 1971), 95–9, 425–30, 436–40. Though such doctrines persisted, they never achieved general acceptance.

12. It is of some interest that in both the Russian and the Chinese cases the capital was shifted, as a more or less direct result of Mongol rule, to a new site nearer Central Asia than before.

13. See Richard Pipes, 'Communism and Russian History', in Donald W. Treadgold (ed.), *Soviet and Chinese Communism* (Seattle, 1967), for a good brief analysis.

14. The phrase comes from Wittfogel, *Oriental Despotism*, in particular 204–27.

15. Wolfgang Franke, *The Reform and Abolition of the Traditional Chinese Examination System* (Harvard, 1960), 7.

16. Alfred North Whitehead, *Science and the Modern World* (New York, 1948), 208.

Foreword

1. Quoted by F. H. Marshall, 'Byzantine Literature', in Norman H. Baynes and H. St L. B. Moss (eds), *Byzantium: An Introduction to East Roman Civilization* (Oxford, 1948), 243.

2. B. H. Sumner, *Survey of Russian History* (reprint, London, 1961), 157.

3. B. D. Grekov, *Kievskaia Rus'* (2nd ed., Leningrad, 1953), 399–400.

4. George P. Fedotov, *The Russian Religious Mind: Kievan Christianity* (Harvard, 1946), 20.

5. Marshall, 'Byzantine Literature', 243.

6. Norman H. Baynes, *The Thought-World of East Rome* (London, 1947), 27–8.

7. *Ibid.*, 7.

8. Norman H. Baynes, *The Hellenistic Civilization and East Rome* (London, 1946), 36–7.

9. André Mazon, 'Byzance et la Russie', *Revue d'Histoire de la Philosophie et d'Histoire Générale de la Civilisation* n.s., v (1937), 265.

10. It is well known that Mikhailovsky and other Russians pointed to the ambiguous meaning of *pravda* (which could mean either 'truth' or 'what is ethically right') as a virtue of their own language. The first steps in thought require making distinctions; of course the failure to make this one clearly was not a result of the language itself.

11. Prot. Georgii Florovskii, *Puti russkago bogosloviia* (Paris, 1937), 1. See also Georges Florovsky, 'The Problem of Old Russian Culture', in Donald W. Treadgold (ed.), *The Development of the USSR* (Seattle, 1964).

12. Kn. E. N. Trubetskoi, *Umozrienie v kraskakh* (Moscow, 1916).

13. Grekov, *Kievskaia Rus'*, 388.

14. See F. Dvornik, 'The Kiev State and Its Relations with Western Europe', *Transactions of the Royal Historical Society*, fourth series, XXIX (1947), 27–46; Baron Meyendorff and Norman H. Baynes, 'The Byzantine Inheritance in Russia', in Baynes and Moss (eds), *Byzantium*, 369–91.

15. Grekov, *Kievskaia Rus'*, 405.

16. Meyendorff and Baynes, 'Byzantine Inheritance', 378–82.

17. Grekov, *Kievskaia Rus'*, 410.

18. No attempt is made here to assess the serious questions that have been raised concerning the authenticity or date of composition of this remarkable work; the published consensus of specialist opinion seems to continue to lean in the direction of accepting it as a monument of the Kievan period.

19. See Steven Runciman, *The Great Church in Captivity* (Cambridge, England, 1968), 138–58; and Dmitrij Čiževskij, *History of Russian Literature from the Eleventh Century to the End of the Baroque* ('s-Gravenhage, 1960), 150–2.

20. Ernst Benz, *The Eastern Orthodox Church: Its Thought and Life* (Garden City, New York, 1963), 115–17.

21. G. P. Fedotov, in John Meyendorff (ed.), *The Russian Religious Mind*, vol. II: *The Middle Ages* (Harvard, 1966), 26.

22. See I. Mansvetov, *Mitropolit Kipriian v ego liturgicheskoi dieiatel'nosti* (Moscow, 1882); and V. Iablonskii, *Pakhomii Serb i ego agiograficheskiia pisaniia* (St Petersburg, 1908).

23. A. I. Sobolevskii, *Perevodnaia literatura moskovskoi Rusi xiv-xvii vekov* (St Petersburg, 1903), Ch. 1.

24. Nikolai Nikol'skii, 'Opisanie rukopisei Kirillo-Bielozerskago monastyria sostavlennoe v kontsie xv vieka', *Izdaniia obshchestva liubitelei drevnei pismennosti*, CXIII (1897). The contents are summarized in Fedotov, *Middle Ages*, 32ff.

25. Fedotov, *Middle Ages*, 45; the *Izmaragd* is exhaustively discussed 36–112.

26. Ernst Benz, in *Wittenberg und Byzanz: Zur Begegnung und Auseinandersetzung der Reformation und der östlich-orthodoxen Kirche* (Marburg, 1949), explores only a few episodes of Lutheran–Orthodox relations of the middle of the sixteenth century, but in his introduction he squarely calls the view that 'the Reformation halted at the border of Eastern Orthodoxy' a 'fable' (p. 1).

27. See Runciman, *The Great Church in Captivity*, esp. Chs 4–7.

1: The meeting of Rome and Moscow (1472–1533)

1. See A. S. Arkhangel'skii, 'Nil Sorskii i Vassian Patrikeev: ikh literaturnye trudy i idei v drevnei Rusi, Chast' Pervaia: Prepodobnyi Nil Sorskii', *PDPI*, xxv (1881). Translations of his treatises on mystical experience that have survived appear in G. P. Fedotov (ed.), *A Treasury of Russian Spirituality* (New York, 1948), 90–133.

2. J. L. I. Fennell suggests that there was affinity between the Transvolgan and 'Judaizer' religious views, but does not go farther, though he emphasizes the similarity of their political outlooks and the personal ties between them, in 'The Attitude of the Josephians and the Trans-Volga Elders to the Heresy of the Judaizers', *SEER* XXIX, no. 73 (June 1951), esp. 503–9.

3. W. J. Ong defines Renaissance humanism in the narrower and stricter sense as 'a literary and intellectual movement...running from 14th-century Italy through Western culture generally into the 17th century...and marked by devotion to Greek and Latin classics as the central and highest expression of human values'. 'Humanism', *New Catholic Encyclopedia* VII, 215–16. A somewhat more apt formulation for some of the clerics influential in both Russia and China is given by Myron P. Gilmore (speaking of Erasmus) in referring to the central 'humanist conviction that there was nothing incompatible between the Christian and the classic traditions and that man's political and social life could

be improved by the exercise of reason and piety'. 'Humanism', *Encyclopedia Americana* (1969 ed.), XIV, 488. Such belief was characteristic of the best in Roman Catholic education in the fifteenth and sixteenth centuries, as expressed in the maxim *nihil humanum alienum*. It was not necessarily typical of all Roman Catholic influence in Russia, as will soon be clear.

4. See Deno Geanokoplos, 'Michael VIII Palaeologus and the Union of Lyons (1274)', *Harvard Theological Review*, XLVI (April 1953), 79–89.

5. Martin Jugie, *Le schisme byzantin* (Paris, 1941), 268.

6. Oscar Halecki, *From Florence to Brest (1439–1596)* (Rome, 1958), 60–3.

7. See the fine, detailed article by M. Gordillo, 'Russie (Pensée religieuse)' in *Dictionnaire de théologie catholique* (Paris, 1939), XIV, pt 1, cols 207–371.

8. Ivan Vlasovs'kyi, *Narys istorii ukrains'koi pravoslavnoi tserkvy* I (New York, 1955), 118; Ia. S. Lur'e, *Ideologicheskaia bor'ba v russkoi publitsistike kontsa xv-nachala xvi veka* (Moscow, Leningrad, 1960), 371.

9. Constantinople, as far as is known, was not to recognize the Moscow metropolitanate as canonically autocephalous until it was elevated to the status of patriarchate in 1589; the Kievan metropolitanate was to remain under Constantinople's jurisdiction, except for the interval 1596–1620, until 1686, when it would be subordinated to the Moscow patriarch.

10. 'Poslanie velikago kniazia Ivana Vasil'evicha k novgorodskomu arkhiepi-skopu Ionie, o tom, chtob on ne imiel obshcheniia s kievskim lzhemitropolitom Grigoriem', *RIB*, VI (1880), no. 100, col. 711. The quotation '*sia uzhe pravoslavie izrushilo*' is ascribed by Lur'e to Ivan III himself (*Ideol. bor'ba*, 371); Ivan is in fact purporting to quote Patriarch 'Simon' (evidently Simeon of Trebizond, doubtless in 1466, when he was patriarch for a few months; his second and third patriarchates were later, in 1471–4 and 1481–6) who writes from Constantinople, while Gregory III Mammas, who confirmed Metropolitan Gregory's appointment for Kiev, did so in exile at Rome.

11. Arnold Joseph Toynbee, 'Russia's Byzantine Heritage', in *Civilization on Trial* (New York, 1948), 169–70. He also misinterprets Filofei's statement of the notion of Moscow the Third Rome (see p. 19 below) as an affirmation of the Byzantine tradition (171). Dmitri Obolensky has demolished the chief contentions of this essay in 'Russia's Byzantine Heritage', *Oxford Slavonic Papers*, I (1950), 37–63, in passing showing that in other works Toynbee avoids some of his own mistakes here in question. Steven Runciman has also effectively challenged Toynbee in 'Byzantium, Russia and Caesaropapism', *Canadian Slavonic Papers*, II (1957), 1–10.

12. K. V. Bazilevich, *Vneshniaia politika tsentralizovannago gosudarstva* (Moscow, 1952), 75.

13. *Ibid.*, 83.

14. Prot. Georgii Florovskii, *Puti russkago bogosloviia* (Paris, 1937), 12.

15. J. L. I. Fennell in *Ivan the Great of Moscow* (London, 1961) argues that court ceremonial in Moscow changed only as a result of discovering how Western states conducted international relations. Gustave Alef, in his interesting article, 'The Adoption of the Muscovite Two-Headed Eagle: A Discordant View', *Speculum*, XL (January 1966), 1–21, shows that Ivan III's adoption of the two-headed eagle as a seal device in 1497 may have been decided upon as a result of the Habsburg example rather than in direct imitation of Byzantium, though the form of the eagle is Byzantine.

16. The Strigolniki have recently been the subject of portions of important Soviet monographs: N. A. Kazakova and Ia. S. Lur'e, *Antifeodal'nye ereticheskie*

dvizheniia na Rusi xiv-nachala xv veka (Moscow and Leningrad, 1955), 'Chast' pervaia: Novgorodsko-pskovskaia eres' strigol'nikov xiv–xv vv.', by N. A. Kazakova, with sources reproduced 230–55; A. I. Klibanov, *Reformatsionnye dvizheniia v Rossii v xiv-pervoi polovine xvi vv.* (Moscow, 1960), 118–36. Klibanov's opinion is that the term applied to the practice of laymen who assumed clerical or even priestly roles, since a specific sort of haircut served to distinguish certain clerical assistants (*chtetsy* and *pevtsy* or 'readers' and 'singers') at divine service from lay persons; *ibid.*, 135.

17. See discussion by G. P. Fedotov in John Meyendorff (ed.), *The Russian Religious Mind*, vol. II: *The Middle Ages* (Harvard, 1966), 135–8. On various conceptions of Terra Mater, see Mircea Eliade, *The Sacred and the Profane* (New York, 1959), 138–47.

18. The metaphor of the trees belongs to St Stephen of Perm, though 'the tree of life' is a phrase used (with a different meaning) in Genesis 3.22–4. See 'Pouchenie episkopa Stefana protiv strigol'nikov', in Kazakova and Lur'e *Antifeod. dvizh.*, 236ff. Klibanov in referring to this passage uses the phras 'drevo poznaniia', which is a misquotation and means rather 'the tree of knowledge' than 'the tree of thought'; *Ref. dvizh.*, 129–30.

19. Text in Kazakova and Lur'e, *Antifeod. dvizh.*, 253–5. Fedotov gives the date of 1429 in *Middle Ages*, 114–15; but he did not have the benefit of the study of Kazakova and Lur'e.

20. Peter Waldo, a rich merchant of Lyon, gave away his possessions as early as 1170. His followers experienced many vicissitudes before being driven into the Alpine valleys of Vaud, where they survived for over a century longer previous to the decisive crusade against them in 1487.

21. Fedotov, *Middle Ages*, 127.

22. See Klibanov, *Ref. dvizh.*, 169–72. The text of the epistle is given in Kazakova and Lur'e, *Antifeod. dvizh.*, 379–82.

23. Chiefly the 'Epistle to the Laodiceans' ('Laodikiiskoe poslanie') of Fedor Kuritsyn, the addition by Ivan the Black to the *Ellinskii letopisets* of 1485, a few glosses on the latter, and (in Klibanov's opinion) a manuscript he discovered entitled, 'Essay Against Monasticism' ('Sochinenie protiv monashestva'); all are found in Kazakova and Lur'e, *Antifeod. dvizh.*, 256–305. Deriving the Judaizer 'heresy' from them is another matter. To take only one example, the first line of the Kuritsyn Epistle is: '*Dusha samovlastna, zagrada ei vera*'. Klibanov argues very convincingly that this does not mean, as other commentators have argued (e.g., N. Tikhonravov), 'Reason is all-powerful, but faith impedes it', but simply, 'The human spirit has freedom of choice, and faith is its defense', an unimpeachably orthodox statement – see Klibanov, *Ref. dvizh.*, 63–6. Kazakova came to the same conclusion earlier about the second part of the phrase, in Kazakova and Lur'e, *Antifeod. dvizh.*, 174; see also Lur'e, *Ideol. bor'ba*, 173–4. I do not find persuasive the argument of John V. A. Fine, Jr, in 'Fedor Kuritsyn's "Laodikijskoe Poslanie" and the Heresy of the Judaisers', *Speculum*, XLII (July, 1966), 500–4, that the Epistle clearly shows Judaic influences.

24. We possess two versions, analyzed at some length in Lur'e, *Ideol. bor'ba*. The author found 37 manuscripts of a shorter version and 60 of a longer, containing a group of chapters (12–16) omitted in the former. The analyses are found on pp. 96–121 and 458–74. See Marc Szeftel, 'Joseph Volotsky's Political Ideas in a New Historical Perspective', *Jahrbücher für Geschichte Osteuropas*, n.s., vol. XIII (April 1965), pt 1, 19ff. The title was not Joseph's, but was supplied by others, perhaps followers of his, a century or more later.

25. Lur'e, *Ideol. bor'ba*, 154 and elsewhere.

26. *Ibid.*, 213–15.

27. Szeftel, 'Volotsky's Ideas', 26.

28. Lur'e, *Ideol. bor'ba*, 137–8.

29. *Ibid.*, 180.

30. Gennady was twenty years older than Joseph and has often been considered his preceptor, but the evidence suggests that the reverse is more likely. *Ibid.*, 214.

31. *Ibid.*, 400.

32. *Ibid.*, 374.

33. William K. Medlin, *Moscow and East Rome: A Political Study of the Relations of Church and State in Muscovite Russia* (Geneva, 1952), 84. The source given is *Pamiatniki diplomaticheskikh snoshenii drevnei Rusi s derzhavami inostrannymi*, pt 1 (St Petersburg, 1851), cols 15–17.

34. Lorenzo Valla had exposed it as a forgery in 1440, although debates on its origin continued for centuries thereafter.

35. A. I. Sobolevsky, in *Perevodnaia literatura moskovskoi Rusi xiv–xvii vekov* (St Petersburg, 1903), 254–9, concludes that Veniamin must have been Croatian on the basis of an examination of his translations, which contain no traces of Polish or Czech influence but significant ones of Serbo-Croatian. He guesses that Veniamin might have been one of the Croatian monks attracted to the Slavic monastery founded by Emperor Charles IV in 1347 in Prague or that which Jadwiga and Jagiello founded in 1390 in Kraków or perhaps spent time in both.

36. A. D. Sedel'nikov, 'Ocherki katolicheskogo vliiania v Novgorode v kontse xv–nachale xvi veka', *Doklady Akademii Nauk SSSR*, Ser. B (1929), no. 1, 16–19. This abstract of a book 'which has been prepared for the press' was evidently never followed by the promised publication, for Lur'e as recently as 1960 (*Ideol. bor'ba*, 23) refers only to the abstract.

37. *Ibid.*, 17. See also A. D. Sedel'nikov, 'Rasskaz 1490 g. ob inkvizitsii', *Trudy komissii po drevne-russkoi literature*, 1 (Leningrad, 1932), 33–57. The text of the document is given on pp. 49–50.

38. Text given in Kazakova and Lur'e, *Antifeod. dvizh.*, 378. The next sentence is: 'I have sent you an account of these conversations'; the reference is presumably to the work mentioned above, of which Sedel'nikov found a manuscript.

39. See p. 9 below.

40. The authorship has been questioned. V. Malinin, in *Starets Eleazarova monastyria Filofei i ego poslaniia: Istoriko-literaturnoe izsliedovanie* (Kiev, 1901), fns. 1881 and 1889, summarizes previous views and states his own belief that Gerasimov was the author. At least the manuscript is prefaced by a letter from Gerasimov to Gennady in which he claims to be presenting the translation of a manuscript given him during a visit in Rome. See Malinin, *Filofei*, 492–6; A. D. Sedel'nikov, 'Vasilij Kalika: L'histoire et la légende', *RES*, VII (1927), 224–40; N. N. Rozov, 'Povest' o novgorodskom belom klobuke kak pamiatnik obshcherusskoi publitsistiki xv veka', *TODRL*, IX (1953), 178–219; D. Strémooukhoff, 'La tiare de Saint Sylvestre et le klobuk blanc', *RES*, XXXIV (1958), 123–8. The longer version of the work is to be found in *Pamiatniki starinnoi russkoi literatury*, vol. 1 (St Petersburg, 1860), 288–98.

41. It is puzzling that Rome is blamed (by Gerasimov and later Filofei of Pskov) for accepting the heresy of Apollinarius the Younger, bishop of Laodicea, who died about 392. The heresy in question held that Christ lacked human

reason, which was replaced by the Holy Spirit. The heresy was condemned by several councils, including the Council of Rome of 381.

42. Sedeln'ikov, 'Ocherki katol.'

43. Such naive millenarianism had generally been rejected in the Greek Church, but seems to have survived more noticeably in the West. See Henry Chadwick, *The Early Church* (Baltimore, 1967), 78.

44. See A. D. Sedel'nikov, 'K izucheniiu "Slova kratka" i deiatel'nosti dominikantsa Veniamina', *IORIaS*, xxx (1926), 205ff.; Ia. S. Lur'e, 'K voprosu o "latinstve" Gennadievskogo literaturnogo kruzhka', in V. D. Kuz'mina (ed.), *Issledovaniia i materialy po drevnerusskoi literature* (Moscow, 1961), 68–77. The text of *Slovo kratko* is published in *Chteniia OIDR*, book 2 (1902), section 2, pp. i–xxx, 1–68, with foreword by A. D. Grigoriev.

45. Ia. S. Lur'e, '"Sobranie na likhoimtsev" – neizdannyi pamiatnik russkoi publitsistiki kontsa xv v.', *TODRL* xxi (1965), 133, concludes that the *Sobranie na likhoimtsev* is the original version of the *Slovo kratko*.

46. A. A. Zimin, 'O politicheskoi doktrine Iosifa Volotskogo', *TODRL*, ix (1953), 166–7. Ia. S. Lur'e (*Ideol. bor'ba*, 214) questions whether this possible influence can be shown to support the hypothesis that the Gennady–Joseph relationship was one of teacher to pupil. It may well be, as Lur'e holds, that Joseph was in the field of heresy-hunting and the defense of ecclesiastical property before Gennady was, but the point of interest here is simply that the primacy of the church was a Western doctrine which the Josephite party found useful.

47. Sobolevsky, *Perevod. lit.*, 254.

48. I. E. Evseev, *Gennadievskaia Bibliia 1499 g.* (St Petersburg, 1914), 6, quoted in Lur'e, *Ideol. bor'ba*, 282; and Evseev, 16, quoted in Lur'e, 'K voprosu o 'latinstve', 76.

49. Joseph Sanin, *Prosvetitel'*, as quoted by Fennell, 'Attitude of the Josephians', 492.

50. Arkhangel'skii, 'Nil Sorskii', 31–3; Lur'e doubts that they resisted in *Ideol. bor'ba*, 312. There is no direct evidence one way or the other.

51. Lur'e, *Ideol. bor'ba*, 151–4.

52. *Ibid.*, 375–84. See comments of A. A. Zimin, 'Osnovnye problemy reformatsionno-gumanisticheskogo dvizheniia v Rossii xiv–xvi vv.', *Istoriia, fol'klor, iskusstvo slavianskikh narodov: Doklady sovetskoi delegatsii, V Mezhdunarodnyi S"ezd Slavistov* (Moscow, 1963), 117.

53. *Ibid.*, 167–71, 183.

54. Lur'e, *Ideol. bor'ba*, 386–91. On the probable Western influence on the adoption of the two-headed eagle, see n. 15 above.

55. See *ibid.*, 409.

56. A. Ekzempliarskii, 'Kniaz' Vasilii Ivanovich Patrikieev', *RBS*, xiii, 383.

57. Lur'e, *Ideol. bor'ba*, 421.

58. This issue is emphasized by the contemporary *Pis'mo o neliubkakh*; see Fennell, 'Attitude', 488. Kazakova and Lur'e do not include this document in the texts they publish in *Antifeod. dvizh.*, and Lur'e in *Ideol. bor'ba*, 457, dates it to the mid-sixteenth century. In our opinion Lur'e's attempt to argue that the dispute about monastic property began only *after* the heretics were disposed of is unsuccessful (*ibid.*, 426); he himself acknowledges at another point (315–16) that it began precisely during the council of 1503.

59. Élie Denissoff suggests that Joseph himself was inspired by the Inquisition in action, but does not explain how or why, in 'Aux origines de l'église

russe autocéphale', *RES*, XXIII (1947), 81. An English version, 'On the Origins of the Autonomous Russian Church', is found in the *Review of Politics*, XII (April 1950), 225–46.

60. N. P. Popov, 'Afanas'evskii izvod povesti o Varlaame i Ioasafe', *IORIaS*, XXXI (1926), 222–4. Lur'e, *Ideol. bor'ba*, 278, challenges much of his argument but not this point.

61. Lur'e, *Ideol. bor'ba*, 279.

62. Sedel'nikov, 'Ocherki', 16.

63. '*Izhe prezhe nizhe slukhom slyshasia v nashei zemli eres*'...' Kazakova and Lur'e, *Antifeod. dvizh.*, 428; in 'Prostrannaia redaktsiia' of 'Poslanie igumena Iosifa Volotskogo episkopu Nifontu Suz'dalskomu'. The statement requires us to believe that Joseph was not acquainted with Gennady's epistle to the council of 1490 (see n. 22).

64. See p. 19.

65. Denissoff, 'Aux origines', 86–7. On his writings, see Horace W. Dewey and Mateja Matejic, 'The Literary Heritage of Vassian Patrikeev', *SEEJ*, X (Winter, 1966), 140–52.

66. Klibanov, *Ref. dvizh.*, 252.

67. Fennell, 'Attitude', 494; citing Maksim Grek, *Soch.* (Kazan, 1894), I, 42–5.

68. Lur'e considers it 'fully possible' that this Isaac 'was in reality a Jew', and not a 'Judaizer' – *Ideol. bor'ba*, 497.

69. N. A. Kazakova, *Vassian Patrikeev i ego sochineniia* (Moscow–Leningrad, 1960), 57.

70. George Vernadsky, *Russia at the Dawn of the Modern Age* (vol. IV of *A History of Russia* by George Vernadsky and Michael Karpovich) (New Haven, 1959), 156.

71. Élie Denissoff, *Maxime le Grec et l'Occident. Contribution à l'Histoire de la pensée religieuse et philosophique de Michel Trivolis* (Paris–Louvain, 1943).

72. *Ibid.*, 7–8.

73. *Ibid.*, 236.

74. *Ibid.*, 309.

75. *Ibid.*, 336.

76. V. S. Ikonnikov, *Maksim Grek i ego vremia. Istoricheskoe izsliedovanie* (2nd ed., Kiev, 1915), 105–8. Denissoff's study of Trivolis appears to confirm the deduction.

77. *Ibid.*, 561–73.

78. *Sochineniia prepodobnago Maksima Greka v russkom perevode* (Sviato-Troitskaia Sergieva Lavra; 3 parts, 1910–11), Slovo X, 'Slovo pokhval'noe Apostolam Petru i Pavlu', II, 100–20; see discussion in Ikonnikov, *Maksim*, 239; Denissoff, *Maxime*, 376.

79. *Ibid.*, Slovo XVI, 'Poslanie k gospodinu Feodoru Ivanovichu Karpovu', II, 220; see Denissoff, *Maxime*, 376.

80. Ikonnikov, *Maksim*, 222.

81. *Soch. Maksima*, Slovo XXVI, 'Poviest' strashnaia i dostoprimiechatel'naia', III, 133.

82. See p. 7.

83. 'Dmitrii Gerasimov', *RBS*, VIII, 447.

84. See A. A. Zimin, 'Doktor Nikolai Bulev – publitsist i uchenyi medik', in V. D. Kuz'mina (ed.), *Issledovaniia i materialy po drevnerusskoi literature* (Moscow, 1961), 78–86.

85. See V. F. Rzhiga, 'Boiarin-zapadnik xvi veka (F. I. Karpov)', *Rossiiskaia Assotsiatsiia Nauchno-Issledovatel'skikh Institutov Obshchestvennykh Nauk, Institut Istorii, Uchenye Zapiski*, IV (1929), 39–50, as cited in Vernadsky, *Russia*, 164; Ikonnikov, *Maksim*, 233ff.

86. Nikolay Andreyev, 'The Pskov-Pechery Monastery in the 16th Century', *SEER*, XXXII, no. 79 (June 1954), 318–24.

87. See Vasilii Zhmakin, 'Mitropolit Daniil i ego sochineniia', *Chteniia OIDR* (1881), Jan.–Mar. and Apr.–June, bks 1 and 2. Zhmakin counterposes the Josephites as conservatives and formalists to the liberal and critical Transvolgans, standing 'higher than Luther, Calvin, and other renowned Western Reformers' (in the address he gave in defense of the work as a dissertation, 'Bor'ba idei v Rossii v pervoi polovinie xvi vieka', *ZMNP*, CCXX (1882) [March–April], Science section, 150).

88. Sobolevsky, *Perevodnaia lit.*, 260.

89. Denissoff, *Maxime*, 391. Denissoff in 'Maxime le Grec et ses vicissitudes au sein de l'église russe', *RES*, XXXI (1954), 7–20 deals with the treatment of Maxim in Russian literature after his death.

90. *Soch. Maksima*, 1, Slovo xxv, 'Blagovierneiishemu i vyshemu tsariu i Bogokhranimomu Gosudariu Velikomu Kniaziu Vasiliiu Ioannovichu vseia Rusii', 191.

91. Quoted in Ikonnikov, *Maksim.*, 173, 178.

92. *Ibid.*, 182.

93. Makarii, Mitropolit Moskovskii, *Istoriia russkoi tserkvi v period razdieleniia eia na dvie metropolii* (12 vols, Ann Arbor, 1965), VII, 254. (Volumes in this set include reproductions from all three Russian editions. The original was finished in 1882.) For a much more reserved view of Maxim's intellectual sophistication, see Dmitrij Čiževskij, *History of Russian Literature from the Eleventh Century to the End of the Baroque* (*Slavistische Drukken en Herdrukken*, XII; 's-Graven-hage, 1960), 298–9.

94. Ikonnikov, *Maksim*, 580. Sobolevsky (*Perevodnaia lit.*, 279–82) doubts that Kurbsky had much personal contact with Maxim, but does not attempt to minimize Maxim's influence upon him.

95. Denissoff, *Maxime*, 379.

96. N. Kapterev, *Patriarkh Nikon i ego protivniki v dielie ispravleniia tser-kovnykh obriadov: Vremia patriarshestva Iosifa* (2nd ed., Sergiev Posad, 1913), 47.

97. Ikonnikov (*Maksim.*, 593) writes, '[S.M.] Soloviev places his name among the early predecessors of the drawing closer together [*sblizhenie*] of Russia and the West', and footnotes the remark to Soloviev's article, 'Shlëtser i anti-istoricheskoe napravlenie', *Russkii Viestnik* VIII, bk 2 of April, 1857. Soloviev, polemizing with Schlözer, actually writes (after a discussion of Gennady, Maxim the Greek, and others): 'if in the sixteenth century for the correction, direction, and collection of Russian treasures whose value was not realized it was impossible to manage without a pupil of foreign universities, then on what basis can one consider a drawing closer together with foreign universities in the eighteenth century to be some kind of deviation from the rightful path?' (456). This assault on Schlözer's consistency cannot be easily twisted into the positive statement that Ikonnikov puts into Soloviev s mouth, and it may be better to consider the opinion Ikonnikov's own.

98. Florovsky, *Puti*, 13.

99. There has been some scholarly confusion about this man's identity. The

chronicles mention a 'Nikolai Liuev' as present at the time of Vasily's final illness in 1533; the imperial envoy Francisco da Collo writes of a 'Dr. Nikolai Liubchanin [i.e., the man from Lübeck]'; Maxim the Greek writes of a 'Nikolai Nemchin [i.e., the German, or West European]'; Nikolai Shonberg (Nikolaus von Schönberg) was a papal envoy to Russia in 1518. Were there one, two, three, or four men? (There is also an alternative spelling of 'Liuev' as 'Bulev'.) Some time ago it was agreed that Nikolai Shonberg was not to be identified with anyone else, but A. A. Zimin has returned to the conclusion held by several scholars before a confusing document was published in 1868; he holds that there was only one Dr Nikolai Bulev of Lübeck and that he was located by Yury Trakhaniot's mission to Rome in 1490–1 and was persuaded to leave the papal court for Novgorod, where he served with the Gennady circle for a time before coming to Moscow. See Zimin, 'Doktor Nikolai Bulev'.

100. After Vasily's death, when Glinsky reproached his niece for becoming the mistress of I. F. Ovchina-Telepnev-Obolensky, he was punished again by imprisonment and died in 1534. See 'Mikhail Lvovich Glinskii', B-E.

101. Vernadsky, *Russia*, 163. See p. 16–17.

102. See p. 16.

103. Malinin, *Starets Filofei*, 'Poslanie Filofeiia k Munekhinu protiv zvie-zdochettsev i latin', Prilozheniia, VII, 45. This letter and the one to Grand Prince Vasily himself (Malinin, Prilozheniia, IX) were first published in *Pravoslavnyi Sobesednik*, 1861, bk II, 78–98, and 1863, bk I, 337–48.

104. See p. 13.

105. Lur'e, *Ideol. borb'a*, 485, points out that A. S. Pavlov in *Istoricheskii ocherk sekuliarizatsii tserkovnykh zemel' v Rossii*, pt 1, 83, first advanced the notion that Filofei was concerned with the influence of Vassian Patrikeev at court, Lur'e finds Malinin's challenge to this idea in *Starets Filofei*, 645, unconvincing.

106. Dimitri Strémooukhoff, 'Moscow the Third Rome: Sources of the Doctrine', *Speculum*, XXVIII (January 1953), 91–101; Lur'e, 487. See also Hildegard Schaeder, *Moskau das dritte Rom, Studien zur Geschichte der politischen Theorien in der slawischen Welt* (2nd ed., Darmstadt, 1957), and Medlin, *Moscow and East Rome*.

Nikolay Andreyev in 'Filofey and his Epistle to Ivan Vasil'yevich', *SEER*, XXXVIII, no. 90 (December 1959), 1–31, argues that the letter mentioned in the title of the article was written not to Ivan IV, as Malinin held, but to Ivan III, and that it was thus written before the letters to Vasily III and Misiur'-Munekhin. In it the scriptual prophecy used is Revelation 12.1–13 (1). If the letter was indeed addressed to Ivan III, it would appear that Filofei later decided that IV Ezra was preferable as a scriptural basis for the doctrine.

107. See p. 9.

108. N. M. Karamzin, *Istoriia gosudarstva rossiiskago* (5th ed., St Petersburg, 1844), VI, col. 23.

109. See p. 7 above. A contemporary of Filofei's, Nicholas Bulev, wrote that if Constantinople had fallen, it showed that the Byzantines had abandoned the true faith, while if (papal) Rome survived, that proved it was faithful. Filofei in a letter to Misiur'-Munekhin attacked Bulev for advancing this argument, which became well known; Peresvetov a little later writes that the *Catholics* (presumably Bulev) said that Constantinople fell to the Turks because of God's judgment; see V. F. Rzhiga, 'I. S. Peresvetov', *Chteniia OIDR* (1908), 1, pt 2, 77. Strémooukhoff in 'Sources', 95, seems to have missed the point by suggesting that

Filofei was chiefly engaged in *combating* Bulev's contention that Rome survived because it kept the true faith. The most obvious explanation is rather that Filofei simply turned the argument to his own advantage, repeating just what Bulev said about the Greeks: they were faithless and they perished for it. This was quite consonant with the view of the *Tale of the White Cowl*.

110. Malinin, *Starets Filofei*, 'Poslanie Filofeia k Munekhinu o pokorenii razuma Otkroveniiu', Prilozheniia, v, 34.

111. Cited in Strémooukhoff, 'Sources', 97–8.

112. Medlin, *Moscow and East Rome*, 94.

113. See p. 12 above.

114. F. Uspenskii, 'Kak voznik i razvivalsia v Rossii Vostochnyi vopros', *Izvestiia Sanktpeterburgskago slavianskago blagotvoritel'nago obshchestva*, nos 7–8 (1886), 309.

115. *Ibid.*, 314; the document is here quoted at length.

116. *Ibid.*, 315–16.

2: Echoes of the Reformation and Catholic Reform (1533–1615)

1. This hyphenated form, an invention of modern historians, seems more descriptive than the official name of the state after 1569, *Rzecz Pospolita* (literally simply 'Republic') or any other alternative designation.

2. Earl Morse Wilbur, *A History of Unitarianism: in Transylvania, England, and America* (Harvard, 1952), 36ff. The name 'Unitarian' originated at the time of the ten-day-long debate in the palace of Gyulafehérvár (Alba Iulia) in Transylvania, and was soon being used also by (Socinian) Poles in exile, although it was not used in Poland itself. The term is found in print for the first time as the name of a church in 1600.

3. Rudolf M. Mainka C.M.F., 'Die erste Auseinandersetzung der russischen Theologie mit dem Protestantismus', *Ostkirchliche Studien*, XI (September 1962), 131–60. See also Erik Amburger, *Geschichte des Protestantismus in Russland* (Stuttgart, 1961).

4. Ivan Vlasovs'kyi, *Narys istorii ukrain'skoi pravoslavnoi tserkvy*, I (New York, 1955), 182–5.

5. Wilbur, *A History of Unitarianism: Socinianism and its Antecedents* (Boston, 1945), Ch. XIX.

6. *Narys*, 230–1. Vlasovs'kyi, challenging the conclusions of Hrushevs'kyi (see *Z istorii religiinoi dumky na Ukraini* [L'viv, 1925], 64), argues that 'as a religious movement' the Reformation had 'only a very feeble echo' in the Ukraine, but evidently means simply that no large number of Ukrainians underwent formal conversion. His criticism of Hrushevs'kyi on this point is not very persuasive, though his apparent motive of emphasizing the genuinely religious aspects of the picture in opposition to Hrushevs'kyi's attempt to politicalize them may be justifiable.

7. Vlasovs'kyi, *Narys*, 231, writes, 'history has preserved not a single eminent name for among the Ukrainian nobility as a representative of the evangelical [i.e., Protestant] movement'. The statement can be defended against the charge of outright inaccuracy only by interpretation of the word 'eminent' (*viznachii*), which has been omitted by the translator of the English edition. Ivan Wlasowsky, *Outline History of the Ukrainian Orthodox Church*, I (New York, 1956), 223.

8. George Vernadsky, *Russia at the Dawn of the Modern Age* (New Haven,

1959), 276; Volodymyr Kubijovyč (ed.), *Ukraine: A Concise Encyclopedia* (Toronto, 1963), 628.

9. Wilbur, *Socinianism*, 329.

10. Stanislas Kot, *Socinianism in Poland: The Social and Political Ideas of the Polish Antitrinitarians in the Sixteenth and Seventeenth Centuries* (trans., Boston, 1957), 109.

11. Wilbur, *Socinianism*, 368. See Chapter 1 above. He mentions as his authority a monograph whose correct citation is Orest Levitskii, 'Sotsinianstvo v Pol'shie i iugo-zapadnoi Rusi', *Kievskaia Starina* (1882), #4, 5, 6. In #4, p. 40, Levitskii says that there was a '*local* Antitrinitarianism' in Russia which began with the Judaizers of Novgorod and Moscow and was revived by the mid-sixteenth-century Moscow heretics.

12. See p. 41.

13. Quoted by E. Likhach, 'Kniaz' Konstantin (Vasilii) Konstantinovich Ostrozhskii', *RBS*, XII, 463.

14. See p. 42.

15. See itemization in Likhach, 'Ostrozhskii', 464.

16. According to Élie Denissoff, 'Une biographie de Maxime le Grec par Kourbski', *Orientalia Christiana Periodica*, XX (1954), 44–6. The editor of the biography, S. Belokurov, considered that it dated only from the early seventeenth century and contained mainly errors. A. I. Sobolevsky, on the other hand (*Perevodnaia literatura Moskovskoi Rusi xiv–xvii viekov* [St Petersburg, 1903], 260), thought it had been composed immediately after Maxim's death. Belokurov's opinion carried the day at least until Denissoff's article was published. Vernadsky, writing in 1959 (*Russia at the Dawn*, 283), accepted Denissoff's attribution to Kurbsky. On Kurbsky's exile, see Oswald P. Backus, 'A. M. Kurbsky in the Polish-Lithuanian State (1564–1583)', *Acta Balto-Slavica* (Białystok) (1969), 29–50.

17. Wilbur, *Socinianism*, 456. Halecki, *From Florence to Brest*, 209, cites a letter of Ostrozhsky's of 1585 (possibly misdated for 1595) as evidence that the latter leaned to Calvinism. The letter is found in S. Golubev, *Kievskii Mitropolit Petr Mogila i ego spodvizhniki* (2 vols and 2 more of supplement; Kiev, 1883–98), suppl., 1, 27. The only relevant statement in the letter is, however, that the writer recognized as 'true Christian believers' those other than Orthodox (i.e., Protestants) who practiced communion in two kinds; that in itself did not distinguish Calvinists from Antitrinitarians. Further evidence of his sympathy for Protestantism is found *ibid.*, 40–1.

18. N. Liubovich, *Nachalo katolicheskoi reaktsii i upadok reformatsii v Pol'shie* (Warsaw, 1890), 102–4.

19. Le P. Pierling, SJ, *La Russie et le Saint-Siège*, 1 (Paris, 1896), 400–1.

20. Stanislas Polčin, SJ, 'Une tentative d'Union au xvie siècle: La mission religieuse du Père Antoine Possevin S.J. en Moscovie (1581–1582)', *Orientalia Christiana Analecta*, CL (Rome, 1957), 7, 84, 94.

21. There was only one extensive conversation on the subject, summarized in *ibid.*, 36–48.

22. Quoted in Pierling, *La Russie et le Saint-Siège*, II (Paris, 1897), 168, from Possevino's account. Ivan's scriptural reference was to Psalms 67.32.

23. Pierling, *La Russie et le Saint-Siège*, II, 158. See Polčin, 'Une tentative', 25.

24. It is true that in 1581 Possevino reproached Rome with having considered Muscovy ahead of the Ukrainian lands of Poland and emphasized his own belief

that the latter's conversion would serve as an instrument (*validissima macchina*) to bring about the conversion of Muscovites. See O. Halecki, 'Possevino's Last Statement on Polish–Russian Relations', *Orientalia Christiana Periodica*, XIX (1953), 282. In the event, the authors of the Union of Brest adopted Possevino's position, taking what they could get at the moment (the Ukraine) at the risk of making it impossible for them to get any more (Moscow) in the future.

25. In a letter to Stanislaus Gomoliński, Provost of Poznan, reprinted and evaluated in O. Halecki, 'Possevino's Last Statement'.

26. Wilbur, *Socinianism*, 433.

27. The book is reprinted in *RIB*, VII (St Petersburg, 1882), cols 223–526, with the changes of the 2nd edition (1590) identified as such.

28. E. S. Prokoshina, *Meletii Smotritskii* (Minsk, 1966), 89.

29. Vlasovs'kyi, *Narys*, II, 22; Georges Florovsky, 'The Orthodox Churches and the Ecumenical Movement Prior to 1910', in Ruth Rouse and Stephen Charles Neill (eds), *A History of the Ecumenical Movement, 1517–1948* (2nd ed., Philadelphia, 1967), 180. An earlier Orthodox rejoinder was one by the priest Vasily of Ostrog (1588) entitled 'O edinoi istinnoi pravoslavnoi vierie i o sviatoi sobornoi apostol'skoi tserkvi, otkudu nachalo priniala, i kako povsiudu rasprostresia', *RIB*, VII, cols 633–938.

30. Halecki, 'Possevino's Last Statement', 285.

31. Halecki, *From Florence to Brest*, 376.

32. *Ibid.*, 373. Probably Socinian is meant, since there was no sizeable organized body of Anabaptists in Poland at this time.

33. A. V. Florovskii, *Chekhi i Vostochnye Slaviane* (2 vols, Prague, 1935–47) I, 388.

34. Likhach, 'Ostrozhskii', 467.

35. Halecki, *From Florence*, 416–17.

36. Florovskii, *Puti*, 41, paraphrasing or quoting the letter.

37. *Ibid.*, 40.

38. Halecki, *From Florence*, 369 (and also 357, 375, and elsewhere) gives the reasons for considering Nicephorus, protosyncellus of the Patriarch of Constantinople, 'a Turkish agent if not spy'.

39. Quoted in W. E. D. Allen, *The Ukraine: A History* (Cambridge, England, 1940), 84.

40. N. Pavlov-Sil'vanskii, 'Ioann IV Vasil'evich, Groznyi', *RBS*, VIII, esp. 232–3.

41. J. L. I. Fennell in his edition of *Prince A. M. Kurbsky's History of Ivan IV* (Cambridge, England, 1965), 20, notes that Kurbsky was the only contemporary to use the term, and Antony Grobovsky in *The 'Chosen Council' of Ivan IV: A Reinterpretation* (Brooklyn, 1969), 137, plausibly concludes that the term meant nothing more than 'council of the righteous' and did not refer to any political group or administrative body. Grobovsky, however, devotes most of his attention to criticism of previous writings and virtually none to the question of who in fact were most influential among Ivan's advisers in 1547–60.

42. This is A. A. Zimin's view as expressed in his *I. S. Peresvetov i ego sovremenniki; ocherki po istorii russkoi obshchestvenno-politicheskoi mysli serediny xvi veka* (Moscow, 1958), 64. As Zimin points out, it has by no means been the unanimous view of scholars. A number, including Karamzin, Sergeevich, Platonov, Wipper, and I. I. Smirnov, have considered Sylvester and Makary to belong to the same camp. It is very difficult indeed to understand why they were brought to this conclusion. Zimin's predecessors in identifying Sylvester

with the Transvolgans include I. N. Zhdanov, K. Zaustsinsky, and S. V. Bakhrushin. See Zimin, *Peresvetov*, 42.

43. D. P. Golokhvastov and Leonid, 'Blagoveshchenskii ierei Sil'vestr i ego pisaniia', *Chteniia OIDR*, as cited in *ibid.*, 60–71.

44. I. U. Budovnits, *Russkaia publitsistika xvi veka* (Moscow–Leningrad, 1947), 201–2.

45. Zimin, *Peresvetov*, 72–3.

46. *Ibid.*, 74.

47. See p. 5 above.

48. Zimin, *Peresvetov*, 75, 83.

49. *Ibid.*, 56–7. Zimin here reviews the literature which considers the question of authorship, and concludes that Sylvester was either editor or author.

50. That is to say, lands whose tenure was conditional upon state service as distinguished from *votchiny*, hereditary landholdings characteristic of the boyars. *Pomestie* tenure dated from the reign of Ivan III.

51. Zimin, *Peresvetov*, 101.

52. Several investigators have noted the kinship of the two: for example, R. Wipper, *Ivan Grozny* (trans., Moscow, 1947), 59; Florovskii, *Puti*, 24; Zimin, *Peresvetov*, 102. Zimin compares the two unfavorably: Trent strengthened dogma, the Stoglav mainly ritual and discipline, and its protocols 'more than any other publicistic work of the mid-sixteenth century show how Josephite ideology ever more distinctly assumed a reactionary character, becoming a brake on the further development of social thought'.

53. Fennell, *Kurbsky's History*, 89.

54. *Ibid.*, 78–9.

55. I. I. Smirnov, 'Ivan Groznyi i boiarskii "miatezh" 1553 g.', *Istoricheskie Zapiski*, XLIII (1953), 165–6. See also Nikolay Andreyev, 'Interpolations in the 16th Century Muscovite Chronicles', *SEER*, XXXV, no. 84 (December 1956), on Viskovaty.

56. See Nikolay Andreyev, 'The Pskov-Pechery Monastery in the 16th Century', *SEER*, XXXII, no. 79 (June 1954). Kurbsky attributed Bashkin's errors to 'Lutheran heresies' (Fennell, *Kurbsky's History*, 269).

57. Zimin comments: 'Thus the religious views of Artemy, although in many respects they coincided with Russian Orthodoxy of the sixteenth century, nevertheless prepared the ground for the appearance of radical Reformational doctrines, a representative of which was Feodosy Kosoi' (*Peresvetov*, 166). Zimin has just noted that Artemy repeated word for word Nil Sorsky's aphorism: 'There is much that is written, but not all of it is divine (*pisaniia mnogo, no ne vsia bozhestvenna sut'*)'. From what we know of Artemy's views, they were no less orthodox than Nil's, and there is no more or less reason to say, 'The Transvolgans prepared the way for the Judaizers', than there is to make the statement just quoted about Artemy and Feodosy. In a word, there is no justification for either statement. This is not to suggest that Zimin is a particular admirer of Artemy's. On the page following the one cited, he declares that Artemy's demand (similar to that of Sylvester) that the tsar be guided by 'justice' and 'humility' meant a demand 'to renounce an independent policy and submit to such fanatical clerics from the Non-possessors around Sylvester as Artemy' (*ibid.*, 167). It is difficult to consider this an objective statement. Borozdin, after extensive citation of sources, plausibly concludes that Artemy and the Transvolgans had nothing worse than 'a condescending view of the "childish fancies" of Bashkin and a freer attitude toward the letter of the "divine

writings" than was usual among the chiefly Josephite clergy of that time' (A. Borozdin, 'Matviei Semenovich Bashkin', *RBS*, II, 613).

58. Zimin, *Peresvetov*, 199–209.

59. *Ibid.*, 187. See p. 28 above.

60. K. Zdr-v, 'Feodosii (Kosoi)', *RBS*, xxv, 334.

61. Dmitrij Čiževskij, *History of Russian Literature from the Eleventh Century to the End of the Baroque* ('s-Gravenhage, 1960), 304. A recent investigation of the idea of 'Holy Russia' is to be found in Michael Cherniavsky, *Tsar and People: Studies in Russian Myths* (New Haven, 1961), Ch. 4. Cherniavsky concludes that the phrase 'Holy Russia' underwent a 'period of silence' (111) that included the whole sixteenth century, but it is not necessary here to decide whether Čiževskij's and Cherniavsky's statements can be reconciled, since the point for us is only the Josephite glorification of the tsar.

62. Cited by Pavlov-Sil'vanskii, 'Ioann IV', 256.

63. There ensued a remarkable correspondence between Kurbsky and Ivan IV in which the issues between them do not emerge directly, but the Trans-volgan–Josephite struggle is obviously in the background of many of them. The issue in the foreground is alleged personal misconduct on both sides; the political issue between the different kinds of society of which Muscovy and Poland-Lithuania are examples underlies the whole polemic. The letters are translated and edited in J. L. I. Fennell (ed. and trans.), *The Correspondence between Prince A. M. Kurbsky and Tsar Ivan IV of Russia, 1564–1579* (Cambridge, England, 1963). The further fate of Kurbsky is discussed above, p. 29.

64. Zimin, *Peresvetov*, 132.

65. *Ibid.*, 122.

66. This trait has led Soviet writers to go so far as to speak of him as a 'consistent *narodnik*' (R. Iu. Vipper, *Ivan Groznyi*, 1st ed. [Moscow, 1922], 36). Similar statements have been made by V. F. Rzhiga, Budovnits, and others. See Zimin, *Peresvetov*, 112, 133, 136.

67. A. I. Pashkov, *Istoriia russkoi ekonomicheskoi mysli*, I, pt 1 (Moscow, 1955), 148.

68. See p. 20.

69. Cited by Zimin from manuscript, *Peresvetov*, 132.

70. *Ibid.*, 301. See also V. S-kii, 'Ivan Semenovich Peresvietov', *RBS*, XIII, 518–19; Čiževskij, *History of Russian Literature*, 279–82; Werner Philipp, 'Ivan Peresvetov und seine Schriften zur Erneuerung des Moskauer Reiches', *Osteuropäische Forschungen*, n.s., vol. xx (Königsberg–Berlin, 1935). Michael Cherniavsky in 'Ivan the Terrible as Renaissance Prince', *Slavic Review*, xxvii (June 1968), 195–211, points out similarities among the ideas of Peresvetov, Ivan IV, and Machiavelli, without contending that Machiavelli was known by the two Russians.

71. Zimin, *Peresvetov*, 270–1.

72. Cited by Čiževskij, *History*, 281.

73. Mohammed II (1451–81) is idealized and the wish to convert to Christianity is imputed to him by such Italian chroniclers as Paulus Jovius (1483–1522) and Francesco Sansovino (1521–83), as pointed out by V. F. Rzhiga, 'I. S. Peresvietov i zapadnaia kul'turno-istoricheskaia sreda', *IORIaS* (1911), #3, 169–81.

74. It is difficult to see why Zimin believes that the triumph of the Josephites in the 1550's made it necessary for Peresvetov to pass from the scene (*Peresvetov*, 338), since 'he and his humanist [*sic*] views' had no future at such a juncture.

Indeed, despite the great scholarly merits of Zimin's monograph and his objective and judicious handling of a great variety of particular issues, it is puzzling why he regards Peresvetov as the culmination and crown of the Christian teachings of such men as Sylvester, Bashkin, Feodosy, and Ermolai-Erazm, and constructs his entire book on the basis of that interpretation of the social thought of the mid-sixteenth century.

75. See p. 7 above.

76. S. Rozhdestvenskii, 'Filipp', *RBS*, xxi, 116–18; G. P. Fedotov, in *Sviatoi Filipp Mitropolit Moskovskii* (Paris, 1928), declares that Filipp 'embodied the best traditions of the Russian church' (178), but does not identify him with either the Transvolgans or the Josephites.

77. The parallel with the scene of 1931 when Stalin, according to Victor Serge, suggested his own retirement from the leadership after the death of his second wife, and was begged to remain, is striking. Such details, one may add, do not require acceptance of the contentions of George Backer's *The Deadly Parallel* (New York, 1950).

78. *Dictionnaire de théologie catholique*, viii–1 (Paris, 1947), cols 886–95; Halecki, *From Florence*, 223–4.

79. V. Korsakov, 'Feodor Ioannovich', *RBS*, xxv, 286–7.

80. Pierling, *La Russie et le Saint-Siège*, ii (1897), 355.

81. Karamzin (and Pushkin) believed him guilty only of Dmitry's murder. George Vernadsky, 'The Death of the Tsarevich Dimitry: A Reconsideration of the Case', *Oxford Slavonic Papers*, v (1954), 1–19.

82. Pl. Vasenko, 'Lzhedimitrii I–i, *RBS*, x, 370, referring to the investigations of Baudouin de Courtenay and S. L. Ptaszycki.

83. *Ibid.*, 396; Pirling [P. Pierling], 'Nazvannyi Dimitrii i pol'skie ariane', *Russkaia Starina* (April 1908), 1–10. It is not known whether Matthew Tvardokhleb was a Pole or a Russian émigré.

84. V. M-n, 'Lzhedimitrii I', B-E, xvii-A, 622.

85. Vasenko, 'Lzhedimitrii I–i', 390.

86. V. O. Kliuchevskii, *Sochineniia*, iii (Moscow, 1957), 241–2.

87. S. F. Platonov, *Moskva i Zapad* (Berlin, 1926), 72.

88. *Ibid.*, 78; Sergei Zen'kovskii, 'Drug Samozvantsa, eretik i stikhotvorets (Kniaz' Ivan Andreevich Khvorostinin)', *Opyty*, vi (1956), 77.

89. *Ibid.* See also Platonov, *Drevne-russkiia skazaniia i poviesti o Smutnom Vremeni*...(1966 reprint of 2nd ed., St Petersburg, 1913), 230–57.

90. Pierre Pascal, *Avvakum et les débuts du raskol* (Paris, 1938), 20.

91. Like Chaadaev, he was personally vain and often sharp with others; we have, for example, Prince S. I. Shakhovskoi's report on a quarrel that ensued, when he was a guest of Khvorostinin's for dinner, on the latter's denial that the Sixth Council was truly ecumenical. See Platonov, *Moskva i Zapad*, 74.

92. There was no real Peter; he was alleged to have been a son of Fedor Ivanovich.

93. Rome, *Archives Boncompagni*, E, 7, as quoted in Pierling, *La Russie et le Saint-Siège*, iii (1901), 364–6.

3: Moscow and Kiev (1613–1689)

1. His original Rumanian name was Movila; the Ukrainian form is Mohyla. My reluctant choice has been to use, in the text, the Great Russian spellings of Ukrainian names, on the ground that they are likely to be less difficult for

readers who know no Slavic languages and provide easier access to English-language reference books.

2. George Vernadsky, *Russia at the Dawn of the Modern Age* (New Haven, 1959), 251, distinguishes 'inner' from 'outer Cossacks'.

3. Ivan Vlasovs'kyi, *Narys istorii ukrains'koi pravoslavnoi tserkvy*, II (New York, 1956), 18.

4. E. S. Prokoshina, *Meletii Smotritskii* (Minsk, 1966), 138-9. Probably fear of being implicated in the killing of a Uniat clergyman was also important in his conversion.

5. Vlasovs'kyi, *Narys*, II, 218-19; Prot. Georgii Florovskii, *Puti russkago bogosloviia* (Paris, 1937), 43-4.

6. 'Iov (Ivan Matvieevich Boretskii)', *RBS*, VIII, 300-1.

7. There is one very lengthy study by S. Golubev, *Petr Mogila i ego spodvizhniki* (2 vols of text plus 2 vols of supplement; Kiev, 1883-98); unfortunately the planned third volume, to deal chiefly with Mogila's cultural activity, was never published (see Golubev, II, 524). See also E. Shmurlo, *Rimskaia kuriia na russkom pravoslavnom vostokie v 1609-1654 godakh* (Prague, 1928); P. P. Panaitescu, *L'influence de l'œuvre de Pierre Mogila, archevêque de Kiev, dans les Principautés roumaines* (*Mélanges de l'École Roumaine en France*; I (Paris, 1926)), 3-96.

8. I. Zh—tskii, 'Petr Mogila', B-E, XXXIII-A (46), 484-5.

9. Golubev, *Mogila*, I, 14; Panaitescu, *L'influence*, 10-11, shows that he did not give up hope of becoming hospodar himself until 1627 or even later.

10. Golubev, *Mogila*, I, 67.

11. *Ibid.*, 58-9.

12. *Ibid.*, 431.

13. *Ibid.*, 447-52.

14. Florovskii, *Puti*, 45; Golubev, *Mogila*, II, 230.

15. Florovskii, *Puti*, 49.

16. Hrushevs'kyi, *Z istorii religiinoi dumky na Ukraini* (L'viv, 1925), 80. Florovskii more discriminatingly declares that Mogila introduced into the Ukraine not medieval scholasticism but Tridentine scholasticism or 'theological Baroque'. *Puti*, 52.

17. Golubev, *Mogila*, II, 228.

18. Quoted *ibid.*, 263.

19. Quoted *ibid.*, 266.

20. *Ibid.*, 268.

21. *Ibid.*, 366-7.

22. Quoted *ibid.*, 383.

23. *Ibid.*, 369.

24. Florovskii, *Puti*, 48.

25. Michael Hrushevsky, *A History of the Ukraine* (New Haven, 1941), 238.

26. Quoted *ibid.*, 284.

27. C. Bickford O'Brien, *Muscovy and the Ukraine From the Pereiaslavl Agreement to the Truce of Andrusovo, 1654-1667* (Berkeley and Los Angeles, 1963), 28-31.

28. For the terms of the truce, see *ibid.*, 115-19.

29. Florovskii, *Puti*, 54.

30. J. L. H. Keep, 'The Régime of Filaret, 1619-1633', *SEER*, XXXVIII, no. 91 (June 1960), 334. Keep cites as the sole biographical treatment available A.

Smirnov, 'Sviatieishii Patriarkh Filaret Nikitich moskovskii i vseia Rusi', *Chteniia v obshchestvie liubitelei dukhovnago prosvieshcheniia*, x (1873), and II–v (1874) (unavailable to me).

31. Keep, 'Régime', 342.

32. *Ibid.*, 338–9.

33. See Aleksandr Golubtsov, *Preniia o vierie, vyzvannyia dielom korolevicha Val'demara i tsarevny Iriny Mikhailovny* (Moscow, 1891), 77–117, for extended discussion of this work.

34. A. Shilov, 'Ivan Vasil'evich Nasiedka', *RBS*, XI, 105–10.

35. N. F. Kapterev, *Patriarkh Nikon i Tsar' Aleksiei Mikhailovich* (2 vols, Sergiev Posad, 1909–12), I, 3ff.

36. Pierre Pascal, *Avvakum et les débuts du Raskol* (Paris, 1938), 35, fn. 4, gives the basis for doubting the traditional date 1591.

37. *Ibid.*, 74–5, 100–1. For Avvakum's works, see 'Pamiatniki istorii staroo-briadchestva xvii v.', book one, *RIB* xxxix (1927), and N. K. Gudzii (ed.) *Zhitie protopopa Avvakuma, im samim napisannoe i drugie ego sochineniia* (Moscow, 1960). The *Zhitie* is translated as *The Life of the Archpriest Avvakum, by Himself* (reprint, Hamden, Conn., 1963) and *La vie de l'archiprêtre Avvakum écrite par lui-même* (trans., Paris, 1938). A new critical edition of the *Zhitie* with extensive commentary, along with the *Life* of Avvakum's colleague Epifanii, is A. N. Robinson, *Zhizneopisaniia Avvakuma i Epifaniia* (Moscow, 1963). One good older study exists: A. K. Borozdin, *Protopop Avvakum, Ocherk iz istorii umstvennoi zhizni russkago obshchestva v xvii viekie* (St Petersburg, 1898; a 2nd ed., 1900, was unavailable to me).

38. Pascal, *Avvakum*, 122.

39. *Ibid.*, 132.

40. Sergei Belokurov, 'Arsenii Sukhanov', *Chteniia OIDR* ('Biografiia' [1891], I, II; 'Sochineniia' [1894], II) (1891), I, 172–8.

41. See p. 57.

42. Pascal, *Avvakum*, 152.

43. Kapterev, *Nikon i Aleksiei*, I, 48, 69. See Iv. Rotar, 'Epifanii Slavinetskii, literaturnyi dieiatel' xvii v.', *Kievskaia Starina*, LXXI (1900), Oct., 1–38; Nov., 189–217; and Dec., 347–400.

44. Kapterev, *Nikon i Aleksiei*, I, 64–6.

45. *Ibid.*, 85; Pascal, *Avvakum*, 156–60.

46. The Thirty-Nine *Articles of Religion* of the Church of England, xxiv.

47. Kapterev, *Nikon i Aleksiei*, I, 115.

48. *Ibid.*, 128.

49. His account is given in William Palmer, *The Patriarch and the Tsar*, vol. II: *Testimonies Concerning the Patriarch Nicon, the Tsar, and the Boyars, from the Travels of the Patriarch Macarius of Antioch, Written in Arabic by His Son and Archdeacon Paul of Aleppo*...; Abridged from the Translation Printed for the Oriental Translation Fund in 1836 (London, 1873).

50. *Ibid.*, 149–50.

51. Kapterev, *Nikon i Aleksiei*, I, 156.

52. Palmer, *Patriarch*, II, 174–5. See p. 63.

53. Kapterev, *Nikon i Aleksiei*, I, 162–79.

54. Of this popular reaction Kliuchevsky writes: 'Those who opposed the alleged Latin innovations of Nikon asserted in justification of what they were doing that these innovations were *Latin*, but in fact they opposed them because they were *innovations*.' 'Zapadnoe vliianie i tserkovnyi raskol v Rossii xvii v.',

Ocherki i rechi (reprint of 1915 edition; Petrograd, 1918), 413. The question of Latin influence will be examined below.

55. Pascal, *Avvakum*, 299. Pascal meant simply, for the time being; in the event no fully independent ecclesiastical authority was ever to be re-established.

56. Palmer, *Patriarch*, preface to vols II and III, II, xii–xiii; Vernadsky, *The Tsardom of Moscow, 1547–1682* (2 vols, New Haven, 1969), II, 589.

57. Analyses of this document are found in Makarii, mitropolit Moskovskii i Kolomenskii, *Istoriia russkoi Tserkvi*, XII (1965 OP reprint of ed. of St Petersburg, 1882), 382–433 and Kapterev, *Nikon i Aleksiei*, II, 181–208.

58. Quoted in Palmer, *Patriarch*, vol. I: *The Replies of the Humble Nicon, by the Mercy of God Patriarch, against the Questions of the Boyar Simeon Streshneff and the Answers of the Metropolitan of Gaza Paisius Ligarides* (London, 1871), xxi.

59. *Ibid.*, 207, 225, 237, 251.

60. *Ibid.*, 251–4.

61. *Ibid.*, 322, 390, 475.

62. This point is argued strongly in V. K-v, 'Vzgliad Nikona na znachenie patriarshei vlasti', *ZMNP*, CCXII (Dec. 1880), esp. 263.

63. Florovskii, *Puti*, 64.

64. Anonymous article 'Nikon' in B-E, XVI (1897), 140.

65. The subject of a famous painting (1887) by Surikov depicting her last progress through Moscow streets *en route* to interrogation, torture, and death.

66. Pascal, *Avvakum*, 349, relying on Kharlampovich, *Malorossiiskoe vliianie na velikorusskuiu tserkovnuiu zhizn'*, I (Kazan, 1914). A. Borozdin's article, 'Simeon Emel'ianovich Sitnianovich-Petrovskii Polotskii', *RBS*, XVIII, 458–62, was written before Kharlampovich's book appeared.

67. Borozdin, 'Simeon', 459.

68. Pascal, *Avvakum*, 357.

69. Palmer, *Patriarch*, vol. III: *History of the Condemnation of the Patriarch Nicon by a Plenary Council of the Orthodox Catholic Eastern Church, Held at Moscow A.D. 1666–1667; Written by Paisius Ligarides of Scio...* Translated, with Supplements, by William Palmer (London, 1873), 256. Italics original; the Greek terms are omitted here.

70. Pascal, *Avvakum*, 468.

71. See p. 68.

72. Serge A. Zenkovsky, 'The Ideological World of the Denisov Brothers', *Harvard Slavic Studies*, III (Harvard 1957), 54. On Andrei Denisov see also P. S. Usov, 'Pomor-filosof', *Istoricheskii Vestnik*, XXIV (1886), 145–60, and on his brother Semën, Elpidifor Barsov, 'Semën Denisovich Vtorushin, predvoditel' russkago raskola xviii vieka', *TKDA* (1866), II, 174–230.

73. Serge A. Zenkovsky, 'The Old Believer Avvakum: His Role in Russian Literature', *Indiana Slavic Studies*, I (Bloomington, 1956), 34. See also his article 'The Russian Church Schism: Its Background and Repercussions', *Russian Review*, XVI, no. 4 (October 1957).

74. I have discussed this point at greater length in an essay, 'The Peasant and Religion', in Wayne S. Vucinich (ed.), *The Peasant in Nineteenth-Century Russia* (Stanford, 1968).

75. Kapterev, *Nikon i Aleksiei*, II, 537.

76. *Ibid.*, 541, 543, 544.

77. *Ibid.*, 546.

78. Zenkovsky draws this conclusion, perhaps overstating his point, in 'The Old Believer Avvakum', 34. See p. 72 above.

79. For a longer discussion of the cultural significance of dissent in Russian religion, see my article, 'The Peasant and Religion'. Michael Cherniavsky in 'The Old Believers and the New Religion', *Slavic Review*, xxv (March 1966), 1–39, has well developed an interpretation of the Old Believers' movement as a desperate reaction to the theory and practice of the secular state.

80. Borozdin, 'Simeon', 460.

81. See p. 63 above.

82. Pascal, *Avvakum*, 358.

83. *Ibid.*, 458.

84. Ante Kadić, 'Križanić's Formative Years', *American Contributions to the Fifth International Congress of Slavists, II: Literary Criticisms* (The Hague, 1963), 179. Kadić examined the document.

85. Kadić points out (*ibid*, 173ff.) that Croatians had strong influence in the congregation, but that they divided on their objectives. One group, following the Jesuit Bartol Kašić, wished to unite the South Slavs by philological means; the other, following the Franciscan Levaković, envisaged the unification of all of Slavdom by similar methods. Kadić also calls attention to antecedents of such 'pan-Slav' objectives among the Croats as far back as the Dominican friar Vinko Pribojević, who lectured in the same vein in 1525.

86. This did not mean that he had any sympathy for the Old Belief, which he attacked sharply. See 'Sobranie sochinenii Iuriia Krizhanicha. Vyp. 3-i: (Okonchanie) 2) Oblichenie na Solovechskuiu Chelobitnu [*sic*]', *Chteniia OIDR* (1893), book 2, i–xi and 79–167.

87. Michael B. Petrovich, 'Juraj Križanić: A Precursor of Pan-Slavism', *ASEER*, vi, nos. 18–19 (December 1947), 81.

88. Iurii Krizhanich, *Politika*, ed. M. N. Tikhomirov (Moscow, 1965), contains the original and an annotated translation into modern Russian. The only previous editions were those of P. A. Bezsonov: *Russkoe gosudarstvo v polovinie xvii vieka: rukopis' vremen tsaria Alekseiia Mikhailovicha*, pts 1–6, Prilozhenie k *Russkoi Besiede*, 1859; and the more complete *Russkoe gosudarstvo v polovinie xvii vieka* (2 vols, Moscow, 1859–60; unavailable to me). According to A. D. Gol'dberg (Tikhomirov ed., 702–4), the latter version included almost all of the *Politika* and other portions of the collection (*sbornik*) of which the *Politika* forms a part, or about three-fifths of the whole *sbornik*. Though doubtless technically correct, this is somewhat misleading, for it implies that the 1965 edition is more complete than that of 1859–60. However, even in the version published as supplements to *Russkaia Besieda* Bezsonov publishes portions of the manuscript drawn from Chapters 37–59, while the Tikhomirov edition stops after Chapter 36. This explains why some quotations below are drawn from the first Bezsonov edition; the Tikhomirov edition does not include those sections. Cyril Bryner in 'The Political Philosophy of Yuri Krizhanich', *The New Scholasticism*, xiii (April 1939) 142ff., gives an extended discussion of the contents of the treatise, based on Bezsonov.

89. Tikhomirov ed., 497, 505ff.

90. First Bezsonov ed., Prilozhenie k no. 5 *Russkoi Besiede* za 1859 god, 174–6.

91. Tikhomirov ed., 375 and 461.

92. *Ibid.*, 668.

93. *Ibid.*, 574.

94. Soloviev, *Istoriia Rossii*, vii (Moscow, 1962), 162.

95. Tikhomirov's introduction to the *Politika*, 5–8.

96. A. L. Gol'dberg's commentary to *Politika*, 701.

97. Bezsonov, title-page.

98. L. R. Lewitter, 'Poland, the Ukraine and Russia in the 17th Century', *SEER*, XXVII, no. 68 (Dec. 1948) and no. 69 (May 1949); text of the charter of Fedor is found in *Drevniaia Russkaia Vivliofika*, VI (2nd ed.; Moscow, 1788), 397–420.

99. See *ibid.*, 390ff. On Medvedev, see Aleksandr Prozorovskii, 'Sil'vestr Medviedev: ego zhizn' i dieiatel'nost', *Chteniia OIDR* (1896), no. 2, 1–148, no. 3, 149–377, no. 4, 379–606.

100. See p. 66 above. The text of the book may be found in Prozorovskii, no. 4, 419–30.

101. P. N. Miliukov, *Outlines of Russian Culture* (trans., Philadelphia, 1943), I, 137–8.

102. Sergei Smirnov, *Istoriia Moskovskoi Slaviano-Greko-Latinskoi Akademii* (Moscow, 1855), 17. From 1700 to 1775 it was called 'Latin' or 'Slavo-Latin'; from 1775 to 1814 it was called 'Slavo-Greco-Latin'.

103. Mikh. Smentsovskii, 'Likhudy, Ioannikii i Sofronii', *RBS*, X, 499–510. See also his earlier monograph, *Brat'ia Likhudy: Opyt izsliedovaniia iz istorii tserkovnago prosvieshcheniia i tserkovnoi zhizni kontsa XVII i nachala XVIII viekov* (St Petersburg, 1899).

104. On the transfer of Kievan allegiance, see L. R. Lewitter, 'The Russo-Polish Treaty of 1686 and its Antecedents', *Polish Review*, IX, nos. 3 and 4: 23–5 (1964); the proscribed books are listed in Lewitter, 'Poland', no. 69, 425–6. Medvedev was accused of participating in the Shaklovity conspiracy of 1689 and was finally executed in 1691.

105. C. Bickford O'Brien, *Russia Under Two Tsars: The Regency of Sophia Alekseevna* (Berkeley, 1952), Ch. III.

106. *Ibid.*, 90.

107. Kliuchevskii, *Sochineniia* III (Moscow, 1957), 353.

108. Čiževskij in his *History of Russian Literature from from the Eleventh Century to the End of the Baroque* gives the 1740's as the time when 'the fate of the Baroque was already determined...' (431), and begins it around 1640 (320).

109. *Ibid.*, 360–1; A. V. Arsen'ev, comp., *Slovar' pisatelei drevniago perioda russkoi literatury, ix-xvii vieka* (St Petersburg, 1882; reprint, Ann Arbor, 1962), 115–17.

110. B. E. Raikov, *Ocherki po istorii geliotsentricheskogo mirovozreniia v Rossii* (2nd ed., Moscow–Leningrad, 1947), 120–32.

111. Smirnov, *Istoriia Moskovskoi Slaviano-Greko-Latinskoi akademii*, 60–3.

112. N. F. Kapterev, *Kharakter otnoshenii Rossii k pravoslavnomu vostoku v xvi i xvii stolietiiakh* (2nd ed., Sergiev Posad, 1913), Ch. XI.

113. Pascal, *Avvakum*, xvi.

4: Russia's quasi-Reformation (1689–1761)

1. P. Pekarskii, *Nauka i literatura v Rossii pri Petrie Velikom* (2 vols, St Petersburg, 1862), I, 6–8.

2. See V. Ger'e, *Sbornik pisem i memorialov Leibnitsa otnosiashchikhsia k Rossii i Petru Velikomu* (St Petersburg, 1873), in particular nos. 13 and 14, pp. 14–20; quotation is on 10.

3. Evidence about both ecclesiastical and non-ecclesiastical schools in the

seventeenth century is scanty and subject to varying interpretation. See M. I. Demkov, *Istoriia russkoi pedagogii* (2 parts, Revel, 1896–7), I, esp. 202–12.

4. Quoted from G. A. Skvortsov, *Patriarkh Adrian* (Kazan, 1912), 15–17, in Rev. Georges Louis Bissonnette, 'Pufendorf and the Church Reforms of Peter the Great' (Columbia University Ph.D. Thesis, University Microfilms, 1962), 19.

5. See p. 69 above.

6. P. E. Shchegolev, 'Stefan Iavorskii', in B-E.

7. Sergei Smirnov, *Istoriia Moskovskoi Slaviano-Greko-Latinskoi akademii* (Moscow, 1855), 80.

8. In 1704 among 34 students in philosophy only 3 were Great Russians; all the rest had 'Belorussian and Polish' names; *ibid.*, 81.

9. Though the Jesuits were expelled from Muscovy in 1689, they soon were back, only to be expelled again in 1719; they were not to be admitted again to Russia until the reign of Catherine II. See Le P. Pierling, SJ, *La Russie et le Saint-Siège*, IV (Paris, 1907), 292.

10. A. Florovskij, 'Palladij Rogovskij, eine Episode aus der Geschichte des Katholizismus in Moskau Ende des 17. Jahrhunderts', *Zeitschrift für osteuropäische Geschichte*, vol. VIII (n.s., vol. IV) (1934), 161–88.

11. Prot. Georgii Florovskii, *Puti russkago bogosloviia* (Paris, 1937), 98.

12. *Ibid.*, 97.

13. See P. Znamenskii, *Dukhovnyia shkoly v Rossii do reformy 1808 goda* (Kazan, 1881), 35–6.

14. Quoted in Bissonnette, 'Pufendorf', 29–32, from Pufendorf's *Einleitung zu der Historie der vornehmsten Staaten in Europa*.

15. *Ibid.*, 37–8. Bissonnette does not mention that the whole plan of studies for Alexis, contained in an order (*nakaz*) of Peter's dated 22 April 1703, is published in I. I. Golikov, *Dieianiia Petra Velikago* (2nd ed., Moscow, 1837), III, 97–106; Pufendorf is mentioned specifically on 103 and 104.

16. D. S. Merezhkovskii, *Antikhrist: Petr i Aleksiei* (the third part of a trilogy, which is in 5 vols; Berlin, 1922).

17. Merezhkovsky recognizes this fact; see *ibid.*, IV, 29.

18. Anonymous article, 'Aleksiei Petrovich', *RBS*, II, 53. The article, a very extensive one, is judicious in tone.

19. Merezhkovskii, V, 304.

20. Iu. F. Samarin, *Sochineniia*, V: *Stefan Iavorskii i Feofan Prokopovich* (Moscow, 1880), 363. Baronius (1538–1607), author of *Annales Ecclesiastici*, which won him a reputation as the foremost church historian for centuries, also became a cardinal. One of the pieces of evidence used against Alexis was that he had made extracts from Baronius in which it was chronicled how various kings who had interfered with the spiritual power had perished. Commynes (*c.* 1447–1511) was an outstanding French historian and statesman.

21. [Stefan Iavorskii], *Kamen' viery* (3 vols, Moscow, 1841–2).

22. Al. Korolev, 'Stefan Iavorskii', *RBS*, XIX, 420.

23. *Ibid.*, 153. Martin Becan (1563–1624) (or Verbreck or van der Breck) was a Jesuit noted for his polemics against Protestants. Robert Francis Romulus Bellarmine (1542–1621) (or Bellarmino), who became a cardinal, was also a powerful foe of Protestantism.

24. *Ibid.*, 35–43. Chaadaev's renowned remark, in his *Philosophical Letter* published in 1836, that Russia had not known the syllogism was inaccurate, not only because of Stefan's writings.

25. *Ibid.*, 51.

26. *Ibid.*, 240–1.

27. *Ibid.*, 265; N. S. Tikhonravov, 'Moskovskie vol'nodumtsy nachala xviii vieka i Stefan Iavorskii', *Russkii Viestnik*, LXXXIX (Sept. 1870), 5–61; XCI (Feb. 1871), 667–720; XCIII (June 1871), 399–446; on this episode LXXXIX, 31. Tomás Malvenda (1566–1628), a Spanish Dominican, published *De antichristo libro XI* in Rome in 1604; he was also author of an outstanding critique of Baronius's *Annales*. It is ironic that Talitsky's outright branding of Peter as Antichrist and support of the boy Alexis anticipated, if it did not already coincide with Stefan's own feelings about the monarch and the heir, yet Stefan was in a position of having to attack Talitsky.

28. Tikhonravov, *Russkii Viestnik*, LXXXIX, 12. See also 'Dmitrii Evdokimovich Tveritinov', B-E.

29. V. O. Kliuchevskii, *Sochineniia* IV, 39–42; Reinhard Wittram, *Peter I. Czar und Kaiser* (2 vols., Göttingen, 1964), I, 106–11.

30. Samarin, *Stefan i Feofan*, 282.

31. I. Chistovich, *Feofan Prokopovich i ego vremia* (n.d., n.p.), 70ff.; B. Titlinov, 'Feodosii (Ianovskii)', *RBS*, XXV, 346–7.

32. Quoted in Chistovich, *Feofan*, 86.

33. *Ibid.*, Ch. 1; B. Titlinov, 'Feofan (Prokopovich)', *RBS*, XXV, 399–448.

34. Quoted in Chistovich, *Feofan*, 9–10.

35. Florovskii, *Puti*, 92. On Protestant scholasticism, see J. A. Weisheipl, 'Scholasticism', in *New Catholic Encyclopedia*, XII (1967), 1153–70. The writer distinguishes three periods of scholasticism: (1) twelfth–thirteenth centuries, in which Aristotelian dialectics was used in theology, philosophy, and canon law and 'scholastics' came to concentrate on metaphysics; (2) 1530–early nineteenth century, with the revival of metaphysics; (3) since the mid-nineteenth century. In the second period characteristics of scholasticism were: distinction between sense and intellect as two modes of knowledge; pluralism, teleological dynamism, emphasis on freedom and responsibility in man; belief in the possibility of normative ethics and metaphysics; belief that the existence of God is demonstrable; distinction between philosophy and theology. The writer traces Protestant scholasticism to Peter Ramus (*Dialecticae institutions*, 1543), but points out how such Protestant writers as Christoph Scheibler (1589–1653) and Polanus von Polansdorf (1561–1610) found it preferable to produce manuals based not on Ramus but rather on Francisco Sáurez (1548–1617), the great Spanish Jesuit theologian who attempted a new synthesis. Protestant scholasticism culminated in 'Leibnizian scholasticism in its Wolanffi form' (p. 1163), using the some forty volumes Wolff produced attempting to put theology into a systematic form in the image of Euclid's work on geometry, and in so doing exalting reason above the senses and experience.

36. Chistovich, *Feofan*, 24.

37. Titlinov, 'Feofan', 403.

38. Translations of these documents appear in Alexander Vilhelm Muller, 'The Spiritual Regulation of Peter the Great', M.A. thesis, University of Washington, 1966.

39. Muller's translation, 123.

40. *Ibid.*, 77.

41. *Ibid.*, 93.

42. *Ibid.*, 126.

43. Samarin, *Stefan i Feofan*, quoting 74–5 from Chapter V of Feofan's *Traktaty* (Leipzig ed., 1782–3).

44. Quoted *ibid.*, 149.

45. Quoted by Chistovich, *Feofan*, 39.

46. Samarin, *Stefan i Feofan*, 144. Philipp Melanchthon (1497–1560), friend and collaborator of Luther, was more of a scholar and systematic theologian than he; Klemens Löffler in the *Catholic Encyclopedia* terms him 'the father of evangelical [i.e., Lutheran] theology'. Martin Chemnitz (1522–86) was a follower of Melanchthon. Johann Gerhard (1582–1637), from 1616 until his death professor at Jena, was renowned as the most outstanding theologian of Protestant Germany in his day.

47. *Ibid.*, 146.

48. Chistovich, *Feofan*, 119.

49. Titlinov, 'Feodosy (Ianovskii)', 353.

50. Chistovich, *Feofan*, 148–50.

51. Jurij Šerech, 'Stefan Yavorsky and the Conflict of Ideologies in the Age of Peter I', *SEER*, xxx, no. 74 (Dec. 1951), 42–3, citing F. Ternovsky, 'Mitropolit Stefan Iavorskii', *TKDA* (1864). Šerech mentions Feodosy only once, when citing Ternovsky, and ignores his crucial role in the ecclesiastical–political and ideological struggle of the time. Feodosy somehow does not seem to have managed to enter eighteenth-century Russian history in versions accessible to students. The roster of extensive treatments of the period which do not even mention his name is long; even such a thorough work as Michael T. Florinsky's *Russia: History and an Interpretation* (2 vols, New York, 1953), although devoting seven pages to Yavorsky and Prokopovich, omits Feodosy altogether.

52. Šerech, 'Stefan', 43–51, believes Yavorsky was 'in spirit' on the side of the Ukraine against Muscovy, instancing his probable sympathy for Mazepa and his unending concern for Nezhin, the Ukrainian monastery which he hoped would help raise the region's cultural level and to which he left all his worldly goods. How far the Ukrainian faction was concerned with the Ukraine's fate is difficult to determine; but the existence of such a group, which came out of the Kievan Academy as reformed by Peter Mogila, can scarcely be disputed.

53. See N. P. Pavlov-Sil'vanskii, 'Pososhkov, Ivan Tikhonovich', in *RBS*, xiv, 604–20; B. B. Kafengauz, *I. T. Pososhkov: Zhizn' i deiatel'nost'* (2nd ed., Moscow, 1951); Kafengauz (ed.), *Kniga o skudosti i bogatstve*, I. T. Pososhkov (Moscow, 1937). The last has a list of Pososhkov's works (86–8).

54. Pavlov-Sil'vanskii, 'Pososhkov', 607.

55. *Kniga o skudosti i bogatstve*, Kafengauz (ed.), 318.

56. *Ibid.*, 259. He uses approximately the same wording several times. Pavlov-Sil'vanskii remarks on the similarities and differences between Pososhkov and the Physiocrats; 'Pososhkov', 618.

57. See John M. Letiche (ed.), *A History of Russian Economic Thought: Ninth through Eighteenth Centuries*, original ed. by A. I. Pashkov (trans., Berkeley, 1964), 318–19. The chapter on Pososhkov was written by Pashkov, who after justifiably denying that Pososhkov was an abolitionist, acknowledges that as between landlord and serf, 'Pososhkov's sympathies are clearly on the side of the peasantry'.

58. *Kniga o skudosti i bogatstve*, 259.

59. Pavlov-Sil'vanskii, 'Pososhkov', 614.

60. Kafengauz in the introduction to *Kniga o skudosti i bogatstve*, 42.

61. See Letiche (ed.), *A History*, Ch. 13.

62. Kafengauz, *Pososhkov: zhizn' i deiatel'nost'*, 131–42.

63. *Ibid.*

64. See Liselotte Richter, *Leibniz und sein Russlandbild* (Berlin, 1946); Ernst Benz, 'Leibniz und Peter der Grosse', *Leibniz zu seinem 300. Geburtstag 1646–1946*, pt 2 (Berlin, 1947); Pekarskii, *Nauka i lit.*, Ch. 3.

65. #240, pp. 348–60, in Ger'e, *Sbornik pisem i memorialov Leibnitsa*.

66. Ger'e, *Sbornik*, xxiii; Richter, *Leibniz*, 137.

67. Benz, 'Leibniz und Peter der Grosse', 62–83.

68. *Ibid.*, 87.

69. Or perhaps it would be more just to say, Orthodox theology to the extent it agreed with Protestant or Protestantizable theology. Leibniz may have overestimated the extent of such agreement.

70. See p. 86 above. After the school moved to St Petersburg to become the Naval Academy, a school continued to operate on the old premises in Moscow until 1752.

71. Znamensky, *Dukhovnyia shkoly*, 52ff.

72. P. N. Miliukov, *Ocherki po istorii russkoi kul'tury* (Paris, 1931), ii, 735–7.

73. Florinsky, *Russia*, i, 408.

74. Florovskii, *Puti*, 104.

75. He was doubtless unqualified for membership, but his qualifications, meager though they were, surpassed those of Prince Alexander Menshikov, his *alter ego*, who managed to get elected to the Royal Society in 1714. The task of informing Menshikov of the scientific achievements by which he had merited that honor fell to the unfortunate Isaac Newton. Alexander Vucinich, *Science in Russian Culture: A History to 1860* (Stanford, 1963), 66–7.

76. Pekarskii, *Nauka i literatura*, i, 33.

77. Or so Blumentrost wrote Schumacher that he had explained to Wolff; *ibid.*, 37–8.

78. Florinsky, *Russia*, i, 409.

79. A. V. Florovskii, 'Pervyi iezuit iz moskovskikh dvorian', *Acta Academiae Velehradensis*, Annus xix (1948), 249–56, describes the career of one Alexis Yurevich Ladyzhensky, who was a pupil of the Jesuits in Moscow in the period 1707–10 and became a Jesuit professor in the Academy in Vilna and other schools. In 1735 he was taken prisoner by the Russian army passing through Vilna; Empress Anna turned him over to Feofan Prokopovich for 'instruction'; he was whipped and sent to Siberia, where he apparently died about 1756 without losing his faith.

80. See p. 96 above.

81. Chistovich, *Feofan*, 229.

82. Robert Stupperich, 'Feofan Prokopovič und Johann Franz Buddeus', *Zeitschrift für osteuropäische Geschichte*, ix (n.s., v) (1935), 341–62.

83. Pierling, *La Russie*, iv, 250–66.

84. Chistovich, *Feofan*, 369; Eduard Winter, in *Halle als Ausgangspunkt der deutschen Russlandkunde im 18. Jahrhundert* (Berlin, 1953), 144, says she was converted in Paris. On Jubé in Russia, see Pierling, *La Russie*, iv, 332–65.

85. Chistovich, *Feofan*, 381.

86. B. Titlinov, 'Feofilakt (Lopatinskii)', *RBS*, xxv, 457–66.

87. Marc Raeff in *Plans for Political Reform in Imperial Russia, 1730–1905* (Englewood Cliffs, New Jersey, 1966). Ch. 1, 'The Succession Crisis of 1730', has translated some of the gentry's memorials to Anna as well as the Conditions themselves.

88. B. Titlinov, 'Feofan', 423.

89. Alexander Lipski, 'A Re-examination of the "Dark Era" of Anna

Ioannovna', *ASEER*, xv (Dec. 1956) 477–88, and 'Some Aspects of Russia's Westernization During the Reign of Anna Ioannovna, 1730–1740', *ASEER*, xviii (Feb. 1959) 1–11.

90. Vucinich, *Science in Russian Culture*, 92–104. Smotritsky's grammar of Church Slavic, published in 1619, was based on the model of the Greek grammar of Lascaris, published in Milan in 1476. It influenced several later grammars, among them Ilia Kopievich's, published in Amsterdam in 1706 (the first grammar of Russian in the Russian language; the first Russian grammar was published in Latin in Oxford in 1698 by Heinrich Wilhelm Ludolf). Adadurov's grammar of Russian was published in German as an appendix to Weisman's German–Latin–Russian Lexicon. Lomonosov's Russian grammar, published in 1755, was the last to be significantly influenced by Smotritsky's. See Prokoshina, *Meletii Smotritskii*, 92–112.

91. J. C. Hoffman, 'Pietism', *New Catholic Encyclopedia* (1967), xi, 355–6; Winter, *Halle als Ausgangspunkt*, 4–8.

92. See p. 103 above.

93. Chistovich, *Feofan*, 617–18. The pietists were unlikely to have been comforted if they had known about such reassurance. As early as the 1690's they had been thinking of missionary activity that would transform not merely the minute Lutheran community in Russia but the Russian Orthodox Church itself in the sense of 'pure' or 'true' Christianity; Winter, *Halle*, 39ff.

94. Winter, *Halle*, 227–40.

95. Lipski, 'Some Aspects of Russia's Westernization', 5–6.

96. Alois Brandl, *Barthold Heinrich Brockes* (Innsbruck, 1878), esp. 13–14 and 41.

97. Lipski, 'Some Aspects of Russia's Westernization', 7.

98. Anna Petrovna, not to be confused with the Empress Anna Ivanovna or the Regent Anna Leopoldovna.

99. Zdr., 'Simon (Todorskii)', *RBS*, xviii, 498.

100. N. A. Astaf'ev, 'Opyt istorii Biblii v Rossii v sviazi s prosvieshcheniem i pravami', *ZMNP* (October 1888), 283.

101. Anon., 'Tikhon Zadonskii', *RBS*, xx, 583–9.

102. Florovskii, *Puti*, 125.

103. O. Erikhsen, 'Grigorii Savvich Skovoroda', *RBS*, xviii, 585–9.

104. V. V. Zenkovsky, *A History of Russian Philosophy* (trans. by George L. Kline; 2 vols., New York and London, 1953), i, 53.

105. Gustav Shpet, *Ocherk razvitiia russkoi filosofii, Pervaia chast'* (Petrograd, 1922), 72.

106. Florovskii, *Puti*, 120; Shpet, *Ocherk*, 79.

107. B. N. Menshutkin, 'Mikhail Vasil'evich Lomonosov', *RBS*, x, 593–628. Menshutkin's first work on Lomonosov was published in 1904. His book, *Russia's Lomonosov*, was translated into English and published in 1952. This work is excessively praised by Professor Tenney L. Davis in a foreword as 'utterly authoritative, a book which will never have to be rewritten'. In fact the book does not raise the question of Lomonosov's intellectual formation at all, and it would be a pity if other scholars were to be deterred from studying the question fully by such expressions. The expertise of Menshutkin is not in doubt, and is much more adequately displayed in the *RBS* article, for example, than in the book mentioned, but he does not raise the question there either.

108. A. P. Topichev, N. A. Figurovskii, and V. L. Chenakal (eds), *Letopis' zhizni i tvorchestva M. V. Lomonosova* (Moscow–Leningrad, 1961), 90.

109. Menshutkin, *Russia's Lomonosov*, 79.
110. Vucinich, *Science in Russian Culture*, 111.
111. Cited by Hans Rogger, *National Consciousness in Eighteenth-Century Russia* (Harvard, 1960), 33.

5: Rationalism and sentimentalism (1761–1825)

1. The non-gentry intelligentsia of the period of the 1750's–70's is thoroughly studied by M. M. Shtrange, *Demokraticheskaia intelligentsiia v XVIII veke* (Moscow, 1965) – without startling results.
2. V. Bogoliubov, *N. I. Novikov i ego vremia* (Moscow, 1916), 257.
3. Such a college was planned under Elizabeth and tentatively approved by her, but as created by Peter III it was to have its own officials and broader powers than those envisaged by the Elizabethan plan. See Marc Raeff's excellent article, 'The Domestic Policies of Peter III and His Overthrow', *AHR*, LXXV (June 1970), 1289–1310.
4. Nicholas A. Hans, *History of Russian Educational Policy 1701–1917* (New York, 1964), 29.
5. P. Znamenskii, *Dukhovnyia shkoly v Rossii do reformy 1808 goda* (Kazan, 1881), 606–9.
6. F. Ternovskii, 'Russkoe vol'nodumstvo pri imper. Ekaterinie II-i i epokha reaktsii', *TKDA* (1868), #3 and #7; #3, 405.
7. Or so she reported to Ségur; quoted *ibid.*, #3, 412.
8. *Ibid.*, #3, 416–27.
9. G. V. Vernadskii, *Russkoe masonstvo v tsarstvovanie Ekateriny II* (Petrograd, 1917), 6. Recent scholarship on Russian Masonry has been scanty. A curious work by various hands entitled *Istoriia russkogo masonstva* (8 vols., Buenos Aires, n.d.), opens with a preface in which the writer, V. F. Ivanov, disclaims any effort to write a 'scholarly book' (1, 6); the work frankly indicts Western influences in Russia as pernicious, and the story of Masonry in Catherine II's reign begins only with pt III, after lengthy attacks on Peter the Great and so forth.
10. It is difficult to agree with the statement of Professor Vernadskii (*Russkoe masonstvo*, 245) that the 'rationalist liberal' current achieved under Alexander a 'decisive predominance, especially after 1815, when the Grand Lodge Astrée was formed', and on the following page he does in fact suggest the importance of the mystical current during the reign.
11. The revelations of Grigory Aronson and Ekaterina Kuskova concerning a Masonic group active in Russian liberal politics before and during the Revolution of 1917 might require a modest qualification of this remark, but not more. There seems to be no evidence that Freemasonry itself provided any intellectual mainsprings of the activities of this group; rather its members, united intellectually by their politically liberal, democratic, and semi-socialist views, found an additional bond of a personal nature in their Masonic circle. See George Katkov, *Russia 1917: The February Revolution* (New York, 1967), 167–73.
12. Vernadskii, *Russkoe masonstvo*, 8.
13. *Ibid.*, 215–17; G. V. Vernadskii, 'Manifest Petra III o vol'nosti dvorianskoi i zakonodatel'naia komissiia 1754–66 gg.', *Istoricheskoe obozrienie*, XX (1915), 51–9; N. L. Rubinshtein, 'Ulozhennaia komissiia 1754–66 gg. i ee proekt novogo ulozheniia "o sostoianii poddannykh voobshche"', *Istoricheskie Zapiski*, XXXVIII (1951), 208–51. Raeff in 'The Domestic Policies of Peter III and

His Overthrow' writes that 'the manifesto can hardly be considered to have expressed the point of view of the Vorontsov group, who wanted to give noble-men a greater stake in private and local concerns', and says that the probable drafter, D. V. Volkov, 'may have expressed the thinking of P. Shuvalov', leader of a rival group which wished 'a small, closed oligarchy' to 'control Russia's economic life by means of monopolies and regalias with rank-and-file nobles continuing to provide most of the military and bureaucratic career personnel'. But since Rubinshtein, in Raeff's words, pointed out that 'the notion of univer-sal exemption from service' was opposed by the Shuvalovs, it is difficult to understand how the manifesto that enacted precisely such exemption can be traced to the Shuvalovs. Raeff correctly points out that 'neither the manifesto itself nor any later legislation' pursued the implications of the Vorontsov view, while some later legislation of Peter III did seem to encourage the simultaneous formation of a new non-compulsory bureaucracy and a non-serving landed nobility (the Shuvalov aim).

14. *Ibid.*, 9.

15. *Ibid.*, 10.

16. *Ibid.*, 86–90.

17. *Ibid.*, 98–9.

18. 'Vol'ter. . . i vol'terianstvo v russkoi literaturie', B-E, VII, 157–9.

19. Ternovskii, 'Russkoe vol'nodumstvo', #3, 431.

20. V. V. Sipovskii, 'Iz istorii russkoi mysli XVIII–XIX vv. (Russkoe vol'ter'ianstvo)', *Golos Minuvshago*, #1 (1914), 114.

21. Marc Raeff speaks of Shcherbatov's 'eighteenth century radical rational-ism'. See his article, 'State and Nobility in the Ideology of M. M. Shcherbatov', *ASEER*, XIX (October 1960), 363–79 (375).

22. *Ibid.*, #3, 446.

23. Vernadskii, *Russkoe masonstvo*, 109.

24. St Martin became the personal secretary of the semi-educated Spanish Jewish convert to Christianity, Don Martinez de Pasqually, in 1770. They worked together only for a short time, but long enough for confusion to arise concerning whether the origin of 'Martinism' as a particular variety of mystical Masonry ought to be ascribed to St Martin or Martinez. M. Kovalevskii, 'Masonstvo vo vremena Ekateriny', *Viestnik Evropy* (Sept. 1915), 108, clearly implies that the term referred to followers of Martinez, and speaks of Schelling's impression that it meant followers of St Martin as a 'mistake'.

25. G. Luchinskii, 'Frank-masonstvo v Rossii', in B-E, XXXVI-A, 509–14.

26. There is a curious lack of scholarship on Novikov, as compared, for example, with his contemporary (surely less influential in their day) Radishchev, on whom four English-language studies have been published during the last few years. Two selections from Novikov's works (one also including a good deal from Sumarokov and Karamzin) have recently been published in the USSR: I. V. Malyshev (ed.), *N. I. Novikov i ego sovremenniki: izbrannye sochineniia* (Moscow, 1961), and P. N. Berkov (ed.), *Satiricheskie zhurnaly N. I. Novikova* (Moscow–Leningrad, 1951), and a biographical study: G. Makogonenko, *Nikolai Novikov i russkoe prosveshchenie xviii veka* (Moscow–Leningrad, 1952). The volume of *RBS* to contain an article on Novikov was not completed. On Schwarz, see V. V. Fursenko, 'Shvarts, Ivan Georgevich (Egorovich, Johann Georg Schwarz)', *RBS*, XXII, 621–9. On both see M. N. Longinov, 'Novikov i Shvarts', *Russkii Viestnik* (October 1857), bk 1, 539–85; and his monograph, *Novikov i moskovskie martinisty* (Moscow, 1867; reprint, Ann Arbor, 1963).

27. Vernadskii, *Russkoe masonstvo*, 231–4.

28. *Ibid.*, 155.

29. *Ibid.*, 180–8.

30. Florovskii, *Puti*, 122.

31. From the diary of S. A. Poroshin; Leo Wiener (ed.), *Anthology of Russian Literature* (New York, 1902), 1, 326.

32. 'Novikov, Nikolai Ivanovich', B-E, xxi, 253–6.

33. Aleksandr Semeka, 'Russkie rozenkreitsery i sochineniia imperatritsy Ekateriny II protiv masonstva', *ZMNP*, cccxxxix, no. 2 (February 1902), 399.

34. Vernadskii, *Russkoe masonstvo*, 240; see also his 'Le Césarévitch Paul et les francs-maçons de Moscou', *RES*, iii (1923), 268–85, and Luchinskii, 'Frank-masonstvo'.

35. N. M. Karamzin, *Letters of a Russian Traveler, 1789–90* (trans., New York, 1957).

36. *Ibid.*, 3.

37. Kliuchevskii, *Kurs russkoi istorii*, v, 201–2.

38. From *Truten'*, 1769 g., List VI; Berkov (ed.), *Satiricheskie zhurnaly Novikova*, 63.

39. Soviet scholars have studied him extensively, especially G. P. Makogonenko, *Radishchev i ego vremia* (Moscow, 1956) and A. I. Startsev, *Universitetskie gody Radishcheva* (Moscow, 1956) and *Radishchev v gody 'Puteshestviia'* (Moscow, 1960). Four English-language studies have been recently published: Roderick Page Thaler (ed.), *Aleksandr Nikolaevich Radishchev's A Journey from St. Petersburg to Moscow* (trans., Harvard, 1958), which has a 37-page introduction; David Marshall Lang, *The First Russian Radical: Alexander Radishchev, 1749–1802* (London, 1959); Jesse V. Clardy, *The Philosophical Ideas of Alexander Radishchev* (New York, 1964); and Allen McConnell, *A Russian Philosophe: Alexander Radishchev, 1749–1802* (The Hague, 1964). McConnell's is the best study; Clardy's is unreliable.

40. Thaler (ed.), *Radishchev's Journey*, 40.

41. Thaler is perhaps misleading on this point in *ibid.*, 28, though he rightly compares it to other quite 'fictitious' contemporary accounts of travels which never took place or whose purely geographical component is nearly missing.

42. On literary sources see *ibid.*, 28–30, and McConnell, *Radishchev*, 69–74. In my view McConnell overstates his point in his article, 'Abbé Raynal and a Russian Philosophe', in *Jahrbücher für Geschichte Osteuropas*, n.s., vol. xii (1964), pt. 4 (Feb. 1965 [*sic*]), 499–512.

43. One can share the annoyance of Soviet scholars who lament the neglect of Radishchev and the failure to bring him into the story of the European Enlightenment and yet deprecate the only slightly veiled ultranationalism which led some in the Stalin era at least to deny Radishchev's debt to the West and made such untenable assertions as that he was 'the foremost economist of the eighteenth century'. See E. V. Prikazchikova's chapter on Radishchev in John M. Letiche (ed.), *A History of Russian Economic Thought: Ninth through Eighteenth Centuries* (orig. ed. by A. I. Pashkov; trans., 1964).

44. V. P. Semennikov, *Radishchev: ocherki i issledovaniia* (Moscow, Petrograd, 1923), 91.

45. McConnell, *Radishchev*, 66–9, has rather missed the point by failing to distinguish St Petersburg Masonry of the 70's from Moscow Masonry of the 80's; rightly indicating Radishchev's distance from the latter, McConnell fails to note his nearness to the former. Already in 1923 Semennikov criticized those

students of Radishchev who wrongly concluded from his hostility to Martinism that he was hostile to all Masonry (*Radishchev*, 102).

46. See Marc Raeff, *Origins of the Russian Intelligentsia: The Eighteenth-Century Nobility* (New York, 1966), 154–7.

47. Thaler, ed., 191. Vl. Orlov, *Russkie prosvetiteli 1790–1800-kh godov* (n. p., 1950), 13–14, cites this passage as a 'not at all veiled summons to peasant revolution'. He and other Soviet scholars follow G. P. Makogonenko on this point; see the latter's *Radishchev i ego vremia* (Moscow, 1956), 460.

48. The empress's notes in an appendix to Thaler, ed., 248.

49. McConnell, 'Abbé Raynal and a Russian Philosophe', 503.

50. Quoted in Thaler, ed., 9.

51. Orlov, *Russkie prosvetiteli 1790–1800-kh godov*, and Vl. Orlov (ed.), *Poety-radishchevtsy* (Leningrad, 1952), an anthology with long introduction.

52. M. N. Longinov, *Novikov i moskovskie martinisty*, 230–1. The work, *Istoriia ordena iezuitov*, was included as a supplement to *Moskovskiia Viedomosti*, and therefore is listed only as such (no. 356, p. 55) in V. P. Semennikov, *Knigoizdatel'skaia dieiatel'nost' N. I. Novikova i Tipograficheskoi kompanii* Peterburg [sic], 1921).

53. Sviashchennik Mikhail Moroshkin, *Iezuity v Rossii s tsarstvovaniia Ekateriny II-i i do nashego vremeni* (2 vols, St Petersburg, 1867–70); Dmitry Tolstoy, *Le Catholicisme Romain en Russie* (2 vols, Paris, 1863–4) – a Russian edition was published in St Petersburg only in 1876–7, though the book was originally written in Russian; Iu. F. Samarin, 'Otvet Iezuitu otsu Martynovu', *Den'*, #45–6, 47–8, 49, 50–1, and 52 (1865). An 1868 edition of the work is reprinted in his *Sochineniia*, VI (Moscow, 1887); P. Stanislas Zalenski, *Les Jésuites de la Russie-Blanche* (trans., 2 vols, Paris [1886]); E. Winter, 'Die Jesuiten in Russland (1772 bis 1820). Ein Beitrag zur Auseinandersetzung zwizchen Aufklärung und Restauration', *Forschen und Wirken: Festshrift zur 150-Jahr-Feier der Humboldt-Universität zu Berlin, 1810–1960*, III (Berlin, 1960), 167–91.

54. Quoted in A. N. Popov, *Razbor sochineniia O. Moroshkina: 'Iezuity v Rossii...'* (St Petersburg, 1869), 8.

55. *Ibid.*, 11.

56. *Ibid.*, 32.

57. Moroshkin, *Iezuity v Rossii*, I, 262.

58. See Tolstoy, *Le Catholicisme Romain en Russie*, II, 96.

59. Moroshkin, *Iezuity*, I, 377; Tolstoy, *Catholicisme*, II, 126.

60. Moroshkin, I, 379.

61. *Ibid.*, 480.

62. A Golitsyn had protected the Jesuits in the reign of Peter I; under Anna another had married an Italian and accepted conversion to Rome; in 1727 Princess Irina Petrovna Dolgorukaia, née Golitsyna, had converted and raised her children as Roman Catholics; under Catherine Prince Dmitry Alexeevich Golitsyn, Russian envoy to Paris and Holland, friend of Voltaire and Diderot, had married a Countess Schmettau and allowed their children to be raised as Catholics, although he himself was an atheist.

63. See Ch. Vol. 2, Ch. 1.

64. Moroshkin, *Iezuity*, II, 4–5; the evidence cited is from *TKDA* (August 1867), *ZMNP* (December 1867), and other sources, including unspecified manuscript material in the author's possession. In a recent study M. J. Rouët de Journel, SJ (*Nonciatures de Russie: d'après les documents authentiques*, vol. v,

Intérim de Benvenuti, 1799–1803 [*Studi e Testi*, no. 194; Vatican City, 1957]), does not mention this account, but does publish a letter in Italian (p. 97) from Papal Secretary of State Consalvi to Gruber, dated 'March 1801' (but before Paul's death occurred or at any rate was known in Rome), in which there is an abrupt and unexplained passage that would tend to confirm that such plans were under way: 'Oh! Would that the Holy Father could have with your cooperation and that of your Institute the consolation of a perfect reunion of His Majesty the Emperor to our communion. Oh! This would therefore smooth all paths, and would crown with endless glory the pontificate of His Holiness and your own immortal work! The Holy Father is unable to give up such glorious hopes, and trusts to the utmost in your religion and zeal and ability to see it one day carried into effect.'

65. Zalenski, *Les Jésuites de la Russie-Blanche*, II, 102, declares: 'It cannot be doubted for a moment that the chief author of the murder, Count Pahlen, governor of St Petersburg, belonged to the [Illuminist; i.e., mystical Masonic] sect and that the sentence of death was passed in a session of the Grand Lodge of Paris.' He acknowledges that the latter supposition cannot be proved.

66. Moroshkin, *Iezuity*, II, 20.

67. Florovskii, *Puti*, 130.

68. See Marc Raeff, *Michael Speransky: Statesman of Imperial Russia, 1772–1839* (The Hague, 1957).

69. There is no proof of the popular supposition that Karamzin's *Memoir on Ancient and Modern Russia* (published in both Russian and English versions, the latter edited by Richard Pipes, by Harvard University Press in 1959) brought about Speransky's downfall, since it is not even certain that Alexander read it. See Pipes's introduction to *Karamzin's Memoir on Ancient and Modern Russia*, 84. Karamzin criticized Speransky's Western-oriented constitutionalism, by indirection; but he himself had been involved in a literary controversy in which he espoused the use of both Western borrowing and popular speech in producing a remolded Russian language suitable for the times, in opposition to Admiral A. S. Shishkov, who defended Church Slavic as the only proper basis for the Russian of the day. Hugh Seton-Watson in *The Russian Empire, 1801–1917* (Oxford, 1967), 107–8, has reminded us that in Greece about the same time a view similar to Shishkov's won out retarding the growth of literature and social development; thus the victory of Karamzin's views on language in Russia appears the more beneficial because it was by no means inevitable.

70. Moroshkin, *Iezuity*, II, 28, writes of the latter group that they were concerned with 'the spread of enlightenment and liberal institutions in Russia, some kind of transcendental unity of mankind, a humanist attitude to every kind of idea, every kind of doctrine, whether it was political or religious, even including all sorts of fantasy; but complete indifference and as it were contempt for popular elements (*narodnyia stikhii*), the history of the fatherland, the ancestral faith, and native traditions, unconsciously clearing the ground for the Jesuits...'

71. M. J. Rouët de Journel, *La compagnie de Jésus en Russie: Un collège de Jésuites à Saint-Pétersbourg, 1800–1816* (Paris, 1922), 52.

72. Nicole returned to France in that year and became rector of the Académie de Paris (that is, in effect, Superintendent of Schools).

73. Not 'de Maistre'; as he himself insisted, 'de' cannot be attached to a proper name beginning with a consonant; see Robert Triomphe, *Joseph de Maistre: Étude sur la vie et sur la doctrine d'un matérialiste mystique* (Geneva, 1968), 9.

74. Dzhuseppe Berti (Giuseppe Berti), *Rossiia i ital'ianskie gosudarstva v period Risordzhimento* (trans., Moscow, 1959), 236–40. The Italian original was unavailable to me.

75. P. B. (ed.), 'Pis'mo Grafa Iosifa de Mestra k Kn. P. B. Kozlovskomu', *Russkii Arkhiv* (1866), col. 1492.

76. Berti, *Rossiia*, 263.

77. In P. B. (ed.), 'Pis'mo', col. 1494.

78. E. Feoktistov, 'Zhozef de-Mestr v Peterburgie', *Russkaia Riech'*, no. 27 (1861).

79. Berti, *Rossiia*, 238.

80. Berti speaks of Maistre's 'reactionary rationalism'; he is careful to point out several times that, much opinion to the contrary, Maistre had little or no mysticism in his make-up.

81. Berti, *Rossiia*, 256.

82. This is the story given by Henri Lutteroth [Nikolai Ivanovich Turgenev], *La Russie et les Jésuites de 1772 à 1820 d'après de documents la plupart inédits* (Paris, 1845), 57–63. Dmitry Tolstoy (*Le Catholicisme*, II, 201–13) tells a slightly different story. He mentions that a number of documents used by 'Lutteroth' were burned in a fire in 1862.

83. Quoted by Tolstoy, *Le Catholicisme Romain*, II, 189; source not given.

84. Actually the ukaz of 20 December 1815/1 January 1816 banned the Jesuits from St Petersburg only; the final act banning the order throughout the Empire was delayed until March 1820, but the expulsion from the capital was decisive in effect.

85. Rouët de Journel, *La compagnie de Jésus*, 220–1.

86. Iu. F. Samarin, 'Otvet Iezuitu otsu Martynovu', Letter IV, #50–1, 1194.

87. Florovskii, *Puti*, 121.

88. 'Razskazy Kniazia Aleksandra Nikolaevicha Golitsyna, zapisannye Iu. N. Bartenevym', *Russkaia Starina* (January 1884), 123–34.

89. 'Golitsyn, Aleksandr Nikolaevich', in B-E, IX, 50–1.

90. V. K., 'Labzin, Aleksandr Fedorovich', B-E, XVII, 176–7.

91. See Judith Cohen Zacek, 'The Russian Bible Society, 1812–1826' (unpublished Columbia University dissertation, 1964; University Microfilms edition, 1967).

92. Quoted Florovskii, *Puti*, 131.

93. 'O sud'be pravoslavnoi tserkvi russkoi v tsarstvovanie imperatora Aleksandra I-go. (Iz zapisok A. S. Sturdzy)', *Russkaia Starina* (February 1876), p. 280.

94. Quoted Florovskii, *Puti*, 149.

95. Sturdza's memoirs in *Russkaia Starina* (February 1876), p. 272.

96. *Ibid.*, p. 279. Sturdza had to edit the text of the ban for transmission to Rome, and knew the circumstances well.

97. See Judith Cohen Zacek, 'The Lancastrian School Movement in Russia', *SEER*, XLV (July 1967), 343–67. It should be noted that virtually identical methods to those of Joseph Lancaster's were used by Andrew Bell. Both introduced them in England, apparently independently, in 1798; Bell had used them in India as early as 1789. But Lancaster's pietist, Bible-without-notes-or-comment approach enabled him to win both in Britain and abroad a fame denied to Bell, whose schools included religious instruction in accordance with the doctrine of the Church of England.

98. 'Tatarinova, Ekaterina Filippovna, née Buksgevden [Buxhövden], B-E, XXXII-A, 666–8.

99. Zacek, 'The Russian Bible Society', Ch. V, contains a good detailed narrative of the end of the ascendancy of Golitsyn and pietism.

100. A recent scholarly reappraisal, prefacing a selection of translated documents, is Marc Raeff, *The Decembrist Movement* (Englewood Cliffs, N.J., 1966). The standard English-language monograph remains Anatole G. Mazour, *The First Russian Revolution, 1825* (reprint, Stanford, 1962). For the literature in Russian, see N. M. Chentsov, *Vosstanie dekabristov, Bibliografiia* (Moscow–Leningrad, 1929), which covers publications to 1928, and M. V. Nechkina (ed.), *Dvizhenie dekabristov, Ukazatel' literatury 1928–1959* (Moscow, 1960). A recent German monograph is Hans Lemberg, *Die nationale Gedankenwelt der Dekabristen* (Köln–Graz, 1963).

101. V. Miakotin, 'Dekabristy', in *Ents. Slovar'* Granat, 7th ed., XVIII, 140.

102. V. I. Semevskii, *Politicheskiia i obshchestvennyia idei dekabristov* (St Petersburg, 1909), 321–2.

103. Quoted in Raeff, *Decembrist Movement*, 56, 54, 51, 49, 46, from the testimony of the arrested Decembrists as given in *Vosstanie dekabristov: Materialy/Dokumenty po istorii vosstaniia dekabristov*, I–IX.

104. Paraphrased in N. Sh[ilder], 'Zagovor dekabristov', B-E, XII, 117–21.

105. See Georges Luciani, *La Société des Slaves Unis, 1823–1825* (Bordeaux, 1963).

106. Masaryk, *The Spirit of Russia*, II, 103.

107. See the two drafts of Nikita Muraviev's constitution (on behalf of the Northern Society) and extracts from Pestel's two drafts of a constitution (on behalf of the Southern Society) which form a part of his *Russkaia Pravda*, in Raeff, *The Decembrist Movement*, 103–18 and 132–56.

108. Semevsky in his introduction to *Politicheskiia i obshchestvennyia idei dekabristov* discusses *inter alia* as forerunners of the Decembrists Catherine II's Legislative Commission, Diderot, the aspirations of N. I. Panin, Prince M. M. Shcherbatov, and Radishchev.

109. This should surprise no one, since the scholastic philosophers (including Jesuits) in the West were in many respects the intellectual ancestors of the *philosophes*, as Carl L. Becker points out in *The Heavenly City of the Eighteenth-Century Philosophers* (New Haven, 1932).

110. On the rumors about conversion, see Père J. Gagarin, SJ, *Tendances catholiques dans la société russe* (Paris, 1860), 37–8; Gagarin is cautious about the purported evidence. A work that takes the story of flight to Siberia seriously is Leonid I. Strakhovsky, *Alexander I of Russia* (New York, 1947).

111. Florovskii, *Puti*, 128.

112. In 1803 a Polish university was founded in Vilna and a German university in Dorpat, in 1804 Russian universities in Kharkov and Kazan, the revived St Petersburg pedagogical school was given university status in 1819, and in 1817 was established the *lycée* Richelieu in Odessa which later became its university.

113. *Ibid.*, 237.

114. Quoted *ibid.*, 166.

115. *Ibid.*, 179; Filaret of Moscow is discussed at some length on pp. 166–85.

6: *German idealism and French anarchism (1825–1855)*

1. A. Nikitenko, *Moia povest' o samom sebe i o tom "chemu svidetel' v zhizni byl."* *Zapiski i dnevnik (1804–1877 gg.)* (2nd ed., St Petersburg, 1905), I, 553, as quoted in Nicholas V. Riasanovsky, *Nicholas I and Official Nationality in Russia, 1825–1855* (Berkeley and Los Angeles, 1959), 266.

2. Michael T. Florinsky, *Russia: A History and an Interpretation* (2 vols, New York, 1953), II, 769, who is by no means inclined to emphasize the positive side of Nicholas's reign, mentions this point.

3. N. Shilder, *Imperator Nikolai Pervyi, ego zhizn' i tsarstvovanie* (2 vols, St Petersburg, 1903), I, 147, as quoted in Riasanovsky, *Nicholas I*, 1.

4. *Ibid.*

5. T. Schiemann, *Geschichte Russlands unter Kaiser Nikolaus I* (4 vols, Berlin, 1904–19), IV, 208–9, as quoted in Riasanovsky, *Nicholas I*, 11.

6. Schiemann, *Geschichte Russlands unter Kaiser Nikolaus I*, II, 114.

7. As quoted in Riasanovsky, *Nicholas I*, 139.

8. Quoted *ibid.*, 71.

9. Florinsky, *Russia*, II, 799.

10. M. Mazaev, 'Grech, Nikolai Ivanovich', in B-E, IX-A, 686–7.

11. Vladimir Botsianovskii, as quoted by Riasanovsky, *Nicholas I*, 68–9.

12. Florinsky, *Russia*, II, 777.

13. Riasanovsky, *Nicholas I*, 181.

14. N. Barsukov, *Zhizn' i trudy M. P. Pogodina* (22 vols, St Petersburg, 1888–1910), II, 17, as quoted in Riasanovsky, *Nicholas I*, 99.

15. Riasanovsky, *Nicholas I*, 105 and 114.

16. In his *Prostaia rech' o mudrenykh veshchakh*; se Riasanovsky, *Nicholas I*, 79–84 for discussion.

17. It ought to be a commonplace, but unfortunately seems far from being one, that modern nationalism, wherever it has appeared in the world, is an intellectual phenomenon borrowed from the West quite as much as any of the political 'isms' or democracy as a doctrine.

18. Quoted Riasanovsky, *Nicholas I*, 126–7.

19. The similarities and differences are well treated by Nicholas V. Riasanovsky in his article, 'Pogodin and Ševyrëv in Russian Intellectual History', *Harvard Slavic Studies*, IV (Harvard, 1957), 149–67.

20. There still is no adequate study of the circle. See N. P. Pavlov-Sil'vanskii, 'Materialisty dvadtsatykh godov', in *Ocherki po russkoi istorii XVIII–XIX vv.* (St Petersburg, 1910; reprint, 1966); Alexandre Koyré, *La philosophie et le problème national en Russie au début du XIXe siècle* (Paris, 1929), Ch. IV; V. A. Riasanovskii, *Obzor russkoi kul'tury* (New York, 1947), pt II, issue 1, 301–10; P. N. Sakulin, *Iz istorii russkago idealizma: Kniaz' V. F. Odoevskii* (vol. I, 2 pts [no more published]; Moscow, 1913; introductory article by D. D. Blagoi to D. V. Venevitinov, *Polnoe sobranie sochinenii* (Moscow–Leningrad, 1934), 7–46.

21. See W. Sechkarev, *Schellings Einfluss in der russischen Literatur der 20-er und 30-er Jahre des XIX Jahrhunderts* (Berlin, 1939).

22. See p. 151.

23. At the same time the use of Latin as the language of instruction diminished, and by the 1840's it had generally been replaced by Russian.

24. Prot. Georgii Florovskii, *Puti russkago bogosloviia* (Paris, 1937), 242.

25. Quoted *ibid.*, 236.

26. The *BSE* (2nd ed.), entry 'Liubomudry', says: 'The crushing of the Decembrist revolt led to the liquidation of the "Society [of Lovers of Wisdom]". In the conditions of cruel reaction the former members of the circle of the Liubomudry began to publish a magazine, *Moscow Messenger* (*Moskovskii Vestnik*)...' The impression is thus given that the government banned the circle, which is not the case.

27. Isaiah Berlin, 'A Marvellous Decade', *Encounter*, June, Nov., and Dec. 1955 and May 1956; June 1955, 31. The title is taken from P. V. Annenkov's *Zamechatel'noe desiatiletie*, first published in 1880, dealing with the 1840's with the emphasis on Belinsky. An English translation, edited by Arthur P. Mendel, was published in Ann Arbor, 1968.

28. *Ibid.*, Nov. 1955, 25.

29. Stankevich retained his Orthodox faith in early manhood and appears not to have abandoned his religious faith thereafter, unlike a number of his friends such as Belinsky and Bakunin. 'At no point', writes Edward J. Brown, 'does he [Stankevich] attempt to substitute reason for religion, or German idealism for Christianity'– *Stankevich and His Moscow Circle, 1830–1840* (Stanford, 1966), 99. However, Berlin's statement is very much to the point in relation to many of the future Westerners who were members of the Stankevich circle, and later the Westerners as a group (despite some reservations which will be made hereafter).

30. Brown, *Stankevich*, 99.

31. Brown *ibid.*, 130, concludes that Stankevich had 'only a minimal effect on the intellectual life of his times and probably none at all on the development of the Russian intelligentsia or Russian literature'. In so saying Brown is trying to demolish the 'myth' produced chiefly by a single work: P. V. Annenkov's *Nikolai Vladimirovich Stankevich: perepiska ego i biografiia* (Moscow, 1858), but he may be making an overstatement in the opposite direction.

32. Martin Malia, *Alexander Herzen and the Birth of Russian Socialism, 1812–1855* (Harvard, 1961), 34.

33. *Ibid.*, 50.

34. *Ibid.*, esp. 93–5.

35. Georgii V. Florovskii, 'Iskaniia molodogo Gertsena', *Sovremennyia Zapiski*, xxxix and xl (Paris, 1929), xxxix, 302.

36. As quoted *ibid.*, xl, 360. In his generally excellent work on Herzen, Malia seems concerned to explain away his religious searchings of the 1830's (*Herzen*, 168, and in other places). Herzen makes it difficult for that to be done. In Viatka he writes: 'Having awakened, I looked with different eyes on nature, on man, and finally on God; I became a Christian'– and it ought to be noted that this was the kind of a 'conversion' which is experienced by a person who is at least a nominal Christian already.

37. 'Literaturnye mechtaniia', in V. G. Belinskii, *Polnoe sobranie sochinenii*, I (1953), 20ff.

38. I. V. Kirieevskii, 'Deviatnadtsatyi viek', in *Polnoe sobranie sochinenii*, I (Moscow, 1861), 61–85. Kireevsky later, as a Slavophile, was to turn this weakness into a strength for Russia.

39. Wladimir Weidlé, *Pushkin* (trans., Paris, 1949), 6, 7. Recent works include Walter N. Vickery, *Pushkin* (New York, 1970), a brief manual which has a few pages serving as introduction to the vast bibliography to date and Henri Troyat, *Pushkin* (trans., Garden City, New York, 1970), a long, rich, sparsely annotated biography. D. S. Mirsky's *Pushkin* (1926; reprint, New York, 1963) remains fresh and provocative. A good introduction to Soviet

scholarship on Pushkin is B. P. Gorodetskii and others (eds), *Pushkin: itogi i problemy izucheniia* (Moscow, 1966).

40. *The Letters of Alexander Pushkin* (3 vols, trans. [and ed.] by J. Thomas Shaw, Bloomington, Ind., 1963), III, 798. The sentence quoted is from a rough draft to the letter whose text is given 779–81; the letter was not sent.

41. The best works on him include M. Gershenzon, *P. Ia. Chaadaev: zhizn' i myshlenie* (St Petersburg, 1908) and Charles Quénet, *Tchaadaev et les lettres philosophiques* (Paris, 1931). His writings may be found in *Oeuvres choisies de Pierre Tschadaief* (Paris and Leipzig, 1862) and M. Gershenzon (ed.), *Sochineniia i pis'ma P. Ia. Chaadaeva* (2 vols, Moscow, 1913). A Russian translation of all eight of the 'philosophical letters' edited by D. Shakhovskoi is in *Literaturnoe nasledstvo*, vols 22–4 (Moscow, 1936). Two English editions of his works have recently appeared: Mary-Barbara Zeldin's of *Philosophical Letters and Apology of a Madman* (Knoxville, Tenn., 1969), and Raymond T. McNally's of *The Major Works of Peter Chaadaev* (Notre Dame, 1969).

42. According to Katerina Nikolaevna Orlova; M. Zhikharev, 'Petr Iakovlevich Chaadaev. Iz vospominanii sovremennika', *Viestnik Evropy* (July 1871), 190–1. Zhikharev was Chaadaev's nephew and literary executor.

43. Mikhail Longinov gave a popular account of this episode in 'Vospominaniia o P. Ia. Chaadaeva', *Russkii Viestnik* (Nov. 1862), 135–8; Zhikharev questions his account in the *Viestnik Evropy* article, 201–7.

44. *Oeuvres* ed. by Gagarin, 15.

45. Zhikharev in *Viestnik Evropy*, 31, writes that not even the death of Pushkin produced such an effect.

46. *Oeuvres*, Gagarin ed., 150.

47. Alexandre Koyré in his *Études sur l'histoire de la pensée philosophique en Russie* (Paris, 1950), 90, shows his clear perception of this point: 'we shall find in the celebrated *Apology of a Madman* almost no idea that we did not recognize in his earlier writings, and the "retractions" that it contains do not exceed the scope of those we have already met in the letters'. See my article, 'Lu Hsün and Chaadaev: A Comparative Study in Westernization', to appear in another volume; a Chinese translation has been published: 'Lu Hsün yü Ch'ai-ta-yeh-fu', *Ta-hsüeh sheng-huo*, v, no. 6 (June 1970), 6–11, in Hong Kong.

48. Zhikharev, 'Chaadaev', 31.

49. Florovskii, *Puti*, 248.

50. M. K. Afanas'ev, 'Obshchestvenno-politicheskie vzgliady Chaadaeva', *Trudy Voronezhskogo Gosudarstvennogo Universiteta*, XIV, pt 1: *Materialy po istorii russkoi kul'tury* (Voronezh, 1947), 150–1.

51. *Oeuvres*, Gagarin ed., 186.

52. *Ibid.*, 37.

53. *Ibid.*, 78–83. He discussed this theme, without mentioning Protestants, in the eighth *Philosophical Letter*.

54. Berlin, 'A Marvellous Decade', June 1955, 33.

55. See Herbert E. Bowman, *Vissarion Belinski, 1811–1848: A Study in the Origins of Social Criticism in Russia* (Harvard, 1954). A new edition of his work, *Polnoe sobranie sochinenii*, was issued in Moscow in 13 vols, 1953–9.

56. E. H. Carr's biography, *Michael Bakunin* (London, 1937), has not been superseded. Y. M. Steklov (ed.), *M. A. Bakunin, sobranie sochinenii i pisem* (4 vols, Moscow, 1934–6), cover the period to 1861; Max Nettlau (ed.) of vol. I, James Guillaume (ed.) of vols II–VI, Michel Bakounine, *Oeuvres* (Paris, 1895–1913), cover from 1867 to 1876.

57. Bowman, *Belinski*, 171.

58. Quoted *ibid.*, 200, from letter to Botkin, December 1847. Sir Isaiah Berlin in 'A Marvellous Decade' (*Encounter*, Dec. 1955, 28–9) rather misleadingly argues that Belinsky rejected the notion that art has a purpose beyond itself and that he held that art itself gave truth to those who sought it.

59. Malia, *Herzen*, 254.

60. *Ibid.*, 320–5.

61. *Ibid.*, 367.

62. *Ibid.*, 405.

63. Riasanovsky, *Russia and the West in the Teaching of the Slavophiles* (Harvard, 1952), 29, also mentions A. I. Koshelev, D. A. Valuev, and others.

64. *Ibid.*, 170.

65. Quoted in Florovskii, *Puti*, 255–6.

66. See Riasanovsky, *Slavophiles*, 177–80.

67. Florovskii, *Puti*, 252.

68. Russians and Ukrainians are referred to here; the one real revolution in the Russian Empire during Nicholas I's reign was that of the Poles, but it falls outside our subject. See R. F. Leslie, *Polish Politics and the Revolution of November 1830* (London, 1956).

69. V. I. Semevskii, *M. V. Butashevich-Petrashevskii i Petrashevtsy* (*Sobranie sochinenii*, vol. II), pt 1 (only one published; Moscow, 1922), 24. See also P. E. Shchegolev (comp.), *Petrashevtsy v vospominaniiakh sovremennikov, sbornik materialov* (3 pts; Moscow–Leningrad, 1926–8).

70. *Ibid.*, 32–7.

71. *Ibid.*, 55.

72. Franco Venturi, *Roots of Revolution: A History of Populist and Socialist Movements in Nineteenth Century Russia* (trans., New York, 1960), 84.

73. Quoted *ibid.*, 87.

74. V. I. Semevskii, 'Nikolai Ivanovich Kostomarov, 1817–1885', *Russkaia Starina* (January 1886), 181–212.

75. P. A. Zaionchkovskii, *Kirillo-Mefodievskoe obshchestvo (1846–1847)* (Moscow, 1959). The text of *Zakon bozhii* is given, pp. 149–60; parallel passages with Lamennais's essay are given, p. 80. Georges Luciani in *La Société des Slaves Unis (1823–1825)* (Bordeaux, 1963), 29, declares that the program of the Brotherhood of Cyril and Methodius was a direct descendant of that of the Society of United Slavs, in a form 'renewed, more conscious, finished, and with different nuances'. But (*ibid.*, 66) the United Slavs' ideology had no reference to any such people as the Ukrainians.

76. Chaadaev in the sentence used as epigraph to this chapter sounded the keynote of the decade of the 1840's in the history of Russian thought.

77. One is reminded of Pushkin's remark about Belinsky as reported by Annenkov (*Extraordinary Decade*, 5): 'His is no ordinary head, but it always has this way about it that the sounder its first thought, the sillier its second.'

78. As Victor Erlich recognizes, without using exactly this phrase, in his extraordinarily perceptive *Gogol* (New Haven, 1969), 196–8. Gogol wrote to Shevyrev, 'I came to Christ [a characteristic pietist expression] through the Protestant rather than through the Catholic way', not mentioning any Orthodox way at all. Quoted in Florovskii, *Puti*, 261. Other studies of merit on Gogol include V. Setchkarev, *Gogol: His Life and Works* (trans., New York, 1965); Vladimir Nabokov, *Nikolai Gogol* (corrected ed., New York, 1961); Paul Debreczeny, *Nikolay Gogol and His Contemporary Critics* (Philadelphia, 1966).

79. Erlich in *Gogol*, 115–17, reviews the issues raised by the critics and by implication gives the same answer I would. For a Chinese example of victimization by such critical misappraisal sixty years later, see my discussion of Lu Hsün in vol. 2 of this work, Ch. 5.

80. Quoted in Florovskii, *Puti*, 184.

81. *Ibid.*, 166–85 gives an extensive account of him.

82. *Ibid.*, 179.

83. I. Korsunskii, 'Filaret', *RBS*, XXI, 83–93.

84. Florovskii, *Puti*, 176.

85. *Ibid.*, 206.

86. *Ibid.*, 231.

7: Socialism and syncretism (1855–1890)

1. *Kolokol*: Gazeta A. I. Gertsena i N. P. Ogareva, 1857–67, faksimil'noe izdanie (Moscow), pt 2 (1862), 363–4. The title of the article was printed in English, as shown. The issue was 1 June, 1859.

2. Prot. Georgii Florovskii, *Puti russkago bogosloviia* (Paris, 1937), 289.

3. Franco Venturi, *Roots of Revolution: A History of Populist and Socialist Movements in Nineteenth Century Russia* (trans. New York, 1960), Ch. 5. The Soviets have extensively studied Chernyshevsky, whose views are regarded as more important for their own evolution than anyone thus far mentioned and indeed any other Russian before the rise of the Russian Social Democratic Labor Party. His works were published as *Polnoe sobranie sochinenii* (15 vols, Moscow, 1939–51). A recent American study is William F. Woehrlin, *Chernyshevskii: The Man and the Journalist* (Harvard, 1971); Francis B. Randall, *N. G. Chernyshevskii* (New York, 1967) is a good survey with bibliography.

4. As quoted in Venturi, *Roots*, 136.

5. Discussed at length in Randall, *Chernyshevskii*, 38–53.

6. Summarized in Woehrlin, *Chernyshevskii*, 251–9.

7. E. Lampert, *Sons against Fathers* (Oxford, 1965), 105. See Herbert E. Bowman, 'Revolutionary Elitism in Černyševskij', *ASEER*, XIII (April 1954), 185–99.

8. Woehrlin in *Chernyshevskii*, 274–87, concludes that he wrote this item of questioned authorship though perhaps not in the exact form in which it survives.

9. Randall, *Chernyshevskii*, 78.

10. Quoted in Lampert, *Sons Against Fathers*, 141.

11. Woehrlin, *Chernyshevskii*, Ch. IX. The slogan '*zemlia i volia*' was coined by Herzen's collaborator, Ogarev, who also wrote the program of the 1862 group.

12. *Ibid.*, 277.

13. Dobroliubov's works were edited by P. I. Lebedev-Poliansky as *Polnoe sobranie sochinenii* (6 vols, Leningrad, 1934–9). Venturi devotes much of Ch. 6 of *Roots* to him; see also Lampert, *Sons against Fathers*, Ch. 4.

14. Quoted in Venturi, *Roots*, 157.

15. Alan P. Pollard, 'The Russian Intelligentsia: The Mind of Russia', *California Slavic Studies* III (1964), 1–32, esp. 13. In the early 1860's the word was used in both senses, the abstraction referring to culture or consciousness as contrasted with the lack thereof. The literature on the term *intelligentsiia* is substantial; an introduction to that existing at the time is to be found in Richard Pipes (ed.), *The Russian Intelligentsia* (New York, 1961).

16. See Christopher Becker, '*Raznochintsy*: The Development of the Word and of the Concept', *ASEER*, XVIII (February 1959), 63–74. It originated as a legal term about 1720, but acquired the meaning of non-gentry only about 1750. Becker finds its earliest use referring to the men of the 60's in a review by Mikhailovsky published in 1874.

17. Martin Katz, *Mikhail N. Katkov: A Political Biography, 1818–1887* (The Hague, 1966), 31 and 71.

18. A. I. Gertsen, *Sobranie sochinenii* (30 vols, Moscow), XX, pt 1 (1960), 349.

19. Armand Coquart, *Dmitri Pisarev (1840–1868) et l'idéologie du nihilisme russe* (Paris, 1946), 88.

20. As quoted in Lampert, *Sons against Fathers*, 312.

21. *Ibid.*, 288.

22. *Ibid.*, 332.

23. See Coquart, *Pisarev*, 380–3, and Lampert, *Sons against Fathers*, fn. 35, 389.

24. As quoted in Lampert, *Sons against Fathers*, 295.

25. See Richard Pipes, 'Narodnichestvo: A Semantic Inquiry', *Slavic Review*, XXIII (September 1964), 441ff. Pipes dates the use of the term to 1875, and distinguishes its unexceptionable narrow usage to mean a revolutionary movement for and through the people from the broader and doubtful usage to refer to all those who, following Herzen and Chernyshevsky, wished for Russia to avoid capitalism. A. Walicki, in his brilliant though tantalizingly brief Marxist–Leninist study entitled *The Controversy Over Capitalism: Studies in the Social Philosophy* (Oxford, 1969), criticizes Pipes's distinction but does not manage to bring much clarity into the picture. He declares that Struve's use of the term, which Pipes emphasizes, could not include all believing in 'the ability of Russia to by-pass capitalism' because it was never applied to such persons as Leontiev. This is to create quite unnecessary problems; the populists wanted to bypass capitalism in order to reach socialism; conservatives like Leontiev did not and never do, though that did not prevent Leontiev from noting his points of contact with the populists (see p. 213). On the relation of Marx and the populists, Walicki is excellent and authoritative, with two noteworthy exceptions: he fails to come to grips with the religious background of populism and entirely omits (though his quotation from Chernyshevsky [see fn. 29] cries out for it and his reference to Plekhanov's mention of 'Peruvian "sons of the sun"' [155] is incomprehensible without it) to mention the issue of 'Asiatic' institutions in Russia as discussed by Marx and Russian populists or Marxists.

26. There was, as already noted, one significant socialist group, the Petrashevtsy, in the 1840's, but it was dispersed. After the 1860's populism never died despite several successful police round-ups of activist groups.

27. Oscar Jászi's phrasing in 'Anarchism', *Encyclopedia of the Social Sciences* (New York, 1930), II. He lists seven other propositions, mostly 'codified' by the Pittsburgh anarchist congress of 1883, which all anarchists accept. Some of them, such as the goodness of human nature, are shared with other socialists; others are more characteristic of and peculiar to anarchism: the rejection of notions of inevitable historical evolution, the stress on violent revolutionary action (Jászi speaks of the anarchist idea of the individual's moral conscience that entitles him to kill tyrants and oppressors), and insistence that no state shall follow the revolution.

28. Walicki, *Controversy*, 158. The context is his discussion of Tikhomirov's 1884 attack on Plekhanov.

29. *Ibid.*, 20 (with the word 'Asiatic' curiously in lower case).

30. In *ibid.*, 59–62, Walicki convincingly argues Mikhailovsky's indebtedness to *Capital* and Marx generally in this respect.

31. This is not to reproach Marx for failing to discuss the difference between Western political institutions and economic formations and those of Russia; as Karl A. Wittfogel and others have pointed out, he did so clearly and repeatedly (if not in such a fashion as to satisfy all readers); see Wittfogel's essay, 'Russia and the East: A Comparison and Contrast' in the book I edited entitled *The Development of the USSR* (Seattle, 1964). But the fact remains that Marx's great work was on Western capitalism, not Russia's 'Asiatic' order. Among the Russian Marxists Plekhanov was the chief figure to make the latter and not capitalism the main enemy.

32. Of course occupationally not clergy but clergy's sons; but occupationally Herzen or Kropotkin were not gentry either, but journalists.

33. Venturi, *Roots*, 306; see also Florovskii, *Puti*, 294. Walicki writes, 'it was not a political movement. It rather resembled a religious movement, and had all the contagious and absorbing character of one'– *Controversy*, 89.

34. Quoted Florovskii, *Puti*, 294.

35. Deborah Welles Hardy, 'Petr Nikitich Tkachev: A Political Biography', unpublished Ph.D. dissertation, University of Washington, 1968, p. 21.

36. Venturi, *Roots*, 398.

37. See Michael M. Karpovich, 'P. L. Lavrov and Russian Socialism', *California Slavic Studies*, II (1963), 21–38; Robert Alan Kimball, 'The Early Political Career of Peter Lavrovich Lavrov, 1823–1873', unpublished Ph.D. dissertation, University of Washington, 1967.

38. The 1891 edition is translated with a 65-page biographical introduction by James P. Scanlan: Peter Lavrov, *Historical Letters* (Berkeley, 1967).

39. Walicki, *Controversy*, 35–6, points out the closeness of Lavrov's argumentation to the debates of the 40's. Mikhailovsky in his essay, 'What is Progress?' (1870) and Tkachev in 'What is the Party of Progress?' (1870, though not published till 1923), raised the same voluntarist banner even though both disagreed with Lavrov in certain ways.

40. Masaryk justly calls Lavrov an 'absolute westerniser' (*Spirit of Russia*, 2nd ed., II, 135); Walicki terms him the 'most extreme Westernizer and "enlightener" within the Populist movement' (*Controversy*, 36).

41. A. D. Mikhailov, who drew up its 1878 program, declared the group's solidarity with 'the federalist International, that is, the anarchists...' S. N. Valk (ed.), *Arkhiv 'Zemli i Voli' i 'Narodnoi Voli'* (Moscow, 1932), 58.

42. Several people quipped at the time that one faction took the '*Zemlia*' ('Black Partition' meant the desired redistribution of land) and the other took the '*Volia*'. Actually '*Volia*' means both 'liberty' and 'will'. The terrorists might have wished liberty, but they concentrated on their own 'will', whether or not it was also the 'people's'.

43. Richard Wortman's interesting study, *The Crisis of Russian Populism* (Cambridge, 1967), deals chiefly with A. N. Engel'gardt, G. I. Uspensky, and N. N. Zlatovratsky, but as he recognizes the term has much broader applicability.

44. *Ibid.*, 59–60, 92–6, 135, 174.

45. Quoted by B. P. Koz'min, *Iz istorii revoliutsionnoi mysli v Rossii* (Moscow, 1961), 475.

46. Quoted in Walicki, *Controversy*, 167–8.

47. Quoted in Ernest J. Simmons, *Leo Tolstoy* (London, 1946), 692–3.

48. It is not a new discovery; D. N. Ovsianiko-Kulikovsky already called *War and Peace* 'the nihilist epos'. Sir Isaiah Berlin, in his lucid essay 'Tolstoy and Enlightenment', mentions that Tolstoy acquired 'the reputation of being a "nihilist"'. Yet he certainly had no wish to destroy for the sake of destruction. He only wanted, more than anything else in the world, to know the truth' – Ralph E. Matlaw (ed.), *Tolstoy: A Collection of Critical Essays* (Englewood Cliffs, N.J., 1967), 29. What Berlin says is perfectly true, or even understated, for Tolstoy did not want to destroy at all, let alone for the sake of destruction; but the nihilism of his *thought* is the point here.

49. For biographical data, see the large two-volume work of N. N. Gusev, *Letopis' zhizni i tvorchestva L'va Nikolaevicha Tolstogo* (Moscow, 1958–60).

50. Quoted in Berlin, 'Tolstoy and Enlightenment', 37.

51. Quoted in Simmons, *Tolstoy*, 148.

52. *Ibid.*, 689–91.

53. *Ibid.*, 184.

54. Cited *ibid.*, 214.

55. *Ibid.*, 304. Simmons does not draw this conclusion explicitly.

56. Isaiah Berlin, *The Hedgehog and the Fox: An Essay on Tolstoy's View of History* (New York, 1953).

57. According to his wife; Simmons, *Tolstoy*, 362.

58. Cited in *ibid.*, 715.

59. Cited in *ibid.*, 700. Compare Engels on the Russian revolutionaries: 'a group of half-baked students, who, uttering grandiloquent cant-phrases, swell up like frogs and devour each other'. Quoted by Walicki, *Controversy*, 144.

60. Cited in *ibid.*, 736.

61. To A. B. Goldenweizer; cited in *ibid.*, 636.

62. D. N. Ovsianiko-Kulikovskii, *L. N. Tolstoi, K 80-lietiiu velikago pisatelia* (St Petersburg, 1908), 24, as quoted in Florovskii, *Puti*, 404.

63. Florovskii, *Puti*, 404–5.

64. *Ibid.*, 409. Sir Isaiah Berlin also emphasizes the eighteenth-century rationalism in Tolstoy; 'Tolstoy and Enlightenment', especially 44, 51. He terms Tolstoy 'martyr and a hero in the central tradition of the European enlightenment'.

Florovskii notes that for many Tolstoyanism was a route back to the Orthodox Church, despite Tolstoy's intentions, and terms his great strength 'a call to repentance, a certain alarm bell of conscience', in which he has in mind by no means only Tolstoy's religious impact.

65. Quoted in Michael Boro Petrovich, *The Emergence of Russian Panslavism, 1856–1870* (New York, 1956), 25–6.

66. P. Miliukov, 'Slavianofil'stvo', B-E, LIX, 312.

67. Quoted in Stephen Lukashevich, *Ivan Aksakov, 1823–1886* (Harvard, 1965), 37. The chapter heading is, aptly, 'A Reluctant Slavophile'.

68. In his last years he was responsible for publishing the falsified Crémieux letter, attributed to a Jewish leader in France, which had been published in France and then Germany, and was a precursor of the forged 'Protocols of the Elders of Zion' (about 1905). *Ibid.*, 105–8.

69. Petrovich, *Russian Panslavism*, 132–45.

70. Lukashevich, *Aksakov*, 132.

71. N. Ia. Danilevskii, *Rossia i Evropa*, vstupitel'naia stat'ia Iu. Ivaska (reprint, New York, 1966), v.

72. *Ibid.*, 91.

73. Petrovich (*Russian Panslavism*, 74) writes that he did this 'probably because he believed that it had not yet come into its own in world history'.

74. Danilevskii, *Rossiia i Evropa*, 133.

75. Robert E. Macmaster, *Danilevsky: A Russian Totalitarian Philosopher* (Harvard, 1967), 110. Macmaster's study has a great number of admirable qualities, and for that very reason many regret his unconvincing attempt to make the category of 'totalitarian' the basis of his interpretation of Danilevsky.

76. Danilevskii, *Rossiia i Evropa*, 423–4.

77. Martin Katz, *Mikhail N. Katkov*, 15.

78. *Ibid.*, 156.

79. *Ibid.*, 127.

80. See Robert F. Byrnes, *Pobedonostsev: His Life and Thought* (Bloomington, Ind., 1968), esp. 28. Much of the preparatory work for the *Course* was actually done before this time. In 1858–68 Pobedonostsev published 32 books and articles.

81. *Ibid.*, 140–3. Byrnes's suggestion that the appointment pleased 'most churchmen' is, however, questionable.

82. *Ibid.*, 191–2.

83. *Ibid.*, 346.

84. Florovskii, *Puti*, 413–14.

85. Thomas Garrigue Masaryk, *The Spirit of Russia*, III (2nd ed., New York, 1967), 5.

86. *Ibid.*, 69, 80.

87. *Ibid.*, 77, 54.

88. *Ibid.*, 86, 92. Note that he later reproaches Tolstoy for not stopping smoking for a year after he stopped using alcohol (*ibid.*, 199). One can scarcely refrain from speculating that if Dostoevsky were to say that Orthodox tell fewer lies than Protestants, Masaryk would find the statement to be a revolting example of Russian chauvinism.

89. Konstantin Mochulsky, *Dostoevsky: His Life and Work* (trans., Princeton, 1967), x. The original is *Dostoevskii: zhizn' i tvorchestvo* (Paris, 1947). The translator has generally done well; there are mistakes, however, some of which obscure the sense, and some of which show insufficient checking – the 'Gadarene swine' (Matthew 8), a reference of some importance to Dostoevsky's thought, appears more than once as the Gadarene 'man', which is unintelligible both to those who know their Bible and those who do not.

90. *Ibid.*, 17.

91. See Ch. 6.

92. Mochulsky, *Dostoevsky*, 115.

93. Quoted in *ibid.*, 132.

94. Edward C. Thaden, *Conservative Nationalism in Nineteenth-Century Russia* (Seattle, 1964), 65.

95. Quoted in *ibid.*, 68. 'Tushino' was a reference to the kind of stance taken by the Second False Dmitry; see Ch. 2.

96. Mochulsky, *Dostoevsky*, 220; Zenkovsky, *History of Russian Philosophy*, I, Ch. xiv.

97. See Robert Louis Jackson, *Dostoevsky's Quest for Form* (New Haven, 1966), Ch. 9, which deals with the writer's objections to Chernyshevsky and Dobroliubov.

98. Mochulsky, *Dostoevsky*, 254.

99. Mochul'skii, *Dostoevskii*, 210.

100. *Ibid.*, 255.

101. See *ibid.*, 409–11 and 442, for evidence that these statements are not merely titillating critical formulae but accounts of Dostoevsky's purpose.

102. René Wellek (ed.), *Dostoevsky: A Collection of Critical Essays* (Englewood Cliffs, N.J., 1962); see Wellek's fine introduction.

103. V. V. Zenkovsky, 'Dostoevsky's Religious and Philosophical Views', in *ibid.*, 144.

104. Dmitri Chizhevsky, 'The Theme of the Double in Dostoevsky', in *ibid.*, 123.

105. Quoted in Mochulsky, *Dostoevsky*, 592.

106. Ernest J. Simmons, *Dostoevsky: The Making of a Novelist* (reprint, New York, 1962), 273.

107. *Ibid.*, 272.

108. He was not referring to 'populism', as the translator wrongly says in Mochulsky, *Dostoevsky*, 645; see the original, 531.

109. Florovskii, *Puti*, 300.

110. That is, the holy Wisdom of God. The basic scriptural text for the interpretation of Sophia as a feminine being is Proverbs 8.22–31.

111. Quoted in K. Mochul'skii, *Vladimir Solov'ev: zhizn' i uchenie* (Paris, 1936), 19.

112. *Ibid.*, 22, citing S. M. Lukianov.

113. Quoted *ibid.*, 45.

114. *Ibid.*, 53.

115. *Ibid.*, 131.

116. *Ibid.*, 148.

117. Michel d'Herbigny, *Vladimir Soloviev: A Russian Newman (1853–1900)* (trans.; London, 1918). But Soloviev passed out of that period, as the monsignor seems not to recognize.

118. See Zenkovsky, *History of Russian Philosophy*, II, 529.

119. Mochul'skii, *Solov'ev*, 150. In 1897 Leontiev wrote to a friend that Soloviev had not shaken his faith in the Eastern Church but had shaken his 'cultural faith in Russia'. Sviashch. I. Fudel', 'K. Leont'ev i Vl. Solov'ev v ikh vzaimnykh otnosheniiakh', *Russkaia Mysl'* (Nov.–Dec. 1917), 30.

120. Zenkovsky, *History of Russian Philosophy*, II, 603.

121. Florovskii, *Puti*, 327.

122. See quotation in Stephen Lukashevich, *Konstantin Leontiev (1831–1891): A Study in Russian 'Heroic Vitalism'* (New York, 1967), 57.

123. *Ibid.*, 86.

124. Quoted *ibid.*, 130.

125. Quoted in Nicolas Berdyaev, *Leontiev* (reprint, Orono, Maine, 1968), 76.

126. Quoted in Lukashevich, *Leontiev*, 162.

127. Berdyaev, *Leontiev*, 198.

128. Quoted *ibid.*, 198.

129. Edward C. Thaden in his in many ways admirable study, *Conservative Nationalism in Nineteenth-Century Russia*, discusses the Pan-Slavists, Katkov, and Pobedonostsev, who became conservative nationalists, and the *pochvenniki*, Strakhov, Dostoevsky, Soloviev, and Leontiev, who do not fit easily into such a rubric at all – Soloviev and Leontiev, in particular, were if anything anti-nationalists. The difficulty comes from trying to classify figures from cultural history in political categories.

8: The partial reconciliation with the West (1890–1917)

1. Ia. I. Teitel, as quoted in Arthur P. Mendel, *Dilemmas of Progress in Tsarist Russia: Legal Marxism and Legal Populism* (Harvard, 1961), 4–5.

2. James H. Billington, *Mikhailovsky and Russian Populism* (Oxford, 1958), 22–3, 38–9, 129–30.

3. Quoted in Mendel, *Dilemmas*, 10.

4. In 1893 Mikhailovsky declared that he was not a populist (*ibid.*, 78). Evidently he meant that he did not place his faith unequivocally in the peasantry – and neither did many other 'populists'. Marx also declared that he was not a Marxist. Both may have been right in some sense; in any case, both were certainly socialists.

5. See A. Walicki, *The Controversy Over Capitalism: Studies in the Social Philosophy* (Oxford, 1969), esp. 115–21, 176.

6. See *ibid.*, 121–6. The Danielson passage is criticized by B. P. Koz'min, *Iz istorii revoliutsionnoi mysli v Rossii* (Moscow, 1961), 722.

7. Though Plekhanov concluded that Danielson meant that the tsarist state would do this job – 'socialism being introduced by Russian policemen – what a chimera!' Quoted Walicki, *Controversy*, 127.

8. See p. 187 above.

9. Mendel, *Dilemmas*, 38ff.

10. Immediately after writing these lines, I encountered Richard Pipes, *Struve: Liberal on the Left, 1870–1905* (Harvard, 1970), 29–30, which convincingly attacks the 'uncritical' literature that has given us the dubious historiographic scheme in which 'populism' is superseded at a certain point by 'Marxism'.

11. Samuel H. Baron, *Plekhanov: The Father of Russian Marxism* (Stanford, 1963), 7–8.

12. Pipes, *Struve*, 66–8.

13. *Ibid.*, 95. In Pipes's view he was thereby responsible for the misleading usage that has bedeviled us ever since.

14. *Ibid.*, 153.

15. A. A. Kizevetter, *Na rubezhe dvukh stoletii* (Prague, 1929), 211–12.

16. Nicolas Berdyaev, *Dream and Reality* (trans., New York, 1951), 117.

17. *Ibid.*, and Prot. Sergii Bulgakov, *Avtobiograficheskiia zametki* (Paris, 1946), 32.

18. Berdyaev, *Dream and Reality*, 122.

19. His analysis was set forth at length in his *Istoriia russkoi obshchestvennoi mysli*; it was to be seven volumes in length, but only three had been completed by the time of his death. The completed portion is well discussed in Baron, *Plekhanov*, 295–307. The now-classic study of the phenomenon on a world-wide scale is Karl A. Wittfogel, *Oriental Despotism* (reprint, New Haven, 1963), which also provides a guide to the relevant literature, Marxist and non-Marxist.

20. Writing in *Novoe Slovo* (June 1897), as quoted in Mendel, *Dilemmas*, 140. The reference, as Mendel does not point out, was doubtless to an essay of Vladimir Soloviev's.

21. See Richard Pipes, *Social Democracy and the St. Petersburg Labor Movement, 1885–1897* (Harvard, 1963).

22. Good brief sketches of the early lives of each are given by Richard Kindersley in *The First Russian Revisionists* (Oxford, 1962), Ch. II. In its main lines of analysis, the book needs correctives supplied by Pipes's *Struve*, but its scholarship is generally careful.

23. Gleb Struve has repeatedly challenged the phrase 'Silver Age', and cited with approval Mirsky's use of the term 'Second Golden Age'. It is worth noting that Mirsky acknowledged that the 'Second Golden Age' was 'inferior' to the first; one may urge that although silver is inferior to gold, it still is valuable and beautiful far beyond the ordinary run of elements, and that as in the case of a number of other dubious but common historical usages of the kind, it is probably too late to change this one. See Struve, 'The Cultural Renaissance', in Theofanis George Stavrou (ed.), *Russia Under the Last Tsar* (Minneapolis, 1969), 179.

24. D. S. Mirsky, *Contemporary Russian Literature, 1881–1925* (London, 1926), 151.

25. Camilla Gray, *The Great Experiment: Russian Art, 1863–1922* (New York, 1962), 9–21.

26. D. S. Merezhkovskii, *O prichinakh upadka i o novykh techeniiakh sovremennoi russkoi literatury* (St Petersburg, 1893), 100. See James P. Scanlan, 'The New Religious Consciousness: Merezhkovskii and Berdiaev', *Canadian Slavic Studies*, IV (Spring 1970), 17–35, for an interesting discussion of Merezhkovsky's subsequent work.

27. Mirsky, *Contemporary Russian Literature*, 158.

28. She paints an effective picture of these years in *Dmitrii Merezhkovskii* (Paris, 1951).

29. Vladimir Markov, 'Balmont: A Reappraisal', *Slavic Review* (June 1969); Oleg A. Maslenikov, *The Frenzied Poets: Andrey Biely and the Russian Symbolists* (Berkeley, 1952).

30. For example, Briusov's one-line 'poem', 'O zakroi svoi blednye nogi!' Briusov defended the notion of brevity as a poetic virtue *per se* in relation to this 'poem'. One questioner then wondered if reducing the poem to its initial 'O!' might not have improved it still further; Briusov was willing to take the suggestion quite seriously. Maslenikov, *The Frenzied Poets*, 17–18.

31. James West, *Russian Symbolism: A Study of Viacheslav Ivanov and the Russian Symbolist Aesthetic* (London, 1970), 4, 57.

32. Quoted in Maslenikov, *The Frenzied Poets*, 208.

33. Leonid I. Strakhovsky, *Craftsmen of the World: Three Poets of Modern Russia* (Harvard, 1949), 23.

34. Jews made a contribution to all aspects of the artistic and cultural revival of the period including religious thought (though not, of course, to the Orthodox revival directly).

35. The debt of the Russian Futurists to the Italian Futurists is examined at several points by Vladimir Markov in *Russian Futurism: A History* (Berkeley, 1968). Though that debt must not be brushed aside, it is clear that many of the Russians concerned knew little of Marinetti and developed their own ideas. As for Marinetti's reaction to his Russian counterparts, after a scandalous visit to Russia in 1914 he declared that they lived not in the future but in the pluperfect (Markov, 158).

36. *Ibid.*, 211.

37. In 1914 David Burliuk and V. G. Shershenevich criticized both Marxists and liberals for persecuting Futurists, declaring that they violated the very ideals of freedom they claimed to uphold and that they were in truth heirs of 'spiritual enslavers' such as Belinsky, Pisarev, and Chernyshevsky. *Ibid.*, 177.

38. Quoted *ibid.*, 226–7.

39. Compare the collection of 'artists' statements' in Camilla Gray, *The Great*

Experiment, 281–7 (and also the manifestoes reproduced in Markov, *Russian Futurism* – for example, 45–6, 65, 345–6) with the rich stock of plates throughout the Gray book.

40. Renato Poggioli, *The Poets of Russia, 1890–1930* (Harvard, 1960), 62.

41. Mirsky, *Contemporary Russian Literature*, 154; see also Arnold L. Haskell in collaboration with Walter Nouvel, *Diaghileff: His Artistic and Private Life* (New York, 1935), and Camilla Gray, *The Great Experiment*, Ch. Two.

42. Haskell, *Diaghileff*, 102.

43. Gray, *The Great Experiment*, 47–8.

44. Both his name and Nijinsky's have passed into international use in the French form, a result of the artistic history here summarized. The transliteration should be Shaliapin and Nizhinsky.

45. Nicolas Berdyaev, *The Russian Idea* (reprint, Boston, 1962), 220.

46. Nicolas Zernov, *The Russian Religious Renaissance of the Twentieth Century* (New York, 1963), 57–60.

47. This is also the justification for deferring until this chapter reference to some of the ecclesiastical developments of the 1860's, which made their consequences felt in the general realm of culture only as the monopoly of atheism weakened among the intelligentsia toward the end of the century.

48. Prot. Georgii Florovskii, *Puti russkago bogosloviia* (Paris, 1937), 340. The following pages use the section 332–502 extensively.

49. Tolstoy was named Procurator of the Synod in 1865 and minister of education in 1866.

50. Byrnes's study, *Pobedonostsev*, regrettably neglects to make this point clear. See, for example, 165–70.

51. Florovskii, *Puti*, 453–4.

52. Zernov, *Russian Religious Renaissance*, 90–7; Florovskii, *Puti*, 470–1.

53. The story of the parties is partially told in Donald W. Treadgold, *Lenin and His Rivals* (New York, 1955); Leopold H. Haimson, *The Russian Marxists and the Origins of Bolshevism* (Harvard, 1955); and George Fischer, *Russian Liberalism* (Harvard, 1958). On the Revolution of 1905, see Sidney Harcave, *First Blood* (New York, 1964).

54. I have used *Viekhi* (4th ed., Moscow, 1909); an English translation by Marshall Shatz and Judith Zimmerman was published in *Canadian Slavic Studies*, beginning in summer 1968 and ending in fall 1971. This quotation was a note to the second edition of the book. *CSS*, II, 173.

55. *Ibid.*, 151–74.

56. *Ibid.*, 291–310, 447–63. An article of his in *Russkaia Mysl'*, no. 3 (1908), had already voiced this opinion.

57. *CSS*, II, 298.

58. *Ibid.*, III, 1–21.

59. Translation by Norbert Gutermann in *Partisan Review* (September 1948), XV, 1047.

60. P. B. Struve, 'Intelligentsiia i revoliutsiia', *Viekhi*, 162–3, 167.

61. From 23 March to 6 September 1909 alone, 158 reviews or commentaries appeared in the periodical press. *Viekhi* (4th ed.) lists them, 213–17.

62. Quoted in Leonard Schapiro, 'The *Vekhi* Group and the Mystique of Revolution', *SEER*, XXXIV (December 1955), 67. See also Nikolai P. Poltoratzky, 'The *Vekhi* Dispute and the Significance of *Vekhi*', *Canadian Slavonic Papers*, IX (Spring 1967), 86–106 and Arthur Levin, 'M. O. Gershenzon and *Vekhi*', *Canadian Slavic Studies*, IV (Spring 1970), 60–73.

63. Quoted in Zernov, *Russian Religious Renaissance*, 129, from Gessen's 1937 autobiography.

64. Mirsky, *Contemporary Russian Literature*, 179.

65. Gleb Struve, 'The Cultural Renaissance', in Stavrou (ed.), *Russia Under the Last Tsar*, 197–8.

66. Alexander Vucinich, 'Politics, Universities, and Science', in Stavrou (ed.), *Russia Under the Last Tsar*, 159.

67. Alexander Vucinich, *Science in Russian Culture, 1861–1917* (Stanford, 1970), 245–8 and elsewhere, mentions without criticizing them several distinguished scientists of the period, including Vernadsky, Nicholas Beketov, Ivan Pavlov, and others who regarded science and religion as fully compatible. It is therefore puzzling that he attacks Berdiaev for conducting an 'unrelenting war on science and democracy' shortly after quoting Berdiaev's own retort to such contemporary charges in which he writes that such charges do 'not deserve a serious rejoinder. In actuality, we are not against science but against rationalism – against encroachments of positivism on the unity and totality of human nature... in the final analysis science itself would benefit if its applicability were clearly delimited...' (*Sub specie aeternitatis*, 1907). Berdiaev's views may be severely criticized on a variety of grounds, but he does not deserve to be regarded as an opponent of science.

68. Mirsky, *Contemporary Russian Literature*, 89.

69. Schapiro declares the intellectual level of *Smena vekh* to have been about the same as 'that of the arguments used by Vichy supporters to justify collaboration with the Germans'. 'The *Vekhi* Group', 71.

9: The West and the Russian tradition

1. *New York Times* interview with Harrison E. Salisbury, 16 September 1969, p. 12. The quoted matter is in Salisbury's paraphrase.

ADDITIONAL BIBLIOGRAPHY

Andreyev, Nikolay. 'Kurbsky's Letters to Vas'yan Muromtsev'. *SEER*, XXXIII, no. 81 (June 1955), 414–36.
  'Was the Pskov-Pechery Monastery a Citadel of the Non-Possessors?' *Jahrbücher für Geschichte Osteuropas*. New series, vol. 17, pt 4, December 1969.
Avrich, Paul. *The Russian Anarchists*. Princeton, 1967.
Berry, Lloyd E., and Robert O. Crummey (eds). *Rude & Barbarous Kingdom: Russia in the Accounts of Sixteenth-Century English Voyagers*. Madison, 1968.
Betiaev, Ia. D. *Obshchestvenno-politicheskaia i filosofskaia mysl' v Rossii v pervoi polovine XVIII veka*. Saransk, 1959.
Bulgakov, Sergei N. *Ot Marksizma k idealizmu, sbornik statei (1896–1903)*. St Petersburg, 1903.
Chadwick, Henry, *The Early Church* (vol. 1 of *The Pelican History of the Church*). Baltimore, 1967.
Chambre, Henri, SJ. *From Karl Marx to Mao Tse-tung*. Trans. by Robert J. Olsen. New York, 1963.
Cherniavsky, Michael. *Tsar and People: Studies in Russian Myths*. New Haven 1961.
Chernyshevskii, N. G., 1828–1929. Neizdannye teksty, materialy i stat'i, ed. S. Z. Katsenbogena. Saratov, 1928.
Clarke, Oliver Fielding. *Introduction to Berdyaev*. London, 1950.
Conybeare, Frederick C. *Russian Dissenters*. Harvard, 1921.
Crummey, Robert O. *The Old Believers and the World of Anti-Christ (1694–1855)*. Madison, 1970.
Dan, Theodore. *The Origins of Bolshevism*, ed. and trans. Joel Carmichael. New York, 1964.
David, Georgius, SJ. *Status Modernus Magnae Russiae seu Moscoviae (1690)*. The Hague, 1965.
Dekabrist M. I. Murav'ev-Apostol. Vospominaniia i pis'ma, ed. S. Ia. Straikh. Petrograd, 1922.
Dewey, Horace W., and Mateja Matejic. 'The Literary Arsenal of Vassian Patrikeev'. *SEEJ*, x (Winter 1966), 400–52.
Eliade, Mircea. *Patterns in Comparative Religion*. Trans. Rosemary Sheed. New York, 1958.
  The Sacred and the Profane: The Nature of Religion. Trans. Willard R. Trask. New York, 1959.
Evgen'ev-Maksimov, V. and D. Maksimov. *Iz proshlogo russkoi zhurnalistiki*. Leningrad, 1930.
Fanger, Donald. *Dostoevsky and Romantic Realism: A Study of Dostoevsky in Relation to Balzac, Dickens, and Gogol*. Harvard, 1965.
Fedotov, G. P. *Novyi Grad*. New York, 1952.
Fine, John V. A., Jr. 'Fedor Kuritsyn's "Laodikijskoe Poslanie" and the Heresy of the Judaisers'. *Speculum*, LXI (July 1966), 500–4.
Fischer, Louis. *The Life of Lenin*. New York, 1964.
Florovskii, A. V. 'Pervyi iezuit iz moskovskikh dvorian'. *Acta Academiae Velehradensis*. Olomouc. Annus XIX, 249–56.
Florovsky, Georges. 'Vladimir Solov'ev and Dante: The Problem of Christian Empire'. In *For Roman Jakobson*. The Hague, 1956.

'The Predicament of the Christian Historian', in Walter Leibrecht (ed.), *Religion and Culture: Essays in Honor of Paul Tillich*. New York, 1959.

'Three Masters: The Quest for Religion in Nineteenth-Centry Russian Literature'. *Comparative Literature Studies* III (1966), 119–37. (On Gogol, Dostoevsky, and Tolstoy.)

Frank, Viktor (ed.). *Russisches Christentum*. Paderborn, 1889.

Gershenzon, M. *Istoricheskie zapiski*. 2nd ed., Berlin, 1923.

Istoriia molodoi Rossii. Moscow–Petrograd, 1923.

Gordillo, M. 'Russie (Pensée réligieuse)'. In *Dictionnaire de théologie catholique*. Vol. 14, pt 1, cols 207–371, Paris, 1939.

Gregg, Richard A. *Fedor Tiutchev: The Evolution of a Poet*. New York, 1965.

Haumant, Émile. *La culture française en Russie (1700–1900)*. 2nd ed., Paris, 1913.

Hingley, Ronald. *The Undiscovered Dostoevsky*. London, 1962.

Iovchuk, M. T. *Formirovanie filosofskoi i obshchestvenno-politicheskoi mysli v Rossii XV–XVIII vekov*. Moscow, 1946.

Kirpichnikov, A. I. *Ocherki po istorii novoi russkoi literatury*. 2nd ed., 2 vols, Moscow, 1903.

Kogan, Iu. Ia. *Ocherki po istorii russkoi ateisticheskoi mysli XVIII v*. Moscow, 1962.

Koretskii, V. I. 'Vnov' naidennoe protivoereticheskoe proizvedenie Zinoviia Otenskogo'. *TODRL*, XXI, Moscow–Leningrad, 1965.

Kozlov, N. S. *Razvitie obshchestvenno-politicheskoi i filosofskoi mysli v epokhu russkogo srednevekov'ia IX–XVI vv*. Moscow, 1961.

Kurland, Jordan E. 'Leont'ev's Views on the Course of Russian Literature'. *ASEER*, XVI (October 1957), 260–74.

Lenin, V. I. 'K kharakteristike ekonomicheskogo romantizma. Sismondi i nashi otechestvennye sismondisty'. *Polnoe sobranie sochinenii*. 5th ed., II (Moscow, 1958), 119–262.

Likhachev, D. S. *Kul'tura russkogo naroda X–XVII vv*. Moscow–Leningrad, 1961.

Lipski, Alexander. 'A Russian Mystic Faces the Age of Rationalism and Revolution: Thought and Activity of Ivan Vladimirovich Lopukhin'. *Church History*, XXXVI, no. 2 (June, 1967), 1–19.

Mathewson, Rufus W., Jr. *The Positive Hero in Russian Literature*. New York, 1958.

Miliukov, P. N. *Glavnyia techeniia russkoi istoricheskoi mysli*. 3rd ed., St Petersburg, 1913.

Munzer, Egbert. *Solovyev: Prophet of Russian–Western Unity*. London, 1956.

Nadezhdin. [sic] 'Evropeizm i narodnost' v otnoshenii k russkoi slovesnosti'. *Teleskop*, XXXI (Moscow, 1836), 5–60, 203–64.

Picchio, Riccardo. '"Prerinascimento esteuropeo" e "Rinascita slava ortodossa"'. *Ricerche Slavistiche*, VI (1958), 185–99.

Pobedonostsev, Konstantin P. *Reflections of a Russian Statesman*. Ann Arbor, 1965.

Pollard, A. F. *The Jesuits in Poland*. Oxford, 1892.

Predtechenskii, A. V. *Ocherki obshchestvenno-politicheskoi istorii Rossii v pervoi chetverti XIX veka*. Moscow–Leningrad, 1957.

Pypin, A. N. *Istoricheskie ocherki: kharakteristiki literaturnykh mnenii ot dvadtsatykh do piatidesiatykh godov*. 2nd ed., St Petersburg, 1890.

Obshchestvennoe dvizhenie v Rossi pri Aleksandrie I. 4th ed., St Petersburg, 1908.

Pyziur, Eugene. 'Mikhail N. Katkov: Advocate of English Liberalism in Russia, 1856–1863'. *SEER*, XLV, no. 105 (July 1967), 439–56.

Roberts, Spencer E. (ed.) *Essays in Russian Literature, the Conservative View: Leontiev, Rozanov, Shestov*. Athens, Ohio, 1968.

Runciman, Steven. 'Byzantium, Russia and Caesaropapism'. *Canadian Slavonic Papers*, II (1957), 1–10.

Rzhiga, V. F. 'I. S. Peresvietov i zapadnaia kul'turno-istoricheskaia sreda'. *IORIaS*, no. 3(1911), 169–81.

Scanlan, James P. 'Nicholas Chernyshevsky and Philosophical Materialism in Russia'. *Journal of the History of Philosophy*, VIII (January 1970), 65–86.

Schmemann, Alexander (ed. and intro.). *Ultimate Questions: An Anthology of Modern Russian Religious Thought*. New York, 1965.

Setschkareff, Wsewolod. *Schellings Einfluss in der russischen Literatur der 20-er und 30-er Jahre des XIX. Jahrhunderts*. Leipzig, 1939.

Ševčenko, Ihor. 'A Neglected Byzantine Source of Muscovite Political Ideology'. *Harvard Slavic Studies*, II (1954), 141–79.

Shein, Louis J. 'Pushkin's Political Weltanschauung'. *Canadian Slavonic Papers*, vol. X, no. 1 (1968), 68–78.

Shestov, Lev. *Athens and Jerusalem*. Trans. w. intro. by Bernard Martin. Athens, Ohio, 1966.

   Dostoevsky, Tolstoy and Nietzsche. Trans. Bernard Martin and Spencer Roberts; intro. by Bernard Martin. Athens, Ohio, 1969.

Shmurlo, E. 'Katolitsizm v Rossii'. B-E, XIV-A, 735–9.

Shtrange, M. M. *Russkoe obshchestvo i frantsuzskaia revoliutsiia 1789–1794 gg*. Moscow, 1956.

Simon, Gerhard. *Konstantin Petrovic Pobedonostsev und die Kirchenpolitik des heiligen Sinod, 1880–1905*. Göttingen, 1969.

[Soloviev, V. S.] *A Solovyov Anthology*. Arranged by S. L. Frank. Trans. from Russian by Natalie Duddington. New York, 1950.

Sushkov, N. V. *Moskovskii Universitetskii Blagorodnyi Pansion i vospominaniia Moskovskago Universiteta, gimnazii ego, universitetskago blagorodnago pansiona i druzheskago obshchestva*. Moscow, 1858.

Sverbeev, Dmitrii Nikolaevich. *Zapiski (1799–1826)*. 2 vols, Moscow, 1899.

Vakar, Nicholas. *The Taproot of Soviet Society*. New York, 1961.

Veselovskii, Aleksiei. *Etiudy i kharakteristiki*. 3rd ed., Moscow, 1907.

   Zapadnoe vliianie v novoi russkoi literaturie. 4th ed., Moscow, 1910.

Vinogradov, V. V. *Ocherki po istorii russkogo literaturnogo iazyka XVII–XIX vv*. 2nd ed., Moscow, 1938.

Wilson, Francesca. *Muscovy: Russia Through Foreign Eyes, 1553–1900*. London, 1970.

Zacek, Judith Cohen. 'The Russian Bible Society and the Russian Orthodox Church'. *Church History*, XXXV, no. 4 (December 1966), 3–29.

   'The Lancastrian School Movement in Russia'. *SEER*, XLV, no. 105 (July 1967), 343–67.

Znamensky, P. *Prikhodnoe dukhovenstvo v Rossii so vremeni reformy Petra*. Kazan, 1873.

INDEX